The Daily New Testament with Psalms and Proverbs

*A One Year Reading Plan for Catholic
from the New American Bible*

Introductions by
David E. Rosage

SERVANT BOOKS
Ann Arbor, Michigan

THE REVISED NEW TESTAMENT
Nihil obstat: Stephen J. Hartdegen, O.F.M., S.S.L.
             Censor Deputatus
Imprimatur: James A. Hickey, S.T.D., J.C.D.
             Archbishop of Washington
Imprimatur: † August 27, 1986

PSALMS AND PROVERBS
Nihil obstat: Stephen J. Hartdegen, O.F.M., S.S.L.
             Christian P. Ceroke, O. Carm., S.T.D.
Imprimatur: Patrick Cardinal O'Boyle, D.D.
             Archbishop of Washington
Imprimatur: † July 27, 1970

INTRODUCTIONS BY DAVID E. ROSAGE
Nihil obstat: Father Oscar L. Benzinger, S.J.
Imprimatur: Lawrence H. Welsh, D.D.
             Bishop of Spokane
Imprimatur: † July 29, 1987

Published by Servant Books
P.O. Box 8617
Ann Arbor, Michigan 48107

Cover design by Michael P. Andaloro
Cover photograph © Four By Five, Inc.

87 88 89 90 91 10 9 8 7 6 5 4 3 2 1

Printed in the United States of America

ISBN 0-89283-346-7

Introduction

THIS SYSTEMATIC ARRANGEMENT of the Psalter and the Book of Proverbs into the whole New Testament has the potential to make a major contribution to our devotional life. A regular reading of, reflecting on, listening to, and praying with these suggested passages of Scripture will develop an ever-growing appreciation of the richness of the Word of God.

Jesus is the focal point of our whole Christian way of life. Our spiritual maturation must be christological. Jesus is the heart and core around which all the Scriptures center. His life, presence, and teaching make all the Scriptures more understandable. Jesus gives them meaning and clarity.

As we go first to the gospel, we there discover Jesus as the central figure toward which all the messages of Psalms and Proverbs gravitate. The Old Testament writings flow up and point to Jesus and find their meaning and fulfillment in him. Everything which was written after Jesus walked the face of the earth flows down from him and fulfills the promises which he made.

Overview

How apt are the words of the sacred writer when he says: "Jesus Christ is the same yesterday, today, and forever" (Heb 13:8). Let us reflect momentarily on the books of the Bible which are incorporated in the *Daily New Testament*.

In the Psalter and Book of Proverbs we see Jesus "yesterday." These were written before the Incarnation. They are better understood and fulfilled in the gospel proclaimed by Jesus. Their messages for the most part lead up to Jesus.

We discover the "today" of Jesus in the Gospels. Not only are his teachings recorded there, but Jesus himself is present in his Word, as the Second Vatican Council reminds us.

The same Jesus "forever" is evident in the teaching of the church in the first century and down through all the ages until our own day. Jesus is faithful to his promise when he said: "And behold, I am with you always, until the end of the age" (Mt

28:20). In the books of the Bible presented in this volume, we find Jesus "yesterday, today and forever."

Gospel

The four different accounts of the Good News interspersed throughout the *Daily New Testament* are the heart and core of this scriptural presentation. A Gospel is not a life of Jesus. In the process of his teaching, he revealed very much about himself as a person.

He gives us some direct statements about his identity. "I am the good shepherd" (Jn 10:1ff); "I am the vine, you are the branches" (Jn 15:1ff); "I am the way and the truth and the life. No one comes to the Father except through me" (Jn 14:6ff).

Jesus also discloses much about his personality by his actions and attitudes. He loves the poor, the downtrodden, the outcasts. He is infinitely patient with the "slow to believe" disciples. He takes time to minister to individuals even though the crowd presses upon him.

Jesus is a teacher *par excellence*. He is a healer. He healed not so much to prove his divine power, but rather to manifest his love.

In the prologue of his Gospel, John introduces Jesus as the Word of God. "In the beginning was the Word, and the Word was with God, and the Word was God" (Jn 1:1). And John continues: "And the Word became flesh and made his dwelling among us" (Jn 1:14). Jesus came into the world not only to proclaim the Word, but also to live and to fulfill the Word.

Jesus came to teach us his way of life, to redeem us by his passion and death, to continue to sanctify us by sharing his risen life with us. He is the focal point of the Old Testament, which prepared the way for him. He is our Savior and Redeemer as presented in the Gospels. His teaching continues down through the ages with the writings of the apostles as an explanation and adaptation of his teaching for us until the end of time. Therefore, he is the heart and center of all our scriptural prayer.

Book of the Psalms

From the vantage point of the Gospels, let us take a brief look at Jesus "yesterday." Many of the Psalms are prophetic. They prepare us for the coming of the Messiah and tell us something of the nature of the kingdom he would establish.

Psalm 2 informs us about the universal reign of the Messiah, while Psalm 22 foretells the suffering and death which he had to endure in order to establish his kingdom. Psalm 110 outlines the principal offices of the Messiah as Lord, King, and Priest. In addition to his "princely power" he is also a priest. "You are a priest forever, according to the order of Melchizedek" (Ps 110:4).

God clothes himself in mystery beyond our human comprehension. Jesus came into the world to reveal to us more about the Father. He went to great lengths to inform us of the Father's mercy and compassion. These teachings of Jesus give us a greater appreciation of those Psalms which praise the providential care and merciful love of God. Jesus' words help us to pray the Psalms more fervently and more gratefully.

By his own example, Jesus taught us the prayer of praise and how important it should be in our devotional life (Mt 11:25ff). Praise is the highest form of vocal prayer. Many of the Psalms are spontaneous hymns of praise. The Psalms are a prayerful effort to understand more about God, to sing his praises, to glorify his name, to express gratitude, and to cry out for help from above.

The Psalms lead us to Jesus, who not only fulfills their prophetic message but also gives them a deeper meaning in our lives.

Book of Proverbs

If we read the Proverbs as disciples of Jesus, we enjoy a deeper and richer appreciation of the many norms and guidelines set forth. By insisting that our primary focus should be our love for God, for our neighbor, and also for ourselves, Jesus added a new dimension to this ethical code with its directives, admonitions, hints, and urgings. This enables us to translate them into guidelines for our daily living according to the standards set down by Jesus.

Acts of the Apostles

Jesus promised the disciples that after they received the Holy Spirit, they would be his witnesses "to the ends of the earth" (Acts 1:8). In this first history of the church, we see that promise being miraculously fulfilled as Peter, Paul, and all their companions carried the news of salvation far and wide. Even though Luke ended his account with the imprisonment of Paul, the history of the church continues two thousand years later.

Jesus is present in the church as he promised. His divine power is manifest now on many occasions, as it was through his first ambassadors. "Jesus Christ is the same . . . forever."

The Epistles

In his farewell discourse, Jesus promised to send his Holy Spirit, who "will teach you everything and remind you of all that

[I] told you . . . . when he comes, the Spirit of truth, he will guide you to all truth" (Jn 14:26; 16:13). The divine influence of the Holy Spirit is apparent in the letters embodying the teachings of Peter, Paul, James, John, and Jude. These divinely inspired authors guide us to the truths taught by Jesus and make them applicable for our life and times. This obviously is the work of the Holy Spirit.

A reflective reading and devout praying with their words will inspire, encourage, and guide us as we daily pursue the way which Jesus mapped out for us on our journey through life.

By way of example, Jesus told us repeatedly that love is the essential element for our Christian living. Paul, in turn, specifies the qualities that our love must have. "Love is patient, love is kind . . ."(1 Cor 13:4ff). John helps us when he assures us that God first loved us and continues to love us just as we are (1 Jn 4:7ff). Each letter offers many opportunities to know Jesus better and to have him guide us to a holy and happy life. Since Jesus is present in his Word, these letters are a way of his speaking to us here and now.

Revelation

The Book of Revelation could be considered a summation of all the books of the New Testament. First, we are warned against falling into either mediocrity or deviation in our Christian commitment and lives (see chapters two and three of Revelation). Next, we are led into some unique prayers of praise and adoration of God in chapters four and five. Finally, our hope and trust is rekindled by the promise of a new creation in the heavenly Jerusalem.

Blending the Psalms and Proverbs with all the New Testament writings has produced a practical reading and prayer guide for our spiritual growth and devotional maturation. Fidelity to the suggested readings for each day will bring us into a better understanding of God's Word. It will effect a powerful transformation within us and will lead us into a deeper, richer love-relationship with the Lord.

JANUARY

Jesus the Teacher

IN THE GOSPEL OF MATTHEW, Jesus is portrayed as a prominent and popular teacher. Jesus came into the world to proclaim the Good News of salvation and to lead his followers into a new way of life.

Methods of Teaching

Jesus was a teacher *par excellence* and employed various teaching methods. By means of parables he explained the most sublime truths in a way that they could be understood by his hearers. He often used allegories or metaphors to present insights into profound mysteries. He used picturesque language as he pointed out scenes with which his hearers were familiar—the farmer sowing seed, the shepherd tending his flock, the lilies of the field, the storm at sea. He appealed to the intellect by offering reasons and proofs to substantiate the truths he was propounding.

He also used one of the most powerful methods, and in fact the only successful method, in teaching spiritual truth. Jesus lived what he taught. He put into practice in his own life everything he advocated. He pleaded: ". . . learn from me, for I am meek and humble of heart" (Mt 11:29).

Some of the teaching of Jesus' day was done peripatetically. Walking was the main means of getting from one location to another. Since walking was time-consuming, many of the rabbis instructed their devotees as they walked along. People often traveled in groups for their own protection and convenience. The rabbis usually had a crowd of eager listeners following them. As they passed through a village, the local inhabitants lined up along the roadway to catch some snatches of the teacher's wisdom. As we read in the Gospel, Jesus followed the same practice as he journeyed up and down the countryside.

Jesus also taught more formally. When his disciples or a large crowd gathered around him, Jesus took the occasion to announce the Good News and to invite his would-be disciples to follow his way of life. This understanding of Jesus' teaching gives us a deeper insight into the format of Matthew's Gospel. The evangelist presented Jesus in five different teaching settings. The makeup of his audience determined the subject on which Jesus dwelt.

Teaching Settings

In the Sermon on the Mount, Jesus intended his teaching for the disciples, even though the crowd swelled as he went on. As a recognized teacher, Jesus sat down as any professional teacher was expected to do. Even though a crowd gathered, Jesus continued to direct his teaching primarily to the disciples. Matthew is careful to note that Jesus taught on the Mount. A mountain signified the place where God would manifest himself and where his divine revelations are made.

In this lengthy discourse Jesus revealed very much about his personality, his mind and heart. In the Beatitudes Jesus was really saying: "This is what I am like. If you want to be my disciples, you must be like me—poor in spirit, single-hearted, merciful," and so on.

Second, Jesus prepared his disciples for their missionary apostolate by instructing them in towns and villages in order to give them a sense of evangelization. He had chosen his disciples from various ranks of life so that they could identify more readily with the diverse types of people they were to evangelize.

Upon arrival in some town or village, Jesus would call the disciples aside to instruct them before sending them among the residents to proclaim the Good News of salvation—like sheep among wolves. The disciples were to be "shrewd as serpents and simple as doves" (Mt 10:16).

Third, Jesus taught by the lakeshore. This teaching was intended for the huge crowd which had gathered to hear him. He sat in a boat so that he could be seen and heard by everyone. In this discourse we find a collection of parables about the kingdom of heaven. Jesus used illustrations from the rural setting around them.

Fourth, when Jesus wanted to school his disciples in a more dedicated way of life and to draw them into a greater conversion and transformation of life, he called them together in a home in Capernaum. There he pointed out some of their weaknesses. He called a little child over to him and reminded the disciples that unless they had the heart and mind of a child they could not enter the kingdom of heaven (Mt 18:2ff).

From this more private setting we can visualize a community or an extended family gathering. In the intimacy of such a group, there can be a process of reconciliation and recommitment.

Finally, Jesus taught on Mt. Olivet overlooking Jerusalem. From this vantage point they could see the temple and the imposing walls of the Holy City. Jesus foretold that all of this would be destroyed with the coming cataclysm because the people had rejected him and his teachings. Jesus intended this pronouncement as a warning for all future ages. The destruction of Jerusalem is also a reminder of our own mortality. We are destined for the heavenly Jerusalem which will be our permanent home.

As we read and reflect on the Good News as presented to us in Matthew's Gospel, what should we expect to glean from our prayerful ponderings? In the first place, we must go to the mountain of our own inner being to sit at the feet of Jesus with a listening heart, to absorb his message as well as his mentality and heart.

Second, we are called to a teaching ministry. We witness by word and example, by our actions and attitudes. Jesus commissioned us as he did his disciples: "Go, therefore, and make disciples of all nations. . . . teaching them to observe all that I have commanded you" (Mt 28:19-20).

JANUARY 1

MATTHEW 1:1-25

The book of the genealogy of Jesus Christ, the son of David, the son of Abraham.

Abraham became the father of Isaac, Isaac the father of Jacob, Jacob the father of Judah and his brothers. Judah became the father of Perez and Zerah, whose mother was Tamar. Perez became the father of Hezron, Hezron the father of Ram, Ram the father of Amminadab. Amminadab became the father of Nahshon, Nahshon the father of Salmon, Salmon the father of Boaz, whose mother was Rahab. Boaz became the father of Obed, whose mother was Ruth. Obed became the father of Jesse, Jesse the father of David the king.

David became the father of Solomon, whose mother had been the wife of Uriah. Solomon became the father of Rehoboam, Rehoboam the father of Abijah, Abijah the father of Asaph. Asaph became the father of Jehoshaphat, Jehoshaphat the father of Joram, Joram the father of Uzziah. Uzziah became the father of Jotham, Jotham the father of Ahaz, Ahaz the father of Hezekiah. Hezekiah became the father of Manasseh, Manasseh the father of Amos, Amos the father of Josiah. Josiah became the father of Jechoniah and his brothers at the time of the Babylonian exile.

After the Babylonian exile, Jechoniah became the father of Shealtiel, Shealtiel the father of Zerubbabel, Zerubbabel the father of Abiud. Abiud became the father of Eliakim, Eliakim the father of Azor, Azor the father of Zadok. Zadok became the father of Achim, Achim the father of Eliud, Eliud the father of Eleazar. Eleazar became the father of Matthan, Matthan the father of Jacob, Jacob the father of Joseph, the husband of Mary. Of her was born Jesus who is called the Messiah.

Thus the total number of generations from Abraham to David is fourteen generations; from David to the Babylonian exile, fourteen generations; from the Babylonian exile to the Messiah, fourteen generations.

Now this is how the birth of Jesus Christ came about. When his mother Mary was betrothed to Joseph, but before they lived together, she was found with child through the holy Spirit. Joseph her husband, since he was a righteous man, yet unwilling to expose her to shame, decided to divorce her quietly. Such was his intention when, behold, the angel of the Lord appeared to him in a dream and said, "Joseph, son of David, do not be afraid to take Mary your wife into your home. For it is through the holy Spirit that this child has been conceived in her. She will bear a son and you are to name him Jesus, because he will save his people from their sins." All this took place to fulfill what the Lord had said through the prophet:

"Behold, the virgin shall be
with child and bear a son,
and they shall name him
Emmanuel,"

which means "God is with us." When Joseph awoke, he did as the angel of the Lord had commanded him and took his wife into his home. He had no relations with her until she bore a son, and he named him Jesus.

PSALM 1:1-6

Happy the man who follows not
the counsel of the wicked

Nor walks in the way of sinners,
nor sits in the company of the
insolent,
But delights in the law of the
LORD
and meditates on his law day
and night.
He is like a tree
planted near running water,
That yields its fruit in due season,
and whose leaves never fade.
[Whatever he does, prospers.]
Not so the wicked, not so;
they are like chaff which the
wind drives away.
Therefore in judgment the
wicked shall not stand,
nor shall sinners, in the
assembly of the just.
For the LORD watches over the
way of the just,
but the way of the wicked
vanishes.

PROVERBS 1:1-6

The proverbs of Solomon, the son of David, / king of Israel: / That men may appreciate wisdom and discipline, / may understand words of intelligence; / May receive training in wise conduct, / in what is right, just and honest; / That resourcefulness may be imparted to the simple, / to the young man knowledge and discretion. / A wise man by hearing them will advance in learning, / an intelligent man will gain sound guidance, / That he may comprehend proverb and parable, / the words of the wise and their riddles.

JANUARY 2

MATTHEW 2:1-23

When Jesus was born in Bethlehem of Judea, in the days of King Herod, behold, magi from the east arrived in Jerusalem, saying, "Where is the newborn king of the Jews? We saw his star at its rising and have come to do him homage." When King Herod heard this, he was greatly troubled, and all Jerusalem with him. Assembling all the chief priests and the scribes of the people, he inquired of them where the Messiah was to be born. They said to him, "In Bethlehem of Judea, for thus it has been written through the prophet:

'And you, Bethlehem, land of
Judah,
 are by no means least among
 the rulers of Judah;
since from you shall come a
ruler,
 who is to shepherd my
 people Israel.' "

Then Herod called the magi secretly and ascertained from them
the time of the star's appearance.
He sent them to Bethlehem and
said, "Go and search diligently for
the child. When you have found
him, bring me word, that I too
may go and do him homage." After their audience with the king
they set out. And behold, the star
that they had seen at its rising pre-
ceded them, until it came and
stopped over the place where the
child was. They were overjoyed at
seeing the star, and on entering
the house they saw the child with
Mary his mother. They prostrated
themselves and did him homage.
Then they opened their treasures
and offered him gifts of gold,
frankincense, and myrrh. And
having been warned in a dream
not to return to Herod, they departed for their country by another way.

When they had departed, behold, the angel of the Lord appeared to Joseph in a dream and
said, "Rise, take the child and his
mother, flee to Egypt, and stay
there until I tell you. Herod is going to search for the child to destroy him." Joseph rose and took
the child and his mother by night
and departed for Egypt. He
stayed there until the death of Herod, that what the Lord had said
through the prophet might be fulfilled, "Out of Egypt I called my
son."

When Herod realized that he
had been deceived by the magi,
he became furious. He ordered
the massacre of all the boys in
Bethlehem and its vicinity two
years old and under, in accordance with the time he had ascertained from the magi. Then was
fulfilled what had been said
through Jeremiah the prophet:

"A voice was heard in Ramah,
 sobbing and loud
 lamentation;
Rachel weeping for her
 children,
 and she would not be
 consoled,
 since they were no more."

When Herod had died, behold,
the angel of the Lord appeared in
a dream to Joseph in Egypt and
said, "Rise, take the child and his
mother and go to the land of Israel, for those who sought the
child's life are dead." He rose,
took the child and his mother,
and went to the land of Israel. But
when he heard that Archelaus
was ruling over Judea in place of
his father Herod, he was afraid to
go back there. And because he
had been warned in a dream, he
departed for the region of Galilee.
He went and dwelt in a town
called Nazareth, so that what had
been spoken through the prophets might be fulfilled, "He shall be
called a Nazorean."

PSALM 2:1-6

Why do the nations rage
 and the peoples utter folly?
The kings of the earth rise up,
 and the princes conspire
 together
 against the LORD and against
 his anointed:
"Let us break their fetters
 and cast their bonds from us!"

He who is throned in heaven
  laughs;
  the LORD derides them.
Then in anger he speaks to them;

he terrifies them in his wrath:
"I myself have set up my king
  on Zion, my holy mountain."

PROVERBS 1:7-9

The fear of the LORD is the beginning of knowledge; / wisdom and instruction fools despise. / Hear, my son, your father's instruction, / and reject not your mother's teaching; / A graceful diadem will they be for your head; / a torque for your neck.

JANUARY 3

MATTHEW 3:1-17

In those days John the Baptist appeared, preaching in the desert of Judea [and] saying, "Repent, for the kingdom of heaven is at hand!" It was of him that the prophet Isaiah had spoken when he said:

"A voice of one crying out in
  the desert,
'Prepare the way of the LORD,
  make straight his paths.' "

John wore clothing made of camel's hair and had a leather belt around his waist. His food was locusts and wild honey. At that time Jerusalem, all Judea, and the whole region around the Jordan were going out to him and were being baptized by him in the Jordan River as they acknowledged their sins.

When he saw many of the Pharisees and Sadducees coming to his baptism, he said to them, "You brood of vipers! Who warned you to flee from the coming wrath? Produce good fruit as evidence of your repentance. And do not presume to say to yourselves, 'We have Abraham as our father.' For I

tell you, God can raise up children to Abraham from these stones. Even now the ax lies at the root of the trees. Therefore every tree that does not bear good fruit will be cut down and thrown into the fire. I am baptizing you with water, for repentance, but the one who is coming after me is mightier than I. I am not worthy to carry his sandals. He will baptize you with the holy Spirit and fire. His winnowing fan is in his hand. He will clear his threshing floor and gather his wheat into his barn, but the chaff he will burn with unquenchable fire."

Then Jesus came from Galilee to John at the Jordan to be baptized by him. John tried to prevent him, saying, "I need to be baptized by you, and yet you are coming to me?" Jesus said to him in reply, "Allow it now, for thus it is fitting for us to fulfill all righteousness." Then he allowed him. After Jesus was baptized, he came up from the water and behold, the heavens were opened [for him], and he saw the Spirit of God descending like a dove [and] coming upon him. And a voice came from the heavens, saying, "This is my beloved Son, with whom I am well pleased."

PSALM 2:7-12

I will proclaim the decree of the LORD:
The LORD said to me, "You are my son;
this day I have begotten you.
Ask of me and I will give you
the nations for an inheritance
and the ends of the earth for your possession.
You shall rule them with an iron rod;
you shall shatter them like an earthen dish."
And now, O kings, give heed;
take warning, you rulers of the earth.
Serve the LORD with fear, and rejoice before him;
with trembling pay homage to him,
Lest he be angry and you perish from the way,
when his anger blazes suddenly.
Happy are all who take refuge in him!

PROVERBS 1:10-19

My son, should sinners entice you, and say, / "Come along with us! / Let us lie in wait for the honest man, / let us, unprovoked, set a trap for the innocent; / Let us swallow them up, as the nether world does, alive, / in the prime of life, like those who go down to the pit! / All kinds of precious wealth shall we gain, / we shall fill our houses with booty; / Cast in your lot with us, / we shall all have one purse!"—/ My son, walk not in the way with them, / hold back your foot from their path! / [For their feet run to evil, / they hasten to shed blood.] / It is in vain that a net is spread / before the eyes of any bird—/ These men lie in wait for their own blood, / they set a trap for their own lives. / This is the fate of everyone greedy of loot: / unlawful gain takes away the life of him who acquires it.

JANUARY 4

MATTHEW 4:1-25

Then Jesus was led by the Spirit into the desert to be tempted by the devil. He fasted for forty days and forty nights, and afterwards he was hungry. The tempter approached and said to him, "If you are the Son of God, command that these stones become loaves of bread." He said in reply, "It is written:

'One does not live by bread alone,
but by every word that comes forth from the mouth of God.' "

Then the devil took him to the holy city, and made him stand on the parapet of the temple, and said to him, "If you are the Son of God, throw yourself down. For it is written:

'He will command his angels concerning you'
and 'with their hands they will support you,

lest you dash your foot against
a stone.' "

Jesus answered him, "Again it is
written, 'You shall not put the
Lord, your God, to the test.' "
Then the devil took him up to a
very high mountain, and showed
him all the kingdoms of the world
in their magnificence, and he said
to him, "All these I shall give to
you, if you will prostrate yourself
and worship me." At this, Jesus
said to him, "Get away, Satan! It
is written:

'The Lord, your God, shall you
worship
and him alone shall you
serve.' "

Then the devil left him and, behold, angels came and ministered
to him.

When he heard that John had
been arrested, he withdrew to
Galilee. He left Nazareth and
went to live in Capernaum by the
sea, in the region of Zebulun and
Naphtali, that what had been said
through Isaiah the prophet might
be fulfilled:

"Land of Zebulun and land of
Naphtali,
the way to the sea, beyond
the Jordan,
Galilee of the Gentiles,
the people who sit in darkness
have seen a great light,
on those dwelling in a land
overshadowed by death
light has arisen."

From that time on, Jesus began to
preach and say, "Repent, for the
kingdom of heaven is at hand."

As he was walking by the Sea
of Galilee, he saw two brothers,
Simon who is called Peter, and
his brother Andrew, casting a net
into the sea; they were fishermen. He said to them, "Come after me, and I will make you fishers of men." At once they left
their nets and followed him. He
walked along from there and saw
two other brothers, James, the
son of Zebedee, and his brother
John. They were in the boat, with
their father Zebedee, mending
their nets. He called them, and
immediately they left their boat
and their father and followed
him.

He went around all of Galilee,
teaching in their synagogues, proclaiming the gospel of the kingdom, and curing every disease
and illness among the people. His
fame spread to all of Syria, and
they brought to him all who were
sick with various diseases and
racked with pain, those who were
possessed, lunatics, and paralyt-
ics, and he cured them. And great
crowds from Galilee, the Decapolis, Jerusalem, and Judea, and
from beyond the Jordan followed
him.

PSALM 3:1-4

*A psalm of David, when he fled from
his son Absolom.*

O LORD, how many are my
adversaries!
Many rise up against me!
Many are saying of me,
"There is no salvation for him
in God."
But you, O LORD, are my shield;
my glory, you lift up my head!

PROVERBS 1:20-23

Wisdom cries aloud in the street, / in the open squares she raises her voice; / Down the crowded ways she calls out, / at the city gates she utters her words: / "How long, you simple ones, will you love inanity, / how long will you turn away at my reproof? / Lo! I will pour out to you my spirit, / I will acquaint you with my words."

JANUARY 5

MATTHEW 5:1-48

When he saw the crowds, he went up the mountain, and after he had sat down, his disciples came to him. He began to teach them, saying:

"Blessed are the poor in spirit,
  for theirs is the kingdom of
    heaven.
Blessed are they who mourn,
  for they will be comforted.
Blessed are the meek,
  for they will inherit the land.
Blessed are they who hunger
  and thirst for
    righteousness,
  for they will be satisfied.
Blessed are the merciful,
  for they will be shown
    mercy.
Blessed are the clean of heart,
  for they will see God.
Blessed are the peacemakers,
  for they will be called
    children of God.
Blessed are they who are
  persecuted for the sake of
    righteousness,
  for theirs is the kingdom of
    heaven.

Blessed are you when they insult you and persecute you and utter every kind of evil against you [falsely] because of me. Rejoice and be glad, for your reward will be great in heaven. Thus they persecuted the prophets who were before you.

"You are the salt of the earth. But if salt loses its taste, with what can it be seasoned? It is no longer good for anything but to be thrown out and trampled underfoot. You are the light of the world. A city set on a mountain cannot be hidden. Nor do they light a lamp and then put it under a bushel basket; it is set on a lampstand, where it gives light to all in the house. Just so, your light must shine before others, that they may see your good deeds and glorify your heavenly Father.

"Do not think that I have come to abolish the law or the prophets. I have come not to abolish but to fulfill. Amen, I say to you, until heaven and earth pass away, not the smallest letter or the smallest part of a letter will pass from the law, until all things have taken place. Therefore, whoever breaks one of the least of these commandments and teaches others to do so will be called least in the kingdom of heaven. But whoever obeys and teaches these commandments will be called greatest in the kingdom of heaven. I tell you, unless your righteousness surpasses that of the scribes and Pharisees, you will not enter into the kingdom of heaven.

"You have heard that it was said to your ancestors, 'You shall not kill; and whoever kills will be liable to judgment.' But I say to you, whoever is angry with his brother will be liable to judgment, and whoever says to his brother, 'Raqa,' will be answerable to the Sanhedrin, and whoever says, 'You fool,' will be liable to fiery Gehenna. Therefore, if you bring your gift to the altar, and there recall that your brother has anything against you, leave your gift there at the altar, go first and be reconciled with your brother, and then come and offer your gift. Settle with your opponent quickly while on the way to court with him. Otherwise your opponent will hand you over to the judge, and the judge will hand you over to the guard, and you will be thrown into prison. Amen, I say to you, you will not be released until you have paid the last penny.

"You have heard that it was said, 'You shall not commit adultery.' But I say to you, everyone who looks at a woman with lust has already committed adultery with her in his heart. If your right eye causes you to sin, tear it out and throw it away. It is better for you to lose one of your members than to have your whole body thrown into Gehenna. And if your right hand causes you to sin, cut it off and throw it away. It is better for you to lose one of your members than to have your whole body go into Gehenna.

"It was also said, 'Whoever divorces his wife must give her a bill of divorce.' But I say to you, whoever divorces his wife (unless the marriage is unlawful) causes her to commit adultery, and whoever marries a divorced woman commits adultery.

"Again you have heard that it was said to your ancestors, 'Do not take a false oath, but make good to the Lord all that you vow.' But I say to you, do not swear at all; not by heaven, for it is God's throne; nor by the earth, for it is his footstool; nor by Jerusalem, for it is the city of the great King. Do not swear by your head, for you cannot make a single hair white or black. Let your 'Yes' mean 'Yes,' and your 'No' mean 'No.' Anything more is from the evil one.

"You have heard that it was said, 'An eye for an eye and a tooth for a tooth.' But I say to you, offer no resistance to one who is evil. When someone strikes you on [your] right cheek, turn the other one to him as well. If anyone wants to go to law with you over your tunic, hand him your cloak as well. Should anyone press you into service for one mile, go with him for two miles. Give to the one who asks of you, and do not turn your back on one who wants to borrow.

"You have heard that it was said, 'You shall love your neighbor and hate your enemy.' But I say to you, love your enemies, and pray for those who persecute you, that you may be children of your heavenly Father, for he makes his sun rise on the bad and the good, and causes rain to fall on the just and the unjust. For if you love those who love you, what recompense will you have? Do not the tax collectors do the same? And if you greet your brothers only, what is unusual about that? Do not the pagans do the same? So be perfect, just as your heavenly Father is perfect."

PSALM 3:5-9

When I call out to the LORD,
  he answers me from his holy
    mountain.
When I lie down in sleep,
  I wake again, for the LORD
    sustains me.
I fear not the myriads of people
  arrayed against me on every
    side.

Rise up, O LORD!
  Save me, my God!
For you strike all my enemies on
    the cheek;
  the teeth of the wicked you
    break.
Salvation is the LORD's!
  Upon your people be your
    blessing!

PROVERBS 1:24-27

"Because I called and you refused, / I extended my hand and no one took notice; / Because you disdained all my counsel, / and my reproof you ignored—/ I, in my turn, will laugh at your doom; / I will mock when terror overtakes you; / When terror comes upon you like a storm, / and your doom approaches like a whirlwind; / when distress and anguish befall you."

JANUARY 6

MATTHEW 6:1-34

"[But] take care not to perform righteous deeds in order that people may see them; otherwise, you will have no recompense from your heavenly Father. When you give alms, do not blow a trumpet before you, as the hypocrites do in the synagogues and in the streets to win the praise of others. Amen, I say to you, they have received their reward. But when you give alms, do not let your left hand know what your right is doing, so that your almsgiving may be secret. And your Father who sees in secret will repay you.

"When you pray, do not be like the hypocrites, who love to stand and pray in the synagogues and on street corners so that others may see them. Amen, I say to you, they have received their reward. But when you pray, go to your inner room, close the door, and pray to your Father in secret. And your Father who sees in secret will repay you. In praying, do not babble like the pagans, who think that they will be heard because of their many words. Do not be like them. Your Father knows what you need before you ask him.

"This is how you are to pray:

Our Father in heaven,
  hallowed be your name,
  your kingdom come,
  your will be done,
    on earth as in heaven.
  Give us today our daily
    bread;
  and forgive us our debts,
    as we forgive our debtors;
  and do not subject us to the
    final test,
    but deliver us from the evil
    one.

If you forgive others their transgressions, your heavenly Father will forgive you. But if you do not forgive others, neither will your Father forgive your transgressions.

"When you fast, do not look gloomy like the hypocrites. They neglect their appearance, so that they may appear to others to be fasting. Amen, I say to you, they have received their reward. But when you fast, anoint your head and wash your face, so that you may not appear to be fasting, except to your Father who is hidden. And your Father who sees what is hidden will repay you.

"Do not store up for yourselves treasures on earth, where moth and decay destroy, and thieves break in and steal. But store up treasures in heaven, where neither moth nor decay destroys, nor thieves break in and steal. For where your treasure is, there also will your heart be.

"The lamp of the body is the eye. If your eye is sound, your whole body will be filled with light; but if your eye is bad, your whole body will be in darkness. And if the light in you is darkness, how great will the darkness be.

"No one can serve two masters. He will either hate one and love the other, or be devoted to one and despise the other. You cannot serve God and mammon.

"Therefore I tell you, do not worry about your life, what you will eat [or drink], or about your body, what you will wear. Is not life more than food and the body more than clothing? Look at the birds in the sky; they do not sow or reap, they gather nothing into barns, yet your heavenly Father feeds them. Are not you more important than they? Can any of you by worrying add a single moment to your life-span? Why are you anxious about clothes? Learn from the way the wild flowers grow. They do not work or spin. But I tell you that not even Solomon in all his splendor was clothed like one of them. If God so clothes the grass of the field, which grows today and is thrown into the oven tomorrow, will he not much more provide for you, O you of little faith? So do not worry and say, 'What are we to eat?' or 'What are we to drink?' or 'What are we to wear?' All these things the pagans seek. Your heavenly Father knows that you need them all. But seek first the kingdom [of God] and his righteousness, and all these things will be given you besides. Do not worry about tomorrow; tomorrow will take care of itself. Sufficient for a day is its own evil."

PSALM 4:1-6

For the leader; with stringed
instruments. A psalm of David.
When I call, answer me, O my
    just God,
  you who relieve me when I am
    in distress;
  Have pity on me, and hear my
    prayer!
Men of rank, how long will you
    be dull of heart?
  Why do you love what is vain
    and seek after falsehood?
Know that the LORD does
    wonders for his faithful one;
  the LORD will hear me when I
    call upon him.
Tremble, and sin not;
  reflect, upon your beds, in
    silence.
Offer just sacrifices,
  and trust in the LORD.

PROVERBS 1:28-33

"Then they call me, but I answer not; / they seek me, but find me not; / Because they hated knowledge, / and chose not the fear of the LORD; / They ignored my counsel, / they spurned all my reproof; / And in their arrogance they preferred arrogance, / and like fools they hated knowledge: / "Now they must eat the fruit of their own way, / and with their own devices be glutted. / For the self-will of the simple kills them, / the smugness of fools destroys them. / But he who obeys me dwells in security, / in peace, without fear of harm."

JANUARY 7

MATTHEW 7:1-29

"Stop judging, that you may not be judged. For as you judge, so will you be judged, and the measure with which you measure will be measured out to you. Why do you notice the splinter in your brother's eye, but do not perceive the wooden beam in your own eye? How can you say to your brother, 'Let me remove that splinter from your eye,' while the wooden beam is in your eye? You hypocrite, remove the wooden beam from your eye first; then you will see clearly to remove the splinter from your brother's eye.

"Do not give what is holy to dogs, or throw your pearls before swine, lest they trample them underfoot, and turn and tear you to pieces.

"Ask and it will be given to you; seek and you will find; knock and the door will be opened to you. For everyone who asks, receives; and the one who seeks, finds; and to the one who knocks, the door will be opened. Which one of you would hand his son a stone when he asks for a loaf of bread, or a snake when he asks for a fish? If you then, who are wicked, know how to give good gifts to your children, how much more will your heavenly Father give good things to those who ask him.

"Do to others whatever you would have them do to you. This is the law and the prophets.

"Enter through the narrow gate; for the gate is wide and the road broad that leads to destruction, and those who enter through it are many. How narrow the gate and constricted the road that leads to life. And those who find it are few.

"Beware of false prophets, who come to you in sheep's clothing, but underneath are ravenous wolves. By their fruits you will know them. Do people pick grapes from thornbushes, or figs from thistles? Just so, every good tree bears good fruit, and a rotten tree bears bad fruit. A good tree cannot bear bad fruit, nor can a rotten tree bear good fruit. Every tree that does not bear good fruit will be cut down and thrown into the fire. So by their fruits you will know them.

"Not everyone who says to me, 'Lord, Lord,' will enter the kingdom of heaven, but only the one who does the will of my Father in heaven. Many will say to me on that day, 'Lord, Lord, did we not prophesy in your name? Did we not drive out demons in your name? Did we not do mighty deeds in your name?' Then I will declare to them solemnly, 'I never knew you. Depart from me, you evildoers.'

"Everyone who listens to these words of mine and acts on them will be like a wise man who built his house on rock. The rain fell, the floods came, and the winds blew and buffeted the house. But it did not collapse; it had been set solidly on rock. And everyone who listens to these words of mine but does not act on them will be like a fool who built his house on sand. The rain fell, the floods came, and the winds blew and buffeted the house. And it collapsed and was completely ruined."

When Jesus finished these words, the crowds were astonished at his teaching, for he taught them as one having authority, and not as their scribes.

PSALM 4:7-9

Many say, "Oh, that we might
　　see better times!"
　O LORD, let the light of your
　　countenance shine upon us!
You put gladness into my heart,
　　more than when grain and
　　wine abound.
As soon as I lie down, I fall
　　peacefully asleep,
　for you alone, O LORD,
　bring security to my dwelling.

PROVERBS 2:1-8

My son, if you receive my words / and treasure my commands, / Turning your ear to wisdom, / inclining your heart to understanding; / Yes, if you call to intelligence, / and to understanding raise your voice; / If you seek her like silver, / and like hidden treasures search her out: / Then will you understand the fear of the LORD; / the knowledge of God you will find; / For the LORD gives wisdom, / from his mouth come knowledge and understanding; / He has counsel in store for the upright, / he is the shield of those who walk honestly, / Guarding the paths of justice, / protecting the way of his pious ones.

JANUARY 8

MATTHEW 8:1-34

When Jesus came down from the mountain, great crowds followed him. And then a leper approached, did him homage, and said, "Lord, if you wish, you can make me clean." He stretched out his hand, touched him, and said, "I will do it. Be made clean." His leprosy was cleansed immediately. Then Jesus said to him,

"See that you tell no one, but go show yourself to the priest, and offer the gift that Moses prescribed; that will be proof for them."

When he entered Capernaum, a centurion approached him and appealed to him, saying, "Lord, my servant is lying at home paralyzed, suffering dreadfully." He said to him, "I will come and cure him." The centurion said in reply, "Lord, I am not worthy to have you enter under my roof; only say the word and my servant will be healed. For I too am a person subject to authority, with soldiers subject to me. And I say to one, 'Go,' and he goes; and to another, 'Come here,' and he comes; and to my slave, 'Do this,' and he does it." When Jesus heard this, he was amazed and said to those following him, "Amen, I say to you, in no one in Israel have I found such faith. I say to you, many will come from the east and the west, and will recline with Abraham, Isaac, and Jacob at the banquet in the kingdom of heaven, but the children of the kingdom will be driven out into the outer darkness, where there will be wailing and grinding of teeth." And Jesus said to the centurion, "You may go; as you have believed, let it be done for you." And at that very hour [his] servant was healed.

Jesus entered the house of Peter, and saw his mother-in-law lying in bed with a fever. He touched her hand, the fever left her, and she rose and waited on him.

When it was evening, they brought him many who were possessed by demons, and he drove out the spirits by a word and cured all the sick, to fulfill what had been said by Isaiah the prophet:

"He took away our infirmities
and bore our diseases."

When Jesus saw a crowd around him, he gave orders to cross to the other side. A scribe approached and said to him, "Teacher, I will follow you wherever you go." Jesus answered him, "Foxes have dens and birds of the sky have nests, but the Son of Man has nowhere to rest his head." Another of [his] disciples said to him, "Lord, let me go first and bury my father." But Jesus answered him, "Follow me, and let the dead bury their dead."

He got into a boat and his disciples followed him. Suddenly a violent storm came up on the sea, so that the boat was being swamped by waves; but he was asleep. They came and woke him, saying, "Lord, save us! We are perishing!" He said to them, "Why are you terrified, O you of little faith?" Then he got up, rebuked the winds and the sea, and there was great calm. The men were amazed and said, "What sort of man is this, whom even the winds and the sea obey?"

When he came to the other side, to the territory of the Gadarenes, two demoniacs who were coming from the tombs met him. They were so savage that no one could travel by that road. They cried out, "What have you to do with us, Son of God? Have you come here to torment us before the appointed time?" Some distance away a herd of many swine was feeding. The demons pleaded with him, "If you drive us out, send us into the herd of swine." And he said to them, "Go then!" They came out and entered the swine, and the whole herd rushed down the steep bank into the sea where they drowned. The swineherds ran away, and when they came to the town they reported everything, including what had happened to the demoniacs. Thereupon the whole town came out to meet Jesus, and when they saw him they begged him to leave their district.

PSALM 5:1-7

For the leader; with wind
*   instruments. A psalm of David.*
Hearken to my words, O LORD,
    attend to my sighing.
Heed my call for help,
    my king and my God!
To you I pray, O LORD;
    at dawn you hear my voice;
    at dawn I bring my plea
        expectantly before you.

For you, O God, delight not in
    wickedess;
    no evil man remains with you;
    the arrogant may not stand in
        your sight.
You hate all evildoers;
    you destroy all who speak
        falsehood;
The bloodthirsty and the deceitful
    the LORD abhors.

PROVERBS 2:9-19

Then you will understand rectitude and justice, / honesty, every good path; / For wisdom will enter your heart, / knowledge will please your soul, / Discretion will watch over you, / understanding will guard you; / Saving you from the way of evil men, / from men of perverse speech, / Who leave the straight paths / to walk in ways of darkness, / Who delight in doing evil, / rejoice in perversity; / Whose ways are crooked, / and devious their paths; / Saving you from the wife of another, / from the adulteress with her smooth words, / Who forsakes the companion of her youth / and forgets the pact with her God; / For her path sinks down to death, / and her footsteps lead to the shades; / None who enter thereon come back again, / or gain the paths of life.

JANUARY 9

MATTHEW 9:1-38

He entered a boat, made the crossing, and came into his own town. And there people brought to him a paralytic lying on a stretcher. When Jesus saw their faith, he said to the paralytic, "Courage, child, your sins are forgiven." At that, some of the scribes said to themselves, "This man is blaspheming." Jesus knew what they were thinking, and said, "Why do you harbor evil thoughts? Which is easier to say, 'Your sins are forgiven,' or to say, 'Rise and walk'? But that you may know that the Son of Man has authority on earth to forgive sins"— he then said to the paralytic, "Rise, pick up your stretcher, and go home." He rose and went home. When the crowds saw this they were struck with awe and glorified God who had given such authority to human beings.

As Jesus passed on from there, he saw a man named Matthew sitting at the customs post. He said to him, "Follow me." And he got up and followed him. While he was at table in his house, many tax collectors and sinners came and sat with Jesus and his disciples. The Pharisees saw this and said to his disciples, "Why does your teacher eat with tax collectors and sinners?" He heard this and said, "Those who are well do not need a physician, but the sick do. Go and learn the meaning of the words, 'I desire mercy, not sacrifice.' I did not come to call the righteous but sinners."

Then the disciples of John approached him and said, "Why do we and the Pharisees fast [much], but your disciples do not fast?" Jesus answered them, "Can the wedding guests mourn as long as the bridegroom is with them? The days will come when the bridegroom is taken away from them, and then they will fast. No one patches an old cloak with a piece of unshrunken cloth, for its fullness pulls away from the cloak and the tear gets worse. People do not put new wine into old wineskins. Otherwise the skins burst, the wine spills out, and the skins are ruined. Rather, they pour new wine into fresh wineskins, and both are preserved."

While he was saying these things to them, an official came forward, knelt down before him, and said, "My daughter has just died. But come, lay your hand on her, and she will live." Jesus rose and followed him, and so did his disciples. A woman suffering hemorrhages for twelve years came up behind him and touched the tassel on his cloak. She said to herself, "If only I can touch his cloak, I shall be cured." Jesus turned around and saw her, and said, "Courage, daughter! Your faith has saved you." And from that hour the woman was cured.

When Jesus arrived at the official's house and saw the flute players and the crowd who were making a commotion, he said, "Go away! The girl is not dead but sleeping." And they ridiculed him. When the crowd was put out, he came and took her by the hand, and the little girl arose. And news of this spread throughout all that land.

And as Jesus passed on from there, two blind men followed [him], crying out, "Son of David, have pity on us!" When he entered the house, the blind men approached him and Jesus said to them, "Do you believe that I can do this?" "Yes, Lord," they said to him. Then he touched their eyes and said, "Let it be done for you according to your faith." And their eyes were opened. Jesus warned them sternly, "See that no one knows about this." But they went out and spread word of him through all that land.

As they were going out, a demoniac who could not speak was brought to him, and when the demon was driven out the mute person spoke. The crowds were amazed and said, "Nothing like this has ever been seen in Israel." But the Pharisees said, "He drives out demons by the prince of demons."

Jesus went around to all the towns and villages, teaching in their synagogues, proclaiming the gospel of the kingdom, and curing every disease and illness. At the sight of the crowds, his heart was moved with pity for them because they were troubled and abandoned, like sheep without a shepherd. Then he said to his disciples, "The harvest is abundant but the laborers are few; so ask the master of the harvest to send out laborers for his harvest."

PSALM 5:8-13

But I, because of your abundant
    kindness,
    will enter your house;
I will worship at your holy
    temple

in fear of you, O LORD;
Because of my enemies, guide me
    in your justice;
    make straight your way before
    me.
For in their mouth there is no
    sincerity;
    their heart teems with
    treacheries.
Their throat is an open grave;
    they flatter with their tongue.
Punish them, O God;
    let them fall by their own
    devices;

For their many sins, cast them
    out
    because they have rebelled
    against you.
But let all who take refuge in you
    be glad and exult forever.
Protect them, that you may be
    the joy
    of those who love your name.
For you, O LORD, bless the just
    man;
    you surround him with the
    shield of your good will.

PROVERBS 2:20-22

Thus you may walk in the way of good men, / and keep to the paths of the just. /
For the upright will dwell in the land, / the honest will remain in it; / But the
wicked will be cut off from the land, / the faithless will be rooted out of it.

JANUARY 10

MATTHEW 10:1-42

Then he summoned his twelve disciples and gave them authority over unclean spirits to drive them out and to cure every disease and every illness. The names of the twelve apostles are these: first, Simon called Peter, and his brother Andrew; James, the son of Zebedee, and his brother John; Philip and Bartholomew, Thomas and Matthew the tax collector; James, the son of Alphaeus, and Thaddeus; Simon the Cananean, and Judas Iscariot who betrayed him.

Jesus sent out these twelve after instructing them thus, "Do not go into pagan territory or enter a Samaritan town. Go rather to the lost sheep of the house of Israel. As you go, make this proclamation: 'The kingdom of heaven is at hand.' Cure the sick, raise the dead, cleanse lepers, drive out demons. Without cost you have received; without cost you are to give. Do not take gold or silver or copper for your belts; no sack for the journey, or a second tunic, or sandals, or walking stick. The laborer deserves his keep. Whatever town or village you enter, look for a worthy person in it, and stay there until you leave. As you enter a house, wish it peace. If the house is worthy, let your peace come upon it; if not, let your peace return to you. Whoever will not receive you or listen to your words—go outside that house or town and shake the dust from your feet. Amen, I say to you, it will be more tolerable for the land of Sodom and Gomorrah on the day of judgment than for that town.

"Behold, I am sending you like

sheep in the midst of wolves; so be shrewd as serpents and simple as doves. But beware of people, for they will hand you over to courts and scourge you in their synagogues, and you will be led before governors and kings for my sake as a witness before them and the pagans. When they hand you over, do not worry about how you are to speak or what you are to say. You will be given at that moment what you are to say. For it will not be you who speak but the Spirit of your Father speaking through you. Brother will hand over brother to death, and the father his child; children will rise up against parents and have them put to death. You will be hated by all because of my name, but whoever endures to the end will be saved. When they persecute you in one town, flee to another. Amen, I say to you, you will not finish the towns of Israel before the Son of Man comes. No disciple is above his teacher, no slave above his master. It is enough for the disciple that he become like his teacher, for the slave that he become like his master. If they have called the master of the house Beelzebul, how much more those of his household!

"Therefore do not be afraid of them. Nothing is concealed that will not be revealed, nor secret that will not be known. What I say to you in the darkness, speak in the light; what you hear whispered, proclaim on the housetops. And do not be afraid of those who kill the body but cannot kill the soul; rather, be afraid of the one who can destroy both soul and body in Gehenna. Are not two sparrows sold for a small coin? Yet not one of them falls to the ground without your Father's knowledge. Even all the hairs of your head are counted. So do not be afraid; you are worth more than many sparrows. Everyone who acknowledges me before others I will acknowledge before my heavenly Father. But whoever denies me before others, I will deny before my heavenly Father.

"Do not think that I have come to bring peace upon the earth. I have come to bring not peace but the sword. For I have come to set

a man 'against his father,
  a daughter against her
    mother,
and a daughter-in-law against
    her mother-in-law;
  and one's enemies
  will be those of his household.'

"Whoever loves father or mother more than me is not worthy of me, and whoever loves son or daughter more than me is not worthy of me; and whoever does not take up his cross and follow after me is not worthy of me. Whoever finds his life will lose it, and whoever loses his life for my sake will find it.

"Whoever receives you receives me, and whoever receives me receives the one who sent me. Whoever receives a prophet because he is a prophet will receive a prophet's reward, and whoever receives a righteous man because he is righteous will receive a righteous man's reward. And whoever gives only a cup of cold water to one of these little ones to drink because he is a disciple—amen, I say to you, he will surely not lose his reward."

PSALM 6:1-4

*For the leader; with stringed
    instruments, "upon the eighth."
    A psalm of David.*

O LORD, reprove me not in your
   anger,
   nor chastise me in your wrath.
Have pity on me, O LORD, for I
   am languishing;
heal me, O LORD, for my body
   is in terror;
My soul, too, is utterly terrified;
   but you, O LORD, how
   long . . . ?

PROVERBS 3:1-4

*My son, forget not my teaching, / keep in mind my commands; / For many days,
and years of life, / and peace, will they bring you. / Let not kindness and fidelity
leave you; / bind them around your neck; / Then will you win favor and good
esteem / before God and man.*

JANUARY 11

MATTHEW 11:1-30

When Jesus finished giving
these commands to his twelve disciples, he went away from that
place to teach and to preach in
their towns.

When John heard in prison of
the works of the Messiah, he sent
his disciples to him with this
question, "Are you the one who
is to come, or should we look for
another?" Jesus said to them in
reply, "Go and tell John what
you hear and see: the blind regain their sight, the lame walk,
lepers are cleansed, the deaf
hear, the dead are raised, and the
poor have the good news proclaimed to them. And blessed is
the one who takes no offense at
me."

As they were going off, Jesus
began to speak to the crowds
about John, "What did you go out
to the desert to see? A reed
swayed by the wind? Then what
did you go out to see? Someone
dressed in fine clothing? Those
who wear fine clothing are in
royal palaces. Then why did you
go out? To see a prophet? Yes, I
tell you, and more than a prophet.

This is the one about whom it is
written;

> 'Behold, I am sending my
>   messenger ahead of you;
>   he will prepare your way
>   before you.'

Amen, I say to you, among those
born of women there has been
none greater than John the Baptist; yet the least in the kingdom
of heaven is greater than he. From
the days of John the Baptist until
now, the kingdom of heaven suffers violence, and the violent are
taking it by force. All the prophets
and the law prophesied up to the
time of John. And if you are willing to accept it, he is Elijah, the
one who is to come. Whoever has
ears ought to hear.

"To what shall I compare this
generation? It is like children who
sit in marketplaces and call to one
another, 'We played the flute for
you, but you did not dance, we
sang a dirge but you did not
mourn.' For John came neither eating nor drinking, and they said,
'He is possessed by a demon.' The
Son of Man came eating and drink-

ing and they said, 'Look, he is a glutton and a drunkard, a friend of tax collectors and sinners.' But wisdom is vindicated by her works."

Then he began to reproach the towns where most of his mighty deeds had been done, since they had not repented. "Woe to you, Chorazin! Woe to you, Bethsaida! For if the mighty deeds done in your midst had been done in Tyre and Sidon, they would long ago have repented in sackcloth and ashes. But I tell you, it will be more tolerable for Tyre and Sidon on the day of judgment than for you. And as for you, Capernaum:

'Will you be exalted to heaven?
    You will go down to the
    netherworld.'

For if the mighty deeds done in your midst had been done in Sodom, it would have remained until this day. But I tell you, it will be more tolerable for the land of Sodom on the day of judgment than for you."

At that time Jesus said in reply, "I give praise to you, Father, Lord of heaven and earth, for although you have hidden these things from the wise and the learned you have revealed them to the childlike. Yes, Father, such has been your gracious will. All things have been handed over to me by my Father. No one knows the Son except the Father, and no one knows the Father except the Son and anyone to whom the Son wishes to reveal him.

"Come to me, all you who labor and are burdened, and I will give you rest. Take my yoke upon you and learn from me, for I am meek and humble of heart; and you will find rest for yourselves. For my yoke is easy, and my burden light."

PSALM 6:5-11

Return, O LORD, save my life;
    rescue me because of your
        kindness,
For among the dead no one
        remembers you;
    in the nether world who gives
        you thanks?
I am wearied with sighing;
    every night I flood my bed with
        weeping;
    I drench my couch with my
        tears.
My eyes are dimmed with
        sorrow;
    they have aged because of all
        my foes.
Depart from me, all evildoers,
    for the LORD has heard the
        sound of my weeping;
The LORD has heard my plea;
    the LORD has accepted my
        prayer.
All my enemies shall be put to
        shame in utter terror;
    they shall fall back in sudden
        shame.

PROVERBS 3:5-8

Trust in the LORD with all your heart, / on your own intelligence rely not; / In all your ways be mindful of him, / and he will make straight your paths. / Be not wise in your own eyes, / fear the LORD and turn away from evil; / This will mean health for your flesh / and vigor for your bones.

MATTHEW 12:1-50

At that time Jesus was going through a field of grain on the sabbath. His disciples were hungry and began to pick the heads of grain and eat them. When the Pharisees saw this, they said to him, "See, your disciples are doing what is unlawful to do on the sabbath." He said to them, "Have you not read what David did when he and his companions were hungry, how he went into the house of God and ate the bread of offering, which neither he nor his companions but only the priests could lawfully eat? Or have you not read in the law that on the sabbath the priests serving in the temple violate the sabbath and are innocent? I say to you, something greater than the temple is here. If you knew what this meant, 'I desire mercy, not sacrifice,' you would not have condemned these innocent men. For the Son of Man is Lord of the sabbath."

Moving on from there, he went into their synagogue. And behold, there was a man there who had a withered hand. They questioned him, "Is it lawful to cure on the sabbath?" so that they might accuse him. He said to them, "Which one of you who has a sheep that falls into a pit on the sabbath will not take hold of it and lift it out? How much more valuable a person is than a sheep. So it is lawful to do good on the sabbath." Then he said to the man, "Stretch out your hand." He stretched it out, and it was restored as sound as the other. But the Pharisees went out and took counsel against him to put him to death.

When Jesus realized this, he withdrew from that place. Many [people] followed him, and he cured them all, but he warned them not to make him known. This was to fulfill what had been spoken through Isaiah the prophet:

"Behold, my servant whom I
  have chosen,
    my beloved in whom I
    delight;
I shall place my spirit upon
  him,
    and he will proclaim justice
    to the Gentiles.
He will not contend or cry out,
  nor will anyone hear his
  voice in the streets.
A bruised reed he will not
  break,
    a smoldering wick he will not
    quench,
until he brings justice to
  victory.
    And in his name the Gentiles
    will hope."

Then they brought to him a demoniac who was blind and mute. He cured the mute person so that he could speak and see. All the crowd was astounded, and said, "Could this perhaps be the Son of David?" But when the Pharisees heard this, they said, "This man drives out demons only by the power of Beelzebul, the prince of demons." But he knew what they were thinking and said to them, "Every kingdom divided against itself will be laid waste, and no town or house divided against itself will stand. And if Satan drives out Satan, he is divided against himself; how, then, will his kingdom stand? And if I drive out demons by Beelzebul, by whom do your own people drive them out? Therefore they will be your judges. But if it is by the Spirit of God that I drive out demons, then the kingdom of God has come upon you. How can anyone enter a strong man's house and steal his property, unless he first ties up the strong man? Then he can plunder his house. Whoever is not with me is against me, and whoever does not gather with me scatters. Therefore, I say to you, every sin and blasphemy will be forgiven people, but blasphemy against the Spirit will not be forgiven. And whoever speaks a word against the Son of Man will be forgiven; but whoever speaks against the holy Spirit will not be forgiven, either in this age or in the age to come.

"Either declare the tree good and its fruit is good, or declare the tree rotten and its fruit is rotten, for a tree is known by its fruit. You brood of vipers, how can you say good things when you are evil? For from the fullness of the heart the mouth speaks. A good person brings forth good out of a store of goodness, but an evil person brings forth evil out of a store of evil. I tell you, on the day of judgment people will render an account for every careless word they speak. By your words you will be acquitted, and by your words you will be condemned."

Then some of the scribes and Pharisees said to him, "Teacher, we wish to see a sign from you." He said to them in reply, "An evil and unfaithful generation seeks a sign, but no sign will be given it except the sign of Jonah the prophet. Just as Jonah was in the belly of the whale three days and three nights, so will the Son of Man be in the heart of the earth three days and three nights. At the judgment, the men of Nineveh will arise with this generation and condemn it, because they repented at the preaching of Jonah; and there is something greater than Jonah here. At the judgment the queen of the south will arise with this generation and condemn it, because she came from the ends of the earth to hear the wisdom of Solomon; and there is something greater than Solomon here.

"When an unclean spirit goes out of a person it roams through arid regions searching for rest but finds none. Then it says, 'I will return to my home from which I came.' But upon returning, it finds it empty, swept clean, and put in order. Then it goes and brings back with itself seven other spirits more evil than itself, and they move in and dwell there; and the last condition of that person is worse than the first. Thus it will be with this evil generation."

While he was still speaking to the crowds, his mother and his brothers appeared outside, wishing to speak with him. [Someone told him, "Your mother and your brothers are standing outside, asking to speak with you."] But he said in reply to the one who told him, "Who is my mother? Who are my brothers?" And stretching out his hand toward his disciples, he said, "Here are my mother and my brothers. For whoever does the will of my heavenly Father is my brother, and sister, and mother."

PSALM 7:1-6

*A plaintive song of David, which he
    sang to the LORD because of
    Cush the Benjaminite.*

O LORD, my God, in you I take
    refuge;
    save me from my pursuers and
    rescue me,
Lest I become like the lion's prey,
    to be torn to pieces, with no
    one to rescue me.
O LORD, my God, if I am at fault
    in this,
    if there is guilt on my hands,
If I have repaid my friend with
    evil,
    I who spared those who
    without cause were my
    foes—
Let the enemy pursue and
    overtake me;
    let him trample my life to the
    ground,
    and lay my glory in the dust.

PROVERBS 3:9-10

*Honor the LORD with your wealth, / with first fruits of all your produce; / Then
will your barns be filled with grain, / with new wine your vats will overflow.*

JANUARY 13

MATTHEW 13:1-30

On that day, Jesus went out of
the house and sat down by the
sea. Such large crowds gathered
around him that he got into a boat
and sat down, and the whole
crowd stood along the shore. And
he spoke to them at length in parables, saying: "A sower went out to
sow. And as he sowed, some seed
fell on the path, and birds came
and ate it up. Some fell on rocky
ground, where it had little soil. It
sprang up at once because the soil
was not deep, and when the sun
rose it was scorched, and it withered for lack of roots. Some seed
fell among thorns, and the thorns
grew up and choked it. But some
seed fell on rich soil, and produced fruit, a hundred or sixty or
thirtyfold. Whoever has ears
ought to hear."

The disciples approached him
and said, "Why do you speak to
them in parables?" He said to
them in reply, "Because knowledge of the mysteries of the kingdom of heaven has been granted
to you, but to them it has not been
granted. To anyone who has,
more will be given and he will
grow rich; from anyone who has
not, even what he has will be
taken away. This is why I speak to
them in parables, because 'they
look but do not see and hear but
do not listen or understand.'
Isaiah's prophecy is fulfilled in
them, which says:

'You shall indeed hear but not
    understand,
    you shall indeed look but
    never see.
Gross is the heart of this
    people,
    they will hardly hear with
    their ears,

they have closed their
eyes,
  lest they see with their
  eyes
and hear with their ears
and understand with their
    hearts and be converted,
  and I heal them.'

"But blessed are your eyes, because they see, and your ears, because they hear. Amen, I say to you, many prophets and righteous people longed to see what you see but did not see it, and to hear what you hear but did not hear it.

"Hear then the parable of the sower. The seed sown on the path is the one who hears the word of the kingdom without understanding it, and the evil one comes and steals away what was sown in his heart. The seed sown on rocky ground is the one who hears the word and receives it at once with joy. But he has no root and lasts only for a time. When some tribulation or persecution comes because of the word, he immediately falls away. The seed sown among thorns is the one who hears the word, but then worldly anxiety and the lure of riches choke the word and it bears no fruit. But the seed sown on rich soil is the one who hears the word and understands it, who indeed bears fruit and yields a hundred or sixty or thirtyfold."

He proposed another parable to them. "The kingdom of heaven may be likened to a man who sowed good seed in his field. While everyone was asleep his enemy came and sowed weeds all through the wheat, and then went off. When the crop grew and bore fruit, the weeds appeared as well. The slaves of the householder came to him and said, 'Master, did you not sow good seed in your field? Where have the weeds come from?' He answered, 'An enemy has done this.' His slaves said to him, 'Do you want us to go and pull them up?' He replied, 'No, if you pull up the weeds you might uproot the wheat along with them. Let them grow together until harvest; then at harvest time I will say to the harvesters, "First collect the weeds and tie them in bundles for burning; but gather the wheat into my barn." ' "

PSALM 7:7-10

Rise up, O LORD, in your anger;
  rise against the fury of my foes;
  wake to the judgment you have
    decreed.
Let the assembly of the peoples
    surround you;
  above them on high be
    enthroned.
[The LORD judges the nations.]
Do me justice, O LORD, because I
    am just,
  and because of the innocence
    that is mine.
Let the malice of the wicked come
    to an end,
  but sustain the just,
  O searcher of heart and soul, O
    just God.

PROVERBS 3:11-12

The discipline of the LORD, my son, disdain not; / spurn not his reproof; / For whom the LORD loves he reproves, / and he chastises the son he favors.

MATTHEW 13:31-58

He proposed another parable to them. "The kingdom of heaven is like a mustard seed that a person took and sowed in a field. It is the smallest of all the seeds, yet when full-grown it is the largest of plants. It becomes a large bush, and the 'birds of the sky come and dwell in its branches.' "

He spoke to them another parable. "The kingdom of heaven is like yeast that a woman took and mixed with three measures of wheat flour until the whole batch was leavened."

All these things Jesus spoke to the crowds in parables. He spoke to them only in parables, to fulfill what had been said through the prophet:

"I will open my mouth in
   parables,
   I will announce what has lain
   hidden from the foundation
   [of the world]."

Then, dismissing the crowds, he went into the house. His disciples approached him and said, "Explain to us the parable of the weeds in the field." He said in reply, "He who sows good seed is the Son of Man, the field is the world, the good seed the children of the kingdom. The weeds are the children of the evil one, and the enemy who sows them is the devil. The harvest is the end of the age, and the harvesters are angels. Just as weeds are collected and burned [up] with fire, so will it be at the end of the age. The Son of Man will send his angels, and they will collect out of his kingdom all who cause others to sin and all evildoers. They will throw them into the fiery furnace, where there will be wailing and grinding of teeth. Then the righteous will shine like the sun in the kingdom of their Father. Whoever has ears ought to hear.

"The kingdom of heaven is like treasure buried in a field, which a person finds and hides again, and out of joy goes and sells all that he has and buys that field. Again, the kingdom of heaven is like a merchant searching for fine pearls. When he finds a pearl of great price, he goes and sells all that he has and buys it. Again, the kingdom of heaven is like a net thrown into the sea, which collects fish of every kind. When it is full they haul it ashore and sit down to put what is good into buckets. What is bad they throw away. Thus it will be at the end of the age. The angels will go out and separate the wicked from the righteous and throw them into the fiery furnace, where there will be wailing and grinding of teeth.

"Do you understand all these things?" They answered, "Yes." And he replied, "Then every scribe who has been instructed in the kingdom of heaven is like the head of a household who brings from his storeroom both the new and the old." When Jesus finished these parables, he went away from there.

He came to his native place and taught the people in their synagogue. They were astonished and said, "Where did this man get such wisdom and mighty deeds? Is he not the carpenter's son? Is not his mother named Mary and his brothers James, Joseph, Simon, and Judas? Are not his sisters all with us? Where did this man get all this?" And they took offense at him. But Jesus said to them, "A prophet is not without honor except in his native place and in his own house." And he did not work many mighty deeds there because of their lack of faith.

PSALM 7:11-18

A shield before me is God,
    who saves the upright of heart;
A just judge is God,
    a God who punishes day by
      day.
Unless they be converted, God
    will sharpen his sword;

    he will bend and aim his bow,
Prepare his deadly weapons
    against them,
    and use fiery darts for arrows.
He who conceived iniquity and
    was pregnant with mischief,
    brings forth failure.
He has opened a hole, he has
    dug it deep,
    but he falls into the pit which
      he has made.
His mischief shall recoil upon his
    own head;
    upon the crown of his head his
    violence shall rebound.
I will give thanks to the LORD for
    his justice,
    and sing praise to the name of
    the LORD Most High.

PROVERBS 3:13-18

Happy the man who finds wisdom, / the man who gains understanding! / For her profit is better than profit in silver, / and better than gold is her revenue; / She is more precious than corals, / and none of your choice possessions can compare with her. / Long life is in her right hand, / in her left are riches and honor; / Her ways are pleasant ways, / and all her paths are peace; / She is a tree of life to those who grasp her, / and he is happy who holds her fast.

JANUARY 15

MATTHEW 14:1-36

At that time Herod the tetrarch heard of the reputation of Jesus and said to his servants, "This man is John the Baptist. He has been raised from the dead; that is why mighty powers are at work in him."

Now Herod had arrested John, bound [him], and put him in prison on account of Herodias, the wife of his brother Philip, for John had said to him, "It is not lawful for you to have her." Although he wanted to kill him, he feared the people, for they re-

garded him as a prophet. But at a birthday celebration for Herod, the daughter of Herodias performed a dance before the guests and delighted Herod so much that he swore to give her whatever she might ask for. Prompted by her mother, she said, "Give me here on a platter the head of John the Baptist." The king was distressed, but because of his oaths and the guests who were present, he ordered that it be given, and he had John beheaded in the prison. His head was brought in on a platter and given to the girl, who took it to her mother. His disciples came and took away the corpse and buried him; and they went and told Jesus.

When Jesus heard of it, he withdrew in a boat to a deserted place by himself. The crowds heard of this and followed him on foot from their towns. When he disembarked and saw the vast crowd, his heart was moved with pity for them, and he cured their sick. When it was evening, the disciples approached him and said, "This is a deserted place and it is already late; dismiss the crowds so that they can go to the villages and buy food for themselves." [Jesus] said to them, "There is no need for them to go away; give them some food yourselves." But they said to him, "Five loaves and two fish are all we have here." Then he said, "Bring them here to me," and he ordered the crowds to sit down on the grass. Taking the five loaves and the two fish, and looking up to heaven, he said the blessing, broke the loaves, and gave them to the disciples, who in turn gave them to the crowds. They all ate and were satisfied, and they picked up the fragments left over—twelve wicker baskets full. Those who ate were about five thousand men, not counting women and children.

Then he made the disciples get into the boat and precede him to the other side, while he dismissed the crowds. After doing so, he went up on the mountain by himself to pray. When it was evening he was there alone. Meanwhile the boat, already a few miles offshore, was being tossed about by the waves, for the wind was against it. During the fourth watch of the night, he came toward them, walking on the sea. When the disciples saw him walking on the sea they were terrified. "It is a ghost," they said, and they cried out in fear. At once [Jesus] spoke to them, "Take courage, it is I; do not be afraid." Peter said to him in reply, "Lord, if it is you, command me to come to you on the water." He said, "Come." Peter got out of the boat and began to walk on the water toward Jesus. But when he saw how [strong] the wind was he became frightened; and, beginning to sink, he cried out, "Lord, save me!" Immediately Jesus stretched out his hand and caught him, and said to him, "O you of little faith, why did you doubt?" After they got into the boat, the wind died down. Those who were in the boat did him homage, saying, "Truly, you are the Son of God."

After making the crossing, they came to land at Gennesaret. When the men of that place recognized him, they sent word to all the surrounding country. People brought to him all those who were sick and begged him that they might touch only the tassel on his cloak, and as many as touched it were healed.

PSALM 8:1-5

For the leader; "upon the gittith." A psalm of David.

O LORD, our Lord,
   how glorious is your name
      over all the earth!
   You have exalted your majesty
      above the heavens.
Out of the mouths of babes and
      sucklings
   you have fashioned praise
      because of your foes,
   to silence the hostile and the
      vengeful.
When I behold your heavens, the
      work of your fingers,

the moon and the stars which
you set in place—
What is man that you should be
mindful of him,

or the son of man that you
should care for him?"

PROVERBS 3:19-20

The LORD by wisdom founded the earth, / established the heavens by understanding; / By his knowledge the depths break open, / and the clouds drop down dew.

JANUARY 16

MATTHEW 15:1-39

Then Pharisees and scribes came to Jesus from Jerusalem and said, "Why do your disciples break the tradition of the elders? They do not wash [their] hands when they eat a meal." He said to them in reply, "And why do you break the commandment of God for the sake of your tradition? For God said, 'Honor your father and your mother,' and 'Whoever curses father or mother shall die.' But you say, 'Whoever says to father or mother, "Any support you might have had from me is dedicated to God," need not honor his father.' You have nullified the word of God for the sake of your tradition. Hypocrites, well did Isaiah prophesy about you when he said:

'This people honors me with
their lips,
but their hearts are far from
me;
in vain do they worship me,
teaching as doctrines human
precepts.' "

He summoned the crowd and said to them, "Hear and understand. It is not what enters one's mouth that defiles that person; but what comes out of the mouth is what defiles one." Then his disciples approached and said to him, "Do you know that the Pharisees took offense when they heard what you said?" He said in reply, "Every plant that my heavenly Father has not planted will be uprooted. Let them alone; they are blind guides [of the blind]. If a blind person leads a blind person, both will fall into a pit." Then Peter said to him in reply, "Explain [this] parable to us." He said to them, "Are even you still without understanding? Do you not realize that everything that enters the mouth passes into the stomach and is expelled into the latrine? But the things that come out of the mouth come from the heart, and they defile. For from the heart come evil thoughts, murder, adultery, unchastity, theft, false witness, blasphemy. These are what defile a person, but to eat with unwashed hands does not defile."

Then Jesus went from that place and withdrew to the region of Tyre and Sidon. And behold, a Canaanite woman of that district came and called out, "Have pity on me, Lord, Son of David! My daughter is tormented by a demon." But he did not say a word in answer to her. His disciples came and asked him, "Send her away, for she keeps calling out after us." He said in reply, "I was sent only to the lost sheep of the house of Israel." But the woman came and did him homage, saying, "Lord, help me." He said in reply, "It is not right to take the food of the children and throw it to the dogs." She said, "Please, Lord, for even the dogs eat the scraps that fall from the table of their masters." Then Jesus said to her in reply, "O woman, great is your faith! Let it be done for you as you wish." And her daughter was healed from that hour.

Moving on from there Jesus walked by the Sea of Galilee, went up on the mountain, and sat down there. Great crowds came to him, having with them the lame, the blind, the deformed, the mute, and many others. They placed them at his feet, and he cured them. The crowds were amazed when they saw the mute speaking, the deformed made whole, the lame walking, and the blind able to see, and they glorified the God of Israel.

Jesus summoned his disciples and said, "My heart is moved with pity for the crowd, for they have been with me now for three days and have nothing to eat. I do not want to send them away hungry, for fear they may collapse on the way." The disciples said to him, "Where could we ever get enough bread in this deserted place to satisfy such a crowd?" Jesus said to them, "How many loaves do you have?" "Seven," they replied, "and a few fish." He ordered the crowd to sit down on the ground. Then he took the seven loaves and the fish, gave thanks, broke the loaves, and gave them to the disciples, who in turn gave them to the crowds. They all ate and were satisfied. They picked up the fragments left over—seven baskets full. Those who ate were four thousand men, not counting women and children. And when he had dismissed the crowds, he got into the boat and came to the district of Magadan.

PSALM 8:6-10

You have made him little less
    than the angels,
    and crowned him with glory
    and honor.
You have given him rule over the
    works of your hands,
    putting all things under his
    feet:
All sheep and oxen,
    yes, and the beasts of the field,
The birds of the air, the fishes of
    the sea,
    and whatever swims the paths
    of the seas.
O LORD, our LORD,
    how glorious is your name
    over all the earth!

PROVERBS 3:21-24, 35, 25-26

My son, let not these slip out of your sight; / keep advice and counsel in view; / So will they be life to your soul, / and an adornment for your neck. / Then you may securely go your way; / your foot will never stumble; / When you lie down, you need not be afraid, / when you rest, your sleep will be sweet. / Honor is the possession of wise men, / but fools inherit shame. / Be not afraid of sudden terror, / of the ruin of the wicked when it comes; / For the LORD will be your confidence, / and will keep your foot from the snare.

MATTHEW 16:1-28

The Pharisees and Sadducees came and, to test him, asked him to show them a sign from heaven. He said to them in reply, "[In the evening you say, 'Tomorrow will be fair, for the sky is red'; and, in the morning, 'Today will be stormy, for the sky is red and threatening.' You know how to judge the appearance of the sky, but you cannot judge the signs of the times.] An evil and unfaithful generation seeks a sign, but no sign will be given it except the sign of Jonah." Then he left them and went away.

In coming to the other side of the sea, the disciples had forgotten to bring bread. Jesus said to them, "Look out, and beware of the leaven of the Pharisees and Sadducees." They concluded among themselves, saying, "It is because we have brought no bread." When Jesus became aware of this he said, "You of little faith, why do you conclude among yourselves that it is because you have no bread? Do you not yet understand, and do you not remember the five loaves for the five thousand, and how many wicker baskets you took up? Or the seven loaves for the four thousand, and how many baskets you took up? How do you not comprehend that I was not speaking to you about bread? Beware of the leaven of the Pharisees and Sadducees." Then they understood that he was not telling them to beware of the leaven of bread, but of the teaching of the Pharisees and Sadducees.

When Jesus went into the region of Caesarea Philippi he asked his disciples, "Who do people say that the Son of Man is?" They replied, "Some say John the Baptist, others Elijah, still others Jeremiah or one of the prophets." He said to them, "But who do you say that I am?" Simon Peter said in reply, "You are the Messiah, the Son of the living God." Jesus said to him in reply, "Blessed are you, Simon son of Jonah. For flesh and blood has not revealed this to you, but my heavenly Father. And so I say to you, you are Peter, and upon this rock I will build my church, and the gates of the netherworld shall not prevail against it. I will give you the keys to the kingdom of heaven. Whatever you bind on earth shall be bound in heaven; and whatever you loose on earth shall be loosed in heaven." Then he strictly ordered his disciples to tell no one that he was the Messiah.

From that time on, Jesus began to show his disciples that he must go to Jerusalem and suffer greatly from the elders, the chief priests, and the scribes, and be killed and on the third day be raised. Then Peter took him aside and began to rebuke him, "God forbid, Lord! No such thing shall ever happen to you." He turned and said to Peter, "Get behind me, Satan! You are an obstacle to me. You are thinking not as God does, but as human beings do."

Then Jesus said to his disciples, "Whoever wishes to come after me must deny himself, take up his cross, and follow me. For whoever wishes to save his life will lose it, but whoever loses his life for my sake will find it. What profit would there be for one to gain the whole world and forfeit his life? Or what can one give in exchange for his life? For the Son of Man will come with his angels in his Father's glory, and then he will repay everyone according to his conduct. Amen, I say to you, there are some standing here who will not taste death until they see the Son of Man coming in his kingdom."

PSALM 9:1-7

For the leader; according to Muth labben. A psalm of David.
I will give thanks to you, O
  LORD, with all my heart;
  I will declare all your
    wondrous deeds.

I will be glad and exult in you;
  I will sing praise to your name,
    Most High,
Because my enemies are turned
    back,
  overthrown and destroyed
    before you.
For you upheld my right and my
    cause,
  seated on your throne, judging
    justly.
You rebuked the nations and
    destroyed the wicked;
  their name you blotted out
    forever and ever.
The enemies are ruined
    completely forever;
  the remembrance of the cities
    you uprooted has perished.

PROVERBS 3:27-32

Refuse no one the good on which he has a claim / when it is in your power to do it for him. / Say not to your neighbor, "Go, and come again, / tomorrow I will give," when you can give at once. / Plot no evil against your neighbor, / against him who lives at peace with you. / Quarrel not with a man without cause, / with one who has done you no harm. / Envy not the lawless man / and choose none of his ways: / To the LORD the perverse man is an abomination, / but with the upright is his friendship.

JANUARY 18

MATTHEW 17:1-27

After six days Jesus took Peter, James, and John his brother, and led them up a high mountain by themselves. And he was transfigured before them; his face shone like the sun and his clothes became white as light. And behold, Moses and Elijah appeared to them, conversing with him. Then Peter said to Jesus in reply, "Lord, it is good that we are here. If you wish, I will make three tents here, one for you, one for Moses, and one for Elijah." While he was still speaking, behold, a bright cloud cast a shadow over them, then from the cloud came a voice that said, "This is my beloved Son, with whom I am well pleased; listen to him." When the disciples heard this, they fell prostrate and were very much afraid. But Jesus came and touched them, saying, "Rise, and do not be afraid." And when the disciples raised their eyes, they saw no one else but Jesus alone.

As they were coming down from the mountain, Jesus charged them, "Do not tell the vision to anyone until the Son of Man has been raised from the dead." Then the disciples asked him, "Why do the scribes say that Elijah must come first?" He said in reply, "Elijah will indeed come and restore all things; but I tell you that Elijah has already come, and they did not recognize him but did to him whatever they pleased. So also will the Son of Man suffer at their hands." Then the disciples understood that he was speaking to them of John the Baptist.

When they came to the crowd a man approached, knelt down before him, and said, "Lord, have pity on my son, for he is a lunatic and suffers severely; often he falls into fire, and often into water. I brought him to your disciples, but they could not cure him." Jesus said in reply, "O faithless and perverse generation, how long will I be with you? How long will I endure you? Bring him here to me." Jesus rebuked him and the demon came out of him, and from that hour the boy was cured. Then the disciples approached Jesus in private and said, "Why could we not drive it out?" He said to them, "Because of your little faith. Amen, I say to you, if you have faith the size of a mustard seed, you will say to this mountain, 'Move from here to there,' and it will move. Nothing will be impossible for you."

As they were gathering in Galilee, Jesus said to them, "The Son of Man is to be handed over to men, and they will kill him, and he will be raised on the third day." And they were overwhelmed with grief.

When they came to Capernaum, the collectors of the temple tax approached Peter and said, "Doesn't your teacher pay the temple tax?" "Yes," he said. When he came into the house, before he had time to speak, Jesus asked him, "What is your opinion, Simon? From whom do the kings of the earth take tolls or census tax? From their subjects or from foreigners?" When he said, "From foreigners," Jesus said to him, "Then the subjects are exempt. But that we may not offend them, go to the sea, drop in a hook, and take the first fish that comes up. Open its mouth and you will find a coin worth twice the temple tax. Give that to them for me and for you."

PSALM 9:8-11

But the LORD sits enthroned
    forever;
  he has set up his throne for
    judgment.
He judges the world with justice;
  he governs the peoples with
    equity.
The LORD is a stronghold for the
    oppressed,
  a stronghold in times of
    distress.
They trust in you who cherish
    your name,
  for you forsake not those who
    seek you, O LORD.

PROVERBS 3:33-34

The curse of the LORD is on the house of the wicked, / but the dwelling of the just he blesses; / When he is dealing with the arrogant, he is stern, / but to the humble he shows kindness.

JANUARY 19

MATTHEW 18:1-35

At that time the disciples approached Jesus and said, "Who is the greatest in the kingdom of heaven?" He called a child over, placed it in their midst, and said, "Amen, I say to you, unless you turn and become like children, you will not enter the kingdom of heaven. Whoever humbles himself like this child is the greatest in the kingdom of heaven. And whoever receives one child such as this in my name receives me.

"Whoever causes one of these little ones who believe in me to sin, it would be better for him to have a great millstone hung around his neck and to be drowned in the depths of the sea. Woe to the world because of things that cause sin! Such things must come, but woe to the one through whom they come! If your hand or foot causes you to sin, cut it off and throw it away. It is better for you to enter into life maimed or crippled than with two hands or two feet to be thrown into eternal fire. And if your eye causes you to sin, tear it out and throw it away. It is better for you to enter into life with one eye than with two eyes to be thrown into fiery Gehenna.

"See that you do not despise one of these little ones, for I say to you that their angels in heaven always look upon the face of my heavenly Father. What is your opinion? If a man has a hundred sheep and one of them goes astray, will he not leave the ninety-nine in the hills and go in search of the stray? And if he finds it, amen, I say to you, he rejoices more over it than over the ninety-nine that did not stray. In just the same way, it is not the will of your heavenly Father that one of these little ones be lost.

"If your brother sins [against you], go and tell him his fault between you and him alone. If he listens to you, you have won over your brother. If he does not listen, take one or two others along with you, so that 'every fact may be established on the testimony of two or three witnesses.' If he refuses to listen to them, tell the church. If he refuses to listen even to the church, then treat him as you would a Gentile or a tax collector. Amen, I say to you, whatever you bind on earth shall be bound in heaven, and whatever you loose on earth shall be loosed in heaven. Again, [amen,] I say to you, if two of you agree on earth about anything for which they are to pray, it shall be granted to them by my heavenly Father. For where two or three are gathered together in my name, there am I in the midst of them."

Then Peter approaching asked him, "Lord, if my brother sins against me, how often must I forgive him? As many as seven times?" Jesus answered, "I say to you, not seven times but seventy-seven times. That is why the kingdom of heaven may be likened to a king who decided to settle accounts with his servants. When he began the accounting, a debtor was brought before him who owed him a huge amount. Since he had no way of paying it back, his master ordered him to be sold, along with his wife, his children, and all his property, in payment of the debt. At that, the servant fell down, did him homage, and said, 'Be patient with me, and I will pay you back in full.' Moved with compassion the master of that servant let him go and forgave him the loan. When that servant had left, he found one of his fellow servants who owed him a much smaller amount. He seized him and started to choke him, demanding, 'Pay back what you owe.' Falling to his knees, his fellow servant begged him, 'Be patient with me, and I will pay you back.' But he refused. Instead, he had him put in prison until he paid back the debt. Now when his fellow servants saw what had happened, they were deeply disturbed, and went to their master and reported the whole affair. His master summoned him and said to him, 'You wicked servant! I forgave you your entire debt because you begged me to. Should you not have had pity on your fellow servant, as I had pity on you?' Then in anger his master handed him over to the torturers until he should pay back the whole debt. So will my heavenly Father do to you, unless each of you forgives his brother from his heart."

PSALM 9:12-21

Sing praise to the LORD
   enthroned in Zion;
    proclaim among the nations his
     deeds;
For the avenger of blood has
   remembered;
   he has not forgotten the cry of
    the afflicted.
Have pity on me, O LORD; see
   how I am afflicted by my
   foes,
   you who have raised me up
    from the gates of death,
That I may declare all your
   praises
   and, in the gates of the
    daughter of Zion, rejoice in
    your salvation.
The nations are sunk in the pit
   they have made;
   in the snare they set, their foot
    is caught;
In passing sentence, the LORD is
   manifest;
   the wicked are trapped by the
    work of their own hands.
To the nether world the wicked
   shall turn back,
   all the nations that forget God.
For the needy shall not always be
   forgotten,
   nor shall the hope of the
    afflicted forever perish.
Rise, O LORD, let not man
   prevail;
   let the nations be judged in
    your presence.
Strike them with terror, O LORD;
   let the nations know that they
    are but men.

PROVERBS 4:1-2

Hear, O children, a father's instruction, / be attentive, that you may gain understanding! / Yes, excellent advice I give you; / my teaching do not forsake.

MATTHEW 19:1-30

When Jesus finished these words, he left Galilee and went to the district of Judea across the Jordan. Great crowds followed him, and he cured them there. Some Pharisees approached him, and tested him, saying, "Is it lawful for a man to divorce his wife for any cause whatever?" He said in reply, "Have you not read that from the beginning the Creator 'made them male and female' and said, 'For this reason a man shall leave his father and mother and be joined to his wife, and the two shall become one flesh'? So they are no longer two, but one flesh. Therefore, what God has joined together, no human being must separate." They said to him, "Then why did Moses command that the man give the woman a bill of divorce and dismiss [her]?" He said to them, "Because of the hardness of your hearts Moses allowed you to divorce your wives, but from the beginning it was not so. I say to you, whoever divorces his wife (unless the marriage is unlawful) and marries another commits adultery." [His] disciples said to him, "If that is the case of a man with his wife, it is better not to marry." He answered, "Not all can accept [this] word, but only those to whom that is granted. Some are incapable of marriage because they were born so; some, because they were made so by others; some, because they have renounced marriage for the sake of the kingdom of heaven. Whoever can accept this ought to accept it."

Then children were brought to him that he might lay his hands on them and pray. The disciples rebuked them, but Jesus said, "Let the children come to me, and do not prevent them; for the kingdom of heaven belongs to such as these." After he placed his hands on them, he went away.

Now someone approached him and said, "Teacher, what good must I do to gain eternal life?" He answered him, "Why do you ask me about the good? There is only one who is good. If you wish to enter into life, keep the commandments." He asked him, "Which ones?" And Jesus replied, " 'You shall not kill; you shall not commit adultery; you shall not steal; you shall not bear false witness; honor your father and your mother'; and 'you shall love your neighbor as yourself.' " The young man said to him, "All of these I have observed. What do I still lack?" Jesus said to him, "If you wish to be perfect, go, sell what you have and give to [the] poor, and you will have treasure in heaven. Then come, follow me." When the young man heard this statement, he went away sad, for he had many possessions. Then Jesus said to his disciples, "Amen, I say to you, it will be hard for one who is rich to enter the kingdom of heaven. Again I say to you, it is easier for a camel to pass through the eye of a needle than for one who is rich to enter the kingdom of God." When the disciples heard this, they were greatly astonished and said, "Who then can be saved?" Jesus looked at them and said, "For human beings this is impossible, but for God all things are possible." Then Peter said to him in reply, "We have given up everything and followed you. What will there be for us?" Jesus said to them, "Amen, I say to you that you who have followed me, in the new age, when the Son of Man is seated on his throne of glory, will yourselves sit on twelve thrones, judging the twelve tribes of Israel. And everyone who has given up houses or brothers or sisters or father or mother or children or lands for the sake of my name will receive a hundred times more, and will inherit eternal life. But many who are first will be last, and the last will be first."

PSALM 10:1-6

Why, O LORD, do you stand
  aloof?
Why hide in times of distress?
Proudly the wicked harass the
  afflicted,
  who are caught in the devices
  the wicked have contrived.
For the wicked man glories in his
  greed,
  and the covetous blasphemes,
  sets the LORD at nought.
The wicked man boasts, "He will
  not avenge it";
  "There is no God," sums up
  his thoughts.
His ways are secure at all times;
  your judgments are far from
  his mind;
  all his foes he scorns.
He says in his heart, "I shall not
  be disturbed;
  from age to age I shall be
  without misfortune."

PROVERBS 4:3-6

When I was my father's child, / frail, yet the darling of my mother, / He taught me, and said to me: / "Let your heart hold fast my words: / keep my commands, that you may live! / Get wisdom, get understanding! / Do not forget or turn aside from the words I utter. / Forsake her not, and she will preserve you; / love her, and she will safeguard you."

JANUARY 21

MATTHEW 20:1-34

"The kingdom of heaven is like a landowner who went out at dawn to hire laborers for his vineyard. After agreeing with them for the usual daily wage, he sent them into his vineyard. Going out about nine o'clock, he saw others standing idle in the marketplace, and he said to them, 'You too go into my vineyard, and I will give you what is just.' So they went off. [And] he went out again around noon, and around three o'clock, and did likewise. Going out about five o'clock, he found others standing around, and said to them, 'Why do you stand here idle all day?' They answered, 'Because no one has hired us.' He said to them, 'You too go into my vineyard.' When it was evening the owner of the vineyard said to his foreman, 'Summon the laborers and give them their pay, beginning with the last and ending with the first.' When those who had started about five o'clock came, each received the usual daily wage. So when the first came, they thought that they would receive more, but each of them also got the usual wage. And on receiving it they grumbled against the landowner, saying, 'These last ones worked only one hour, and you have made them equal to us, who bore the day's burden and the heat.' He said to one of them in reply, 'My friend, I am not cheating you. Did you not agree with me for the usual daily wage? Take what is yours and go. What if I wish to give this last one the same as you? [Or] am I not free to do as I wish with my own money? Are you envious because I am generous?' Thus, the last will be first, and the first will be last."

As Jesus was going up to Jerusalem, he took the twelve [disciples] aside by themselves, and said to them on the way, "Behold, we are going up to Jerusalem, and the Son of Man will be handed over to the chief priests and the scribes, and they will condemn him to death, and hand him over to the Gentiles to be mocked and scourged and crucified, and he will be raised on the third day."

Then the mother of the sons of Zebedee approached him with her sons and did him homage, wishing to ask him for something. He said to her, "What do you wish?" She answered him, "Command that these two sons of mine sit, one at your right and the other at your left, in your kingdom." Jesus said in reply, "You do not know what you are asking. Can you drink the cup that I am going to drink?" They said to him, "We can." He replied, "My cup you will indeed drink, but to sit at my right and at my left [this] is not mine to give but is for those for whom it has been prepared by my Father." When the ten heard this, they became indignant at the two brothers. But Jesus summoned them and said, "You know that the rulers of the Gentiles lord it over them, and the great ones make their authority over them felt. But it shall not be so among you. Rather, whoever wishes to be great among you shall be your servant; whoever wishes to be first among you shall be your slave. Just so, the Son of Man did not come to be served but to serve and to give his life as a ransom for many."

As they left Jericho, a great crowd followed him. Two blind men were sitting by the roadside, and when they heard that Jesus was passing by, they cried out, "[Lord,] Son of David, have pity on us!" The crowd warned them to be silent, but they called out all the more, "Lord, Son of David, have pity on us!" Jesus stopped and called them and said, "What do you want me to do for you?" They answered him, "Lord, let our eyes be opened." Moved with pity, Jesus touched their eyes. Immediately they received their sight, and followed him.

PSALM 10:7-11

His mouth is full of cursing, guile
    and deceit;
    under his tongue are mischief
      and iniquity.
He lurks in ambush near the
    villages;
    in hiding he murders the
      innocent;
    his eyes spy upon the
      unfortunate.
He waits in secret like a lion in
    his lair;
    he lies in wait to catch the
      afflicted;
    he catches the afflicted and
      drags them off in his net.

He stoops and lies prone
    till by his violence fall the
      unfortunate.
He says in his heart, "God has
    forgotten;

he hides his face, he never
    sees."

PROVERBS 4:7-9

"The beginning of wisdom is: get wisdom; / at the cost of all you have, get understanding. / Extol her, and she will exalt you; / she will bring you honors if you embrace her; / She will put on your head a graceful diadem; / a glorious crown will she bestow on you."

JANUARY 22

MATTHEW 21:1-46

When they drew near Jerusalem and came to Bethphage on the Mount of Olives, Jesus sent two disciples, saying to them, "Go into the village opposite you, and immediately you will find an ass tethered, and a colt with her. Untie them and bring them here to me. And if anyone should say anything to you, reply, 'The Master has need of them.' Then he will send them at once." This happened so that what had been spoken through the prophet might be fulfilled:

"Say to daughter Zion,
'Behold, your king comes to
    you,
    meek and riding on an ass,
      and on a colt, the foal of a
      beast of burden.' "

The disciples went and did as Jesus had ordered them. They brought the ass and the colt and laid their cloaks over them, and he sat upon them. The very large crowd spread their cloaks on the road, while others cut branches from the trees and strewed them on the road. The crowds preceding him and those following kept crying out and saying:

"Hosanna to the Son of David;
    blessed is he who comes in
      the name of the LORD;
hosanna in the highest."

And when he entered Jerusalem the whole city was shaken and asked, "Who is this?" And the crowds replied, "This is Jesus the prophet, from Nazareth in Galilee."

Jesus entered the temple area and drove out all those engaged in selling and buying there. He overturned the tables of the money changers and the seats of those who were selling doves. And he said to them, "It is written:

'My house shall be a house of
    prayer,'
    but you are making it a den
      of thieves."

The blind and the lame approached him in the temple area, and he cured them. When the chief priests and the scribes saw the wondrous things he was doing, and the children crying out in the temple area, "Hosanna to the Son of David," they were indignant and said to him, "Do you hear what they are saying?" Jesus said to them, "Yes; and have you never read the text, 'Out of the mouths of infants and nurslings you have brought forth praise'?" And leaving them, he went out of the city to Bethany, and there he spent the night.

When he was going back to the city in the morning, he was hungry. Seeing a fig tree by the road, he went over to it, but found nothing on it except leaves. And he said to it, "May no fruit ever come from you again." And immediately the fig tree withered. When the disciples saw this, they were amazed and said, "How was it that the fig tree withered immediately?" Jesus said to them in reply, "Amen, I say to you, if you have faith and do not waver, not only will you do what has been done to the fig tree, but even if you say to this mountain, 'Be lifted up and thrown into the sea,' it will be done. Whatever you ask for in prayer with faith, you will receive."

When he had come into the temple area, the chief priests and the elders of the people approached him as he was teaching and said, "By what authority are you doing these things? And who gave you this authority?" Jesus said to them in reply, "I shall ask you one question, and if you answer it for me, then I shall tell you by what authority I do these things. Where was John's baptism from? Was it of heavenly or of human origin?" They discussed this among themselves and said, "If we say 'Of heavenly origin,' he will say to us,

'Then why did you not believe him?' But if we say, 'Of human origin,' we fear the crowd, for they all regard John as a prophet." So they said to Jesus in reply, "We do not know." He himself said to them, "Neither shall I tell you by what authority I do these things.

"What is your opinion? A man had two sons. He came to the first and said, 'Son, go out and work in the vineyard today.' He said in reply, 'I will not,' but afterwards he changed his mind and went. The man came to the other son and gave the same order. He said in reply, 'Yes, sir,' but did not go. Which of the two did his father's will?" They answered, "The first." Jesus said to them, "Amen, I say to you, tax collectors and prostitutes are entering the kingdom of God before you. When John came to you in the way of righteousness, you did not believe him; but tax collectors and prostitutes did. Yet even when you saw that, you did not later change your minds and believe him.

"Hear another parable. There was a landowner who planted a vineyard, put a hedge around it, dug a wine press in it, and built a tower. Then he leased it to tenants and went on a journey. When vintage time drew near, he sent his servants to the tenants to obtain his produce. But the tenants seized the servants and one they beat, another they killed, and a third they stoned. Again he sent other servants, more numerous than the first ones, but they treated them in the same way. Finally, he sent his son to them, thinking, 'They will respect my son.' But when the tenants saw the son, they said to one another, 'This is the heir. Come, let us kill him and acquire his inheritance.' They seized him, threw him out of the vineyard, and killed him. What will the owner of the vineyard do to those tenants when he comes?" They answered him, "He will put those wretched men to a wretched death and lease his vineyard to other tenants who will give him the produce at the proper times." Jesus said to them, "Did you never read in the scriptures:

'The stone that the builders rejected
has become the cornerstone;
by the LORD has this been done,
and it is wonderful in our eyes'?

Therefore, I say to you, the kingdom of God will be taken away from you and given to a people that will produce its fruit. [The one who falls on this stone will be dashed to pieces; and it will crush anyone on whom it falls.]" When the chief priests and the Pharisees heard his parables, they knew that he was speaking about them. And although they were attempting to arrest him, they feared the crowds, for they regarded him as a prophet.

PSALM 10:12-18

Rise, O LORD! O God, lift up your hand!
Forget not the afflicted!
Why should the wicked man despise God,
saying in his heart, "He will not avenge it"?
You do see, for you behold misery and sorrow,
taking them in your hands.
On you the unfortunate man depends;
of the fatherless you are the helper.
Break the strength of the wicked and of the evildoer;
punish their wickedness; let them not survive.
The LORD is king forever and ever;
the nations have perished out of his land.
The desire of the afflicted you hear, O LORD;
strengthening their hearts, you pay heed
To the defense of the fatherless and the oppressed,
that man, who is of earth, may terrify no more.

PROVERBS 4:10-13

Hear, my son, and receive my words, / and the years of your life shall be many. / On the way of wisdom I direct you, / I lead you on straightforward paths. / When you walk, your step will not be impeded, / and should you run, you will not stumble. / Hold fast to instruction, never let her go; / keep her, for she is your life.

MATTHEW 22:1-46

Jesus again in reply spoke to them in parables, saying, "The kingdom of heaven may be likened to a king who gave a wedding feast for his son. He dispatched his servants to summon the invited guests to the feast, but they refused to come. A second time he sent other servants, saying, 'Tell those invited: "Behold, I have prepared my banquet, my calves and fattened cattle are killed, and everything is ready; come to the feast." ' Some ignored the invitation and went away, one to his farm, another to his business. The rest laid hold of his servants, mistreated them, and killed them. The king was enraged and sent his troops, destroyed those murderers, and burned their city. Then he said to his servants, 'The feast is ready, but those who were invited were not worthy to come. Go out, therefore, into the main roads and invite to the feast whomever you find.' The servants went out into the streets and gathered all they found, bad and good alike, and the hall was filled with guests. But when the king came in to meet the guests he saw a man there not dressed in a wedding garment. He said to him, 'My friend, how is it that you came in here without a wedding garment?' But he was reduced to silence. Then the king said to his attendants, 'Bind his hands and feet, and cast him into the darkness outside, where there will be wailing and grinding of teeth.' Many are invited, but few are chosen."

Then the Pharisees went off and plotted how they might entrap him in speech. They sent their disciples to him, with the Herodians, saying, "Teacher, we know that you are a truthful man and that you teach the way of God in accordance with the truth. And you are not concerned with anyone's opinion, for you do not regard a person's status. Tell us, then, what is your opinion: Is it lawful to pay the census tax to Caesar or not?" Knowing their malice, Jesus said, "Why are you testing me, you hypocrites? Show me the coin that pays the census tax." Then they handed him the Roman coin. He said to them, "Whose image is this and whose inscription?" They replied, "Caesar's." At that he said to them, "Then repay to Caesar what belongs to Caesar and to God what belongs to God." When they heard this they were amazed, and leaving him they went away.

On that day Sadducees approached him, saying that there is no resurrection. They put this question to him, saying, "Teacher, Moses said, 'If a man dies without children, his brother shall marry his wife and raise up descendants for his brother.' Now there were seven brothers among us. The first married and died and, having no descendants, left his wife to his brother. The same happened with the second and the third, through all seven. Finally the woman died. Now at the resurrection, of the seven, whose wife will she be? For they all had been married to her." Jesus said to them in reply, "You are misled because you do not know the scriptures or the power of God. At the resurrection they neither marry nor are given in marriage but are like the angels in heaven. And concerning the resurrection of the dead, have you not read what was said to you by God, 'I am the God of Abraham, the God of Isaac, and the God of Jacob'? He is not the God of the dead but of the living." When the crowds heard this, they were astonished at his teaching.

When the Pharisees heard that he had silenced the Sadducees, they gathered together, and one of them [a scholar of the law] tested him by asking, "Teacher, which commandment in the law is the greatest?" He said to him, "You shall love the Lord, your God, with all your heart, with all your soul, and with all your mind. This is the greatest and the first commandment. The second is like it: You shall love your neighbor as yourself. The whole law and the prophets depend on these two commandments."

While the Pharisees were gathered together, Jesus questioned them, saying, "What is your opinion about the Messiah? Whose son is he?" They replied, "David's." He said to them, "How, then, does David, inspired by the Spirit, call him 'lord,' saying:

'The LORD said to my lord,
"Sit at my right hand
until I place your enemies
under your feet"'?

If David calls him 'lord,' how can he be his son?" No one was able to answer him a word, nor from that day on did anyone dare to ask him any more questions.

PSALM 11:1-7

For the leader. Of David.
In the LORD I take refuge; how
can you say to me,
"Flee to the mountain like a
bird!
For, see, the wicked bend the
bow;
they place the arrow on the
string
to shoot in the dark at the
upright of heart.
When the pillars are overthrown,
what can the just man do?"
The LORD is in his holy temple;
the LORD's throne is in heaven.
His eyes behold,
his searching glance is on
mankind.
The LORD searches the just and
the wicked;
the lover of violence he hates.
He rains upon the wicked fiery
coals and brimstone;
a burning blast is their allotted
cup.
For the LORD is just, he loves just
deeds;
the upright shall see his face.

PROVERBS 4:14-19

The path of the wicked enter not, / walk not on the way of evil men; / Shun it, cross it not, / turn aside from it, and pass on. / For they cannot rest unless they have done evil; / to have made no one stumble steals away their sleep. / For they eat the bread of wickedness / and drink the wine of violence. / The way of the wicked is like darkness; / they know not on what they stumble. / But the path of the just is like shining light, / that grows in brilliance till perfect day.

MATTHEW 23:1-39

Then Jesus spoke to the crowds and to his disciples, saying, "The scribes and the Pharisees have taken their seat on the chair of Moses. Therefore, do and observe all things whatsoever they tell you, but do not follow their example. For they preach but they do not practice. They tie up heavy burdens [hard to carry] and lay them on people's shoulders, but they will not lift a finger to move them. All their works are performed to be seen. They widen their phylacteries and lengthen their tassels. They love places of honor at banquets, seats of honor in synagogues, greetings in marketplaces, and the salutation 'Rabbi.' As for you, do not be called 'Rabbi.' You have but one teacher, and you are all brothers. Call no one on earth your father; you have but one Father in heaven. Do not be called 'Master'; you have but one master, the Messiah. The greatest among you must be your servant. Whoever exalts himself will be humbled; but whoever humbles himself will be exalted.

"Woe to you, scribes and Pharisees, you hypocrites. You lock the kingdom of heaven before human beings. You do not enter yourselves, nor do you allow entrance to those trying to enter.

"Woe to you, scribes and Pharisees, you hypocrites. You traverse sea and land to make one convert, and when that happens you make him a child of Gehenna twice as much as yourselves.

"Woe to you, blind guides, who say, 'If one swears by the temple, it means nothing, but if one swears by the gold of the temple, one is obligated.' Blind fools, which is greater, the gold, or the temple that made the gold sacred? And you say, 'If one swears by the altar, it means nothing, but if one swears by the gift on the altar, one is obligated.' You blind ones, which is greater, the gift, or the altar that makes the gift sacred? One who swears by the altar swears by it and all that is upon it; one who swears by the temple swears by it and by him who dwells in it; one who swears by heaven swears by the throne of God and by him who is seated on it.

"Woe to you, scribes and Pharisees, you hypocrites. You pay tithes of mint and dill and cummin, and have neglected the weightier things of the law: judgment and mercy and fidelity. [But] these you should have done, without neglecting the others. Blind guides, who strain out the gnat and swallow the camel!

"Woe to you, scribes and Pharisees, you hypocrites. You cleanse the outside of cup and dish, but inside they are full of plunder and self-indulgence. Blind Pharisee, cleanse first the inside of the cup, so that the outside also may be clean.

"Woe to you, scribes and Pharisees, you hypocrites. You are like whitewashed tombs, which appear beautiful on the outside, but inside are full of dead men's bones and every kind of filth. Even so, on the outside you appear righteous, but inside you are filled with hypocrisy and evildoing.

"Woe to you, scribes and Pharisees, you hypocrites. You build the tombs of the prophets and adorn the memorials of the righteous, and you say, 'If we had lived in the days of our ancestors, we would not have joined them in shedding the prophets' blood.' Thus you bear witness against yourselves that you are the children of those who murdered the prophets; now fill up what your ancestors measured out! You serpents, you brood of vipers, how can you flee from the judgment of Gehenna? Therefore, behold, I send to you prophets and wise men and scribes; some of them you will kill and crucify, some of them you will scourge in your synagogues and pursue from town to town, so that there may come upon you all the righteous blood shed upon earth, from the righteous blood of Abel to the blood of Zechariah, the son of Barachiah, whom you murdered between the sanctuary and the altar. Amen, I say to you, all these things will come upon this generation.

"Jerusalem, Jerusalem, you who kill the prophets and stone those sent to you, how many times I yearned to gather your children together, as a hen gathers her young under her wings, but you were unwilling! Behold, your house will be abandoned, desolate. I tell you, you will not see me again until you say, 'Blessed is he who comes in the name of the Lord.' "

PSALM 12:1-5

For the leader; "upon the eighth." A psalm of David.

Help, O LORD! for no one now is dutiful;
  faithfulness has vanished from among men.
Everyone speaks falsehood to his neighbor;
  with smooth lips they speak, and double heart.
May the LORD destroy all smooth lips,
  every boastful tongue,
Those who say, "We are heroes with our tongues;
  our lips are our own; who is lord over us?"

PROVERBS 4:20-22

My son, to my words be attentive, / to my sayings incline your ear; / Let them not slip out of your sight, / keep them within your heart; / For they are life to those who find them, / to man's whole being they are health.

JANUARY 25

MATTHEW 24:1-51

Jesus left the temple area and was going away, when his disciples approached him to point out the temple buildings. He said to them in reply, "You see all these things, do you not? Amen, I say to you, there will not be left here a stone upon another stone that will not be thrown down."

As he was sitting on the Mount of Olives, the disciples approached him privately and said, "Tell us, when will this happen, and what sign will there be of your coming, and of the end of the age?" Jesus said to them in reply, "See that no one deceives you. For many will come in my name, saying, 'I am the Messiah,' and they will deceive many. You will hear of wars and reports of wars; see that you are not alarmed, for these things must happen, but it will not yet be the end. Nation will rise against nation, and kingdom against kingdom; there will be famines and earthquakes from place to place. All these are the beginning of the labor pains. Then they will hand you over to persecution, and they will kill you. You will be hated by all nations because of my name. And then many will be led into sin; they will betray and hate one another. Many false prophets will arise and deceive many; and because of the increase of evildoing, the love of many will grow cold. But the one who perseveres to the end will be saved. And this gospel of the kingdom will be preached throughout the world as a witness to all nations, and then the end will come.

"When you see the desolating abomination spoken of through Daniel the prophet standing in the holy place (let the reader understand), then those in Judea must flee to the mountains, a person on the housetop must not go down to get things out of his house, a person in the field must not return to get his cloak. Woe to pregnant women and nursing mothers in those days. Pray that your flight not be in winter or on the sabbath, for at that time there will be great tribulation, such as has not been since the beginning of the world until now, nor ever will be. And if those days had not been shortened, no one would be saved; but for the sake of the elect they will be shortened. If anyone says to you then, 'Look, here is the Messiah!' or, 'There he is!' do not believe it. False messiahs and false prophets will arise, and they will perform signs and wonders so great as to deceive, if that were possible, even the elect. Behold, I have told it to you beforehand. So if they say to you, 'He is in the desert,' do not go out there; if they say, 'He is in the inner rooms,' do not believe it. For just as lightning comes from the east and is seen as far as the west, so will the coming of the Son of Man be. Wherever the corpse is, there the vultures will gather.

"Immediately after the tribulation of those days,

the sun will be darkened,
and the moon will not give
its light,
and the stars will fall from the
sky,
and the powers of the
heavens will be shaken.

And then the sign of the Son of Man will appear in heaven, and all the tribes of the earth will mourn, and they will see the Son of Man coming upon the clouds of heaven with power and great glory. And he will send out his angels with a trumpet blast, and they will gather his elect from the four winds, from one end of the heavens to the other.

"Learn a lesson from the fig tree. When its branch becomes tender and sprouts leaves, you know that summer is near. In the same way, when you see all these things, know that he is near, at the gates. Amen, I say to you, this generation will not pass away until all these things have taken place. Heaven and earth will pass away, but my words will not pass away.

"But of that day and hour no one knows, neither the angels of heaven, nor the Son, but the Father alone. For as it was in the days of Noah, so it will be at the coming of the Son of Man. In [those] days before the flood, they were eating and drinking, marrying and giving in marriage, up to the day that Noah entered the ark. They did not know until the flood came and carried them all away. So will it be [also] at the coming of the Son of Man. Two men will be out in the field; one will be taken, and one will be left. Two women will be grinding at the mill; one will be taken, and one will be left. Therefore, stay awake! For you do not know on which day your Lord will come. Be sure of this: if the master of the house had known the hour of night when the thief was coming, he would have stayed awake and not let his house be broken into. So too, you also must be prepared, for at an hour you do not expect, the Son of Man will come.

"Who, then, is the faithful and prudent servant, whom the master has put in charge of his household to distribute to them their food at the proper time? Blessed is that servant whom his master on his arrival finds doing so. Amen, I say to you, he will put him in charge of all his property. But if that wicked servant says to himself, 'My master is long delayed,' and begins to beat his fellow servants, and eat and drink with drunkards, the servant's master will come on an unexpected day and at an unknown hour and will punish him severely and assign him a place with the hypocrites, where there will be wailing and grinding of teeth."

PSALM 12:6-9

"Because they rob the afflicted,
    and the needy sigh,
    now will I arise," says the
        LORD;
"I will grant safety to him who
    longs for it."
The promises of the LORD are
    sure,
    like tried silver, freed from
        dross, sevenfold refined.
You, O LORD, will keep us
    and preserve us always from
        this generation,
While about us the wicked strut
    and in high place are the basest
        of men.

PROVERBS 4:23-27

With closest custody, guard your heart, / for in it are the sources of life. / Put away from you dishonest talk, / deceitful speech put far from you. / Let your eyes look straight ahead / and your glance be directly forward. / Survey the path for your feet, / and let all your ways be sure. / Turn neither to right nor to left, / keep your foot far from evil.

JANUARY 26

MATTHEW 25:1-46

"Then the kingdom of heaven will be like ten virgins who took their lamps and went out to meet the bridegroom. Five of them were foolish and five were wise. The foolish ones, when taking their lamps, brought no oil with them, but the wise brought flasks of oil with their lamps. Since the bridegroom was long delayed, they all became drowsy and fell asleep. At midnight, there was a cry, 'Behold, the bridegroom! Come out to meet him!' Then all those virgins got up and trimmed their lamps. The foolish ones said to the wise, 'Give us some of your oil, for our lamps are going out.' But the wise ones replied, 'No, for there may not be enough for us and you. Go instead to the merchants and buy some for yourselves.' While they went off to buy it, the bridegroom came and those who were ready went into the wedding feast with him. Then the door was locked. Afterwards the other virgins came and said, 'Lord, Lord, open the door for us!' But he said in reply, 'Amen, I say to you, I do not know you.' Therefore, stay awake, for you know neither the day nor the hour.

"It will be as when a man who was going on a journey called in his servants and entrusted his possessions to them. To one he gave five talents; to another, two; to a third, one—to each according to his ability. Then he went away. Immediately the one who received five talents went and traded with them, and made another five. Likewise, the one who received two made another two. But the man who received one went off and dug a hole in the ground and buried his master's money. After a long time the master of those servants came back and settled accounts with them. The one who had received five talents came forward bringing the additional five. He said, 'Master, you gave me five talents. See, I have made five more.' His master said to him, 'Well done, my good and faithful servant. Since you were faithful in small matters, I will give you great responsibilities. Come, share your master's joy.' [Then] the one who had received two talents also came forward and said, 'Master, you gave me two talents. See, I have made two more.' His master said to him, 'Well done, my good and faithful servant. Since you were faithful in small matters, I will give you great responsibilities. Come, share your master's joy.' Then the one who had received the one talent came forward and said, 'Master, I knew you were a demanding person, harvesting where you did not plant and gathering where you did not scatter; so out of fear I went off and buried your talent in the ground. Here it is back.' His master said to him in reply, 'You wicked, lazy servant! So you knew that I harvest where I did not plant and gather where I did not scatter? Should you not then have put my money in the bank so that I could have got it back with interest on my return? Now then! Take the talent from him and give it to the one with ten. For to everyone who has, more will be given and he will grow rich; but from the one who has not, even what he has will be taken away. And throw this useless servant into the darkness outside, where there will be wailing and grinding of teeth.'

"When the Son of Man comes in his glory, and all the angels with him, he will sit upon his glorious throne, and all the nations will be assembled before him. And he will separate them one from another, as a shepherd separates the sheep from the goats. He will place the sheep on his right and the goats on his left. Then the king will say to those on his right, 'Come, you who are blessed by my Father. Inherit the kingdom prepared for you from the foundation of the world. For I was hungry and you gave me food, I was thirsty and you gave me drink, a stranger and you welcomed me, naked and you clothed me, ill and you cared for me, in prison and you visited me.' Then the righteous will answer him and say, 'Lord, when did we see you hungry and feed you, or thirsty and give you drink? When did we see you a stranger and welcome you, or naked and clothe you? When did we see you ill or in prison, and visit you?' And the king will say to them in reply, 'Amen, I say to you, whatever you did for one of these least brothers of mine, you did for me.' Then he will say to those on his left, 'Depart from me, you accursed, into the eternal fire prepared for the devil and his angels. For I was hungry and you gave me no food, I was thirsty and you gave me no drink, a stranger and you gave me no welcome, naked and you gave me no clothing, ill and in prison, and you did not care for me.' Then they will answer and say, 'Lord, when did we see you hungry or thirsty or a stranger or naked or ill or in prison, and not minister to your needs?' He will answer them, 'Amen, I say to you, what you did not do for one of these least ones, you did not do for me.' And these will go off to eternal punishment, but the righteous to eternal life."

PSALM 13:1-6

For the leader. A psalm of David.

How long, O LORD? Will you
  utterly forget me?
  How long will you hide your
  face from me
How long shall I harbor sorrow
  in my soul,
  grief in my heart day after day?
How long will my enemy
  triumph over me?
  Look, answer me, O LORD, my
  God!
Give light to my eyes that I may
  not sleep in death
  lest my enemy say, "I have
  overcome him";
Lest my foes rejoice at my
  downfall
  though I trusted in your
  kindness.
Let my heart rejoice in your
  salvation;
  let me sing of the LORD, "He
  has been good to me."

PROVERBS 5:1-6

My son, to my wisdom be attentive, / to my knowledge incline your ear, / That discretion may watch over you, / and understanding may guard you. / The lips of an adulteress drip with honey, / and her mouth is smoother than oil; / But in the end she is as bitter as wormwood, / as sharp as a two-edged sword. / Her feet

JANUARY 27

MATTHEW 26:1-30

When Jesus finished all these words, he said to his disciples, "You know that in two days' time it will be Passover, and the Son of Man will be handed over to be crucified." Then the chief priests and the elders of the people assembled in the palace of the high priest, who was called Caiaphas, and they consulted together to arrest Jesus by treachery and put him to death. But they said, "Not during the festival, that there may not be a riot among the people."

Now when Jesus was in Bethany in the house of Simon the leper, a woman came up to him with an alabaster jar of costly perfumed oil, and poured it on his head while he was reclining at table. When the disciples saw this, they were indignant and said, "Why this waste? It could have been sold for much, and the money given to the poor." Since Jesus knew this, he said to them, "Why do you make trouble for the woman? She has done a good thing for me. The poor you will always have with you; but you will not always have me. In pouring this perfumed oil upon my body, she did it to prepare me for burial. Amen, I say to you, wherever this gospel is proclaimed in the whole world, what she has done will be spoken of, in memory of her."

Then one of the Twelve, who was called Judas Iscariot, went to the chief priests and said, "What

are you willing to give me if I hand him over to you?" They paid him thirty pieces of silver, and from that time on he looked for an opportunity to hand him over.

On the first day of the feast of Unleavened Bread, the disciples approached Jesus and said, "Where do you want us to prepare for you to eat the Passover?" He said, "Go into the city to a certain man and tell him, 'The teacher says, "My appointed time draws near; in your house I shall celebrate the Passover with my disciples." ' " The disciples then did as Jesus had ordered, and prepared the Passover.

When it was evening, he reclined at table with the Twelve. And while they were eating, he said, "Amen, I say to you, one of you will betray me." Deeply distressed at this, they began to say to him one after another, "Surely it is not I, Lord?" He said in reply, "He who has dipped his hand into the dish with me is the one who will betray me. The Son of Man indeed goes, as it is written of him, but woe to that man by whom the Son of Man is betrayed. It would be better for that man if he had never been born." Then Judas, his betrayer, said in reply, "Surely it is not I, Rabbi?" He answered, "You have said so."

While they were eating, Jesus took bread, said the blessing, broke it, and giving it to his disciples said, "Take and eat; this is my body." Then he took a cup, gave thanks, and gave it to them, saying, "Drink from it, all of you, for this is my blood of the covenant, which will be shed on behalf of many for the forgiveness of sins. I tell you, from now on I shall not drink this fruit of the vine until the day when I drink it with you new in the kingdom of my Father." Then, after singing a hymn, they went out to the Mount of Olives.

PSALM 14:1-3

For the leader. Of David.
The fool says in his heart,

"There is no God."
Such are corrupt; they do
  abominable deeds;
  there is not one who does
    good.
The LORD looks down from
    heaven upon the children of
    men,
  to see if there be one who is
    wise and seeks God.
All alike have gone astray;
  they have become perverse;
there is not one who does good,
    not even one.

PROVERBS 5:7-14

So now, O children, listen to me, / go not astray from the words of my mouth. / Keep your way far from her, / approach not the door of her house, / Lest you give your honor to others, / and your years to a merciless one; / Lest strangers have their fill of your wealth, / your hard-won earnings go to an alien's house; / And you groan in the end, / when your flesh and your body are consumed; / And you say, "Oh, why did I hate instruction, / and my heart spurn reproof! / Why did I not listen to the voice of my teachers, / nor to my instructors incline my ear! / I have all but come to utter ruin, / condemned by the public assembly!"

JANUARY 28

MATTHEW 26:31-75

Then Jesus said to them, "This night all of you will have your faith in me shaken, for it is written:

'I will strike the shepherd,
  and the sheep of the flock
  will be dispersed';

but after I have been raised up, I shall go before you to Galilee." Peter said to him in reply, "Though all may have their faith in you shaken, mine will never be." Jesus said to him, "Amen, I say to you, this very night before the cock crows, you will deny me three times." Peter said to him, "Even though I should have to die with you, I will not deny you." And all the disciples spoke likewise.

Then Jesus came with them to a place called Gethsemane, and he said to his disciples, "Sit here while I go over there and pray." He took along Peter and the two sons of Zebedee, and began to feel sorrow and distress. Then he said to them, "My soul is sorrowful even to death. Remain here and keep watch with me." He advanced a little and fell prostrate in prayer, saying, "My Father, if it is possible, let this cup pass from me; yet, not as I will, but as you will." When he returned to his disciples he found them asleep. He said to Peter, "So you could not keep watch with me for one hour? Watch and pray that you may not undergo the test. The spirit is willing, but the flesh is weak." Withdrawing a second time, he prayed again, "My Father, if it is not possible that this cup pass without my drinking it, your will be done!" Then he returned once more and found them asleep, for they could not keep their eyes open. He left them and withdrew again and prayed a third time, saying the same thing again. Then he returned to his disciples and said to them, "Are you still sleeping and taking your rest? Behold, the hour is at hand when the Son of Man is to be handed over to sinners. Get up, let us go. Look, my betrayer is at hand."

While he was still speaking, Judas, one of the Twelve, arrived, accompanied by a large crowd, with swords and clubs, who had come from the chief priests and the elders of the people. His betrayer had arranged a sign with them, saying, "The man I shall kiss is the one; arrest him." Immediately he went over to Jesus and said, "Hail, Rabbi!" and he kissed him. Jesus answered him, "Friend, do what you have come for." Then stepping forward they laid hands on Jesus and arrested him. And behold, one of those who accompanied Jesus put his hand to his sword, drew it, and struck the high priest's servant, cutting off his ear. Then Jesus said to him, "Put your sword back into its sheath, for all who take the sword will perish by the sword. Do you think that I cannot call upon my Father and he will not provide me at this moment with more than twelve legions of angels? But then how would the scriptures be fulfilled which say that it must come to pass in this way?" At that hour Jesus said to the crowds, "Have you come out as against a robber, with swords and clubs to seize me? Day after day I sat teaching in the temple area, yet you did not arrest me. But all this has come to pass that the writings of the prophets may be fulfilled." Then all the disciples left him and fled.

Those who had arrested Jesus led him away to Caiaphas the high priest, where the scribes and the elders were assembled. Peter was following him at a distance as far as the high priest's courtyard, and going inside he sat down with the servants to see the outcome. The chief priests and the entire Sanhedrin kept trying to obtain false testimony against Jesus in order to put him to death, but they found none, though many false witnesses came forward. Finally two came forward who stated, "This man said, 'I can destroy the temple of God and within three days rebuild it.' " The high priest rose and addressed him, "Have you no answer? What are these men testifying against you?" But Jesus was silent. Then the high priest said to him, "I order you to tell us under oath before the living God whether you are the Messiah, the Son of God." Jesus said to him in reply, "You have said so. But I tell you:

From now on you will see 'the Son of Man
seated at the right hand of the Power'

and 'coming on the clouds of heaven.' "

Then the high priest tore his robes and said, "He has blasphemed! What further need have we of witnesses? You have now heard the blasphemy; what is your opinion?" They said in reply, "He deserves to die!" Then they spat in his face and struck him, while some slapped him, saying, "Prophesy for us, Messiah: who is it that struck you?"

Now Peter was sitting outside in the courtyard. One of the maids came over to him and said, "You too were with Jesus the Galilean." But he denied it in front of everyone, saying, "I do not know what you are talking about!" As he went out to the gate, another girl saw him and said to those who were there, "This man was with Jesus the Nazorean." Again he denied it with an oath, "I do not know the man!" A little later the bystanders came over and said to Peter, "Surely you too are one of them; even your speech gives you away." At that he began to curse and to swear, "I do not know the man." And immediately a cock crowed. Then Peter remembered the word that Jesus had spoken: "Before the cock crows you will deny me three times." He went out and began to weep bitterly.

PSALM 14:4-7

Will all these evildoers never learn,
    they who eat up my people
    just as they eat bread?
They have not called upon the LORD;
    then they shall be in great fear,
    for God is with the just generation.
You would confound the plans of the afflicted,
    but the LORD is his refuge.
Oh, that out of Zion would come the salvation of Israel!
    When the LORD restores the well-being of his people,
    then shall Jacob exult and Israel be glad.

PROVERBS 5:15-23

Drink water from your own cistern, / running water from your own well. / How may your water sources be dispersed abroad, / streams of water in the streets? / Let your fountain be yours alone, / not one shared with strangers; / And have joy of the wife of your youth, / your lovely hind, your graceful doe. / Her love will invigorate you always, / through her love you will flourish continually, / When you lie down she will watch over you, / and when you wake, she will share your concerns; / wherever you turn, she will guide you. / Why then, my son, should you go astray for another's wife / and accept the embraces of an adulteress? / For each man's ways are plain to the LORD's sight; / all their paths he surveys; / By his own iniquities the wicked man will be caught, / in the meshes of his own sin he will be held fast; / He will die from lack of discipline, / through the greatness of his folly he will be lost.

JANUARY 29

MATTHEW 27:1-31

When it was morning, all the chief priests and the elders of the people took counsel against Jesus to put him to death. They bound him, led him away, and handed him over to Pilate, the governor.

Then Judas, his betrayer, seeing that Jesus had been condemned, deeply regretted what he had done. He returned the thirty pieces of silver to the chief priests and elders, saying, "I have sinned in betraying innocent blood." They said, "What is that to us? Look to it yourself." Flinging the money into the temple, he departed and went off and hanged himself. The chief priests gathered up the money, but said, "It is not lawful to deposit this in the temple treasury, for it is the price of blood." After consultation, they used it to buy the potter's field as a burial place for foreigners. That is why that field even today is called the Field of Blood. Then was fulfilled what had been said through Jeremiah the prophet, "And they took the thirty pieces of silver, the value of a man with a price on his head, a price set by some of the Israelites, and they paid it out for the potter's field just as the Lord had commanded me."

Now Jesus stood before the governor, and he questioned him, "Are you the king of the Jews?" Jesus said, "You say so." And when he was accused by the chief priests and elders, he made no answer. Then Pilate said to him, "Do you not hear how many things they are testifying against you?" But he did not answer him one word, so that the governor was greatly amazed.

Now on the occasion of the feast the governor was accustomed to release to the crowd one prisoner whom they wished. And at that time they had a notorious prisoner called [Jesus] Barabbas. So when they had assembled, Pilate said to them, "Which one do you want me to release to you, [Jesus] Barabbas, or Jesus called Messiah?" For he knew that it was out of envy that they had handed him over. While he was still seated on the bench, his wife sent him a message, "Have nothing to do with that righteous man. I suffered much in a dream today because of him." The chief priests and the elders persuaded the crowds to ask for Barabbas but to destroy Jesus. The governor said to them in reply, "Which of the two do you want me to release to you?" They answered, "Barabbas!" Pilate said to them, "Then what shall I do with Jesus called Messiah?" They all said, "Let him be crucified!" But he said, "Why? What evil has he done?" They only shouted the louder, "Let him be crucified!" When Pilate saw that he was not succeeding at all, but that a riot was breaking out instead, he took water and washed his hands in the sight of the crowd, saying, "I am innocent of this man's blood. Look to it yourselves." And the whole people said in reply, "His blood be upon us and upon our children." Then he released Barabbas to them, but after he had Jesus scourged, he handed him over to be crucified.

Then the soldiers of the governor took Jesus inside the praetorium and gathered the whole cohort around him. They stripped off his clothes and threw a scarlet military cloak about him. Weaving a crown out of thorns, they placed it on his head, and a reed in his right hand. And kneeling before him, they mocked him, saying, "Hail, King of the Jews!" They spat upon him and took the reed and kept striking him on the head. And when they had mocked him, they stripped him of the cloak, dressed him in his own clothes, and led him off to crucify him.

PSALM 15:1-5

A psalm of David.

O Lord, who shall sojourn in your tent?
  Who shall dwell on your holy mountain?
He who walks blamelessly and does justice;
  who thinks the truth in his heart
  and slanders not with his tongue;
Who harms not his fellow man,
  nor takes up a reproach against his neighbor;
By whom the reprobate is despised,
  while he honors those who fear the Lord;
Who, though it be to his loss, changes not his pledged word;
  who lends not his money at usury
  and accepts no bribe against the innocent.
He who does these things
  shall never be disturbed.

PROVERBS 6:1-5

My son, if you have become surety to your neighbor, / given your hand in pledge to another, / You have been snared by the utterance of your lips, / caught by the words of your mouth; / So do this, my son, to free yourself, / since you have fallen into your neighbor's power: / Go, hurry, stir up your neighbor! / Give no sleep to your eyes, / nor slumber to your eyelids; / Free yourself as a gazelle from the snare, / or as a bird from the hand of the fowler.

JANUARY 30

MATTHEW 27:32-66

As they were going out, they met a Cyrenian named Simon; this man they pressed into service to carry his cross.

And when they came to a place called Golgotha (which means Place of the Skull), they gave Jesus wine to drink mixed with gall. But when he had tasted it, he refused to drink. After they had cru- cified him, they divided his garments by casting lots; then they sat down and kept watch over him there. And they placed over his head the written charge against him: This is Jesus, the King of the Jews. Two revolution- aries were crucified with him, one on his right and the other on his left. Those passing by reviled him, shaking their heads and saying, "You who would destroy the temple and rebuild it in three days, save yourself, if you are the Son of God, [and] come down from the cross!" Likewise the chief priests with the scribes and elders mocked him and said, "He saved others; he cannot save himself. So he is the king of Israel! Let him come down from the cross now, and we will believe in him. He trusted in God; let him deliver him now if he wants him. For he said, 'I am the Son of God.' " The revolutionaries who were crucified with him also kept abusing him in the same way.

From noon onward, darkness came over the whole land until three in the afternoon. And about three o'clock Jesus cried out in a loud voice, *"Eli, Eli, lema sabachthani?"* which means, "My God, my God, why have you forsaken me?" Some of the bystanders who heard it said, "This one is calling for Elijah." Immediately one of them ran to get a sponge; he soaked it in wine, and putting it on a reed, gave it to him to drink. But the rest said, "Wait, let us see if Elijah comes to save him." But Jesus cried out again in a loud voice, and gave up his spirit. And behold, the veil of the sanctuary was torn in two from top to bottom. The earth quaked, rocks were split, tombs were opened, and the bodies of many saints who had fallen asleep were raised. And coming forth from their tombs after his resurrection, they entered the holy city and appeared to many. The centurion and the men with him who were keeping watch over Jesus feared greatly when they saw the earthquake and all that was happening, and they said, "Truly, this was the Son of God!" There were many women there, looking on from a distance, who had followed Jesus from Galilee, ministering to him. Among them were Mary Magdalene and Mary the mother of James and Joseph, and the mother of the sons of Zebedee.

When it was evening, there came a rich man from Arimathea named Joseph, who was himself a disciple of Jesus. He went to Pilate and asked for the body of Jesus; then Pilate ordered it to be handed over. Taking the body, Joseph wrapped it [in] clean linen and laid it in his new tomb that he had hewn in the rock. Then he rolled a huge stone across the entrance to the tomb and departed. But Mary Magdalene and the other Mary remained sitting there, facing the tomb.

The next day, the one following the day of preparation, the chief priests and the Pharisees gathered before Pilate and said, "Sir, we remember that this impostor while still alive said, 'After three days I will be raised up.' Give orders, then, that the grave be secured until the third day, lest his disciples come and steal him and say to the people, 'He has been raised from the dead.' This last imposture would be worse than the first." Pilate said to them, "The guard is yours; go secure it as best you can." So they went and secured the tomb by fixing a seal to the stone and setting the guard.

PSALM 16:1-6

A miktam of David.

Keep me, O God, for in you I
    take refuge;
  I say to the LORD, "My LORD
    are you.
  Apart from you I have no
    good."

How wonderfully has he made
   me cherish
    the holy ones who are in his
    land!
They multiply their sorrows
   who court other gods.
Blood libations to them I will not
   pour out,
    nor will I take their names
    upon my lips.

O LORD, my allotted portion and
   my cup,
   you it is who hold fast my lot.
For me the measuring lines have
   fallen on pleasant sites;
   fair to me indeed is my
   inheritance.

PROVERBS 6:6-11

Go to the ant, O sluggard, / study her ways and learn wisdom; / For though she has no chief, / no commander or ruler, / She procures her food in the summer, / stores up her provisions in the harvest. / How long, O sluggard, will you rest? / when will you rise from your sleep? / A little sleep, a little slumber, / a little folding of the arms to rest—/ Then will poverty come upon you like a highwayman, / and want like an armed man.

JANUARY 31

MATTHEW 28:1-20

After the sabbath, as the first day of the week was dawning, Mary Magdalene and the other Mary came to see the tomb. And behold, there was a great earthquake; for an angel of the Lord descended from heaven, approached, rolled back the stone, and sat upon it. His appearance was like lightning and his clothing was white as snow. The guards were shaken with fear of him and became like dead men. Then the angel said to the women in reply, "Do not be afraid! I know that you are seeking Jesus the crucified. He is not here, for he has been raised just as he said. Come and see the place where he lay. Then go quickly and tell his disciples, 'He has been raised from the dead, and he is going before you to Galilee; there you will see him.' Behold, I have told you." Then they went away quickly from the tomb, fearful yet overjoyed, and ran to announce this to his disciples. And behold, Jesus met them on their way and greeted them. They approached, embraced his feet, and did him homage. Then Jesus said to them, "Do not be afraid. Go tell my brothers to go to Galilee, and there they will see me."

While they were going, some of the guard went into the city and told the chief priests all that had happened. They assembled with the elders and took counsel; then they gave a large sum of money to the soldiers, telling them, "You are to say, 'His disciples came by night and stole him while we were asleep.' And if this gets to the ears of the governor, we will satisfy [him] and keep you out of trouble." The soldiers took the money and did as they were instructed. And this story has circulated among the Jews to the present [day].

The eleven disciples went to Galilee, to the mountain to which Jesus had ordered them. When they saw him, they worshiped, but they doubted. Then Jesus approached and said to them, "All power in heaven and on earth has been given to me. Go, therefore, and make disciples of all nations, baptizing them in the name of the Father, and of the Son, and of the holy Spirit, teaching them to observe all that I have commanded you. And behold, I am with you always, until the end of the age."

even in the night my heart
    exhorts me.
I set the LORD ever before me;
    with him at my right hand I
    shall not be disturbed.
Therefore my heart is glad and
    my soul rejoices,
    my body, too, abides in
    confidence;
Because you will not abandon my
    soul to the nether world,
    nor will you suffer your faithful
    one to undergo corruption.
You will show me the path to
    life,
    fullness of joys in your
    presence,
    the delights at your right hand
    forever.

PSALM 16:7-11

I bless the LORD who counsels
    me;

PROVERBS 6:12-15

A scoundrel, a villain, is he / who deals in crooked talk. / He winks his eyes, / shuffles his feet, / makes signs with his fingers; / He has perversity in his heart, / is always plotting evil, / sows discord. / Therefore suddenly ruin comes upon him; / in an instant he is crushed beyond cure.

FEBRUARY

Your Kingdom Come

THE BOOK WHICH WE COMMONLY CALL "The Acts of the Apostles" is a kind of history of the establishment and the spread of the primitive church. It is an important book since without it we would have very little information of this important period after the ascension. We would have only some few facts from the letters of St. Paul which were written many years after the resurrection and ascension of Jesus into heaven.

There are two ways of writing history. One way is to chronicle events in order as they occurred and add a few details surrounding or causing these events. This was the method which Josephus followed in writing the history of the Jews.

A second method is to record certain great moments and personalities of any period. This presentation can be compared to a number of windows through which we get some glimpses into the events of that time. This is the method which Luke followed in describing the early years of the church in Acts. Luke is more preoccupied with the theological developments of this period rather than a strictly historical presentation.

The Book of Acts is sometimes called the Gospel of the Holy Spirit because the power and influence of the Holy Spirit is patently evident in the events recorded in this historical work. Throughout Acts, Luke makes it quite clear that the decisions and actions of the infant church were not human ideas and programs, but a response to the guidance and direction given by the Holy Spirit.

Promise

During his farewell address at the Last Supper, Jesus promised that we could recognize the work of the Holy Spirit "because it remains with you, and will be in you" (Jn 14:17). One of the principal functions of the Holy Spirit was to enlighten and guide the establishment and spread of the church throughout the known world. Jesus said: "The Advocate, the Holy Spirit . . . will teach you everything and remind you of all that [I] told you" (Jn 14:26).

The Spirit continues to enlighten and guide us today as we try daily to live out all that Jesus taught us. The Spirit continues his work of giving us the insights and the understanding we need to interpret the mind of Jesus in our daily encounters in life.

Jesus gave us even more reassurance when he repeated that the Paraclete would accompany and direct us in this valley of fear. "But when he comes, the Spirit of truth, he will guide you to all truth" (Jn 16:12ff).

After the ascension of Jesus into heaven, the only directives which the first followers of Jesus had came from the Holy Spirit. We must remember that there was lapse of at least twenty years before Paul wrote his Letters and forty or more years before Matthew, Mark, Luke, or John would write their Gospels. All that the Apostles could teach was what they recalled from memory that Jesus had taught and all that the Spirit was teaching them through his divine revelation.

This gives much more credibility to the influence and guidance of the Holy Spirit. The church is the mystery of the presence of the Holy Trinity introduced into history through the apostolic teaching. The divine nature of the church is even more apparent as these first evangelists were able to adapt the teaching of Jesus for the Gentiles of the Roman Empire.

Pentecost

The powerful workings of the Holy Spirit are quite evident from the external manifestations of his presence and power. Jesus promised his apostles that the Holy Spirit would come upon them and transform them into fearless witnesses for him. "But you will receive power when the Holy Spirit comes upon you, and you will be my witnesses in Jerusalem, throughout Judea and Samaria, and to the ends of the earth" (Acts 1:8).

This promise was fulfilled a few days later when the Holy Spirit manifested himself publicly with "a noise like a strong driving wind . . . tongues as of fire" (Acts 2:1ff). This was the great day of Pentecost, the birthday of the church.

Other Pentecosts

After the first coming of the Holy Spirit upon the Apostles on the day of the resurrection (Jn 20:22) and this great public manifestation, (Acts 2:1ff), there were at least three other similar, though lesser, outpourings of the Holy Spirit recorded by Luke.

Peter and John went to Samaria after the Samaritans had accepted the word. They prayed that these disciples might receive the Holy Spirit. Luke's words are few and simple: ". . . they received the Holy Spirit" (Acts 8:14ff).

At Caesarea, Peter had not yet finished his message when the Holy Spirit descended upon all who were listening to him. Some of the Judeo-Christians were surprised since Cornelius and his household were Gentiles.

Another outpouring of the Holy Spirit took place when Paul went down to Ephesus. He found some disciples to whom he explained the mission of the Holy Spirit. Luke reports: "And when Paul laid [his] hands on them, the Holy Spirit came upon them and they spoke in tongues and prophesied" (Acts 19:1ff).

These few facts recorded by Luke are proof sufficient of how powerfully the Holy Spirit was inspiring, motivating, and guiding the primitive church. Frequently Luke remarks that "the word of God continued to spread" (Acts 6:7). This took place regardless of the persecutions and other cultural obstacles that got in the way. This miraculous spread of the church can be attributed only to the divine presence and the power of the Holy Spirit.

An awareness that the Holy Spirit is dynamic and operative in the same way in the church today is the source of much peace and joy for us. Jesus is confirming his promise: ". . . upon this rock I will build my church, and the gates of the netherworld shall not prevail against it" (Mt 16:18). "Your ways, O Lord, make known to me; teach me your paths" (Ps 25:4).

FEBRUARY 1

ACTS 1:1-26

In the first book, Theophilus, I dealt with all that Jesus did and taught until the day he was taken up, after giving instructions through the holy Spirit to the apostles whom he had chosen. He presented himself alive to them by many proofs after he had suffered, appearing to them during forty days and speaking about the kingdom of God. While meeting with them, he enjoined them not to depart from Jerusalem, but to wait for "the promise of the Father about which you have heard me speak; for John baptized with water, but in a few days you will be baptized with the holy Spirit."

When they had gathered together they asked him, "Lord, are you at this time going to restore the kingdom to Israel?" He answered them, "It is not for you to know the times or seasons that the Father has established by his own authority. But you will receive power when the holy Spirit comes upon you, and you will be my witnesses in Jerusalem, throughout Judea and Samaria, and to the ends of the earth." When he had said this, as they were looking on, he was lifted up, and a cloud took him from their sight. While they were looking intently at the sky as he was going, suddenly two men dressed in white garments stood beside them. They said, "Men of Galilee, why are you standing there looking at the sky? This Jesus who has been taken up from you into heaven will return in the same way as you have seen him going into heaven." Then they returned to Jerusalem from the mount called Olivet, which is near Jerusalem, a sabbath day's journey away.

When they entered the city they went to the upper room where they were staying, Peter and John and James and Andrew, Philip and Thomas, Bartholomew and Matthew, James son of Alphaeus, Simon the Zealot, and Judas son of James. All these devoted themselves with one accord to prayer, together with some women, and Mary the mother of Jesus, and his brothers.

During those days Peter stood up in the midst of the brothers (there was a group of about one hundred and twenty persons in the one place). He said, "My brothers, the scripture had to be fulfilled which the holy Spirit spoke beforehand through the mouth of David, concerning Judas, who was the guide for those who arrested Jesus. He was numbered among us and was allotted a share in this ministry. He bought a parcel of land with the wages of his iniquity, and falling headlong, he burst open in the middle, and all his insides spilled out. This became known to everyone who lived in Jerusalem, so that the parcel of land was called in their language 'Akeldama', that is, Field of Blood. For it is written in the Book of Psalms:

> 'Let his encampment become desolate,
>> and may no one dwell in it.'

And:

> 'May another take his office.'

Therefore, it is necessary that one of the men who accompanied us the whole time the Lord Jesus came and went among us, beginning from the baptism of John until the day on which he was taken up from us, become with us a witness to his resurrection." So they proposed two, Joseph called Barsabbas, who was also known as Justus, and Matthias. Then they prayed, "You, Lord, who know the hearts of all, show which one of these two you have chosen to take the place in this apostolic ministry from which Judas turned away to go to his own place." Then they gave lots to them, and the lot fell upon Matthias, and he was counted with the eleven apostles.

PSALM 17:1-5

A prayer of David.

Hear, O LORD, a just suit;
    attend to my outcry;
    hearken to my prayer from lips
        without deceit.
From you let my judgment come;
    your eyes behold what is right.
Though you test my heart,
    searching it in the night,
    though you try me with fire,
        you shall find no malice in
        me.
My mouth has not transgressed
    after the manner of man;
    according to the words of your
        lips I have kept the ways of
        the law.
My steps have been steadfast in
        your paths,
    my feet have not faltered.

PROVERBS 6:16-19

There are six things the LORD hates, / yes, seven are an abomination to him; / Haughty eyes, a lying tongue, / and hands that shed innocent blood; / A heart that plots wicked schemes, / feet that run swiftly to evil, / The false witness who utters lies, / and he who sows discord among brothers.

FEBRUARY 2

ACTS 2:1-13

When the time for Pentecost was fulfilled, they were all in one place together. And suddenly there came from the sky a noise like a strong driving wind, and it filled the entire house in which they were. Then there appeared to them tongues as of fire, which parted and came to rest on each one of them. And they were all filled with the holy Spirit and began to speak in different tongues, as the Spirit enabled them to proclaim.

Now there were devout Jews from every nation under heaven staying in Jerusalem. At this sound, they gathered in a large crowd, but they were confused because each one heard them speaking in his own language. They were astounded, and in amazement they asked, "Are not all these people who are speaking Galileans? Then how does each of us hear them in his own native language? We are Parthians, Medes, and Elamites, inhabitants of Mesopotamia, Judea and Cappadocia, Pontus and Asia, Phrygia and Pamphylia, Egypt and the districts of Libya near Cyrene, as well as travelers from Rome, both Jews and converts to Judaism, Cretans and Arabs, yet we hear them speaking in our own tongues of the mighty acts of God." They were all astounded and bewildered, and said to one another, "What does this mean?" But others said, scoffing, "They have had too much new wine."

PSALM 17:6-12

I call upon you, for you will
    answer me, O God;
  incline your ear to me; hear my
    word.
Show your wondrous kindness,
  O savior of those who flee
  from their foes to refuge at
    your right hand.
Keep me as the apple of your
    eye;
  hide me in the shadow of your
    wings
  from the wicked who use
    violence against me.
My ravenous enemies beset me;
  they shut up their cruel hearts,
  their mouths speak proudly.
Their steps even now surround
    me;
  crouching to the ground, they
    fix their gaze,
Like lions hungry for prey,
  like young lions lurking in
    hiding.

PROVERBS 6:20-26

Observe, my son, your father's bidding, / and reject not your mother's teaching; / Keep them fastened over your heart always, / put them around your neck; / For the bidding is a lamp, and the teaching a light, / and a way to life are the reproofs of discipline; / To keep you from your neighbor's wife, / from the smooth tongue of the adulteress. / Lust not in your heart after her beauty, / let her not captivate you with her glance! / For the price of a loose woman / may be scarcely a loaf of bread, / But if she is married, / she is a trap for your precious life.

FEBRUARY 3

ACTS 2:14-36

Then Peter stood up with the Eleven, raised his voice, and proclaimed to them, "You who are Jews, indeed all of you staying in Jerusalem. Let this be known to you, and listen to my words. These people are not drunk, as you suppose, for it is only nine o'clock in the morning. No, this is what was spoken through the prophet Joel:

'It will come to pass in the last
    days,' God says,
    'that I will pour out a portion
    of my spirit
    upon all flesh.
Your sons and your daughters
    shall prophesy,
    your young men shall see
    visions,
    your old men shall dream
    dreams.
Indeed, upon my servants and
    my handmaids
    I will pour out a portion of
    my spirit in those days,
    and they shall prophesy.
And I will work wonders in the
    heavens above
    and signs on the earth below:
    blood, fire, and a cloud of
    smoke.
The sun shall be turned to
    darkness,
    and the moon to blood,
    before the coming of the
    great and splendid day of
    the LORD,
and it shall be that everyone
    shall be saved who calls on
    the name of the LORD.'

You who are Israelites, hear these words. Jesus the Nazorean was a man commended to you by God with mighty deeds, wonders, and signs, which God worked through him in your midst, as you yourselves know. This man, delivered up by the set plan and foreknowledge of God, you killed, using lawless men to crucify him. But God raised him up, releasing him from the throes of death, because it was impossible for him to be held by it. For David says of him:

'I saw the LORD ever before me,
    with him at my right hand I
    shall not be disturbed.
Therefore my heart has been
    glad and my tongue has
    exulted;
    my flesh, too, will dwell in
    hope,
because you will not abandon
    my soul to the nether
    world,
    nor will you suffer your holy
    one to see
    corruption.
You have made known to me
    the paths of life;
    you will fill me with joy in
    your presence.'

My brothers, one can confidently say to you about the patriarch David that he died and was buried, and his tomb is in our midst to this day. But since he was a prophet and knew that God had sworn an oath to him that he would set one of his descendants upon his throne, he foresaw and spoke of the resurrection of the Messiah, that neither was he abandoned to the netherworld nor did his flesh see corruption. God raised this Jesus; of this we are all witnesses. Exalted at the right hand of God, he received the promise of the holy Spirit from the Father and poured it forth, as you [both] see and hear. For David did not go up into heaven, but he himself said:

'The Lord said to my Lord,
"Sit at my right hand
    until I make your enemies
    your footstool." '

Therefore let the whole house of Israel know for certain that God has made him both Lord and Messiah, this Jesus whom you crucified."

PSALM 17:13-15

Rise, O LORD, confront them and
    cast them down;
  rescue me by your sword from
    the wicked,
  by your hand, O LORD, from
    mortal men:
From mortal men whose portion
  in life is in this world,
where with your treasures you
    fill their bellies.
Their sons are enriched
  and bequeath their abundance
    to their little ones.
But I in justice shall behold your
    face;
  on waking, I shall be content in
    your presence.

PROVERBS 6:27-35

Can a man take fire to his bosom, / and his garments not be burned? / Or can a man walk on live coals, / and his feet not be scorched? / So with him who goes in to his neighbor's wife—/ none who touches her shall go unpunished. / Men despise not the thief if he steals / to satisfy his appetite when he is hungry; / Yet if he be caught he must pay back sevenfold; / all the wealth of his house he may yield up. / But he who commits adultery is a fool; / he who would destroy himself does it. / A degrading beating will he get, / and his disgrace will not be wiped away; / For vindictive is the husband's wrath, / he will have no pity on the day of vengeance; / He will not consider any restitution, / nor be satisfied with the greatest gifts.

FEBRUARY 4

ACTS 2:37-47

Now when they heard this, they were cut to the heart, and they asked Peter and the other apostles, "What are we to do, my brothers?" Peter [said] to them, "Repent and be baptized, every one of you, in the name of Jesus Christ for the forgiveness of your sins; and you will receive the gift of the holy Spirit. For the promise is made to you and to your children and to all those far off, whomever the Lord our God will call." He testified with many other arguments, and was exhorting them, "Save yourselves from this corrupt generation." Those who accepted his message were baptized, and about three thousand persons were added that day.

They devoted themselves to the teaching of the apostles and to the communal life, to the breaking of the bread and to the prayers. Awe came upon everyone, and many wonders and signs were done through the apostles. All who believed were together and had all things in common; they would sell their property and possessions and divide them among all according to each one's need. Every day they devoted themselves to meeting together in the temple area and to breaking bread in their homes. They ate their meals with exultation and sincerity of heart, praising God and enjoying favor with all the people. And every day the Lord added to their number those who were being saved.

PSALM 18:1-7

For the leader. Of David, the servant of the LORD, who sang to the LORD the words of this song when the LORD had rescued him from the grasp of all his enemies and from the hand of Saul.

I love you, O LORD, my strength,
O LORD, my rock, my fortress, my deliverer.
My God, my rock of refuge, my shield, the horn of my salvation, my stronghold!
Praised be the LORD, I exclaim, and I am safe from my enemies.
The breakers of death surged round about me, the destroying floods overwhelmed me;
The cords of the nether world enmeshed me, the snares of death overtook me.
In my distress I called upon the LORD and cried out to my God;
From his temple he heard my voice, and my cry to him reached his ears.

PROVERBS 7:1-5

My son, keep my words, / and treasure my commands. / Keep my commands and live, / my teaching as the apple of your eye; / Bind them on your fingers, / write them on the tablet of your heart. / Say to Wisdom, "You are my sister!" / call Understanding, "Friend!" / That they may keep you from another's wife, / from the adulteress with her smooth words.

FEBRUARY 5

ACTS 3:1-26

Now Peter and John were going up to the temple area for the three o'clock hour of prayer. And a man crippled from birth was carried and placed at the gate of the temple called "the Beautiful Gate" every day to beg for alms from the people who entered the temple. When he saw Peter and John about to go into the temple, he asked for alms. But Peter looked intently at him, as did John, and said, "Look at us." He paid attention to them, expecting to receive something from them. Peter said, "I have neither silver nor gold, but what I do have I give you: in the name of Jesus Christ the Nazorean, [rise and] walk." Then Peter took him by the right hand and raised him up, and immediately his feet and ankles grew strong. He leaped up, stood, and walked around, and went into the temple with them, walking and jumping and praising God. When all the people saw him walking and praising God, they recognized him as the one who used to sit begging at the Beautiful Gate of the temple, and they were filled with amazement and astonishment at what had happened to him.

As he clung to Peter and John,

all the people hurried in amazement toward them in the portico called "Solomon's Portico." When Peter saw this, he addressed the people, "You Israelites, why are you amazed at this, and why do you look so intently at us as if we had made him walk by our own power or piety? The God of Abraham, [the God] of Isaac, and [the God] of Jacob, the God of our ancestors, has glorified his servant Jesus whom you handed over and denied in Pilate's presence, when he had decided to release him. You denied the Holy and Righteous One and asked that a murderer be released to you. The author of life you put to death, but God raised him from the dead; of this we are witnesses. And by faith in his name, this man, whom you see and know, his name has made strong, and the faith that comes through it has given him this perfect health, in the presence of all of you. Now I know, brothers, that you acted out of ignorance, just as your leaders did; but God has thus brought to fulfillment what he had announced beforehand through the mouth of all the prophets, that his Messiah would suffer. Repent, therefore, and be converted, that your sins may be wiped away, and that the Lord may grant you times of refreshment and send you the Messiah already appointed for you, Jesus, whom heaven must receive until the times of universal restoration of which God spoke through the mouth of his holy prophets from of old. For Moses said:

'A prophet like me will the
　　Lord, your God, raise up
　　for you
　from among your own
　　kinsmen;

to him you shall listen in all
　　that he may say to you.
Everyone who does not listen
　　to that prophet
　will be cut off from the
　　people.'

Moreover, all the prophets who spoke, from Samuel and those afterwards, also announced these days. You are the children of the prophets and of the covenant that God made with your ancestors when he said to Abraham, 'In your offspring all the families of the earth shall be blessed.' For you first, God raised up his servant and sent him to bless you by turning each of you from your evil ways."

PSALM 18:8-16

The earth swayed and quaked;
　the foundations of the
　　mountains trembled
　and shook when his wrath
　　flared up.
Smoke rose from his nostrils,
　and a devouring fire from his
　　mouth
　that kindled coals into flame.
And he inclined the heavens and
　　came down,
　with dark clouds under his
　　feet.
He mounted a cherub and flew,
　borne on the wings of the
　　wind.
And he made darkness the cloak
　　about him;
　dark, misty rain-clouds his
　　wrap.
From the brightness of his
　　presence
　coals were kindled to flame.
And the LORD thundered from
　　heaven,
　the Most High gave forth his
　　voice;

He sent forth his arrows to put
    them to flight,
  with frequent lightnings he
    routed them.
Then the bed of the sea
    appeared,

and the foundations of the
    world were laid bare,
At the rebuke of the LORD,
  and the blast of the wind of his
    wrath.

PROVERBS 7:6-23

For at the window of my house, / through my lattice I looked out—/ And I saw among the simple ones, / I observed among the young men, / a youth with no sense, / Going along the street near the corner, / then walking in the direction of her house—/ In the twilight, at dusk of day, / at the time of the dark of night. / And lo! the woman comes to meet him, / robed like a harlot, with secret designs—/ She is fickle and unruly, / in her home her feet cannot rest; / Now she is in the streets, now in the open squares, / and at every corner she lurks in ambush—/ When she seizes him, she kisses him, / and with an impudent look says to him: / "I owed peace offerings, / and today I have fulfilled my vows; / So I came out to meet you, / to look for you, and I have found you! / With coverlets I have spread my couch, / with brocaded cloths of Egyptian linen; / I have sprinkled my bed with myrrh, / with aloes, and with cinnamon. / Come, let us drink our fill of love, / until morning, let us feast on love! / For my husband is not at home, / he has gone on a long journey; / A bag of money he took with him, / not till the full moon will he return home." / She wins him over by her repeated urging, / with her smooth lips she leads him astray; / He follows her stupidly, / like an ox that is led to slaughter; / Like a stag that minces toward the net, / till an arrow pierces its liver; / Like a bird that rushes into a snare, / unaware that its life is at stake.

FEBRUARY 6

ACTS 4:1-22

While they were still speaking to the people, the priests, the captain of the temple guard, and the Sadducees confronted them, disturbed that they were teaching the people and proclaiming in Jesus the resurrection of the dead. They laid hands on them and put them in custody until the next day, since it was already evening. But many of those who heard the word came to believe and [the] number of men grew to [about] five thousand.

On the next day, their leaders, elders, and scribes were assembled in Jerusalem, with Annas the high priest, Caiaphas, John, Alexander, and all who were of the high-priestly class. They brought them into their presence and questioned them, "By what power or by what name have you done this?" Then Peter, filled with the holy Spirit, answered them, "Leaders of the people and elders: If we are being examined today about a good deed done to a cripple, namely, by what means he was saved, then all of you and all the people of Israel should know that it was in the name of Jesus Christ the Nazorean whom you crucified, whom God raised from the dead; in his name this man stands before you healed. He is 'the stone rejected by you, the builders, which has become the cornerstone.' There is no salvation through anyone else, nor is there any other name under heaven given to the human race by which we are to be saved."

Observing the boldness of Peter and John and perceiving them to be uneducated, ordinary men, they were amazed, and they recognized them as the companions of Jesus. Then when they saw the man who had been cured standing there with them, they could say nothing in reply. So they ordered them to leave the Sanhedrin, and conferred with one another, saying, "What are we to do with these men? Everyone living in Jerusalem knows that a remarkable sign was done through them, and we cannot deny it. But so that it may not be spread any further among the people, let us give them a stern warning never again to speak to anyone in this name."

So they called them back and ordered them not to speak or teach at all in the name of Jesus. Peter and John, however, said to them in reply, "Whether it is right in the sight of God for us to obey you rather than God, you be the judges. It is impossible for us not to speak about what we have seen and heard." After threatening them further, they released them, finding no way to punish them, on account of the people who were all praising God for what had happened. For the man on whom this sign of healing had been done was over forty years old.

PSALM 18:17-31

He reached out from on high and
    grasped me;
  he drew me out of the deep
    waters.
He rescued me from my mighty
    enemy
  and from my foes, who were
    too powerful for me.
They attacked me in the day of
    my calamity,
  but the LORD came to my
    support.
He set me free in the open,
  and rescued me, because he
    loves me.
The LORD rewarded me according
    to my justice;
  according to the cleanness of
    my hands he requited me;
For I kept the ways of the LORD
  and was not disloyal to my
    God;
For his ordinances were all
    present to me,
  and his statutes I put not from
    me,
But I was wholehearted toward
    him,
  and I was on my guard against
    guilt.
And the LORD requited me
    according to my justice,
  according to the cleanness of
    my hands in his sight.
Toward the faithful you are
    faithful,
  toward the wholehearted you
    are wholehearted,
Toward the sincere you are
    sincere,
  but toward the crooked you are
    astute;
For lowly people you save
  but haughty eyes you bring
    low;
You indeed, O LORD, give light to
    my lamp;
  O my God, you brighten the
    darkness about me;

For with your aid I run against an
  armed band,
    and by the help of my God I
    leap over a wall.
God's way is unerring,

the promise of the LORD is fire-
  tried,
he is a shield to all who take
  refuge in him.

PROVERBS 7:24-27

So now, O children, listen to me, / be attentive to the words of my mouth! / Let not your heart turn to her ways, / go not astray in her paths; / For many are those she has struck down dead, / numerous, those she has slain. / Her house is made up of ways to the nether world, / leading down into the chambers of death.

FEBRUARY 7

ACTS 4:23-37

After their release they went back to their own people and reported what the chief priests and elders had told them. And when they heard it, they raised their voices to God with one accord and said, "Sovereign Lord, maker of heaven and earth and the sea and all that is in them, you said by the holy Spirit through the mouth of our father David, your servant:

'Why did the Gentiles rage
  and the peoples entertain
  folly?
The kings of the earth took
  their stand
  and the princes gathered
  together
  against the Lord and against
  his anointed.'

Indeed they gathered in this city against your holy servant Jesus whom you anointed, Herod and Pontius Pilate, together with the Gentiles and the peoples of Israel, to do what your hand and [your] will had long ago planned to take place. And now, Lord, take note of their threats, and enable your servants to speak your word with all boldness, as you stretch forth [your] hand to heal, and signs and wonders are done through the name of your holy servant Jesus." As they prayed, the place where they were gathered shook, and they were all filled with the holy Spirit and continued to speak the word of God with boldness.

The community of believers was of one heart and mind, and no one claimed that any of his possessions was his own, but they had everything in common. With great power the apostles bore witness to the resurrection of the Lord Jesus, and great favor was accorded them all. There was no needy person among them, for those who owned property or houses would sell them, bring the proceeds of the sale, and put them at the feet of the apostles, and they were distributed to each according to need.

Thus Joseph, also named by the apostles Barnabas (which is translated "son of encouragement"), a Levite, a Cypriot by birth, sold a piece of property that he owned, then brought the money and put it at the feet of the apostles.

PSALM 18:32-35

For who is God except the LORD?
  Who is a rock, save our God?
The God who girded me with
  strength
and kept my way unerring;
Who made my feet swift as those
  of hinds
and set me on the heights;
Who trained my hands for war
  and my arms to bend a bow of
  brass.

PROVERBS 8:1-11

Does not Wisdom call, / and Understanding raise her voice? / On the top of the heights along the road, / at the crossroads she takes her stand; / By the gates at the approaches of the city, / in the entryways she cries aloud: / "To you, O men, I call; / my appeal is to the children of men. / You simple ones, gain resource, / you fools, gain sense. / Give heed! for noble things I speak; / honesty opens my lips. / Yes, the truth my mouth recounts, / but wickedness my lips abhor. / Sincere are all the words of my mouth, / no one of them is wily or crooked; / All of them are plain to the man of intelligence, / and right to those who attain knowledge. / Receive my instruction in preference to silver, / and knowledge rather than choice gold. / [For Wisdom is better than corals, / and no choice possession can compare with her.]"

FEBRUARY 8

ACTS 5:1-16

A man named Ananias, however, with his wife Sapphira, sold a piece of property. He retained for himself, with his wife's knowledge, some of the purchase price, took the remainder, and put it at the feet of the apostles. But Peter said, "Ananias, why has Satan filled your heart so that you lied to the holy Spirit and retained part of the price of the land? While it remained unsold, did it not remain yours? And when it was sold, was it not still under your control? Why did you contrive this deed? You have lied not to human beings, but to God." When Ananias heard these words, he fell down and breathed his last, and great fear came upon all who heard of it. The young men came and wrapped him up, then carried him out and buried him.

After an interval of about three hours, his wife came in, unaware of what had happened. Peter said to her, "Tell me, did you sell the land for this amount?" She answered, "Yes, for that amount." Then Peter said to her, "Why did you agree to test the Spirit of the Lord? Listen, the footsteps of those who have buried your husband are at the door, and they will carry you out." At once, she fell down at his feet and breathed her last. When the young men entered they found her dead, so they carried her out and buried her beside her husband. And great fear came upon the whole church and upon all who heard of these things.

Many signs and wonders were done among the people at the hands of the apostles. They were all together in Solomon's portico. None of the others dared to join them, but the people esteemed them. Yet more than ever, believers in the Lord, great numbers of men and women, were added to them. Thus they even carried the sick out into the streets and laid them on cots and mats so that when Peter came by, at least his shadow might fall on one or another of them. A large number of people from the towns in the vicinity of Jerusalem also gathered, bringing the sick and those disturbed by unclean spirits, and they were all cured.

PSALM 18:36-43

You have given me your saving shield;
   your right hand has upheld me,
and you have stooped to make me great.
You made room for my steps;
   unwavering was my stride.
I pursued my enemies and overtook them,
   nor did I turn again till I made an end of them.
I smote them and they could not rise;
   they fell beneath my feet.
And you girded me with strength for war;
   you subdued my adversaries beneath me.
My enemies you put to flight before me,
   and those who hated me you destroyed.
They cried for help—but no one saved them;
   to the LORD—but he answered them not.
I ground them fine as the dust before the wind;
   like the mud in the streets I trampled them down.

PROVERBS 8:12-13

"I, Wisdom, dwell with experience, / and judicious knowledge I attain. / [The fear of the LORD is to hate evil;] / Pride, arrogance, the evil way, / and the perverse mouth I hate."

FEBRUARY 9

ACTS 5:17-42

Then the high priest rose up and all his companions, that is, the party of the Sadducees, and, filled with jealousy, laid hands upon the apostles and put them in the public jail. But during the night, the angel of the Lord opened the doors of the prison, led them out, and said, "Go and take your place in the temple area, and tell the people everything about this life." When they heard this, they went to the temple early in the morning and taught. When the high priest and his companions arrived, they convened the Sanhedrin, the full senate of the

Israelites, and sent to the jail to have them brought in. But the court officers who went did not find them in the prison, so they came back and reported, "We found the jail securely locked and the guards stationed outside the doors, but when we opened them, we found no one inside." When they heard this report, the captain of the temple guard and the chief priests were at a loss about them, as to what this would come to. Then someone came in and reported to them, "The men whom you put in prison are in the temple area and are teaching the people." Then the captain and the court officers went and brought them in, but without force, because they were afraid of being stoned by the people.

When they had brought them in and made them stand before the Sanhedrin, the high priest questioned them, "We gave you strict orders [did we not?] to stop teaching in that name. Yet you have filled Jerusalem with your teaching and want to bring this man's blood upon us." But Peter and the apostles said in reply, "We must obey God rather than men. The God of our ancestors raised Jesus, though you had him killed by hanging him on a tree. God exalted him at his right hand as leader and savior to grant Israel repentance and forgiveness of sins. We are witnesses of these things, as is the holy Spirit that God has given to those who obey him."

When they heard this, they became infuriated and wanted to put them to death. But a Pharisee in the Sanhedrin named Gamaliel, a teacher of the law, respected by all the people, stood up, ordered the men to be put outside for a short time, and said to them, "Fellow Israelites, be careful what you are about to do to these men. Some time ago, Theudas appeared, claiming to be someone important, and about four hundred men joined him, but he was killed, and all those who were loyal to him were disbanded and came to nothing. After him came Judas the Galilean at the time of the census. He also drew people after him, but he too perished and all who were loyal to him were scattered. So now I tell you, have nothing to do with these men, and let them go. For if this endeavor or this activity is of human origin, it will destroy itself. But if it comes from God, you will not be able to destroy them; you may even find yourselves fighting against God." They were persuaded by him. After recalling the apostles, they had them flogged, ordered them to stop speaking in the name of Jesus, and dismissed them. So they left the presence of the Sanhedrin, rejoicing that they had been found worthy to suffer dishonor for the sake of the name. And all day long, both at the temple and in their homes, they did not stop teaching and proclaiming the Messiah, Jesus.

PSALM 18:44-51

You rescued me from the strife of
    the people;
  you made me head over
    nations;
A people I had not known
    became my slaves;
  as soon as they heard me they
    obeyed.
The foreigners fawned and
    cringed before me;
  they staggered forth from their
    fortresses.
The LORD live! And blessed be
    my Rock!

Extolled be God my savior.
O God, who granted me
    vengeance,
    who made peoples subject to
    me
    and preserved me from my
    enemies,
Truly above my adversaries you
    exalt me
    and from the violent man you
    have rescued me.

Therefore will I proclaim you, O
    LORD, among the nations,
    and I will sing praise to your
    name,
You who gave great victories to
    your king
    and showed kindness to your
    anointed,
to David and his posterity
    forever.

PROVERBS 8:14-21

"Mine are counsel and advice; / Mine is strength; I am understanding. / By me kings reign, / and lawgivers establish justice; / By me princes govern, / and nobles; all the rulers of earth. / Those who love me I also love, / and those who seek me find me. / With me are riches and honor, / enduring wealth and prosperity. / My fruit is better than gold, yes, than pure gold, / and my revenue than choice silver. / On the way of duty I walk, / along the paths of justice, / Granting wealth to those who love me, / and filling their treasuries."

FEBRUARY 10

ACTS 6:1-15

At that time, as the number of disciples continued to grow, the Hellenists complained against the Hebrews because their widows were being neglected in the daily distribution. So the Twelve called together the community of the disciples and said, "It is not right for us to neglect the word of God to serve at table. Brothers, select from among you seven reputable men, filled with the Spirit and wisdom, whom we shall appoint to this task, whereas we shall devote ourselves to prayer and to the ministry of the word." The proposal was acceptable to the whole community, so they chose Stephen, a man filled with faith and the holy Spirit, also Philip, Prochorus, Nicanor, Timon, Parmenas, and Nicholas of Antioch, a convert to Judaism. They presented these men to the apostles who prayed and laid hands on them. The word of God continued to spread, and the number of the disciples in Jerusalem increased greatly; even a large group of priests were becoming obedient to the faith.

Now Stephen, filled with grace and power, was working great wonders and signs among the people. Certain members of the so-called Synagogue of Freedmen, Cyrenians, and Alexandrians, and people from Cilicia and Asia, came forward and debated with Stephen, but they could not withstand the wisdom and the spirit with which he spoke. Then they instigated some men to say, "We have heard him speaking blasphemous words against Moses and God." They stirred up the people, the elders, and the scribes, accosted him, seized him, and brought him before the Sanhedrin. They presented false witnesses who testified, "This man never stops saying things against [this] holy place and the law. For we have heard him claim that this Jesus the Nazorean will destroy this place and change the customs that Moses handed down to us." All those who sat in the Sanhedrin looked intently at him and saw that his face was like the face of an angel.

PSALM 19:1-7

For the leader. A psalm of David.
The heavens declare the glory of
    God,
    and the firmament proclaims
    his handiwork.
Day pours out the word to day,
    and night to night imparts
    knowledge;
Not a word nor a discourse
    whose voice is not heard;
Through all the earth their voice
    resounds,
    and to the ends of the world,
    their message.
He has pitched a tent there for
    the sun,
    which comes forth like the
    groom from his bridal
    chamber
    and, like a giant, joyfully runs
    its course.
At one end of the heavens it
    comes forth,
    and its course is to their other
    end;
    nothing escapes its heat.

PROVERBS 8:22-31

"The LORD begot me, the firstborn of his ways, / the forerunner of his prodigies of long ago; / From of old I was poured forth, / at the first, before the earth. / When there were no depths I was brought forth, / when there were no fountains or springs of water; / Before the mountains were settled into place, / before the hills, I was brought forth; / While as yet the earth and the fields were not made, / nor the first clods of the world. / When he established the heavens I was there, / when he marked out the vault over the face of the deep; / When he made firm the skies above, / when he fixed fast the foundations of the earth; / When he set for the sea its limit, / so that the waters should not transgress his command; / Then was I beside him as his craftsman, / and I was his delight day by day, / Playing before him all the while, / playing on the surface of his earth; / and I found delight in the sons of men."

FEBRUARY 11

ACTS 7:1-34

Then the high priest asked, "Is this so?" And he replied, "My brothers and fathers, listen. The God of glory appeared to our father Abraham while he was in Mesopotamia, before he had settled in Haran, and said to him, 'Go forth from your land and [from] your kinsfolk to the land that I will show you.' So he went forth from the land of the Chaldeans and settled in Haran. And from there, after his father died, he made him migrate to this land where you now dwell. Yet he gave him no inheritance in it, not even a foot's length, but he did promise to give it to him and his descendants as a possession, even though he was childless. And God spoke thus, 'His descendants shall be aliens in a land not their own, where they shall be enslaved and oppressed for four hundred years; but I will bring judgment on the nation they serve,' God said, 'and after that they will come out and worship me in this place.' Then he gave him the covenant of circumcision, and so he became the father of Isaac, and circumcised him on the eighth day, as Isaac did Jacob, and Jacob the twelve patriarchs.

"And the patriarchs, jealous of Joseph, sold him into slavery in Egypt; but God was with him and rescued him from all his afflictions. He granted him favor and wisdom before Pharaoh, the king of Egypt, who put him in charge of Egypt and [of] his entire household. Then a famine and great affliction struck all Egypt and Canaan, and our ancestors could find no food; but when Jacob heard that there was grain in Egypt, he sent our ancestors there a first time. The second time, Joseph made himself known to his brothers, and Joseph's family became known to Pharaoh. Then Joseph sent for his father Jacob, inviting him and his whole clan, seventy-five persons; and Jacob went down to Egypt. And he and our ancestors died and were brought back to Shechem and placed in the tomb that Abraham had purchased for a sum of money from the sons of Hamor at Shechem.

"When the time drew near for the fulfillment of the promise that God pledged to Abraham, the people had increased and become very numerous in Egypt, until another king who knew nothing of Joseph came to power [in Egypt]. He dealt shrewdly with our people and oppressed [our] ancestors by forcing them to expose their infants, that they might not survive. At this time Moses was born, and he was extremely beautiful. For three months he was nursed in his father's house; but when he was exposed, Pharaoh's daughter adopted him and brought him up as her own son. Moses was educated [in] all the wisdom of the Egyptians and was powerful in his words and deeds.

"When he was forty years old, he decided to visit his kinsfolk, the Israelites. When he saw one of them treated unjustly, he defended and avenged the oppressed man by striking down the Egyptian. He assumed [his] kinsfolk would understand that God was offering them deliverance through him, but they did not understand. The next day he appeared to them as they were fighting and tried to reconcile them peacefully, saying, 'Men, you are brothers. Why are you harming one another?' Then the one who was harming his neighbor pushed him aside, saying, 'Who appointed you ruler and judge over us? Are you thinking of killing me as you killed the Egyptian yesterday?' Moses fled when he heard this and settled as an alien in the land of Midian, where he became the father of two sons.

"Forty years later, an angel appeared to him in the desert near Mount Sinai in the flame of a burning bush. When Moses saw it, he was amazed at the sight, and as he drew near to look at it, the voice of the Lord came, 'I am the God of your fathers, the God of Abraham, of Isaac, and of Jacob.' Then Moses, trembling, did not dare to look at it. But the Lord said to him, 'Remove the sandals from your feet, for the place where you stand is holy ground. I have witnessed the affliction of my people in Egypt and have heard their groaning, and I have come down to rescue them. Come now, I will send you to Egypt.' "

PSALM 19:8-15

The law of the LORD is perfect,
    refreshing the soul;
The decree of the LORD is
        trustworthy,
    giving wisdom to the simple.
The precepts of the LORD are
    right,
    rejoicing the heart;
The command of the LORD is
    clear,
    enlightening the eye;
The fear of the LORD is pure,
    enduring forever;
The ordinances of the LORD are
    true,
    all of them just;
They are more precious than
        gold,
    than a heap of purest gold;
Sweeter also than syrup
    or honey from the comb.
Though your servant is careful of
    them,
    very diligent in keeping them,
Yet who can detect failings?
    Cleanse me from my unknown
    faults!
From wanton sin especially,
        restrain your servant;
    let it not rule over me.
Then shall I be blameless and
    innocent of serious sin.
Let the words of my mouth and
    the thought of my heart
    find favor before you,
O LORD, my rock and my
    redeemer.

PROVERBS 8:32-36

"So now, O children, listen to me; / instruction and wisdom do not reject! / Happy the man who obeys me, / and happy those who keep my ways, / Happy the man watching daily at my gates, / waiting at my doorposts; / For he who finds me finds life, / and wins favor from the LORD; / But he who misses me harms himself; / all who hate me love death."

FEBRUARY 12

ACTS 7:35-60; 8:1a

"This Moses, whom they had rejected with the words, 'Who appointed you ruler and judge?' God sent as [both] ruler and deliverer, through the angel who appeared to him in the bush. This man led them out, performing wonders and signs in the land of Egypt, at the Red Sea, and in the desert for forty years. It was this Moses who said to the Israelites, 'God will raise up for you, from among your own kinsfolk, a prophet like me.' It was he who, in the assembly in the desert, was with the angel who spoke to him on Mount Sinai and with our ancestors, and he received living utterances to hand on to us.

"Our ancestors were unwilling to obey him; instead, they pushed him aside and in their hearts turned back to Egypt, saying to Aaron, 'Make us gods who will be our leaders. As for that Moses who led us out of the land of Egypt, we do not know what has happened to him.' So they made a calf in those days, offered sacrifice to the idol, and reveled in the works of their hands. Then God turned and handed them over to worship the host of heaven, as it is written in the book of the prophets;

'Did you bring me sacrifices
    and offerings
    for forty years in the desert,
    O house of Israel?
No, you took up the tent of
    Moloch
    and the star of [your] god
    Rephan,
    the images that you made to
    worship.
So I shall take you into exile
    beyond Babylon.'

"Our ancestors had the tent of testimony in the desert just as the One who spoke to Moses directed him to make it according to the pattern he had seen. Our ancestors who inherited it brought it with Joshua when they dispossessed the nations that God drove out from before our ancestors, up to the time of David, who found favor in the sight of God and asked that he might find a dwelling place for the house of Jacob. But Solomon built a house for him. Yet the Most High does not dwell in houses made by human hands. As the prophet says:

'The heavens are my throne,
    the earth is my footstool.
What kind of house can you
    build for me? says the
    LORD,
    or what is to be my resting
    place?
Did not my hand make all
    these things?'

"You stiff-necked people, uncircumcised in heart and ears, you always oppose the holy Spirit; you are just like your ancestors. Which of the prophets did your ancestors not persecute? They put to death those who foretold the coming of the righteous one, whose betrayers and murderers you have now become. You received the law as transmitted by angels, but you did not observe it."

When they heard this, they were infuriated, and they ground their teeth at him. But he, filled with the holy Spirit, looked up intently to heaven and saw the glory of God and Jesus standing at the right hand of God, and he said, "Behold, I see the heavens opened and the Son of Man standing at the right hand of God." But they cried out in a loud voice, covered their ears, and rushed upon him together. They threw him out of the city, and began to stone him. The witnesses laid down their cloaks at the feet of a young man named Saul. As they were stoning Stephen, he called out, "Lord Jesus, receive my spirit." Then he fell to his knees and cried out in a loud voice, "Lord, do not hold this sin against them"; and when he said this, he fell asleep. Now Saul was consenting to his execution.

PSALM 20:1-10

For the leader. A psalm of David.

The LORD answer you in time of distress;
  the name of the God of Jacob defend you!
May he send you help from the sanctuary,
  from Zion may he sustain you.
May he remember all your offerings
  and graciously accept your holocaust.
May he grant you what is in your heart
  and fulfill your every plan.
May we shout for joy at your victory
  and raise the standards in the name of our God.
The LORD grant all your requests!
Now I know that the LORD has given victory to his anointed,
  that he has answered him from his holy heaven
with the strength of his victorious right hand.
Some are strong in chariots; some, in horses;
  but we are strong in the name of the LORD, our God.
Though they bow down and fall, yet we stand erect and firm.
O LORD, grant victory to the king,
  and answer us when we call upon you.

PROVERBS 9:1-6, 11

Wisdom has built her house, / she has set up her seven columns; / She has dressed her meat, mixed her wine, / yes, she has spread her table. / She has sent out her maidens; she calls / from the heights out over the city: / "Let whoever is simple turn in here; / to him who lacks understanding, I say, / Come, eat of my food, / and drink of the wine I have mixed! / Forsake foolishness that you may live; / advance in the way of understanding. / For by me your days will be multiplied / and the years of your life increased."

FEBRUARY 13

ACTS 8:1b-24

On that day, there broke out a severe persecution of the church in Jerusalem, and all were scattered throughout the countryside of Judea and Samaria, except the apostles. Devout men buried Stephen and made a loud lament over him. Saul, meanwhile, was trying to destroy the church; entering house after house and dragging out men and women, he handed them over for imprisonment.

Now those who had been scattered went about preaching the word. Thus Philip went down to [the] city of Samaria and proclaimed the Messiah to them. With one accord, the crowds paid attention to what was said by Philip when they heard it and saw the signs he was doing. For unclean spirits, crying out in a loud voice, came out of many possessed people, and many paralyzed and crippled people were cured. There was great joy in that city.

A man named Simon used to practice magic in the city and astounded the people of Samaria, claiming to be someone great. All of them, from the least to the greatest, paid attention to him, saying, "This man is the 'Power of God' that is called 'Great.' " They paid attention to him because he had astounded them by his magic for a long time, but once they began to believe Philip as he preached the good news about the kingdom of God and the name of Jesus Christ, men and women alike were baptized. Even Simon himself believed and, after being baptized, became devoted to Philip; and when he saw the signs and mighty deeds that were occurring, he was astounded.

Now when the apostles in Jerusalem heard that Samaria had accepted the word of God, they sent them Peter and John, who went down and prayed for them, that they might receive the holy Spirit, for it had not yet fallen upon any of them; they had only been baptized in the name of the Lord Jesus. Then they laid hands on them and they received the holy Spirit.

When Simon saw that the Spirit was conferred by the laying on of the apostles' hands, he offered them money and said, "Give me this power too, so that anyone upon whom I lay my hands may receive the holy Spirit." But Peter said to him, "May your money perish with you, because you thought that you could buy the gift of God with money. You have no share or lot in this matter, for your heart is not upright before God. Repent of this wickedness of yours and pray to the Lord that, if possible, your intention may be forgiven. For I see that you are filled with bitter gall and are in the bonds of iniquity." Simon said in reply, "Pray for me to the Lord, that nothing of what you have said may come upon me."

PSALM 21:1-8

For the leader. A psalm of David.

O LORD, in your strength the
    king is glad;
    in your victory how greatly he
      rejoices!
You have granted him his heart's
    desire;
    you refused not the wish of his
      lips.
For you welcomed him with
    goodly blessings,
    you placed on his head a crown
      of pure gold.
He asked life of you: you gave
    him length of days forever
      and ever.
Great is his glory in your victory;
    majesty and splendor you
      conferred upon him.
For you made him a blessing
    forever;
    you gladdened him with the
      joy of your presence.
For the king trusts in the LORD,
    and through the kindness of
      the Most High
    he stands unshaken.

PROVERBS 9:7-10, 12

He who corrects an arrogant man earns insult; / and he who reproves a wicked man incurs opprobrium. / Reprove not an arrogant man, lest he hate you; / reprove a wise man, and he will love you. / Instruct a wise man, and he becomes still wiser; / teach a just man, and he advances in learning. / The beginning of wisdom is the fear of the LORD, / and knowledge of the Holy One is understanding. . . . / If you are wise, it is to your own advantage; / and if you are arrogant, you alone shall bear it.

FEBRUARY 14

ACTS 8:25-40

So when they had testified and proclaimed the word of the Lord, they returned to Jerusalem and preached the good news to many Samaritan villages.

Then the angel of the Lord spoke to Philip, "Get up and head south on the road that goes down from Jerusalem to Gaza, the desert route." So he got up and set out. Now there was an Ethiopian eunuch, a court official of the Candace, that is, the queen of the Ethiopians, in charge of her entire treasury, who had come to Jerusalem to worship, and was returning home. Seated in his chariot, he was reading the prophet Isaiah. The Spirit said to Philip, "Go and join up with that chariot." Philip ran up and heard him reading Isaiah the prophet and said, "Do you understand what you are reading?" He replied, "How can I, unless someone instructs me?" So he invited Philip to get in and sit with him. This was the scripture passage he was reading:

"Like a sheep he was led to the slaughter,
and as a lamb before its shearer is silent,
so he opened not his mouth.
In [his] humiliation justice was denied him.
Who will tell of his posterity?
For his life is taken from the earth."

Then the eunuch said to Philip in reply, "I beg you, about whom is the prophet saying this? About himself, or about someone else?" Then Philip opened his mouth and, beginning with this scripture passage, he proclaimed Jesus to him. As they traveled along the road they came to some water, and the eunuch said, "Look, there is water. What is to prevent my being baptized?" Then he ordered the chariot to stop, and Philip and the eunuch both went down into the water, and he baptized him. When they came out of the water, the Spirit of the Lord snatched Philip away, and the eunuch saw him no more, but continued on his way rejoicing. Philip came to Azotus, and went about proclaiming the good news to all the towns until he reached Caesarea.

PSALM 21:9-14

May your hand reach all your enemies,
may your right hand reach your foes!
Make them burn as though in a fiery furnace,
when you appear.
May the LORD consume them in his anger;
let fire devour them.
Destroy their fruit from the earth and their posterity from among men.
Though they intend evil against you,
devising plots, they cannot succeed,
For you shall put them to flight; you shall aim your shafts against them.
Be extolled, O LORD, in your strength!
We will sing, chant the praise of your might.

PROVERBS 9:13-18

The woman Folly is fickle, / she is inane, and knows nothing. / She sits at the door of her house / upon a seat on the city heights, / Calling to passers-by / as they go on their straight way: / "Let whoever is simple turn in here, / or who lacks understanding; for to him I say, / Stolen water is sweet, / and bread gotten secretly is pleasing!" / Little he knows that the shades are there, / that in the depths of the nether world are her guests!

FEBRUARY 15

ACTS 9:1-25

Now Saul, still breathing murderous threats against the disciples of the Lord, went to the high priest and asked him for letters to the synagogues in Damascus, that, if he should find any men or women who belonged to the Way, he might bring them back to Jerusalem in chains. On his journey, as he was nearing Damascus, a light from the sky suddenly flashed around him. He fell to the ground and heard a voice saying to him, "Saul, Saul, why are you persecuting me?" He said, "Who are you, sir?" The reply came, "I am Jesus, whom you are persecuting. Now get up and go into the city and you will be told what you must do." The men who were traveling with him stood speechless, for they heard the voice but could see no one. Saul got up from the ground, but when he opened his eyes he could see nothing; so they led him by the hand and brought him to Damascus. For three days he was unable to see, and he neither ate nor drank.

There was a disciple in Damascus named Ananias, and the Lord said to him in a vision, "Ananias." He answered, "Here I am, Lord." The Lord said to him, "Get up and go to the street called Straight and ask at the house of Judas for a man from Tarsus named Saul. He is there praying, and [in a vision] he has seen a man named Ananias come in and lay [his] hands on him, that he may regain his sight." But Ananias replied, "Lord, I have heard from many sources about this man, what evil things he has done to your holy ones in Jerusalem. And here he has authority from the chief priests to imprison all who call upon your name." But the Lord said to him, "Go, for this man is a chosen instrument of mine to carry my name before Gentiles, kings, and Israelites, and I will show him what he will have to suffer for my name." So Ananias went and entered the house; laying his hands on him, he said, "Saul, my brother, the Lord has sent me, Jesus who appeared to you on the way by which you came, that you may regain your sight and be filled with the holy Spirit." Immediately things like scales fell from his eyes and he regained his sight. He got up and was baptized, and when he had eaten, he recovered his strength.

He stayed some days with the disciples in Damascus, and he began at once to proclaim Jesus in the synagogues, that he is the Son of God. All who heard him were astounded and said, "Is not this the man who in Jerusalem ravaged those who call upon this name, and came here expressly to take them back in chains to the chief priests?" But Saul grew all the stronger and confounded [the] Jews who lived in Damascus, proving that this is the Messiah.

After a long time had passed, the Jews conspired to kill him, but their plot became known to Saul. Now they were keeping watch on the gates day and night so as to kill him, but his disciples took him one night and let him down through an opening in the wall, lowering him in a basket.

PSALM 22:1-12

For the leader; according to "The hind of the dawn." A psalm of David.

My God, my God, why have you forsaken me,
  far from my prayer, from the words of my cry?
O my God, I cry out by day, and you answer not;
  by night, and there is no relief for me.
Yet you are enthroned in the holy place,
  O glory of Israel!
In you our fathers trusted;
  they trusted, and you delivered them.
To you they cried, and they escaped;
  in you they trusted, and they were not put to shame.
But I am a worm, not a man;
  the scorn of men, despised by the people.
All who see me scoff at me;
  they mock me with parted lips, they wag their heads:
"He relied on the LORD; let him deliver him,
  let him rescue him, if he loves him."
You have been my guide since I was first formed,
  my security at my mother's breast.
To you I was committed at birth,
  from my mother's womb you are my God.
Be not far from me, for I am in distress,
  be near, for I have no one to help me.

PROVERBS 10:1-2

A wise son makes his father glad, / but a foolish son is a grief to his mother. / Ill-gotten treasures profit nothing, / but virtue saves from death.

FEBRUARY 16

ACTS 9:26-43

When he arrived in Jerusalem he tried to join the disciples, but they were all afraid of him, not believing that he was a disciple. Then Barnabas took charge of him and brought him to the apostles, and he reported to them how on the way he had seen the Lord and that he had spoken to him, and how in Damascus he had spoken out boldly in the name of Jesus.

He moved about freely with them in Jerusalem, and spoke out boldly in the name of the Lord. He also spoke and debated with the Hellenists, but they tried to kill him. And when the brothers learned of this, they took him down to Caesarea and sent him on his way to Tarsus.

The church throughout all Judea, Galilee, and Samaria was at peace. It was being built up and walked in the fear of the Lord, and with the consolation of the holy Spirit it grew in numbers.

As Peter was passing through every region, he went down to the holy ones living in Lydda. There he found a man named Aeneas, who had been confined to bed for eight years, for he was paralyzed. Peter said to him, "Aeneas, Jesus Christ heals you. Get up and make your bed." He got up at once. And all the inhabitants of Lydda and Sharon saw him, and they turned to the Lord.

Now in Joppa there was a disciple named Tabitha (which translated means Dorcas). She was completely occupied with good deeds and almsgiving. Now during those days she fell sick and died, so after washing her, they laid [her] out in a room upstairs. Since Lydda was near Joppa, the disciples, hearing that Peter was there, sent two men to him with the request, "Please come to us without delay." So Peter got up and went with them. When he arrived, they took him to the room upstairs where all the widows came to him weeping and showing him the tunics and cloaks that Dorcas had made while she was with them. Peter sent them all out and knelt down and prayed. Then he turned to her body and said, "Tabitha, rise up." She opened her eyes, saw Peter, and sat up. He gave her his hand and raised her up, and when he had called the holy ones and the widows, he presented her alive. This became known all over Joppa, and many came to believe in the Lord. And he stayed a long time in Joppa with Simon, a tanner.

PSALM 22:13-19

Many bullocks surround me;
    the strong bulls of Bashan
        encircle me.
They open their mouths against
    me
    like ravening and roaring lions.
I am like water poured out;
    all my bones are racked.
My heart has become like wax
    melting away within my
        bosom.
My throat is dried up like baked
    clay,
    my tongue cleaves to my jaws;
    to the dust of death you have
        brought me down.
Indeed, many dogs surround me,
    a pack of evildoers closes in
        upon me;
They have pierced my hands and
    my feet;
    I can count all my bones.
They look on and gloat over me;
    they divide my garments
        among them,
    and for my vesture they cast
        lots.

PROVERBS 10:3

The LORD permits not the just to hunger, / but the craving of the wicked he thwarts.

ACTS 10:1-23

Now in Caesarea there was a man named Cornelius, a centurion of the Cohort called the Italica, devout and God-fearing along with his whole household, who used to give alms generously to the Jewish people and pray to God constantly. One afternoon about three o'clock, he saw plainly in a vision an angel of God come in to him and say to him, "Cornelius." He looked intently at him and, seized with fear, said, "What is it, sir?" He said to him, "Your prayers and almsgiving have ascended as a memorial offering before God. Now send some men to Joppa and summon one Simon who is called Peter. He is staying with another Simon, a tanner, who has a house by the sea." When the angel who spoke to him had left, he called two of his servants and a devout soldier from his staff, explained everything to them, and sent them to Joppa.

The next day, while they were on their way and nearing the city, Peter went up to the roof terrace to pray at about noontime. He was hungry and wished to eat, and while they were making preparations he fell into a trance. He saw heaven opened and something resembling a large sheet coming down, lowered to the ground by its four corners. In it were all the earth's four-legged animals and reptiles and the birds of the sky. A voice said to him, "Get up, Peter. Slaughter and eat." But Peter said, "Certainly not, sir. For never have I eaten anything profane and unclean." The voice spoke to him again, a second time, "What God has made clean, you are not to call profane." This happened three times, and then the object was taken up into the sky.

While Peter was in doubt about the meaning of the vision he had seen, the men sent by Cornelius asked for Simon's house and arrived at the entrance. They called out inquiring whether Simon, who is called Peter, was staying there. As Peter was pondering the vision, the Spirit said [to him], "There are three men here looking for you. So get up, go downstairs, and accompany them without hesitation, because I have sent them." Then Peter went down to the men and said, "I am the one you are looking for. What is the reason for your being here?" They answered, "Cornelius, a centurion, an upright and God-fearing man, respected by the whole Jewish nation, was directed by a holy angel to summon you to his house and to hear what you have to say." So he invited them in and showed them hospitality.

PSALM 22:20-22

But you, O LORD, be not far from
  me;
  O my help, hasten to aid me.
Rescue my soul from the sword,
  my loneliness from the grip of
    the dog.
Save me from the lion's mouth;
  from the horns of the wild
    bulls, my wretched life.

FEBRUARY 18

ACTS 10:24-49

The next day he got up and went with them, and some of the brothers from Joppa went with him. On the following day he entered Caesarea. Cornelius was expecting them and had called together his relatives and close friends. When Peter entered, Cornelius met him and, falling at his feet, paid him homage. Peter, however, raised him up, saying, "Get up. I myself am also a human being." While he conversed with him, he went in and found many people gathered together and said to them, "You know that it is unlawful for a Jewish man to associate with, or visit, a Gentile, but God has shown me that I should not call any person profane or unclean. And that is why I came without objection when sent for. May I ask, then, why you summoned me?"

Cornelius replied, "Four days ago at this hour, three o'clock in the afternoon, I was at prayer in my house when suddenly a man in dazzling robes stood before me and said, 'Cornelius, your prayer has been heard and your almsgiving remembered before God. Send therefore to Joppa and summon Simon, who is called Peter. He is a guest in the house of Simon, a tanner, by the sea.' So I sent for you immediately, and you were kind enough to come. Now therefore we are all here in the presence of God to listen to all that you have been commanded by the Lord."

Then Peter proceeded to speak and said, "In truth, I see that God shows no partiality. Rather, in every nation whoever fears him and acts uprightly is acceptable to him. You know the word [that] he sent to the Israelites as he proclaimed peace through Jesus Christ, who is Lord of all, what has happened all over Judea, beginning in Galilee after the baptism that John preached, how God anointed Jesus of Nazareth with the holy Spirit and power. He went about doing good and healing all those oppressed by the devil, for God was with him. We are witnesses of all that he did both in the country of the Jews and [in] Jerusalem. They put him to death by hanging him on a tree. This man God raised [on] the third day and granted that he be visible, not to all the people, but to us, the witnesses chosen by God in advance, who ate and drank with him after he rose from the dead. He commissioned us to preach to the people and testify that he is the one appointed by God as judge of the living and the dead. To him all the prophets bear witness, that everyone who believes in him will receive forgiveness of sins through his name."

While Peter was still speaking these things, the holy Spirit fell upon all who were listening to the word. The circumcised believers who had accompanied Peter were astounded that the gift of the holy Spirit should have been poured out on the Gentiles also, for they could hear them speaking in tongues and glorifying God. Then Peter responded, "Can anyone withhold the water for baptizing these people, who have received the holy Spirit even as we have?" He ordered them to be baptized in the name of Jesus Christ. Then they invited him to stay for a few days.

PSALM 22:23-27

I will proclaim your name to my brethren;
in the midst of the assembly I will praise you:
"You who fear the LORD, praise him;
all you descendants of Jacob, give glory to him;
revere him, all you descendants of Israel!
For he has not spurned nor disdained
the wretched man in his misery,
Nor did he turn his face away from him,
but when he cried out to him, he heard him."
So by your gift will I utter praise in the vast assembly;
I will fulfill my vows before those who fear him.
The lowly shall eat their fill;
they who seek the LORD shall praise him:
"May your hearts be ever merry!"

PROVERBS 10:5

A son who fills the granaries in summer is a credit; / a son who slumbers during harvest, a disgrace.

FEBRUARY 19

ACTS 11:1-18

Now the apostles and the brothers who were in Judea heard that the Gentiles too had accepted the word of God. So when Peter went up to Jerusalem the circumcised believers confronted him, saying, "You entered the house of uncircumcised people and ate with them." Peter began and explained it to them step by step, saying, "I was at prayer in the city of Joppa when in a trance I had a vision, something resembling a large sheet coming down, lowered from the sky by its four corners, and it came to me. Looking intently into it, I observed and saw the four-legged animals of the earth, the wild beasts, the reptiles, and the birds of the sky. I also heard a voice say to me, 'Get up, Peter. Slaughter and eat.' But I said, 'Certainly not, sir, because nothing profane or unclean has ever entered my mouth.' But a second time a voice from heaven answered, 'What God has made clean, you are not to call profane.' This happened three times, and then everything was drawn up again into the sky. Just then three men appeared at the house where we were, who had been sent to me from Caesarea. The Spirit told me to accompany them without discriminating. These six brothers also went with me, and we entered the man's house. He related to us how he had seen [the] angel standing in his house, saying, 'Send someone to Joppa and summon Simon, who is called Peter, who will speak words to you by which you and all your household will be saved.' As I began to speak, the holy Spirit fell upon them as it had upon us at the beginning, and I remembered the word of the Lord, how he had said, 'John baptized with water but you will be baptized with the holy Spirit.' If then God gave them the same gift he gave to us when we came to believe in the Lord Jesus Christ, who was I to be able to hinder God?" When they heard this, they stopped objecting and glorified God, saying, "God has then granted life-giving repentance to the Gentiles too."

PSALM 22:28-32

All the ends of the earth
   shall remember and turn to the
   LORD;
All the families of the nations
   shall bow down before him.
For dominion is the LORD's,
   and he rules the nations.
To him alone shall bow down
   all who sleep in the earth;
Before him shall bend
   all who go down into the dust.
And to him my soul shall live;
   my descendants shall serve
   him.
Let the coming generation be told
   of the LORD
   that they may proclaim to a
   people yet to be born
   the justice he has shown.

PROVERBS 10:6
Blessings are for the head of the just, / but a rod for the back of the fool.

FEBRUARY 20

ACTS 11:19-30

Now those who had been scattered by the persecution that arose because of Stephen went as far as Phoenicia, Cyprus, and Antioch, preaching the word to no one but Jews. There were some Cypriots and Cyrenians among them, however, who came to Antioch and began to speak to the Greeks as well, proclaiming the Lord Jesus. The hand of the Lord was with them and a great number who believed turned to the Lord. The news about them reached the ears of the church in Jerusalem, and they sent Barnabas [to go] to Antioch. When he arrived and saw the grace of God, he rejoiced and encouraged them all to remain faithful to the Lord in firmness of heart, for he was a good man, filled with the holy Spirit and faith. And a large number of people was added to the Lord. Then he went to Tarsus to look for Saul, and when he had found him he brought him to Antioch. For a whole year they met with the church and taught a large number of people, and it was in Antioch that the disciples were first called Christians.

At that time some prophets came down from Jerusalem to Antioch, and one of them named Agabus stood up and predicted by the Spirit that there would be a severe famine all over the world, and it happened under Claudius. So the disciples determined that, according to ability, each should send relief to the brothers who lived in Judea. This they did, sending it to the presbyters in care of Barnabas and Saul.

PSALM 23:1-6

A psalm of David.
The LORD is my shepherd; I shall not want.

In verdant pastures he gives me repose;
Beside restful waters he leads me; he refreshes my soul.
He guides me in right paths for his name's sake.
Even though I walk in the dark valley
I fear no evil; for you are at my side
With your rod and your staff that give me courage.
You spread the table before me in the sight of my foes;
You anoint my head with oil; my cup overflows.
Only goodness and kindness follow me
all the days of my life;
And I shall dwell in the house of the LORD
for years to come.

PROVERBS 10:7

The memory of the just will be blessed, / but the name of the wicked will rot.

FEBRUARY 21

ACTS 12:1-25

About that time King Herod laid hands upon some members of the church to harm them. He had James, the brother of John, killed by the sword, and when he saw that this was pleasing to the Jews he proceeded to arrest Peter also. (It was [the] feast of Unleavened Bread.) He had him taken into custody and put in prison under the guard of four squads of four soldiers each. He intended to bring him before the people after Passover. Peter thus was being kept in prison, but

prayer by the church was fervently being made to God on his behalf.

On the very night before Herod was to bring him to trial, Peter, secured by double chains, was sleeping between two soldiers, while outside the door guards kept watch on the prison. Suddenly the angel of the Lord stood by him and a light shone in the cell. He tapped Peter on the side and awakened him, saying, "Get up quickly." The chains fell from his wrists. The angel said to him, "Put on your belt and your sandals." He did so. Then he said to him, "Put on your cloak and follow me." So he followed him out, not realizing that what was happening through the angel was real; he thought he was seeing a vision. They passed the first guard, then the second, and came to the iron gate leading out to the city, which opened for them by itself. They emerged and made their way down an alley, and suddenly the angel left him. Then Peter recovered his senses and said, "Now I know for certain that [the] Lord sent his angel and rescued me from the hand of Herod and from all that the Jewish people had been expecting." When he realized this, he went to the house of Mary, the mother of John who is called Mark, where there were many people gathered in prayer. When he knocked on the gateway door, a maid named Rhoda came to answer it. She was so overjoyed when she recognized Peter's voice that, instead of opening the gate, she ran in and announced that Peter was standing at the gate. They told her, "You are out of your mind," but she insisted that it was so. But they kept saying, "It is his angel." But Peter continued to knock, and when the opened it, they saw him and were astounded. He motioned to them with his hand to be quiet and explained [to them] how the Lord had led him out of the prison, and said, "Report this to James and the brothers." Then he left and went to another place. At daybreak there was no small commotion among the soldiers over what had become of Peter. Herod, after instituting a search but not finding him, ordered the guards tried and executed. Then he left Judea to spend some time in Caesarea.

He had long been very angry with the people of Tyre and Sidon, who now came to him in a body. After winning over Blastus, the king's chamberlain, they sued for peace because their country was supplied with food from the king's territory. On an appointed day, Herod, attired in royal robes, [and] seated on the rostrum, addressed them publicly. The assembled crowd cried out, "This is the voice of a god, not of a man." At once the angel of the Lord struck him down because he did not ascribe the honor to God, and he was eaten by worms and breathed his last. But the word of God continued to spread and grow.

After Barnabas and Saul completed their relief mission, they returned to Jerusalem, taking with them John, who is called Mark.

PSALM 24:1-6

A psalm of David.

The LORD's are the earth and its
    fullness;
    the world and those who dwell
        in it.
For he founded it upon the seas
    and established it upon the
        rivers.
Who can ascend the mountain of
    the LORD?
    or who may stand in his holy
        place?
He whose hands are sinless,
    whose heart is clean,
    who desires not what is vain,
    nor swears deceitfully to his
        neighbor.
He shall receive a blessing from
    the LORD,
    a reward from God his savior.
Such is the race that seeks for
    him,
    that seeks the face of the God
    of Jacob.

FEBRUARY 22

ACTS 13:1-15

Now there were in the church at Antioch prophets and teachers: Barnabas, Symeon who was called Niger, Lucius of Cyrene, Manaen who was a close friend of Herod the tetrarch, and Saul. While they were worshiping the Lord and fasting, the holy Spirit said, "Set apart for me Barnabas and Saul for the work to which I have called them." Then, completing their fasting and prayer, they laid hands on them and sent them off.

So they, sent forth by the holy Spirit, went down to Seleucia and from there sailed to Cyprus. When they arrived in Salamis, they proclaimed the word of God in the Jewish synagogues. They had John also as their assistant. When they had traveled through the whole island as far as Paphos, they met a magician named Bar-Jesus who was a Jewish false prophet. He was with the proconsul Sergius Paulus, a man of intelligence, who had summoned Barnabas and Saul and wanted to hear the word of God. But Elymas the magician (for that is what his name means) opposed them in an attempt to turn the proconsul away from the faith. But Saul, also known as Paul, filled with the holy Spirit, looked intently at him and said, "You son of the devil, you enemy of all that is right, full of every sort of deceit and fraud. Will you not stop twisting the straight paths of [the] Lord? Even now the hand of the Lord is upon you. You will be blind, and unable to see the sun for a time." Immediately a dark mist fell upon him, and he went about seeking people to lead him by the hand. When the proconsul saw what had happened, he came to believe, for he was astonished by the teaching about the Lord.

From Paphos, Paul and his companions set sail and arrived at Perga in Pamphylia. But John left them and returned to Jerusalem. They continued on from Perga and reached Antioch in Pisidia. On the sabbath they entered [into] the synagogue and took their seats. After the reading of the law and the prophets, the synagogue officials sent word to them, "My brothers, if one of you has a word of exhortation for the people, please speak."

PSALM 24:7-10

Lift up, O gates, your lintels;
  reach up, you ancient portals,
  that the king of glory may
    come in!
Who is this king of glory?
  The LORD, strong and mighty,
  the LORD, mighty in battle.
Lift up, O gates, your lintels;
  reach up, you ancient portals,
  that the king of glory may
    come in!
Who is this king of glory?
  The LORD of hosts; he is the
    king of glory.

PROVERBS 10:9-10

He who walks honestly walks securely, / but he whose ways are crooked will fare badly. / He who winks at a fault causes trouble, / but he who frankly reproves promotes peace.

FEBRUARY 23

ACTS 13:16-43

So Paul got up, motioned with his hand, and said, "Fellow Israelites and you others who are God-fearing, listen. The God of this people Israel chose our ancestors and exalted the people during their sojourn in the land of Egypt. With uplifted arms he led them out of it and for about forty years he put up with them in the desert. When he had destroyed seven nations in the land of Canaan, he gave them their land as an inheritance at the end of about four hundred and fifty years. After these things he provided judges up to Samuel [the] prophet. Then they asked for a king. God gave them Saul, son of Kish, a man from the tribe of Benjamin, for forty years. Then he removed him and raised up David as their king; of him he testified, 'I have found David, son of Jesse, a man after my own heart; he will carry out my every wish.' From this man's descendants God, according to his promise, has brought to Israel a savior, Jesus. John heralded his coming by proclaiming a baptism of repentance to all the people of Israel; and as John was completing his course, he would say, 'What do you suppose that I am? I am not he. Behold, one is coming after me; I am not worthy to unfasten the sandals of his feet.' "

"My brothers, children of the family of Abraham, and those others among you who are God-fearing, to us this word of salvation has been sent. The inhabitants of Jerusalem and their leaders failed to recognize him, and by condemning him they fulfilled the oracles of the prophets that are read sabbath after sabbath. For even though they found no grounds for a death sentence, they asked Pilate to have him put to death, and when they had accomplished all that was written about him, they took him down from the tree and placed him in a tomb. But God raised him from the dead, and for many days he appeared to those who had come up with him from Galilee to Jerusalem. These are [now] his witnesses before the people. We ourselves are proclaiming this good news to you that what God promised our ancestors he has brought to fulfillment for us, [their] children, by raising up Jesus, as it is written in the second psalm, 'You are my son; this day I have begotten you.' And that he raised him from the dead never to return to corruption he declared in this way, 'I shall give you the benefits assured to David.' That is why he also says in another psalm, 'You will not suffer your holy one to see corruption.' Now David, after he had served the will of God in his lifetime, fell asleep, was gathered to his ancestors, and did see corruption. But the one whom God raised up did not see corruption. You must know, my brothers, that through him forgiveness of sins is being proclaimed to you, [and] in regard to everything from which you could not be justified under the law of Moses, in him every believer is justified. Be careful, then, that what was said in the prophets not come about:

'Look on, you scoffers,
    be amazed and disappear.
For I am doing a work in your days,
    a work that you will never believe even if someone tells you.' "

As they were leaving, they invited them to speak on these subjects the following sabbath. After the congregation had dispersed, many Jews and worshipers who were converts to Judaism followed Paul and Barnabas, who spoke to them and urged them to remain faithful to the grace of God.

In you I trust; let me not be put to shame,
    let not my enemies exult over me.
No one who waits for you shall be put to shame;
    those shall be put to shame who heedlessly break faith.
Your ways, O LORD, make known to me;
    teach me your paths,
Guide me in your truth and teach me,
    for you are God my savior,
    and for you I wait all the day.
Remember that your compassion, O LORD,
    and your kindness are from of old.
The sins of my youth and my frailties remember not;
    in your kindness remember me,
    because of your goodness, O LORD.
Good and upright is the LORD;
    thus he shows sinners the way.
He guides the humble to justice,
    he teaches the humble his way.
All the paths of the LORD are kindness and constancy
    toward those who keep his covenant and his decrees.
For your name's sake, O LORD,
    you will pardon my guilt, great as it is.

PSALM 25:1-11
Of David.
To you I lift up my soul,
    O LORD, my God.

PROVERBS 10:11-12
A fountain of life is the mouth of the just, / but the mouth of the wicked conceals violence. / Hatred stirs up disputes, / but love covers all offenses.

FEBRUARY 24

ACTS 13:44-52

On the following sabbath almost the whole city gathered to hear the word of the Lord. When the Jews saw the crowds, they were filled with jealousy and with violent abuse contradicted what Paul said. Both Paul and Barnabas spoke out boldly and said, "It was necessary that the word of God be spoken to you first, but since you reject it and condemn yourselves as unworthy of eternal life, we now turn to the Gentiles. For so the Lord has commanded us, 'I have made you a light to the Gentiles, that you may be an instrument of salvation to the ends of the earth.' "

The Gentiles were delighted when they heard this and glorified the word of the Lord. All who were destined for eternal life came to believe, and the word of the Lord continued to spread through the whole region. The Jews, however, incited the women of prominence who were worshipers and the leading men of the city, stirred up a persecution against Paul and Barnabas, and expelled them from their territory. So they shook the dust from their feet in protest against them and went to Iconium. The disciples were filled with joy and the holy Spirit.

PSALM 25:12-22

When a man fears the LORD,
    he shows him the way he
      should choose.
He abides in prosperity,
    and his descendants inherit the
      land.
The friendship of the LORD is
      with those who fear him,
    and his covenant, for their
      instruction.
My eyes are ever toward the
    LORD,
    for he will free my feet from
      the snare.
Look toward me, and have pity
    on me,
    for I am alone and afflicted.
Relieve the troubles of my heart,
    and bring me out of my
      distress.
Put an end to my affliction and
    my suffering,
    and take away all my sins.
Behold, my enemies are many,
    and they hate me violently.
Preserve my life, and rescue me;
    let me not be put to shame, for
      I take refuge in you.
Let integrity and uprightness
    preserve me,
    because I wait for you, O LORD.
Redeem Israel, O God,
    from all its distress!

PROVERBS 10:13-14

On the lips of the intelligent is found wisdom, / [but the mouth of the wicked conceals violence]. / Wise men store up knowledge, / but the mouth of a fool is imminent ruin.

ACTS 14:1-28

In Iconium they entered the Jewish synagogue together and spoke in such a way that a great number of both Jews and Greeks came to believe, although the disbelieving Jews stirred up and poisoned the minds of the Gentiles against the brothers. So they stayed for a considerable period, speaking out boldly for the Lord, who confirmed the word about his grace by granting signs and wonders to occur through their hands. The people of the city were divided: some were with the Jews; others, with the apostles. When there was an attempt by both the Gentiles and the Jews, together with their leaders, to attack and stone them, they realized it and fled to the Lycaonian cities of Lystra and Derbe and to the surrounding countryside, where they continued to proclaim the good news.

At Lystra there was a crippled man, lame from birth, who had never walked. He listened to Paul speaking, who looked intently at him, saw that he had the faith to be healed, and called out in a loud voice, "Stand up straight on your feet." He jumped up and began to walk about. When the crowds saw what Paul had done, they cried out in Lycaonian, "The gods have come down to us in human form." They called Barnabas "Zeus" and Paul "Hermes," because he was the chief speaker. And the priest of Zeus, whose temple was at the entrance to the city, brought oxen and garlands to the gates, for he together with the people intended to offer sacrifice.

The apostles Barnabas and Paul tore their garments when they heard this and rushed out into the crowd, shouting, "Men, why are you doing this? We are of the same nature as you, human beings. We proclaim to you good news that you should turn from these idols to the living God, 'who made heaven and earth and sea and all that is in them.' In past generations he allowed all Gentiles to go their own ways; yet, in bestowing his goodness, he did not leave himself without witness, for he gave you rains from heaven and fruitful seasons, and filled you with nourishment and gladness for your hearts." Even with these words, they scarcely restrained the crowds from offering sacrifice to them.

However, some Jews from Antioch and Iconium arrived and won over the crowds. They stoned Paul and dragged him out of the city, supposing that he was dead. But when the disciples gathered around him, he got up and entered the city. On the following day he left with Barnabas for Derbe.

After they had proclaimed the good news to that city and made a considerable number of disciples, they returned to Lystra and to Iconium and to Antioch. They strengthened the spirits of the disciples and exhorted them to persevere in the faith, saying, "It is necessary for us to undergo many hardships to enter the kingdom of God." They appointed presbyters for them in each church and, with prayer and fasting, commended them to the Lord in whom they had put their faith. Then they traveled through Pisidia and reached Pamphylia. After proclaiming the word at Perga they went down to Attalia. From there they sailed to Antioch, where they had been commended to the grace of God for the work they had now accomplished. And when they arrived, they called the church together and reported what God had done with them and how he had opened the door of faith to the Gentiles. Then they spent no little time with the disciples.

PSALM 26:1-8

Of David.

Do me justice, O LORD! for I have
walked in integrity,
and in the LORD I trust without
wavering.

Search me, O LORD, and try me;
test my soul and my heart.
For your kindness is before my
eyes,
and I walk in your truth.
I stay not with worthless men,
nor do I consort with
hypocrites.
I hate the assembly of evildoers,
and with the wicked I will not
stay.
I wash my hands in innocence,
and I go around your altar, O
LORD,
Giving voice to my thanks,
and recounting all your
wondrous deeds.
O Lord, I love the house in which
you dwell,
the tenting-place of your glory.

PROVERBS 10:15-16

The rich man's wealth is his strong city; / the ruination of the lowly is their poverty. / The just man's recompense leads to life, / the gains of the wicked, to sin.

FEBRUARY 26

ACTS 15:1-21

Some who had come down from Judea were instructing the brothers, "Unless you are circumcised according to the Mosaic practice, you cannot be saved." Because there arose no little dissension and debate by Paul and Barnabas with them, it was decided that Paul, Barnabas, and some of the others should go up to Jerusalem to the apostles and presbyters about this question. They were sent on their journey by the church, and passed through Phoenicia and Samaria telling of the conversion of the Gentiles, and brought great joy to all the broth-

ers. When they arrived in Jerusalem, they were welcomed by the church, as well as by the apostles and the presbyters, and they reported what God had done with them. But some from the party of the Pharisees who had become believers stood up and said, "It is necessary to circumcise them and direct them to observe the Mosaic law."

The apostles and the presbyters met together to see about this matter. After much debate had taken place, Peter got up and said to them, "My brothers, you are well aware that from early days God made his choice among you that through my mouth the Gentiles would hear the word of the gospel and believe. And God, who knows the heart, bore witness by granting them the holy Spirit just as he did us. He made no distinction between us and them, for by faith he purified their hearts. Why, then, are you now putting God to the test by placing on the shoulders of the disciples a yoke that neither our ancestors nor we have been able to bear? On the contrary, we believe that we are saved through the grace of the Lord Jesus, in the same way as they." The whole assembly fell silent, and they listened while Paul and Barnabas described the signs and wonders God had worked among the Gentiles through them.

After they had fallen silent, James responded, "My brothers, listen to me. Symeon has described how God first concerned himself with acquiring from among the Gentiles a people for his name. The words of the prophets agree with this, as is written:

'After this I shall return
  and rebuild the fallen hut of
    David;
  from its ruins I shall rebuild it
  and raise it up again,

so that the rest of humanity
  may seek out the LORD,
  even all the Gentiles on
    whom my name is
    invoked.
Thus says the LORD who
  accomplishes these things,
  known from of old.'

It is my judgment, therefore, that we ought to stop troubling the Gentiles who turn to God, but tell them by letter to avoid pollution from idols, unlawful marriage, the meat of strangled animals, and blood. For Moses, for generations now, has had those who proclaim him in every town, as he has been read in the synagogues every sabbath."

PSALM 26:9-12

Gather not my soul with those of
    sinners,
  nor with men of blood my life.
On their hands are crimes,
  and their right hands are full of
    bribes.
But I walk in integrity;
  redeem me, and have pity on
    me.
My foot stands on level ground;
  in the assemblies I will bless
    the LORD.

PROVERBS 10:17

A path to life is his who heeds admonition, / but he who disregards reproof goes astray.

FEBRUARY 27

ACTS 15:22-41

Then the apostles and presbyters, in agreement with the whole church, decided to choose representatives and to send them to Antioch with Paul and Barnabas.

The ones chosen were Judas, who was called Barsabbas, and Silas, leaders among the brothers. This is the letter delivered by them: "The apostles and the presbyters, your brothers, to the brothers in Antioch, Syria, and Cilicia of Gentile origin: greetings. Since we have heard that some of our number [who went out] without any mandate from us have upset you with their teachings and disturbed your peace of mind, we have with one accord decided to choose representatives and to send them to you along with our beloved Barnabas and Paul, who have dedicated their lives to the name of our Lord Jesus Christ. So we are sending Judas and Silas who will also convey this same message by word of mouth: 'It is the decision of the holy Spirit and of us not to place on you any burden beyond these necessities, namely, to abstain from meat sacrificed to idols, from blood, from meats of strangled animals, and from unlawful marriage. If you keep free of these, you will be doing what is right. Farewell.' "

And so they were sent on their journey. Upon their arrival in Antioch they called the assembly together and delivered the letter. When the people read it, they were delighted with the exhortation. Judas and Silas, who were themselves prophets, exhorted and strengthened the brothers with many words. After they had spent some time there, they were sent off with greetings of peace from the brothers to those who had commissioned them. But Paul and Barnabas remained in Antioch, teaching and proclaiming with many others the word of the Lord.

After some time, Paul said to Barnabas, "Come, let us make a return visit to see how the brothers are getting on in all the cities where we proclaimed the word of the Lord." Barnabas wanted to take with them also John, who was called Mark, but Paul insisted that they should not take with them someone who had deserted them at Pamphylia and who had not continued with them in their work. So sharp was their disagreement that they separated. Barnabas took Mark and sailed to Cyprus. But Paul chose Silas and departed after being commended by the brothers to the grace of the Lord. He traveled through Syria and Cilicia bringing strength to the churches.

PSALM 27:1-6

Of David.
The LORD is my light and my
    salvation;
    whom should I fear?
The LORD is my life's refuge;
    of whom should I be afraid?
When evildoers come at me
    to devour my flesh,
My foes and my enemies
    themselves stumble and fall.
Though an army encamp against
    me,
    my heart will not fear;
Though war be waged upon me,
    even then will I trust.
One thing I ask of the LORD;
    this I seek:
To dwell in the house of the LORD
    all the days of my life,
That I may gaze on the loveliness
    of the LORD
    and contemplate his temple.
For he will hide me in his abode
    in the day of trouble;
He will conceal me in the shelter
    of his tent,
    he will set me high upon a
    rock.
Even now my head is held high

above my enemies on every
side.
And I will offer in his tent
sacrifices with shouts of
gladness;

I will sing and chant praise to the
LORD.

PROVERBS 10:18

It is the lips of the liar that conceal hostility; / but he who spreads accusations is a fool.

FEBRUARY 28

ACTS 16:1-15

He reached [also] Derbe and Lystra where there was a disciple named Timothy, the son of a Jewish woman who was a believer, but his father was a Greek. The brothers in Lystra and Iconium spoke highly of him, and Paul wanted him to come along with him. On account of the Jews of that region, Paul had him circumcised, for they all knew that his father was a Greek. As they traveled from city to city, they handed on to the people for observance the decisions reached by the apostles and presbyters in Jerusalem. Day after day the churches grew stronger in faith and increased in number.

They traveled through the Phrygian and Galatian territory because they had been prevented by the holy Spirit from preaching the message in the province of Asia. When they came to Mysia, they tried to go on into Bithynia, but the Spirit of Jesus did not allow them, so they crossed through Mysia and came down to Troas. During [the] night Paul had a vision. A Macedonian stood before him and implored him with these words, "Come over to Macedonia and help us." When he had seen the vision, we sought passage to Macedonia at once, concluding that God had called us to proclaim the good news to them.

We set sail from Troas, making a straight run for Samothrace, and on the next day to Neapolis, and from there to Philippi, a leading city in that district of Macedonia and a Roman colony. We spent some time in that city. On the sabbath we went outside the city gate along the river where we thought there would be a place of prayer. We sat and spoke with the women who had gathered there. One of them, a woman named Lydia, a dealer in purple cloth, from the city of Thyatira, a worshiper of God, listened, and the Lord opened her heart to pay attention to what Paul was saying. After she and her household had been baptized, she offered us an invitation, "If you consider me a believer in the Lord, come and stay at my home," and she prevailed on us.

PSALM 27:7-14

Hear, O LORD, the sound of my
call;

have pity on me, and answer
me.
Of you my heart speaks; you my
glance seeks;
your presence, O LORD, I seek.
Hide not your face from me;
do not in anger repel your
servant.
You are my helper: cast me not
off;
forsake me not, O God my
savior.
Though my father and mother
forsake me,
yet will the LORD receive me.

Show me, O LORD, your way,
and lead me on a level path,
because of my adversaries.
Give me not up to the wishes of
my foes;
for false witnesses have risen
up against me,
and such as breathe out
violence.
I believe that I shall see the
bounty of the LORD
in the land of the living.
Wait for the LORD with courage;
be stouthearted, and wait for
the LORD.

PROVERBS 10:19

Where words are many, sin is not wanting; / but he who restrains his lips does well.

FEBRUARY 29

ACTS 16:16-40

As we were going to the place of prayer, we met a slave girl with an oracular spirit, who used to bring a large profit to her owners through her fortune-telling. She began to follow Paul and us, shouting, "These people are slaves of the Most High God, who proclaim to you a way of salvation." She did this for many days. Paul became annoyed, turned, and said to the spirit, "I command you in the name of Jesus Christ to come out of her." Then it came out at that moment.

When her owners saw that their hope of profit was gone, they seized Paul and Silas and dragged them to the public square before the local authorities. They brought them before the magistrates and said, "These people are Jews and are disturbing our city

and are advocating customs that are not lawful for us Romans to adopt or practice." The crowd joined in the attack on them, and the magistrates had them stripped and ordered them to be beaten with rods. After inflicting many blows on them, they threw them into prison and instructed the jailer to guard them securely. When he received these instructions, he put them in the innermost cell and secured their feet to a stake.

About midnight, while Paul and Silas were praying and singing hymns to God as the prisoners listened, there was suddenly such a severe earthquake that the foundations of the jail shook; all the doors flew open, and the chains of all were pulled loose. When the jailer woke up and saw the prison doors wide open, he drew [his] sword and was about to kill himself, thinking that the prisoners had escaped. But Paul shouted out in a loud voice, "Do no harm to yourself; we are all here." He asked for a light and rushed in and, trembling with fear, he fell down before Paul and Silas. Then he brought them out and said, "Sirs, what must I do to be saved?" And they said, "Believe in the Lord Jesus and you and your household will be saved." So they spoke the word of the Lord to him and to everyone in his house. He took them in at that hour of the night and bathed their wounds; then he and all his family were baptized at once. He brought them up into his house and provided a meal and with his household rejoiced at having come to faith in God.

But when it was day, the magistrates sent the lictors with the order, "Release those men." The jailer reported the[se] words to Paul, "The magistrates have sent orders that you be released. Now, then, come out and go in peace." But Paul said to them, "They have beaten us publicly, even though we are Roman citizens and have not been tried, and have thrown us into prison. And now, are they going to release us secretly? By no means. Let them come themselves and lead us out." The lictors reported these words to the magistrates, and they became alarmed when they heard that they were Roman citizens. So they came and placated them, and led them out and asked that they leave the city. When they had come out of the prison, they went to Lydia's house where they saw and encouraged the brothers, and then they left.

PSALM 28:1-5

Of David.
To you, O LORD, I call;
  O my Rock, be not deaf to me,
Lest, if you heed me not,
  I become one of those going
    down into the pit.
Hear the sound of my pleading,
    when I cry to you,
  lifting up my hands toward
    your holy shrine.

PROVERBS 10:20

Like choice silver is the just man's tongue; / the heart of the wicked is of little worth.

MARCH

Psalms

"THE FAVORS OF THE LORD I will sing forever." (Ps 89:2)
The Book of Psalms is a precious anthology of some of the most magnificent prayers we know. It is a collection of the only divinely inspired prayers available to us. The Psalter has a universal appeal since it contains prayers to fit our every mood and occasion, every circumstance and event.

These prayers express our basic relationship toward God—our praise and gratitude, our faith and trust, repentance and sorrow for our sinfulness, our doubts and fears, our happiness and joy in the Lord.

In order to appreciate more fully the richness of these Psalm prayers, we need to recall how and why they were composed. In the first place the ancient Hebrew did not think and speak only in abstract concepts as we are inclined to do. His language and expressions were rich in imagery and pictorially enchanting.

Second, the Psalms were an attempt to verbalize the Hebrew's experiential awareness of the presence and power, the goodness and fidelity of the Lord. We can understand how difficult, if not impossible, it is to express in words, or to set down in writing, our deepest and most personal experiences in life. How could a mother verbalize her feelings for the newborn babe in her arms? The psalmist found himself in the same predicament, yet he felt impelled to record his experience of God so that the whole community could join in praising and rejoicing in the Lord's goodness.

In the marvels of creation, the psalmist beheld the creative love and power of God. He rejoiced in the beauty and wonders of creation and tried to put into words his deep personal experience and to verbalize his praise of God the Creator (Ps 104). Our first duty toward God is to praise and glorify him for who he is and what he is. Many of the Psalms will help us to express our heartfelt sentiments of praise to our loving Father.

The ancient psalmist recognized the providential care and concern of God in the life-giving rain, sunshine, and bountiful harvest. The harvest songs reflect his gratefulness and joy (Ps 145). We owe God our gratitude and appreciation for all his countless blessings showered upon us moment by moment. Again we will find powerful expressions of thankfulness in the Psalms.

The composer of the Psalms realized that he needed the Lord's help and protection at all times. With joyful confidence he cries out to the Lord, knowing that he will receive the help he implores.

In the Psalms we discover many moving expressions of faith and trust in God. The faith of the psalmist is an expectant faith by which he knows that God will respond to his need. Praying the Psalms will increase and strengthen our own faith and trust in our heavenly Father's loving care.

The chosen people knew that God was always with them. They visualized him as abiding on the tops of the mountains. It was their firm belief that God was especially present in the temple. They longed to go to the temple. They felt that their prayers were far more powerful if poured out in the sacred precincts of the temple. On their pilgrimages to the temple they joyously sang the songs of ascent (Ps 121).

As we journey down the road of life we are often beset with doubts and fears. The sentiments expressed in the Psalms will do much to help us dispel all the worries and anxieties which disturb our equilibrium. They will help us recall the presence of Jesus on the road to Emmaus and also his parting words to us: "And behold, I am with you always, until the end of the age" (Mt 28:20).

Coming before the Lord we acknowledge our dire need of his help in all the circumstances of life. The Psalm prayers aid us in crying out to the Lord to come to our rescue with his divine assistance. The confidence and trust of the psalmist assures us that the Lord will never turn a deaf ear to our humble pleading.

The Israelites witnessed the might and power of God in a violent storm or in the storm-tossed sea. In awe and wonder they sang of the immensity of God's power and praised him for it (Ps 148).

When the people turned away from God, they gradually became aware of God's method and plan for recalling them back to him. They understood that various calamities, such as war, famine, pestilence, and exile, were means that God was using to bring them to repentance and conversion (Ps 130).

In our day we have lost our sense of sin. Perhaps God is

sending us some messages by means of the disasters which take place from time to time—earthquakes, drought, epidemics, upheavals, sickness. Hopefully the prayers of the Psalms might help us discern our waywardness and lead us back to the arms of our eternal Father. In the penitential psalms we find many ways of asking the Lord's healing and forgiveness if we approach him, like the people of old, with a humble, contrite spirit.

The joy exuding from the Psalms lifts our hearts and our spirits. With the psalmist we want to call upon the whole assembly to raise their voices and play their instruments to praise the Lord of heaven and earth (Ps 150).

"Oh, that today you would hear his voice: 'Harden not your hearts . . .' " (Ps 95:7-8).

ACTS 17:1-15

When they took the road through Amphipolis and Apollonia, they reached Thessalonica, where there was a synagogue of the Jews. Following his usual custom, Paul joined them, and for three sabbaths he entered into discussions with them from the scriptures, expounding and demonstrating that the Messiah had to suffer and rise from the dead, and that "This is the Messiah, Jesus, whom I proclaim to you." Some of them were convinced and joined Paul and Silas; so, too, a great number of Greeks who were worshipers, and not a few of the prominent women. But the Jews became jealous and recruited some worthless men loitering in the public square, formed a mob, and set the city in turmoil. They marched on the house of Jason, intending to bring them before the people's assembly. When they could not find them, they dragged Jason and some of the brothers before the city magistrates, shouting, "These people who have been creating a disturbance all over the world have now come here, and Jason has welcomed them. They all act in opposition to the decrees of Caesar and claim instead that there is another king, Jesus." They stirred up the crowd and the city magistrates who, upon hearing these charges, took a surety payment from Jason and the others before releasing them.

The brothers immediately sent Paul and Silas to Beroea during the night. Upon arrival they went to the synagogue of the Jews. These Jews were more fair-minded than those in Thessalonica, for they received the word with all willingness and examined the scriptures daily to determine whether these things were so. Many of them became believers, as did not a few of the influential Greek women and men. But when the Jews of Thessalonica learned that the word of God had now been proclaimed by Paul in Beroea also, they came there too to cause a commotion and stir up the crowds. So the brothers at once sent Paul on his way to the seacoast, while Silas and Timothy remained behind. After Paul's escorts had taken him to Athens, they came away with instructions for Silas and Timothy to join him as soon as possible.

PSALM 28:6-9

Blessed be the LORD,
    for he has heard the sound of
      my pleading;
    the LORD is my strength and
      my shield.

In him my heart trusts, and I find
    help;
    then my heart exults, and with
      my song I give him thanks.
The LORD is the strength of his
    people,
the saving refuge of his
    anointed.
Save your people, and bless your
    inheritance;
    feed them, and carry them
      forever!

PROVERBS 10:21

The just man's lips nourish many, / but fools die for want of sense.

MARCH 2

ACTS 17:16-34

While Paul was waiting for them in Athens, he grew exasperated at the sight of the city full of idols. So he debated in the synagogue with the Jews and with the worshipers, and daily in the public square with whoever happened to be there. Even some of the Epicurean and Stoic philosophers engaged him in discussion. Some asked, "What is this scavenger trying to say?" Others said, "He sounds like a promoter of foreign deities," because he was preaching about 'Jesus' and 'Resurrection.' They took him and led him to the Areopagus and said, "May we learn what this new teaching is that you speak of? For you bring some strange notions to our ears; we should like to know what these things mean." Now all the Athenians as well as the foreigners residing there used their time for nothing else but telling or hearing something new.

Then Paul stood up at the Areopagus and said: "You Athenians, I see that in every respect you are very religious. For as I walked around looking carefully at your shrines, I even discovered an altar inscribed, 'To an Unknown God.' What therefore you unknowingly worship, I proclaim to you. The God who made the world and all that is in it, the Lord of heaven and earth, does not dwell in sanctuaries made by human hands, nor is he served by human hands because he needs anything. Rather it is he who gives to everyone life and breath and everything. He made from one the whole human race to dwell on the entire surface of the earth, and he fixed the ordered seasons and the boundaries of their regions, so that people might seek God, even perhaps grope for him and find him, though indeed he is not far from any one of us. For 'In him we live and move and have our being,' as even some of your poets have said, 'For we too are his offspring.' Since therefore we are the offspring of God, we ought not to think that the divinity is like an image fashioned from gold, silver, or stone by human art and imagination. God has overlooked the times of ignorance, but now he demands that all people everywhere repent because he has established a day on which he will 'judge the world with justice' through a man he has appointed, and he has provided confirmation for all by raising him from the dead."

When they heard about resurrection of the dead, some began to scoff, but others said, "We should like to hear you on this some other time." And so Paul left them. But some did join him, and became believers. Among them were Dionysius, a member of the Court of the Areopagus, a woman named Damaris, and others with them.

PSALM 29:1-11

A psalm of David.
Give to the LORD, you sons of God,
    give to the LORD glory and praise;
Give to the LORD the glory due his name;
    adore the LORD in holy attire.
The voice of the LORD is over the waters,
    the God of glory thunders,
    the LORD, over vast waters.
The voice of the LORD is mighty;
    the voice of the LORD is majestic.
The voice of the LORD breaks the cedars,
    the LORD breaks the cedars of Lebanon.
He makes Lebanon leap like a calf
    and Sirion like a young bull.
The voice of the LORD strikes fiery flames;
    the voice of the LORD shakes the desert,
    the LORD shakes the wilderness of Kadesh.
the voice of the LORD twists the oaks and strips the forests,
    and in his temple all say, "Glory!"
The LORD is enthroned above the flood;
    the LORD is enthroned as king forever.
May the LORD give strength to his people;
    may the LORD bless his people with peace!

PROVERBS 10:22

It is the LORD's blessing that brings wealth, / and no effort can substitute for it.

MARCH 3

ACTS 18:1-28

After this he left Athens and went to Corinth. There he met a Jew named Aquila, a native of Pontus, who had recently come from Italy with his wife Priscilla because Claudius had ordered all the Jews to leave Rome. He went to visit them and, because he practiced the same trade, stayed with them and worked, for they were tentmakers by trade. Every sabbath, he entered into discussions in the synagogue, attempting to convince both Jews and Greeks.

When Silas and Timothy came down from Macedonia, Paul began to occupy himself totally with preaching the word, testifying to the Jews that the Messiah was Jesus. When they opposed him and reviled him, he shook out his garments and said to them, "Your blood be on your heads! I am clear of responsibility. From now on I will go to the Gentiles." So he left there and went to a house belonging to a man named Titus Justus, a worshiper of God; his house was next to a synagogue. Crispus, the synagogue official, came to believe in the Lord along with his entire household, and many of the Corinthians who heard believed and were baptized. One night in a vision the Lord said to Paul, "Do not be afraid. Go on speaking, and do not be silent, for I am with you. No one will attack and harm you, for I have many people in this city." He settled there for a year and a half and taught the word of God among them.

But when Gallio was proconsul of Achaia, the Jews rose up together against Paul and brought him to the tribunal, saying, "This man is inducing people to worship God contrary to the law." When Paul was about to reply, Gallio spoke to the Jews, "If it were a matter of some crime or malicious fraud, I should with reason hear the complaint of you Jews; but since it is a question of arguments over doctrine and titles and your own law, see to it yourselves. I do not wish to be a judge of such matters." And he drove them away from the tribunal. They all seized Sosthenes, the synagogue official, and beat him in full view of the tribunal. But none of this was of concern to Gallio.

Paul remained for quite some time, and after saying farewell to the brothers he sailed for Syria, together with Priscilla and Aquila. At Cenchreae he had his hair cut because he had taken a vow. When they reached Ephesus, he left them there, while he entered the synagogue and held discussions with the Jews. Although they asked him to stay for a longer time, he did not consent, but as he said farewell he promised, "I shall come back to you again, God willing." Then he set sail from Ephesus. Upon landing at Caesarea, he went up and greeted the church and then went down to Antioch. After staying there some time, he left and traveled in orderly sequence through the Galatian country and Phrygia, bringing strength to all the disciples.

A Jew named Apollos, a native of Alexandria, an eloquent speaker, arrived in Ephesus. He was an authority on the scriptures. He had been instructed in the Way of the Lord and, with ardent spirit, spoke and taught accurately about Jesus, although he knew only the baptism of John. He began to speak boldly in the synagogue; but when Priscilla and Aquila heard him, they took him aside and explained to him the Way [of God] more accurately. And when he wanted to cross to Achaia, the brothers encouraged him and wrote to the disciples there to welcome him. After his arrival he gave great assistance to those who had come to believe through grace. He vigorously refuted the Jews in public, establishing from the scriptures that the Messiah is Jesus.

PSALM 30:1-6

A psalm. A song for the dedication of the temple. Of David.

I will extol you, O LORD, for you drew me clear
  and did not let my enemies rejoice over me.
O LORD, my God,

I cried out to you and you
  healed me.
O LORD, you brought me up from
  the nether world;
  you preserved me from among
  those going down into the
  pit.
Sing praise to the LORD, you his
  faithful ones,

and give thanks to his holy
  name.
For his anger lasts but a moment;
  a lifetime, his good will.
At nightfall, weeping enters in,
  but with the dawn, rejoicing.

PROVERBS 10:23

Crime is the entertainment of the fool; / so is wisdom for the man of sense.

MARCH 4

ACTS 19:1-20

While Apollos was in Corinth, Paul traveled through the interior of the country and came [down] to Ephesus where he found some disciples. He said to them, "Did you receive the holy Spirit when you became believers?" They answered him, "We have never even heard that there is a holy Spirit." He said, "How were you baptized?" They replied, "With the baptism of John." Paul then said, "John baptized with a baptism of repentance, telling the people to believe in the one who was to come after him, that is, in Jesus." When they heard this, they were baptized in the name of the Lord Jesus. And when Paul laid [his] hands on them, the holy Spirit came upon them, and they spoke in tongues and prophesied. Altogether there were about twelve men.

He entered the synagogue, and for three months debated boldly with persuasive arguments about the kingdom of God. But when some in their obstinacy and disbelief disparaged the Way before the assembly, he withdrew and took his disciples with him and began to hold daily discussions in the lecture hall of Tyrannus. This continued for two years with the result that all the inhabitants of the province of Asia heard the word of the Lord, Jews and Greeks alike. So extraordinary were the mighty deeds God accomplished at the hands of Paul that when face cloths or aprons that touched his skin were applied to the sick, their diseases left them and the evil spirits came out of them.

Then some itinerant Jewish exorcists tried to invoke the name of the Lord Jesus over those with evil spirits, saying, "I adjure you by the Jesus whom Paul preaches." When the seven sons of Sceva, a Jewish high priest, tried to do this, the evil spirit said to them in reply, "Jesus I recognize, Paul I know, but who are you?" The person with the evil spirit then sprang at them and subdued them all. He so overpowered them that they fled naked and wounded from that house. When this became known to all the Jews and Greeks who lived in Ephesus, fear fell upon them all, and the name of the Lord Jesus was held in great esteem. Many of those who had become believers came forward and openly acknowledged their former practices. Moreover, a large number of those who had practiced magic collected their books and burned them in public. They calculated their value and found it to be fifty thousand silver pieces. Thus did the word of the Lord continue to spread with influence and power.

PSALM 30:7-13

Once, in my security, I said,
"I shall never be disturbed."
O LORD, in your good will you had
endowed me with majesty and strength;
but when you hid your face I was terrified.
To you, O LORD, I cried out;
with the LORD I pleaded:
"What gain would there be from my lifeblood,
from my going down into the grave?
Would dust give you thanks
or proclaim your faithfulness?
Hear, O LORD, and have pity on me;
O LORD, be my helper."
You changed my mourning into dancing;
you took off my sackcloth and clothed me with gladness,
That my soul might sing praise to you without ceasing;
O LORD, my God, forever will I give you thanks.

PROVERBS 10:24-25

What the wicked man fears will befall him, / but the desire of the just will be granted. / When the tempest passes, the wicked man is no more; / but the just man is established forever.

MARCH 5

ACTS 19:21-40

When this was concluded, Paul made up his mind to travel through Macedonia and Achaia, and then to go on to Jerusalem, saying, "After I have been there, I must visit Rome also." Then he sent to Macedonia two of his assistants, Timothy and Erastus, while he himself stayed for a while in the province of Asia.

About that time a serious disturbance broke out concerning the Way. There was a silversmith named Demetrius who made miniature silver shrines of Artemis and provided no little work for the craftsmen. He called a meeting of these and other workers in related crafts and said, "Men, you know well that our prosperity derives from this work. As you can now see and hear, not only in Ephesus but throughout most of the province of Asia this Paul has persuaded and misled a great number of people by saying that gods made by hands are not gods at all. The danger grows, not only that our business will be discredited, but also that the temple of the great goddess Artemis will be of no account, and that she whom the whole province of Asia and all the world worship will be stripped of her magnificence."

When they heard this, they were filled with fury and began to shout, "Great is Artemis of the Ephesians!" The city was filled with confusion, and the people rushed with one accord into the theater, seizing Gaius and Aristarchus, the Macedonians, Paul's traveling companions. Paul wanted to go before the crowd, but the disciples would not let him, and even some of the Asiarchs who were friends of his sent word to him advising him not to venture into the theater. Meanwhile, some were shouting one thing, others something else; the assembly was in chaos, and most of the people had no idea why they had come together. Some of the crowd prompted Alexander, as the Jews pushed him forward, and Alexander signaled with his hand that he wished to explain something to the gathering. But when they recognized that he was a Jew, they all shouted in unison, for about two hours, "Great is Artemis of the Ephesians!" Finally the town clerk restrained the crowd and said, "You Ephesians, what person is there who does not know that the city of the Ephesians is the guardian of the temple of the great Artemis and of her image that fell from the sky? Since these things are undeniable, you must calm yourselves and not do anything rash. The men you brought here are not temple robbers, nor have they insulted our goddess. If Demetrius and his fellow craftsmen have a complaint against anyone, courts are in session, and there are proconsuls. Let them bring charges against one another. If you have anything further to investigate, let the matter be settled in the lawful assembly, for as it is, we are in danger of being charged with rioting because of today's conduct. There is no cause for it. We shall [not] be able to give a reason for this demonstration." With these words he dismissed the assembly.

PSALM 31:1-9

For the leader. A psalm of David.
In you, O LORD, I take refuge;
　　let me never be put to shame.
In your justice rescue me,
　　incline your ear to me,
　　make haste to deliver me!
Be my rock of refuge,
　　a stronghold to give me safety.
You are my rock and my fortress;
　　for your name's sake you will
　　lead and guide me.
You will free me from the snare
　　they set for me,
　　for you are my refuge.
Into your hands I commend my
　　spirit;
　　you will redeem me, O LORD,
　　O faithful God.
Into your hands I commend my
　　spirit;
　　you will redeem me, O LORD,
　　O faithful God.
You hate those who worship vain
　　idols,
　　but my trust is in the LORD.
I will rejoice and be glad of your
　　kindness,
　　when you have seen my
　　affliction
　　and watched over me in my
　　distress,
Not shutting me up in the grip of
　　the enemy
　　but enabling me to move about
　　at large.

PROVERBS 10:26

As vinegar to the teeth, and smoke to the eyes, / is the sluggard to those who use him as a messenger.

MARCH 6

ACTS 20:1-12

When the disturbance was over, Paul had the disciples summoned and, after encouraging them, he bade them farewell and set out on his journey to Macedonia. As he traveled throughout those regions, he provided many words of encouragement for them. Then he arrived in Greece, where he stayed for three months. But when a plot was made against him by the Jews as he was about to set sail for Syria, he decided to return by way of Macedonia.

Sopater, the son of Pyrrhus, from Beroea, accompanied him, as did Aristarchus and Secundus from Thessalonica, Gaius from Derbe, Timothy, and Tychicus and Trophimus from Asia who went on ahead and waited for us at Troas. We sailed from Philippi after the feast of Unleavened Bread, and rejoined them five days later in Troas, where we spent a week.

On the first day of the week when we gathered to break bread, Paul spoke to them because he was going to leave on the next day, and he kept on speaking until midnight. There were many lamps in the upstairs room where we were gathered, and a young man named Eutychus who was sitting on the window sill was sinking into a deep sleep as Paul talked on and on. Once overcome by sleep, he fell down from the third story and when he was picked up, he was dead. Paul went down, threw himself upon him, and said as he embraced him, "Don't be alarmed; there is life in him." Then he returned upstairs, broke the bread, and ate; after a long conversation that lasted until daybreak, he departed. And they took the boy away alive and were immeasurably comforted.

PSALM 31:10-13

Have pity on me, O LORD, for I
　　am in distress;
　　with sorrow my eye is
　　　　consumed; my soul also, and
　　　　my body.
For my life is spent with grief
　　and my years with sighing;
My strength has failed through
　　affliction,
　　and my bones are consumed.
For all my foes I am an object of
　　reproach,
　　a laughingstock to my
　　　　neighbors, and a dread to my
　　　　friends;
　　they who see me abroad flee
　　　　from me.
I am forgotten like the
　　unremembered dead;
　　I am like a dish that is broken.

PROVERBS 10:27-28

The fear of the LORD *prolongs life, / but the years of the wicked are brief. / The hope of the just brings them joy, / but the expectation of the wicked comes to nought.*

MARCH 7

ACTS 20:13-38

We went ahead to the ship and set sail for Assos where we were to take Paul on board, as he had arranged, since he was going overland. When he met us in Assos, we took him aboard and went on to Mitylene. We sailed away from there on the next day and reached a point off Chios, and a day later we reached Samos, and on the following day we arrived at Miletus. Paul had decided to sail past Ephesus in order not to lose time in the province of Asia, for he was hurrying to be in Jerusalem, if at all possible, for the day of Pentecost.

From Miletus he had the presbyters of the church at Ephesus summoned. When they came to him, he addressed them, "You know how I lived among you the whole time from the day I first came to the province of Asia. I served the Lord with all humility and with the tears and trials that came to me because of the plots of the Jews, and I did not at all shrink from telling you what was for your benefit, or from teaching you in public or in your homes. I earnestly bore witness for both Jews and Greeks to repentance before God and to faith in our Lord Jesus. But now, compelled by the Spirit, I am going to Jerusalem. What will happen to me there I do not know, except that in one city after another the holy Spirit has been warning me that imprisonment and hardships await me. Yet I consider life of no importance to me, if only I may finish my course and the ministry that I received from the Lord Jesus, to bear witness to the gospel of God's grace.

"But now I know that none of you to whom I preached the kingdom during my travels will ever see my face again. And so I solemnly declare to you this day that I am not responsible for the blood of any of you, for I did not shrink from proclaiming to you the entire plan of God. Keep watch over yourselves and over the whole flock of which the holy Spirit has appointed you overseers, in which you tend the church of God that he acquired with his own blood. I know that after my departure savage wolves will come among you, and they will not spare the flock. And from your own group, men will come forward perverting the truth to draw the disciples away after them. So be vigilant and remember that for three years, night and day, I unceasingly admonished each of you with tears. And now I commend you to God and to that gracious word of his that can build you up and give you the inheritance among all who are consecrated. I have never wanted anyone's silver or gold or clothing. You know well that these very hands have served my needs and my companions. In every way I have shown you that by hard work of that sort we must help the weak, and keep in mind the words of the Lord Jesus who himself said, 'It is more blessed to give than to receive.' "

When he had finished speaking he knelt down and prayed with them all. They were all weeping loudly as they threw their arms around Paul and kissed him, for they were deeply distressed that he had said that they would never see his face again. Then they escorted him to the ship.

PSALM 31:14-19

I hear the whispers of the crowd,
    that frighten me from every
    side,
as they consult together against
    me, plotting to take my life.
But my trust is in you, O LORD;
    I say, "You are my God."
In your hands is my destiny;
    rescue me
    from the clutches of my
    enemies and my persecutors.
Let your face shine upon your
    servant;
    save me in your kindness.
O LORD, let me not be put to
    shame, for I call upon you;
    let the wicked be put to shame;
    let them be reduced to
    silence in the
    nether world.
Let dumbness strike their lying
    lips
    that speak insolence against
    the just in
    pride and scorn.

PROVERBS 10:29-30

The LORD is a stronghold to him who walks honestly, / but to evildoers, their downfall. / The just man will never be disturbed, / but the wicked will not abide in the land.

MARCH 8

ACTS 21:1-26

When we had taken leave of them we set sail, made a straight run for Cos, and on the next day for Rhodes, and from there to Patara. Finding a ship crossing to Phoenicia, we went on board and put out to sea. We caught sight of Cyprus but passed by it on our left and sailed on toward Syria and put in at Tyre where the ship was to unload cargo. There we sought out the disciples and stayed for a week. They kept telling Paul through the Spirit not to embark for Jerusalem. At the end of our stay we left and resumed our journey. All of them, women and children included, escorted us out of the city, and after kneeling on the beach to pray, we bade farewell to one another. Then we boarded the ship, and they returned home.

We continued the voyage and came from Tyre to Ptolemais, where we greeted the brothers and stayed a day with them. On the next day we resumed the trip and came to Caesarea, where we went to the house of Philip the evangelist, who was one of the

Seven, and stayed with him. He had four virgin daughters gifted with prophecy. We had been there several days when a prophet named Agabus came down from Judea. He came up to us, took Paul's belt, bound his own feet and hands with it, and said, "Thus says the holy Spirit: This is the way the Jews will bind the owner of this belt in Jerusalem, and they will hand him over to the Gentiles." When we heard this, we and the local residents begged him not to go up to Jerusalem. Then Paul replied, "What are you doing, weeping and breaking my heart? I am prepared not only to be bound but even to die in Jerusalem for the name of the Lord Jesus." Since he would not be dissuaded we let the matter rest, saying, "The Lord's will be done."

After these days we made preparations for our journey, then went up to Jerusalem. Some of the disciples from Caesarea came along to lead us to the house of Mnason, a Cypriot, a disciple of long standing, with whom we were to stay. When we reached Jerusalem the brothers welcomed us warmly. The next day, Paul accompanied us on a visit to James, and all the presbyters were present. He greeted them, then proceeded to tell them in detail what God had accomplished among the Gentiles through his ministry. They praised God when they heard it but said to him, "Brother, you see how many thousands of believers there are from among the Jews, and they are all zealous observers of the law. They have been informed that you are teaching all the Jews who live among the Gentiles to abandon Moses and that you are telling them not to circumcise their children or to observe their customary practices.

What is to be done? They will surely hear that you have arrived. So do what we tell you. We have four men who have taken a vow. Take these men and purify yourself with them, and pay their expenses that they may have their heads shaved. In this way everyone will know that there is nothing to the reports they have been given about you but that you yourself live in observance of the law. As for the Gentiles who have come to believe, we sent them our decision that they abstain from meat sacrificed to idols, from blood, from the meat of strangled animals, and from unlawful marriage." So Paul took the men, and on the next day after purifying himself together with them entered the temple to give notice of the day when the purification would be completed and the offering made for each of them.

PSALM 31:20-25

How great is the goodness, O
LORD,
    which you have in store for
      those who fear you,
And which, toward those who
    take refuge in you,
    you show in the sight of men.
You hide them in the shelter of
    your presence
    from the plottings of men;
You screen them within your
    abode
    from the strife of tongues.
Blessed be the LORD whose
    wondrous kindness
    he has shown me in a fortified
    city.
Once I said in my anguish,
    "I am cut off from your sight";
Yet you heard the sound of my
    pleading
    when I cried out to you.

Love the LORD, all you his
  faithful ones!
The LORD keeps those who are
  constant,
but more than requites those
  who act proudly.

Take courage and be
  stouthearted,
all you who hope in the LORD.

PROVERBS 10:31-32

The mouth of the just yields wisdom, / but the perverse tongue will be cut off. /
The lips of the just know how to please, / but the mouth of the wicked, how to
pervert.

MARCH 9

ACTS 21:27-40

When the seven days were nearly completed, the Jews from the province of Asia noticed him in the temple, stirred up the whole crowd, and laid hands on him, shouting, "Fellow Israelites, help us. This is the man who is teaching everyone everywhere against the people and the law and this place, and what is more, he has even brought Greeks into the temple and defiled this sacred place." For they had previously seen Trophimus the Ephesian in the city with him and supposed that Paul had brought him into the temple. The whole city was in turmoil with people rushing together. They seized Paul and dragged him out of the temple, and immediately the gates were closed. While they were trying to kill him, a report reached the cohort commander that all Jerusalem was rioting. He immediately took soldiers and centurions and charged down on them. When they saw the commander and the soldiers they stopped beating Paul. The cohort commander came forward, arrested him, and ordered him to be secured with two chains; he tried to find out who he might be and what he had done. Some in the mob shouted one thing, others something else; so, since he was unable to ascertain the truth because of the uproar, he ordered Paul to be brought into the compound. When he reached the steps, he was carried by the soldiers because of the violence of the mob, for a crowd of people followed and shouted, "Away with him!"

Just as Paul was about to be taken into the compound, he said to the cohort commander, "May I say something to you?" He replied, "Do you speak Greek? So then you are not the Egyptian who started a revolt some time ago and led the four thousand assassins into the desert?" Paul answered, "I am a Jew, of Tarsus in Cilicia, a citizen of no mean city; I request you to permit me to speak to the people." When he had given his permission, Paul stood on the steps and motioned with his hand to the people; and when all was quiet he addressed them in Hebrew.

PSALM 32:1-7

Of David. A maskil.

Happy is he whose fault is taken
away,
  whose sin is covered.
Happy the man to whom the
  LORD imputes not guilt,
  in whose spirit there is no
  guile.
As long as I would not speak, my
  bones wasted away
  with my groaning all the day,
For day and night your hand was
  heavy upon me,
  my strength was dried up as by
  the heat of summer.

Then I acknowledged my sin to
  you,
  my guilt I covered not.
I said, "I confess my faults to the
  LORD,"
  and you took away the guilt of
  my sin.
For this shall every faithful man
  pray to you
  in time of stress.
Though deep waters overflow,
  they shall not reach him.
You are my shelter; from distress
  you will preserve me;
  with glad cries of freedom you
  will ring me round.

PROVERBS 11:1

False scales are an abomination to the LORD, / but a full weight is his delight.

MARCH 10

ACTS 22:1-29

"My brothers and fathers, listen to what I am about to say to you in my defense." When they heard him addressing them in Hebrew they became all the more quiet. And he continued, "I am a Jew, born in Tarsus in Cilicia, but brought up in this city. At the feet of Gamaliel I was educated strictly in our ancestral law and was zealous for God, just as all of you are today. I persecuted this Way to death, binding both men and women and delivering them to prison. Even the high priest and the whole council of elders can testify on my behalf. For from them I even received letters to the brothers and set out for Damascus to bring back to Jerusalem in chains for punishment those there as well.

"On that journey as I drew near to Damascus, about noon a great light from the sky suddenly shone around me. I fell to the ground and heard a voice saying to me, 'Saul, Saul, why are you persecuting me?' I replied, 'Who are you, sir?' And he said to me, 'I am Jesus the Nazorean whom you are persecuting.' My companions saw the light but did not hear the voice of the one who spoke to me. I asked, 'What shall I do, sir?' The Lord answered me, 'Get up and go into Damascus, and there you will be told about everything appointed for you to do.' Since I could see nothing because of the brightness of that light, I was led by hand by my companions and entered Damascus.

"A certain Ananias, a devout observer of the law, and highly spoken of by all the Jews who lived there, came to me and stood there and said, 'Saul, my brother, regain your sight.' And at that very moment I regained my sight and saw him. Then he said, 'The God of our ancestors designated you to know his will, to see the Righteous One, and to hear the sound of his voice; for you will be his witness before all to what you have seen and heard. Now, why delay? Get up and have yourself baptized and your sins washed away, calling upon his name.'

"After I had returned to Jerusalem and while I was praying in the temple, I fell into a trance and saw the Lord saying to me, 'Hurry, leave Jerusalem at once, because they will not accept your testimony about me.' But I replied, 'Lord, they themselves know that from synagogue to synagogue I used to imprison and beat those who believed in you. And when the blood of your witness Stephen was being shed, I myself stood by giving my approval and keeping guard over the cloaks of his murderers.' Then he said to me, 'Go, I shall send you far away to the Gentiles.' "

They listened to him until he said this, but then they raised their voices and shouted, "Take such a one as this away from the earth. It is not right that he should live." And as they were yelling and throwing off their cloaks and flinging dust into the air, the cohort commander ordered him to be brought into the compound and gave instruction that he be interrogated under the lash to determine the reason why they were making such an outcry against him. But when they had stretched him out for the whips, Paul said to the centurion on duty, "Is it lawful for you to scourge a man who is a Roman citizen and has not been tried?" When the centurion heard this, he went to the cohort commander and reported it, saying, "What are you going to do? This man is a Roman citizen." Then the commander came and said to him, "Tell me, are you a Roman citizen?" "Yes," he answered. The commander replied, "I acquired this citizenship for a large sum of money." Paul said, "But I was born one." At once those who were going to interrogate him backed away from him, and the commander became alarmed when he realized that he was a Roman citizen and that he had had him bound.

PSALM 32:8-11

I will instruct you and show you
　　the way you should walk;
　I will counsel you, keeping my
　　eye on you.
Be not senseless like horses or
　　mules:
　with bit and bridle their temper
　　must be curbed,
　else they will not come near
　　you.
Many are the sorrows of the
　　wicked.
　but kindness surrounds him
　　who trusts in the LORD.
Be glad in the LORD and rejoice,
　　you just;
　exult, all you upright of heart.

PROVERBS 11:2-3

When pride comes, disgrace comes; / but with the humble is wisdom. / The honesty of the upright guides them; / the faithless are ruined by their duplicity.

MARCH 11

ACTS 22:30; 23:1-11

The next day, wishing to determine the truth about why he was being accused by the Jews, he freed him and ordered the chief priests and the whole Sanhedrin to convene. Then he brought Paul down and made him stand before them.

Paul looked intently at the Sanhedrin and said, "My brothers, I have conducted myself with a perfectly clear conscience before God to this day." The high priest Ananias ordered his attendants to strike his mouth. Then Paul said to him, "God will strike you, you whitewashed wall. Do you indeed sit in judgment upon me according to the law and yet in violation of the law order me to be struck?" The attendants said, "Would you revile God's high priest?" Paul answered, "Brothers, I did not realize he was the high priest. For it is written, 'You shall not curse a ruler of your people.' "

Paul was aware that some were Sadducees and some Pharisees, so he called out before the Sanhedrin, "My brothers, I am a Pharisee, the son of Pharisees; [I] am on trial for hope in the resurrection of the dead." When he said this, a dispute broke out between the Pharisees and Sadducees, and the group became divided. For the Sadducees say that there is no resurrection or angels or spirits, while the Pharisees acknowledge all three. A great uproar occurred, and some scribes belonging to the Pharisee party stood up and sharply argued, "We find nothing wrong with this man. Suppose a spirit or an angel has spoken to him?" The dispute was so serious that the commander, afraid that Paul would be torn to pieces by them, ordered his troops to go down and rescue him from their midst and take him into the compound. The following night the Lord stood by him and said, "Take courage. For just as you have borne witness to my cause in Jerusalem, so you must also bear witness in Rome."

PSALM 33:1-5

Exult, you just, in the LORD;
   praise from the upright is
     fitting.
Give thanks to the LORD on the
   harp;
   with the ten-stringed lyre chant
     his praises.
Sing to him a new song;
   pluck the strings skillfully,
     with shouts of gladness.
For upright is the word of the
   LORD,
   and all his works are
     trustworthy.
He loves justice and right;
   of the kindness of the LORD the
     earth is full.

PROVERBS 11:4-6

Wealth is useless on the day of wrath, / but virtue saves from death. / The honest man's virtue makes his way straight, / but by his wickedness the wicked man falls. / The virtue of the upright saves them, / but the faithless are caught in their own intrigue.

MARCH 12

ACTS 23:12-35

When day came, the Jews made a plot and bound themselves by oath not to eat or drink until they had killed Paul. There were more than forty who formed this conspiracy. They went to the chief priests and elders and said, "We have bound ourselves by a solemn oath to taste nothing until we have killed Paul. You, together with the Sanhedrin, must now make an official request to the commander to have him bring him down to you, as though you meant to investigate his case more thoroughly. We on our part are prepared to kill him before he arrives." The son of Paul's sister, however, heard about the ambush; so he went and entered the compound and reported it to Paul. Paul then called one of the centurions and requested, "Take this young man to the commander; he has something to report to him." So he took him and brought him to the commander and explained, "The prisoner Paul called me and asked that I bring this young man to you; he has something to say to you." The commander took him by the hand, drew him aside, and asked him privately, "What is it you have to report to me?" He replied, "The Jews have conspired to ask you to bring Paul down to the Sanhedrin tomorrow, as though they meant to inquire about him more thoroughly, but do not believe them. More than forty of them are lying in wait for him; they have bound themselves by oath not to eat or drink until they have killed him. They are now ready and only wait for your consent." As the commander dismissed the young man he directed him, "Tell no one that you gave me this information."

Then he summoned two of the centurions and said, "Get two hundred soldiers ready to go to Caesarea by nine o'clock tonight, along with seventy horsemen and two hundred auxiliaries. Provide mounts for Paul to ride and give him safe conduct to Felix the governor." Then he wrote a letter with this content: "Claudius Lysias to his excellency the governor Felix, greetings. This man, seized by the Jews and about to be murdered by them, I rescued after intervening with my troops when I learned that he was a Roman citizen. I wanted to learn the reason for their accusations against him so I brought him down to their Sanhedrin. I discovered that he was accused in matters of controversial questions of their law and not of any charge deserving death or imprisonment. Since it was brought to my attention that there will be a plot against the man, I am sending him to you at once, and have also notified his accusers to state [their case] against him before you."

So the soldiers, according to their orders, took Paul and escorted him by night to Antipatris. The next day they returned to the compound, leaving the horsemen to complete the journey with him. When they arrived in Caesarea they delivered the letter to the governor and presented Paul to him. When he had read it and asked to what province he belonged, and learned that he was from Cilicia, he said, "I shall hear your case when your accusers arrive." Then he ordered that he be held in custody in Herod's praetorium.

PSALM 33:6-12

By the word of the LORD the
    heavens were made;
  by the breath of his mouth all
    their host.
He gathers the waters of the sea
    as in a flask;
  in cellars he confines the deep.
Let all the earth fear the LORD;
  let all who dwell in the world
    revere him.

For he spoke, and it was made;
  he commanded, and it stood
    forth.
The LORD brings to nought the
    plans of nations;
  he foils the designs of peoples.
But the plan of the LORD stands
    forever;
  the design of his heart, through
    all generations.
Happy the nation whose God is
    the LORD,
  the people he has chosen for
    his own inheritance.

PROVERBS 11:7

When a wicked man dies his hope perishes, / and what is expected from strength comes to nought.

MARCH 13

ACTS 24:1-27

Five days later the high priest Ananias came down with some elders and an advocate, a certain Tertullus, and they presented formal charges against Paul to the governor. When he was called, Tertullus began to accuse him, saying, "Since we have attained much peace through you, and reforms have been accomplished in this nation through your provident care, we acknowledge this in every way and everywhere, most excellent Felix, with all gratitude. But in order not to detain you further, I ask you to give us a brief hearing with your customary graciousness. We found this man to be a pest; he creates dissension among Jews all over the world and is a ringleader of the sect of the Nazoreans. He even tried to desecrate our temple, but we arrested him. If you examine him you will be able to learn from him for yourself about everything of which we are accusing him." The Jews also joined in the attack and asserted that these things were so.

Then the governor motioned to him to speak and Paul replied, "I know that you have been a judge over this nation for many years and so I am pleased to make my defense before you. As you can verify, not more than twelve days have passed since I went up to Jerusalem to worship. Neither in the temple, nor in the synagogues, nor anywhere in the city did they find me arguing with anyone or instigating a riot among the people. Nor can they prove to you the accusations they are now making against me. But this I do admit to you, that according to the Way, which they call a sect, I worship the God of our ancestors and I believe everything that is in accordance with the law and written in the prophets. I have the same hope in God as they themselves have that there will be a resurrection of the righteous and the unrighteous. Because of this, I always strive to keep my conscience clear before God and man. After many years, I came to bring alms for my nation and offerings. While I was so engaged, they found me, after my purification, in the temple without a crowd or disturbance. But some Jews from the province of Asia, who should be here before you to make whatever accusation they might have against me—or let these men themselves state what crime they discovered when I stood before the Sanhedrin, unless it was my one outcry as I stood among them, that 'I am on trial before you today for the resurrection of the dead.' "

Then Felix, who was accurately informed about the Way, postponed the trial, saying, "When Lysias the commander comes down, I shall decide your case." He gave orders to the centurion that he should be kept in custody but have some liberty, and that he should not prevent any of his friends from caring for his needs.

Several days later Felix came with his wife Drusilla, who was Jewish. He had Paul summoned and listened to him speak about faith in Christ Jesus. But as he spoke about righteousness and self-restraint and the coming judgment, Felix became frightened and said, "You may go for now; when I find an opportunity I shall summon you again." At the same time he hoped that a bribe would be offered him by Paul, and so he sent for him very often and conversed with him.

Two years passed and Felix was succeeded by Porcius Festus. Wishing to ingratiate himself with the Jews, Felix left Paul in prison.

PSALM 33:13-19

From heaven the LORD looks
    down;
  he sees all mankind.
From his fixed throne he beholds
  all who dwell on the earth,
He who fashioned the heart of
    each,
  he who knows all their works.
A king is not saved by a mighty
    army,
  nor is a warrior delivered by
    great strength.
Useless is the horse for safety;
  great though its strength, it
    cannot provide escape.
But see, the eyes of the LORD are
  upon those who fear him.
  upon those who hope for his
    kindness,
To deliver them from death
  and preserve them in spite of
    famine.

PROVERBS 11:8

The just man escapes trouble, / and the wicked man falls into it on his stead.

ACTS 25:1-27

Three days after his arrival in the province, Festus went up from Caesarea to Jerusalem where the chief priests and Jewish leaders presented him their formal charges against Paul. They asked him as a favor to have him sent to Jerusalem, for they were plotting to kill him along the way. Festus replied that Paul was being held in custody in Caesarea and that he himself would be returning there shortly. He said, "Let your authorities come down with me, and if this man has done something improper, let them accuse him."

After spending no more than eight or ten days with them, he went down to Caesarea, and on the following day took his seat on the tribunal and ordered that Paul be brought in. When he appeared, the Jews who had come down from Jerusalem surrounded him and brought many serious charges against him, which they were unable to prove. In defending himself Paul said, "I have committed no crime either against the Jewish law or against the temple or against Caesar." Then Festus, wishing to ingratiate himself with the Jews, said to Paul in reply, "Are you willing to go up to Jerusalem and there stand trial before me on these charges?" Paul answered, "I am standing before the tribunal of Caesar; this is where I should be tried. I have committed no crime against the Jews, as you very well know. If I have committed a crime or done anything deserving death, I do not seek to escape the death penalty; but if there is no substance to the charges they are bringing against me, then no one has the right to hand me over to them. I appeal to Caesar." Then Festus, after conferring with his council, replied, "You have appealed to Caesar. To Caesar you will go."

When a few days had passed, King Agrippa and Bernice arrived in Caesarea on a visit to Festus. Since they spent several days there, Festus referred Paul's case to the king, saying, "There is a man here left in custody by Felix. When I was in Jerusalem the chief priests and the elders of the Jews brought charges against him and demanded his condemnation. I answered them that it was not Roman practice to hand over an accused person before he has faced his accusers and had the opportunity to defend himself against their charge. So when [they] came together here, I made no delay; the next day I took my seat on the tribunal and ordered the man to be brought in. His accusers stood around him, but did not charge him with any of the crimes I suspected. Instead they had some issues with him about their own religion and about a certain Jesus who had died but who Paul claimed was alive. Since I was at a loss how to investigate this controversy, I asked if he were willing to go to Jerusalem and there stand trial on these charges. And when Paul appealed that he be held in custody for the Emperor's decision, I ordered him held until I could send him to Caesar." Agrippa said to Festus, "I too should like to hear this man." He replied, "Tomorrow you will hear him."

The next day Agrippa and Bernice came with great ceremony

and entered the audience hall in the company of cohort commanders and the prominent men of the city and, by command of Festus, Paul was brought in. And Festus said, "King Agrippa and all you here present with us, look at this man about whom the whole Jewish populace petitioned me here and in Jerusalem, clamoring that he should live no longer. I found, however, that he had done nothing deserving death, and so when he appealed to the Emperor, I decided to send him. But I have nothing definite to write about him to our sovereign; therefore I have brought him before all of you, and particularly before you, King Agrippa, so that I may have something to write as a result of this investigation. For it seems senseless to me to send up a prisoner without indicating the charges against him."

PSALM 33:20-22

Our soul waits for the LORD,
who is our help and our shield,
For in him our hearts rejoice;
in his holy name we trust.
May your kindness, O LORD, be
upon us
who have put our hope in you.

PROVERBS 11:9-11

With his mouth the impious man would ruin his neighbor, / but through their knowledge the just make their escape. / When the just prosper, the city rejoices; / and when the wicked perish, there is jubilation. / Through the blessing of the righteous the city is exalted, / but through the mouth of the wicked it is overthrown.

MARCH 15

ACTS 26:1-32

Then Agrippa said to Paul, "You may now speak on your own behalf." So Paul stretched out his hand and began his defense. "I count myself fortunate, King Agrippa, that I am to defend myself before you today against all the charges made against me by the Jews, especially since you are an expert in all the Jewish customs and controversies. And therefore I beg you to listen patiently. My manner of living from my youth, a life spent from the beginning among my people and in Jerusalem, all [the] Jews know. They have known about me from the start, if they are willing to testify, that I have lived my life as a Pharisee, the strictest party of our religion. But now I am standing trial because of my hope in the promise made by God to our ancestors. Our twelve tribes hope to attain to that promise as they fervently worship God day and night; and on account of this hope I am accused by Jews, O king. Why is it thought unbelievable among you that God raises the dead? I myself once thought that I had to do many things against the name of Jesus the Nazorean, and I did so in Jerusalem. I imprisoned many of the holy ones with the authorization I received from the chief priests, and when they were to be put to death I cast my vote against them. Many times, in synagogue after synagogue, I punished them in an attempt to force them to blaspheme; I was so enraged against them that I pursued them even to foreign cities.

"On one such occasion I was traveling to Damascus with the authorization and commission of the chief priests. At midday, along the way, O king, I saw a light from the sky, brighter than the sun, shining around me and my traveling companions. We all fell to the ground and I heard a voice saying to me in Hebrew, 'Saul, Saul, why are you persecuting me? It is hard for you to kick against the goad.' And I said, 'Who are you, sir?' And the Lord replied, 'I am Jesus whom you are persecuting. Get up now, and stand on your feet. I have appeared to you for this purpose, to appoint you as a servant and witness of what you have seen [of me] and what you will be shown. I shall deliver you from this people and from the Gentiles to whom I send you, to open their eyes that they may turn from darkness to light and from the power of Satan to God, so that they may obtain forgiveness of sins and an inheritance among those who have been consecrated by faith in me.'

"And so, King Agrippa, I was not disobedient to the heavenly vision. On the contrary, first to those in Damascus and in Jerusalem and throughout the whole country of Judea, and then to the Gentiles, I preached the need to repent and turn to God, and to do works giving evidence of repentance. That is why the Jews seized me [when I was] in the temple and tried to kill me. But I have enjoyed God's help to this very day, and so I stand here testifying to small and great alike, saying nothing different from what the prophets and Moses foretold, that the Messiah must suffer and that, as the first to rise from the dead, he would proclaim light both to our people and to the Gentiles."

While Paul was so speaking in his defense, Festus said in a loud voice, "You are mad, Paul; much learning is driving you mad." But Paul replied, "I am not mad, most excellent Festus; I am speaking words of truth and reason. The king knows about these matters and to him I speak boldly, for I cannot believe that [any] of this has escaped his notice; this was not done in a corner. King Agrippa, do you believe the prophets? I know you believe." Then Agrippa said to Paul, "You will soon persuade me to play the Christian." Paul replied, "I would pray to God that sooner or later not only you but all who listen to me today might become as I am except for these chains."

Then the king rose, and with him the governor and Bernice and the others who sat with them. And after they had withdrawn they said to one another, "This man is doing nothing [at all] that deserves death or imprisonment." And Agrippa said to Festus, "This man could have been set free if he had not appealed to Caesar."

PSALM 34:1-4

Of David, when he feigned madness before Abimelech, who forced him to depart.

I will bless the LORD at all times;
   his praise shall be ever in my
     mouth.
Let my soul glory in the LORD;

the lowly will hear me and be
glad.

Glorify the LORD with me,
let us together extol his name.

PROVERBS 11:12-13

He who reviles his neighbor has no sense, / but the intelligent man keeps silent. /
A newsmonger reveals secrets, / but a trustworthy man keeps a confidence.

MARCH 16

ACTS 27:1-17

When it was decided that we should sail to Italy, they handed Paul and some other prisoners over to a centurion named Julius of the Cohort Augusta. We went on board a ship from Adramyttium bound for ports in the province of Asia and set sail. Aristarchus, a Macedonian from Thessalonica, was with us. On the following day we put in at Sidon where Julius was kind enough to allow Paul to visit his friends who took care of him. From there we put out to sea and sailed around the sheltered side of Cyprus because of the headwinds, and crossing the open sea off the coast of Cilicia and Pamphylia we came to Myra in Lycia.

There the centurion found an Alexandrian ship that was sailing to Italy and put us on board. For many days we made little headway, arriving at Cnidus only with difficulty, and because the wind would not permit us to continue our course we sailed for the sheltered side of Crete off Salmone. We sailed past it with difficulty and reached a place called Fair Havens, near which was the city of Lasea.

Much time had now passed and sailing had become hazardous because the time of the fast had already gone by, so Paul warned them, "Men, I can see that this voyage will result in severe damage and heavy loss not only to the cargo and the ship, but also to our lives." The centurion, however, paid more attention to the pilot and to the owner of the ship than to what Paul said. Since the harbor was unfavorably situated for spending the winter, the majority planned to put out to sea from there in the hope of reaching Phoenix, a port in Crete facing westnorthwest, there to spend the winter.

A south wind blew gently, and thinking they had attained their objective, they weighed anchor and sailed along close to the coast of Crete. Before long an offshore wind of hurricane force called a "Northeaster" struck. Since the ship was caught up in it and could not head into the wind we gave way and let ourselves be driven. We passed along the sheltered side of an island named Cauda and managed only with difficulty to get the dinghy under control. They hoisted it aboard, then used cables to undergird the ship. Because of their fear that they would run aground on the shoal of Syrtis, they lowered the drift anchor and were carried along in this way.

PSALM 34:5-11

I sought the LORD, and he
answered me
and delivered me from all my
fears.
Look to him that you may be
radiant with joy,
and your faces may not blush
with shame.
When the afflicted man called
out, the LORD heard,
and from all his distress he
saved him.
The angel of the LORD encamps
around those who fear him,
and delivers them.
Taste and see how good the LORD
is;
happy the man who takes
refuge in him.
Fear the LORD, you his holy ones,
for nought is lacking to those
who fear him.
The great grow poor and hungry;
but those who seek the LORD
want for no good thing.

PROVERBS 11:14

For lack of guidance a people falls; / security lies in many counselors.

MARCH 17

ACTS 27:18-44

We were being pounded by the storm so violently that the next day they jettisoned some cargo, and on the third day with their own hands they threw even the ship's tackle overboard. Neither the sun nor the stars were visible for many days, and no small storm raged. Finally, all hope of our surviving was taken away.

When many would no longer eat, Paul stood among them and said, "Men, you should have taken my advice and not have set sail from Crete and you would have avoided this disastrous loss. I urge you now to keep up your courage; not one of you will be lost, only the ship. For last night an angel of the God to whom [I] belong and whom I serve stood by me and said, 'Do not be afraid, Paul. You are destined to stand before Caesar; and behold, for your sake, God has granted safety to all

who are sailing with you.' Therefore, keep up your courage, men; I trust in God that it will turn out as I have been told. We are destined to run aground on some island."

On the fourteenth night, as we were still being driven about on the Adriatic Sea, toward midnight the sailors began to suspect that they were nearing land. They took soundings and found twenty fathoms; a little farther on, they again took soundings and found fifteen fathoms. Fearing that we would run aground on a rocky coast, they dropped four anchors from the stern and prayed for day to come. The sailors then tried to abandon ship; they lowered the dinghy to the sea on the pretext of going to lay out anchors from the bow. But Paul said to the centurion and the soldiers, "Unless these men stay with the ship, you cannot be saved." So the soldiers cut the ropes of the dinghy and set it adrift.

Until the day began to dawn, Paul kept urging all to take some food. He said, "Today is the fourteenth day that you have been waiting, going hungry and eating nothing. I urge you, therefore, to take some food; it will help you survive. Not a hair of the head of anyone of you will be lost." When he said this, he took bread, gave thanks to God in front of them all, broke it, and began to eat. They were all encouraged, and took some food themselves. In all, there were two hundred seventy-six of us on the ship. After they had eaten enough, they lightened the ship by throwing the wheat into the sea.

When day came they did not recognize the land, but made out a bay with a beach. They planned to run the ship ashore on it, if they could. So they cast off the anchors and abandoned them to the sea, and at the same time they unfastened the lines of the rudders, and hoisting the foresail into the wind, they made for the beach. But they struck a sandbar and ran the ship aground. The bow was wedged in and could not be moved, but the stern began to break up under the pounding [of the waves]. The soldiers planned to kill the prisoners so that none might swim away and escape, but the centurion wanted to save Paul and so kept them from carrying out their plan. He ordered those who could swim to jump overboard first and get to the shore, and then the rest, some on planks, others on debris from the ship. In this way, all reached shore safely.

PSALM 34:12-23

Come, children, hear me;
  I will teach you the fear of the
    LORD.
Which of you desires life,
  and takes delight in prosperous
    days?
Keep your tongue from evil
  and your lips from speaking
    guile;
Turn from evil, and do good;
  seek peace, and follow after it.
The LORD has eyes for the just,
  and ears for their cry.
The LORD confronts the
    evildoers,
  to destroy remembrance of
    them from the earth.
When the just cry out, the LORD
    hears them,
  and from all their distress he
    rescues them.
The LORD is close to the
    brokenhearted;
  and those who are crushed in
    spirit he saves.
Many are the troubles of the just
    man,
  but out of them all the LORD
    delivers him;
He watches over all his bones;
  not one of them shall be
    broken.
Vice slays the wicked,
  and the enemies of the just pay
    for their guilt.
But the LORD redeems the lives of
    his servants;
  no one incurs guilt who takes
    refuge in him.

PROVERBS 11:15

He is in a bad way who becomes surety for another, / but he who hates giving pledges is safe.

ACTS 28:1-15

Once we had reached safety we learned that the island was called Malta. The natives showed us extraordinary hospitality; they lit a fire and welcomed all of us because it had begun to rain and was cold. Paul had gathered a bundle of brushwood and was putting it on the fire when a viper, escaping from the heat, fastened on his hand. When the natives saw the snake hanging from his hand, they said to one another, "This man must certainly be a murderer; though he escaped the sea, Justice has not let him remain alive." But he shook the snake off into the fire and suffered no harm. They were expecting him to swell up or suddenly to fall down dead but, after waiting a long time and seeing nothing unusual happen to him, they changed their minds and began to say that he was a god. In the vicinity of that place were lands belonging to a man named Publius, the chief of the island. He welcomed us and received us cordially as his guests for three days. It so happened that the father of Publius was sick with a fever and dysentery. Paul visited him and, after praying, laid his hands on him and healed him. After this had taken place, the rest of the sick on the island came to Paul and were cured. They paid us great honor and when we eventually set sail they brought us the provisions we needed.

Three months later we set sail on a ship that had wintered at the island. It was an Alexandrian ship with the Dioscuri as its figurehead. We put in at Syracuse and stayed there three days, and from there we sailed round the coast and arrived at Rhegium. After a day, a south wind came up and in two days we reached Puteoli. There we found some brothers and were urged to stay with them for seven days. And thus we came to Rome. The brothers from there heard about us and came as far as the Forum of Appius and Three Taverns to meet us. On seeing them, Paul gave thanks to God and took courage.

PSALM 35:1-12

Of David.

Fight, O LORD, against those who
    fight me;
  war against those who make
    war upon me.
Take up the shield and buckler,
  and rise up in my defense.
Brandish the lance, and block the
    way
  in the face of my pursuers;
Say to my soul,
  "I am your salvation."
Let those be put to shame and
    disgraced
  who seek my life;
Let those be turned back and
    confounded
  who plot evil against me.
Let them be like chaff before the
    wind,
  with the angel of the LORD
    driving them on.
Let their way be dark and
    slippery,
  with the angel of the LORD
    pursuing them.
For without cause they set their
    snare for me,
  without cause they dug a pit
    against my life.

Let ruin come upon them
unawares,
and let the snare they have set
catch them;
into the pit they have dug let
them fall.
But I will rejoice in the LORD,
I will be joyful because of his
salvation.
All my being shall say,
"O LORD, who is like you,
The rescuer of the afflicted man
from those too strong for
him,
of the afflicted and the needy
from their despoilers?"
Unjust witnesses have risen up;
things I knew not of, they lay
to my charge.
They have repaid me evil for
good,
bringing bereavement to my
soul.

PROVERBS 11:16

A gracious woman wins esteem, / but she who hates virtue is covered with shame. / [The slothful become impoverished, / but the diligent gain wealth.]

MARCH 19

ACTS 28:16-31

When he entered Rome, Paul was allowed to live by himself, with the soldier who was guarding him.

Three days later he called together the leaders of the Jews. When they had gathered he said to them, "My brothers, although I had done nothing against our people or our ancestral customs, I was handed over to the Romans as a prisoner from Jerusalem. After trying my case the Romans wanted to release me, because they found nothing against me deserving the death penalty. But when the Jews objected, I was obliged to appeal to Caesar, even though I had no accusation to make against my own nation. This is the reason, then, I have requested to see you and to speak with you, for it is on account of the hope of Israel that I wear these chains." They answered him, "We have received no letters from Judea about you, nor has any of the brothers arrived with a damaging report or rumor about you. But we should like to hear you present your views, for we know that this sect is denounced everywhere."

So they arranged a day with him and came to his lodgings in great numbers. From early morning until evening, he expounded his position to them, bearing witness to the kingdom of God and trying to convince them about Jesus from the law of Moses and the prophets. Some were convinced by what he had said, while others did not believe. Without reaching any agreement among themselves they began to leave; then Paul made one final statement. "Well did the holy Spirit speak to your ancestors through the prophet Isaiah, saying:

'Go to this people and say:

You shall indeed hear but not
understand.
You shall indeed look but
never see.
Gross is the heart of this
people;
they will not hear with their
ears;
they have closed their eyes,
so they may not see with their
eyes
and hear with their ears
and understand with their
heart and be converted,
and I heal them.'

Let it be known to you that this
salvation of God has been sent to
the Gentiles; they will listen."

He remained for two full years
in his lodgings. He received all
who came to him, and with complete assurance and without hindrance he proclaimed the kingdom of God and taught about the
Lord Jesus Christ.

PSALM 35:13-16

But I, when they were ill, put on
sackcloth;
I afflicted myself with fasting
and poured forth prayers
within my bosom.
As though it were a friend of
mine, or a brother, I went
about;
like one bewailing a mother, I
was bowed down in
mourning.
Yet when I stumbled they were
glad and gathered together;
they gathered together striking
me unawares.
They tore at me without ceasing;
they put me to the test; they
mocked me,
gnashing their teeth at me.

PROVERBS 11:17-19

A kindly man benefits himself, / but a merciless man harms himself. / The
wicked man makes empty profits, / but he who sows virtue has a sure reward. /
Virtue directs toward life, / but he who pursues evil does so to his death.

MARCH 20

ROMANS 1:1-32

Paul, a slave of Christ Jesus,
called to be an apostle and set
apart for the gospel of God, which
he promised previously through
his prophets in the holy scriptures, the gospel about his Son,
descended from David according
to the flesh, but established as
Son of God in power according to
the spirit of holiness through resurrection from the dead, Jesus
Christ our Lord. Through him we
have received the grace of apostleship, to bring about the obedience
of faith, for the sake of his name,
among all the Gentiles, among
whom are you also, who are
called to belong to Jesus Christ; to
all the beloved of God in Rome,
called to be holy. Grace to you
and peace from God our Father
and the Lord Jesus Christ.

First, I give thanks to my God
through Jesus Christ for all of
you, because your faith is heralded throughout the world. God
is my witness, whom I serve with

my spirit in proclaiming the gospel of his Son, that I remember you constantly, always asking in my prayers that somehow by God's will I may at last find my way clear to come to you. For I long to see you, that I may share with you some spiritual gift so that you may be strengthened, that is, that you and I may be mutually encouraged by one another's faith, yours and mine. I do not want you to be unaware, brothers, that I often planned to come to you, though I was prevented until now, that I might harvest some fruit among you, too, as among the rest of the Gentiles. To Greeks and non-Greeks alike, to the wise and the ignorant, I am under obligation; that is why I am eager to preach the gospel also to you in Rome.

For I am not ashamed of the gospel. It is the power of God for the salvation of everyone who believes: for Jew first, and then Greek. For in it is revealed the righteousness of God from faith to faith; as it is written, "The one who is righteous by faith will live."

The wrath of God is indeed being revealed from heaven against every impiety and wickedness of those who suppress the truth by their wickedness. For what can be known about God is evident to them, because God made it evident to them. Ever since the creation of the world, his invisible attributes of eternal power and divinity have been able to be understood and perceived in what he has made. As a result, they have no excuse; for although they knew God they did not accord him glory as God or give him thanks. Instead, they became vain in their reasoning, and their senseless minds were darkened. While claiming to be wise, they became fools and exchanged the glory of the immortal God for the likeness of an image of mortal man or of birds or of four-legged animals or of snakes.

Therefore, God handed them over to impurity through the lusts of their hearts for the mutual degradation of their bodies. They exchanged the truth of God for a lie and revered and worshiped the creature rather than the creator, who is blessed forever. Amen. Therefore, God handed them over to degrading passions. Their females exchanged natural relations for unnatural, and the males likewise gave up natural relations with females and burned with lust for one another. Males did shameful things with males and thus received in their own persons the due penalty for their perversity. And since they did not see fit to acknowledge God, God handed them over to their undiscerning mind to do what is improper. They are filled with every form of wickedness, evil, greed, and malice; full of envy, murder, rivalry, treachery, and spite. They are gossips and scandalmongers and they hate God. They are insolent, haughty, boastful, ingenious in their wickedness, and rebellious toward their parents. They are senseless, faithless, heartless, ruthless. Although they know the just decree of God that all who practice such things deserve death, they not only do them but give approval to those who practice them.

PSALM 35:17-28

O LORD, how long will you look on?
  Save me from the roaring

beasts; from the lions, my
only life.
I will give you thanks in the vast
assembly,
in the mighty throng I will
praise you.
Let not my unprovoked enemies
rejoice over me;
let not my undeserved foes
wink knowingly.
For civil words they speak not,
but against the peaceful in the
land
they fashion treacherous
speech.
And they open wide their
mouths against me,
saying, "Aha, aha! We saw him
with our own eyes!"
You, O LORD, have seen; be not
silent;
LORD, be not far from me!
Awake, and be vigilant in my
defense;
in my cause, my God and my
LORD.

Do me justice, because you are
just, O LORD;
my God, let them not rejoice
over me.
Let them not say in their hearts,
"Aha! This is what we
wanted!"
Let them not say, "We have
swallowed him up!"
Let all be put to shame and
confounded
who are glad at my misfortune.
Let those be clothed with shame
and disgrace
who glory over me.
But let those shout for joy and be
glad
who favor my just cause;
And may they ever say, "The
LORD be glorified;
he wills the prosperity of his
servant!"
Then my tongue shall recount
your justice,
your praise, all the day.

PROVERBS 11:20-21

The depraved in heart are an abomination to the LORD, / but those who walk
blamelessly are his delight. / Truly the evil man shall not go unpunished, / but
those who are just shall escape.

MARCH 21

ROMANS 2:1-29

Therefore, you are without excuse, every one of you who
passes judgment. For by the standard by which you judge another
you condemn yourself, since you,
the judge, do the very same
things. We know that the judgment of God on those who do
such things is true. Do you suppose, then, you who judge those
who engage in such things and
yet do them yourself, that you
will escape the judgment of God?
Or do you hold his priceless kindness, forbearance, and patience in
low esteem, unaware that the
kindness of God would lead you
to repentance? By your stubborn-
ness and impenitent heart, you
are storing up wrath for yourself
for the day of wrath and revelation of the just judgment of God,
who will repay everyone accord-

ing to his works: eternal life to those who seek glory, honor, and immortality through perseverance in good works, but wrath and fury to those who selfishly disobey the truth and obey wickedness. Yes, affliction and distress will come upon every human being who does evil, Jew first and then Greek. But there will be glory, honor, and peace for everyone who does good, Jew first and then Greek. There is no partiality with God.

All who sin outside the law will also perish without reference to it, and all who sin under the law will be judged in accordance with it. For it is not those who hear the law who are just in the sight of God; rather, those who observe the law will be justified. For when the Gentiles who do not have the law by nature observe the prescriptions of the law, they are a law for themselves even though they do not have the law. They show that the demands of the law are written in their hearts, while their conscience also bears witness and their conflicting thoughts accuse or even defend them on the day when, according to my gospel, God will judge people's hidden works through Jesus Christ.

Now if you call yourself a Jew and rely on the law and boast of God and know his will and are able to discern what is important since you are instructed from the law, and if you are confident that you are a guide for the blind and a light for those in darkness, that you are a trainer of the foolish and teacher of the simple, because in the law you have the formulation of knowledge and truth—then you who teach another, are you failing to teach yourself? You who preach against stealing, do you steal? You who forbid adultery, do you commit adultery? You who detest idols, do you rob temples? You who boast of the law, do you dishonor God by breaking the law? For, as it is written, "Because of you the name of God is reviled among the Gentiles."

Circumcision, to be sure, has value if you observe the law; but if you break the law, your circumcision has become uncircumcision. Again, if an uncircumcised man keeps the precepts of the law, will he not be considered circumcised? Indeed, those who are physically uncircumcised but carry out the law will pass judgment on you, with your written law and circumcision, who break the law. One is not a Jew outwardly. True circumcision is not outward, in the flesh. Rather, one is a Jew inwardly, and circumcision is of the heart, in the spirit, not the letter; his praise is not from human beings but from God.

PSALM 36:1-10

For the leader. Of David, the servant
of the LORD.

Sin speaks to the wicked man in
    his heart;
  there is no dread of God before
    his eyes,
For he beguiles himself with the
    thought
  that his guilt will not be found
    out or hated.
The words of his mouth are
    empty and false;
  he has ceased to understand
    how to do good.
He plans wickedness in his bed;
  he sets out on a way that is not
    good, with no repugnance
    for evil.
O LORD, your kindness reaches to
    heaven;
  your faithfulness, to the
    clouds.

Your justice is like the mountains
    of God;
  your judgments, like the
    mighty deep;
  man and beast you save, O
    LORD.
How precious is your kindness,
    O God!
  the children of men take refuge
    in the shadow of your wings.

They have their fill of the prime
    gifts of your house;
  from your delightful stream
    you give them to drink.
For with you is the fountain of
    life,
  and in your light we see light.

PROVERBS 11:22
*Like a golden ring in a swine's snout / is a beautiful woman with a rebellious
disposition.*

MARCH 22

ROMANS 3:1-31

What advantage is there then in
being a Jew? Or what is the value
of circumcision? Much, in every respect. [For] in the first place, they
were entrusted with the utterances of God. What if some were
unfaithful? Will their infidelity nullify the fidelity of God? Of course
not! God must be true, though every human being is a liar, as it is
written:

  "That you may be justified in
    your words,
    and conquer when you are
      judged."

But if our wickedness provides
proof of God's righteousness,
what can we say? Is God unjust,
humanly speaking, to inflict his
wrath? Of course not! For how
else is God to judge the world?
But if God's truth redounds to his
glory through my falsehood, why
am I still being condemned as a
sinner? And why not say—as we
are accused and as some claim we

say—that we should do evil that
good may come of it? Their penalty is what they deserve.

Well, then, are we better off?
Not entirely, for we have already
brought the charge against Jews
and Greeks alike that they are all
under the domination of sin, as it
is written:

  "There is no one just, not one,
    there is no one who
      understands, there is no
      one who seeks God.
  All have gone astray; all alike
    are worthless;
    there is not one who does
      good, [there is not] even
      one.
  Their throats are open graves;
    they deceive with their
      tongues;
  the venom of asps is on their
    lips;
    their mouths are full of bitter
      cursing.
  Their feet are quick to shed
    blood;

ruin and misery are in their
ways,
and the way of peace they
know not.
There is no fear of God
before their eyes."

Now we know that what the law says is addressed to those under the law, so that every mouth may be silenced and the whole world stand accountable to God, since no human being will be justified in his sight by observing the law; for through the law comes consciousness of sin.

But now the righteousness of God has been manifested apart from the law, though testified to by the law and the prophets, the righteousness of God through faith in Jesus Christ for all who believe. For there is no distinction; all have sinned and are deprived of the glory of God. They are justified freely by his grace through the redemption in Christ Jesus, whom God set forth as an expiation, through faith, by his blood, to prove his righteousness because of the forgiveness of sins previously committed, through the forbearance of God—to prove his righteousness in the present

time, that he might be righteous and justify the one who has faith in Jesus.

What occasion is there then for boasting? It is ruled out. On what principle, that of works? No, rather on the principle of faith. For we consider that a person is justified by faith apart from works of the law. Does God belong to Jews alone? Does he not belong to Gentiles, too? Yes, also to Gentiles, for God is one and will justify the circumcised on the basis of faith and the uncircumcised through faith. Are we then annulling the law by this faith? Of course not! On the contrary, we are supporting the law.

PSALM 36:11-13

Keep up your kindness toward
your friends,
your just defense of the upright
of heart.
Let not the foot of the proud
overtake me
nor the hand of the wicked
disquiet me.
See how the evildoers have
fallen;
they are thrust down and
cannot rise.

PROVERBS 11:23

The desire of the just ends only in good; / the expectation of the wicked is wrath.

MARCH 23

ROMANS 4:1-25

What then can we say that Abraham found, our ancestor according to the flesh? Indeed, if Abraham was justified on the basis of his works, he has reason to boast;

but this was not so in the sight of God. For what does the scripture say? "Abraham believed God, and it was credited to him as righteousness." A worker's wage is credited not as a gift, but as something due. But when one does not work, yet believes in the one who justifies the ungodly, his faith is credited as righteousness. So also David declares the blessedness of the person to whom God credits righteousness apart from works:

"Blessed are they whose
iniquities are forgiven
and whose sins are covered.
Blessed is the man whose sin
the Lord does not record."

Does this blessedness apply only to the circumcised, or to the uncircumcised as well? Now we assert that "faith was credited to Abraham as righteousness." Under what circumstances was it credited? Was he circumcised or not? He was not circumcised, but uncircumcised. And he received the sign of circumcision as a seal on the righteousness received through faith while he was uncircumcised. Thus he was to be the father of all the uncircumcised who believe, so that to them [also] righteousness might be credited, as well as the father of the circumcised who not only are circumcised, but also follow the path of faith that our father Abraham walked while still uncircumcised.

It was not through the law that the promise was made to Abraham and his descendants that he would inherit the world, but through the righteousness that comes from faith. For if those who adhere to the law are the heirs, faith is null and the promise is void. For the law produces wrath; but where there is no law, neither is there violation. For this reason, it depends on faith, so that it may be a gift, and the promise may be guaranteed to all his descendants, not to those who only adhere to the law but to those who follow

the faith of Abraham, who is the father of all of us, as it is written, "I have made you father of many nations." He is our father in the sight of God, in whom he believed, who gives life to the dead and calls into being what does not exist. He believed, hoping against hope, that he would become "the father of many nations," according to what was said, "Thus shall your descendants be." He did not weaken in faith when he considered his own body as [already] dead (for he was almost a hundred years old) and the dead womb of Sarah. He did not doubt God's promise in unbelief; rather, he was empowered by faith and gave glory to God and was fully convinced that what he had promised he was also able to do. That is why "it was credited to him;" it was also for us, to whom it will be credited, who believe in the one who raised Jesus our Lord from the dead, who was handed over for our transgressions and was raised for our justification.

PSALM 37:1-6

Of David.

Be not vexed over evildoers,
    nor jealous of those who do
        wrong;
For like grass they quickly wither,
    and like green herbs they wilt.
Trust in the LORD and do good,
    that you may dwell in the land
        and enjoy security.
Take delight in the LORD,
    and he will grant you your
        hearts requests.
Commit to the LORD your way;
    trust in him, and he will act.
He will make justice dawn for
        you like the light;
    bright as the noonday shall be
        your vindication.

One man is lavish yet grows still richer; / another is too sparing, yet is the poorer. / He who confers benefits will be amply enriched, / and he who refreshes others will himself be refreshed. / Him who monopolizes grain, the people curse—/ but blessings upon the head of him who distributes it!

MARCH 24

ROMANS 5:1-21

Therefore, since we have been justified by faith, we have peace with God through our Lord Jesus Christ, through whom we have gained access [by faith] to this grace in which we stand, and we boast in hope of the glory of God. Not only that, but we even boast of our afflictions, knowing that affliction produces endurance, and endurance, proven character, and proven character, hope, and hope does not disappoint, because the love of God has been poured out into our hearts through the holy Spirit that has been given to us. For Christ, while we were still helpless, yet died at the appointed time for the ungodly. Indeed, only with difficulty does one die for a just person, though perhaps for a good person one might even find courage to die. But God proves his love for us in that while we were still sinners Christ died for us. How much more then, since we are now justified by his blood, will we be saved through him from the wrath. Indeed, if, while we were enemies, we were reconciled to God through the death of his Son, how much more, once reconciled, will we be saved by his life. Not only that, but we also boast of God through our Lord Jesus Christ, through whom we have now received reconciliation.

Therefore, just as through one person sin entered the world, and through sin, death, and thus death came to all, inasmuch as all sinned—for up to the time of the law, sin was in the world, though sin is not accounted when there is no law. But death reigned from Adam to Moses, even over those who did not sin after the pattern of the trespass of Adam, who is the type of the one who was to come.

But the gift is not like the transgression. For if by that one person's transgression the many died, how much more did the grace of God and the gracious gift of the one person Jesus Christ overflow for the many. And the gift is not like the result of the one person's sinning. For after one sin there was the judgment that brought condemnation; but the gift, after many transgressions, brought acquittal. For if, by the transgression of one person, death came to reign through that one, how much more will those who receive the abundance of grace and of the gift of justification come to reign in life through the one person Jesus Christ. In conclusion, just as through one transgression condemnation came upon all, so through one righteous act acquittal and life came to all. For just as through the disobedience of one person the many were made sinners, so through the obedience of one the many will be made righteous. The law entered in so that transgression might increase but, where sin increased, grace overflowed all the more, so that, as sin reigned in death, grace also might reign through justification for eternal life through Jesus Christ our Lord.

PSALM 37:7-11

Leave it to the LORD,
  and wait for him;
Be not vexed at the successful
  path
  of the man who does malicious
  deeds.
Give up your anger, and forsake
  wrath;
  be not vexed, it will only harm
  you.
For evildoers shall be cut off,
  but those who wait for the
  LORD shall possess the land.
Yet a little while, and the wicked
  man shall be no more;
  though you mark his place he
  will not be there.
But the meek shall possess the
  land,
  they shall delight in abounding
  peace.

PROVERBS 11:27

He who seeks the good commands favor, / but he who pursues evil will have evil befall him.

MARCH 25

ROMANS 6:1-23

What then shall we say? Shall we persist in sin that grace may abound? Of course not! How can we who died to sin yet live in it? Or are you unaware that we who were baptized into Christ Jesus were baptized into his death? We were indeed buried with him through baptism into death, so that, just as Christ was raised from the dead by the glory of the Father, we too might live in newness of life.

For if we have grown into union with him through a death like his, we shall also be united with him in the resurrection. We know that our old self was crucified with him, so that our sinful body might be done away with, that we might no longer be in slavery to sin. For a dead person has been absolved from sin. If, then, we have died with Christ, we believe that we shall also live with him. We know that Christ, raised from the dead, dies no more; death no longer has power over him. As to his death, he died to sin once and for all; as to his life, he lives for God. Consequently, you too must think of yourselves as [being] dead to sin and living for God in Christ Jesus.

Therefore, sin must not reign over your mortal bodies so that you obey their desires. And do not present the parts of your bodies to sin as weapons for wickedness, but present yourselves to

God as raised from the dead to life and the parts of your bodies to God as weapons for righteousness. For sin is not to have any power over you, since you are not under the law but under grace.

What then? Shall we sin because we are not under the law but under grace? Of course not! Do you not know that if you present yourselves to someone as obedient slaves, you are slaves of the one you obey, either of sin, which leads to death, or of obedience, which leads to righteousness? But thanks be to God that, although you were once slaves of sin, you have become obedient from the heart to the pattern of teaching to which you were entrusted. Freed from sin, you have become slaves of righteousness. I am speaking in human terms because of the weakness of your nature. For just as you presented the parts of your bodies as slaves to impurity and to lawlessness for lawlessness, so now present them as slaves to righteousness for sanctification. For when you were slaves of sin,

you were free from righteousness. But what profit did you get then from the things of which you are now ashamed? For the end of those things is death. But now that you have been freed from sin and have become slaves of God, the benefit that you have leads to sanctification, and its end is eternal life. For the wages of sin is death, but the gift of God is eternal life in Christ Jesus our Lord.

PSALM 37:12-15

The wicked man plots against the just
    and gnashes his teeth at them;
But the Lord laughs at him,
    for he sees that his day is coming.
A sword the wicked draw; they bend their bow
    to bring down the afflicted and the poor,
    to slaughter those whose path is right.
But their swords shall pierce their own hearts,
    and their bows shall be broken.

PROVERBS 11:28

He who trusts in his riches will fall, / but like green leaves the just flourish.

MARCH 26

ROMANS 7:1-6

Are you unaware, brothers (for I am speaking to people who know the law), that the law has jurisdiction over one as long as one lives? Thus a married woman is bound by law to her living husband; but if her husband dies, she is released from the law in respect to her husband. Consequently,

while her husband is alive she will be called an adulteress if she consorts with another man. But if her husband dies she is free from that law, and she is not an adulteress if she consorts with another man.

In the same way, my brothers, you also were put to death to the law through the body of Christ, so that you might belong to another, to the one who was raised from the dead in order that we might bear fruit for God. For when we were in the flesh, our sinful passions, awakened by the law, worked in our members to bear fruit for death. But now we are released from the law, dead to what held us captive, so that we may serve in the newness of the spirit and not under the obsolete letter.

PSALM 37:16-22

Better is the scanty store of the
    just
  than the great wealth of the
    wicked,
For the power of the wicked shall
    be broken,
but the LORD supports the just.
The LORD watches over the lives
    of the wholehearted;
  their inheritance lasts forever.
They are not put to shame in an
    evil time;
  in days of famine they have
    plenty.
But the wicked perish,
  and the enemies of the LORD,
    like the beauty of the
    meadows,
  vanish; like smoke they vanish.
The wicked man borrows and
    does not repay;
  the just man is kindly and
    gives,
But those whom he blesses shall
    possess the land,
  while those he curses shall be
    cut off.

PROVERBS 11:29-31

He who upsets his household has empty air for a heritage; / and the fool will become slave to the wise man. / The fruit of virtue is a tree of life, / but violence takes lives away. / If the just man is punished on earth, / how much more the wicked and the sinner!

MARCH 27

ROMANS 7:7-25

What then can we say? That the law is sin? Of course not! Yet I did not know sin except through the law, and I did not know what it is to covet except that the law said, "You shall not covet." But sin, finding an opportunity in the commandment, produced in me every kind of covetousness. Apart from the law sin is dead. I once lived outside the law, but when the commandment came, sin became alive; then I died, and the commandment that was for life turned out to be death for me. For sin, seizing an opportunity in the commandment, deceived me and through it put me to death. So then the law is holy, and the commandment is holy and righteous and good.

Did the good, then, become death for me? Of course not! Sin, in order that it might be shown to be sin, worked death in me through the good, so that sin might become sinful beyond measure through the commandment. We know that the law is spiritual; but I am carnal, sold into slavery to sin. What I do, I do not understand. For I do not do what I want, but I do what I hate. Now if I do what I do not want, I concur that the law is good. So now it is no longer I who do it, but sin that dwells in me. For I know that good does not dwell in me, that is, in my flesh. The willing is ready at hand, but doing the good is not. For I do not do the good I want, but I do the evil I do not want. Now if [I] do what I do not want, it is no longer I who do it, but sin that dwells in me. So, then, I discover the principle that when I want to do right, evil is at hand. For I take delight in the law of God, in my inner self, but I see in my members another principle at war with the law of my mind, taking me captive to the law of sin that dwells in my members. Miserable one that I am! Who will deliver me from this mortal body?

Thanks be to God through Jesus Christ our Lord. Therefore, I myself, with my mind, serve the law of God but, with my flesh, the law of sin.

PSALM 37:23-26

By the LORD are the steps of a
    man made firm,
    and he approves his way.
Though he fall, he does not lie
    prostrate,
    for the hand of the LORD
    sustains him.
Neither in my youth, nor now
    that I am old,
    have I seen a just man forsaken
    nor his descendants begging
    bread.
All the day he is kindly and
    lends,
    and his descendants shall be
    blessed.

PROVERBS 12:1

He who loves correction loves knowledge, / but he who hates reproof is stupid.

MARCH 28

ROMANS 8:1-10

Hence, now there is no condemnation for those who are in Christ Jesus. For the law of the spirit of life in Christ Jesus has freed you from the law of sin and death. For what the law, weakened by the flesh, was powerless to do, this God has done: by sending his own Son in the likeness of sinful flesh and for the sake of sin, he condemned sin in the flesh, so that the righteous decree of the law might be fulfilled in us, who live not according to the flesh but according to the spirit. For those who live according to the flesh are concerned with the things of the flesh, but those who live according to the spirit with the things of the spirit. The concern of the flesh is death, but the concern of the spirit is life and peace. For the concern of the flesh is hostility toward God; it does not submit to the law of God, nor can it; and those who are in the flesh cannot please God. But you are not in the flesh; on the contrary, you are in the spirit, if only the Spirit of God dwells in you. Whoever does not have the Spirit of Christ does not belong to him. But if Christ is in you, although the body is dead because of sin, the spirit is alive because of righteousness.

PSALM 37:27-34

Turn from evil and do good,
    that you may abide forever;
For the LORD loves what is right,
    and forsakes not his faithful
        ones.
Criminals are destroyed,
    and the posterity of the wicked
        is cut off.
The just shall possess the land
    and dwell in it forever.
The mouth of the just man tells of
    wisdom
and his tongue utters what is
    right.
The law of his God is in his heart,
    and his steps do not falter.
The wicked man spies on the
    just,
    and seeks to slay him.
The LORD will not leave him in
    his power
    nor let him be condemned
        when he is on trial.
Wait for the LORD,
    and keep his way;
He will promote you to
    ownership of the land;
    when the wicked are
        destroyed, you shall look on.

PROVERBS 12:2-3

The good man wins favor from the LORD, / but the schemer is condemned by him. / No man is built up by wickedness, / but the root of the just will never be disturbed.

MARCH 29

ROMANS 8:11-25

If the Spirit of the one who raised Jesus from the dead dwells in you, the one who raised Christ from the dead will give life to your mortal bodies also, through his Spirit that dwells in you. Consequently, brothers, we are not debtors to the flesh, to live according to the flesh. For if you live according to the flesh, you will die, but if by the spirit you put to death the deeds of the body, you will live.

For those who are led by the Spirit of God are children of God. For you did not receive a spirit of slavery to fall back into fear, but you received a spirit of adoption, through which we cry, "*Abba*, Father!" The Spirit itself bears witness with our spirit that we are children of God, and if children, then heirs, heirs of God and joint heirs with Christ, if only we suffer with him so that we may also be glorified with him.

I consider that the sufferings of this present time are as nothing compared with the glory to be revealed for us. For creation awaits with eager expectation the revelation of the children of God; for creation was made subject to futility, not of its own accord but because of the one who subjected it, in hope that creation itself would be set free from slavery to corruption and share in the glorious freedom of the children of God. We know that all creation is groaning in labor pains even until now; and not only that, but we ourselves, who have the firstfruits of the Spirit, we also groan within ourselves as we wait for adoption, the redemption of our bodies. For in hope we were saved. Now hope that sees for itself is not hope. For who hopes for what one sees? But if we hope for what we do not see, we wait with endurance.

PSALM 37:35-40

I saw a wicked man, fierce,
　and stalwart as a flourishing,
　　age-old tree.
Yet as I passed by, lo! he was no
　more;
I sought him, but he could not
　be found.
Watch the wholehearted man,
　and mark the upright;
　for there is a future for the man
　　of peace.
Sinners shall all alike be
　destroyed;
　the future of the wicked shall
　be cut off.
The salvation of the just is from
　the LORD;
　he is their refuge in time of
　distress.
And the LORD helps them and
　delivers them;
　he delivers them from the
　wicked and saves them,
　because they take refuge in
　him.

PROVERBS 12:4

A worthy wife is the crown of her husband, / but a disgraceful one is like rot in his bones.

MARCH 30

ROMANS 8:26-39

In the same way, the Spirit too comes to the aid of our weakness; for we do not know how to pray as we ought, but the Spirit itself intercedes with inexpressive groanings. And the one who searches hearts knows what is the intention of the Spirit, because it intercedes for the holy ones according to God's will.

We know that all things work for good for those who love God, who are called according to his purpose. For those he foreknew he also predestined to be conformed to the image of his Son, so that he might be the firstborn among many brothers. And those he predestined he also called; and those he called he also justified; and those he justified he also glorified.

What then shall we say to this? If God is for us, who can be against us? He who did not spare his own Son but handed him over for us all, how will he not also give us everything else along with him? Who will bring a charge against God's chosen ones? It is God who acquits us. Who will condemn? It is Christ [Jesus] who died, rather, was raised, who also is at the right hand of God, who indeed intercedes for us. What will separate us from the love of Christ? Will anguish, or distress, or persecution, or famine, or nakedness, or peril, or the sword? As it is written:

> "For your sake we are being
>   slain all the day;
>   we are looked upon as sheep
>   to be slaughtered."

No, in all these things we conquer overwhelmingly through him who loved us. For I am convinced that neither death, nor life, nor angels, nor principalities, nor present things, nor future things, nor powers, nor height, nor depth, nor any other creature will be able to separate us from the love of God in Christ Jesus our Lord.

PSALM 38:1-5

A psalm of David. For remembrance.
O LORD, in your anger punish me
    not,
    in your wrath chastise me not;
For your arrows have sunk deep
    in me,
    and your hand has come down
    upon me.
There is no health in my flesh
    because of your indignation;
    there is no wholeness in my
    bones because of my sin,
For my iniquities have
    overwhelmed me;
    they are like a heavy burden,
    beyond my strength.

PROVERBS: 12:5-7

The plans of the just are legitimate; / the designs of the wicked are deceitful. / The words of the wicked are a deadly ambush, / but the speech of the upright saves them. / The wicked are overthrown and are no more, / but the house of the just stands firm.

MARCH 31

ROMANS 9:1-33

I speak the truth in Christ, I do not lie; my conscience joins with the holy Spirit in bearing me witness that I have great sorrow and constant anguish in my heart. For I could wish that I myself were accursed and separated from Christ for the sake of my brothers, my kin according to the flesh. They are Israelites; theirs the adoption, the glory, the covenants, the giving of the law, the worship, and the promises; theirs the patriarchs, and from them, according to the flesh, is the Messiah. God

who is over all be blessed forever. Amen.

But it is not that the word of God has failed. For not all who are of Israel are Israel, nor are they all children of Abraham because they are his descendants; but "It is through Isaac that descendants shall bear your name." This means that it is not the children of the flesh who are the children of God, but the children of the promise are counted as descendants. For this is the wording of the promise, "About this time I shall return and Sarah will have a son."

And not only that, but also when Rebecca had conceived children by one husband, our father Isaac—before they had yet been born or had done anything, good or bad, in order that God's elective plan might continue, not by works but by his call—she was told, "The older shall serve the younger." As it is written:

"I loved Jacob
but hated Esau."

What then are we to say? Is there injustice on the part of God? Of course not! For he says to Moses:

"I will show mercy to whom I
will,
I will take pity on whom I
will."

So it depends not upon a person's will or exertion, but upon God, who shows mercy. For the scripture says to Pharaoh, "This is why I have raised you up, to show my power through you that my name may be proclaimed throughout the earth." Consequently, he has mercy upon whom he wills, and he hardens whom he wills.

You will say to me then, "Why [then] does he still find fault? For who can oppose his will?" But who indeed are you, a human being, to talk back to God? Will what is made say to its maker, "Why have you created me so?" Or does not the potter have a right over the clay, to make out of the same lump one vessel for a noble purpose and another for an ignoble one? What if God, wishing to show his wrath and make known his power, has endured with much patience the vessels of wrath made for destruction? This was to make known the riches of his glory to the vessels of mercy, which he has prepared previously for glory, namely, us whom he has called, not only from the Jews but also from the Gentiles.

As indeed he says in Hosea:

"Those who were not my
people I will call 'my
people,'
and her who was not
beloved I will call
'beloved.'
And in the very place where it
was said to them, 'You are
not my
people,'
there they shall be called
children of the living
God."

And Isaiah cries out concerning Israel, "Though the number of the Israelites were like the sand of the sea, only a remnant will be saved; for decisively and quickly will the Lord execute sentence upon the earth." And as Isaiah predicted:

"Unless the Lord of hosts had
left us descendants,
we would have become like
Sodom
and have been made like
Gomorrah."

What then shall we say? That Gentiles, who did not pursue righteousness, have achieved it, that is, righteousness that comes from faith; but that Israel, who pursued the law of righteousness, did not attain to that law? Why not? Because they did it not by faith, but as if it could be done by works. They stumbled over the stone that causes stumbling, as it is written:

"Behold, I am laying a stone in
Zion

that will make people
stumble
and a rock that will make
them fall,
and whoever believes in him
shall not be put to shame."

PSALM 38:6-13

Noisome and festering are my
sores
because of my folly,
I am stooped and bowed down
profoundly;
all the day I go in mourning,
For my loins are filled with
burning pains;
there is no health in my flesh.
I am numbed and severely
crushed;
I roar with anguish of heart.
O LORD, all my desire is before
you;
from you my groaning is not
hid.
My heart throbs; my strength
forsakes me;
the very light of my eyes has
failed me.
My friends and my
companions stand back
because of my affliction;
my neighbors stand afar off.
Men lay snares for me seeking
my life;
they look to my misfortune,
they speak of ruin,
treachery they talk of all the
day.

PROVERBS 12:8-9

According to his good sense a man is praised, / but one with a warped mind is despised. / Better a lowly man who supports himself / than one of assumed importance who lacks bread.

APRIL

Mark's Message

THE GOSPEL OF MARK is placed second in the order of the books of the New Testament. It is a vitally important book and perhaps the most important of the four Gospels.

Mark's background prepared him well to write the Gospel. The circumstances surrounding his life contributed greatly to the authenticity and importance of this Gospel. Mark's mother was a wealthy woman, and her home in Jerusalem was the meeting place for the early Christian community. From the very beginning Mark lived in the center of the early church's activity. The followers of Jesus gathered to share their memories of what Jesus had done and taught. Mark was well versed in the life and works of Jesus as it was recalled and shared by these eyewitnesses.

Second, Mark was an associate and interpreter for Peter as he evangelized in Rome. Mark reflected and embodied some of Peter's teaching and personal experiences of the Lord in his writing. Because Mark's Gospel was the first one written, his account of Jesus is the nearest we will ever have to an eyewitness record of Jesus' ministry and teaching. All these factors make this Gospel a reliable document.

Mark frequently refers to Jesus as "Christ." This term was rapidly becoming a part of Jesus' proper name since the Gospel was reaching out to the Gentiles who could not understand nor appreciate the name "Messiah," which referred to a strictly Jewish concept. The name Christ reveals more accurately to the Gentiles the mission of Jesus as Savior and Redeemer.

Humanity of Jesus

Mark portrays the human side of Jesus more than any of the other three Gospels. Jesus is depicted with an unaffected naturalness. He reacts to circumstances and events with authentic human emotions. Jesus sharply rebuked the unclean spirit (Mk 1:25-26). He manifested anger at the Jewish leaders who refused to accept him (Mk 3:5). Jesus must have felt elated that he could inspire some faith in the disciples when he calmed the storm at sea (Mk 4:40). The heart of Jesus was filled with empathy when he raised the dead girl and gave her back to her parents (Mk 5:36). On one occasion when the disciples tried to prevent the little children from coming to him, Jesus became indignant (Mk 10:14).

Jesus manifested his love on many occasions in his public ministry. Mark alone notes Jesus' love for the rich man who could not give up his possessions to become a disciple (Mk 10:21).

Several times Mark mentions the discouragement Jesus felt when his disciples could not comprehend his mission (Mk 8:14).

Mark reveals the humanness of Jesus in order that we might understand that Jesus is approachable because he experienced life as we do with all its disappointments and problems, with all its love, peace, and joy.

Jesus Asks for Trust

The Jesus of Mark's Gospel asks for an implicit trust in him. As Jesus challenged the people of his own day, he also challenges us to trust him, to accept his way of life even though it may seem to lead us into the "dark valley."

When Jesus invited his followers, they appeared "slow-witted," even "blind." Jesus asked for their complete trust in the mystery which would unfold if they believed, but when they witnessed the wonders he performed, they responded with "amazement and fear" rather than trust.

The disciples began to accept Jesus as the divine wonder-worker who could miraculously multiply bread, but they were totally blind to the possibility of his mission of suffering and death. The disciples were eyewitnesses to Jesus restoring physical sight to the blind (Mk 8:22ff), yet he could not give them an understanding or insight into his redemptive suffering. This blindness of the disciples is related frequently in Mark's Gospel.

In our own day, there is a definite lack of faith. Our intellectual pride and technological efficiency have robbed us of the simple faith in accepting the Lord and his message at face value.

As we pray with Mark's Gospel, may we ask for a deeper faith and a limitless trust.

"Serve the Needs of All"

In Mark's Gospel Jesus spelled out by his own example the way he wants his followers to pursue. "For the Son of Man did not come to be served but to serve and to give his life as a ransom for many." Jesus said plainly: "You must serve the needs of all" (Mk 10:43ff).

In Mark's Gospel Jesus did not detail the ways and means to serve God and others, but his own example shines forth as the ideal path to follow. Jesus is our model. Just as he used every opportunity to serve others, we too may not ignore any occasion to reach out in loving concern. As we ponder the words of Mark, this challenge becomes quite clear.

When we can honestly and sincerely say with the psalmist: "A lamp to my feet is your word, a light to my path" (Ps 119:105), then we will be better enabled to fulfill Jesus' urgent request to trust him completely and entirely, come what may. "Do not be afraid; just have faith" (Mk 5:36).

APRIL 1

MARK 1:1-20

The beginning of the gospel of Jesus Christ [the Son of God].

As it is written in Isaiah the prophet:

"Behold, I am sending my
    messenger ahead of you;
he will prepare your way.
A voice of one crying out in the
    desert:
    'Prepare the way of the
    LORD,
make straight his paths.' "

John [the] Baptist appeared in the desert proclaiming a baptism of repentance for the forgiveness of sins. People of the whole Judean countryside and all the inhabitants of Jerusalem were going out to him and were being baptized by him in the Jordan River as they acknowledged their sins. John was clothed in camel's hair, with a leather belt around his waist. He fed on locusts and wild honey. And this is what he proclaimed: "One mightier than I is coming after me. I am not worthy to stoop and loosen the thongs of his sandals. I have baptized you with water; he will baptize you with the holy Spirit."

It happened in those days that Jesus came from Nazareth of Galilee and was baptized in the Jordan by John. On coming up out of the water he saw the heavens being torn open and the Spirit, like a dove, descending upon him. And a voice came from the heavens, "You are my beloved Son; with you I am well pleased."

At once the Spirit drove him out into the desert, and he remained in the desert for forty days, tempted by Satan. He was among wild beasts, and the angels ministered to him.

After John had been arrested, Jesus came to Galilee proclaiming the gospel of God: "This is the time of fulfillment. The kingdom of God is at hand. Repent, and believe in the gospel."

As he passed by the Sea of Galilee, he saw Simon and his brother Andrew casting their nets into the sea; they were fishermen. Jesus said to them, "Come after me, and I will make you fishers of men." Then they left their nets and followed him. He walked along a little farther and saw James, the son of Zebedee, and his brother John. They too were in a boat mending their nets. Then he called them. So they left their father Zebedee in the boat along with the hired men and followed him.

PSALM 38:14-23

But I am like a deaf man, hearing
    not,
    like a dumb man who opens
        not his mouth.
I am become like a man who
        neither hears
    nor has in his mouth a retort.
Because for you, O LORD, I wait;
    you, O LORD my God, will
        answer
When I say, "Let them not be
        glad on my account
    who, when my foot slips, glory
        over me."

For I am very near to falling,
    and my grief is with me
        always.
Indeed, I acknowledge my guilt;
    I grieve over my sin.
But my undeserved enemies are
        strong;
    many are my foes without
        cause.
Those who repay evil for good
    harass me for pursuing good.
Forsake me not, O LORD;
    my God, be not far from me!
Make haste to help me,
    O LORD my salvation!

PROVERBS 12:10

The just man takes care of his beast, / but the heart of the wicked is merciless.

APRIL 2

MARK 1:21-45

Then they came to Capernaum, and on the sabbath he entered the synagogue and taught. The people were astonished at his teaching, for he taught them as one having authority and not as the scribes. In their synagogue was a man with an unclean spirit; he cried out, "What have you to do with us, Jesus of Nazareth? Have you come to destroy us? I know who you are—the Holy One of God!" Jesus rebuked him and said, "Quiet! Come out of him!" The unclean spirit convulsed him and with a loud cry came out of him. All were amazed and asked one another, "What is this? A new teaching with authority. He commands even the unclean spirits and they obey him." His fame spread everywhere throughout the whole region of Galilee.

On leaving the synagogue he entered the house of Simon and Andrew with James and John. Simon's mother-in-law lay sick with a fever. They immediately told him about her. He approached, grasped her hand, and helped her up. Then the fever left her and she waited on them.

When it was evening, after sunset, they brought to him all who were ill or possessed by demons. The whole town was gathered at the door. He cured many who were sick with various diseases, and he drove out many demons, not permitting them to speak because they knew him.

Rising very early before dawn, he left and went off to a deserted place, where he prayed. Simon and those who were with him pursued him and on finding him said, "Everyone is looking for you." He told them, "Let us go on to the nearby villages that I may preach there also. For this purpose have I come." So he went into their synagogues, preaching and driving out demons throughout the whole of Galilee.

A leper came to him [and kneeling down] begged him and said, "If you wish, you can make me clean." Moved with pity, he stretched out his hand, touched him, and said to him, "I do will it. Be made clean." The leprosy left him immediately, and he was made clean. Then, warning him sternly, he dismissed him at once. Then he said to him, "See that you tell no one anything, but go, show yourself to the priest and offer for your cleansing what Moses prescribed; that will be proof for them." The man went away and began to publicize the whole matter. He spread the report abroad so that it was impossible for Jesus to enter a town openly. He remained outside in deserted places, and people kept coming to him from everywhere.

I said, "I will watch my ways,
    so as not to sin with my
        tongue;
I will set a curb on my mouth."
While the wicked man was before
    me
    I kept dumb and silent;
    I refrained from rash speech.
But my grief was stirred up;
    hot grew my heart within me;
    in my thoughts, a fire blazed
        forth.
I spoke out with my tongue:
Let me know, O LORD, my end
    and what is the number of my
        days,
    that I may learn how frail I am.
A short span you have made my
        days,
    and my life is as nought before
        you;
    only a breath is any human
        existence.
A phantom only, man goes his
        ways;
    like vapor only are his restless
        pursuits;
    he heaps up stores, and knows
        not who will use them.

PSALM 39:1-7

For the leader, for Jeduthun. A psalm of David.

PROVERBS 12:11

He who tills his own land has food in plenty, / but he who follows idle pursuits is a fool.

APRIL 3

MARK 2:1-28

When Jesus returned to Capernaum after some days, it became known that he was at home.

Many gathered together so that there was no longer room for them, not even around the door, and he preached the word to them. They came bringing to him a paralytic carried by four men. Unable to get near Jesus because of the crowd, they opened up the roof above him. After they had broken through, they let down the mat on which the paralytic was lying. When Jesus saw their faith, he said to the paralytic, "Child, your sins are forgiven." Now some of the scribes were sitting there asking themselves, "Why does this man speak that way? He is blaspheming. Who but God alone can forgive sins?" Jesus immediately knew in his mind what they were thinking to themselves, so he said, "Why are you thinking such things in your hearts? Which is easier, to say to the paralytic, 'Your sins are forgiven,' or to say, 'Rise, pick up your mat and walk'? But that you may know that the Son of Man has authority to forgive sins on earth"—he said to the paralytic, "I say to you, rise, pick up your mat, and go home." He rose, picked up his mat at once, and went away in the sight of everyone. They were all astounded and glorified God, saying, "We have never seen anything like this."

Once again he went out along the sea. All the crowd came to him and he taught them. As he passed by, he saw Levi, son of Alphaeus, sitting at the customs post. He said to him, "Follow me." And he got up and followed him. While he was at table in his house, many tax collectors and sinners sat with Jesus and his disciples; for there were many who followed him. Some scribes who were Pharisees saw that he was eating with sinners and tax collectors and said to his disciples, "Why does he eat with tax collectors and sinners?" Jesus heard this and said to them [that], "Those who are well do not need a physician, but the sick do. I did not come to call the righteous but sinners."

The disciples of John and of the Pharisees were accustomed to fast. People came to him and objected, "Why do the disciples of John and the disciples of the Pharisees fast, but your disciples do not fast?" Jesus answered them, "Can the wedding guests fast while the bridegroom is with them? As long as they have the bridegroom with them they cannot fast. But the days will come when the bridegroom is taken away from them, and then they will fast on that day. No one sews a piece of unshrunken cloth on an old cloak. If he does, its fullness pulls away, the new from the old, and the tear gets worse. Likewise, no one pours new wine into old wineskins. Otherwise, the wine will burst the skins, and both the wine and the skins are ruined. Rather, new wine is poured into fresh wineskins."

As he was passing through a field of grain on the sabbath, his disciples began to make a path while picking the heads of grain. At this the Pharisees said to him, "Look, why are they doing what is unlawful on the sabbath?" He said to them, "Have you never read what David did when he was in need and he and his companions were hungry? How he went into the house of God when Abiathar was high priest and ate the bread of offering that only the priests could lawfully eat, and shared it with his companions?" Then he said to them, "The sabbath was made for man, not man for the sabbath. That is why the Son of Man is lord even of the sabbath."

PSALM 39:8-14

And now, for what do I wait, O
    LORD?
  In you is my hope.
From all my sins deliver me;
  a fool's taunt let me not suffer.
I was speechless and opened not
    my mouth,
  because it was your doing;
Take away your scourge from me;
  at the blow of your hand I
    wasted away.
With rebukes for guilt you
    chasten man;
you dissolve like a cobweb all
    that is dear to him;
  only a breath is any man.
Hear my prayer, O LORD;
  to my cry give ear;
  to my weeping be not deaf!
For I am but a wayfarer before
    you,
  a pilgrim like all my fathers.
Turn your gaze from me, that I
    may find respite
  ere I depart and be no more.

PROVERBS 12:12-13

*The stronghold of evil men will be demolished, / but the root of the just is
enduring. / In the sin of his lips the evil man is ensnared, / but the just comes
free of trouble.*

APRIL 4

MARK 3:1-35

Again he entered the synagogue. There was a man there who had a withered hand. They watched him closely to see if he would cure him on the sabbath so that they might accuse him. He said to the man with the withered hand, "Come up here before us." Then he said to them, "Is it lawful to do good on the sabbath rather than to do evil, to save life rather than to destroy it?" But they remained silent. Looking around at them with anger and grieved at their hardness of heart, he said to the man, "Stretch out your hand." He stretched it out and his hand was restored. The Pharisees went out and immediately took counsel with the Herodians against him to put him to death.

Jesus withdrew toward the sea with his disciples. A large number of people [followed] from Galilee and from Judea. Hearing what he was doing, a large number of people came to him also from Jerusalem, from Idumea, from beyond the Jordan, and from the neighborhood of Tyre and Sidon. He told his disciples to have a boat ready for him because of the crowd, so that they would not crush him. He had cured many and, as a result, those who had diseases were pressing upon him to touch him. And whenever unclean spirits saw him they would fall down before him and shout, "You are the Son of God." He warned them sternly not to make him known.

He went up the mountain and summoned those whom he wanted and they came to him. He appointed twelve [whom he also named apostles] that they might be with him and he might send them forth to preach and to have authority to drive out demons: [he appointed the twelve:] Simon, whom he named Peter; James, son of Zebedee, and John the brother of James, whom he named Boanerges, that is, sons of thunder; Andrew, Philip, Bartholomew, Matthew, Thomas, James the son of Alphaeus; Thaddeus, Simon the Cananean, and Judas Iscariot who betrayed him.

He came home. Again [the] crowd gathered, making it impossible for them even to eat. When his relatives heard of this they set out to seize him, for they said, "He is out of his mind." The scribes who had come from Jerusalem said, "He is possessed by Beelzebul," and "By the prince of demons he drives out demons."

Summoning them, he began to speak to them in parables, "How can Satan drive out Satan? If a kingdom is divided against itself, that kingdom cannot stand. And if a house is divided against itself, that house will not be able to stand. And if Satan has risen up against himself and is divided, he cannot stand; that is the end of him. But no one can enter a strong man's house to plunder his property unless he first ties up the strong man. Then he can plunder his house. Amen, I say to you, all sins and all blasphemies that people utter will be forgiven them. But whoever blasphemes against the holy Spirit will never have forgiveness, but is guilty of an everlasting sin." For they had said, "He has an unclean spirit."

His mother and his brothers arrived. Standing outside they sent word to him and called him. A crowd seated around him told him, "Your mother and your brothers [and your sisters] are outside asking for you." But he said to them in reply, "Who are my mother and [my] brothers?" And looking around at those seated in the circle he said, "Here are my mother and my brothers. [For] whoever does the will of God is my brother and sister and mother."

PSALM 40:1-4

For the leader. A psalm of David.
I have waited, waited for the
    LORD,
    and he stooped toward me and
      heard my cry.
He drew me out of the pit of
    destruction,
    out of the mud of the swamp;
He set my feet upon a crag;
    he made firm my steps.
And he put a new song into my
    mouth,
    a hymn to our God.
Many shall look on in awe
    and trust in the LORD.

PROVERBS 12:14

From the fruit of his words a man has his fill of good things, / and the work of his hands comes back to reward him.

APRIL 5

MARK 4:1-20

On another occasion he began to teach by the sea. A very large crowd gathered around him so that he got into a boat on the sea and sat down. And the whole crowd was beside the sea on land. And he taught them at length in parables, and in the course of his instruction he said to them, "Hear this! A sower went out to sow. And as he sowed, some seed fell on the path, and the birds came and ate it up. Other seed fell on rocky ground where it had little soil. It sprang up at once because the soil was not deep. And when the sun rose, it was scorched and it withered for lack of roots. Some seed fell among thorns, and the thorns grew up and choked it and it produced no grain. And some seed fell on rich soil and produced fruit. It came up and grew and yielded thirty, sixty, and a hundredfold." He added, "Whoever has ears to hear ought to hear."

And when he was alone, those present along with the Twelve questioned him about the parables. He answered them, "The mystery of the kingdom of God has been granted to you. But to those outside everything comes in parables, so that

'they may look and see but not perceive,
  and hear and listen but not understand,
in order that they may not be converted and be forgiven.' "

Jesus said to them, "Do you not understand this parable? Then how will you understand any of the parables? The sower sows the word. These are the ones on the path where the word is sown. As soon as they hear, Satan comes at once and takes away the word sown in them. And these are the ones sown on rocky ground who, when they hear the word, receive it at once with joy. But they have no root; they last only for a time. Then when tribulation or persecution comes because of the word, they quickly fall away. Those sown among thorns are another sort. They are the people who hear the word, but worldly anxiety, the lure of riches, and the craving for other things intrude and choke the word, and it bears no fruit. But those sown on rich soil are the ones who hear the word and accept it and bear fruit thirty and sixty and a hundredfold."

PSALM 40:5-11

Happy the man who makes the
    LORD his trust;
  who turns not to idolatry
  or to those who stray after
    falsehood.
How numerous have you made,
  O LORD, my God, your
    wondrous deeds!
And in your plans for us
  there is none to equal you;
Should I wish to declare or to tell
    them,
  they would be too many to
    recount.
Sacrifice or oblation you wished
    not,
  but ears open to obedience you
    gave me.
Holocausts or sin-offerings you
    sought not;

then said I, "Behold I come;
in the written scroll it is
prescribed for me.
To do your will, O my God, is my
delight,
and your law is within my
heart!"
I announced your justice in the
vast assembly;
I did not restrain my lips, as
you, O LORD, know.
Your justice I kept not hid within
my heart;
your faithfulness and your
salvation I have spoken of;
I have made no secret of your
kindness and your truth
in the vast assembly.

PROVERBS 12:15-18

The way of the fool seems right in his own eyes, / but he who listens to advice is wise. / The fool immediately shows his anger, / but the shrewd man passes over an insult. / He tells the truth who states what he is sure of, / but a lying witness speaks deceitfully. / The prating of some men is like sword thrusts, / but the tongue of the wise is healing.

APRIL 6

MARK 4:21-41

He said to them, "Is a lamp brought in to be placed under a bushel basket or under a bed, and not to be placed on a lampstand? For there is nothing hidden except to be made visible; nothing is secret except to come to light. Anyone who has ears to hear ought to hear." He also told them, "Take care what you hear. The measure with which you measure will be measured out to you, and still more will be given to you. To the one who has, more will be given; from the one who has not, even what he has will be taken away."

He said, "This is how it is with the kingdom of God; it is as if a man were to scatter seed on the land and would sleep and rise night and day and the seed would sprout and grow, he knows not how. Of its own accord the land yields fruit, first the blade, then the ear, then the full grain in the ear. And when the grain is ripe,

he wields the sickle at once, for the harvest has come."

He said, "To what shall we compare the kingdom of God, or what parable can we use for it? It is like a mustard seed that, when it is sown in the ground, is the smallest of all the seeds on the earth. But once it is sown, it springs up and becomes the largest of plants and puts forth large branches, so that the birds of the sky can dwell in its shade." With many such parables he spoke the word to them as they were able to understand it. Without parables he did not speak to them, but to his own disciples he explained everything in private.

On that day, as evening drew on, he said to them, "Let us cross to the other side." Leaving the crowd, they took him with them in the boat just as he was. And other boats were with him. A violent squall came up and waves were breaking over the boat, so that it was already filling up. Jesus was in the stern, asleep on a cushion. They woke him and said to him, "Teacher, do you not care that we are perishing?" He woke up, rebuked the wind, and said to the sea, "Quiet! Be still!" The wind ceased and there was great calm. Then he asked them, "Why are you terrified? Do you not yet have faith?" They were filled with great awe and said to one another, "Who then is this whom even wind and sea obey?"

PSALM 40:12-18

Withhold not, O LORD, your
 compassion from me;
 may your kindness and your
 truth ever preserve me.
For all about me are evils beyond
 reckoning;
 my sins so overcome me that I
 cannot see;
They are more numerous than
 the hairs of my head,
and my heart fails me.
Deign, O LORD, to rescue me;
 O LORD, make haste to help
 me.
Let all be put to shame and
 confusion
 who seek to snatch away my
 life.
Let them be turned back in
 disgrace
 who desire my ruin.
Let them be dismayed in their
 shame
 who say to me, "Aha, aha!"
But may all who seek you
 exult and be glad in you,
And may those who love your
 salvation
 say ever, "The LORD be
 glorified."
Though I am afflicted and poor,
 yet the LORD thinks of me.
You are my help and my
 deliverer;
 O my God, hold not back!

PROVERBS 12:19-20

Truthful lips endure forever, / the lying tongue, for only a moment. / Deceit is in the hands of those who plot evil, / but those who counsel peace have joy.

APRIL 7

MARK 5:1-20

They came to the other side of the sea, to the territory of the Gerasenes. When he got out of the boat, at once a man from the tombs who had an unclean spirit met him. The man had been dwelling among the tombs, and no one could restrain him any longer, even with a chain. In fact, he had frequently been bound with shackles and chains, but the chains had been pulled apart by him and the shackles smashed, and no one was strong enough to subdue him. Night and day among the tombs and on the hillsides he was always crying out and bruising himself with stones. Catching sight of Jesus from a distance, he ran up and prostrated himself before him, crying out in a loud voice, "What have you to do with me, Jesus, Son of the Most High

God? I adjure you by God, do not torment me!" (He had been saying to him, "Unclean spirit, come out of the man!") He asked him, "What is your name?" He replied, "Legion is my name. There are many of us." And he pleaded earnestly with him not to drive them away from that territory.

Now a large herd of swine was feeding there on the hillside. And they pleaded with him, "Send us into the swine. Let us enter them." And he let them, and the unclean spirits came out and entered the swine. The herd of about two thousand rushed down a steep bank into the sea, where they were drowned. The swineherds ran away and reported the incident in the town and throughout the countryside. And people came out to see what had happened. As they approached Jesus, they caught sight of the man who had been possessed by Legion, sitting there clothed and in his right mind. And they were seized with fear. Those who witnessed the incident explained to them what had happened to the possessed man and to the swine. Then they began to beg him to leave their district. As he was getting into the boat, the man who had been possessed pleaded to remain with him. But he would not permit him but told him instead, "Go home to your family and announce to them all that the Lord in his pity has done for you." Then the man went off and began to proclaim in the Decapolis what Jesus had done for him; and all were amazed.

PSALM 41:1-4

For the leader. A psalm of David.
Happy is he who has regard for
    the lowly and the poor;
    in the day of misfortune the
      LORD will deliver him.
The LORD will keep and preserve
    him;
    he will make him happy on the
      earth,
    and not give him over to the
      will of his enemies.
The LORD will help him on his
    sickbed,
    he will take away all his
      ailment when he is ill.

PROVERBS 12:21-23

No harm befalls the just, / but the wicked are overwhelmed with misfortune. / Lying lips are an abomination to the LORD, / but those who are truthful are his delight. / A shrewd man conceals his knowledge, / but the hearts of fools gush forth folly.

APRIL 8

MARK 5:21-43

When Jesus had crossed again [in the boat] to the other side, a large crowd gathered around him, and he stayed close to the sea. One of the synagogue officials, named Jairus, came forward. Seeing him he fell at his feet and pleaded earnestly with him, saying, "My daughter is at the point of death. Please, come lay your hands on her that she may get well and live." He went off with him, and a large crowd followed him and pressed upon him.

There was a woman afflicted with hemorrhages for twelve years. She had suffered greatly at the hands of many doctors and had spent all that she had. Yet she was not helped but only grew worse. She had heard about Jesus and came up behind him in the crowd and touched his cloak. She said, "If I but touch his clothes, I shall be cured." Immediately her flow of blood dried up. She felt in her body that she was healed of her affliction. Jesus, aware at once that power had gone out from him, turned around in the crowd and asked, "Who has touched my clothes?" But his disciples said to him, "You see how the crowd is pressing upon you, and yet you ask, 'Who touched me?' " And he looked around to see who had done it. The woman, realizing what had happened to her, approached in fear and trembling. She fell down before Jesus and told him the whole truth. He said to her, "Daughter, your faith has saved you. Go in peace and be cured of your affliction."

While he was still speaking, people from the synagogue official's house arrived and said, "Your daughter has died; why trouble the teacher any longer?" Disregarding the message that was reported, Jesus said to the synagogue official, "Do not be afraid; just have faith." He did not allow anyone to accompany him inside except Peter, James, and John, the brother of James. When they arrived at the house of the synagogue official, he caught sight of a commotion, people weeping and wailing loudly. So he went in and said to them, "Why this commotion and weeping? The child is not dead but asleep." And they ridiculed him. Then he put them all out. He took along the child's father and mother and those who were with him and entered the room where the child was. He took the child by the hand and said to her, "*Talitha koum*," which means, "Little girl, I say to you, arise!" The girl, a child of twelve, arose immediately and walked around. [At that] they were utterly astounded. He gave strict orders that no one should know this and said that she should be given something to eat.

PSALM 41:5-14

Once I said, "O LORD, have pity on me;
  heal me, though I have sinned against you.
My enemies say the worst of me:
  'When will he die and his name perish?'
When one comes to see me, he speaks without sincerity;
  his heart stores up malice;
  when he leaves he gives voice to it outside.
All my foes whisper together against me;
  against me they imagine the worst:
'A malignant disease fills his frame';
  and 'Now that he lies ill, he will not rise again.'
Even my friend who had my trust and partook of my bread, has raised his heel against me.
But you, O LORD, have pity on me, and raise me up,
  that I may repay them."
That you love me I know by this, that my enemy does not triumph over me,

But because of my integrity you
 sustain me
and let me stand before you
 forever.

Blessed be the LORD, the God of
 Israel,
from all eternity and forever.
 Amen. Amen.

PROVERBS 12:24
The diligent hand will govern, / but the slothful will be enslaved.

APRIL 9

MARK 6:1-13

He departed from there and came to his native place, accompanied by his disciples. When the sabbath came he began to teach in the synagogue, and many who heard him were astonished. They said, "Where did this man get all this? What kind of wisdom has been given him? What mighty deeds are wrought by his hands! Is he not the carpenter, the son of Mary, and the brother of James and Joses and Judas and Simon? And are not his sisters here with us?" And they took offense at him. Jesus said to them, "A prophet is not without honor except in his native place and among his own kin and in his own house." So he was not able to perform any mighty deed there, apart from curing a few sick people by laying his hands on them. He was amazed at their lack of faith.

He went around to the villages in the vicinity teaching. He summoned the Twelve and began to send them out two by two and gave them authority over unclean spirits. He instructed them to take nothing for the journey but a walk-ing stick—no food, no sack, no money in their belts. They were, however, to wear sandals but not a second tunic. He said to them, "Wherever you enter a house, stay there until you leave from there. Whatever place does not welcome you or listen to you, leave there and shake the dust off your feet in testimony against them." So they went off and preached repentance. They drove out many demons, and they anointed with oil many who were sick and cured them.

PSALM 42:1-4

*For the leader. A maskil of the sons of
 Korah.*
As the hind longs for the running
 waters,
 so my soul longs for you, O
 God.
Athirst is my soul for God, the
 living God.
 When shall I go and behold the
 face of God?
My tears are my food day and
 night,
 as they say to me day after day,
 "Where is your God?"

APRIL 10

MARK 6:14-44

King Herod heard about it, for his fame had become widespread, and people were saying, "John the Baptist has been raised from the dead; that is why mighty powers are at work in him." Others were saying, "He is Elijah"; still others, "He is a prophet like any of the prophets." But when Herod learned of it, he said, "It is John whom I beheaded. He has been raised up."

Herod was the one who had John arrested and bound in prison on account of Herodias, the wife of his brother Philip, whom he had married. John had said to Herod, "It is not lawful for you to have your brother's wife." Herodias harbored a grudge against him and wanted to kill him but was unable to do so. Herod feared John, knowing him to be a righteous and holy man, and kept him in custody. When he heard him speak he was very much perplexed, yet he liked to listen to him. She had an opportunity one day when Herod, on his birthday, gave a banquet for his courtiers, his military officers, and the leading men of Galilee. Herodias's own daughter came in and performed a dance that delighted Herod and his guests. The king said to the girl, "Ask of me whatever you wish and I will grant it to you." He even swore [many things] to her, "I will grant you whatever you ask of me, even to half of my kingdom." She went out and said to her mother, "What shall I ask for?" She replied, "The head of John the Baptist." The girl hurried back to the king's presence and made her request, "I want you to give me at once on a platter the head of John the Baptist." The king was deeply distressed, but because of his oaths and the guests he did not wish to break his word to her. So he promptly dispatched an executioner with orders to bring back his head. He went off and beheaded him in the prison. He brought in the head on a platter and gave it to the girl. The girl in turn gave it to her mother. When his disciples heard about it, they came and took his body and laid it in a tomb.

The apostles gathered together with Jesus and reported all they had done and taught. He said to them, "Come away by yourselves to a deserted place and rest a while." People were coming and going in great numbers, and they had no opportunity even to eat. So they went off in the boat by themselves to a deserted place. People saw them leaving and many came to know about it. They hastened there on foot from all the towns and arrived at the place before them.

When he disembarked and saw the vast crowd, his heart was moved with pity for them, for they were like sheep without a shepherd; and he began to teach them many things. By now it was already late and his disciples approached him and said, "This is a deserted place and it is already very late. Dismiss them so that they can go to the surrounding farms and villages and buy themselves something to eat." He said to them in reply, "Give them some food yourselves." But they said to him, "Are we to buy two hundred days' wages worth of food and give it to them to eat?" He asked them, "How many loaves do you have? Go and see." And when they had found out they said, "Five loaves and two fish." So he gave orders to have them sit down in groups on the green grass. The people took their places in rows by hundreds and by fifties. Then, taking the five loaves and the two fish and looking up to heaven, he said the blessing, broke the loaves, and gave them to [his] disciples to set before the people; he also divided the two fish among them all. They all ate and were satisfied. And they picked up twelve wicker baskets full of fragments and what was left of the fish. Those who ate [of the loaves] were five thousand men.

PSALM 42:5-8

Those times I recall,
    now that I pour out my soul
        within me,
When I went with the throng
    and led them in procession to
        the house of God,
Amid loud cries of joy and
        thanksgiving,
    with the multitude keeping
        festival.
    Why are you so downcast, O
        my soul?
    Why do you sigh within me?
    Hope in God! For I shall again
        be thanking him,
    in the presence of my savior
        and my God.
Within me my soul is downcast;
    so will I remember you
From the land of the Jordan and
        of Hermon,
    from Mount Mizar.
Deep calls unto deep
    in the roar of your cataracts;
All your breakers and your
        billows
    pass over me.

PROVERBS 12:26

The just man surpasses his neighbor, / but the way of the wicked leads them astray.

APRIL 11

MARK 6:45-56

Then he made his disciples get into the boat and precede him to the other side toward Bethsaida, while he dismissed the crowd. And when he had taken leave of them, he went off to the mountain to pray. When it was evening, the boat was far out on the sea and he was alone on shore. Then he saw that they were tossed about while rowing, for the wind was against them. About the fourth watch of the night, he came toward them walking on the sea. He meant to pass by them. But when they saw him walking on the sea, they thought it was a ghost and cried out. They had all seen him and were terrified. But at once he spoke with them, "Take courage, it is I, do not be afraid!" He got into the boat with them and the wind died down. They were [completely] astounded. They had not understood the incident of the loaves. On the contrary, their hearts were hardened.

After making the crossing, they came to land at Gennesaret and tied up there. As they were leaving the boat, people immediately recognized him. They scurried about the surrounding country and began to bring in the sick on mats to wherever they heard he was. Whatever villages or towns or countryside he entered, they laid the sick in the marketplaces and begged him that they might touch only the tassel on his cloak; and as many as touched it were healed.

PSALM 42:9-12

By day the LORD bestows his
   grace,
  and at night I have his song,
  a prayer to my living God.
I sing to God, my rock;
  "Why do you forget me?
Why must I go about in
   mourning,
  with the enemy oppressing
  me?"
It crushes my bones that my foes
   mock me,
  as they say to me day after day,
  "Where is your God?"
Why are you so downcast, O
  my soul?
Why do you sigh within me?
Hope in God! For I shall again
  be thanking him,
in the presence of my savior
  and my God.

PROVERBS 12:27-28

The slothful man catches not his prey, / but the wealth of the diligent man is great. / In the path of justice there is life, / but the abominable way leads to death.

APRIL 12

MARK 7:1-37

Now when the Pharisees with some scribes who had come from Jerusalem gathered around him, they observed that some of his disciples ate their meals with unclean, that is, unwashed, hands. (For the Pharisees and, in fact, all Jews, do not eat without carefully washing their hands, keeping the tradition of the elders. And on coming from the marketplace they do not eat without purifying themselves. And there are many other things that they have traditionally observed, the purification of cups and jugs and kettles [and beds].) So the Pharisees and scribes questioned him, "Why do your disciples not follow the tradition of the elders but instead eat a meal with unclean hands?" He responded, "Well did Isaiah prophesy about you hypocrites, as it is written:

'This people honors me with their lips,
but their hearts are far from me;
In vain do they worship me,
teaching as doctrines human precepts.'

You disregard God's commandment but cling to human tradition." He went on to say, "How well you have set aside the commandment of God in order to uphold your tradition! For Moses said, 'Honor your father and your mother,' and 'Whoever curses father or mother shall die.' Yet you say, 'If a person says to father or mother, "Any support you might have had from me is *qorban*" ' (meaning, dedicated to God), you allow him to do nothing more for his father or mother. You nullify the word of God in favor of your tradition that you have handed on. And you do many such things." He summoned the crowd again and said to them, "Hear me, all of you, and understand. Nothing that enters one from outside can defile that person; but the things that come out from within are what defile."

When he got home away from the crowd his disciples questioned him about the parable. He said to them, "Are even you likewise without understanding? Do you not realize that everything that goes into a person from outside cannot defile, since it enters not the heart but the stomach and passes out into the latrine?" (Thus he declared all foods clean.) "But what comes out of a person, that is what defiles. From within peo-

ple, from their hearts, come evil thoughts, unchastity, theft, murder, adultery, greed, malice, deceit, licentiousness, envy, blasphemy, arrogance, folly. All these evils come from within and they defile."

From that place he went off to the district of Tyre. He entered a house and wanted no one to know about it, but he could not escape notice. Soon a woman whose daughter had an unclean spirit heard about him. She came and fell at his feet. The woman was a Greek, a Syrophoenician by birth, and she begged him to drive the demon out of her daughter. He said to her, "Let the children be fed first. For it is not right to take the food of the children and throw it to the dogs." She replied and said to him, "Lord, even the dogs under the table eat the children's scraps." Then he said to her, "For saying this, you may go. The demon has gone out of your daughter." When the woman went home, she found the child lying in bed and the demon gone.

Again he left the district of Tyre and went by way of Sidon to the Sea of Galilee, into the district of the Decapolis. And people brought to him a deaf man who had a speech impediment and begged him to lay his hand on him. He took him off by himself away from the crowd. He put his finger into the man's ears and, spitting, touched his tongue; then he looked up to heaven and groaned, and said to him, "*Ephphatha!*" (that is, "Be opened!") And [immediately] the man's ears were opened, his speech impediment was removed, and he spoke plainly. He ordered them not to tell anyone. But the more he ordered them not to, the more they proclaimed it. They were exceedingly astonished and they said, "He has done all things well. He makes the deaf hear and [the] mute speak."

PSALM 43:1-5

Do me justice, O God, and fight my fight
    against a faithless people;
    from the deceitful and impious man rescue me.
For you, O God, are my strength.
    Why do you keep me so far away?
Why must I go about in mourning,
    with the enemy oppressing me?

Send forth your light and your fidelity;
    they shall lead me on
And bring me to your holy mountain,
    to your dwelling-place,
Then will I go in to the altar of God,
    the God of my gladness and joy;
Then will I give you thanks upon the harp,
    O God, my God!
Why are you so downcast, O my soul?
    Why do you sigh within me?
Hope in God! For I shall again be thanking him,
    in the presence of my savior and my God.

PROVERBS 13:1

A wise son loves correction, / but the senseless one heeds no rebuke.

APRIL 13

MARK 8:1-26

In those days when there again was a great crowd without anything to eat, he summoned the disciples and said, "My heart is moved with pity for the crowd, because they have been with me now for three days and have nothing to eat. If I send them away hungry to their homes, they will collapse on the way, and some of them have come a great distance." His disciples answered him, "Where can anyone get enough bread to satisfy them here in this deserted place?" Still he asked them, "How many loaves to you have?" "Seven," they replied. He ordered the crowd to sit down on the ground. Then, tak-

ing the seven loaves he gave thanks, broke them, and gave them to his disciples to distribute, and they distributed them to the crowd. They also had a few fish. He said the blessing over them and ordered them distributed also. They ate and were satisfied. They picked up the fragments left over—seven baskets. There were about four thousand people.

He dismissed them and got into the boat with his disciples and came to the region of Dalmanutha.

The Pharisees came forward and began to argue with him, seeking from him a sign from heaven to test him. He sighed from the depth of his spirit and said, "Why does this generation seek a sign? Amen, I say to you, no sign will be given to this generation." Then he left them, got into the boat again, and went off to the other shore.

They had forgotten to bring bread, and they had only one loaf with them in the boat. He enjoined them, "Watch out, guard against the leaven of the Pharisees and the leaven of Herod." They concluded among themselves that it was because they had no bread. When he became aware of this he said to them, "Why do you conclude that it is because you have no bread? Do you not yet understand or comprehend? Are your hearts hardened? Do you have eyes and not see, ears and not hear? And do you not remember, when I broke the five loaves for the five thousand, how many wicker baskets full of fragments you picked up?" They answered him, "Twelve." "When I broke the seven loaves for the four thousand, how many full baskets of fragments did you pick up?" They answered [him], "Seven." He said to them, "Do you still not understand?"

When they arrived at Bethsaida, they brought to him a blind man and begged him to touch him. He took the blind man by the hand and led him outside the village. Putting spittle on his eyes he laid his hands on him and asked, "Do you see anything?" Looking up he replied, "I see people looking like trees and walking." Then he laid hands on his eyes a second time and he saw clearly; his sight was restored and he could see everything distinctly. Then he sent him home and said, "Do not even go into the village."

PSALM 44:1-4

For the leader. A maskil of the sons of Korah.

O God, our ears have heard,
　　our fathers have declared to us,
The deeds you did in their days,
　　in days of old:
How with your own hand you
　　　rooted out the nations and
　　　planted them;
　　you smashed the peoples, but
　　　for them you made room.
For not with their own sword did
　　　they conquer the land,
　　nor did their own arm make
　　　them victorious,
But it was your arm and your
　　　right hand
　　and the light of your
　　　countenance, in your love for
　　　them.

PROVERBS 13:2-3

From the fruit of his words a man eats good things, / but the treacherous one craves violence. / He who guards his mouth protects his life; / to open wide one's lips brings downfall.

APRIL 14

MARK 8:27-38; 9:1

Now Jesus and his disciples set out for the villages of Caesarea Philippi. Along the way he asked his disciples, "Who do people say that I am?" They said in reply, "John the Baptist, others Elijah, still others one of the prophets." And he asked them, "But who do you say that I am?" Peter said to him in reply, "You are the Messiah." Then he warned them not to tell anyone about him.

He began to teach them that the Son of Man must suffer greatly and be rejected by the elders, the chief priests, and the scribes, and be killed, and rise after three days. He spoke this openly. Then Peter took him aside and began to rebuke him. At this he turned around and, looking at his disciples, rebuked Peter and said, "Get behind me, Satan. You are thinking not as God does, but as human beings do."

He summoned the crowd with his disciples and said to them, "Whoever wishes to come after me must deny himself, take up his cross, and follow me. For whoever wishes to save his life will lose it, but whoever loses his life for my sake and that of the gospel will save it. What profit is there for one to gain the whole world and forfeit his life? What could one give in exchange for his life? Whoever is ashamed of me and of my words in this faithless and sinful generation, the Son of Man will be ashamed of when he comes in his Father's glory with the holy angels." He also said to them, "Amen, I say to you, there are some standing here who will not taste death until they see that the kingdom of God has come in power."

PSALM 44:5-9

You are my king and my God,
    who bestowed victories on
      Jacob.
Our foes through you we struck
    down;
    through your name we
      trampled down our
      adversaries.
For not in my bow did I trust,
    nor did my sword save me;
But you saved us from our foes,
    and those who hated us you
      put to shame.
In God we gloried day by day;
    your name we praised always.

PROVERBS 13:4

The soul of the sluggard craves in vain, / but the diligent soul is amply satisfied.

APRIL 15

MARK 9:2-29

After six days Jesus took Peter, James, and John and led them up a high mountain apart by themselves. And he was transfigured before them, and his clothes became dazzling white, such as no fuller on earth could bleach them. Then Elijah appeared to them along with Moses, and they were conversing with Jesus. Then Peter said to Jesus in reply, "Rabbi, it is good that we are here! Let us make three tents: one for you, one for Moses, and one for Elijah." He hardly knew what to say, they were so terrified. Then a cloud came, casting a shadow over them; then from the cloud came a voice, "This is my beloved Son. Listen to him." Suddenly, looking around, they no longer saw anyone but Jesus alone with them.

As they were coming down from the mountain, he charged them not to relate what they had seen to anyone, except when the Son of Man had risen from the dead. So they kept the matter to themselves, questioning what rising from the dead meant. Then they asked him, "Why do the scribes say that Elijah must come first?" He told them, "Elijah will indeed come first and restore all things, yet how is it written regarding the Son of Man that he must suffer greatly and be treated with contempt? But I tell you that Elijah has come and they did to him whatever they pleased, as it is written of him."

When they came to the disciples, they saw a large crowd around them and scribes arguing with them. Immediately on seeing him, the whole crowd was utterly amazed. They ran up to him and greeted him. He asked them, "What are you arguing about with them?" Someone from the crowd answered him, "Teacher, I have brought to you my son possessed by a mute spirit. Wherever it seizes him, it throws him down; he foams at the mouth, grinds his teeth, and becomes rigid. I asked your disciples to drive it out, but they were unable to do so." He said to them in reply, "O faithless generation, how long will I be with you? How long will I endure you? Bring him to me." They brought the boy to him. And when he saw him, the spirit immediately threw the boy into convulsions. As he fell to the ground, he began to roll around and foam at the mouth. Then he questioned his father, "How long has this been happening to him?" He replied, "Since childhood. It has often thrown him into fire and into water to kill him. But if you can do anything, have compassion on us and help us." Jesus said to him, " 'If you can!' Everything is possible to one who has faith." Then the boy's father cried out, "I do believe, help my unbelief!" Jesus, on seeing a crowd rapidly gathering, rebuked the unclean spirit and said to it, "Mute and deaf spirit, I command you: come out of him and never enter him again!" Shouting and throwing the boy into convulsions, it came out. He became like a corpse, which caused many to say, "He is dead!" But Jesus took him by the hand, raised him, and he stood up. When he entered the house, his disciples asked him in private, "Why could we not drive it out?"

He said to them, "This kind can only come out through prayer."

PSALM 44:10-17

Yet now you have cast us off and put us in disgrace,
and you go not forth with our armies.
You have let us be driven back by our foes;
those who hated us plundered us at will.
You marked us out as sheep to be slaughtered;
among the nations you scattered us.
You sold your people for no great price;
you made no profit from the sale of them.
You made us the reproach of our neighbors,
the mockery and the scorn of those around us.
You made us a byword among the nations,
a laughingstock among the peoples.
All the day my disgrace is before me,
and shame covers my face
At the voice of him who mocks and blasphemes,
and in the presence of the enemy and the avenger.

PROVERBS 13:5-6

Anything deceitful the just man hates, / but the wicked brings shame and disgrace. / Virtue guards one who walks honestly, / but the downfall of the wicked is sin.

APRIL 16

MARK 9:30-50

They left from there and began a journey through Galilee, but he did not wish anyone to know about it. He was teaching his disciples and telling them, "The Son of Man is to be handed over to men and they will kill him, and three days after his death he will rise." But they did not understand the saying, and they were afraid to question him.

They came to Capernaum and, once inside the house, he began to ask them, "What were you arguing about on the way?" But they remained silent. They had been discussing among themselves on the way who was the greatest.

Then he sat down, called the Twelve, and said to them, "If anyone wishes to be first, he shall be the last of all and the servant of all." Taking a child he placed it in their midst, and putting his arms around it he said to them, "Whoever receives one child such as this in my name, receives me; and whoever receives me, receives not me but the one who sent me."

John said to him, "Teacher, we saw someone driving out demons in your name, and we tried to prevent him because he does not follow us." Jesus replied, "Do not prevent him. There is no one who performs a mighty deed in my name who can at the same time speak ill of me. For whoever is not against us is for us. Anyone who gives you a cup of water to drink because you belong to Christ, amen, I say to you, will surely not lose his reward.

"Whoever causes one of these little ones who believe [in me] to sin, it would be better for him if a great millstone were put around his neck and he were thrown into the sea. If your hand causes you to sin, cut it off. It is better for you to enter into life maimed than with two hands to go into Gehenna, into the unquenchable fire. And if your foot causes you to sin, cut it off. It is better for you to enter into life crippled than with two feet to be thrown into Gehenna. And if your eye causes you to sin, pluck it out. Better for you to enter into the kingdom of God with one eye than with two eyes to be thrown into Gehenna, where 'their worm does not die, and the fire is not quenched.'

"Everyone will be salted with fire. Salt is good, but if salt becomes insipid, with what will you restore its flavor? Keep salt in yourselves and you will have peace with one another."

nor have we been disloyal to
    your covenant;
Our hearts have not shrunk back,
    nor our steps turned aside
    from your path,
Though you thrust us down into
    a place of misery
    and covered us over with
    darkness.
If we had forgotten the name of
    our God
    and stretched out our hands to
    a strange god,
Would not God have discovered
    this?
    For he knows the secrets of the
    heart.
Yet for your sake we are being
    slain all the day;
    we are looked upon as sheep to
    be slaughtered.
Awake! Why are you asleep, O
    LORD?
    Arise! Cast us not off forever!
Why do you hide your face,
    forgetting our woe and our
    oppression?
For our souls are bowed down to
    the dust,
    our bodies are pressed to the
    earth.
Arise, help us!
    Redeem us for your kindness'
    sake.

PSALM 44:18-27

All this has come upon us,
    though we have not
    forgotten you,

PROVERBS 13:7-8

One man pretends to be rich, yet has nothing; / another pretends to be poor, yet has great wealth. / A man's riches serve as ransom for his life, / but the poor man heeds no rebuke.

APRIL 17

MARK 10:1-16

He set out from there and went into the district of Judea [and] across the Jordan. Again crowds gathered around him and, as was his custom, he again taught them. The Pharisees approached and asked, "Is it lawful for a husband to divorce his wife?" They were testing him. He said to them in reply, "What did Moses command you?" They replied, "Moses permitted him to write a bill of divorce and dismiss her." But Jesus told them, "Because of the hardness of your hearts he wrote you this commandment. But from the beginning of creation, 'God made them male and female. For this reason a man shall leave his father and mother [and be joined to his wife], and the two shall become one flesh.' So they are no longer two but one flesh. Therefore what God has joined together, no human being must separate." In the house the disciples again questioned him about this. He said to them, "Whoever divorces his wife and marries another commits adultery against her; and if she divorces her husband and marries another, she commits adultery."

And people were bringing children to him that he might touch them, but the disciples rebuked them. When Jesus saw this he became indignant and said to them, "Let the children come to me; do not prevent them, for the kingdom of God belongs to such as these. Amen, I say to you, whoever does not accept the kingdom of God like a child will not enter it." Then he embraced them and blessed them, placing his hands on them.

PSALM 45:1-10

For the leader; according to "Lilies."
A maskil of the sons of Korah. A
love song.

My heart overflows with a goodly theme;
as I sing my ode to the king,
my tongue is nimble as the pen of a skillful scribe.
Fairer in beauty are you than the sons of men;
grace is poured out upon your lips;
thus God has blessed you forever.
Gird your sword upon your thigh, O mighty one!
In your splendor and your majesty ride on triumphant
In the cause of truth and for the sake of justice;
and may your right hand show you wondrous deeds.
Your arrows are sharp; peoples are subject to you;
the king's enemies lose heart.
Your throne, O God, stands forever and ever;
a tempered rod is your royal scepter.
You love justice and hate wickedness;
therefore God, your God, has anointed you
with the oil of gladness above your fellow kings.
With myrrh and aloes and cassia your robes are fragrant;
from ivory palaces string music brings you joy.
The daughters of kings come to meet you;
the queen takes her place at your right hand in gold of Ophir.

PROVERBS 13:9-10

The light of the just shines gaily, / but the lamp of the wicked goes out. / The stupid man sows discord by his insolence, / but with those who take counsel is wisdom.

APRIL 18

MARK 10:17-52

As he was setting out on a journey, a man ran up, knelt down before him, and asked him, "Good teacher, what must I do to inherit eternal life?" Jesus answered him, "Why do you call me good? No one is good but God alone. You know the commandments: 'You shall not kill; you shall not commit adultery; you shall not steal; you shall not bear false witness; you shall not defraud; honor your father and your mother.' " He replied and said to him, "Teacher, all of these I have observed from my youth." Jesus, looking at him, loved him and said to him, "You are lacking in one thing. Go, sell what you have, and give to [the] poor and you will have treasure in heaven; then come, follow me." At that statement his face fell, and he went away sad, for he had many possessions.

Jesus looked around and said to his disciples, "How hard it is for those who have wealth to enter the kingdom of God!" The disciples were amazed at his words. So Jesus again said to them in reply, "Children, how hard it is to enter the kingdom of God! It is easier for a camel to pass through [the] eye of [a] needle than for one who is rich to enter the kingdom of God." They were exceedingly astonished and said among themselves, "Then who can be saved?" Jesus looked at them and said, "For human beings it is impossible, but not for God. All things are possible for God." Peter began to say to him, "We have given up everything and followed you." Jesus said, "Amen, I say to you, there is no one who has given up house or brothers or sisters or mother or father or children or lands for my sake and for the sake of the gospel who will not receive a hundred times more now in this present age: houses and brothers and sisters and mothers and children and lands, with persecutions, and eternal life in the age to come. But many that are first will be last, and [the] last will be first."

They were on the way, going up to Jerusalem, and Jesus went ahead of them. They were amazed, and those who followed were afraid. Taking the Twelve aside again, he began to tell them what was going to happen to him. "Behold, we are going up to Jerusalem, and the Son of Man will be handed over to the chief priests and the scribes, and they will condemn him to death and hand him over to the Gentiles who will mock him, spit upon him, scourge him, and put him to death, but after three days he will rise."

Then James and John, the sons of Zebedee, came to him and said to him, "Teacher, we want you to do for us whatever we ask of you." He replied, "What do you wish [me] to do for you?" They answered him, "Grant that in your glory we may sit one at your right and the other at your left." Jesus said to them, "You do not know what you are asking. Can you drink the cup that I drink or be baptized with the baptism with which I am baptized?" They said to him, "We can." Jesus said to them, "The cup that I drink, you will drink, and with the baptism with which I am baptized, you will be baptized; but to sit at my right or at my left is not mine to give but is for those for whom it has been prepared." When the ten heard this, they became indignant at James and John. Jesus summoned them and said to them, "You know that those who are recognized as rulers over the Gentiles lord it over them, and their great ones make their authority over them felt. But it shall not be so among you. Rather, whoever wishes to be great among you will be your servant; whoever wishes to be first among you will be the slave of all. For the Son of Man did not come to be served but to serve and to give his life as a ransom for many."

They came to Jericho. And as he was leaving Jericho with his disciples and a sizable crowd, Bartimaeus, a blind man, the son of Timaeus, sat by the roadside begging. On hearing that it was Jesus of Nazareth, he began to cry out and say, "Jesus, son of David, have pity on me." And many rebuked him, telling him to be silent. But he kept calling out all the more, "Son of David, have pity on me." Jesus stopped and said, "Call him." So they called the blind man, saying to him, "Take courage; get up, he is calling you." He threw aside his cloak, sprang up, and came to Jesus. Jesus said to him in reply, "What do you want me to do for you?" The blind man replied to him, "Master, I want to see." Jesus told him, "Go your way; your faith has saved you." Immediately he received his sight and followed him on the way.

PSALM 45:11-18

Hear, O daughter, and see; turn your ear,
    forget your people and your father's house.
So shall the king desire your beauty;
    for he is your lord, and you must worship him.
And the city of Tyre is here with gifts;
    the rich among the people seek your favor.
All glorious is the king's daughter as she enters;
    her raiment is threaded with spun gold.
In embroidered apparel she is borne in to the king;
    behind her the virgins of her train are brought to you.
They are borne in with gladness and joy;
    they enter the palace of the king.
The place of your fathers your sons shall have;
    you shall make them princes through all the land.
I will make your name memorable through all generations;
    therefore shall nations praise you forever and ever.

PROVERBS 13:11-12

*Wealth quickly gotten dwindles away, / but amassed little by little, it grows. /
Hope deferred makes the heart sick, / but a wish fulfilled is a tree of life.*

APRIL 19

MARK 11:1-33

When they drew near to Jerusalem, to Bethphage and Bethany at the Mount of Olives, he sent two of his disciples and said to them, "Go into the village opposite you, and immediately on entering it, you will find a colt tethered on which no one has ever sat. Untie it and bring it here. If anyone should say to you, 'Why are you doing this?' reply, 'The Master has need of it and will send it back here at once.' " So they went off and found a colt tethered at a gate outside on the street, and they untied it. Some of the bystanders said to them, "What are you doing, untying the colt?" They answered them just as Jesus had told them to, and they permitted them to do it. So they brought the colt to Jesus and put their cloaks over it. And he sat on it. Many people spread their cloaks on the road, and others spread leafy branches that they had cut from the fields. Those preceding him as well as those following kept crying out:

"Hosanna!
Blessed is he who comes in
the name of the LORD!
Blessed is the kingdom of
our father David that is to
come!
Hosanna in the highest!"

He entered Jerusalem and went into the temple area. He looked around at everything and, since it was already late, went out to Bethany with the Twelve.

The next day as they were leaving Bethany he was hungry. Seeing from a distance a fig tree in leaf, he went over to see if he could find anything on it. When he reached it he found nothing but leaves; it was not the time for figs. And he said to it in reply, "May no one ever eat of your fruit again!" And his disciples heard it.

They came to Jerusalem, and on entering the temple area he began to drive out those selling and buying there. He overturned the tables of the money changers and the seats of those who were selling doves. He did not permit anyone to carry anything through the temple area. Then he taught them saying, "Is it not written:

'My house shall be called a
house of prayer for all
peoples'?
But you have made it a den
of thieves."

The chief priests and the scribes came to hear of it and were seeking a way to put him to death, yet they feared him because the whole crowd was astonished at his teaching. When evening came, they went out of the city.
Early in the morning, as they

were walking along, they saw the fig tree withered to its roots. Peter remembered and said to him, "Rabbi, look! The fig tree that you cursed has withered." Jesus said to them in reply, "Have faith in God. Amen, I say to you, whoever says to this mountain, 'Be lifted up and thrown into the sea,' and does not doubt in his heart but believes that what he says will happen, it shall be done for him. Therefore I tell you, all that you ask for in prayer, believe that you will receive it and it shall be yours. When you stand to pray, forgive anyone against whom you have a grievance, so that your heavenly Father may in turn forgive you your transgressions."

They returned once more to Jerusalem. As he was walking in the temple area, the chief priests, the scribes, and the elders approached him and said to him, "By what authority are you doing these things? Or who gave you this authority to do them?" Jesus said to them, "I shall ask you one question. Answer me, and I will tell you by what authority I do these things. Was John's baptism of heavenly or of human origin? Answer me." They discussed this among themselves and said, "If we say, 'Of heavenly origin,' he will say, '[Then] why did you not believe him?' But shall we say, 'Of human origin'?"—they feared the crowd, for they all thought John really was a prophet. So they said to Jesus in reply, "We do not know." Then Jesus said to them, "Neither shall I tell you by what authority I do these things."

PSALM 46:1-8

For the leader. A song of the sons of Korah; according to "Virgins."
God is our refuge and our strength,
    an ever-present help in distress.
Therefore we fear not, though the earth be shaken
    and mountains plunge into the depths of the sea;
Though its waters rage and foam
    and the mountains quake at its surging.
    The LORD of hosts is with us;
    our stronghold is the God of Jacob.
There is a stream whose runlets gladden the city of God,
    the holy dwelling of the Most High.
God is in its midst; it shall not be disturbed;
    God will help it at the break of dawn.
Though nations are in turmoil, kingdoms totter,
    his voice resounds, the earth melts away,
    The LORD of hosts is with us;
    our stronghold is the God of Jacob.

PROVERBS 13:13-14

He who despises the word must pay for it, / but he who reveres the commandment will be rewarded. / The teaching of the wise is a fountain of life, / that a man may avoid the snares of death.

APRIL 20

MARK 12:1-27

He began to speak to them in parables. "A man planted a vineyard, put a hedge around it, dug a wine press, and built a tower. Then he leased it to tenant farmers and left on a journey. At the proper time he sent a servant to the tenants to obtain from them some of the produce of the vineyard. But they seized him, beat him, and sent him away empty-handed. Again he sent them another servant. And that one they beat over the head and treated shamefully. He sent yet another whom they killed. So, too, many others; some they beat, others they killed. He had one other to send, a beloved son. He sent him to them last of all, thinking, 'They will respect my son.' But those tenants said to one another, 'This is the heir. Come, let us kill him, and the inheritance will be ours.' So they seized him and killed him, and threw him out of the vineyard. What [then] will the owner of the vineyard do? He will come, put the tenants to death, and give the vineyard to others. Have you not read this scripture passage:

'The stone that the builders
    rejected
   has become the cornerstone;
by the LORD has this been
    done,
   and it is wonderful in our
   eyes'?"

They were seeking to arrest him, but they feared the crowd, for they realized that he had addressed the parable to them. So they left him and went away.

They sent some Pharisees and Herodians to him to ensnare him in his speech. They came and said to him, "Teacher, we know that you are a truthful man and that you are not concerned with anyone's opinion. You do not regard a person's status but teach the way of God in accordance with the truth. Is it lawful to pay the census tax to Caesar or not? Should we pay or should we not pay?" Knowing their hypocrisy he said to them, "Why are you testing me? Bring me a denarius to look at." They brought one to him and he said to them, "Whose image and inscription is this?" They replied to him, "Caesar's." So Jesus said to them, "Repay to Caesar what belongs to Caesar and to God what belongs to God." They were utterly amazed at him.

Some Sadducees, who say there is no resurrection, came to him and put this question to him, saying, "Teacher, Moses wrote for us, 'If someone's brother dies, leaving a wife but no child, his brother must take the wife and raise up descendants for his brother.' Now there were seven brothers. The first married a woman and died, leaving no descendants. So the second married her and died, leaving no descendants, and the third likewise. And the seven left no descendants. Last of all the woman also died. At the resurrection [when they arise] whose wife will she be? For all seven had been married to her." Jesus said to them, "Are you not misled because you do not know the scriptures or the power of God? When they rise from the dead, they neither marry nor are given in marriage, but they are like the angels in heaven. As for the dead being raised, have you not read in the Book of Moses, in the passage about the bush, how God told him, 'I am the God of Abraham, [the] God of Isaac, and [the] God of Jacob'? He is not God of the dead but of the living. You are greatly misled."

PSALM 46:9-12

Come! behold the deeds of the LORD,

the astounding things he has wrought on earth:
He has stopped wars to the end of the earth:
the bow he breaks; he splinters the spears;
he burns the shields with fire.
Desist! and confess that I am God,
exalted among the nations, exalted upon the earth.
The LORD of hosts is with us;
our stronghold is the God of Jacob.

PROVERBS 13:15-16

Good sense brings favor, / but the way of the faithless is their ruin. / The shrewd man does everything with prudence, / but the fool peddles folly.

APRIL 21

MARK 12:28-44

One of the scribes, when he came forward and heard them disputing and saw how well he had answered them, asked him, "Which is the first of all the commandments?" Jesus replied, "The first is this: 'Hear, O Israel! The Lord our God is Lord alone! You shall love the Lord your God with all your heart, with all your soul, with all your mind, and with all your strength.' The second is this: 'You shall love your neighbor as yourself.' There is no other commandment greater than these." The scribe said to him, "Well said, teacher. You are right in saying, 'He is One and there is no other than he.' And 'to love him with all your heart, with all your understanding, with all your strength, and to love your neighbor as yourself' is worth more than all burnt

offerings and sacrifices." And when Jesus saw that [he] answered with understanding, he said to him, "You are not far from the kingdom of God." And no one dared to ask him any more questions.

As Jesus was teaching in the temple area he said, "How do the scribes claim that the Messiah is the son of David? David himself, inspired by the holy Spirit, said:

'The Lord said to my lord,
"Sit at my right hand
until I place your enemies
under your feet." '

David himself calls him 'lord'; so how is he his son?" [The] great crowd heard this with delight.

In the course of his teaching he said, "Beware of the scribes, who like to go around in long robes and accept greetings in the market-places, seats of honor in synagogues, and places of honor at banquets. They devour the houses of widows and, as a pretext, recite lengthy prayers. They will receive a very severe condemnation."

He sat down opposite the treasury and observed how the crowd put money into the treasury. Many rich people put in large sums. A poor widow also came and put in two small coins worth a few cents. Calling his disciples to himself, he said to them, "Amen, I say to you, this poor widow put in more than all the other contributors to the treasury. For they have all contributed from their surplus wealth, but she, from her poverty, has contributed all she had, her whole livelihood."

PSALM 47:1-10

For the leader. A psalm of the sons of Korah.
All you peoples, clap your hands,
shout to God with cries of gladness,
For the LORD, the Most High, the awesome,
is the great king over all the earth.
He brings peoples under us;
nations under our feet.
He chooses for us our inheritance,
the glory of Jacob, whom he loves.
God mounts his throne amid shouts of joy;
the LORD, amid trumpet blasts.
Sing praise to God, sing praise;
sing praise to our king, sing praise.
For king of all the earth is God;
sing hymns of praise.
God reigns over the nations,
God sits upon his holy throne.
The princes of the peoples are gathered together
with the people of the God of Abraham.
For God's are the guardians of the earth;
he is supreme.

PROVERBS 13:17-19

A wicked messenger brings on disaster, / but a trustworthy envoy is a healing remedy. / Poverty and shame befall the man who disregards correction, / but he who heeds reproof is honored. / Lust indulged starves the soul, / but fools hate to turn from evil.

APRIL 22

MARK 13:1-23

As he was making his way out of the temple area one of his disciples said to him, "Look, teacher, what stones and what buildings!" Jesus said to him, "Do you see these great buildings? There will not be one stone left upon another that will not be thrown down."

As he was sitting on the Mount of Olives opposite the temple area, Peter, James, John, and Andrew asked him privately, "Tell us, when will this happen, and what sign will there be when all these things are about to come to an end?" Jesus began to say to them, "See that no one deceives you. Many will come in my name saying, 'I am he,' and they will deceive many. When you hear of wars and reports of wars do not be alarmed; such things must happen, but it will not yet be the end. Nation will rise against nation and kingdom against kingdom. There will be earthquakes from place to place and there will be famines. These are the beginnings of the labor pains.

"Watch out for yourselves. They will hand you over to the courts. You will be beaten in synagogues. You will be arraigned before governors and kings because of me, as a witness before them. But the gospel must first be preached to all nations. When they lead you away and hand you over, do not worry beforehand about what you are to say. But say whatever will be given to you at that hour. For it will not be you who are speaking but the holy Spirit. Brother will hand over brother to death, and the father his child; children will rise up against parents and have them put to death. You will be hated by all because of my name. But the one who perseveres to the end will be saved.

"When you see the desolating abomination standing where he should not (let the reader understand), then those in Judea must flee to the mountains, [and] a person on a housetop must not go down or enter to get anything out of his house, and a person in a field must not return to get his cloak. Woe to pregnant women and nursing mothers in those days. Pray that this does not happen in winter. For those times will have tribulation such as has not been since the beginning of God's creation until now, nor ever will be. If the Lord had not shortened those days, no one would be saved; but for the sake of the elect whom he chose, he did shorten the days. If anyone says to you then, 'Look, here is the Messiah! Look, there he is!' do not believe it. False messiahs and false prophets will arise and will perform signs and wonders in order to mislead, if that were possible, the elect. Be watchful! I have told it all to you beforehand."

PSALM 48:1-8

A psalm of the sons of Korah; a song.

Great is the LORD and wholly to
> be praised
> in the city of our God.
His holy mountain, fairest of
> heights,
> is the joy of all the earth;
Mount Zion, "the recesses of the
> North,"
> is the city of the great King.
God is with her castles;
> renowned is he as a
> stronghold.
For lo! the kings assemble,
> they come on together;
They also see, and at once are
> stunned,
> terrified, routed;
Quaking seizes them there;
> anguish, like a woman's in
> labor,
As though a wind from the east
> were shattering ships of
> Tarshish.

PROVERBS 13:20-23

Walk with wise men and you will become wise, / but the companion of fools will fare badly. / Misfortune pursues sinners, / but the just shall be recompensed with good. / The good man leaves an inheritance to his children's children, / but the wealth of the sinner is stored up for the just. / A lawsuit devours the tillage of the poor, / but some men perish for lack of a law court.

APRIL 23

MARK 13:24-37

"But in those days after that tribulation

the sun will be darkened,
and the moon will not give
its light,
and the stars will be falling
from the sky,
and the powers in the
heavens will be shaken.

And then they will see 'the Son of Man coming in the clouds' with great power and glory, and then he will send out the angels and gather [his] elect from the four winds, from the end of the earth to the end of the sky.

"Learn a lesson from the fig tree. When its branch becomes tender and sprouts leaves, you know that summer is near. In the same way, when you see these things happening, know that he is near, at the gates. Amen, I say to you, this generation will not pass away until all these things have taken place. Heaven and earth will pass away, but my words will not pass away.

"But of that day or hour, no one knows, neither the angels in heaven, nor the Son, but only the Father. Be watchful! Be alert! You do not know when the time will come. It is like a man traveling abroad. He leaves home and places his servants in charge, each with his work, and orders the gatekeeper to be on the watch. Watch, therefore; you do not know when the lord of the house is coming, whether in the evening, or at midnight, or at cockcrow, or in the morning. May he not come suddenly and find you sleeping. What I say to you, I say to all: 'Watch!' "

PSALM 48:9-15

As we had heard, so have we
seen
in the city of the LORD of hosts,
In the city of our God;
God makes it firm forever.
O God, we ponder your kindness
within your temple.
As your name, O God, so also
your praise
reaches to the ends of the
earth.
Of justice your right hand is full;
let Mount Zion be glad,
Let the cities of Judah rejoice,
because of your judgments.
Go about Zion, make the round;
count her towers.
Consider her ramparts,
examine her castles,
That you may tell a future
generation
that such is God,
Our God forever and ever;
he will guide us.

He who spares his rod hates his son, / but he who loves him takes care to chastise him. / When the just man eats, his hunger is appeased; / but the belly of the wicked suffers want.

APRIL 24

MARK 14:1-21

The Passover and the feast of Unleavened Bread were to take place in two days' time. So the chief priests and the scribes were seeking a way to arrest him by treachery and put him to death. They said, "Not during the festival, for fear that there may be a riot among the people."

When he was in Bethany reclining at table in the house of Simon the leper, a woman came with an alabaster jar of perfumed oil, costly genuine spikenard. She broke the alabaster jar and poured it on his head. There were some who were indignant. "Why has there been this waste of perfumed oil? It could have been sold for more than three hundred days' wages and the money given to the poor." They were infuriated with her. Jesus said, "Let her alone. Why do you make trouble for her? She has done a good thing for me. The poor you will always have with you, and whenever you wish you can do good to them, but you will not always have me. She has done what she could. She has anticipated anointing my body for burial. Amen, I say to you, wherever the gospel is proclaimed to the whole world, what she has done will be told in memory of her."

Then Judas Iscariot, one of the Twelve, went off to the chief priests to hand him over to them. When they heard him they were pleased and promised to pay him money. Then he looked for an opportunity to hand him over.

On the first day of the Feast of Unleavened Bread, when they sacrificed the Passover lamb, his disciples said to him, "Where do you want us to go and prepare for you to eat the Passover?" He sent two of his disciples and said to them, "Go into the city and a man will meet you, carrying a jar of water. Follow him. Wherever he enters, say to the master of the house, 'The Teacher says, "Where is my guest room where I may eat the Passover with my disciples?"' Then he will show you a large upper room furnished and ready. Make the preparations for us there." The disciples then went off, entered the city, and found it just as he had told them; and they prepared the Passover.

When it was evening, he came with the Twelve. And as they reclined at table and were eating, Jesus said, "Amen, I say to you, one of you will betray me, one who is eating with me." They began to be distressed and to say to him, one by one, "Surely it is not I?" He said to them, "One of the Twelve, the one who dips with me into the dish. For the Son of Man indeed goes, as it is written of him, but woe to that man by whom the Son of Man is betrayed. It would be better for that man if he had never been born."

PSALM 49:1-13

For the leader. A psalm of the sons of Korah.

Hear this, all you peoples;
hearken, all who dwell in the world,
Of lowly birth or high degree,
rich and poor alike.
My mouth shall speak wisdom;
prudence shall be the utterance of my heart.
My ear is intent upon a proverb;
I will set forth my riddle to the music of the harp.
Why should I fear in evil days
when my wicked ensnarers ring me round?

They trust in their wealth;
the abundance of their riches is their boast.
Yet in no way can a man redeem himself,
or pay his own ransom to God;
Too high is the price to redeem one's life; he would never have enough
to remain alive always and not see destruction.
For he can see that wise men die,
and likewise the senseless and the stupid pass away,
leaving to others their wealth.
Tombs are their homes forever,
their dwellings through all generations,
though they have called lands by their names.
Thus man, for all his splendor, does not abide;
he resembles the beasts that perish.

PROVERBS 14:1-2

Wisdom builds her house, / but Folly tears hers down with her own hands. / He who walks uprightly fears the LORD, / but he who is devious in his ways spurns him.

APRIL 25

MARK 14:22-42

While they were eating, he took bread, said the blessing, broke it, and gave it to them, and said, "Take it; this is my body." Then he took a cup, gave thanks, and gave it to them, and they all drank from it. He said to them, "This is my blood of the covenant, which will be shed for many. Amen, I say to you, I shall not drink again the fruit of

the vine until the day when I drink it new in the kingdom of God." Then, after singing a hymn, they went out to the Mount of Olives.

Then Jesus said to them, "All of you will have your faith shaken, for it is written:

'I will strike the shepherd,
and the sheep will be dispersed.'

But after I have been raised up, I shall go before you to Galilee." Peter said to him, "Even though all should have their faith shaken, mine will not be." Then Jesus said to him, "Amen, I say to you, this very night before the cock crows twice you will deny me three times." But he vehemently replied, "Even though I should have to die with you, I will not deny you." And they all spoke similarly.

Then they came to a place named Gethsemane, and he said to his disciples, "Sit here while I pray." He took with him Peter, James, and John, and began to be troubled and distressed. Then he said to them, "My soul is sorrowful even to death. Remain here and keep watch." He advanced a little and fell to the ground and prayed that if it were possible the hour might pass by him; he said, "Abba, Father, all things are possible to you. Take this cup away from me, but not what I will but what you will." When he returned he found them asleep. He said to Peter, "Simon, are you asleep? Could you not keep watch for one hour? Watch and pray that you may not undergo the test. The spirit is willing but the flesh is weak." Withdrawing again, he prayed, saying the same thing. Then he returned once more and found them asleep, for they could not keep their eyes open and did not know what to answer him. He returned a third time and said to them, "Are you still sleeping and taking your rest? It is enough. The hour has come. Behold, the Son of Man is to be handed over to sinners. Get up, let us go. See, my betrayer is at hand."

PSALM 49:14-21

This is the way of those whose
    trust is folly,
  the end of those contented
    with their lot:
Like sheep they are herded into
    the nether world;
  death is their shepherd, and
    the upright rule over them.
Quickly their form is consumed;
  the nether world is their
    palace.
But God will redeem me
  from the power of the nether
    world by receiving me.
Fear not when a man grows rich,
    when the wealth of his house
    becomes great,
For when he dies, he shall take
    none of it;
  his wealth shall not follow him
    down.
Though in his lifetime he counted
    himself blessed,
  "They will praise you for doing
    well for yourself,"
He shall join the circle of his
    forebears
  who shall never more see light.
Man, for all his splendor, if he
    have not prudence,
  resembles the beasts that
    perish.

PROVERBS 14:3-4

In the mouth of the fool is a rod for his back, / but the lips of the wise preserve them. / Where there are no oxen, the crib remains empty; / but large crops come through the strength of the bull.

APRIL 26

MARK 14:43-65

Then, while he was still speaking, Judas, one of the Twelve, arrived, accompanied by a crowd with swords and clubs who had come from the chief priests, the scribes, and the elders. His betrayer had arranged a signal with them, saying, "The man I shall kiss is the one; arrest him and lead him away securely." He came and immediately went over to him and said, "Rabbi." And he kissed him. At this they laid hands on him and arrested him. One of the bystanders drew his sword, struck the high priest's servant, and cut off his ear. Jesus said to them in reply, "Have you come out as against a robber, with swords and clubs, to seize me? Day after day I was with you teaching in the temple area, yet you did not arrest me; but that the scriptures may be fulfilled." And they all left him and fled. Now a young man followed him wearing nothing but a linen cloth about his body. They seized him, but he left the cloth behind and ran off naked.

They led Jesus away to the high priest, and all the chief priests and the elders and the scribes came together. Peter followed him at a distance into the high priest's courtyard and was seated with the guards, warming himself at the fire. The chief priests and the entire Sanhedrin kept trying to obtain testimony against Jesus in order to put him to death, but they found none. Many gave false witness against him, but their testimony did not agree. Some took the stand and testified falsely against him, alleging, "We heard him say, 'I will destroy this temple made with hands and within three days I will build another not made with hands.'" Even so their testimony did not agree. The high priest rose before the assembly and questioned Jesus, saying, "Have you no answer? What are these men testifying against you?" But he was silent and answered nothing. Again the high priest asked him and said to him, "Are you the Messiah, the son of the Blessed One?" Then Jesus answered, "I am;

and 'you will see the Son of Man
　　seated at the right hand of the Power
　　and coming with the clouds of heaven.'"

At that the high priest tore his garments and said, "What further need have we of witnesses? You have heard the blasphemy. What do you think?" They all condemned him as deserving to die. Some began to spit on him. They blindfolded him and struck him and said to him, "Prophesy!" And the guards greeted him with blows.

PSALM 50:1-6

A psalm of Asaph.
God the LORD has spoken and
　　summoned the earth,
　　from the rising of the sun to its
　　　setting.
From Zion, perfect in beauty,
　　God shines forth.
May our God come and not be
　　deaf to us!
　　Before him is a devouring fire;

around him is a raging storm.
He summons the heavens from
above,
and the earth, to the trial of his
people:
"Gather my faithful ones before
me,

those who have made a
covenant with me by
sacrifice."
And the heavens proclaim his
justice;
for God himself is the judge.

PROVERBS 14:5-6

A truthful witness does not lie, / but a false witness utters lies. / The senseless man seeks in vain for wisdom, / but knowledge is easy to the man of intelligence.

APRIL 27

MARK 14:66-72

While Peter was below in the courtyard, one of the high priest's maids came along. Seeing Peter warming himself, she looked intently at him and said, "You too were with the Nazarene, Jesus." But he denied it saying, "I neither know nor understand what you are talking about." So he went out into the outer court. [Then the cock crowed.] The maid saw him and began again to say to the bystanders, "This man is one of them." Once again he denied it. A little later the bystanders said to Peter once more, "Surely you are one of them; for you too are a Galilean." He began to curse and to swear, "I do not know this man about whom you are talking." And immediately a cock crowed a second time. Then Peter remembered the word that Jesus had said to him, "Before the cock crows twice you will deny me three times." He broke down and wept.

PSALM 50:7-15

"Hear, my people, and I will
speak;
Israel, I will testify against you;
God, your God, am I.
Not for your sacrifices do I
rebuke you,
for your holocausts are before
me always.
I take from your house no
bullock,
no goats out of your fold.
For mine are all the animals of
the forests,
beasts by the thousand on my
mountains.
I know all the birds of the air,
and whatever stirs in the
plains, belongs to me.
If I were hungry, I should not tell
you,
for mine are the world and its
fullness.
Do I eat the flesh of strong bulls,
or is the blood of goats my
drink?
Offer to God praise as your
sacrifice

and fulfill your vows to the
  Most High;
Then call upon me in time of

distress;
I will rescue you, and you shall
  glorify me."

PROVERBS 14:7-8

To avoid the foolish man, take steps! / But knowing lips one meets with by surprise. / The shrewd man's wisdom gives him knowledge of his way, / but the folly of fools is their deception.

APRIL 28

MARK 15:1-28

As soon as morning came, the chief priests with the elders and the scribes, that is, the whole Sanhedrin, held a council. They bound Jesus, led him away, and handed him over to Pilate. Pilate questioned him, "Are you the king of the Jews?" He said to him in reply, "You say so." The chief priests accused him of many things. Again Pilate questioned him, "Have you no answer? See how many things they accuse you of." Jesus gave him no further answer, so that Pilate was amazed.

Now on the occasion of the feast he used to release to them one prisoner whom they requested. A man called Barabbas was then in prison along with the rebels who had committed murder in a rebellion. The crowd came forward and began to ask him to do for them as he was accustomed. Pilate answered, "Do you want me to release to you the king of the Jews?" For he knew that it was out of envy that the chief priests had handed him over. But the chief priests stirred up the crowd to have him release Barabbas for them instead. Pilate again said to them in reply, "Then what [do you want] me to do with [the man you call] the king of the

Jews?" They shouted again, "Crucify him." Pilate said to them, "Why? What evil has he done?" They only shouted the louder, "Crucify him." So Pilate, wishing to satisfy the crowd, released Barabbas to them and, after he had Jesus scourged, handed him over to be crucified.

The soldiers led him away inside the palace, that is, the praetorium, and assembled the whole cohort. They clothed him in purple and, weaving a crown of thorns, placed it on him. They began to salute him with, "Hail, King of the Jews!" and kept striking his head with a reed and spitting upon him. They knelt before him in homage. And when they had mocked him, they stripped him of the purple cloak, dressed him in his own clothes, and led him out to crucify him.

They pressed into service a passer-by, Simon, a Cyrenian, who was coming in from the country, the father of Alexander and Rufus, to carry his cross.

They brought him to the place of Golgotha (which is translated Place of the Skull). They gave him wine drugged with myrrh, but he did not take it. Then they crucified him and divided his garments by casting lots for them to see what each should take. It was nine o'clock in the morning when they crucified him. The inscription of the charge against him read, "The King of the Jews." With him they crucified two revolutionaries, one on his right and one on his left.

PSALM 50:16-23

But to the wicked man God says:
    "Why do you recite my
        statutes,
    and profess my covenant with
        your mouth,
Though you hate discipline
    and cast my words behind
        you?
When you see a thief, you keep
        pace with him,
    and with adulterers you throw
        in your lot.

To your mouth you give free rein
        for evil,
    you harness your tongue to
        deceit.
You sit speaking against your
        brother;
    against your mother's son you
        spread rumors.
When you do these things, shall I
        be deaf to it?
    Or do you think that I am like
        yourself?
I will correct you by drawing
        them up before your eyes.
"Consider this, you who forget
        God,
    lest I rend you and there be no
        one to rescue you.
He that offers praise as a sacrifice
        glorifies me;
    and to him that goes the right
        way I will show the salvation
        of God."

PROVERBS 14:9-10

Guilt lodges in the tents of the arrogant, / but favor in the house of the just. / The heart knows its own bitterness, / and in its joy no one else shares.

APRIL 29

MARK 15:29-47

Those passing by reviled him, shaking their heads and saying, "Aha! You who would destroy the temple and rebuild it in three days, save yourself by coming down from the cross." Likewise the chief priests, with the scribes, mocked him among themselves and said, "He saved others; he cannot save himself. Let the Messiah, the King of Israel, come down now from the cross that we may see and believe." Those who were crucified with him also kept abusing him.

At noon darkness came over the whole land until three in the afternoon. And at three o'clock Jesus cried out in a loud voice, "*Eloi, Eloi, lema sabachthani?*" which is translated, "My God, my God, why have you forsaken me?" Some of the bystanders who heard it said, "Look, he is calling Elijah." One of them ran, soaked a sponge with wine, put it on a reed, and gave it to him to drink, saying, "Wait, let us see if Elijah comes to take him down." Jesus gave a loud cry and breathed his last. The veil of the sanctuary was torn in two from top to bottom. When the centurion who stood facing him saw how he breathed his last he said, "Truly this man was the Son of God!" There were also women looking on from a distance. Among them were Mary Magdalene, Mary the mother of the younger James and of Joses, and Salome. These women had followed him when he was in Galilee and ministered to him. There were also many other women who had come up with him to Jerusalem.

When it was already evening, since it was the day of preparation, the day before the sabbath, Joseph of Arimathea, a distinguished member of the council, who was himself awaiting the kingdom of God, came and courageously went to Pilate and asked for the body of Jesus. Pilate was amazed that he was already dead. He summoned the centurion and asked him if Jesus had already died. And when he learned of it from the centurion, he gave the body to Joseph. Having bought a linen cloth, he took him down, wrapped him in the linen cloth and laid him in a tomb that had been hewn out of the rock. Then he rolled a stone against the entrance to the tomb. Mary Magdalene and Mary the mother of Joses watched where he was laid.

to him after his sin with Bathsheba.

Have mercy on me, O God, in your goodness;
in the greatness of your compassion wipe out my offense.
Thoroughly wash me from my guilt
and of my sin cleanse me.
For I acknowledge my offense,
and my sin is before me always:
"Against you only have I sinned, and done what is evil in your sight"—
That you may be justified in your sentence,
vindicated when you condemn.
Indeed, in guilt was I born,
and in sin my mother conceived me;
Behold, you are pleased with sincerity of heart,
and in my inmost being you teach me wisdom.
Cleanse me of sin with hyssop, that I may be purified;
wash me, and I shall be whiter than snow.
Let me hear the sounds of joy and gladness;
the bones you have crushed shall rejoice.
Turn away your face from my sins,
and blot out all my guilt.

PSALM 51:1-11
For the leader. A psalm of David, when Nathan the prophet came

PROVERBS 14:11-12
The house of the wicked will be destroyed, / but the tent of the upright will flourish. / Sometimes a way seems right to a man, / but the end of it leads to death!

APRIL 30

MARK 16:1-20

When the sabbath was over, Mary Magdalene, Mary, the mother of James, and Salome bought spices so that they might go and anoint him. Very early when the sun had risen, on the first day of the week, they came to the tomb. They were saying to one another, "Who will roll back the stone for us from the entrance to the tomb?" When they looked up, they saw that the stone had been rolled back; it was very large. On entering the tomb they saw a young man sitting on the right side, clothed in a white robe, and they were utterly amazed. He said to them, "Do not be amazed! You seek Jesus of Nazareth, the crucified. He has been raised; he is not here. Behold the place where they laid him. But go and tell his disciples and Peter, 'He is going before you to Galilee; there you will see him, as he told you.' " Then they went out and fled from the tomb, seized with trembling and bewilderment. They said nothing to anyone, for they were afraid.

[When he had risen, early on the first day of the week, he appeared first to Mary Magdalene, out of whom he had driven seven demons. She went and told his companions who were mourning and weeping. When they heard that he was alive and had been seen by her, they did not believe.

After this he appeared in another form to two of them walking along on their way to the country. They returned and told the others; but they did not believe them either.

[But] later, as the eleven were at table, he appeared to them and rebuked them for their unbelief and hardness of heart because they had not believed those who saw him after he had been raised. He said to them, "Go into the whole world and proclaim the gospel to every creature. Whoever believes and is baptized will be saved; whoever does not believe will be condemned. These signs will accompany those who believe: in my name they will drive out demons, they will speak new languages. They will pick up serpents [with their hands], and if they drink any deadly thing, it will not harm them. They will lay hands on the sick, and they will recover."

So then the Lord Jesus, after he spoke to them, was taken up into heaven and took his seat at the right hand of God. But they went forth and preached everywhere, while the Lord worked with them and confirmed the word through accompanying signs.]

[And they reported all the instructions briefly to Peter's companions. Afterwards Jesus himself, through them, sent forth from east to west the sacred and imperishable proclamation of eternal salvation. Amen.]

PSALM 51:12-21

A clean heart create for me, O God,
    and a steadfast spirit renew within me.
Cast me not out from your presence,
    and your holy spirit take not from me.
Give me back the joy of your salvation,

and a willing spirit sustain in
me.
I will teach transgressors your
ways,
and sinners shall return to you.
Free me from blood guilt, O God,
my saving God;
then my tongue shall revel in
your justice.
O LORD, open my lips,
and my mouth shall proclaim
your praise.
For you are not pleased with
sacrifices;
should I offer a holocaust, you
would not accept it.

My sacrifice, O God, is a contrite
spirit;
a heart contrite and humbled,
O God, you will not spurn.
Be bountiful, O LORD, to Zion in
your kindness
by rebuilding the walls of
Jerusalem;
Then shall you be pleased with
due sacrifices,
burnt offerings and holocausts;
then shall they offer up
bullocks on your altar.

PROVERBS 14:13-14

Even in laughter the heart may be sad / and the end of joy may be sorrow. / The scoundrel suffers the consequences of his ways, / and the good man reaps the fruit of his paths.

MAY

Spirit-filled

WE ARE LIVING IN THE AGE of the Holy Spirit. The Second Vatican Council has dutifully reminded us of the presence and dynamism of the Holy Spirit in our lives. Through this renewed assurance of his presence, the Holy Spirit continues to draw us by his divine influence and power into a deeper awareness of his work of sanctification within us.

When Jesus redeemed our human nature, he gave us the potential and capacity to receive his divine life and love. He rose triumphantly from the dead that he might endow us with his glorified, exalted life.

At the moment of our baptism, this tremendous transformation takes place within us. When we were baptized we were able to breach that immense chasm which existed between our broken, sinful nature and the transcendent God, the Lord and Master of the entire universe. Through the divine power inherent in the baptismal rite, we were enabled to receive the indwelling of the Holy Spirit who is the fullness of Jesus living with us.

We became the temples of the Holy Spirit. Paul earnestly strives to make us aware of this unique privilege and urges us to respond generously to the Spirit's presence. Three separate times in his letters to the Corinthians, Paul reminds us of our real dignity as the dwelling place of the Holy Spirit. He asks us:

Do you not know that you are the temple of God, and that the Spirit of God dwells in you? If anyone destroys God's temple, God will destroy that person; for the temple of God, which you are, is holy. (1 Cor 3:16-17)

Not long after this solemn pronouncement, Paul comes back to the same sublime truth lest we lack genuine appreciation of our identity as members of the Body of Christ. Once again he says;

> Do you not know that your body is a temple of the holy
> Spirit within you, whom you have from God, and that you
> are not your own? For you have been purchased at a price.
> Therefore glorify God in your body. (1 Cor 6:19-20)

This is what makes us a Christian. We are Christian not because we believe certain truths, nor because we pray and worship in a special way, not because we adhere to a prescribed moral code. Rather we are Christian because Christ is dwelling within us through the power of his Spirit. Since we are privileged persons by virtue of his call to follow him, then we believe, pray, and live according to his way of life.

God's Family

At the moment of our baptism the Father adopts us as his daughters and sons. "For those who are led by the Spirit of God are children of God. . . . The Spirit itself bears witness with our spirit that we are children of God . . . " (Rom 8:14 and 16). The Lord himself tells us: ". . . I will receive you and I will be a father to you, and you shall be sons and daughters to me . . ." (2 Cor 6:18).

This gives us our true dignity as persons. Since we have a common Father, we are in every sense of the term brothers and sisters to one another. ". . . if children, then heirs, heirs of God and joint heirs with Christ . . ." (Rom 8:14ff).

Jesus already had confirmed this indwelling when he exhorted us to reach out in loving care and concern for those less fortunate than we are. In his discourse on the last judgment, Jesus left no doubt about this mysterious relationship. "Amen, I say to you, whatever you did for one of these least brothers of mine, you did for me" (Mt 25:40). Jesus did not imply that our loving concern for others would simply be a nice thing to do, but whatever we did for another person we would be doing for him personally. This is ample proof that we form one Body with Christ.

The Holy Spirit does not come to rest within us in some sort of dormant or static state. On the contrary, he comes laden with his many gratuitous gifts to help each one of us to grow and mature spiritually. With his divine power, he helps us put on the new man and to have this mind in us which was in Christ Jesus.

Called to Serve

The Holy Spirit endows us with those personal gifts which we need to complete the special ministry to which we are called—be that to the members of our family, to our friends, to our acquaintances, in our work place, in the church and community, to our brothers and sisters throughout the world.

The Spirit of God reminds us that as members of the Body of Christ, we are effective channels through which his divine life and love can touch our brothers and sisters. Through us he can bring reconciliation and peace to our weary world. We can convey his love to many others, especially to those who do not know or have never experienced his love for them. This is what Paul meant when he said: "To each individual the manifestation of the Spirit is given for some benefit" (1 Cor 12:7). In other words, we are gifted by the Spirit in order to build up the Body of Christ. We can accomplish this mission in life by becoming holy ourselves and radiating the love, peace, and joy of the Lord to all who are journeying with us through this land of exile.

In all our endeavors the Holy Spirit will guide and direct us. He will give us a discerning spirit to recognize and respond to his inspirations. In order to respond graciously and courageously, we must release ourselves to the power and presence of the Holy Spirit within us. We can draw motivation and strength from the treasury of his divine Word, as we daily read, ponder, and pray with his Word. "Do not quench the Spirit" (1 Thes 5:19).

MAY 1

ROMANS 10:1-21

Brothers, my heart's desire and prayer to God on their behalf is for salvation. I testify with regard to them that they have zeal for God, but it is not discerning. For, in their unawareness of the righteousness that comes from God and their attempt to establish their own [righteousness], they did not submit to the righteousness of God. For Christ is the end of the law for the justification of everyone who has faith.

Moses writes about the righteousness that comes from [the] law, "The one who does these things will live by them." But the righteousness that comes from faith says, "Do not say in your heart, 'Who will go up into heaven?' (that is, to bring Christ down) or 'Who will go down into the abyss?' (that is, to bring Christ up from the dead)." But what does it say?

"The word is near you,
in your mouth and in your
heart"

(that is, the word of faith that we preach), for, if you confess with your mouth that Jesus is Lord and believe in your heart that God raised him from the dead, you will be saved. For one believes with the heart and so is justified, and one confesses with the mouth and so is saved. For the scripture says, "No one who believes in him will be put to shame." For there is no distinction between Jew and Greek; the same Lord is Lord of all, enriching all who call upon him. For "everyone who calls on the name of the Lord will be saved."

But how can they call on him in whom they have not believed? And how can they believe in him of whom they have not heard? And how can they hear without someone to preach? And how can people preach unless they are sent? As it is written, "How beautiful are the feet of those who bring [the] good news!" But not everyone has heeded the good news; for Isaiah says, "Lord, who has believed what was heard from us?" Thus faith comes from what is heard, and what is heard comes through the word of Christ. But I ask, did they not hear? Certainly they did; for

"Their voice has gone forth to
all the earth,
and their words to the ends
of the world."

But I ask, did not Israel understand? First Moses says:

"I will make you jealous of
those who are not a
nation;
with a senseless nation I will
make you angry."

Then Isaiah speaks boldly and
says:

"I was found [by] those who
were not seeking me;
I revealed myself to those
who were not asking for
me."

But regarding Israel he says, "All
day long I stretched out my hands
to a disobedient and contentious
people."

PSALM 52:1-11

*For the leader. A maskil of David,
when Doeg the Edomite went
and told Saul, "David went to
the house of Ahimelech."*
Why do you glory in evil,
you champion of infamy?
All the day you plot harm;
your tongue is like a sharpened

razor, you practiced
deceiver!
You love evil rather than good,
falsehood rather than honest
speech.
You love all that means ruin,
you of the deceitful tongue!
God himself shall demolish you;
forever he shall break you;
He shall pluck you from your
tent,
and uproot you from the land
of the living.
The just shall look on with awe;
then they shall laugh at him:
"This is the man who made not
God the source of his strength,
But put his trust in his great
wealth,
and his strength in harmful
plots."
But I, like a green olive tree
in the house of God.
Trust in the kindness of God
forever and ever.
I will thank you always for what
you have done,
and proclaim the goodness of
your name
before your faithful ones.

PROVERBS 14:15-16

*The simpleton believes everything, / but the shrewd man measures his steps. /
The wise man is cautious and shuns evil; / the fool is reckless and sure of
himself.*

MAY 2

ROMANS 11:1-18

I ask, then, has God rejected his
people? Of course not! For I too
am an Israelite, a descendant of
Abraham, of the tribe of Benjamin. God has not rejected his people whom he foreknew. Do you
not know what the scripture says
about Elijah, how he pleads with
God against Israel? "Lord, they
have killed your prophets, they
have torn down your altars, and I
alone am left, and they are seeking my life." But what is God's response to him? "I have left for myself seven thousand men who

have not knelt to Baal." So also at the present time there is a remnant, chosen by grace. But if by grace, it is no longer because of works; otherwise grace would no longer be grace. What then? What Israel was seeking it did not attain, but the elect attained it; the rest were hardened, as it is written:

"God gave them a spirit of
    deep sleep,
  eyes that should not see
  and ears that should not
    hear,
down to this very day."

And David says:

"Let their table become a snare
    and a trap,
  a stumbling block and a
    retribution for them;
let their eyes grow dim so that
    they may not see,
  and keep their backs bent
    forever."

Hence I ask, did they stumble so as to fall? Of course not! But through their transgression salvation has come to the Gentiles, so as to make them jealous. Now if their transgression is enrichment for the world, and if their diminished number is enrichment for the Gentiles, how much more their full number.

Now I am speaking to you Gentiles. Inasmuch then as I am the apostle to the Gentiles, I glory in my ministry in order to make my race jealous and thus save some of them. For if their rejection is the reconciliation of the world, what will their acceptance be but life from the dead? If the firstfruits are holy, so is the whole batch of dough; and if the root is holy, so are the branches.

But if some of the branches were broken off, and you, a wild olive shoot, were grafted in their place and have come to share in the rich root of the olive tree, do not boast against the branches. If you do boast, consider that you do not support the root; the root supports you.

PSALM 53:1-7

*For the leader; according to
    Mahalath. A maskil of David.*
The fool says in his heart,
    "There is no God."
Such are corrupt; they do
    abominable deeds;
  there is not one who does
    good.
God looks down from heaven
    upon the children of men
  to see if there be one who is
    wise and seeks God.
All alike have gone astray; they
    have become perverse;
  there is not one who does
    good, not even one.
Will all these evildoers never
    learn,
  they who eat up my people
    just as they eat bread,
  who call not upon God?
There they were in great fear,
    where no fear was,
For God has scattered the bones
    of your besiegers;
  they are put to shame, because
    God has rejected them.
Oh, that out of Zion would come
    the salvation of Israel!
  When God restores the well-
    being of his people,
  then shall Jacob exalt and Israel
    be glad.

PROVERBS 14:17-19

The quick-tempered man makes a fool of himself, / but the prudent man is at peace. / The adornment of simpletons is folly, / but shrewd men gain the crown of knowledge. / Evil men must bow down before the good, / and the wicked, at the gates of the just.

MAY 3

ROMANS 11:19-36

Indeed you will say, "Branches were broken off so that I might be grafted in." That is so. They were broken off because of unbelief, but you are there because of faith. So do not become haughty, but stand in awe. For if God did not spare the natural branches, [perhaps] he will not spare you either. See, then, the kindness and severity of God: severity toward those who fell, but God's kindness to you, provided you remain in his kindness; otherwise you too will be cut off. And they also, if they do not remain in unbelief, will be grafted in, for God is able to graft them in again. For if you were cut from what is by nature a wild olive tree, and grafted, contrary to nature, into a cultivated one, how much more will they who belong to it by nature be grafted back into their own olive tree.

I do not want you to be unaware of this mystery, brothers, so that you will not become wise [in] your own estimation: a hardening has come upon Israel in part, until the full number of the Gentiles comes in, and thus all Israel will be saved, as it is written:

"The deliverer will come out of Zion,
    he will turn away
        godlessness from Jacob;

and this is my covenant with them
    when I take away their sins."

In respect to the gospel, they are enemies on your account; but in respect to election, they are beloved because of the patriarchs. For the gifts and the call of God are irrevocable.

Just as you once disobeyed God but have now received mercy because of their disobedience, so they have now disobeyed in order that, by virtue of the mercy shown to you, they too may [now] receive mercy. For God delivered all to disobedience, that he might have mercy upon all.

Oh the depth of the riches and wisdom and knowledge of God! How inscrutable are his judgments and how unsearchable his ways!

"For who has known the mind of the Lord
    or who has been his counselor?"
"Or who has given him anything
    that he may be repaid?"

For from him and through him and for him are all things. To him be glory forever. Amen.

PSALM 54:1-9

*For the leader; with stringed
    instruments. A maskil of David,
    when the Ziphites went and said
    to Saul, "David is hiding among
    us."*

O God, by your name save me,
    and by your might defend my
    cause.
O God, hear my prayer;
    hearken to the words of my
    mouth.
For haughty men have risen up
    against me,
    and fierce men seek my life;
they set not God before their
    eyes.
Behold, God is my helper;
    the Lord sustains my life.
Turn back the evil upon my foes;
    in your faithfulness destroy
    them.
Freely will I offer you sacrifice;
    I will praise your name, O
    LORD, for its goodness,
Because from all distress you
    have rescued me,
    and my eyes look down upon
    my enemies.

PROVERBS 14:20-21

*Even by his neighbor the poor man is hated, / but the friends of the rich are
many. / He sins who despises the hungry; / but happy is he who is kind to the
poor!*

MAY 4

ROMANS 12:1-21

I urge you therefore, brothers,
by the mercies of God, to offer
your bodies as a living sacrifice,
holy and pleasing to God, your
spiritual worship. Do not conform
yourself to this age but be transformed by the renewal of your
mind, that you may discern what
is the will of God, what is good
and pleasing and perfect.

For by the grace given to me I
tell everyone among you not to
think of himself more highly than
one ought to think, but to think
soberly, each according to the
measure of faith that God has apportioned. For as in one body we
have many parts, and all the parts
do not have the same function, so
we, though many, are one body
in Christ and individually parts of
one another. Since we have gifts
that differ according to the grace
given to us, let us exercise them: if
prophecy, in proportion to the
faith; if ministry, in ministering; if
one is a teacher, in teaching; if one
exhorts, in exhortation; if one con-
tributes, in generosity; if one is
over others, with diligence; if one
does acts of mercy, with cheerful-
ness.

Let love be sincere; hate what is
evil, hold on to what is good; love
one another with mutual affection; anticipate one another in
showing honor. Do not grow
slack in zeal, be fervent in spirit,
serve the Lord. Rejoice in hope,
endure in affliction, persevere in
prayer. Contribute to the needs of
the holy ones, exercise hospitality. Bless those who persecute

[you], bless and do not curse them. Rejoice with those who rejoice, weep with those who weep. Have the same regard for one another; do not be haughty but associate with the lowly; do not be wise in your own estimation. Do not repay anyone evil for evil; be concerned for what is noble in the sight of all. If possible, on your part, live at peace with all. Beloved, do not look for revenge but leave room for the wrath; for it is written, "Vengeance is mine, I will repay, says the Lord." Rather, "if your enemy is hungry, feed him; if he is thirsty, give him something to drink; for by so doing you will heap burning coals upon his head." Do not be conquered by evil but conquer evil with good.

PSALM 55:1-9

For the leader; with stringed instruments. A maskil of David.

Hearken, O God, to my prayer;
    turn not away from my
        pleading;
    give heed to me, and answer
        me.
I rock with grief, and am troubled
    at the voice of the enemy and
        the clamor of the wicked.
For they bring down evil upon
        me,
    and with fury they persecute
        me.
My heart quakes within me;
    the terror of death has fallen
        upon me.
Fear and trembling come upon
        me,
    and horror overwhelms me,
And I say, "Had I but wings like
        a dove,
    I would fly away and be at rest.
Far away I would flee;
    I would lodge in the
        wilderness.
I would hasten to find shelter
    from the violent storm and the
        tempest."

PROVERBS 14:22-23

Do not those who plot evil go astray? / But those intent on good gain kindness and constancy. / In all labor there is profit, / but mere talk tends only to penury.

MAY 5

ROMANS 13:1-14

Let every person be subordinate to the higher authorities, for there is no authority except from God, and those that exist have been established by God. Therefore, whoever resists authority opposes what God has appointed, and those who oppose it will bring judgment upon themselves. For rulers are not a cause of fear to good conduct, but to evil. Do you wish to have no fear of authority? Then do what is good and you will receive approval from it, for it is a servant of God for your good. But if you do evil, be afraid, for it does not bear the sword without purpose; it is the servant of God to inflict wrath on the evildoer. Therefore, it is necessary to be subject not only because of the wrath but also because of conscience. This is why you also pay taxes, for the authorities are ministers of God, devoting themselves to this very thing. Pay to all their dues, taxes to whom taxes are due, toll to whom toll is due, respect to whom respect is due, honor to whom honor is due.

Owe nothing to anyone, except to love one another; for the one who loves another has fulfilled the law. The commandments, "You shall not commit adultery; you shall not kill; you shall not steal; you shall not covet," and whatever other commandment there may be, are summed up in this saying, [namely] "You shall love your neighbor as yourself." Love does no evil to the neighbor; hence, love is the fulfillment of the law.

And do this because you know the time; it is the hour now for you to awake from sleep. For our salvation is nearer now than when we first believed; the night is advanced, the day is at hand. Let us then throw off the works of darkness [and] put on the armor of light; let us conduct ourselves properly as in the day, not in orgies and drunkenness, not in promiscuity and licentiousness, not in rivalry and jealousy. But put on the Lord Jesus Christ, and make no provision for the desires of the flesh.

PSALM 55:10-15

Engulf them, O Lord; divide their counsels,
 for in the city I see violence and strife;
 day and night they prowl about upon its walls.
Evil and mischief are in its midst;
 [treachery is in its midst;]
 oppression and fraud never depart from its streets.
If an enemy had reviled me,
 I could have borne it;
If he who hates me had vaunted himself against me,
 I might have hidden from him.
But you, my other self,
 my companion and my bosom friend!
You, whose comradeship I enjoyed;
 at whose side I walked in procession in the house of God!

PROVERBS 14:24-25

The crown of the wise is resourcefulness; / the diadem of fools is folly. / The truthful witness saves lives, / but he who utters lies is a betrayer.

MAY 6

ROMANS 14:1-23

Welcome anyone who is weak in faith, but not for disputes over opinions. One person believes that one may eat anything, while the weak person eats only vegetables. The one who eats must not despise the one who abstains, and the one who abstains must not pass judgment on the one who eats; for God has welcomed him. Who are you to pass judgment on someone else's servant? Before his own master he stands or falls.

And he will be upheld, for the Lord is able to make him stand. [For] one person considers one day more important than another, while another person considers all days alike. Let everyone be fully persuaded in his own mind. Whoever observes the day, observes it for the Lord. Also whoever eats, eats for the Lord, since he gives thanks to God; while whoever abstains, abstains for the Lord and gives thanks to God. None of us lives for oneself, and no one dies for oneself. For if we live, we live for the Lord, and if we die, we die for the Lord; so then, whether we live or die, we are the Lord's. For this is why Christ died and came to life, that he might be Lord of both the dead and the living. Why then do you judge your brother? Or you, why do you look down on your brother? For we shall all stand before the judgment seat of God; for it is written:

"As I live, says the Lord, every knee shall bend before me, and every tongue shall give praise to God."

So [then] each of us shall give an account of himself [to God].

Then let us no longer judge one another, but rather resolve never to put a stumbling block or hindrance in the way of a brother. I know and am convinced in the Lord Jesus that nothing is unclean in itself; still, it is unclean for someone who thinks it unclean. If your brother is being hurt by what you eat, your conduct is no longer in accord with love. Do not because of your food destroy him for whom Christ died. So do not let your good be reviled. For the kingdom of God is not a matter of food and drink, but of righteousness, peace, and joy in the holy Spirit; whoever serves Christ in this way is pleasing to God and approved by others. Let us then pursue what leads to peace and to building up one another. For the sake of food, do not destroy the work of God. Everything is indeed clean, but it is wrong for anyone to become a stumbling block by eating; it is good not to eat meat or drink wine or do anything that causes your brother to stumble. Keep the faith [that] you have to yourself in the presence of God; blessed is the one who does not condemn himself for what he approves. But whoever has doubts is condemned if he eats, because this is not from faith; for whatever is not from faith is sin.

PSALM 55:16-24

Let death surprise them;
   let them go down alive to the
      nether world,
   for evil is in their dwellings, in
      their very midst.
But I will call upon God,
   and the LORD will save me.
In the evening, and at dawn, and
      at noon,
   I will grieve and moan,
   and he will hear my voice.
He will give me freedom and
      peace
   from those who war against
      me,
   for many there are who oppose
      me.
God will hear me and will
      humble them
   from his eternal throne;
For improvement is not in them,
   nor do they fear God.
Each one lays hands on his
      associates,
   and violates his pact.
Softer than butter is his speech,
   but war is in his heart;
His words are smoother than oil,

but they are drawn swords.
Cast your care upon the LORD,
    and he will support you;
    never will he permit the just
    man to be disturbed.
And you, O God, will bring them
    down
into the pit of destruction;
Men of blood and deceit shall not
    live out half their days.
But I trust in you, O LORD.

PROVERBS 14:26-27

In the fear of the LORD is a strong defense; / even for one's children he will be a refuge. / The fear of the LORD is a fountain of life, / that a man may avoid the snares of death.

MAY 7

ROMANS 15:1-13

We who are strong ought to put up with the failings of the weak and not to please ourselves; let each of us please our neighbor for the good, for building up. For Christ did not please himself; but, as it is written, "The insults of those who insult you fall upon me." For whatever was written previously was written for our instruction, that by endurance and by the encouragement of the scriptures we might have hope. May the God of endurance and encouragement grant you to think in harmony with one another, in keeping with Christ Jesus, that with one accord you may with one voice glorify the God and Father of our Lord Jesus Christ.

Welcome one another, then, as Christ welcomed you, for the glory of God. For I say that Christ became a minister of the circumcised to show God's truthfulness, to confirm the promises to the patriarchs, but so that the Gentiles might glorify God for his mercy. As it is written:

"Therefore, I will praise you
    among the Gentiles
and sing praises to your
    name."

And again it says:

"Rejoice, O Gentiles, with his
    people."

And again:

"Praise the LORD, all you
    Gentiles,
and let all the peoples praise
    him."

And again Isaiah says:

"The root of Jesse shall come,
    raised up to rule the
    Gentiles;
in him shall the Gentiles
    hope."

May the God of hope fill you with all joy and peace in believing, so that you may abound in hope by the power of the holy Spirit.

PSALM 56:1-5

*For the leader; according to
Jonath . . . rehokim. A miktam
of David, when the Philistines
held him in Gath.*

Have pity on me, O God; for men
trample upon me;
all the day they press their
attack against me.
My adversaries trample upon me
all the day;

yes, many fight against me.
O Most High, when I begin to
fear,
in you will I trust.
In God, in whose promise I
glory,
in God I trust without fear;
what can flesh do against me?

PROVERBS 14:28-29

*In many subjects lies the glory of the king; / but if his people are few, it is the
prince's ruin. / The patient man shows much good sense, / but the quick-
tempered man displays folly at its height.*

MAY 8

ROMANS 15:14-33

I myself am convinced about
you, my brothers, that you yourselves are full of goodness, filled
with all knowledge, and able to
admonish one another. But I have
written to you rather boldly in
some respects to remind you, because of the grace given me by
God to be a minister of Christ Jesus to the Gentiles in performing
the priestly service of the gospel
of God, so that the offering up of
the Gentiles may be acceptable,
sanctified by the holy Spirit. In
Christ Jesus, then, I have reason
to boast in what pertains to God.
For I will not dare to speak of anything except what Christ has accomplished through me to lead
the Gentiles to obedience by word
and deed, by the power of signs
and wonders, by the power of the
Spirit [of God], so that from Jerusalem all the way around to
Illyricum I have finished preach-

ing the gospel of Christ. Thus I
aspire to proclaim the gospel not
where Christ has already been
named, so that I do not build on
another's foundation, but as it is
written:

"Those who have never been
told of him shall see,
and those who have never
heard of him shall
understand."

That is why I have so often been
prevented from coming to you.
But now, since I no longer have
any opportunity in these regions
and since I have desired to come
to you for many years, I hope to
see you in passing as I go to Spain
and to be sent on my way there by
you, after I have enjoyed being
with you for a time. Now, however, I am going to Jerusalem to
minister to the holy ones. For
Macedonia and Achaia have de-

cided to make some contribution for the poor among the holy ones in Jerusalem; they decided to do it, and in fact they are indebted to them, for if the Gentiles have come to share in their spiritual blessings, they ought also to serve them in material blessings. So when I have completed this and safely handed over this contribution to them, I shall set out by way of you to Spain; and I know that in coming to you I shall come in the fullness of Christ's blessing.

I urge you, [brothers,] by our Lord Jesus Christ and by the love of the Spirit, to join me in the struggle by your prayers to God on my behalf, that I may be delivered from the disobedient in Judea, and that my ministry for Jerusalem may be acceptable to the holy ones, so that I may come to you with joy by the will of God and be refreshed together with you. The God of peace be with all of you. Amen.

PSALM 56:6-14

All the day they molest me in my
    efforts;

their every thought is of evil
    against me.
They gather together in hiding,
    they watch my steps.
As they have waited for my life,
    because of their wickedness
    keep them in view:
    in your wrath bring down the
    peoples, O God.
My wanderings you have
    counted;
    my tears are stored in your
    flask;
    are they not recorded in your
    book?
Then do my enemies turn back,
    when I call upon you;
    now I know that God is with
    me.
In God, in whose promise I
    glory,
    in God I trust without fear;
    what can flesh do against me?
I am bound, O God, by vows to
    you;
    your thank offerings I will
    fulfill.
For you have rescued me from
    death,
    my feet, too, from stumbling;
    that I may walk before God in
    the light of the living.

PROVERBS 14:30-31

A tranquil mind gives life to the body, / but jealousy rots the bones. / He who oppresses the poor blasphemes his Maker, / but he who is kind to the needy glorifies him.

MAY 9

ROMANS 16:1-27

I commend to you Phoebe our sister, who is [also] a minister of the church at Cenchreae, that you may receive her in the Lord in a manner worthy of the holy ones, and help her in whatever she may need from you, for she has been a benefactor to many and to me as well.

Greet Prisca and Aquila, my co-workers in Christ Jesus, who

risked their necks for my life, to whom not only I am grateful but also all the churches of the Gentiles; greet also the church at their house. Greet my beloved Epaenatus, who was the firstfruits in Asia for Christ. Greet Mary, who has worked hard for you. Greet Andronicus and Junia, my relatives and my fellow prisoners; they are prominent among the apostles and they were in Christ before me. Greet Ampliatus, my beloved in the Lord. Greet Urbanus, our co-worker in Christ, and my beloved Stachys. Greet Apelles, who is approved in Christ. Greet those who belong to the family of Aristobulus. Greet my relative Herodion. Greet those in the Lord who belong to the family of Narcissus. Greet those workers in the Lord, Tryphaena and Tryphosa. Greet the beloved Persis, who has worked hard in the Lord. Greet Rufus, chosen in the Lord, and his mother and mine. Greet Asyncritus, Phlegon, Hermes, Patrobas, Hermas, and the brothers who are with them. Greet Philologus, Julia, Nereus and his sister, and Olympas, and all the holy ones who are with them. Greet one another with a holy kiss. All the churches of Christ greet you.

I urge you, brothers, to watch out for those who create dissensions and obstacles, in opposition to the teaching that you learned; avoid them. For such people do not serve our Lord Christ but their own appetites, and by fair and flattering speech they deceive the hearts of the innocent. For while your obedience is known to all, so that I rejoice over you, I want you to be wise as to what is good, and simple as to what is evil; then the God of

peace will quickly crush Satan under your feet. The grace of our Lord Jesus be with you.

Timothy, my co-worker, greets you; so do Lucius and Jason and Sosipater, my relatives. I, Tertius, the writer of this letter, greet you in the Lord. Gaius, who is host to me and to the whole church, greets you. Erastus, the city treasurer, and our brother Quartus greet you.

[Now to him who can strengthen you, according to my gospel and the proclamation of Jesus Christ, according to the revelation of the mystery kept secret for long ages but now manifested through the prophetic writings and, according to the command of the eternal God, made known to all nations to bring about the obedience of faith, to the only wise God, through Jesus Christ be glory forever and ever. Amen.]

PSALM 57:1-6

For the leader. (Do not destroy!) A miktam of David, when he fled away from Saul into the cave.
Have pity on me, O God; have pity on me,
    for in you I take refuge.
In the shadow of your wings I take refuge,
    till harm pass by.
I call to God the Most High,
    to God, my benefactor.
May he send from heaven and save me;
    may he make those a reproach who trample upon me;
    may God send his kindness and his faithfulness.
I lie prostrate in the midst of lions which devour men;

Their teeth are spears and arrows,	Be exalted above the heavens, O God;
their tongue is a sharp sword.	above all the earth be your glory!

PROVERBS 14:32-33

The wicked man is overthrown by his wickedness, / but the just man finds a refuge in his honesty. / In the heart of the intelligent wisdom abides, / but in the bosom of fools it is unknown.

MAY 10

1 CORINTHIANS 1:1-31

Paul, called to be an apostle of Christ Jesus by the will of God, and Sosthenes our brother, to the church of God that is in Corinth, to you who have been sanctified in Christ Jesus, called to be holy, with all those everywhere who call upon the name of our Lord Jesus Christ, their Lord and ours. Grace to you and peace from God our Father and the Lord Jesus Christ.

I give thanks to my God always on your account for the grace of God bestowed on you in Christ Jesus, that in him you were enriched in every way, with all discourse and all knowledge, as the testimony to Christ was confirmed among you, so that you are not lacking in any spiritual gift as you wait for the revelation of our Lord Jesus Christ. He will keep you firm to the end, irreproachable on the day of our Lord Jesus [Christ]. God is faithful, and by him you were called to fellowship with his Son, Jesus Christ our Lord.

I urge you, brothers, in the name of our Lord Jesus Christ, that all of you agree in what you say, and that there be no divisions among you, but that you be united in the same mind and in the same purpose. For it has been reported to

me about you, my brothers, by Chloe's people, that there are rivalries among you. I mean that each of you is saying, "I belong to Paul," or "I belong to Apollos," or "I belong to Kephas," or "I belong to Christ." Is Christ divided? Was Paul crucified for you? Or were you baptized in the name of Paul? I give thanks [to God] that I baptized none of you except Crispus and Gaius, so that no one can say you were baptized in my name. (I baptized the household of Stephanas also; beyond that I do not know whether I baptized anyone else.) For Christ did not send me to baptize but to preach the gospel, and not with the wisdom of human eloquence, so that the cross of Christ might not be emptied of its meaning.

The message of the cross is foolishness to those who are perishing, but to us who are being saved it is the power of God. For it is written:

"I will destroy the wisdom of the wise,
and the learning of the learned I will set aside."

Where is the wise one? Where is the scribe? Where is the debater of this age? Has not God made the wisdom of the world foolish? For since in the wisdom of God the world did not come to know God through wisdom, it was the will of God through the foolishness of the proclamation to save those who have faith. For Jews demand signs and Greeks look for wisdom, but we proclaim Christ crucified, a stumbling block to Jews and foolishness to Gentiles, but to those who are called, Jews and Greeks alike, Christ the power of God and the wisdom of God. For the foolishness of God is wiser than human wisdom, and the weakness of God is stronger than human strength.

Consider your own calling, brothers. Not many of you were wise by human standards, not many were powerful, not many were of noble birth. Rather, God chose the foolish of the world to shame the wise, and God chose the weak of the world to shame the strong, and God chose the lowly and despised of the world, those who count for nothing, to reduce to nothing those who are something, so that no human being might boast before God. It is due to him that you are in Christ Jesus, who became for us wisdom from God, as well as righteousness, sanctification, and redemption, so that, as it is written, "Whoever boasts, should boast in the Lord."

PSALM 57:7-12

They have prepared a net for my feet;
    they have bowed me down;
They have dug a pit before me,
    but they fall into it.
My heart is steadfast, O God; my heart is steadfast;
    I will sing and chant praise.
Awake, O my soul; awake, lyre and harp!
    I will wake the dawn.
I will give thanks to you among the peoples, O Lord,
    I will chant your praise among the nations,
For your kindness towers to the heavens,
    and your faithfulness to the skies.
Be exalted above the heavens, O God;
    above all the earth be your glory!

PROVERBS 14:34-35

Virtue exalts a nation, / but sin is a people's disgrace. / The king favors the intelligent servant, / but the worthless one incurs his wrath.

MAY 11

1 CORINTHIANS 2:1-16

When I came to you, brothers, proclaiming the mystery of God, I did not come with sublimity of words or of wisdom. For I resolved to know nothing while I was with you except Jesus Christ, and him crucified. I came to you in weakness and fear and much trembling, and my message and my proclamation were not with persuasive [words of] wisdom, but with a demonstration of spirit and power, so that your faith might rest not on human wisdom but on the power of God.

Yet we do speak a wisdom to those who are mature, but not a wisdom of this age, nor of the rulers of this age who are passing away. Rather, we speak God's wisdom, mysterious, hidden, which God predetermined before the ages for our glory and which none of the rulers of this age knew for, if they had known it, they would not have crucified the Lord of glory. But as it is written:

"What eye has not seen and ear has not heard,
and what has not entered the human heart,
what God has prepared for those who love him,"
this God has revealed to us through the Spirit.

For the Spirit scrutinizes everything, even the depths of God. Among human beings, who knows what pertains to a person except the spirit of the person that is within? Similarly, no one knows what pertains to God except the Spirit of God. We have not received the spirit of the world but the Spirit that is from God, so that we may understand the things freely given us by God. And we speak about them not with words taught by human wisdom, but with words taught by the Spirit, describing spiritual realities in spiritual terms.

Now the natural person does not accept what pertains to the Spirit of God, for to him it is foolishness, and he cannot understand it, because it is judged spiritually. The spiritual person, however, can judge everything but is not subject to judgment by anyone.

For "who has known the mind of the Lord, so as to counsel him?" But we have the mind of Christ.

PSALM 58:1-12

For the leader. (Do not destroy!) A miktam of David.

Do you indeed like gods
    pronounce justice
  and judge fairly, you men of
    rank?
Nay, you willingly commit
    crimes;
  on earth you look to the fruits
    of extortion.
From the womb the wicked are
    perverted;
  astray from birth have the liars
    gone.
Theirs is poison like a serpent's,
  like that of a stubborn snake
    that stops its ears,
That it may not hear the voice of
    enchanters
  casting cunning spells.
O God, smash their teeth in their
    mouths;
  the jaw-teeth of the lions,
    break, O LORD!
Let them vanish like water
    flowing off;
  when they draw the bow, let
    their arrows be headless
    shafts.
Let them dissolve like a melting
    snail,
  like an untimely birth that
    never sees the sun.
Unexpectedly, like a thorn-bush,
    or like thistles, let the
    whirlwind carry them away.
The just man shall be glad when
    he sees vengeance;

he shall bathe his feet in the
blood of the wicked.
And men shall say, "Truly there
is a reward for the just;

truly there is a God who is
judge on earth!"

PROVERBS 15:1-3

A mild answer calms wrath, / but a harsh word stirs up anger. / The tongue of the wise pours out knowledge, / but the mouth of fools spurts forth folly. / The eyes of the LORD are in every place, / keeping watch on the evil and the good.

MAY 12

1 CORINTHIANS 3:1-23

Brothers, I could not talk to you as spiritual people but as fleshly people, as infants in Christ. I fed you milk, not solid food, because you were unable to take it. Indeed, you are still not able, even now, for you are still of the flesh. While there is jealousy and rivalry among you, are you not of the flesh and behaving in an ordinary human way? Whenever someone says, "I belong to Paul," and another, "I belong to Apollos," are you not merely human?

What is Apollos, after all, and what is Paul? Ministers through whom you became believers, just as the Lord assigned each one. I planted, Apollos watered, but God caused the growth. Therefore, neither the one who plants nor the one who waters is anything, but only God, who causes the growth. The one who plants and the one who waters are equal, and each will receive wages in proportion to his labor. For we are God's co-workers; you are God's field, God's building.

According to the grace of God given to me, like a wise master builder I laid a foundation, and another is building upon it. But each one must be careful how he builds upon it, for no one can lay a foundation other than the one that is there, namely, Jesus Christ. If anyone builds on this foundation with gold, silver, precious stones, wood, hay, or straw, the work of each will come to light, for the Day will disclose it. It will be revealed with fire, and the fire [itself] will test the quality of each one's work. If the work stands that someone built upon the foundation, that person will receive a wage. But if someone's work is burned up, that one will suffer loss; the person will be saved, but only as through fire. Do you not know that you are the temple of God and that the Spirit of God dwells in you? If anyone destroys God's temple, God will destroy that person; for the temple of God, which you are, is holy.

Let no one deceive himself. If anyone among you considers himself wise in this age, let him become a fool so as to become wise. For the wisdom of this world is foolishness in the eyes of God, for it is written:

"He catches the wise in their
own ruses,"

and again:

"The Lord knows the thoughts
of the wise, that they are
vain."

So let no one boast about human beings, for everything belongs to you, Paul or Apollos or Kephas, or the world or life or death, or the present or the future: all belong to you, and you to Christ, and Christ to God.

PSALM 59:1-11

For the leader, (Do not destroy!) A miktam of David when Saul sent men to watch his house and put him to death.

Rescue me from my enemies, O my God;
from my adversaries defend me.
Rescue me from evildoers;
from bloodthirsty men save me.
For behold, they lie in wait for my life;
mighty men come together against me.
Not for any offense or sin of mine, O LORD;
for no guilt of mine they hurry to take up arms.
Rouse yourself to see it, and aid me,
for you are the LORD of hosts, the God of Israel.
Arise; punish all the nations;
have no pity on any worthless traitors.
Each evening they return, they snarl like dogs
and prowl about the city.
Though they bay with their mouths,
and blasphemies are on their lips—
"Who is there to listen?"—
You, O LORD, laugh at them;
you deride all the nations.
O my strength! for you I watch;
for you, O God, are my stronghold,
my gracious God!
May God come to my aid;
may he show me the fall of my foes.

PROVERBS 15:4

A soothing tongue is a tree of life, / but a perverse one crushes the spirit.

MAY 13

1 CORINTHIANS 4:1-21

Thus should one regard us: as servants of Christ and stewards of the mysteries of God. Now it is of course required of stewards that they be found trustworthy. It does not concern me in the least that I be judged by you or any human tribunal; I do not even pass judgment on myself; I am not conscious of anything against me, but I do not thereby stand acquitted; the one who judges me is the Lord. Therefore, do not make any judgment before the appointed time, until the Lord comes, for he will bring to light what is hidden in darkness and will manifest the motives of our hearts, and then everyone will receive praise from God.

I have applied these things to myself and Apollos for your benefit, brothers, so that you may learn from us not to go beyond what is written, so that none of you will be inflated with pride in favor of one person over against another. Who confers distinction upon you? What do you possess that you have not received? But if you have received it, why are you boasting as if you did not receive it? You are already satisfied; you have already grown rich; you have become kings without us! Indeed, I wish that you had become kings, so that we also might become kings with you.

For as I see it, God has exhibited us apostles as the last of all, like people sentenced to death, since we have become a spectacle to the world, to angels and human beings alike. We are fools on Christ's account, but you are wise in Christ; we are weak, but you are strong; you are held in honor, but we in disrepute. To this very hour we go hungry and thirsty, we are poorly clad and roughly treated, we wander about homeless and we toil, working with our own hands. When ridiculed, we bless; when persecuted, we endure; when slandered, we respond gently. We have become like the world's rubbish, the scum of all, to this very moment.

I am writing you this not to shame you, but to admonish you as my beloved children. Even if you should have countless guides to Christ, yet you do not have many fathers, for I became your father in Christ Jesus through the gospel. Therefore, I urge you, be imitators of me. For this reason I am sending you Timothy, who is my beloved and faithful son in the Lord; he will remind you of my ways in Christ [Jesus], just as I teach them everywhere in every church.

Some have become inflated with pride, as if I were not coming to you. But I will come to you soon, if the Lord is willing, and I shall ascertain not the talk of these inflated people but their power. For the kingdom of God is not a matter of talk but of power. Which do you prefer? Shall I come to you with a rod, or with love and a gentle spirit?

PSALM 59:12-18

O God, slay them, lest they
    beguile my people;
  shake them by your power,
    and bring them down,
  O Lord our shield!
By the sin of their mouths and
    the word of their lips
  let them be caught in their
    arrogance,
  for the lies they have told
    under oath.
Consume them in wrath;
    consume, till they are no
    more;
  that men may know that God
    is the ruler of Jacob,
  yes, to the ends of the earth.
  Each evening they return, they
    snarl like dogs
  and prowl about the city;
They wander about as
    scavengers;
  if they are not filled, they howl.
But I will sing of your strength
  and revel at dawn in your
    kindness;
You have been my stronghold,
  my refuge in the day of
    distress.
  O my strength! your praise will
    I sing;
  for you, O God, are my
    stronghold,
    my gracious God!

PROVERBS 15:5-7

The fool spurns his father's admonition, / but prudent is he who heeds reproof. / In the house of the just there are ample resources, / but the earnings of the wicked are in turmoil. / The lips of the wise disseminate knowledge, / but the heart of fools is perverted.

MAY 14

1 CORINTHIANS 5:1-13

It is widely reported that there is immorality among you, and immorality of a kind not found even among pagans—a man living with his father's wife. And you are inflated with pride. Should you not rather have been sorrowful? The one who did this deed should be expelled from your midst. I, for my part, although absent in body but present in spirit, have already, as if present, pronounced judgment on the one who has committed this deed, in the name of [our] Lord Jesus: when you have gathered together and I am with you in spirit with the power of the Lord Jesus, you are to deliver this man to Satan for the destruction of his flesh, so that his spirit may be saved on the day of the Lord.

Your boasting is not appropriate. Do you not know that a little yeast leavens all the dough? Clear out the old yeast, so that you may become a fresh batch of dough, inasmuch as you are unleavened. For our paschal lamb, Christ, has been sacrificed. Therefore, let us celebrate the feast, not with the old yeast, the yeast of malice and wickedness, but with the unleavened bread of sincerity and truth.

I wrote you in my letter not to associate with immoral people, not at all referring to the immoral of this world or the greedy and robbers or idolaters; for you would then have to leave the world. But I now write to you not to associate with anyone named a brother, if he is immoral, greedy, an idolater, a slanderer, a drunkard, or a robber, not even to eat with such a person. For why should I be judging outsiders? Is it not your business to judge those within? God will judge those outside. "Purge the evil person from your midst."

PSALM 60:1-14

For the leader; according to "The Lily of . . . " A miktam of David (for teaching) when he fought against Aram Naharaim and Aramzobah; and Joab, coming back, killed twelve thousand Edomites in the "valley of salt."

O God, you have rejected us and broken our defenses;
　you have been angry; rally us!
You have rocked the country and split it open;
　repair the cracks in it, for it is tottering.
You have made your people feel hardships;
　you have given us stupefying wine.
You have raised for those who fear you a banner

to which they may flee out of
bowshot
That your loved ones may escape;
help us by your right hand,
and answer us!
God promised in his sanctuary:
"Exultantly I will apportion
Shechem,
and measure off the valley of
Succoth.
Mine is Gilead, and mine
Manasseh;
Ephraim is the helmet for my
head; Judah, my scepter;
Moab shall serve as my
washbowl;

upon Edom I will set my shoe;
I will triumph over Philistia."
Who will bring me into the
fortified city?
Who will lead me into Edom?
Have not you, O God, rejected
us,
so that you go not forth, O
God, with our armies?
Give us aid against the foe,
for worthless is the help of
men.
Under God we shall do valiantly;
it is he who will tread down
our foes.

PROVERBS 15:8-10

*The sacrifice of the wicked is an abomination to the LORD, / but the prayer of the
upright is his delight. / The way of the wicked is an abomination to the LORD, /
but he loves the man who pursues virtue. / Severe punishment is in store for the
man who goes astray; / he who hates reproof will die.*

MAY 15

1 CORINTHIANS 6:1-20

How can any one of you with
a case against another dare to
bring it to the unjust for judgment instead of to the holy
ones? Do you not know that the
holy ones will judge the world?
If the world is to be judged by
you, are you unqualified for the
lowest law courts? Do you not
know that we will judge angels?
Then why not everyday matters?
If, therefore, you have courts for
everyday matters, do you seat as
judges people of no standing in
the church? I say this to shame
you. Can it be that there is not
one among you wise enough to
be able to settle a case between
brothers? But rather brother goes

to court against brother, and that
before unbelievers?

Now indeed [then] it is, in any
case, a failure on your part that
you have lawsuits against one another. Why not rather put up with
injustice? Why not rather let yourselves be cheated? Instead, you inflict injustice and cheat, and this
to brothers. Do you not know that
the unjust will not inherit the kingdom of God? Do not be deceived;
neither fornicators nor idolaters
nor adulterers nor boy prostitutes
nor practicing homosexuals nor
thieves nor the greedy nor drunkards nor slanderers nor robbers
will inherit the kingdom of God.
That is what some of you used to
be; but now you have had yourselves washed, you were sancti-

fied, you were justified in the name of the Lord Jesus Christ and in the Spirit of our God.

"Everything is lawful for me," but not everything is beneficial. "Everything is lawful for me," but I will not let myself be dominated by anything. "Food for the stomach and the stomach for food," but God will do away with both the one and the other. The body, however, is not for immorality but for the Lord, and the Lord is for the body; God raised the Lord and will also raise us by his power.

Do you not know that your bodies are members of Christ? Shall I then take Christ's members and make them the members of a prostitute? Of course not! [Or] do you not know that anyone who joins himself to a prostitute becomes one body with her? For "the two," it says, "will become one flesh." But whoever is joined to the Lord becomes one spirit with him. Avoid immorality. Every other sin a person commits is outside the body, but the immoral person sins against his own body. Do you not know that your body is a temple of the holy Spirit within you, whom you have from God, and that you are not your own? For you have been purchased at a price. Therefore, glorify God in your body.

PSALM 61:1-9

For the leader; with stringed instruments. Of David.

Hear, O God, my cry;
   listen to my prayer!
From the earth's end I call to you
   as my heart grows faint.
You will set me high upon a rock;
   you will give me rest,
   for you are my refuge,
   a tower of strength against the
   enemy.
Oh, that I might lodge in your
   tent forever,
   take refuge in the shelter of
   your wings!
You indeed, O God, have
   accepted my vows;
   you granted me the heritage of
   those who fear your name.
Add to the days of the king's life;
   let his years be many
   generations;
Let him sit enthroned before God
   forever;
   bid kindness and faithfulness
   preserve him.
So will I sing the praises of your
   name forever,
   fulfilling my vows day by day.

PROVERBS 15:11

The nether world and the abyss lie open before the LORD; / how much more the hearts of men!

MAY 16

1 CORINTHIANS 7:1-16

Now in regard to the matters about which you wrote: "It is a good thing for a man not to touch a woman," but because of cases of immorality every man should have his own wife, and every woman her own husband. The husband should fulfill his duty toward his wife, and likewise the wife toward her husband. A wife does not have authority over her own body, but rather her husband, and similarly a husband does not have authority over his own body, but rather his wife. Do not deprive each other, except perhaps by mutual consent for a time, to be free for prayer, but then return to one another, so that Satan may not tempt you through your lack of self-control. This I say by way of concession, however, not as a command. Indeed, I wish everyone to be as I am, but each has a particular gift from God, one of one kind and one of another.

Now to the unmarried and to widows I say: it is a good thing for them to remain as they are, as I do, but if they cannot exercise self-control they should marry, for it is better to marry than to be on fire. To the married, however, I give this instruction (not I, but the Lord): a wife should not separate from her husband—and if she does separate she must either remain single or become reconciled to her husband—and a husband should not divorce his wife.

To the rest I say (not the Lord): if any brother has a wife who is an unbeliever, and she is willing to go on living with him, he should not divorce her; and if any woman has a husband who is an unbeliever, and he is willing to go on living with her, she should not divorce her husband. For the unbelieving husband is made holy through his wife, and the unbelieving wife is made holy through the brother. Otherwise your children would be unclean, whereas in fact they are holy.

If the unbeliever separates, however, let him separate. The brother or sister is not bound in such cases; God has called you to peace. For how do you know, wife, whether you will save your husband; or how do you know, husband, whether you will save your wife?

PSALM 62:1-5

For the leader; 'al Jeduthun. A psalm of David.

Only in God is my soul at rest;
from him comes my salvation.
He only is my rock and my salvation,
my stronghold; I shall not be disturbed at all.
How long will you set upon a man and all together beat him down
as though he were a sagging fence, a battered wall?
Truly from my place on high they plan to dislodge me;
they delight in lies;
They bless with their mouths,
but inwardly they curse.

PROVERBS 15:12-14

The senseless man loves not to be reproved; / to wise men he will not go. / A glad heart lights up the face, / but by mental anguish the spirit is broken. / The mind of the intelligent man seeks knowledge, / but the mouth of fools feeds on folly.

MAY 17

1 CORINTHIANS 7:17-40

Only, everyone should live as the Lord has assigned, just as God called each one. I give this order in all the churches. Was someone called after he had been circumcised? He should not try to undo his circumcision. Was an uncircumcised person called? He should not be circumcised. Circumcision means nothing, and uncircumcision means nothing; what matters is keeping God's commandments. Everyone should remain in the state in which he was called.

Were you a slave when you were called? Do not be concerned but, even if you can gain your freedom, make the most of it. For the slave called in the Lord is a freed person in the Lord, just as the free person who has been called is a slave of Christ. You have been purchased at a price. Do not become slaves to human beings. Brothers, everyone should continue before God in the state in which he was called.

Now in regard to virgins I have no commandment from the Lord, but I give my opinion as one who by the Lord's mercy is trustworthy. So this is what I think best because of the present distress: that it is a good thing for a person to remain as he is. Are you bound to a wife? Do not seek a separation. Are you free of a wife? Then do not look for a wife. If you marry, however, you do not sin, nor does an unmarried woman sin if she marries; but such people will experience affliction in their earthly life, and I would like to spare you that.

I tell you, brothers, the time is running out. From now on, let those having wives act as not having them, those weeping as not weeping, those rejoicing as not rejoicing, those buying as not owning, those using the world as not using it fully. For the world in its present form is passing away.

I should like you to be free of anxieties. An unmarried man is anxious about the things of the Lord, how he may please the Lord. But a married man is anxious about the things of the world, how he may please his wife, and he is divided. An unmarried woman or a virgin is anxious about the things of the Lord, so that she may be holy in both body and spirit. A married woman, on the other hand, is anxious about the things of the world, how she may please her husband. I am telling you this for your own benefit, not to impose a restraint upon you, but for the sake of propriety and adherence to the Lord without distraction.

If anyone thinks he is behaving improperly toward his virgin, and if a critical moment has come and so it has to be, let him do as he wishes. He is committing no sin; let them get married. The one who stands firm in his resolve, however, who is not under compulsion but has power over his own will, and has made up his mind to keep his virgin, will be doing well. So then, the one who marries his virgin does well; the one who does not marry her will do better.

A wife is bound to her husband as long as he lives. But if her husband dies, she is free to be married to whomever she wishes, provided that it be in the Lord. She is more blessed, though, in my opinion, if she remains as she is, and I think that I too have the Spirit of God.

PSALM 62:6-9

Only in God be at rest, my
  soul,
for from him comes my hope.
He only is my rock and my
  salvation,
my stronghold; I shall not be
  disturbed.
With God is my safety and my
  glory,
he is the rock of my strength;
  my refuge is in God.
Trust in him at all times, O my
  people!
Pour out your hearts before
  him;
God is our refuge!

PROVERBS 15:15-17

Every day is miserable for the depressed, / but a lighthearted man has a continual feast. / Better a little with fear of the LORD / than a great fortune with anxiety. / Better a dish of herbs where love is / than a fatted ox and hatred with it.

MAY 18

1 CORINTHIANS 8:1-13

Now in regard to meat sacrificed to idols: we realize that "all of us have knowledge"; knowledge inflates with pride, but love builds up. If anyone supposes he knows something, he does not yet know as he ought to know. But if one loves God, one is known by him.

So about the eating of meat sacrificed to idols: we know that "there is no idol in the world," and that "there is no God but one." Indeed, even though there are so-called gods in heaven and on earth (there are, to be sure, many "gods" and many "lords"), yet for us there is

one God, the Father,
  from whom all things are
    and for whom we exist,
and one Lord, Jesus Christ,
through whom all things are
  and through whom we
  exist.

But not all have this knowledge. There are some who have been so used to idolatry up until now that, when they eat meat sacrificed to idols, their conscience, which is weak, is defiled.

Now food will not bring us closer to God. We are no worse off if we do not eat, nor are we better off if we do. But make sure that this liberty of yours in no way becomes a stumbling block to the weak. If someone sees you, with your knowledge, reclining at table in the temple of an idol, may not his conscience too, weak as it is, be "built up" to eat the meat sacrificed to idols? Thus through your knowledge, the weak person is brought to destruction, the brother for whom Christ died. When you sin in this way against your brothers and wound their consciences, weak as they are, you are sinning against Christ. Therefore, if food causes my brother to sin, I will never eat meat again, so that I may not cause my brother to sin.

PSALM 62:10-12

Only a breath are mortal men;
  an illusion are men of rank;
In a balance they prove lighter,
  all together, than a breath.
Trust not in extortion; in plunder
  take no empty pride;
  though wealth abound, set not
  your heart upon it.
One thing God said; these two
  things which I heard:
  that power belongs to God,
  and yours, O LORD, is
  kindness;
  and that you render to
  everyone according to his
  deeds.

PROVERBS 15:18-19

An ill-tempered man stirs up strife, / but a patient man allays discord. / The way of the sluggard is hemmed in as with thorns, / but the path of the diligent is a highway.

MAY 19

1 CORINTHIANS 9:1-27

Am I not free? Am I not an apostle? Have I not seen Jesus our Lord? Are you not my work in the Lord? Although I may not be an apostle for others, certainly I am for you, for you are the seal of my apostleship in the Lord.

My defense against those who would pass judgment on me is this. Do we not have the right to eat and drink? Do we not have the right to take along a Christian wife, as do the rest of the apostles, and the brothers of the Lord, and Kephas? Or is it only myself and Barnabas who do not have the right not to work? Who ever serves as a soldier at his own expense? Who plants a vineyard without eating its produce? Or who shepherds a flock without using some of the milk from the flock? Am I saying this on human authority, or does not the law also speak of these things? It is written in the law of Moses, "You shall not muzzle an ox while it is treading out the grain." Is God concerned about oxen, or is he not really speaking for our sake? It was written for our sake, because the plowman should plow in hope, and the thresher in hope of receiving a share. If we have sown spiritual seed for you, is it a great thing that we reap a material harvest from you? If others share this rightful claim on you, do not we still more?

Yet we have not used this right. On the contrary, we endure everything so as not to place an obstacle to the gospel of Christ. Do you not know that those who perform the temple services eat [what] belongs to the temple, and those who minister at the altar share in the sacrificial offerings? In the same way, the Lord ordered that those who preach the gospel should live by the gospel.

I have not used any of these rights, however, nor do I write this that it be done so in my case. I would rather die. Certainly no one is going to nullify my boast. If I preach the gospel, this is no reason for me to boast, for an obligation has been imposed on me, and woe to me if I do not preach it! If I do so willingly, I have a recompense, but if unwillingly, then I have been entrusted with a stewardship. What then is my recompense? That, when I preach, I offer the gospel free of charge so as not to make full use of my right in the gospel.

Although I am free in regard to all, I have made myself a slave to all so as to win over as many as possible. To the Jews I became like a Jew to win over Jews; to those under the law I became like one under the law—though I myself am not under the law—to win over those under the law. To those outside the law I became like one outside the law—though I am not outside God's law but within the law of Christ—to win over those outside the law. To the weak I became weak, to win over the weak. I have become all things to all, to save at least some. All this I do for the sake of the gospel, so that I too may have a share in it.

Do you not know that the runners in the stadium all run in the race, but only one wins the prize? Run so as to win. Every athlete exercises discipline in every way. They do it to win a perishable crown, but we an imperishable one. Thus I do not run aimlessly; I do not fight as if I were shadow-boxing. No, I drive my body and train it, for fear that, after having preached to others, I myself should be disqualified.

PSALM 63:1-4

A psalm of David, when he was in the wilderness of Judah.

O God, you are my God whom I seek;
  for you my flesh pines and my soul thirsts
  like the earth, parched, lifeless and without water.
Thus have I gazed toward you in the sanctuary
  to see your power and your glory,
For your kindness is a greater good than life;
  my lips shall glorify you.

PROVERBS 15:20-21

A wise son makes his father glad, / but a fool of a man despises his mother. / Folly is joy to the senseless man, / but the man of understanding goes the straight way.

MAY 20

1 CORINTHIANS 10:1-13

I do not want you to be unaware, brothers, that our ancestors were all under the cloud and all passed through the sea, and all of them were baptized into Moses in the cloud and in the sea. All ate the same spiritual food, and all drank the same spiritual drink, for they drank from a spiritual rock that followed them, and the rock was the Christ. Yet God was not pleased with most of them, for they were struck down in the desert.

These things happened as examples for us, so that we might not desire evil things, as they did. And do not become idolaters, as some of them did, as it is written, "The people sat down to eat and drink, and rose up to revel." Let us not indulge in immorality as some of them did, and twenty-three thousand fell within a single day. Let us not test Christ as some of them did, and suffered death by serpents. Do not grumble as some of them did, and suffered death by the destroyer. These things happened to them as an example, and they have been written down as a warning to us, upon whom the end of the ages has come. Therefore, whoever thinks he is standing secure should take care not to fall. No trial has come to you but what is human. God is faithful and will not let you be tried beyond your strength; but with the trial he will also provide a way out, so that you may be able to bear it.

PSALM 63:5-12

Thus will I bless you while I live;
lifting up my hands, I will call
upon your name.
As with the riches of a banquet
shall my soul be satisfied,
and with exultant lips my
mouth shall praise you.
I will remember you upon my
couch,
and through the night-watches
I will meditate on you:
That you are my help,
and in the shadow of your
wings I shout for joy.
My soul clings fast to you;
your right hand upholds me.
But they shall be destroyed who
seek my life,
they shall go into the depths of
the earth;
They shall be delivered over to
the sword,
and shall be the prey of jackals.
The king, however, shall rejoice
in God;
everyone who swears by him
shall glory,
but the mouths of those who
speak falsely shall be
stopped.

PROVERBS 15:22-23

Plans fail when there is no counsel, / but they succeed when counselors are many. / There is joy for a man in his utterance; / a word in season, how good it is!

1 CORINTHIANS 10:14-33; 11:1

Therefore, my beloved, avoid idolatry. I am speaking as to sensible people; judge for yourselves what I am saying. The cup of blessing that we bless, is it not a participation in the blood of Christ? The bread that we break, is it not a participation in the body of Christ? Because the loaf of bread is one, we, though many, are one body, for we all partake of the one loaf.

Look at Israel according to the flesh; are not those who eat the sacrifices participants in the altar? So what am I saying? That meat sacrificed to idols is anything? Or that an idol is anything? No, I mean that what they sacrifice, [they sacrifice] to demons, not to God, and I do not want you to become participants with demons. You cannot drink the cup of the Lord and also the cup of demons. You cannot partake of the table of the Lord and of the table of demons. Or are we provoking the Lord to jealous anger? Are we stronger than he?

"Everything is lawful," but not everything is beneficial. "Everything is lawful," but not everything builds up. No one should seek his own advantage, but that of his neighbor. Eat anything sold in the market, without raising questions on grounds of conscience, for "the earth and its fullness are the Lord's." If an unbeliever invites you and you want to go, eat whatever is placed before you, without raising questions on grounds of conscience. But if someone says to you, "This was offered in sacrifice," do not eat it on account of the one who called attention to it and on account of conscience; I mean not your own conscience, but the other's. For why should my freedom be determined by someone else's conscience? If I partake thankfully, why am I reviled for that over which I give thanks?

So whether you eat or drink, or whatever you do, do everything for the glory of God. Avoid giving offense, whether to Jews or Greeks or the church of God, just as I try to please everyone in every way, not seeking my own benefit but that of the many, that they may be saved.

Be imitators of me, as I am of Christ.

PSALM 64:1-11

For the leader. A psalm of David.

Hear, O God, my voice in my
  lament;
    from the dread enemy preserve
    my life.
Shelter me against the council of
  malefactors,
    against the tumult of evildoers,
Who sharpen their tongues like
  swords,
    who aim like arrows their bitter
    words,
Shooting from ambush at the
  innocent man,
    suddenly shooting at him
    without fear.
They resolve on their wicked
  plan;
    they conspire to set snares,
    saying, "Who will see us?"
They devise a wicked scheme,
  and conceal the scheme they
  have devised;
    deep are the thoughts of each
    heart.

But God shoots his arrows at
  them;
  suddenly they are struck.
He brings them down by their
  own tongues;
  all who see them nod their
  heads.

And all men fear and proclaim
  the work of God,
  and ponder what he has done.
The just man is glad in the LORD
  and takes refuge in him;
  in him glory all the upright of
  heart.

PROVERBS 15:24-26

The path of life leads the prudent man upward, / that he may avoid the nether world below. / The LORD overturns the house of the proud, / but he preserves intact the widow's landmark. / The wicked man's schemes are an abomination to the LORD, / but the pure speak what is pleasing to him.

MAY 22

1 CORINTHIANS 11:2-16

I praise you because you remember me in everything and hold fast to the traditions, just as I handed them on to you.

But I want you to know that Christ is the head of every man, and a husband the head of his wife, and God the head of Christ. Any man who prays or prophesies with his head covered brings shame upon his head. But any woman who prays or prophesies with her head unveiled brings shame upon her head, for it is one and the same thing as if she had had her head shaved. For if a woman does not have her head veiled, she may as well have her hair cut off. But if it is shameful for a woman to have her hair cut off or her head shaved, then she should wear a veil.

A man, on the other hand, should not cover his head, because he is the image and glory of God, but woman is the glory of man. For man did not come from woman, but woman from man; nor was man created for woman,

but woman for man; for this reason a woman should have a sign of authority on her head, because of the angels. Woman is not independent of man or man of woman in the Lord. For just as woman came from man, so man is born of woman; but all things are from God.

Judge for yourselves: is it proper for a woman to pray to God with her head unveiled? Does not nature itself teach you that if a man wears his hair long it is a disgrace to him, whereas if a woman has long hair it is her glory, because long hair has been given [her] for a covering? But if anyone is inclined to be argumentative, we do not have such a custom, nor do the churches of God.

PSALM 65:1-5

For the leader. A psalm of David. A song.
To you we owe our hymn of
  praise,
  O God, in Zion;
To you must vows be fulfilled,

you who hear prayers.
To you all flesh must come
  because of wicked deeds.
We are overcome by our sins;
  it is you who pardon them.
Happy the man you choose,

and bring to dwell in your
  courts.
May we be filled with the good
  things of your house,
  the holy things of your temple!

PROVERBS 15:27-28

He who is greedy of gain brings ruin on his own house, / but he who hates bribes will live. / The just man weighs well his utterance, / but the mouth of the wicked pours out evil.

MAY 23

1 CORINTHIANS 11:17-34

In giving this instruction, I do not praise the fact that your meetings are doing more harm than good. First of all, I hear that when you meet as a church there are divisions among you, and to a degree I believe it; there have to be factions among you in order that [also] those who are approved among you may become known. When you meet in one place, then, it is not to eat the Lord's supper, for in eating, each one goes ahead with his own supper, and one goes hungry while another gets drunk. Do you not have houses in which you can eat and drink? Or do you show contempt for the church of God and make those who have nothing feel ashamed? What can I say to you? Shall I praise you? In this matter I do not praise you.

For I received from the Lord what I also handed on to you, that the Lord Jesus, on the night he was handed over, took bread and, after he had given thanks, broke it and said, "This is my body that is for you. Do this in remembrance of me." In the same way also the cup, after supper, saying, "This cup is the new covenant in my blood. Do this, as often as you drink it, in remembrance of me." For as often as you eat this bread and drink the cup, you proclaim the death of the Lord until he comes.

Therefore, whoever eats the bread or drinks the cup of the Lord unworthily will have to answer for the body and blood of the Lord. A person should examine himself, and so eat the bread and drink the cup. For anyone who eats and drinks without discerning the body, eats and drinks judgment on himself. That is why many among you are ill and infirm, and a considerable number are dying. If we discerned ourselves, we would not be under judgment; but since we are judged by [the] Lord, we are being disciplined so that we may not be condemned along with the world.

Therefore, my brothers, when you come together to eat, wait for one another. If anyone is hungry, he should eat at home, so that your meetings may not result in judgment. The other matters I shall set in order when I come.

PSALM 65:6-9

With awe-inspiring deeds of
   justice you answer us,
   O God our savior,
The hope of all the ends of the
      earth
   and of the distant seas.

You set the mountains in place
      by your power,
   you who are girt with might;
You still the roaring of the seas,
   the roaring of their waves and
      the tumult of the peoples.
And the dwellers at the earth's
      ends are in fear at your
      marvels;
   the farthest east and west you
      make resound with joy.

PROVERBS 15:29-30

The LORD is far from the wicked, / but the prayer of the just he hears. / A cheerful glance brings joy to the heart; / good news invigorates the bones.

MAY 24

1 CORINTHIANS 12:1-11

Now in regard to spiritual gifts, brothers, I do not want you to be unaware. You know how, when you were pagans, you were constantly attracted and led away to mute idols. Therefore, I tell you that nobody speaking by the spirit of God says, "Jesus be accursed." And no one can say, "Jesus is Lord," except by the holy Spirit.

There are different kinds of spiritual gifts but the same Spirit; there are different forms of service but the same Lord; there are different workings but the same God who produces all of them in everyone. To each individual the manifestation of the Spirit is given for some benefit. To one is given through the Spirit the expression of wisdom; to another the expression of knowledge according to the same Spirit; to another faith by the same Spirit; to another gifts of healing by the one Spirit; to another mighty deeds; to another

prophecy; to another discernment of spirits; to another varieties of tongues; to another interpretation of tongues. But one and the same Spirit produces all of these, distributing them individually to each person as he wishes.

PSALM 65:10-14

You have visited the land and
      watered it;
   greatly have you enriched it.
God's watercourses are filled;
   you have prepared the grain.
Thus have you prepared the land:
      drenching its furrows,
   breaking up its clods,
Softening it with showers,
   blessing its yield.
You have crowned the year with
      your bounty,
   and your paths overflow with a
      rich harvest;
The untilled meadows overflow
      with it,

and rejoicing clothes the hills.
The fields are garmented with
    flocks

and the valleys blanketed with
    grain.
They shout and sing for joy.

PROVERBS 15:31-32

He who listens to salutary reproof / will abide among the wise. / He who rejects admonition despises his own soul, / but he who heeds reproof gains understanding.

MAY 25

1 CORINTHIANS 12:12-31

As a body is one though it has many parts, and all the parts of the body, though many, are one body, so also Christ. For in one Spirit we were all baptized into one body, whether Jews or Greeks, slaves or free persons, and we were all given to drink of one Spirit.

Now the body is not a single part, but many. If a foot should say, "Because I am not a hand I do not belong to the body," it does not for this reason belong any less to the body. Or if an ear should say, "Because I am not an eye I do not belong to the body," it does not for this reason belong any less to the body. If the whole body were an eye, where would the hearing be? If the whole body were hearing, where would the sense of smell be? But as it is, God placed the parts, each one of them, in the body as he intended. If they were all one part, where would the body be? But as it is, there are many parts, yet one body. The eye cannot say to the hand, "I do not need you," nor again the head to the feet, "I do not need you." Indeed, the parts of the body that seem to be weaker are all the more necessary, and those parts of the body that we consider less honorable we surround with greater honor, and our less presentable parts are treated with greater propriety, whereas our more presentable parts do not need this. But God has so constructed the body as to give greater honor to a part that is without it, so that there may be no division in the body, but that the parts may have the same concern for one another. If [one] part suffers, all the parts suffer with it; if one part is honored, all the parts share its joy.

Now you are Christ's body, and individually parts of it. Some people God has designated in the church to be, first, apostles; second, prophets; third, teachers; then, mighty deeds; then, gifts of healing, assistance, administration, and varieties of tongues. Are all apostles? Are all prophets? Are all teachers? Do all work mighty deeds? Do all have gifts of healing? Do all speak in tongues? Do all interpret? Strive eagerly for the greatest spiritual gifts.

But I shall show you a still more excellent way.

PSALM 66:1-4

For the leader. A psalm; a song.

Shout joyfully to God, all you on
    earth,
    sing praise to the glory of his
    name;
    proclaim his glorious praise.
Say to God, "How tremendous
    are your deeds!

for your great strength your
    enemies fawn upon you.
Let all on earth worship and sing
    praise to you,
    sing praise to your name!"

PROVERBS 15:33

The fear of the LORD is training for wisdom, / and humility goes before honors.

MAY 26

1 CORINTHIANS 13:1-13

If I speak in human and angelic tongues but do not have love, I am a resounding gong or a clashing cymbal. And if I have the gift of prophecy and comprehend all mysteries and all knowledge; if I have all faith so as to move mountains but do not have love, I am nothing. If I give away everything I own, and if I hand my body over so that I may boast but do not have love, I gain nothing.

Love is patient, love is kind. It is not jealous, [love] is not pompous, it is not inflated, it is not rude, it does not seek its own interests, it is not quick-tempered, it does not brood over injury, it does not rejoice over wrongdoing but rejoices with the truth. It bears all things, believes all things, hopes all things, endures all things.

Love never fails. If there are prophecies, they will be brought to nothing; if tongues, they will cease; if knowledge, it will be brought to nothing. For we know

partially and we prophesy partially, but when the perfect comes, the partial will pass away. When I was a child, I used to talk as a child, think as a child, reason as a child; when I became a man, I put aside childish things. At present we see indistinctly, as in a mirror, but then face to face. At present I know partially; then I shall know fully, as I am fully known. So faith, hope, love remain, these three; but the greatest of these is love.

PSALM 66:5-7

Come and see the works of God,
    his tremendous deeds among
    men.
He has changed the sea into dry
    land;
    through the river they passed
    on foot;
    therefore let us rejoice in him.
He rules by his might forever;
    his eyes watch the nations;
    rebels may not exalt
    themselves.

Man may make plans in his heart, / but what the tongue utters is from the LORD. / All the ways of a man may be pure in his own eyes, / but it is the LORD who proves the spirit. / Entrust your works to the LORD, / and your plans will succeed.

MAY 27

---

1 CORINTHIANS 14:1-19

Pursue love, but strive eagerly for the spiritual gifts, above all that you may prophesy. For one who speaks in a tongue does not speak to human beings but to God, for no one listens; he utters mysteries in spirit. On the other hand, one who prophesies does speak to human beings, for their building up, encouragement, and solace. Whoever speaks in a tongue builds himself up, but whoever prophesies builds up the church. Now I should like all of you to speak in tongues, but even more to prophesy. One who prophesies is greater than one who speaks in tongues, unless he interprets, so that the church may be built up.

Now, brothers, if I should come to you speaking in tongues, what good will I do you if I do not speak to you by way of revelation, or knowledge, or prophecy, or instruction? Likewise, if inanimate things that produce sound, such as flute or harp, do not give out the tones distinctly, how will what is being played on flute or harp be recognized? And if the bugle gives an indistinct sound, who will get ready for battle? Similarly, if you, because of speaking in tongues, do not utter intelligible speech, how will any-one know what is being said? For you will be talking to the air. It happens that there are many different languages in the world, and none is meaningless; but if I do not know the meaning of a language, I shall be a foreigner to one who speaks it, and one who speaks it a foreigner to me. So with yourselves: since you strive eagerly for spirits, seek to have an abundance of them for building up the church.

Therefore, one who speaks in a tongue should pray to be able to interpret. [For] if I pray in a tongue, my spirit is at prayer but my mind is unproductive. So what is to be done? I will pray with the spirit, but I will also pray with the mind. I will sing praise with the spirit, but I will also sing praise with the mind. Otherwise, if you pronounce a blessing [with] the spirit, how shall one who holds the place of the uninstructed say the "Amen" to your thanksgiving, since he does not know what you are saying? For you may be giving thanks very well, but the other is not built up. I give thanks to God that I speak in tongues more than any of you, but in the church I would rather speak five words with my mind, so as to instruct others also, than ten thousand words in a tongue.

PSALM 66:8-12

Bless our God, you peoples,
   loudly sound his praise;
He has given life to our souls,
   and has not let our feet slip.
For you have tested us, O God!
   You have tried us as silver is
   tried by fire;

You have brought us into a snare;
   you laid a heavy burden on our
   backs.
You let men ride over our heads;
   we went through fire and
   water,
   but you have led us out to
   refreshment.

PROVERBS 16:4-5

*The LORD has made everything for his ends, / even the wicked for the evil day. /
Every proud man is an abomination to the LORD; / I assure you that he will not
go unpunished.*

MAY 28

1 CORINTHIANS 14:20-40

Brothers, stop being childish in
your thinking. In respect to evil be
like infants, but in your thinking
be mature. It is written in the law:

"By people speaking strange
      tongues
   and by the lips of foreigners
I will speak to this people,
   and even so they will not
      listen to me,

says the Lord." Thus, tongues are
a sign not for those who believe
but for unbelievers, whereas
prophecy is not for unbelievers
but for those who believe.

So if the whole church meets in
one place and everyone speaks in
tongues, and then uninstructed
people or unbelievers should
come in, will they not say that you
are out of your minds? But if
everyone is prophesying, and an
unbeliever or uninstructed person
should come in, he will be convinced by everyone and judged
by everyone, and the secrets of

his heart will be disclosed, and so
he will fall down and worship
God, declaring, "God is really in
your midst."

So what is to be done, brothers?
When you assemble, one has a
psalm, another an instruction, a
revelation, a tongue, or an interpretation. Everything should be
done for building up. If anyone
speaks in a tongue, let it be two or
at most three, and each in turn,
and one should interpret. But if
there is no interpreter, the person
should keep silent in the church
and speak to himself and to God.

Two or three prophets should
speak, and the others discern. But
if a revelation is given to another
person sitting there, the first one
should be silent. For you can all
prophesy one by one, so that all
may learn and all be encouraged.
Indeed, the spirits of prophets are
under the prophets' control, since
he is not the God of disorder but
of peace.

As in all the churches of the
holy ones, women should keep si-

lent in the churches, for they are not allowed to speak, but should be subordinate, as even the law says. But if they want to learn anything, they should ask their husbands at home. For it is improper for a woman to speak in the church. Did the word of God go forth from you? Or has it come to you alone?

If anyone thinks that he is a prophet or a spiritual person, he should recognize that what I am writing to you is a commandment of the Lord. If anyone does not acknowledge this, he is not acknowledged. So, [my] brothers, strive eagerly to prophesy, and do not forbid speaking in tongues, but everything must be done properly and in order.

PSALM 66:13-20

I will bring holocausts to your
  house;
  to you I will fulfill the vows
Which my lips uttered
  and my words promised in my
    distress.
Holocausts of fatlings I will offer
    you,
  with burnt offerings of rams;
  I will sacrifice oxen and goats.
Hear now, all you who fear God,
    while I declare
  what he has done for me.
When I appealed to him in
    words,
  praise was on the tip of my
    tongue.
Were I to cherish wickedness in
    my heart,
  the LORD would not hear;
But God has heard;
  he has hearkened to the sound
    of my prayer.
Blessed be God who refused me
    not
  my prayer or his kindness!

PROVERBS 16:6-7

By kindness and piety guilt is expiated, / and by the fear of the LORD man avoids evil. / When the LORD is pleased with a man's ways, / he makes even his enemies be at peace with him.

MAY 29

1 CORINTHIANS 15:1-29

Now I am reminding you, brothers, of the gospel I preached to you, which you indeed received and in which you also stand. Through it you are also being saved, if you hold fast to the word I preached to you, unless you believed in vain. For I handed on to you as of first importance what I also received: that Christ died for our sins in accordance with the scriptures; that he was buried; that he was raised on the third day in accordance with the scriptures; that he appeared to Kephas, then to the Twelve. After that, he appeared to more than five hundred brothers at once, most of whom are still living, though some have fallen asleep. After that he appeared to James, then to all the apostles. Last of all, as to one born abnormally, he appeared to me. For I am the least of the apostles, not fit to be called an apostle, because I persecuted the church of God. But by the grace of God I am what I am, and his grace to me has not been ineffective. Indeed, I have toiled harder than all of them; not I, however, but the grace of God [that is] with me. Therefore, whether it be I or they, so we preach and so you believed.

But if Christ is preached as raised from the dead, how can some among you say there is no resurrection of the dead? If there is no resurrection of the dead, then neither has Christ been raised. And if Christ has not been raised, then empty [too] is our preaching; empty, too, your faith. Then we are also false witnesses to God, because we testified against God that he raised Christ, whom he did not raise if in fact the dead are not raised. For if the dead are not raised, neither has Christ been raised, and if Christ has not been raised, your faith is vain; you are still in your sins. Then those who have fallen asleep in Christ have perished. If for this life only we have hoped in Christ, we are the most pitiable people of all.

But now Christ has been raised from the dead, the firstfruits of those who have fallen asleep. For since death came through a human being, the resurrection of the dead came also through a human being. For just as in Adam all die, so too in Christ shall all be brought to life, but each one in proper order: Christ the firstfruits; then, at his coming, those who belong to Christ; then comes the end, when he hands over the kingdom to his God and Father, when he has destroyed every sovereignty and every authority and power. For he must reign until he has put all his enemies under his feet. The last enemy to be destroyed is death, for "he subjected everything under his feet." But when it says that everything has been subjected, it is clear that it excludes the one who subjected everything to him. When everything is subjected to him, then the Son himself will [also] be subjected to the one who subjected everything to him, so that God may be all in all.

Otherwise, what will people accomplish by having themselves baptized for the dead? If the dead are not raised at all, then why are they having themselves baptized for them?

PSALM 67:1-8

For the leader; with stringed instruments. A psalm; a song.

May God have pity on us and bless us;
may he let his face shine upon us.
So may your way be known upon earth;
among all nations, your salvation.
May the peoples praise you, O God;
may all the peoples praise you!
May the nations be glad and exult
because you rule the peoples in equity;
the nations on the earth you guide.
May the peoples praise you, O God;
may all the peoples praise you!
The earth has yielded its fruits;
God, our God, has blessed us.
May God bless us,
and may all the ends of the earth fear him!

Better a little with virtue, / than a large income with injustice. / In his mind a man plans his course, / but the LORD *directs his steps.*

MAY 30

---

1 CORINTHIANS 15:30-58

Moreover, why are we endangering ourselves all the time? Every day I face death; I swear it by the pride in you [brothers] that I have in Christ Jesus our Lord. If at Ephesus I fought with beasts, so to speak, what benefit was it to me? If the dead are not raised:

"Let us eat and drink,
    for tomorrow we die."

Do not be led astray:

"Bad company corrupts good
    morals."

Become sober as you ought and stop sinning. For some have no knowledge of God; I say this to your shame.

But someone may say, "How are the dead raised? With what kind of body will they come back?"

You fool! What you sow is not brought to life unless it dies. And what you sow is not the body that is to be but a bare kernel of wheat, perhaps, or of some other kind; but God gives it a body as he chooses, and to each of the seeds its own body. Not all flesh is the same, but there is one kind for human beings, another kind of flesh for animals, another kind of flesh for birds, and another for fish. There are both heavenly bodies and earthly bodies, but the brightness of the heavenly is one kind and that of the earthly another. The brightness of the sun is one kind, the brightness of the moon another, and the brightness of the stars another. For star differs from star in brightness.

So also is the resurrection of the dead. It is sown corruptible; it is raised incorruptible. It is sown dishonorable; it is raised glorious. It is sown weak; it is raised powerful. It is sown a natural body; it is raised a spiritual body. If there is a natural body, there is also a spiritual one.

So, too, it is written, "the first man, Adam, became a living being," the last Adam a life-giving spirit. But the spiritual was not first; rather the natural and then the spiritual. The first man was from the earth, earthly; the second man, from heaven. As was the earthly one, so also are the earthly, and as is the heavenly one, so also are the heavenly. Just as we have borne the image of the earthly one, we shall also bear the image of the heavenly one.

This I declare, brothers: flesh and blood cannot inherit the kingdom of God, nor does corruption inherit incorruption. Behold, I tell you a mystery. We shall not all fall asleep, but we will all be changed, in an instant, in the blink of an eye, at the last trumpet. For the trumpet will sound, the dead will be raised incorruptible, and we shall be changed. For that which is corruptible must clothe itself with incorruptibility, and that which is mortal must clothe itself with immortality. And when this which is corruptible clothes itself with incorruptibility and this which is mortal clothes itself with immortality, then the word that is written shall come about:

"Death is swallowed up in victory.
Where, O death, is your victory?
Where, O death, is your sting?"

The sting of death is sin, and the power of sin is the law. But thanks be to God who gives us the victory through our Lord Jesus Christ.

Therefore, my beloved brothers, be firm, steadfast, always fully devoted to the work of the Lord, knowing that in the Lord your labor is not in vain.

PSALM 68:1-7

For the leader. A psalm of David; a song.

God arises; his enemies are scattered,
  and those who hate him flee before him.
As smoke is driven away, so are they driven;
  as wax melts before the fire,
  so the wicked perish before God.
But the just rejoice and exult before God;
  they are glad and rejoice.
Sing to God, chant praise to his name,
  extol him who rides upon the clouds,
Whose name is the LORD;
  exult before him.
The father of orphans and the defender of widows
  is God in his holy dwelling.
God gives a home to the forsaken;
  he leads forth prisoners to prosperity;
  only rebels remain in the parched land.

PROVERBS 16:10-11

The king's lips are an oracle; / no judgment he pronounces is false. / Balance and scales belong to the LORD; / all the weights used with them are his concern.

MAY 31

1 CORINTHIANS 16:1-24

Now in regard to the collection for the holy ones, you also should do as I ordered the churches of Galatia. On the first day of the week each of you should set aside and save whatever he can afford, so that collections will not be going on when I come. And when I arrive, I shall send those whom you have approved with letters of recommendation to take your gracious gift to Jerusalem. If it seems fitting that I should go also, they will go with me.

I shall come to you after I pass

through Macedonia (for I am going to pass through Macedonia), and perhaps I shall stay or even spend the winter with you, so that you may send me on my way wherever I may go. For I do not wish to see you now just in passing, but I hope to spend some time with you, if the Lord permits. I shall stay in Ephesus until Pentecost, because a door has opened for me wide and productive for work, but there are many opponents.

If Timothy comes, see that he is without fear in your company, for he is doing the work of the Lord just as I am. Therefore, no one should disdain him. Rather, send him on his way in peace that he may come to me, for I am expecting him with the brothers. Now in regard to our brother Apollos, I urged him strongly to go to you with the brothers, but it was not at all his will that he go now. He will go when he has an opportunity.

Be on your guard, stand firm in the faith, be courageous, be strong. Your every act should be done with love.

I urge you, brothers—you know that the household of Stephanas is the firstfruits of Achaia and that they have devoted themselves to the service of the holy ones—be subordinate to such people and to everyone who works and toils with them. I re-joice in the arrival of Stephanas, Fortunatus, and Achaicus, because they made up for your absence, for they refreshed my spirit as well as yours. So give recognition to such people.

The churches of Asia send you greetings. Aquila and Prisca together with the church at their house send you many greetings in the Lord. All the brothers greet you. Greet one another with a holy kiss.

I, Paul, write you this greeting in my own hand. If anyone does not love the Lord, let him be accursed. *Maranatha.* The grace of the Lord Jesus be with you. My love to all of you in Christ Jesus.

PSALM 68:8-11

O God, when you went forth at
    the head of your people,
  when you marched through
    the wilderness,
The earth quaked; it rained from
    heaven at the presence of
    God,
  at the presence of God, the
    God of Israel, the One of
    Sinai,
A bountiful rain you showered
    down, O God, upon your
    inheritance;
  you restored the land when it
    languished;
Your flock settled in it,
  in your goodness, O God, you
    provided it for the needy.

PROVERBS 16:12-13

Kings have a horror of wrongdoing, / for by righteousness the throne endures. / The king takes delight in honest lips, / and the man who speaks what is right he loves.

JUNE

As I Have Loved You

JESUS TOLD US that the love of God takes precedence over every other law. "This is the greatest and the first commandment . . .", but he was quick to add: "The second is like it: You shall love your neighbor as yourself" (Mt 22:38-39).

In the letters recommended for our prayerful reading this month, we discover the basis for this love of neighbor. The Father tells us: "I will live with them and move among them, and I will be their God and they shall be my people. . . . I will receive you and I will be a father to you, and you shall be sons and daughters to me . . ." (2 Cor 6:16ff). Since the Father has adopted us as his sons and daughters, we are in reality brothers and sisters to each other. We are one family.

Furthermore, Jesus is dwelling within each one of us. Did he not say: " 'Amen, I say to you, whatever you did for one of these least brothers of mine, you did for me' " (Mt 25:40). This makes us all members of one body. We form his Body.

Paul confirmed this same truth when he told the Galatians and us: "For through faith you are all children of God in Christ Jesus. For all of you who were baptized into Christ have clothed yourselves with Christ" (Gal 3:26). To be clothed with Christ means forming a close union with Christ and publicly manifesting a commitment to develop the dispositions and outlook which Jesus had.

This mind and heart of Jesus can be formed in us by our faithful practice of the prayer of the heart, or the prayer of listening as it is sometimes called. Paul guarantees this fruit when he tells us: "All of us, gazing with unveiled face on the glory of the Lord, are being transformed into the same image from glory to glory, as from the Lord who is the Spirit" (2 Cor 3:18). This kind of prayer has a tremendous transforming power by virtue of the presence of the Holy Spirit praying within us. As we strive to do so, we will instinctively reach out in loving concern to others. The apostle of the Gentiles summed it up in one brief directive: "Be subordinate to one another out of reverence for Christ" (Eph 5:21).

Paul would have been an efficient chairman of a ways and means committee. He is forever giving directives on how to live a deeper, fuller, more committed Christian life. Many of his directives are stated clearly and briefly, even though the implementation of them in our daily round of duties may be far more difficult.

In his zealous, pastoral enthusiasm, Paul urges us to prove our love of neighbor by being available to others at all times and to do so with the proper motivation. Jesus said that he had come not to be served, but to serve. The apostle of the Gentiles re-states this as a way of life for us: "For the whole law is fulfilled in one statement, namely, 'You shall love your neighbor as yourself' " (Gal 5:13ff).

In his letter to the Ephesians he returns to the same advice. Here Paul says that our motivation must be directed to the Lord: ". . . willingly serving the Lord and not human beings . . ." (Eph 6:7).

Loving our neighbors means accepting them as the kind of persons they are. Too often we have an image of the kind of people we expect others to be. In our judgmental attitude, we criticize others because they do not seem to measure up to the standard that we have set. Our pride frequently does not permit us to see all the good qualities which others may possess.

Without mincing words, Paul makes it quite imperative when he says: ". . . with all humility and gentleness, with patience, bearing with one another through love . . ." (Eph 4:2). His words are few, but his challenge requires a lifetime to attain. If all people possessed these excellent virtues, practically all inter-personal problems would be nonexistent and many of the problems which disrupt a peaceful and tranquil environment would disappear.

Again Paul is an ideal teacher: ". . . striving to preserve the unity of the spirit through the bond of peace . . ." (Eph 4:3). In other words, Christian community is formed not on rules, laws, and regulations but on love.

Sometimes we regard our responsibilities and duties in life as unavoidable obligations. We have a tendency to separate them from our spiritual life. The inspired writers of the Bible would have us understand that each one of these duties is a golden opportunity to love our neighbor and to express that love in action.

Paul singles out a special duty of parents which is an ideal way of expressing love of neighbor. He addresses himself to fathers with no intention of excluding mothers from this privilege. "Fathers, do not provoke your children to anger, but bring them up with the training and instruction of the Lord" (Eph 6:4). Any devoted parent will vouch for the fact that it requires a tolerant, understanding love to guide and train children in the way of the Lord in our materialistic, humanistic society.

As we strive to love God with all our mind, heart, and soul, we will be better enabled to love our neighbor as ourselves. As our desire to do so intensifies within us, we can say with Paul: ". . . yet I live, no longer I, but Christ lives in me . . ." (Gal 2:20).

JUNE 1

2 CORINTHIANS 1:1-24

Paul, an apostle of Christ Jesus by the will of God, and Timothy our brother, to the church of God that is in Corinth, with all the holy ones throughout Achaia: grace to you and peace from God our Father and the Lord Jesus Christ.

Blessed be the God and Father of our Lord Jesus Christ, the Father of compassion and God of all encouragement, who encourages us in our every affliction, so that we may be able to encourage those who are in any affliction with the encouragement with which we ourselves are encouraged by God. For as Christ's sufferings overflow to us, so through Christ does our encouragement also overflow. If we are afflicted, it is for your encouragement and salvation; if we are encouraged, it is for your encouragement, which enables you to endure the same sufferings that we suffer. Our hope for you is firm, for we know that as you share in the sufferings, you also share in the encouragement.

We do not want you to be unaware, brothers, of the affliction that came to us in the province of Asia; we were utterly weighed down beyond our strength, so that we despaired even of life. Indeed, we had accepted within ourselves the sentence of death, that we might trust not in ourselves but in God who raises the dead. He rescued us from such great danger of death, and he will continue to rescue us; in him we have put our hope [that] he will also rescue us again, as you help us with prayer, so that thanks may be given by many on our behalf for the gift granted us through the prayers of many.

For our boast is this, the testimony of our conscience that we have conducted ourselves in the world, and especially toward you, with the simplicity and sincerity of God, [and] not by human wisdom but by the grace of God. For we write you nothing but what you can read and understand, and I hope that you will understand completely, as you have come to understand us partially, that we are your boast as you also are ours, on the day of [our] Lord Jesus.

With this confidence I formerly intended to come to you so that you might receive a double favor, namely, to go by way of you to Macedonia, and then to come to you again on my return from Macedonia, and have you send me on my way to Judea. So when I intended this, did I act lightly? Or do I make my plans according to human considerations, so that with me it is "yes, yes" and "no, no"? As God is faithful, our word to you is not "yes" and "no." For the Son of God, Jesus Christ, who was proclaimed to you by us, Silvanus and Timothy and me, was not "yes" and "no," but "yes" has been in him. For however many are the promises of God, their Yes is in him; therefore, the Amen from us also goes through him to God for glory. But the one who gives us security with you in Christ and who anointed us is God; he has also put his seal upon us and given the Spirit in our hearts as a first installment.

But I call upon God as witness, on my life, that it is to spare you that I have not yet gone to Corinth. Not that we lord it over your faith; rather, we work together for your joy, for you stand firm in the faith.

PSALM 68:12-19

The LORD gives the word;
  women bear the glad tidings, a
    vast army:
"Kings and their hosts are
  fleeing, fleeing,
and the household shall divide
  the spoils.
Though you rested among the
  sheepfolds,
  the wings of the dove shone
    with silver,
  and her pinions with a golden
    hue.
While the Almighty dispersed the
  kings there,
  snow fell on Zalmon."
High the mountains of Bashan;
  rugged the mountains of
    Bashan.
Why look you jealously, you
  rugged mountains,
  at the mountain God has
    chosen for his throne,
  where the LORD himself will
    dwell forever?
The chariots of God are myriad,
  thousands on thousands;
  the LORD advances from Sinai
    to the sanctuary.
You have ascended on high,
  taken captives,
  received men as gifts—
  even rebels; the LORD God
    enters his dwelling.

PROVERBS 16:14-15

The king's wrath is like messengers of death, / but a wise man can pacify it. / In the light of the king's countenance is life, / and his favor is like a rain cloud in spring.

JUNE 2

2 CORINTHIANS 2:1-17

For I decided not to come to you again in painful circumstances. For if I inflict pain upon you, then who is there to cheer me except the one pained by me? And I wrote as I did so that when I came I might not be pained by those in whom I should have rejoiced, confident about all of you that my joy is that of all of you. For out of much affliction and anguish of heart I wrote to you with many tears, not that you might be pained but that you might know the abundant love I have for you.

If anyone has caused pain, he has caused it not to me, but in some measure (not to exaggerate) to all of you. This punishment by the majority is enough for such a person, so that on the contrary you should forgive and encourage him instead, or else the person may be overwhelmed by excessive pain. Therefore, I urge you to reaffirm your love for him. For this is why I wrote, to know your proven character, whether you were obedient in everything. Whomever you forgive anything, so do I. For indeed what I have forgiven, if I have forgiven anything, has been for you in the presence of Christ, so that we might not be taken advantage of by Satan, for we are not unaware of his purposes.

When I went to Troas for the gospel of Christ, although a door was opened for me in the Lord, I had no relief in my spirit because I did not find my brother Titus. So I took leave of them and went on to Macedonia.

But thanks be to God, who always leads us in triumph in Christ and manifests through us the odor of the knowledge of him in every place. For we are the aroma of Christ for God among those who are being saved and among those who are perishing, to the latter an odor of death that leads to death, to the former an odor of life that leads to life. Who is qualified for this? For we are not like the many who trade on the word of God; but as out of sincerity, indeed as from God and in the presence of God, we speak in Christ.

PSALM 68:20-24

Blessed day by day be the LORD,
   who bears our burdens; God,
   who is our salvation.
God is a saving God for us;
   the LORD, my Lord, controls
   the passageways of death.
Surely God crushes the heads of
   his enemies,
   the hairy crowns of those who
   stalk about in their guilt.
The Lord said: "I will fetch them
   back from Bashan;
I will fetch them back from the
   depths of the sea,
So that you will bathe your feet
   in blood;
   the tongues of your dogs will
   have their share of your
   enemies."

PROVERBS 16:16-17

How much better to acquire wisdom than gold! / To acquire understanding is more desirable than silver. / The path of the upright avoids misfortune; / he who pays attention to his way safeguards his life.

JUNE 3

2 CORINTHIANS 3:1-18

Are we beginning to commend ourselves again? Or do we need, as some do, letters of recommendation to you or from you? You are our letter, written on our hearts, known and read by all, shown to be a letter of Christ administered by us, written not in ink but by the Spirit of the living God, not on tablets of stone but on tablets that are hearts of flesh.

Such confidence we have through Christ toward God. Not that of ourselves we are qualified to take credit for anything as coming from us; rather, our qualification comes from God, who has indeed qualified us as ministers of a new covenant, not of letter but of spirit; for the letter brings death, but the Spirit gives life.

Now if the ministry of death, carved in letters on stone, was so glorious that the Israelites could not look intently at the face of Moses because of its glory that was going to fade, how much more will the ministry of the Spirit be glorious? For if the ministry of condemnation was glorious, the ministry of righteousness will abound much more in glory. Indeed, what was endowed with glory has come to have no glory in this respect because of the glory that surpasses it. For if what was going to fade was glorious, how much more will what endures be glorious.

Therefore, since we have such hope, we act very boldly and not like Moses, who put a veil over his face so that the Israelites could not look intently at the cessation of what was fading. Rather, their thoughts were rendered dull, for to this present day the same veil remains unlifted when they read the old covenant, because through Christ it is taken away. To this day, in fact, whenever Moses is read, a veil lies over their hearts, but whenever a person turns to the Lord the veil is removed. Now the Lord is the Spirit, and where the Spirit of the Lord is, there is freedom. All of us, gazing with unveiled face on the glory of the Lord, are being transformed into the same image from glory to glory, as from the Lord who is the Spirit.

PSALM 68:25-32

They view your progress, O God,
   the progress of my God, my
      King, into the sanctuary;
The singers lead, the minstrels
   follow,
   in their midst the maidens play
      on timbrels.
In your choirs bless God;
   bless the LORD, you of Israel's
      wellspring!
There is Benjamin, the youngest,
   leading them;
   the princes of Judah in a body,
   the princes of Zebulun, the
      princes of Naphtali.
Show forth, O God, your power,
   the power, O God, with which
      you took our part;
For your temple in Jerusalem
   let the kings bring you gifts.
Rebuke the wild beast of the
   reeds,
   the herd of strong bulls and the
      bullocks, the nations.
Let them prostrate themselves
   with bars of silver;
   scatter the peoples who delight
      in war.
Let nobles come from Egypt;
   let Ethiopia extend its hands to
      God.

PROVERBS 16:18-19

Pride goes before disaster, / and a haughty spirit before a fall. / It is better to be humble with the meek / than to share plunder with the proud.

JUNE 4

2 CORINTHIANS 4:1-18

Therefore, since we have this ministry through the mercy shown us, we are not discouraged. Rather, we have renounced shameful, hidden things; not acting deceitfully or falsifying the word of God, but by the open declaration of the truth we commend ourselves to everyone's conscience in the sight of God. And even though our gospel is veiled, it is veiled for those who are perishing, in whose case the god of this age has blinded the minds of the unbelievers, so that they may not see the light of the gospel of the glory of Christ, who is the image of God. For we do not preach ourselves but Jesus Christ as Lord, and ourselves as your slaves for the sake of Jesus. For God who said, "Let light shine out of darkness," has shone in our hearts to bring to light the knowledge of the glory of God on the face of [Jesus] Christ.

But we hold this treasure in earthen vessels, that the surpassing power may be of God and not from us. We are afflicted in every way, but not constrained; perplexed, but not driven to despair; persecuted, but not abandoned; struck down, but not destroyed; always carrying about in the body the dying of Jesus, so that the life of Jesus may also be manifested in our body. For we who live are constantly being given up to death for the sake of Jesus, so that the life of Jesus may be manifested in our mortal flesh.

So death is at work in us, but life in you. Since, then, we have the same spirit of faith, according to what is written, "I believed, therefore I spoke," we too believe and therefore speak, knowing that the one who raised the Lord Jesus will raise us also with Jesus and place us with you in his presence. Everything indeed is for you, so that the grace bestowed in abundance on more and more people may cause the thanksgiving to overflow for the glory of God.

Therefore, we are not discouraged; rather, although our outer self is wasting away, our inner self is being renewed day by day. For this momentary light affliction is producing for us an eternal weight of glory beyond all comparison, as we look not to what is seen but to what is unseen; for what is seen is transitory, but what is unseen is eternal.

PSALM 68:33-36

You kingdoms of the earth, sing
    to God,
    chant praise to the LORD
    who rides on the heights of the
    ancient heavens.
Behold, his voice resounds, the
    voice of power;
    "Confess the power of God!"
Over Israel is his majesty;
    his power is in the skies.
Awesome in his sanctuary is
    God, the God of Israel;
    he gives power and strength to
    his people
    Blessed be God!

PROVERBS 16:20

He who plans a thing will be successful; / happy is he who trusts in the LORD!

JUNE 5

2 CORINTHIANS 5:1-21

For we know that if our earthly dwelling, a tent, should be destroyed, we have a building from God, a dwelling not made with hands, eternal in heaven. For in this tent we groan, longing to be further clothed with our heavenly habitation if indeed, when we have taken it off, we shall not be found naked. For while we are in this tent we groan and are weighed down, because we do not wish to be unclothed but to be further clothed, so that what is mortal may be swallowed up by life. Now the one who has prepared us for this very thing is God, who has given us the Spirit as a first installment.

So we are always courageous, although we know that while we are at home in the body we are away from the Lord, for we walk by faith, not by sight. Yet we are courageous, and we would rather leave the body and go home to the Lord. Therefore, we aspire to please him, whether we are at home or away. For we must all appear before the judgment seat of Christ, so that each one may receive recompense, according to what he did in the body, whether good or evil.

Therefore, since we know the fear of the Lord, we try to persuade others; but we are clearly apparent to God, and I hope we are also apparent to your consciousness. We are not commending ourselves to you again but giving you an opportunity to boast of us, so that you may have something to say to those who boast of external appearance rather than of the heart. For if we are out of our minds, it is for God; if we are rational, it is for you. For the love of Christ impels us, once we have come to the conviction that one died for all; therefore, all have died. He indeed died for all, so that those who live might no longer live for themselves but for him who for their sake died and was raised.

Consequently, from now on we regard no one according to the flesh; even if we once knew Christ according to the flesh, yet now we know him so no longer. So whoever is in Christ is a new creation: the old things have passed away; behold, new things have come. And all this is from God, who has reconciled us to himself through Christ and given us the ministry of reconciliation, namely, God was reconciling the world to himself in Christ, not counting their trespasses against them and entrusting to us the message of reconciliation. So we are ambassadors for Christ, as if God were appealing through us. We implore you on behalf of Christ, be reconciled to God. For our sake he made him to be sin who did not know sin, so that we might become the righteousness of God in him.

PSALM 69:1-5

For the leader; according to "Lilies."
Of David.
Save me, O God,
for the waters threaten my life;
I am sunk in the abysmal swamp
where there is no foothold;
I have reached the watery depths;
the flood overwhelms me.
I am wearied with calling,

my throat is parched;
My eyes have failed
with looking for my God.
Those outnumber the hairs of my
head
who hate me without cause.

Too many for my strength
are they who wrongfully are
my enemies.
Must I restore what I did not
steal?

PROVERBS 16:21-23

The wise man is esteemed for his discernment, / yet pleasing speech increases his persuasiveness. / Good sense is a fountain of life to its possessor, / but folly brings chastisement on fools. / The mind of the wise man makes him eloquent, / and augments the persuasiveness of his lips.

JUNE 6

2 CORINTHIANS 6:1-18

Working together, then, we appeal to you not to receive the grace of God in vain. For he says:

"In an acceptable time I heard
you,
and on the day of salvation I
helped you."

Behold, now is a very acceptable time; behold, now is the day of salvation. We cause no one to stumble in anything, in order that no fault may be found with our ministry; on the contrary, in everything we commend ourselves as ministers of God, through much endurance, in afflictions, hardships, constraints, beatings, imprisonments, riots, labors, vigils, fasts; by purity, knowledge, patience, kindness, in a holy spirit, in unfeigned love, in truthful speech, in the power of God; with weapons of righteousness at the right and at the left; through glory and dishonor, insult and praise. We are treated as deceivers and yet are truthful; as unrecognized and yet acknowledged; as dying and behold we live; as chastised and yet not put to death; as sorrowful yet always rejoicing; as poor yet enriching many; as having nothing and yet possessing all things.

We have spoken frankly to you, Corinthians; our heart is open wide. You are not constrained by us; you are constrained by your own affections. As recompense in kind (I speak as to my children), be open yourselves.

Do not be yoked with those who are different, with unbelievers. For what partnership do righteousness and lawlessness have? Or what fellowship does light have with darkness? What accord has Christ with Beliar? Or what has a believer in common with an unbeliever? What agreement has the temple of God with idols? For we are the temple of the living God; as God said:

"I will live with them and move
among them,
and I will be their God
and they shall be my people.

Therefore, come forth from
them
and be separate," says the
LORD,
"and touch nothing unclean;
then I will receive you
and I will be a father to you,
and you shall be sons and
daughters to me,
says the LORD Almighty."

PSALM 69:6-13

O God, you know my folly,
and my faults are not hid from
you.
Let not those who wait for you be
put to shame through me,
O LORD, God of hosts.
Let not those who seek you blush
for me,

O God of Israel,
Since for your sake I bear insult,
and shame covers my face.
I have become an outcast to my
brothers,
a stranger to my mother's sons,
Because zeal for your house
consumes me,
and the insults of those who
blaspheme you fall upon me.
I humbled myself with fasting,
and this was made a reproach
to me.
I made sackcloth my garment,
and I became a byword for
them.
They who sit at the gate gossip
about me,
and drunkards make me the
butt of their songs.

PROVERBS 16:24

Pleasing words are a honeycomb, / sweet to the taste and healthful to the body.

JUNE 7

2 CORINTHIANS 7:1-16

Since we have these promises,
beloved, let us cleanse ourselves
from every defilement of flesh
and spirit, making holiness perfect in the fear of God.

Make room for us; we have not
wronged anyone, or ruined anyone, or taken advantage of anyone. I do not say this in condemnation, for I have already said that
you are in our hearts, that we may
die together and live together. I
have great confidence in you, I
have great pride in you; I am filled
with encouragement, I am overflowing with joy all the more because of all our affliction.

For even when we came into

Macedonia, our flesh had no rest,
but we were afflicted in every
way—external conflicts, internal
fears. But God, who encourages
the downcast, encouraged us by
the arrival of Titus, and not only
by his arrival but also by the encouragement with which he was
encouraged in regard to you, as
he told us of your yearning, your
lament, your zeal for me, so that I
rejoiced even more. For even if I
saddened you by my letter, I do
not regret it; and if I did regret it
([for] I see that that letter saddened you, if only for a while), I
rejoice now, not because you
were saddened, but because you
were saddened into repentance;

for you were saddened in a godly way, so that you did not suffer loss in anything because of us. For godly sorrow produces a salutary repentance without regret, but worldly sorrow produces death. For behold what earnestness this godly sorrow has produced for you, as well as readiness for a defense, and indignation, and fear, and yearning, and zeal, and punishment. In every way you have shown yourselves to be innocent in the matter. So then even though I wrote to you, it was not on account of the one who did the wrong, or on account of the one who suffered the wrong, but in order that your concern for us might be made plain to you in the sight of God. For this reason we are encouraged.

And besides our encouragement, we rejoice even more because of the joy of Titus, since his spirit has been refreshed by all of you. For if I have boasted to him about you, I was not put to shame. No, just as everything we said to you was true, so our boasting before Titus proved to be the truth. And his heart goes out to you all the more, as he remembers the obedience of all of you, when you received him with fear and trembling. I rejoice, because I have confidence in you in every respect.

PSALM 69:14-15

But I pray to you, O LORD,
    for the time of your favor, O God!
In your great kindness answer me
    with your constant help.
Rescue me out of the mire; may I not sink!
    may I be rescued from my foes,
    and from the watery depths.

PROVERBS 16:25

Sometimes a way seems right to a man, / but the end of it leads to death!

JUNE 8

2 CORINTHIANS 8:1-24

We want you to know, brothers, of the grace of God that has been given to the churches of Macedonia, for in a severe test of affliction, the abundance of their joy and their profound poverty overflowed in a wealth of generosity on their part. For according to their means, I can testify, and beyond their means, spontaneously, they begged us insistently for the favor of taking part in the service to the holy ones, and this, not as we expected, but they gave themselves first to the Lord and to us through the will of God, so that we urged Titus that, as he had already begun, he should also complete for you this gracious act also. Now as you excel in every respect, in faith, discourse, knowledge, all earnestness, and in the love we have for you, may you excel in this gracious act also.

I say this not by way of command, but to test the genuineness of your love by your concern for others. For you know the gracious act of our Lord Jesus Christ, that for your sake he became poor although he was rich, so that by his poverty you might become rich. And I am giving counsel in this matter, for it is appropriate for you who began not only to act but to act willingly last year: complete it now, so that your eager willingness may be matched by your completion of it out of what you have. For if the eagerness is there, it is acceptable according to what one has, not according to what one does not have; not that others should have relief while you are burdened, but that as a matter of equality your surplus at the present time should supply their needs, so that their surplus may also supply your needs, that there may be equality. As it is written:

"Whoever had much did not
     have more,
  and whoever had little did
     not have less."

But thanks be to God who put the same concern for you into the heart of Titus, for he not only welcomed our appeal but, since he is very concerned, he has gone to you of his own accord. With him we have sent the brother who is praised in all the churches for his preaching of the gospel. And not only that, but he has also been appointed our traveling companion by the churches in this gracious work administered by us for the glory of the Lord [himself] and for the expression of our eagerness. This we desire to avoid, that anyone blame us about this lavish gift administered by us, for we are concerned for what is honorable not only in the sight of the Lord but also in the sight of others. And with them we have sent our brother whom we often tested in many ways and found earnest, but who is now much more earnest because of his great confidence in you. As for Titus, he is my partner and co-worker for you; as for our brothers, they are apostles of the churches, the glory of Christ. So give proof before the churches of your love and of our boasting about you to them.

PSALM 69:16-22

Let not the flood-waters
     overwhelm me,
  nor the abyss swallow me up,
  nor the pit close its mouth over
     me.
Answer me, O LORD, for
     bounteous is your kindness;
  in your great mercy turn
     toward me.
Hide not your face from your
     servant;
  in my distress, make haste to
     answer me.
Come and ransom my life;
  as an answer for my enemies,
     redeem me.
You know my reproach, my
     shame and my ignominy:
  before you are all my foes.
Insult has broken my heart, and I
     am weak,
  I looked for sympathy, but
     there was none;
  for comforters, and I found
     none.
Rather they put gall in my food,
  and in my thirst they gave me
     vinegar to drink.

PROVERBS 16:26-27

The laborer's appetite labors for him, / for his mouth urges him on. / A scoundrel is a furnace of evil, / and on his lips there is a scorching fire.

JUNE 9

2 CORINTHIANS 9:1-15

Now about the service to the holy ones, it is superfluous for me to write to you, for I know your eagerness, about which I boast of you to the Macedonians, that Achaia has been ready since last year; and your zeal has stirred up most of them. Nonetheless, I sent the brothers so that our boast about you might not prove empty in this case, so that you might be ready, as I said, for fear that if any Macedonians come with me and find you not ready we might be put to shame (to say nothing of you) in this conviction. So I thought it necessary to encourage the brothers to go on ahead to you and arrange in advance for your promised gift, so that in this way it might be ready as a bountiful gift and not as an exaction.

Consider this: whoever sows sparingly will also reap sparingly, and whoever sows bountifully will also reap bountifully. Each must do as already determined, without sadness or compulsion, for God loves a cheerful giver. Moreover, God is able to make every grace abundant for you, so that in all things, always having all you need, you may have an abundance for every good work. As it is written:

"He scatters abroad, he gives to the poor;

his righteousness endures forever."

The one who supplies seed to the sower and bread for food will supply and multiply your seed and increase the harvest of your righteousness.

You are being enriched in every way for all generosity, which through us produces thanksgiving to God, for the administration of this public service is not only supplying the needs of the holy ones but is also overflowing in many acts of thanksgiving to God. Through the evidence of this service, you are glorifying God for your obedient confession of the gospel of Christ and the generosity of your contribution to them and to all others, while in prayer on your behalf they long for you, because of the surpassing grace of God upon you. Thanks be to God for his indescribable gift!

PSALM 69:23-29

Let their own table be a snare before them,
　and a net for their friends.
Let their eyes grow dim so that they cannot see,
　and keep their backs always feeble.
Pour out your wrath upon them;
　let the fury of your anger overtake them.

Let their encampment become
 desolate;
  in their tents let there be no
  one to dwell.
For they kept after him whom
 you smote,
  and added to the pain of him
  you wounded.

Heap guilt upon their guilt,
 and let them not attain to your
 reward.
May they be erased from the
 book of the living,
  and not be recorded with the
  just!

PROVERBS 16:28-30

An intriguer sows discord, / and a talebearer separates bosom friends. / A lawless man allures his neighbor, / and leads him into a way that is not good. / He who winks his eye is plotting trickery; / he who compresses his lips has mischief ready.

JUNE 10

2 CORINTHIANS 10:1-18

Now I myself, Paul, urge you through the gentleness and clemency of Christ, I who am humble when face to face with you, but brave toward you when absent, I beg you that, when present, I may not have to be brave with that confidence with which I intend to act boldly against some who consider us as acting according to the flesh. For, although we are in the flesh, we do not battle according to the flesh, for the weapons of our battle are not of flesh but are enormously powerful, capable of destroying fortresses. We destroy arguments and every pretension raising itself against the knowledge of God, and take every thought captive in obedience to Christ, and we are ready to punish every disobedience, once your obedience is complete.

Look at what confronts you. Whoever is confident of belonging to Christ should consider that as he belongs to Christ, so do we. And even if I should boast a little too much of our authority, which the Lord gave for building you up and not for tearing you down, I shall not be put to shame. May I not seem as one frightening you through letters. For someone will say, "His letters are severe and forceful, but his bodily presence is weak, and his speech contemptible." Such a person must understand that what we are in word through letters when absent, that we also are in action when present.

Not that we dare to class or compare ourselves with some of those who recommend themselves. But when they measure themselves by one another and compare themselves with one another, they are without understanding. But we will not boast beyond measure but will keep to the limits God has apportioned us, namely, to reach even to you. For we are not overreaching ourselves, as though we did not reach you; we indeed first came to you with the gospel of Christ. We are not boasting beyond measure, in other people's labors; yet our hope is that, as your faith increases, our influence among you may be greatly enlarged, within our proper limits, so that we may preach the gospel even beyond you, not boasting of work already done in another's sphere. "Whoever boasts, should boast in the Lord." For it is not the one who recommends himself who is approved, but the one whom the Lord recommends.

PSALM 69:30-37

But I am afflicted and in pain;
　　let your saving help, O God,
　　　protect me.
I will praise the name of God in
　　song,
　　and I will glorify him with
　　thanksgiving;

This will please the LORD more
　　than oxen
　　or bullocks with horns and
　　divided hooves:
"See, you lowly ones, and be
　　glad;
　　you who seek God, may your
　　hearts be merry!
For the LORD hears the poor,
　　and his own who are in bonds
　　he spurns not.
Let the heavens and the earth
　　praise him,
　　the seas and whatever moves
　　in them!"
For God will save Zion
　　and rebuild the cities of Judah.
They shall dwell in the land and
　　own it,
　　and the descendants of his
　　servants shall inherit it,
　　and those who love his name
　　shall inhabit it.

PROVERBS 16:31-33

Gray hair is a crown of glory; / it is gained by virtuous living. / A patient man is better than a warrior, / and he who rules his temper, than he who takes a city. / When the lot is cast into the lap, / its decision depends entirely on the LORD.

JUNE 11

2 CORINTHIANS 11:1-15

If only you would put up with a little foolishness from me! Please put up with me. For I am jealous of you with the jealousy of God, since I betrothed you to one husband to present you as a chaste virgin to Christ. But I am afraid that, as the serpent deceived Eve by his cunning, your thoughts may be corrupted from a sincere [and pure] commitment to Christ. For if someone comes and preaches another Jesus than the one we preached, or if you receive a different spirit from the one you received or a different gospel from the one you accepted, you put up with it well enough. For I think that I am not in any way inferior to these "superapostles." Even if I am untrained in speaking, I am not so in knowledge; in every way we have made this plain to you in all things.

Did I make a mistake when I humbled myself so that you might be exalted, because I preached the gospel of God to you without charge? I plundered other churches by accepting from them in order to minister to you. And when I was with you and in need, I did not burden anyone, for the brothers who came from Macedonia supplied my needs. So I refrained and will refrain from burdening you in any way. By the truth of Christ in me, this boast of mine shall not be silenced in the regions of Achaia. And why? Because I do not love you? God knows I do!

And what I do I will continue to do, in order to end this pretext of those who seek a pretext for being regarded as we are in the mission of which they boast. For such people are false apostles, deceitful workers, who masquerade as apostles of Christ. And no wonder, for even Satan masquerades as an angel of light. So it is not strange that his ministers also masquerade as ministers of righteousness. Their end will correspond to their deeds.

PSALM 70:1-6

For the leader; of David. For remembrance.

Deign, O God, to rescue me;
  O LORD, make haste to help me.
Let them be put to shame and confounded
  who seek my life.
Let them be turned back in disgrace
  who desire my ruin.
Let them retire in their shame
  who say to me, "Aha, aha!"
But may all who seek you
  exult and be glad in you,
And may those who love your salvation
  say ever, "God be glorified!"
But I am afflicted and poor;
  O God, hasten to me!
You are my help and my deliverer;
  O LORD, hold not back!

PROVERBS 17:1

Better a dry crust with peace / than a house full of feasting with strife.

JUNE 12

2 CORINTHIANS 11:16-33

I repeat, no one should consider me foolish; but if you do, accept me as a fool, so that I too may boast a little. What I am saying I am not saying according to the Lord but as in foolishness, in this boastful state. Since many boast according to the flesh, I too will boast. For you gladly put up with fools, since you are wise yourselves. For you put up with it if someone enslaves you, or devours you, or gets the better of you, or puts on airs, or slaps you in the face. To my shame I say that we were too weak!

But what anyone dares to boast of (I am speaking in foolishness) I also dare. Are they Hebrews? So am I. Are they Israelites? So am I. Are they descendants of Abraham? So am I. Are they ministers of Christ? (I am talking like an insane person.) I am still more, with far greater labors, far more imprisonments, far worse beatings, and numerous brushes with death. Five times at the hands of the Jews I received forty lashes minus one. Three times I was beaten with rods, once I was stoned, three times I was shipwrecked, I passed a night and a day on the deep; on frequent journeys, in dangers from rivers, dangers from robbers, dangers from my own race, dangers from Gentiles, dangers in the city, dangers in the wilderness, dangers at sea, dangers among false brothers; in toil and hardship, through many sleepless nights, through hunger and thirst, through frequent fastings, through cold and exposure. And apart from these things, there is the daily pressure upon me of my anxiety for all the churches. Who is weak, and I am not weak? Who is led to sin, and I am not indignant?

If I must boast, I will boast of the things that show my weakness. The God and Father of the Lord Jesus knows, he who is blessed forever, that I do not lie. At Damascus, the governor under King Aretas guarded the city of Damascus, in order to seize me, but I was lowered in a basket through a window in the wall and escaped his hands.

PSALM 71:1-8

In you, O LORD, I take refuge;
   let me never be put to shame.
In your justice rescue me, and
   deliver me;
   incline your ear to me, and
   save me.
Be my rock of refuge,
   a stronghold to give me safety,
   for you are my rock and my
   fortress.
O my God, rescue me from the
   hand of the wicked,
   from the grasp of the criminal
   and the violent.
For you are my hope, O LORD;
   my trust, O God, from my
   youth.
On you I depend from birth;
   from my mother's womb you
   are my strength;
   constant has been my hope in
   you.
A portent am I to many,
   but you are my strong refuge!
My mouth shall be filled with
   your praise,
   with your glory day by day.

PROVERBS 17:2-3

An intelligent servant will rule over a worthless son, / and will share the inheritance with the brothers. / The crucible for silver, and the furnace for gold, / but the tester of hearts is the LORD.

JUNE 13

2 CORINTHIANS 12:1-21

I must boast; not that it is profitable, but I will go on to visions and revelations of the Lord. I know someone in Christ who, fourteen years ago (whether in the body or out of the body I do not know, God knows), was caught up to the third heaven. And I know that this person (whether in the body or out of the body I do not know, God knows) was caught up into Paradise and heard ineffable things, which no one may utter. About this person I will boast, but about myself I will not boast, except about my weaknesses. Although if I should wish to boast, I would not be foolish, for I would be telling the truth. But I refrain, so that no one may think more of me than what he sees in me or hears from me because of the abundance of the revelations. Therefore, that I might not become too elated, a thorn in the flesh was given to me, an angel of Satan, to beat me, to keep me from being too elated. Three times I begged the Lord about this, that it might leave me, but he said to me, "My grace is sufficient for you, for power is made perfect in weakness." I will rather boast most gladly of my weaknesses, in order that the power of Christ may dwell with me. Therefore, I am content with weaknesses, insults, hardships, persecutions, and constraints, for the sake of Christ; for when I am weak, then I am strong.

I have been foolish. You compelled me, for I ought to have been commended by you. For I am in no way inferior to these "superapostles," even though I am nothing. The signs of an apostle were performed among you with all endurance, signs and wonders, and mighty deeds. In what way were you less privileged than the rest of the churches, except that on my part I did not burden you? Forgive me this wrong!

Now I am ready to come to you this third time. And I will not be a burden, for I want not what is yours, but you. Children ought not to save for their parents, but parents for their children. I will most gladly spend and be utterly spent for your sakes. If I love you more, am I to be loved less? But granted that I myself did not burden you, yet I was crafty and got the better of you by deceit. Did I take advantage of you through any of those I sent to you? I urged Titus to go and sent the brother with him. Did Titus take advantage of you? Did we not walk in the same spirit? And in the same steps?

Have you been thinking all along that we are defending ourselves before you? In the sight of God we are speaking in Christ, and all for building you up, beloved. For I fear that when I come I may find you not such as I wish, and that you may find me not as you wish; that there may be rivalry, jealousy, fury, selfishness, slander, gossip, conceit, and disorder. I fear that when I come again my God may humiliate me before you, and I may have to mourn over many of those who sinned earlier and have not repented of the impurity, immorality, and licentiousness they practiced.

PSALM 71:9-16

Cast me not off in my old age;
    as my strength fails, forsake me
      not,
For my enemies speak against
    me,
    and they who keep watch
      against my life take counsel
      together.
They say, "God has forsaken
    him;
    pursue and seize him,
    for there is no one to rescue
      him."
O God, be not far from me;

my God, make haste to help me.
Let them be put to shame and consumed who attack my life;
let them be wrapped in ignominy and disgrace who seek to harm me.
But I will always hope
and praise you ever more and more.

My mouth shall declare your justice,
day by day your salvation,
though I know not their extent.
I will treat of the mighty works of the LORD;
O God, I will tell of your singular justice.

PROVERBS 17:4-5

The evil man gives heed to wicked lips, / and listens to falsehood from a mischievous tongue. / He who mocks the poor blasphemes his Maker; / he who is glad at calamity will not go unpunished.

JUNE 14

2 CORINTHIANS 13:1-13

This third time I am coming to you. "On the testimony of two or three witnesses a fact shall be established." I warned those who sinned earlier and all the others, and I warn them now while absent, as I did when present on my second visit, that if I come again I will not be lenient, since you are looking for proof of Christ speaking in me. He is not weak toward you but powerful in you. For indeed he was crucified out of weakness, but he lives by the power of God. So also we are weak in him, but toward you we shall live with him by the power of God.

Examine yourselves to see whether you are living in faith. Test yourselves. Do you not realize that Jesus Christ is in you—unless, of course, you fail the test. I hope you will discover that we have not failed. But we pray to God that you may not do evil, not that we may appear to have passed the test but that you may do what is right, even though we may seem to have failed. For we cannot do anything against the truth, but only for the truth. For we rejoice when we are weak but you are strong. What we pray for is your improvement.

I am writing this while I am away, so that when I come I may not have to be severe in virtue of the authority that the Lord has given me to build up and not to tear down.

Finally, brothers, rejoice. Mend your ways, encourage one another, agree with one another, live in peace, and the God of love and peace will be with you. Greet one another with a holy kiss. All the holy ones greet you.

The grace of the Lord Jesus Christ and the love of God and the fellowship of the holy Spirit be with all of you.

PSALM 71:17-20

O God, you have taught me from
my youth,
and till the present I proclaim
your wondrous deeds;
And now that I am old and gray,
O God, forsake me not
Till I proclaim your strength
to every generation that is to
come.

Your power and your justice,
O God, reach to heaven.
You have done great things;
O God, who is like you?
Though you have made me feel
many bitter afflictions,
you will again revive me;
from the depths of the earth
you will once more raise me.

PROVERBS 17:6

*Grandchildren are the crown of old men, / and the glory of children is their
parentage.*

JUNE 15

GALATIANS 1:1-24

Paul, an apostle not from human beings nor through a human
being but through Jesus Christ
and God the Father who raised
him from the dead, and all the
brothers who are with me, to the
churches of Galatia: grace to you
and peace from God our Father
and the Lord Jesus Christ, who
gave himself for our sins that he
might rescue us from the present
evil age in accord with the will of
our God and Father, to whom be
glory forever and ever. Amen.

I am amazed that you are so
quickly forsaking the one who
called you by [the] grace [of
Christ] for a different gospel (not
that there is another). But there
are some who are disturbing you
and wish to pervert the gospel of
Christ. But even if we or an angel
from heaven should preach [to
you] a gospel other than the one
that we preached to you, let that
one be accursed! As we have said
before, and now I say again, if anyone preaches to you a gospel
other than the one that you received, let that one be accursed!

Am I now currying favor with
human beings or God? Or am I
seeking to please people? If I were
still trying to please people, I
would not be a slave of Christ.

Now I want you to know, brothers, that the gospel preached by
me is not of human origin. For I
did not receive it from a human
being, nor was I taught it, but it
came through a revelation of Jesus
Christ.

For you heard of my former
way of life in Judaism, how I persecuted the church of God beyond
measure and tried to destroy it,
and progressed in Judaism beyond many of my contemporaries
among my race, since I was even
more a zealot for my ancestral traditions. But when [God], who
from my mother's womb had set
me apart and called me through
his grace, was pleased to reveal
his Son to me, so that I might pro-

claim him to the Gentiles, I did not immediately consult flesh and blood, nor did I go up to Jerusalem to those who were apostles before me; rather, I went into Arabia and then returned to Damascus.

Then after three years I went up to Jerusalem to confer with Kephas and remained with him for fifteen days. But I did not see any other of the apostles, only James the brother of the Lord. (As to what I am writing to you, behold, before God, I am not lying.) Then I went into the regions of Syria and Cilicia. And I was unknown personally to the churches of Judea that are in Christ; they only kept hearing that "the one who once was persecuting us is now preaching the faith he once tried to destroy." So they glorified God because of me.

PSALM 71:21-24

Renew your benefits toward me,
and comfort me over and over.
So will I give you thanks with
music on the lyre,
for your faithfulness, O my
God!
I will sing your praises with the
harp,
O Holy One of Israel!
My lips shall shout for joy
as I sing your praises;
My soul also, which you have
redeemed,
and my tongue day by day
shall discourse on your
justice.
How shamed and how disgraced
are those who sought to harm
me!

PROVERBS 17:7-8

Fine words are out of place in a fool; / how much more, lying words in a noble! / A man who has a bribe to offer rates it a magic stone; / at every turn it brings him success.

JUNE 16

GALATIANS 2:1-21

Then after fourteen years I again went up to Jerusalem with Barnabas, taking Titus along also. I went up in accord with a revelation, and I presented to them the gospel that I preach to the Gentiles—but privately to those of repute—so that I might not be running, or have run, in vain. Moreover, not even Titus, who was with me, although he was a Greek, was compelled to be circumcised, but because of the false

brothers secretly brought in, who slipped in to spy on our freedom that we have in Christ Jesus, that they might enslave us—to them we did not submit even for a moment, so that the truth of the gospel might remain intact for you. But from those who were reputed to be important (what they once were makes no difference to me; God shows no partiality)—those of repute made me add nothing. On the contrary, when they saw that I had been entrusted with the gospel to the uncircumcised, just as Peter to the circumcised, for the one who worked in Peter for an apostolate to the circumcised worked also in me for the Gentiles, and when they recognized the grace bestowed upon me, James and Kephas and John, who were reputed to be pillars, gave me and Barnabas their right hands in partnership, that we should go to the Gentiles and they to the circumcised. Only, we were to be mindful of the poor, which is the very thing I was eager to do.

And when Kephas came to Antioch, I opposed him to his face because he clearly was wrong. For, until some people came from James, he used to eat with the Gentiles; but when they came, he began to draw back and separated himself, because he was afraid of the circumcised. And the rest of the Jews [also] acted hypocritically along with him, with the result that even Barnabas was carried away by their hypocrisy. But when I saw that they were not on the right road in line with the truth of the gospel, I said to Kephas in front of all, "If you, though a Jew, are living like a Gentile and not like a Jew, how can you compel the Gentiles to live like Jews?"

We, who are Jews by nature and not sinners from among the Gentiles, [yet] who know that a person is not justified by works of the law but through faith in Jesus Christ, even we have believed in Christ Jesus that we may be justified by faith in Christ and not by works of the law, because by works of the law no one will be justified. But if, in seeking to be justified in Christ, we ourselves are found to be sinners, is Christ then a minister of sin? Of course not! But if I am building up again those things that I tore down, then I show myself to be a transgressor. For through the law I died to the law, that I might live for God. I have been crucified with Christ; yet I live, no longer I, but Christ lives in me; insofar as I now live in the flesh, I live by faith in the Son of God who has loved me and given himself up for me. I do not nullify the grace of God; for if justification comes through the law, then Christ died for nothing.

PSALM 72:1-7

Of Solomon.
O God, with your judgment
　　endow the king,
　　and with your justice, the
　　　king's son;
He shall govern your people with
　　justice
　　and your afflicted ones with
　　　judgment.
The mountains shall yield peace
　　for the people,
　　and the hills justice.
He shall defend the afflicted
　　among the people,
　　save the children of the poor,
　　and crush the oppressor.
May he endure as long as the
　　sun,
　　and like the moon through all
　　　generations.
He shall be like rain coming
　　down on the meadow,
　　like showers watering the
　　　earth.
Justice shall flower in his days,
　　and profound peace, till the
　　　moon be no more.

PROVERBS 17:9-11

He who covers up a misdeed fosters friendship, / but he who gossips about it separates friends. / A single reprimand does more for a man of intelligence / than a hundred lashes for a fool. / On rebellion alone is the wicked man bent, / but a merciless messenger will be sent against him.

JUNE 17

GALATIANS 3:1-14

O stupid Galatians! Who has bewitched you, before whose eyes Jesus Christ was publicly portrayed as crucified? I want to learn only this from you: did you receive the Spirit from works of the law, or from faith in what you heard? Are you so stupid? After beginning with the Spirit, are you now ending with the flesh? Did you experience so many things in vain?—if indeed it was in vain. Does, then, the one who supplies the Spirit to you and works mighty deeds among you do so from works of the law or from faith in what you heard? Thus Abraham "believed God, and it was credited to him as righteousness."

Realize then that it is those who have faith who are children of Abraham. Scripture, which saw in advance that God would justify the Gentiles by faith, foretold the good news to Abraham, saying, "Through you shall all the nations be blessed." Consequently, those who have faith are blessed along with Abraham who had faith. For all who depend on works of the law are under a curse; for it is written, "Cursed be everyone who does not persevere in doing all the things written in the book of the law." And that no one is justified before God by the law is clear, for "the one who is righteous by faith will live." But the law does not depend on faith; rather, "the one who does these things will live by them." Christ ransomed us from the curse of the law by becoming a curse for us, for it is written, "Cursed be everyone who hangs on a tree," that the blessing of Abraham might be extended to the Gentiles through Christ Jesus, so that we might receive the promise of the Spirit through faith.

PSALM 72:8-14

May he rule from sea to sea,
   and from the River to the ends
     of the earth.
His foes shall bow before him,
   and his enemies shall lick the
     dust.
The kings of Tarshish and the
     Isles shall offer gifts;
   the kings of Arabia and Seba
     shall bring tribute.
All kings shall pay him homage,
   all nations shall serve him.
For he shall rescue the poor man
     when he cries out,
   and the afflicted when he has
     no one to help him.
He shall have pity for the lowly
     and the poor;
   the lives of the poor he shall
     save.
From fraud and violence he shall
     redeem them,
   and precious shall their blood
     be in his sight.

PROVERBS 17:12-13

Face a bear robbed of her cubs, / but never a fool in his folly! / If a man returns evil for good, / from his house evil will not depart.

JUNE 18

GALATIANS 3:15-29

Brothers, in human terms I say that no one can annul or amend even a human will once ratified. Now the promises were made to Abraham and to his descendant. It does not say, "And to descendants," as referring to many, but as referring to one, "And to your descendant," who is Christ. This is what I mean: the law, which came four hundred and thirty years afterward, does not annul a covenant previously ratified by God, so as to cancel the promise. For if the inheritance comes from the law, it is no longer from a promise; but God bestowed it on Abraham through a promise.

Why, then, the law? It was added for transgressions, until the descendant came to whom the promise had been made; it was promulgated by angels at the hand of a mediator. Now there is no mediator when only one party is involved, and God is one. Is the law then opposed to the promises [of God]? Of course not! For if a law had been given that could bring life, then righteousness would in reality come from the law. But scripture confined all things under the power of sin, that through faith in Jesus Christ the promise might be given to those who believe.

Before faith came, we were held in custody under law, con-fined for the faith that was to be revealed. Consequently, the law was our disciplinarian for Christ, that we might be justified by faith. But now that faith has come, we are no longer under a disciplinarian. For through faith you are all children of God in Christ Jesus. For all of you who were baptized into Christ have clothed yourselves with Christ. There is neither Jew nor Greek, there is neither slave nor free person, there is not male and female; for you are all one in Christ Jesus. And if you belong to Christ, then you are Abraham's descendant, heirs according to the promise.

PSALM 72:15-20

May he live to be given the gold
> of Arabia,
>> and to be prayed for
>> continually;
>> day by day shall they bless
>> him.
May there be an abundance of
> grain upon the earth;
>> on the tops of the mountains
>> the crops shall rustle like
>> Lebanon;
>> the city dwellers shall flourish
>> like the verdure of the fields.
May his name be blessed forever;
> as long as the sun his name
> shall remain.

In him shall all the tribes of the earth be blessed;
all the nations shall proclaim his happiness.
Blessed be the LORD, the God of Israel,
who alone does wondrous deeds.

And blessed forever be his glorious name;
may the whole earth be filled with his glory.
Amen. Amen.
The prayers of David the son of Jesse are ended.

PROVERBS 17:14-15

The start of strife is like the opening of a dam; / therefore, check a quarrel before it begins! / He who condones the wicked, he who condemns the just, / are both an abomination to the LORD.

JUNE 19

GALATIANS 4:1-11

I mean that as long as the heir is not of age, he is no different from a slave, although he is the owner of everything, but he is under the supervision of guardians and administrators until the date set by his father. In the same way we also, when we were not of age, were enslaved to the elemental powers of the world. But when the fullness of time had come, God sent his son, born of a woman, born under the law, to ransom those under the law, so that we might receive adoption. As proof that you are children, God sent the spirit of his Son into our hearts, crying out, "Abba, Father!" So you are no longer a slave but a child, and if a child then also an heir, through God.

At a time when you did not know God, you became slaves to things that by nature are not gods; but now that you have come to know God, or rather to be known by God, how can you turn back again to the weak and destitute elemental powers? Do you want to be slaves to them all over again? You are observing days, months, seasons, and years. I am afraid on your account that perhaps I have labored for you in vain.

PSALM 73:1-12

A psalm of Asaph.
How good God is to the upright;
the LORD, to those who are clean of heart!
But, as for me, I almost lost my balance;
my feet all but slipped,
Because I was envious of the arrogant
when I saw them prosper though they were wicked.
For they are in no pain;
their bodies are sound and sleek;
They are free from the burdens of mortals,
and are not afflicted like the rest of men.
So pride adorns them as a necklace;

as a robe violence enwraps them.
Out of their crassness comes iniquity;
their fancies overflow their hearts.
They scoff and speak evil;
outrage from on high they threaten.
They set their mouthings in place of heaven,
and their pronouncements roam the earth:

"So he brings his people to such a pass
that they have not even water!"
And they say, "How does God know?"
And, "Is there any knowledge in the Most High?"
Such, then, are the wicked;
always carefree, while they increase in wealth.

PROVERBS 17:16

Of what use in the fool's hand are the means / to buy wisdom, since he has no mind for it?

JUNE 20

GALATIANS 4:12-31

I implore you, brothers, be as I am, because I have also become as you are. You did me no wrong; you know that it was because of a physical illness that I originally preached the gospel to you, and you did not show disdain or contempt because of the trial caused you by my physical condition, but rather you received me as an angel of God, as Christ Jesus. Where now is that blessedness of yours? Indeed, I can testify to you that, if it had been possible, you would have torn out your eyes and given them to me. So now have I become your enemy by telling you the truth? They show interest in you, but not in a good way; they want to isolate you, so that you may show interest in them. Now it is good to be shown interest for good reason at all times, and not only when I am with you. My children, for whom I am again in labor until Christ be formed in you! I would like to be with you now and to change my tone, for I am perplexed because of you.

Tell me, you who want to be under the law, do you not listen to the law? For it is written that Abraham had two sons, one by the slave woman and the other by the freeborn woman. The son of the slave woman was born naturally, the son of the freeborn through a promise. Now this is an allegory. These women represent two covenants. One was from Mount Sinai, bearing children for slavery; this is Hagar. Hagar represents Sinai, a mountain in Arabia; it corresponds to the present Jerusalem, for she is in slavery along with her children. But the Jerusalem above is freeborn, and she is our mother. For it is written:

"Rejoice, you barren one who bore no children;

break forth and shout, you
who were not in labor;
for more numerous are the
children of the deserted
one
than of her who has a
husband."

Now you, brothers, like Isaac, are children of the promise. But just as then the child of the flesh persecuted the child of the spirit, it is the same now. But what does the scripture say?

"Drive out the slave woman
and her son!
For the son of the slave
woman shall not share the
inheritance
with the son"

of the freeborn. Therefore, brothers, we are children not of the slave woman but of the freeborn woman.

PSALM 73:13-17

Is it but in vain I have kept my
heart clean
and washed my hands as an
innocent man?
For I suffer affliction day after
day
and chastisement with each
new dawn.
Had I thought, "I will speak as
they do,"
I had been false to the
fellowship of your children.
Though I tried to understand this
it seemed to me too difficult,
Till I entered the sanctuary of
God
and considered their final
destiny.

PROVERBS 17:17-18

He who is a friend is always a friend, / and a brother is born for the time of stress. / Senseless is the man who gives his hand in pledge, / who becomes surety for his neighbor.

JUNE 21

GALATIANS 5:1-26

For freedom Christ set us free; so stand firm and do not submit again to the yoke of slavery.

It is I, Paul, who am telling you that if you have yourselves circumcised, Christ will be of no benefit to you. Once again I declare to every man who has himself circumcised that he is bound to observe the entire law. You are separated from Christ, you who are trying to be justified by law; you have fallen from grace. For through the Spirit, by faith, we await the hope of righteousness. For in Christ Jesus, neither circumcision nor uncircumcision counts for anything, but only faith working through love.

You were running well; who hindered you from following [the] truth? That enticement does not come from the one who called you. A little yeast leavens the whole batch of dough. I am confident of you in the Lord that you will not take a different view, and that the one who is troubling you will bear the condemnation, whoever he may be. As for me, brothers, if I am still preaching circumcision, why am I still being persecuted? In that case, the stumbling block of the cross has been abolished. Would that those who are upsetting you might also castrate themselves!

For you were called for freedom, brothers. But do not use this freedom as an opportunity for the flesh; rather, serve one another through love. For the whole law is fulfilled in one statement, namely, "You shall love your neighbor as yourself." But if you go on biting and devouring one another, beware that you are not consumed by one another.

I say, then: live by the Spirit and you will certainly not gratify the desire of the flesh. For the flesh has desires against the Spirit, and the Spirit against the flesh; these are opposed to each other, so that you may not do what you want. But if you are guided by the Spirit, you are not under the law. Now the works of the flesh are obvious: immorality, impurity, licentiousness, idolatry, sorcery, hatreds, rivalry, jealousy, outbursts of fury, acts of selfishness, dissensions, factions, occasions of envy, drinking bouts, orgies, and the like. I warn you, as I warned you before, that those who do such things will not inherit the kingdom of God. In contrast, the fruit of the Spirit is love, joy, peace, patience, kindness, generosity, faithfulness, gentleness, self-control. Against such there is no law. Now those who belong to Christ [Jesus] have crucified their flesh with its passions and desires. If we live in the Spirit, let us also follow the Spirit. Let us not be conceited, provoking one another, envious of one another.

PSALM 73:18-22

You set them, indeed, on a
    slippery road;
  you hurl them down to ruin.
How suddenly they are made
    desolate!
  They are completely wasted
    away amid horrors.
As though they were the dream
    of one who had awakened,
    O LORD,
  so will you, when you arise, set
    at nought these phantoms.
Because my heart was embittered
    and my soul was pierced,
I was stupid and understood not;
  I was like a brute beast in your
    presence.

PROVERBS 17:19-21

He who loves strife loves guilt; / he who builds his gate high courts disaster. / He who is perverse in heart finds no good, / and a double-tongued man falls into trouble. / To be a fool's parent is grief for a man; / the father of a numskull has no joy.

JUNE 22

GALATIANS 6:1-18

Brothers, even if a person is caught in some transgression, you who are spiritual should correct that one in a gentle spirit, looking to yourself, so that you also may not be tempted. Bear one another's burdens, and so you will fulfill the law of Christ. For if anyone thinks he is something when he is nothing, he is deluding himself. Each one must examine his own work, and then he will have reason to boast with regard to himself alone, and not with regard to someone else; for each will bear his own load.

One who is being instructed in the word should share all good things with his instructor. Make no mistake: God is not mocked, for a person will reap only what he sows, because the one who sows for his flesh will reap corruption from the flesh, but the one who sows for the spirit will reap eternal life from the spirit. Let us not grow tired of doing good, for in due time we shall reap our harvest, if we do not give up. So then, while we have the opportunity, let us do good to all, but especially to those who belong to the family of the faith.

See with what large letters I am writing to you in my own hand! It is those who want to make a good appearance in the flesh who are trying to compel you to have yourselves circumcised, only that they may not be persecuted for the cross of Christ. Not even those having themselves circumcised observe the law themselves; they only want you to be circumcised so that they may boast of your flesh. But may I never boast except in the cross of our Lord Jesus Christ, through which the world has been crucified to me, and I to the world. For neither does circumcision mean anything, nor does uncircumcision, but only a new creation. Peace and mercy be to all who follow this rule and to the Israel of God.

From now on, let no one make troubles for me; for I bear the marks of Jesus on my body.

The grace of our Lord Jesus Christ be with your spirit, brothers. Amen.

PSALM 73:23-28

Yet with you I shall always be;
    you have hold of my right
      hand;
With your counsel you guide me,
    and in the end you will receive
      me in glory.
Whom else have I in heaven?
    And when I am with you, the
      earth delights me not.
Though my flesh and my heart
      waste away,
    God is the rock of my heart
      and my portion forever.
For indeed, they who withdraw
      from you perish;
    you destroy everyone who is
      unfaithful to you.
But for me, to be near God is my
      good;
    to make the Lord GOD my
      refuge.
I shall declare all your works
    in the gates of the daughter of
      Zion.

PROVERBS 17:22

A joyful heart is the health of the body, / but a depressed spirit dries up the bones.

JUNE 23

EPHESIANS 1:1-23

Paul, an apostle of Christ Jesus by the will of God, to the holy ones who are [in Ephesus] faithful in Christ Jesus: grace to you and peace from God our Father and the Lord Jesus Christ.

Blessed be the God and Father of our Lord Jesus Christ, who has blessed us in Christ with every spiritual blessing in the heavens, as he chose us in him, before the foundation of the world, to be holy and without blemish before him. In love he destined us for adoption to himself through Jesus Christ, in accord with the favor of his will, for the praise of the glory of his grace that he granted us in the beloved.

In him we have redemption by his blood, the forgiveness of transgressions, in accord with the riches of his grace that he lavished upon us. In all wisdom and insight, he has made known to us the mystery of his will in accord with his favor that he set forth in him as a plan for the fullness of times, to sum up all things in Christ, in heaven and on earth.

In him we were also chosen, destined in accord with the purpose of the One who accomplishes all things according to the intention of his will, so that we might exist for the praise of his glory, we who first hoped in Christ. In him you also, who have heard the word of truth, the gospel of your salvation, and have believed in him, were sealed with the promised holy Spirit, which is the first installment of our inheritance toward redemption as God's possession, to the praise of his glory.

Therefore, I, too, hearing of your faith in the Lord Jesus and of your love for all the holy ones, do not cease giving thanks for you, remembering you in my prayers, that the God of our Lord Jesus Christ, the Father of glory, may give you a spirit of wisdom and revelation resulting in knowledge of him. May the eyes of [your] hearts be enlightened, that you may know what is the hope that belongs to his call, what are the riches of glory in his inheritance among the holy ones, and what is the surpassing greatness of his power for us who believe, in accord with the exercise of his great might, which he worked in Christ, raising him from the dead and seating him at his right hand in the heavens, far above every principality, authority, power, and dominion, and every name that is named not only in this age but also in the one to come. And he put all things beneath his feet and gave him as head over all things to the church, which is his body, the fullness of the one who fills all things in every way.

PSALM 74:1-11

A maskil of Asaph.

Why, O God, have you cast us
off forever?
  Why does your anger smolder
  against the sheep of your
  pasture?
Remember your flock which you
built up of old,
  the tribe you redeemed as your
  inheritance,
  Mount Zion, where you took
  up your abode.
Turn your steps toward the utter
ruins;
  toward all the damage the
  enemy has done in the
  sanctuary.
Your foes roar triumphantly in
your shrine;
  they have set up their tokens of
  victory.
They are like men coming up
  with axes to a clump of trees;
and now with chisel and
  hammer they hack at all its
  paneling.
They set your sanctuary on fire;
  the place where your name
  abides they have razed and
  profaned.
They said in their hearts, "Let us
  destroy them;
  burn all the shrines of God in
  the land."
Deeds on our behalf we do not
  see; there is no prophet now,
  and no one of us knows how
  long . . .
How long, O God, shall the foe
  blaspheme?
  Shall the enemy revile your
  name forever?
Why draw back your hand
  and keep your right hand idle
  beneath your cloak?

PROVERBS 17:23

The wicked man accepts a concealed bribe / to pervert the course of justice.

JUNE 24

EPHESIANS 2:1-22

You were dead in your transgressions and sins in which you once lived following the age of this world, following the ruler of the power of the air, the spirit that is now at work in the disobedient. All of us once lived among them in the desires of our flesh, following the wishes of the flesh and the impulses, and we were by nature children of wrath, like the rest. But God, who is rich in mercy, because of the great love he had for us, even when we were dead in our transgressions, brought us to life with Christ (by grace you have been saved), raised us up with him, and seated us with him in the heavens in Christ Jesus, that in the ages to come he might show the immeasurable riches of his grace in his kindness to us in Christ Jesus. For by grace you have been saved through faith, and this is not from you; it is the gift of God; it is not from works, so no one may boast. For we are his handiwork, created in Christ Jesus for the good works that God has prepared in advance, that we should live in them.

Therefore, remember that at one time you, Gentiles in the flesh, called the uncircumcision by those called the circumcision, which is done in the flesh by human hands, were at that time without Christ, alienated from the community of Israel and strangers to the covenants of promise, without hope and without God in the world. But now in Christ Jesus you who once were far off have become near by the blood of Christ.

For he is our peace, he who made both one and broke down the dividing wall of enmity, through his flesh, abolishing the law with its commandments and legal claims, that he might create in himself one new person in place of the two, thus establishing peace, and might reconcile both with God, in one body, through the cross, putting that enmity to death by it. He came and preached peace to you who were far off and peace to those who were near, for through him we both have access in one Spirit to the Father.

So then you are no longer strangers and sojourners, but you are fellow citizens with the holy ones and members of the household of God, built upon the foundation of the apostles and prophets, with Christ Jesus himself as the capstone. Through him the whole structure is held together and grows into a temple sacred in the Lord; in him you also are being built together into a dwelling place of God in the Spirit.

PSALM 74:12-17

Yet, O God, my king from of old,
   you doer of saving deeds on
     earth,
You stirred up the sea by your
   might;
   you smashed the heads of the
     dragons in the waters.
You crushed the heads of
   Leviathan,
   and made food of him for the
     dolphins.
You released the springs and
   torrents;
   you brought dry land out of the
     primeval waters.
Yours is the day, and yours the
   night;
   you fashioned the moon and
     the sun.
You fixed all the limits of the
   land;
   summer and winter you made.

PROVERBS 17:24-25

The man of intelligence fixes his gaze on wisdom, / but the eyes of a fool are on the ends of the earth. / A foolish son is vexation to his father, / and bitter sorrow to her who bore him.

JUNE 25

EPHESIANS 3:1-21

Because of this, I, Paul, a prisoner of Christ [Jesus] for you Gentiles—if, as I suppose, you have heard of the stewardship of God's grace that was given to me for your benefit, [namely, that] the mystery was made known to me by revelation, as I have written briefly earlier. When you read this you can understand my insight into the mystery of Christ, which was not made known to human beings in other generations as it has now been revealed to his holy apostles and prophets by the Spirit, that the Gentiles are coheirs, members of the same body, and copartners in the promise in Christ Jesus through the gospel.

Of this I became a minister by the gift of God's grace that was granted me in accord with the exercise of his power. To me, the very least of all the holy ones, this grace was given, to preach to the Gentiles the inscrutable riches of Christ, and to bring to light [for all] what is the plan of the mystery hidden from ages past in God who created all things, so that the manifold wisdom of God might now be made known through the church to the principalities and authorities in the heavens. This was according to the eternal purpose that he accomplished in Christ Jesus our Lord, in whom we have boldness of speech and confidence of access through faith in him. So I ask you not to lose heart over my afflictions for you; this is your glory.

For this reason I kneel before the Father, from whom every family in heaven and on earth is named, that he may grant you in accord with the riches of his glory to be strengthened with power through his Spirit in the inner self, and that Christ may dwell in your hearts through faith; that you, rooted and grounded in love, may have strength to comprehend with all the holy ones what is the breadth and length and height and depth, and to know the love of Christ that surpasses knowledge, so that you may be filled with all the fullness of God.

Now to him who is able to accomplish far more than all we ask or imagine, by the power at work within us, to him be glory in the church and in Christ Jesus to all generations, forever and ever. Amen.

PSALM 74:18-23

Remember how the enemy has
    blasphemed you, O LORD,
  and how a stupid people has
    reviled your name.
Give not to the vulture the life of
    your dove;
  be not forever unmindful of the
    lives of your afflicted ones.
Look to your covenant,
  for the hiding places in the
    land and the plains are full of
    violence.
May the humble not retire in
    confusion;
  may the afflicted and the poor
    praise your name.
Arise, O God; defend your cause;
  remember how the fool
    blasphemes you day after
    day.
Be not unmindful of the voice of
    your foes;
  the uproar of those who rebel
    against you is unceasing.

It is wrong to fine an innocent man, / but beyond reason to scourge princes.

JUNE 26

EPHESIANS 4:1-16

I, then, a prisoner for the Lord, urge you to live in a manner worthy of the call you have received, with all humility and gentleness, with patience, bearing with one another through love, striving to preserve the unity of the spirit through the bond of peace: one body and one Spirit, as you were also called to the one hope of your call; one Lord, one faith, one baptism; one God and Father of all, who is over all and through all and in all.

But grace was given to each of us according to the measure of Christ's gift. Therefore, it says:

> "He ascended on high and took
> prisoners captive;
> he gave gifts to men."

What does "he ascended" mean except that he also descended into the lower [regions] of the earth? The one who descended is also the one who ascended far above all the heavens, that he might fill all things.

And he gave some as apostles, others as prophets, others as evangelists, others as pastors and teachers, to equip the holy ones for the work of ministry, for building up the body of Christ, until we all attain to the unity of faith and knowledge of the Son of God, to mature manhood, to the extent of the full stature of Christ, so that we may no longer be infants, tossed by waves and swept along by every wind of teaching arising from human trickery, from their cunning in the interests of deceitful scheming. Rather, living the truth in love, we should grow in every way into him who is the head, Christ, from whom the whole body, joined and held together by every supporting ligament, with the proper functioning of each part, brings about the body's growth and builds itself up in love.

PSALM 75:1-11

For the leader. (Do not destroy!) A
psalm of Asaph; a song.
We give you thanks, O God, we
give thanks,
and we invoke your name; we
declare your wondrous
deeds.
"When I seize the appointed
time,
I will judge with equity.
Though the earth and all who
dwell in it quake,
I have set firm its pillars.
I say to the boastful: Boast not;
and to the wicked: Lift not up
your horns."
Lift not up your horns against the
Most High;
speak not haughtily against the
Rock.

For neither from the east nor
from the west,
neither from the desert nor
from the mountains—
But God is the judge;
one he brings low; another he
lifts up.
For a cup is in the LORD's hand,
full of spiced and foaming
wine,
And he pours out from it; even to
the dregs they shall drain it;
all the wicked of the earth shall
drink.
But as for me, I will exult forever;
I will sing praise to the God of
Jacob.
And I will break off the horns of
all the wicked;
the horns of the just shall be
lifted up.

PROVERBS 17:27-28

He who spares his words is truly wise, / and he who is chary of speech is a man of intelligence. / Even a fool, if he keeps silent, is considered wise; / if he closes his lips, intelligent.

JUNE 27

EPHESIANS 4:17-32

So I declare and testify in the Lord that you must no longer live as the Gentiles do, in the futility of their minds; darkened in understanding, alienated from the life of God because of their ignorance, because of their hardness of heart, they have become callous and have handed themselves over to licentiousness for the practice of every kind of impurity to excess. That is not how you learned Christ, assuming that you have heard of him and were taught in him, as truth is in Jesus, that you should put away the old self of your former way of life, corrupted through deceitful desires, and be renewed in the spirit of your minds, and put on the new self, created in God's way in righteousness and holiness of truth.

Therefore, putting away false-hood, speak the truth, each one to his neighbor, for we are members one of another. Be angry but do not sin; do not let the sun set on your anger, and do not leave room for the devil. The thief must no longer steal, but rather labor, doing honest work with his [own] hands, so that he may have something to share with one in need. No foul language should come out of your mouths, but only such as is good for needed edification, that it may impart grace to those who hear. And do not grieve the holy Spirit of God, with which you were sealed for the day of redemption. All bitterness, fury, anger, shouting, and reviling must be removed from you, along with all malice. [And] be kind to one another, compassionate, forgiving one another as God has forgiven you in Christ.

PSALM 76:1-7

For the leader; a psalm with stringed instruments. A song of Asaph.

God is renowned in Judah,
in Israel great is his name.
In Salem is his abode;
his dwelling is in Zion.
There he shattered the flashing
shafts of the bow,
shield and sword, and
weapons of war.

Resplendent you came, O
powerful One,
from the everlasting
mountains.
Despoiled are the stouthearted;
they sleep their sleep;
the hands of all the mighty
ones have failed.
At your rebuke, O God of Jacob,
chariots and steeds lay stilled.

PROVERBS 18:1

In estrangement one seeks pretexts: / with all persistence he picks a quarrel.

JUNE 28

EPHESIANS 5:1-14

So be imitators of God, as beloved children, and live in love, as Christ loved us and handed himself over for us as a sacrificial offering to God for a fragrant aroma. Immorality or any impurity or greed must not even be mentioned among you, as is fitting among holy ones, no obscenity or silly or suggestive talk, which is out of place, but instead, thanksgiving. Be sure of this, that no immoral or impure or greedy person, that is, an idolater, has any inheritance in the kingdom of Christ and of God.

Let no one deceive you with empty arguments, for because of these things the wrath of God is coming upon the disobedient. So do not be associated with them. For you were once darkness, but now you are light in the Lord. Live as children of light, for light produces every kind of goodness and righteousness and truth. Try to learn what is pleasing to the Lord. Take no part in the fruitless works of darkness; rather expose them, for it is shameful even to mention the things done by them in secret; but everything exposed by the light becomes visible, for everything that becomes visible is light. Therefore, it says:

"Awake, O sleeper,
and arise from the dead,
and Christ will give you light."

PSALM 76:8-13

You are terrible; and who can
withstand you
for the fury of your anger?
From heaven you made your
intervention heard;
the earth feared and was silent
When God arose for judgment,
to save all the afflicted of the
earth.
For wrathful Edom shall glorify
you,
and the survivors of Hamath
shall keep your festivals.

Make vows to the LORD, your
    God, and fulfill them;
  let all round about him bring
    gifts to the terrible Lord

Who checks the pride of princes,
  who is terrible to the kings of
    the earth.

PROVERBS 18:2-3

*The fool takes no delight in understanding, / but rather in displaying what he
thinks. / With wickedness comes contempt, / and with disgrace comes scorn.*

JUNE 29

EPHESIANS 5:15-33

Watch carefully then how you live, not as foolish persons but as wise, making the most of the opportunity, because the days are evil. Therefore, do not continue in ignorance, but try to understand what is the will of the Lord. And do not get drunk on wine, in which lies debauchery, but be filled with the Spirit, addressing one another [in] psalms and hymns and spiritual songs, singing and playing to the Lord in your hearts, giving thanks always and for everything in the name of our Lord Jesus Christ to God the Father.

Be subordinate to one another out of reverence for Christ. Wives should be subordinate to their husbands as to the Lord. For the husband is head of his wife just as Christ is head of the church, he himself the savior of the body. As the church is subordinate to Christ, so wives should be subordinate to their husbands in everything. Husbands, love your wives, even as Christ loved the church and handed himself over for her to sanctify her, cleansing her by the bath of water with the word, that he might present to himself the church in splendor,

without spot or wrinkle or any such thing, that she might be holy and without blemish. So [also] husbands should love their wives as their own bodies. He who loves his wife loves himself. For no one hates his own flesh but rather nourishes and cherishes it, even as Christ does the church, because we are members of his body.

"For this reason a man shall
    leave [his] father and [his]
    mother
  and be joined to his wife,
and the two shall become one
    flesh."

This is a great mystery, but I speak in reference to Christ and the church. In any case, each one of you should love his wife as himself, and the wife should respect her husband.

PSALM 77:1-5

*For the leader; 'al Jeduthun. A psalm
    of Asaph.*
Aloud to God I cry;
  aloud to God, to hear me;
    on the day of my distress I seek
      the LORD.

By night my hands are stretched
out without flagging;
my soul refuses comfort.
When I remember God, I moan;
when I ponder, my spirit
grows faint.
You keep my eyes watchful;
I am troubled and cannot
speak.

PROVERBS 18:4-5

The words from a man's mouth are deep waters, / but the source of wisdom is a flowing brook. / It is not good to be partial to the guilty, / and so to reject a rightful claim.

JUNE 30

EPHESIANS 6:1-24

Children, obey your parents [in the LORD], for this is right. "Honor your father and mother." This is the first commandment with a promise, "that it may go well with you and that you may have a long life on earth." Fathers, do not provoke your children to anger, but bring them up with the training and instruction of the Lord.

Slaves, be obedient to your human masters with fear and trembling, in sincerity of heart, as to Christ, not only when being watched, as currying favor, but as slaves of Christ, doing the will of God from the heart, willingly serving the Lord and not human beings, knowing that each will be requited from the Lord for whatever good he does, whether he is slave or free. Masters, act in the same way towards them, and stop bullying, knowing that both they and you have a Master in heaven and that with him there is no partiality.

Finally, draw your strength from the Lord and from his mighty power. Put on the armor of God so that you may be able to stand firm against the tactics of the devil. For our struggle is not with flesh and blood but with the principalities, with the powers, with the world rulers of this present darkness, with the evil spirits in the heavens. Therefore, put on the armor of God, that you may be able to resist on the evil day and, having done everything, to hold your ground. So stand fast with your loins girded in truth, clothed with righteousness as a breastplate, and your feet shod in readiness for the gospel of peace. In all circumstances, hold faith as a shield, to quench all [the] flaming arrows of the evil one. And take the helmet of salvation and the sword of the Spirit, which is the word of God.

With all prayer and supplication, pray at every opportunity in the Spirit. To that end, be watchful with all perseverance and supplication for all the holy ones and also for me, that speech may be given me to open my mouth, to make known with boldness the mystery of the gospel for which I am an ambassador in chains, so that I may have the courage to speak as I must.

So that you also may have news of me and of what I am doing, Tychicus, my beloved brother and trustworthy minister in the Lord, will tell you everything. I am sending him to you for this very purpose, so that you may know about us and that he may encourage your hearts.

Peace be to the brothers, and love with faith, from God the Father and the Lord Jesus Christ. Grace be with all who love our Lord Jesus Christ in immortality.

PSALM 77:6-13

I consider the days of old;
    the years long past I remember.
In the night I meditate in my
    heart;
  I ponder, and my spirit broods:
"Will the LORD reject forever
and nevermore be favorable?
Will his kindness utterly cease,
  his promise fail for all
  generations?
Has God forgotten pity?
  Does he in anger withhold his
  compassion?"
And I say, "This is my sorrow,
  that the right hand of the Most
  High is changed."
I remember the deeds of the
  LORD,
  yes, I remember your wonders
  of old,
And I meditate on your works;
  your exploits I ponder.

PROVERBS 18:6-7

The fool's lips lead him into strife, / and his mouth provokes a beating. / The fool's mouth is his ruin; / his lips are a snare to his life.

JULY

Dedicate Yourselves to Thankfulness

INTERSPERSED THROUGHOUT THE PAGES of the Bible we find a series of admonitions exhorting us to practice this or that virtue in order to grow and mature spiritually. One of the most frequently repeated recommendations urges us to become a truly grateful person. The Lord endowed each one of us with a sense of gratitude. We must exercise this gift in order to live a good Christian life.

There are many reasons why we should be genuinely grateful. Everything we have and are is a gift. Every gift should stir within us a spirit of gratitude. A grateful attitude enriches our own life and the lives of others.

A prayerful person is usually a grateful person. In fact, prayer is grateful living. When our thoughts turn to an all-good God who continues to bless us daily with his myriad gifts, our hearts are filled with thankfulness. The oxygen for our twenty-five thousand daily respirations is only one of his countless gifts being showered upon us continuously.

Gratefulness admits our dependence upon others who do so very much for us. An expression of our appreciation brings happiness to them because each one of us wants to be needed. Gratitude brings joy to the human heart. It is equally true that joy is an expression of gratefulness. Gratitude is often caused by the extraordinary, but it also helps us to take a fresh look at the ordinary.

Gratitude—a Golden Thread

Throughout the Scriptures we are reminded so frequently of our duty to express a spirit of thankfulness. We owe an incalculable debt of gratitude to our caring, concerned Father. Many of the Psalms are hymns of praise and thanksgiving to our gracious God.

Jesus manifested his gratitude on many occasions. While on location in teaching or healing, he would pause to thank the Father. Jesus expressed his painful disappointment at the lack of gratitude of the nine lepers who did not return to thank him after they had been healed (Lk 17:11ff).

Threaded throughout the voluminous writings of Paul, we discover many pastoral admonitions addressed to the early Christians, encouraging them to be grateful for the gift of faith, for redemption, for life—for all God's blessings. Paul himself expressed his thankfulness for all the Lord was doing for his early converts. Paul also thanked his followers for accepting and living the faith he was proclaiming. In his letters, Paul often thanks God for his graciousness to the Christian family; then he thanks the community for their response in faith. While gratefulness is woven throughout Paul's writings, one letter is especially noteworthy.

Letter to the Colossians

Whether Paul himself or some member of the Pauline school wrote this letter makes little difference to us here and now. The importance of the letter is the emphasis which is placed on thanksgiving.

How pleased the Lord must be with this expression of gratefulness! How welcome to the Christian community are the words of the inspired writer:

> We always *give thanks to God*, the Father of our Lord Jesus Christ, when we pray for you, for we have heard of your faith in Christ Jesus and the love you have for all the holy ones because of the hope reserved for you in heaven.
> (Col 1:3-5)

As we listen to these inspired words, our own hearts too are moved to a deeper appreciation for our own faith and likewise for the support of the community which often stimulates and sustains us in our faith.

Paul commends the Colossians for their persevering faith. He recognized that they are ". . . strengthened with every power, in accord with his glorious might, for all endurance and patience, with joy giving thanks to the Father, who has made you fit to share in the inheritance of the holy ones in light" (Col 1:9ff).

In his pastoral zeal Paul spells out ways and means to develop an appreciative humble spirit of gratitude. Listen to this directive: ". . . teach and admonish one another, singing psalms, hymns, and spiritual songs *with gratitude in your hearts* to God" (Col 3:16). As we hear Paul's fatherly exhortation, many of the Psalms and other expressions of gratitude found in Scripture will become more prayerful for us. These words will instill and stir up within us a deeper sense of gratitude.

All our endeavors, our work, our recreation and relaxation, our loving service to others can become a prayer of gratitude. Again Paul came to the point in a few well-chosen words:

And whatever you do, in word or in deed, do everything in the name of the Lord Jesus, *giving thanks to God* the Father through him. (Col 3:17)

Gratitude must characterize our life of prayer. As we come to appreciate more and more that everything we have and are is a gift to us, thankfulness will naturally permeate our prayer. Using and enjoying God's gifts is another means of expressing our appreciation and giving glory to God.

Before closing his letter we find another exhortation coming from the pen of Paul. It is a brief but accurate method of prayer. "Persevere in prayer, being watchful in it with *thanksgiving* . . ." (Col 4:2).

In the four brief chapters of this letter to the Colossians we discover these repeated exhortations to express and live a life of genuine gratitude. In the other letters we are encouraged in the same way to be a grateful person at prayer and in all the duties of the day.

Listening and reflecting on God's Word will transform our hearts and make them overflow with a spirit of real gratitude. In another brief statement Paul tells us how this can be accomplished in our lives: "Let the word of Christ dwell in you richly . . ." (Col 3:16).

JULY 1

PHILIPPIANS 1:1-11

Paul and Timothy, slaves of Christ Jesus, to all the holy ones in Christ Jesus who are in Philippi, with the overseers and ministers: grace to you and peace from God our Father and the Lord Jesus Christ.

I give thanks to my God at every remembrance of you, praying always with joy in my every prayer for all of you, because of your partnership for the gospel from the first day until now. I am confident of this, that the one who began a good work in you will continue to complete it until the day of Christ Jesus. It is right that I should think this way about all of you, because I hold you in my heart, you who are all partners with me in grace, both in my imprisonment and in the defense and confirmation of the gospel. For God is my witness, how I long for all of you with the affection of Christ Jesus. And this is my prayer: that your love may increase ever more and more in knowledge and every kind of perception, to discern what is of value, so that you may be pure and blameless for the day of Christ, filled with the fruit of righteousness that comes through Jesus Christ for the glory and praise of God.

PSALM 77:14-16

O God, your way is holy;
    what great god is there like our God?
You are the God who works wonders;
    among the peoples you have made known your power.
With your strong arm you redeemed your people,
    the sons of Jacob and Joseph.

PROVERBS 18:8

The words of a talebearer are like dainty morsels / that sink into one's inmost being.

JULY 2

PHILIPPIANS 1:12-30

I want you to know, brothers, that my situation has turned out rather to advance the gospel, so that my imprisonment has become well known in Christ throughout the whole praetorium and to all the rest, and so that the majority of the brothers, having taken encouragement in the Lord from my imprisonment, dare more than ever to proclaim the word fearlessly.

Of course, some preach Christ from envy and rivalry, others from good will. The latter act out of love, aware that I am here for the defense of the gospel; the former proclaim Christ out of selfish ambition, not from pure motives, thinking that they will cause me trouble in my imprisonment. What difference does it make, as long as in every way, whether in pretense or in truth, Christ is being proclaimed? And in that I rejoice. Indeed I shall continue to rejoice, for I know that this will result in deliverance for me through your prayers and support from the Spirit of Jesus Christ. My eager expectation and hope is that I shall not be put to shame in any way, but that with all boldness, now as always, Christ will be magnified in my body, whether by life or by death. For to me life is Christ, and death is gain. If I go on living in the flesh, that means fruitful labor for me. And I do not know which I shall choose. I am caught between the two. I long to depart this life and be with Christ, [for] that is far better. Yet that I remain [in] the flesh is more necessary for your benefit. And this I know with confidence, that I shall remain and continue in the service of all of you for your prog-

ress and joy in the faith, so that your boasting in Christ Jesus may abound on account of me when I come to you again.

Only, conduct yourselves in a way worthy of the gospel of Christ, so that, whether I come and see you or am absent, I may hear news of you, that you are standing firm in one spirit, with one mind struggling together for the faith of the gospel, not intimidated in any way by your opponents. This is proof to them of destruction, but of your salvation. And this is God's doing. For to you has been granted, for the sake of Christ, not only to believe in him but also to suffer for him. Yours is the same struggle as you saw in me and now hear about me.

PSALM 77:17-21

The waters saw you, O God;
  the waters saw you and
    shuddered;
  the very depths were troubled.
The clouds poured down water;
  the skies gave forth their voice;
  your arrows also sped abroad.
Your thunder resounded in the
    whirlwind;
  your lightning illumined the
    world;
  the earth quivered and quaked.
Through the sea was your way,
  and your path through the
    deep waters,
  though your footsteps were not
    seen.
You led your people like a flock
  under the care of Moses and
    Aaron.

PROVERBS 18:9-10

The man who is slack in his work / is own brother to the man who is destructive. / The name of the LORD is a strong tower; / the just man runs to it and is safe.

JULY 3

PHILIPPIANS 2:1-11

If there is any encouragement in Christ, any solace in love, any participation in the Spirit, any compassion and mercy, complete my joy by being of the same mind, with the same love, united in heart, thinking one thing. Do nothing out of selfishness or out of vainglory; rather, humbly regard others as more important than yourselves, each looking out not for his own interests, but [also] everyone for those of others.

Have among yourselves the same attitude that is also yours in Christ Jesus,

> Who, though he was in the
>   form of God,
>   did not regard equality with
>   God
>   something to be grasped.
>   Rather, he emptied himself,
>   taking the form of a slave,
>   coming in human likeness;
>   and found human in
>   appearance,
>   he humbled himself,
>   becoming obedient to death,
>   even death on a cross.
> Because of this, God greatly
>   exalted him
>   and bestowed on him the
>   name
>   that is above every name,
>   that at the name of Jesus
>   every knee should bend,
>   of those in heaven and on
>   earth and under the earth,
>   and every tongue confess
>   that
>   Jesus Christ is Lord,
>   to the glory of God the
>   Father.

PSALM 78:1-8

A maskil of Asaph.

> Hearken, my people, to my
>   teaching;
>   incline your ears to the words
>   of my mouth.
> I will open my mouth in a
>   parable,
>   I will utter mysteries from of
>   old.
> What we have heard and know,
>   and what our fathers have
>   declared to us,
> We will not hide from their sons;
>   we will declare to the
>   generation to come
> The glorious deeds of the LORD
>   and his strength
>   and the wonders that he
>   wrought.
> He set it up as a decree in Jacob,
>   and established it as a law in
>   Israel,
> That what he commanded our
>   fathers
>   they should make known to
>   their sons;
> So that the generation to come
>   might know,
>   their sons yet to be born,
> That they too may rise and
>   declare to their sons
>   that they should put their hope
>   in God,
> And not forget the deeds of God
>   but keep his commands,
> And not be like their fathers,
>   a generation wayward and
>   rebellious,
> A generation that kept not its
>   heart steadfast
>   nor its spirit faithful toward
>   God.

PROVERBS 18:11-12

The rich man's wealth is his strong city; / he fancies it a high wall. / Before his downfall a man's heart is haughty, / but humility goes before honors.

JULY 4

PHILIPPIANS 2:12-30

So then, my beloved, obedient as you have always been, not only when I am present but all the more now when I am absent, work out your salvation with fear and trembling. For God is the one who, for his good purpose, works in you both to desire and to work. Do everything without grumbling or questioning, that you may be blameless and innocent, children of God without blemish in the midst of a crooked and perverse generation, among whom you shine like lights in the world, as you hold on to the word of life, so that my boast for the day of Christ may be that I did not run in vain or labor in vain. But, even if I am poured out as a libation upon the sacrificial service of your faith, I rejoice and share my joy with all of you. In the same way you also should rejoice and share your joy with me.

I hope, in the Lord Jesus, to send Timothy to you soon, so that I too may be heartened by hearing news of you. For I have no one comparable to him for genuine interest in whatever concerns you. For they all seek their own interests, not those of Jesus Christ. But you know his worth, how as a child with a father he served along with me in the cause of the gospel. He it is, then, whom I hope to send as soon as I see how things go with me, but I am confident in the Lord that I myself will also come soon.

With regard to Epaphroditus, my brother and co-worker and fellow soldier, your messenger and minister in my need, I consider it necessary to send him to you. For he has been longing for all of you and was distressed because you heard that he was ill. He was indeed ill, close to death; but God had mercy on him, not just on him but also on me, so that I might not have sorrow upon sorrow. I send him therefore with the greater eagerness, so that, on seeing him, you may rejoice again, and I may have less anxiety. Welcome him then in the Lord with all joy and hold such people in esteem, because for the sake of the work of Christ he came close to death, risking his life to make up for those services to me that you could not perform.

PSALM 78:9-16

The sons of Ephraim, ordered ranks of bowmen,
   retreated in the day of battle.
They kept not the covenant with God;
   according to his law they would not walk;
And they forgot his deeds,
   the wonders he had shown them.
Before their fathers he did wondrous things,

in the land of Egypt, in the
plain of Zoan.
He cleft the sea and brought
them through,
and he made the waters stand
as in a mound.
He led them with a cloud by day,
and all night with a glow of
fire.

He cleft the rocks in the desert
and gave them water in
copious floods.
He made streams flow from the
crag
and brought the waters forth in
rivers.

PROVERBS 18:13

He who answers before he hears—/ his is the folly and the shame.

JULY 5

PHILIPPIANS 3:1-21

Finally, my brothers, rejoice in the Lord. Writing the same things to you is no burden for me but is a safeguard for you.

Beware of the dogs! Beware of the evil-workers! Beware of the mutilation! For we are the circumcision, we who worship through the Spirit of God, who boast in Christ Jesus and do not put our confidence in flesh, although I myself have grounds for confidence even in the flesh.

If anyone else thinks he can be confident in flesh, all the more can I. Circumcised on the eighth day, of the race of Israel, of the tribe of Benjamin, a Hebrew of Hebrew parentage, in observance of the law a Pharisee, in zeal I persecuted the church, in righteousness based on the law I was blameless.

[But] whatever gains I had, these I have come to consider a loss because of Christ. More than that, I even consider everything as a loss because of the supreme good of knowing Christ Jesus my Lord. For his sake I have accepted the loss of all things and I consider them so much rubbish, that I may gain Christ and be found in him, not having any righteousness of my own based on the law but that which comes through faith in Christ, the righteousness from God, depending on faith to know him and the power of his resurrection and [the] sharing of his sufferings by being conformed to his death, if somehow I may attain the resurrection from the dead.

It is not that I have already taken hold of it or have already attained perfect maturity, but I continue my pursuit in hope that I may possess it, since I have indeed been taken possession of by Christ [Jesus]. Brothers, I for my part do not consider myself to have taken possession. Just one thing: forgetting what lies behind but straining forward to what lies ahead, I continue my pursuit toward the goal, the prize of God's upward calling, in Christ Jesus. Let us, then, who are "perfectly mature" adopt this attitude. And if you have a different attitude, this too God will reveal to you. Only, with regard to what we have attained, continue on the same course.

Join with others in being imitators of me, brothers, and observe those who thus conduct themselves according to the model you have in us. For many, as I have often told you and now tell you even in tears, conduct themselves as enemies of the cross of Christ. Their end is destruction. Their God is their stomach; their glory is in their "shame." Their minds are occupied with earthly things. But our citizenship is in heaven, and from it we also await a savior, the Lord Jesus Christ. He will change our lowly body to conform with his glorified body by the power that enables him also to bring all things into subjection to himself.

PSALM 78:17-20

But they sinned yet more against him,
    rebelling against the Most High in the wasteland,
And they tempted God in their hearts
    by demanding the food they craved.
Yes, they spoke against God, saying,
    "Can God spread a table in the desert?
For when he struck the rock, waters gushed forth,
    and the streams overflowed;
Can he also give bread
    and provide meat for his people?"

PROVERBS 18:14-15

A man's spirit sustains him in infirmity—/ but a broken spirit who can bear? / The mind of the intelligent gains knowledge, / and the ear of the wise seeks knowledge.

JULY 6

PHILIPPIANS 4:1-23

Therefore, my brothers, whom I love and long for, my joy and crown, in this way stand firm in the Lord, beloved.

I urge Euodia and I urge Syntyche to come to a mutual understanding in the Lord. Yes, and I ask you also, my true yokemate, to help them, for they have struggled at my side in promoting the gospel, along with Clement and my other co-workers, whose names are in the book of life.

Rejoice in the Lord always. I shall say it again: rejoice! Your kindness should be known to all. The Lord is near. Have no anxiety at all, but in everything, by prayer and petition, with thanksgiving, make your requests known to God. Then the peace of God that surpasses all understanding will guard your hearts and minds in Christ Jesus.

Finally, brothers, whatever is true, whatever is honorable, whatever is just, whatever is pure, whatever is lovely, whatever is gracious, if there is any excellence and if there is anything worthy of praise, think about these things. Keep on doing what you have learned and received and heard and seen in me. Then the God of peace will be with you.

I rejoice greatly in the Lord that now at last you revived your concern for me. You were, of course, concerned about me but lacked an opportunity. Not that I say this because of need, for I have learned, in whatever situation I find myself, to be self-sufficient. I know indeed how to live in humble circumstances; I know also how to live with abundance. In every circumstance and in all things I have learned the secret of being well fed and of going hungry, of living in abundance and of being in need. I have the strength for everything through him who empowers me. Still it was kind of you to share in my distress.

You Philippians indeed know that at the beginning of the gospel, when I left Macedonia, not a single church shared with me in an account of giving and receiving, except you alone. For even when I was at Thessalonica you sent me something for my needs, not only once but more than once. It is not that I am eager for the gift; rather, I am eager for the profit that accrues to your account. I have received full payment and I abound. I am very well supplied because of what I received from you through Epaphroditus, "a fragrant aroma," an acceptable sacrifice, pleasing to God. My God will fully supply whatever you need, in accord with his glorious riches in Christ Jesus. To our God and Father, glory for ever and ever. Amen.

Give my greetings to every holy one in Christ Jesus. The brothers who are with me send you their greetings; all the holy ones send you their greetings, especially those of Caesar's household. The grace of the Lord Jesus Christ be with your spirit.

PSALM 78:21-31

Then the LORD heard and was enraged;
  and fire blazed up against Jacob,
  and anger rose against Israel,
Because they believed not God
  nor trusted in his help.
Yet he commanded the skies above
  and the doors of heaven he opened;
He rained manna upon them for food
  and gave them heavenly bread.
The bread of the mighty was eaten by men;
  even a surfeit of provisions he sent them.
He stirred up the east wind in the heavens,
  and by his power brought on the south wind.
And he rained meat upon them like dust,
  and, like the sand of the sea, winged fowl,
Which fell in the midst of their camp
  round about their tents.
So they ate and were wholly surfeited;
  he had brought them what they craved.
They had not given over their craving,
  and their food was still in their mouths,
When the anger of God rose against them
  and slew their best men,
  and laid low the young men of Israel.

PROVERBS 18:16-18

A man's gift clears the way for him, / and gains him access to great men. / The man who pleads his case first seems to be in the right; / then his opponent comes and puts him to the test. / The lot puts an end to disputes, / and is decisive in a controversy between the mighty.

JULY 7

COLOSSIANS 1:1-14

Paul, an apostle of Christ Jesus by the will of God, and Timothy our brother, to the holy ones and faithful brothers in Christ in Colossae: grace to you and peace from God our Father.

We always give thanks to God, the Father of our Lord Jesus Christ, when we pray for you, for we have heard of your faith in Christ Jesus and the love that you have for all the holy ones because of the hope reserved for you in heaven. Of this you have already heard through the word of truth, the gospel, that has come to you. Just as in the whole world it is bearing fruit and growing, so also among you, from the day you heard it and came to know the grace of God in truth, as you learned it from Epaphras our beloved fellow slave, who is a trustworthy minister of Christ on your behalf and who also told us of your love in the Spirit.

Therefore, from the day we heard this, we do not cease praying for you and asking that you may be filled with the knowledge of his will through all spiritual wisdom and understanding to live in a manner worthy of the Lord, so as to be fully pleasing, in every good work bearing fruit and growing in the knowledge of God, strengthened with every power, in accord with his glorious might, for all endurance and patience, with joy giving thanks to the Father, who has made you fit to share in the inheritance of the holy ones in light. He delivered us from the power of darkness and transferred us to the kingdom of his beloved Son, in whom we have redemption, the forgiveness of sins.

PSALM 78:32-39

Yet for all this they sinned still
 more
 and believed not in his
  wonders
Therefore he quickly ended their
 days
 and their years with sudden
  destruction.
While he slew them they sought
 him
 and inquired after God again,
Remembering that God was their
 rock
 and the Most High God, their
  redeemer.
But they flattered him with their
 mouths
 and lied to him with their
  tongues,
Though their hearts were not
 steadfast toward him,
 nor were they faithful to his
  covenant.

Yet he, being merciful, forgave
their sin
and destroyed them not;
Often he turned back his anger
and let none of his wrath be
roused
He remembered that they were
flesh,
a passing breath that returns
not.

PROVERBS 18:19

*A brother is a better defense than a strong city, / and a friend is like the bars of a
castle.*

JULY 8

COLOSSIANS 1:15-29

He is the image of the invisible
God,
the firstborn of all creation.
For in him were created all
things in heaven and on
earth,
the visible and the invisible,
whether thrones or
dominions or principalities
or powers;
all things were created
through him and for him.
He is before all things,
and in him all things hold
together.
He is the head of the body, the
church.
He is the beginning, the
firstborn from the dead,
that in all things he himself
might be preeminent.
For in him all the fullness was
pleased to dwell,
and through him to reconcile
all things for him,
making peace by the blood of
his cross
[through him], whether
those on earth or those in
heaven.

And you who once were alienated and hostile in mind because
of evil deeds he has now reconciled in his fleshly body through
his death, to present you holy,
without blemish, and irreproachable before him, provided that
you persevere in the faith, firmly
grounded, stable, and not shifting
from the hope of the gospel that
you heard, which has been
preached to every creature under
heaven, of which I, Paul, am a
minister.
Now I rejoice in my sufferings
for your sake, and in my flesh I
am filling up what is lacking in the
afflictions of Christ on behalf of
his body, which is the church, of
which I am a minister in accordance with God's stewardship
given to me to bring to completion
for you the word of God, the mystery hidden from ages and from
generations past. But now it has
been manifested to his holy ones,
to whom God chose to make
known the riches of the glory of
this mystery among the Gentiles;
it is Christ in you, the hope for
glory. It is he whom we proclaim,
admonishing everyone and teaching everyone with all wisdom,

that we may present everyone perfect in Christ. For this I labor and struggle, in accord with the exercise of his power working within me.

PSALM 78:40-55

How often they rebelled against him in the desert
  and grieved him in the wilderness!
Again and again they tempted God
  and provoked the Holy One of Israel.
They remembered not his hand
  nor the day he delivered them from the foe,
When he wrought his signs in Egypt
  and his marvels in the plain of Zoan,
And changed into blood their streams—
  their running water, so that they could not drink;
He sent among them flies that devoured them
  and frogs that destroyed them.
He gave their harvest to the caterpillar,
  the fruits of their toil to the locust.
He killed their vines with hail
  and their sycamores with frost.

He gave over to the hail their beasts
  and their flocks to the lightning.
He loosed against them his fierce anger,
  wrath and fury and strife,
  a detachment of messengers of doom.
When he measured the course of his anger
  he spared them not from death,
  and delivered their beasts to the plague.
He smote every first-born in Egypt,
  the first fruits of manhood in the tents of Ham;
But his people he led forth like sheep
  and guided them like a herd in the desert.
He led them on secure and unafraid,
  while he covered their enemies with the sea.
And he brought them to his holy land,
  to the mountains his right hand had won.
And he drove out nations before them;
  he distributed their inheritance by lot,
  and settled the tribes of Israel in their tents.

PROVERBS 18:20-21

From the fruit of his mouth a man has his fill; / with the yield of his lips he sates himself. / Death and life are in the power of the tongue; / those who make it a friend shall eat its fruit.

JULY 9

COLOSSIANS 2:1-23

For I want you to know how great a struggle I am having for you and for those in Laodicea and all who have not seen me face to face, that their hearts may be encouraged as they are brought together in love, to have all the richness of fully assured understanding, for the knowledge of the mystery of God, Christ, in whom are hidden all the treasures of wisdom and knowledge.

I say this so that no one may deceive you by specious arguments. For even if I am absent in the flesh, yet I am with you in spirit, rejoicing as I observe your good order and the firmness of your faith in Christ. So, as you received Christ Jesus the Lord, walk in him, rooted in him and built upon him and established in the faith as you were taught, abounding in thanksgiving. See to it that no one captivate you with an empty, seductive philosophy according to human tradition, according to the elemental powers of the world and not according to Christ.

For in him dwells the whole fullness of the deity bodily, and you share in this fullness in him, who is the head of every principality and power. In him you were also circumcised with a circumcision not administered by hand, by stripping off the carnal body, with the circumcision of Christ. You were buried with him in baptism, in which you were also raised with him through faith in the power of God, who raised him from the dead. And even when you were dead [in] transgressions and the uncircumcision of your flesh, he brought you to life along with him, having forgiven us all our transgressions; obliterating the bond against us, with its legal claims, which was opposed to us, he also removed it from our midst, nailing it to the cross; despoiling the principalities and the powers, he made a public spectacle of them, leading them away in triumph by it.

Let no one, then, pass judgment on you in matters of food and drink or with regard to a festival or new moon or sabbath. These are shadows of things to come; the reality belongs to Christ. Let no one disqualify you, delighting in self-abasement and worship of angels, taking his stand on visions, inflated without reason by his fleshly mind, and not holding closely to the head, from whom the whole body, supported and held together by its ligaments and bonds, achieves the growth that comes from God.

If you died with Christ to the elemental powers of the world, why do you submit to regulations as if you were still living in the world? "Do not handle! Do not taste! Do not touch!" These are all things destined to perish with use; they accord with human precepts and teachings. While they have a semblance of wisdom in rigor of devotion and self-abasement [and] severity to the body, they are of no value against gratification of the flesh.

PSALM 78:56-64

But they tempted and rebelled
　　against God the Most High,
　　and kept not his decrees.

They turned back and were
   faithless like their fathers;
   they recoiled like a treacherous
   bow.
They angered him with their high
   places
   and with their idols roused his
   jealousy.
God heard and was enraged
   and utterly rejected Israel.
And he forsook the tabernacle in
   Shiloh,
   the tent where he dwelt among
   men.

And he surrendered his strength
   into captivity,
   his glory into the hands of the
   foe.
He abandoned his people to the
   sword
   and was enraged against his
   inheritance.
Fire consumed their young men,
   and their maidens were not
   betrothed.
Their priests fell by the sword,
   and their widows sang no
   dirges.

PROVERBS 18:22

He who finds a wife finds happiness; / it is a favor he receives from the LORD.

JULY 10

COLOSSIANS 3:1-17

If then you were raised with Christ, seek what is above, where Christ is seated at the right hand of God. Think of what is above, not of what is on earth. For you have died, and your life is hidden with Christ in God. When Christ your life appears, then you too will appear with him in glory.

Put to death, then, the parts of you that are earthly: immorality, impurity, passion, evil desire, and the greed that is idolatry. Because of these the wrath of God is coming [upon the disobedient]. By these you too once conducted yourselves, when you lived in that way. But now you must put them all away: anger, fury, malice, slander, and obscene language out of your mouths. Stop lying to one another, since you have taken off the old self with its practices and have put on the new self, which is being renewed, for knowledge, in the image of its creator. Here there is not Greek and Jew, circumcision and uncircumcision, barbarian, Scythian, slave, free; but Christ is all and in all.

Put on then, as God's chosen ones, holy and beloved, heartfelt compassion, kindness, humility, gentleness, and patience, bearing with one another and forgiving one another, if one has a grievance against another; as the Lord has forgiven you, so must you also do. And over all these put on love, that is, the bond of perfection. And let the peace of Christ control your hearts, the peace into which you were also called in one body. And be thankful. Let the word of Christ dwell in you richly, as in all wisdom you teach and admonish one another, singing psalms, hymns, and spiritual songs with gratitude in your hearts to God. And whatever you do, in word or in deed, do everything in the name of the Lord Jesus, giving thanks to God the Father through him.

PSALM 78:65-72

Then the Lord awoke, as wakes
    from sleep
  a champion overcome with
    wine;
And he put his foes to flight
  and cast them into everlasting
    disgrace.
And he rejected the tent of
    Joseph,
  and the tribe of Ephraim he
    chose not;

But he chose the tribe of Judah,
    Mount Zion which he loved.
And he built his shrine like
    heaven,
  like the earth which he
    founded forever.
And he chose David, his servant,
  and took him from the
    sheepfolds;
From following the ewes he
    brought him
  to shepherd Jacob, his people,
  and Israel, his inheritance.
And he tended them with a
    sincere heart,
  and with skillful hands he
    guided them.

PROVERBS 18:23-24

The poor man implores, / but the rich man answers harshly. / Some friends bring ruin on us, / but a true friend is more loyal than a brother.

JULY 11

COLOSSIANS 3:18-25

Wives, be subordinate to your husbands, as is proper in the Lord. Husbands, love your wives, and avoid any bitterness toward them. Children, obey your parents in everything, for this is pleasing to the Lord. Fathers, do not provoke your children, so they may not become discouraged.

Slaves, obey your human masters in everything, not only when being watched, as currying favor, but in simplicity of heart, fearing the Lord. Whatever you do, do from the heart, as for the Lord and not for others, knowing that you will receive from the Lord the due payment of the inheritance; be slaves of the Lord Christ. For the wrongdoer will receive recompense for the wrong he committed, and there is no partiality.

PSALM 79:1-8

A psalm of Asaph.
O God, the nations have come
    into your inheritance;
  they have defiled your holy
    temple,
  they have laid Jerusalem in
    ruins.
They have given the corpses of
    your servants
  as food to the birds of heaven,
  the flesh of your faithful ones
    to the beasts of the earth.
They have poured out their blood
    like water
  round about Jerusalem,
  and there is no one to bury
    them.

We have become the reproach of
  our neighbors,
  the scorn and derision of those
  around us.
O LORD, how long? Will you be
  angry forever?
  Will your jealousy burn like
  fire?
Pour out your wrath upon the
  nations that acknowledge
  you not,
upon the kingdoms that call
  not upon your name;
For they have devoured Jacob
  and laid waste his dwelling.
Remember not against us the
  iniquities of the past;
  may your compassion quickly
  come to us,
  for we are brought very low.

PROVERBS 19:1-3

Better a poor man who walks in his integrity / than he who is crooked in his ways and rich. / Without knowledge even zeal is not good; / and he who acts hastily, blunders. / A man's own folly upsets his way, / but his heart is resentful against the LORD.

JULY 12

COLOSSIANS 4:1-18

Masters, treat your slaves justly and fairly, realizing that you too have a Master in heaven.

Persevere in prayer, being watchful in it with thanksgiving; at the same time, pray for us, too, that God may open a door to us for the word, to speak of the mystery of Christ, for which I am in prison, that I may make it clear, as I must speak. Conduct yourselves wisely toward outsiders, making the most of the opportunity. Let your speech always be gracious, seasoned with salt, so that you know how you should respond to each one.

Tychicus, my beloved brother, trustworthy minister, and fellow slave in the Lord, will tell you all the news of me. I am sending him to you for this very purpose, so that you may know about us and that he may encourage your hearts, together with Onesimus, a trustworthy and beloved brother, who is one of you. They will tell you about everything here.

Aristarchus, my fellow prisoner, sends you greetings, as does Mark the cousin of Barnabas (concerning whom you have received instructions; if he comes to you, receive him), and Jesus, who is called Justus, who are of the circumcision; these alone are my coworkers for the kingdom of God, and they have been a comfort to me. Epaphras sends you greetings; he is one of you, a slave of Christ [Jesus], always striving for you in his prayers so that you may be perfect and fully assured in all the will of God. For I can testify that he works very hard for you and for those in Laodicea and those in Hierapolis. Luke the beloved physician sends greetings, as does Demas.

Give greetings to the brothers in Laodicea and to Nympha and to the church in her house. And when this letter is read before you, have it read also in the church of the Laodiceans, and you yourselves read the one from Laodicea. And tell Archippus, "See that you fulfill the ministry that you received in the Lord."

The greeting is in my own hand, Paul's. Remember my chains. Grace be with you.

PSALM 79:9-13

Help us, O God our savior,
  because of the glory of your
    name;
Deliver us and pardon our sins
  for your name's sake.

Why should the nations say,
  "Where is their God?"
Let it be known among the
    nations in our sight
  that you avenge the shedding
    of your servants' blood.
Let the prisoners' sighing come
    before you;
  with your great power free
    those doomed to death.
And repay our neighbors
    sevenfold into their bosoms
  the disgrace they have inflicted
    on you, O Lord.
Then we, your people and the
    sheep of your pasture,
  will give thanks to you forever;
  through all generations we will
    declare your praise.

PROVERBS 19:4-5

Wealth adds many friends, / but the friend of the poor man deserts him. / The false witness will not go unpunished, / and he who utters lies will not escape.

JULY 13

1 THESSALONIANS 1:1-10

Paul, Silvanus, and Timothy to the church of the Thessalonians in God the Father and the Lord Jesus Christ: grace to you and peace.

We give thanks to God always for all of you, remembering you in our prayers, unceasingly calling to mind your work of faith and labor of love and endurance in hope of our Lord Jesus Christ, before our God and Father, knowing, brothers loved by God, how you were chosen. For our gospel did not come to you in word alone, but also in power and in the holy Spirit and [with] much conviction. You know what sort of people we were [among] you for your sake. And

you became imitators of us and of the Lord, receiving the word in great affliction, with joy from the holy Spirit, so that you became a model for all the believers in Macedonia and in Achaia. For from you the word of the Lord has sounded forth not only in Macedonia and [in] Achaia, but in every place your faith in God has gone forth, so that we have no need to say anything. For they themselves openly declare about us what sort of reception we had among you, and how you turned to God from idols to serve the living and true God and to await his Son from heaven, whom he raised from [the] dead, Jesus, who delivers us from the coming wrath.

PSALM 80:1-8

For the leader; according to "Lilies."
Eduth. A psalm of Asaph.

O shepherd of Israel, hearken,
  O guide of the flock of Joseph!
From your throne upon the
    cherubim, shine forth
before Ephraim, Benjamin and
    Manasseh.
Rouse your power,
  and come to save us.
O LORD of hosts, restore us;
  if your face shine upon us,
    then we shall be safe.

O LORD of hosts, how long will
  you burn with anger
while your people pray?
You have fed them with the
    bread of tears
  and given them tears to drink
    in ample measure.
You have left us to be fought
    over by our neighbors,
  and our enemies mock us.
O LORD of hosts, restore us;
  if your face shine upon us,
    then we shall be safe.

PROVERBS 19:6-7

Many curry favor with a noble; / all are friends of the man who has something to give. / All the poor man's brothers hate him; / how much more do his friends shun him!

JULY 14

1 THESSALONIANS 2:1-20

For you yourselves know, brothers, that our reception among you was not without effect. Rather, after we had suffered and been insolently treated, as you know, in Philippi, we drew courage through our God to speak to you the gospel of God with much struggle. Our exhortation was not from delusion or impure motives, nor did it work through deception. But as we were judged worthy by God to be entrusted with the gospel, that is how we speak, not as trying to please human beings, but rather God, who judges our hearts. Nor, indeed, did we ever appear with flattering speech, as you know, or with a pretext for greed—God is witness—nor did we seek praise from human beings, either from you or from others, although we were able to impose our weight as apostles of Christ. Rather, we were gentle among you, as a nursing mother cares for her children. With such affection for you, we were determined to share with you not only the gospel of God, but our very selves as well, so dearly beloved had you become to us. You recall, brothers, our toil and drudgery. Working night and day in order not to burden any of you, we proclaimed to you the gospel of God. You are witnesses, and so is God, how devoutly and justly and blamelessly we behaved toward you believers. As you know, we treated each one of you as a father treats his children, exhorting and encouraging you and insisting that you conduct yourselves as worthy of the God who calls you into his kingdom and glory.

And for this reason we too give thanks to God unceasingly, that, in receiving the word of God from hearing us, you received not a human word but, as it truly is, the word of God, which is now at work in you who believe. For you, brothers, have become imitators of the churches of God that are in Judea in Christ Jesus. For you suffer the same things from your compatriots as they did from the Jews, who killed both the Lord Jesus and the prophets and persecuted us; they do not please God, and are opposed to everyone, trying to prevent us from speaking to the Gentiles that they may be saved, thus constantly filling up the measure of their sins. But the wrath of God has finally begun to come upon them.

Brothers, when we were bereft of you for a short time, in person, not in heart, we were all the more eager in our great desire to see you in person. We decided to go to you—I, Paul, not only once but more than once—yet Satan thwarted us. For what is our hope or joy or crown to boast of in the presence of our Lord Jesus at his coming if not you yourselves? For you are our glory and joy.

PSALM 80:9-14

A vine from Egypt you
    transplanted;
  you drove away the nations
    and planted it.
You cleared the ground for it.
  and it took root and filled the
    land.
The mountains were hidden in its
    shadow;
  by its branches, the cedars of
    God.
It put forth its foliage to the Sea,
  its shoots as far as the River.
Why have you broken down its
    walls,
  so that every passer-by plucks
    its fruit,
The boar from the forest lays it
    waste,
  and the beasts of the field feed
    upon it?

PROVERBS 19:8-9

He who gains intelligence is his own best friend; / he who keeps understanding will be successful. / The false witness will not go unpunished, / and he who utters lies will perish.

JULY 15

1 THESSALONIANS 3:1-13

That is why, when we could bear it no longer, we decided to remain alone in Athens and sent Timothy, our brother and co-worker for God in the gospel of Christ, to strengthen and encourage you in your faith, so that no one be disturbed in these afflictions. For you yourselves know that we are destined for this. For even when we were among you, we used to warn you in advance that we would undergo affliction, just as has happened, as you know. For this reason, when I too could bear it no longer, I sent to learn about your faith, for fear that somehow the tempter had put you to the test and our toil might come to nothing.

But just now Timothy has returned to us from you, bringing us the good news of your faith and love, and that you always think kindly of us and long to see us as we long to see you. Because of this, we have been reassured about you, brothers, in our every distress and affliction, through your faith. For we now live, if you stand firm in the Lord.

What thanksgiving, then, can we render to God for you, for all the joy we feel on your account before our God? Night and day we pray beyond measure to see you in person and to remedy the deficiencies of your faith. Now may God himself, our Father, and our Lord Jesus direct our way to you, and may the Lord make you increase and abound in love for one another and for all, just as we have for you, so as to strengthen your hearts, to be blameless in holiness before our God and Father at the coming of our Lord Jesus with all his holy ones. [Amen.]

PSALM 80:15-20

Once again, O LORD of hosts,
  look down from heaven, and
    see;
Take care of this vine,
  and protect what your right
    hand has planted
  [the son of man whom you
    yourself made strong].
Let those who would burn it with
  fire or cut it down
  perish before you at your
    rebuke.
May your help be with the man
  of your right hand,
  with the son of man whom you
    yourself made strong.
Then we will no more withdraw
  from you;
  give us new life, and we will
    call upon your name.
O LORD of hosts, restore us;
  if your face shine upon us then
    we shall be safe.

PROVERBS 19:10-12

Luxury is not befitting a fool; / much less should a slave rule over princes. / It is good sense in a man to be slow to anger, / and it is his glory to overlook an offense. / The king's wrath is like the roaring of a lion, / but his favor, like dew on the grass.

JULY 16

1 THESSALONIANS 4:1-18

Finally, brothers, we earnestly ask and exhort you in the Lord Jesus that, as you received from us how you should conduct yourselves to please God—and as you are conducting yourselves—you do so even more. For you know what instructions we gave you through the Lord Jesus.

This is the will of God, your holiness: that you refrain from immorality, that each of you know how to acquire a wife for himself in holiness and honor, not in lustful passion as do the Gentiles who do not know God; not to take advantage of or exploit a brother in this matter, for the Lord is an avenger in all these things, as we told you before and solemnly affirmed. For God did not call us to impurity but to holiness. Therefore, whoever disregards this, disregards not a human being but God, who [also] gives his holy Spirit to you.

On the subject of mutual charity you have no need for anyone to write you, for you yourselves have been taught by God to love one another. Indeed, you do this for all the brothers throughout Macedonia. Nevertheless we urge you, brothers, to progress even more, and to aspire to live a tranquil life, to mind your own affairs, and to work with your [own] hands, as we instructed you, that you may conduct yourselves properly toward outsiders and not depend on anyone.

We do not want you to be unaware, brothers, about those who have fallen asleep, so that you may not grieve like the rest, who have no hope. For if we believe that Jesus died and rose, so too will God, through Jesus, bring with him those who have fallen asleep. Indeed, we tell you this, on the word of the Lord, that we who are alive, who are left until the coming of the Lord, will surely not precede those who have fallen asleep. For the Lord himself, with a word of command, with the voice of an archangel and with the trumpet of God, will come down from heaven, and the dead in Christ will rise first. Then we who are alive, who are left, will be caught up together with them in the clouds to meet the Lord in the air. Thus we shall always be with the Lord. Therefore, console one another with these words.

PSALM 81:1-6

For the leader; "upon the gittith." Of Asaph.

Sing joyfully to God our strength;
acclaim the God of Jacob.
Take up a melody, and sound the timbrel,
the pleasant harp and the lyre.
Blow the trumpet at the new moon,
at the full moon, on our solemn feast;
For it is a statute in Israel,
an ordinance of the God of Jacob,
Who made it a decree for Joseph when he came forth from the land of Egypt.

PROVERBS 19:13-14

The foolish son is ruin to his father, / and the nagging of a wife is a persistent leak. / Home and possessions are an inheritance from parents, / but a prudent wife is from the LORD.

JULY 17

1 THESSALONIANS 5:1-28

Concerning times and seasons, brothers, you have no need for anything to be written to you. For you yourselves know very well that the day of the Lord will come like a thief at night. When people are saying, "Peace and security," then sudden disaster comes upon them, like labor pains upon a pregnant woman, and they will not escape.

But you, brothers, are not in darkness, for that day to overtake you like a thief. For all of you are children of the light and children of the day. We are not of the night or of darkness. Therefore, let us not sleep as the rest do, but let us stay alert and sober. Those who sleep go to sleep at night, and those who are drunk get drunk at night. But since we are of the day, let us be sober, putting on the breastplate of faith and love and the helmet that is hope for salvation. For God did not destine us for wrath, but to gain salvation through our Lord Jesus Christ, who died for us, so that whether we are awake or asleep we may live together with him. Therefore, encourage one another and build one another up, as indeed you do.

We ask you, brothers, to respect those who are laboring among you and who are over you in the Lord and who admonish you, and to show esteem for them with special love on account of their work. Be at peace among yourselves.

We urge you, brothers, admonish the idle, cheer the fainthearted, support the weak, be patient with all. See that no one returns evil for evil; rather, always seek what is good [both] for each other and for all. Rejoice always. Pray without ceasing. In all circumstances give thanks, for this is the will of God for you in Christ Jesus. Do not quench the Spirit. Do not despise prophetic utterances. Test everything; retain what is good. Refrain from every kind of evil.

May the God of peace himself make you perfectly holy and may you entirely, spirit, soul, and body, be preserved blameless for the coming of our Lord Jesus Christ. The one who calls you is faithful, and he will also accomplish it. Brothers, pray for us [too].

Greet all the brothers with a holy kiss. I adjure you by the Lord that this letter be read to all the brothers. The grace of our Lord Jesus Christ be with you.

PSALM 81:7-11

An unfamiliar speech I hear:
> "I relieved his shoulder of the burden;
> his hands were freed from the basket.
In distress you called, and I rescued you;
> Unseen, I answered you in thunder;
> I tested you at the waters of Meribah.
Hear, my people, and I will admonish you;
> O Israel, will you not hear me?
There shall be no strange god among you
> nor shall you worship any alien god.

I, the LORD, am your God
who led you forth from the
land of Egypt;

open wide your mouth, and I
will fill it.

PROVERBS 19:15-16

Laziness plunges a man into deep sleep, / and the sluggard must go hungry. /
He who keeps the precept keeps his life, / but the despiser of the word will die.

JULY 18

2 THESSALONIANS 1:1-12

Paul, Silvanus, and Timothy to the church of the Thessalonians in God our Father and the Lord Jesus Christ: grace to you and peace from God [our] Father and the Lord Jesus Christ.

We ought to thank God always for you, brothers, as is fitting, because your faith flourishes ever more, and the love of every one of you for one another grows ever greater. Accordingly, we ourselves boast of you in the churches of God regarding your endurance and faith in all your persecutions and the afflictions you endure.

This is evidence of the just judgment of God, so that you may be considered worthy of the kingdom of God for which you are suffering. For it is surely just on God's part to repay with afflictions those who are afflicting you, and to grant rest along with us to you who are undergoing afflictions, at the revelation of the Lord Jesus from heaven with his mighty angels, in blazing fire, inflicting punishment on those who do not acknowledge God and on those who do not obey the gospel of our Lord Jesus. These will pay the penalty of eternal ruin, separated from the presence of the Lord and from the glory of his power, when he comes to be glorified among his holy ones and to be marveled at on that day among all who have believed, for our testimony to you was believed.

To this end, we always pray for you, that our God may make you worthy of his calling and powerfully bring to fulfillment every good purpose and every effort of faith, that the name of our Lord Jesus may be glorified in you, and you in him, in accord with the grace of our God and Lord Jesus Christ.

PSALM 81:12-17

"But my people heard not my
voice,
and Israel obeyed me not;
So I gave them up to the
hardness of their hearts;
they walked according to their
own counsels.
If only my people would hear
me,
and Israel walk in my ways,
Quickly would I humble their
enemies;
against their foes I would turn
my hand.
Those who hated the LORD would
seek to flatter me,

but their fate would endure
  forever,
While Israel I would feed with
  the best of wheat,

and with honey from the rock I
  would fill them."

PROVERBS 19:17

He who has compassion on the poor lends to the LORD, / and he will repay him for his good deed.

JULY 19

---

2 THESSALONIANS 2:1-17

We ask you, brothers, with regard to the coming of our Lord Jesus Christ and our assembling with him, not to be shaken out of your minds suddenly, or to be alarmed either by a "spirit," or by an oral statement, or by a letter allegedly from us to the effect that the day of the Lord is at hand. Let no one deceive you in any way. For unless the apostasy comes first and the lawless one is revealed, the one doomed to perdition, who opposes and exalts himself above every so-called god and object of worship, so as to seat himself in the temple of God, claiming that he is a god—do you not recall that while I was still with you I told you these things? And now you know what is restraining, that he may be revealed in his time. For the mystery of lawlessness is already at work. But the one who restrains is to do so only for the present, until he is removed from the scene. And then the lawless one will be revealed, whom the Lord [Jesus] will kill with the breath of his mouth and render powerless by the manifestation of his coming, the one whose coming springs from the power of Satan in every mighty deed and in signs and wonders that lie, and in every wicked deceit for those who are perishing because they have not accepted the love of truth so that they may be saved. Therefore, God is sending them a deceiving power so that they may believe the lie, that all who have not believed the truth but have approved wrongdoing may be condemned.

But we ought to give thanks to God for you always, brothers loved by the Lord, because God chose you as the firstfruits for salvation through sanctification by the Spirit and belief in truth. To this end he has [also] called you through our gospel to possess the glory of our Lord Jesus Christ. Therefore, brothers, stand firm and hold fast to the traditions that you were taught, either by an oral statement or by a letter of ours.

May our Lord Jesus Christ himself and God our Father, who has loved us and given us everlasting encouragement and good hope through his grace, encourage your hearts and strengthen them in every good deed and word.

PSALM 82:1-8

A psalm of Asaph.
God arises in the divine
  assembly;

he judges in the midst of the
gods.
"How long will you judge
unjustly
and favor the cause of the
wicked?
Defend the lowly and the
fatherless;
render justice to the afflicted
and the destitute.
Rescue the lowly and the poor;
from the hand of the wicked
deliver them.

"They know not, neither do they
understand;
they go about in darkness;
all the foundations of the earth
are shaken.
I said: You are gods,
all of you sons of the Most
High;
Yet like men you shall die,
and fall like any prince."
Rise, O God; judge the earth,
for yours are all the nations.

PROVERBS 19:18-19

Chastise your son, for in this there is hope; / but do not desire his death. / The man of violent temper pays the penalty; / even if you rescue him, you will have it to do again.

JULY 20

2 THESSALONIANS 3:1-18

Finally, brothers, pray for us, so that the word of the Lord may speed forward and be glorified, as it did among you, and that we may be delivered from perverse and wicked people, for not all have faith. But the Lord is faithful; he will strengthen you and guard you from the evil one. We are confident of you in the Lord that what we instruct you, you [both] are doing and will continue to do. May the Lord direct your hearts to the love of God and to the endurance of Christ.

We instruct you, brothers, in the name of [our] Lord Jesus Christ, to shun any brother who conducts himself in a disorderly way and not according to the tradition they received from us. For you know how one must imitate us. For we did not act in a disor-

derly way among you, nor did we eat food received free from anyone. On the contrary, in toil and drudgery, night and day we worked, so as not to burden any of you. Not that we do not have the right. Rather, we wanted to present ourselves as a model for you, so that you might imitate us. In fact, when we were with you, we instructed you that if anyone was unwilling to work, neither should that one eat. We hear that some are conducting themselves among you in a disorderly way, by not keeping busy but minding the business of others. Such people we instruct and urge in the Lord Jesus Christ to work quietly and to eat their own food. But you, brothers, do not be remiss in doing good. If anyone does not obey our word as expressed in this letter, take note of this person not to associate with him, that he may be put to shame. Do not regard him as an enemy but admonish him as a brother. May the Lord of peace himself give you peace at all times and in every way. The Lord be with all of you.

This greeting is in my own hand, Paul's. This is the sign in every letter; this is how I write. The grace of our Lord Jesus Christ be with all of you.

PSALM 83: 1-9

A song; a psalm of Asaph.
O God, do not remain unmoved;
  be not silent, O God, and be
    not still!
For behold, your enemies raise a
  tumult,
  and they who hate you lift up
    their heads.

Against your people they plot
  craftily;
  they conspire against those
    whom you protect.
They say, "Come, let us destroy
  their nation;
  let the name of Israel be
    remembered no more!"
Yes, they consult together with
  one mind,
  and against you they are allied:
The tents of Edom and the
  Ishmaelites,
  Moab and the people of Hagar,
Gebal and Ammon and Amalek,
  Philistia with the inhabitants of
    Tyre;
The Assyrians, too, are leagued
  with them;
  they are the forces of the sons
    of Lot.

PROVERBS 19:20-21

Listen to counsel and receive instruction, / that you may eventually become wise. / Many are the plans in a man's heart, / but it is the decision of the LORD that endures.

JULY 21

1 TIMOTHY 1:1-11

Paul, an apostle of Christ Jesus by command of God our savior and of Christ Jesus our hope, to Timothy, my true child in faith: grace, mercy, and peace from God the Father and Christ Jesus our Lord.

I repeat the request I made of you when I was on my way to Macedonia, that you stay in Ephesus to instruct certain people not to teach false doctrines or to concern themselves with myths and endless genealogies, which promote speculations rather than the plan of God that is to be received by faith. The aim of this instruction is love from a pure heart, a good conscience, and a sincere faith. Some people have deviated from these and turned to meaningless talk, wanting to be teachers of the law, but without understanding either what they are saying or what they assert with such assurance.

We know that the law is good, provided that one uses it as law, with the understanding that law is meant not for a righteous person but for the lawless and unruly, the godless and sinful, the unholy and profane, those who kill their fathers or mothers, murderers, the unchaste, practicing homosexuals, kidnapers, liars, perjurers, and whatever else is opposed to sound teaching, according to the glorious gospel of the blessed God, with which I have been entrusted.

PSALM 83:10-13

Deal with them as with Midian;

as with Sisera and Jabin at the torrent Kishon,
Who perished at Endor;
  they became dung on the ground.
Make their nobles like Oreb and Zeeb;
  all their chiefs like Zebah and Zalmunna,
Who said, "Let us take for ourselves
  the dwelling place of God."

PROVERBS 19:22

From a man's greed comes his shame; / rather be a poor man than a liar.

JULY 22

1 TIMOTHY 1:12-20

I am grateful to him who has strengthened me, Christ Jesus our Lord, because he considered me trustworthy in appointing me to the ministry. I was once a blasphemer and a persecutor and an arrogant man, but I have been mercifully treated because I acted out of ignorance in my unbelief. Indeed, the grace of our Lord has been abundant, along with the faith and love that are in Christ Jesus. This saying is trustworthy and deserves full acceptance: Christ Jesus came into the world to save sinners. Of these I am the foremost. But for that reason I was mercifully treated, so that in me, as the foremost, Christ Jesus might display all his patience as an example for those who would come to believe in him for everlasting life. To the king of ages, incorruptible, invisible, the only God,

honor and glory forever and ever. Amen.

I entrust this charge to you, Timothy, my child, in accordance with the prophetic words once spoken about you. Through them may you fight a good fight by having faith and a good conscience. Some, by rejecting conscience, have made a shipwreck of their faith, among them Hymenaeus and Alexander, whom I have handed over to Satan to be taught not to blaspheme.

PSALM 83:14-19

O my God, make them like leaves in a whirlwind,
  like chaff before the wind.
As a fire raging in a forest,
  as a flame setting the mountains ablaze,
So pursue them with your tempest

and rout them with your
 storm.
Darken their faces with disgrace,
 that men may seek your name,
 O LORD.
Let them be shamed and put to
 rout forever;

let them be confounded and
 perish,
Knowing that you alone are the
 LORD,
 the Most High over all the
 earth.

PROVERBS 19:23

The fear of the LORD is an aid to life; / one eats and sleeps without being visited by misfortune.

JULY 23

1 TIMOTHY 2:1-15

First of all, then, I ask that supplications, prayers, petitions, and thanksgivings be offered for everyone, for kings and for all in authority, that we may lead a quiet and tranquil life in all devotion and dignity. This is good and pleasing to God our savior, who wills everyone to be saved and to come to knowledge of the truth.

For there is one God. There is also one mediator between God and the human race, Christ Jesus, himself human, who gave himself as ransom for all.

This was the testimony at the proper time. For this I was appointed preacher and apostle (I am speaking the truth, I am not lying), teacher of the Gentiles in faith and truth.

It is my wish, then, that in every place the men should pray, lifting up holy hands, without anger or argument. Similarly, [too,] women should adorn themselves with proper conduct, with modesty and self-control, not with braided hairstyles and gold ornaments, or pearls, or expensive clothes, but rather, as befits

women who profess reverence for God, with good deeds. A woman must receive instruction silently and under complete control. I do not permit a woman to teach or to have authority over a man. She must be quiet. For Adam was formed first, then Eve. Further, Adam was not deceived, but the woman was deceived and transgressed. But she will be saved through motherhood, provided women persevere in faith and love and holiness, with self-control.

PSALM 84:1-8

*For the leader; "upon the gittith." A
 psalm of the sons of Korah.*
How lovely is your dwelling
 place,
 O LORD of hosts!
My soul yearns and pines
 for the courts of the LORD.
My heart and my flesh
 cry out for the living God.
Even the sparrow finds a home,
 and the swallow a nest
 in which she puts her young—
Your altars, O LORD of hosts,
 my king and my God!

Happy they who dwell in your house!
continually they praise you.
Happy the men whose strength you are!
their hearts are set upon the pilgrimage:
When they pass through the valley of the mastic trees,
they make a spring of it;
the early rain clothes it with generous growth.
They go from strength to strength;
they shall see the God of gods in Zion.

PROVERBS 19:24-26

The sluggard loses his hand in the dish; / he will not even lift it to his mouth. / If you beat an arrogant man, the simple learn a lesson; / if you rebuke an intelligent man, he gains knowledge. / He who mistreats his father, or drives away his mother, / is a worthless and disgraceful son.

JULY 24

1 TIMOTHY 3:1-16

This saying is trustworthy: whoever aspires to the office of bishop desires a noble task. Therefore, a bishop must be irreproachable, married only once, temperate, self-controlled, decent, hospitable, able to teach, not a drunkard, not aggressive, but gentle, not contentious, not a lover of money. He must manage his own household well, keeping his children under control with perfect dignity; for if a man does not know how to manage his own household, how can he take care of the church of God? He should not be a recent convert, so that he may not become conceited and thus incur the devil's punishment. He must also have a good reputation among outsiders, so that he may not fall into disgrace, the devil's trap.

Similarly, deacons must be dignified, not deceitful, not addicted to drink, not greedy for sordid gain, holding fast to the mystery of the faith with a clear conscience. Moreover, they should be tested first; then, if there is nothing against them, let them serve as deacons. Women, similarly, should be dignified, not slanderers, but temperate and faithful in everything. Deacons may be married only once and must manage their children and their households well. Thus those who serve well as deacons gain good standing and much confidence in their faith in Christ Jesus.

I am writing you about these matters, although I hope to visit you soon. But if I should be delayed, you should know how to behave in the household of God, which is the church of the living God, the pillar and foundation of truth. Undeniably great is the mystery of devotion,

Who was manifest in the flesh,
vindicated in the spirit,
seen by angels,
proclaimed to the Gentiles,

believed in throughout the
world,
taken up in glory.

PSALM 84:9-13

O LORD of hosts, hear my prayer;
hearken, O God of Jacob!
O God, behold our shield,
and look upon the face of your
anointed.
I had rather one day in your
courts
than a thousand elsewhere;

I had rather lie at the threshhold
of the house of my God
than dwell in the tents of the
wicked.
For a sun and a shield is the
LORD God;
grace and glory he bestows;
The LORD withholds no good
thing
from those who walk in
sincerity.
O LORD of hosts,
happy the men who trust in
you!

PROVERBS 19:27-29

If a son ceases to hear instruction, / he wanders from words of knowledge. / An unprincipled witness perverts justice, / and the mouth of the wicked pours out iniquity. / Rods are prepared for the arrogant, / and blows for the backs of fools.

JULY 25

1 TIMOTHY 4:1-16

Now the Spirit explicitly says that in the last times some will turn away from the faith by paying attention to deceitful spirits and demonic instructions through the hypocrisy of liars with branded consciences. They forbid marriage and require abstinence from foods that God created to be received with thanksgiving by those who believe and know the truth. For everything created by God is good, and nothing is to be rejected when received with thanksgiving, for it is made holy by the invocation of God in prayer.

If you will give these instructions to the brothers, you will be a good minister of Christ Jesus, nourished on the words of the faith and of the sound teaching you have followed. Avoid profane and silly myths. Train yourself for devotion, for, while physical training is of limited value, devotion is valuable in every respect, since it holds a promise of life both for the present and for the future. This saying is trustworthy and deserves full acceptance. For this we toil and struggle, because we have set our hope on the living God, who is the savior of all, especially of those who believe.

Command and teach these things. Let no one have contempt for your youth, but set an example for those who believe, in speech, conduct, love, faith, and purity. Until I arrive, attend to the reading, exhortation, and teaching. Do not neglect the gift you have, which was conferred on you through the prophetic word with the imposition of hands of the presbyterate. Be diligent in these matters, be absorbed in them, so that your progress may be evident to everyone. Attend to yourself and to your teaching; persevere in both tasks, for by doing so you will save both yourself and those who listen to you.

PSALM 85:1-8

*For the leader. A psalm of the sons of
    Korah.*
You have favored, O LORD, your
    land;
  you have restored the well-
    being of Jacob.
You have forgiven the guilt of
    your people;

you have covered all their sins.
You have withdrawn all your
    wrath;
  you have revoked your burning
    anger.
Restore us, O God our savior,
  and abandon your displeasure
    against us.
Will you be ever angry with us,
  prolonging your anger to all
    generations?
Will you not instead give us life;
  and shall not your people
    rejoice in you?
Show us, O LORD, your
    kindness,
  and grant us your salvation.

PROVERBS 20:1

Wine is arrogant, strong drink is riotous; / none who goes astray for it is wise.

JULY 26

1 TIMOTHY 5:1-25

Do not rebuke an older man, but appeal to him as a father. Treat younger men as brothers, older women as mothers, and younger women as sisters with complete purity.

Honor widows who are truly widows. But if a widow has children or grandchildren, let these first learn to perform their religious duty to their own family and to make recompense to their parents, for this is pleasing to God. The real widow, who is all alone, has set her hope on God and continues in supplications and prayers night and day. But the one who is self-indulgent is dead while she lives. Command this, so that they may be irreproachable. And whoever does

not provide for relatives and especially family members has denied the faith and is worse than an unbeliever.

Let a widow be enrolled if she is not less than sixty years old, married only once, with a reputation for good works, namely, that she has raised children, practiced hospitality, washed the feet of the holy ones, helped those in distress, involved herself in every good work. But exclude younger widows, for when their sensuality estranges them from Christ, they want to marry and will incur condemnation for breaking their first pledge. And furthermore, they learn to be idlers, going about from house to house, and not only idlers but gossips and busybodies as well, talking about things that ought not to be mentioned. So I would like younger widows to marry, have children, and manage a home, so as to give the adversary no pretext for maligning us. For some have already turned away to follow Satan. If any woman believer has widowed relatives, she must assist them; the church is not to be burdened, so that it will be able to help those who are truly widows.

Presbyters who preside well deserve double honor, especially those who toil in preaching and teaching. For the scripture says, "You shall not muzzle an ox when it is threshing," and, "A worker deserves his pay." Do not accept an accusation against a presbyter unless it is supported by two or three witnesses. Reprimand publicly those who do sin, so that the rest also will be afraid. I charge you before God and Christ Jesus and the elect angels to keep these rules without prejudice, doing nothing out of favoritism. Do not lay hands too readily on anyone, and do not share in another's sins. Keep yourself pure. Stop drinking only water, but have a little wine for the sake of your stomach and your frequent illnesses.

Some people's sins are public, preceding them to judgment; but other people are followed by their sins. Similarly, good works are also public; and even those that are not cannot remain hidden.

PSALM 85:9-14

I will hear what God proclaims;
   the LORD—for he proclaims
    peace.
To his people, and to his faithful
   ones,
   and to those who put in him
    their hope.
Near indeed is his salvation to
   those who fear him,
   glory dwelling in our land.
Kindness and truth shall meet;
   justice and peace shall kiss.
Truth shall spring out of the
   earth,
   and justice shall look down
    from heaven.
The LORD himself will give his
   benefits;
   our land shall yield its increase.
Justice shall walk before him,
   and salvation, along the way of
    his steps.

PROVERBS 20:2-3

The dread of the king is as when a lion roars; / he who incurs his anger forfeits his life. / It is honorable for a man to shun strife, / while every fool starts a quarrel.

JULY 27

1 TIMOTHY 6:1-21

Those who are under the yoke of slavery must regard their masters as worthy of full respect, so that the name of God and our teaching may not suffer abuse. Those whose masters are believers must not take advantage of them because they are brothers but must give better service because those who will profit from their work are believers and are beloved.

Teach and urge these things. Whoever teaches something different and does not agree with the sound words of our Lord Jesus Christ and the religious teaching is conceited, understanding nothing, and has a morbid disposition for arguments and verbal disputes. From these come envy, rivalry, insults, evil suspicions, and mutual friction among people with corrupted minds, who are deprived of the truth, supposing religion to be a means of gain. Indeed, religion with contentment is a great gain. For we brought nothing into the world, just as we shall not be able to take anything out of it. If we have food and clothing, we shall be content with that. Those who want to be rich are falling into temptation and into a trap and into many foolish and harmful desires, which plunge them into ruin and destruction. For the love of money is the root of all evils, and some people in their desire for it have strayed from the faith and have pierced themselves with many pains.

But you, man of God, avoid all this. Instead, pursue righteousness, devotion, faith, love, patience, and gentleness. Compete well for the faith. Lay hold of eternal life, to which you were called when you made the noble confession in the presence of many witnesses. I charge [you] before God, who gives life to all things, and before Christ Jesus, who gave testimony under Pontius Pilate for the noble confession, to keep the commandment without stain or reproach until the appearance of our Lord Jesus Christ that the blessed and only ruler will make manifest at the proper time, the King of kings and Lord of lords, who alone has immortality, who dwells in unapproachable light, and whom no human being has seen or can see. To him be honor and eternal power. Amen.

Tell the rich in the present age not to be proud and not to rely on so uncertain a thing as wealth but rather on God, who richly provides us with all things for our enjoyment. Tell them to do good, to be rich in good works, to be generous, ready to share, thus accumulating as treasure a good foundation for the future, so as to win the life that is true life.

O Timothy, guard what has been entrusted to you. Avoid profane babbling and the absurdities of so-called knowledge. By professing it, some people have deviated from the faith.

Grace be with all of you.

PSALM 86:1-10

A prayer of David.

Incline your ear, O LORD; answer
   me,
   for I am afflicted and poor.
Keep my life, for I am devoted to
   you;
   save your servant who trusts in
   you.
You are my God; have pity on
   me, O Lord,
   for to you I call all the day.
Gladden the soul of your servant,
   for to you, O Lord, I lift up my
   soul;
For you, O Lord, are good and
   forgiving,
   abounding in kindness to all
   who call upon you.
Hearken, O LORD, to my prayer
   and attend to the sound of my
   pleading.
In the day of my distress I call
   upon you,
   for you will answer me.

There is none like you among the
gods, O Lord,
and there are no works like
yours.
All the nations you have made
shall come

and worship you, O Lord,
and glorify your name.
For you are great, and you do
wondrous deeds;
you alone are God.

PROVERBS 20:4

*In seedtime the sluggard plows not; / when he looks for the harvest, it is not
there.*

JULY 28

2 TIMOTHY 1:1-18

Paul, an apostle of Christ Jesus
by the will of God for the promise
of life in Christ Jesus, to Timothy,
my dear child: grace, mercy, and
peace from God the Father and
Christ Jesus our Lord.

I am grateful to God, whom I
worship with a clear conscience as
my ancestors did, as I remember
you constantly in my prayers,
night and day. I yearn to see you
again, recalling your tears, so that
I may be filled with joy, as I recall
your sincere faith that first lived in
your grandmother Lois and in
your mother Eunice and that I am
confident lives also in you.

For this reason, I remind you to
stir into flame the gift of God that
you have through the imposition
of my hands. For God did not give
us a spirit of cowardice but rather
of power and love and self-
control. So do not be ashamed of
your testimony to our Lord, nor of
me, a prisoner for his sake; but
bear your share of hardship for
the gospel with the strength that
comes from God.

He saved us and called us to a
holy life, not according to our
works but according to his own
design and the grace bestowed
on us in Christ Jesus before time
began, but now made manifest
through the appearance of our
savior Christ Jesus, who destroyed death and brought life
and immortality to light through
the gospel, for which I was appointed preacher and apostle
and teacher. On this account I
am suffering these things; but I
am not ashamed, for I know him
in whom I have believed and am
confident that he is able to guard
what has been entrusted to me
until that day. Take as your
norm the sound words that you
heard from me, in the faith and
love that are in Christ Jesus.
Guard this rich trust with the
help of the holy Spirit that
dwells within us.

You know that everyone in Asia
deserted me, including Phygelus
and Hermogenes. May the Lord
grant mercy to the family of
Onesiphorus because he often
gave me new heart and was not
ashamed of my chains. But when
he came to Rome, he promptly
searched for me and found me.
May the Lord grant him to find
mercy from the Lord on that day.

And you know very well the services he rendered in Ephesus.

PSALM 86:11-17

Teach me, O Lord, your way
    that I may walk in your truth;
    direct my heart that it may fear
    your name.
I will give thanks to you, O Lord
    my God,
    with all my heart,
    and I will glorify your name
    forever.
Great has been your kindness
    toward me;
    you have rescued me from the
    depths of the nether world.
O God, the haughty have risen
    up against me,
and the company of fierce men
    seeks my life,
    nor do they set you before their
    eyes.
But you, O Lord, are a God
    merciful and gracious,
    slow to anger, abounding in
    kindness and fidelity.
Turn toward me, and have pity
    on me;
    give your strength to your
    servant,
    and save the son of your
    handmaid.
Grant me a proof of your favor,
    that my enemies may see, to
    their confusion,
    that you, O LORD, have helped
    and comforted me.

PROVERBS 20:5-6

The intention in the human heart is like water far below the surface, / but the man of intelligence draws it forth. / Many are declared to be men of virtue: / but who can find one worthy of trust?

JULY 29

2 TIMOTHY 2:1-26

So you, my child, be strong in the grace that is in Christ Jesus. And what you heard from me through many witnesses entrust to faithful people who will have the ability to teach others as well. Bear your share of hardship along with me like a good soldier of Christ Jesus. To satisfy the one who recruited him, a soldier does not become entangled in the business affairs of life. Similarly, an athlete cannot receive the winner's crown except by competing according to the rules. The hardworking farmer ought to have the first share of the crop. Reflect on what I am saying, for the Lord will give you understanding in everything.

Remember Jesus Christ, raised from the dead, a descendant of David: such is my gospel, for which I am suffering, even to the point of chains, like a criminal. But the word of God is not chained. Therefore, I bear with everything for the sake of those who are chosen, so that they too may obtain the salvation that is in Christ Jesus, together with eternal glory. This saying is trustworthy:

If we have died with him

we shall also live with him;
if we persevere
we shall also reign with him.
But if we deny him
he will deny us.
If we are unfaithful
he remains faithful,
for he cannot deny himself.

Remind people of these things and charge them before God to stop disputing about words. This serves no useful purpose since it harms those who listen. Be eager to present yourself as acceptable to God, a workman who causes no disgrace, imparting the word of truth without deviation. Avoid profane, idle talk, for such people will become more and more godless, and their teaching will spread like gangrene. Among them are Hymenaeus and Philetus, who have deviated from the truth by saying that [the] resurrection has already taken place and are upsetting the faith of some. Nevertheless, God's solid foundation stands, bearing this inscription, "The Lord knows those who are his"; and, "Let everyone who calls upon the name of the Lord avoid evil."

In a large household there are vessels not only of gold and silver but also of wood and clay, some for lofty and others for humble use. If anyone cleanses himself of these things, he will be a vessel for lofty use, dedicated, beneficial to the master of the house, ready for every good work. So turn from youthful desires and pursue righteousness, faith, love, and peace, along with those who call on the Lord with purity of heart. Avoid foolish and ignorant debates, for you know that they breed quarrels. A slave of the Lord should not quarrel, but should be gentle with everyone, able to teach, tolerant, correcting opponents with kindness. It may be that God will grant them repentance that leads to knowledge of the truth, and that they may return to their senses out of the devil's snare, where they are entrapped by him, for his will.

PSALM 87:1-7

A psalm of the sons of Korah. A
*   song.*
His foundation upon the holy
    mountains
    the LORD loves,
The gates of Zion,
    more than any dwelling of
    Jacob.
Glorious things are said of you,
    O city of God!
I tell of Egypt and Babylon
    among those that know the
    LORD;
Of Philistia, Tyre, Ethiopia:
    "This man was born there."
And of Zion they shall say:
    "One and all were born in her;
And he who has established her
    is the Most High LORD."
They shall note, when the
    peoples are enrolled:
    "This man was born there."
And all shall sing, in their festive
    dance:
    "My home is within you."

PROVERBS 20:7-8

When a man walks in integrity and justice, / happy are his children after him! /
A king seated on the throne of judgment / dispels all evil with his glance.

JULY 30

2 TIMOTHY 3:1-17

But understand this: there will be terrifying times in the last days. People will be self-centered and lovers of money, proud, haughty, abusive, disobedient to their parents, ungrateful, irreligious, callous, implacable, slanderous, licentious, brutal, hating what is good, traitors, reckless, conceited, lovers of pleasure rather than lovers of God, as they make a pretense of religion but deny its power. Reject them. For some of these slip into homes and make captives of women weighed down by sins, led by various desires, always trying to learn but never able to reach a knowledge of the truth. Just as Jannes and Jambres opposed Moses, so they also oppose the truth—people of depraved mind, unqualified in the faith. But they will not make further progress, for their foolishness will be plain to all, as it was with those two.

You have followed my teaching, way of life, purpose, faith, patience, love, endurance, persecutions, and sufferings, such as happened to me in Antioch, Iconium, and Lystra, persecutions that I endured. Yet from all these things the Lord delivered me. In fact, all who want to live religiously in Christ Jesus will be persecuted. But wicked people and charlatans will go from bad to worse, deceivers and deceived. But you, remain faithful to what you have learned and believed, because you know from whom you learned it, and that from infancy you have known [the] sacred scriptures, which are capable of giving you wisdom for salvation through faith in Christ Jesus. All scripture is inspired by God and is useful for teaching, for refutation, for correction, and for training in righteousness, so that one who belongs to God may be competent, equipped for every good work.

PSALM 88:1-9

A song; a psalm of the sons of Korah.
For the leader; according to
Mahalath. For singing; a maskil
of Heman the Ezrahite.

O LORD, my God, by day I cry out;
at night I clamor in your presence.
Let my prayer come before you;
incline your ear to my call for help,
For my soul is surfeited with troubles
and my life draws near to the nether world.
I am numbered with those who go down into the pit;
I am a man without strength.
My couch is among the dead,
like the slain who lie in the grave,
Whom you remember no longer
and who are cut off from your care.
You have plunged me into the bottom of the pit,
into the dark abyss.
Upon me your wrath lies heavy,
and with all your billows you overwhelm me.
You have taken my friends away from me;
you have made me an abomination to them;
I am imprisoned, and I cannot escape.

JULY 31

2 TIMOTHY 4:1-22

I charge you in the presence of God and of Christ Jesus, who will judge the living and the dead, and by his appearing and his kingly power: proclaim the word; be persistent whether it is convenient or inconvenient; convince, reprimand, encourage through all patience and teaching. For the time will come when people will not tolerate sound doctrine but, following their own desires and insatiable curiosity, will accumulate teachers and will stop listening to the truth and will be diverted to myths. But you, be self-possessed in all circumstances; put up with hardship; perform the work of an evangelist; fulfill your ministry.

For I am already being poured out like a libation, and the time of my departure is at hand. I have competed well; I have finished the race; I have kept the faith. From now on the crown of righteousness awaits me, which the Lord, the just judge, will award to me on that day, and not only to me, but to all who have longed for his appearance.

Try to join me soon, for Demas, enamored of the present world, deserted me and went to Thessalonica, Crescens to Galatia, and Titus to Dalmatia. Luke is the only one with me. Get Mark and bring him with you, for he is helpful to me in the ministry. I have sent Tychicus to Ephesus. When you come, bring the cloak I left with Carpus in Troas, the papyrus rolls, and especially the parchments.

Alexander the coppersmith did me a great deal of harm; the Lord will repay him according to his deeds. You too be on guard against him, for he has strongly resisted our preaching.

At my first defense no one appeared on my behalf, but everyone deserted me. May it not be held against them! But the Lord stood by me and gave me strength, so that through me the proclamation might be completed and all the Gentiles might hear it. And I was rescued from the lion's mouth. The Lord will rescue me from every evil threat and will bring me safe to his heavenly kingdom. To him be glory forever and ever. Amen.

Greet Prisca and Aquila and the family of Onesiphorus. Erastus remained in Corinth, while I left Trophimus sick at Miletus. Try to get here before winter. Eubulus, Pudens, Linus, Claudia, and all the brothers send greetings.

The Lord be with your spirit. Grace be with all of you.

PSALM 88:10-19

My eyes have grown dim
    through affliction;
    daily I call upon you, O LORD;
    to you I stretch out my hands.
Will you work wonders for the
    dead?

Will the shades arise to give
you thanks?
Do they declare your kindness in
the grave,
your faithfulness among those
who have perished?
Are your wonders made known
in the darkness,
or your justice in the land of
oblivion?
But I, O LORD, cry out to you;
with my morning prayer I wait
upon you.
Why, O LORD, do you reject me;
why hide from me your face?
I am afflicted and in agony from
my youth;
I am dazed with the burden of
your dread.
Your furies have swept over me;
your terrors have cut me off.
They encompass me like water all
the day;
on all sides they close in upon
me.
Companion and neighbor you
have taken away from me;
my only friend is darkness.

PROVERBS 20:10-11

*Varying weights, varying measures, / are both an abomination to the LORD. /
Even by his manners the child betrays / whether his conduct is innocent and
right.*

AUGUST

Listening with Luke

L UKE IS A GIFTED WRITER, a gentle physician, a talented artist—all of which is reflected in his account of the Good News. Luke's recording of the Good News of salvation warrants many subtitles. It is called the Gospel of mercy and forgiveness since Luke portrays Jesus' great compassion in ministering to sinners and outcasts. It has also been designated as the Gospel of women, with accounts of great women such as Mary, Elizabeth, Anna, the widow of Nain, Martha, her sister Mary, and Mary Magdalene—to mention only a few.

Another frequent subtitle is the Gospel of praise. In fact, Luke uses the term "praising God" more frequently than the rest of the New Testament writers put together.

A recurring theme in Luke's Gospel is universal salvation. Jesus speaks about the kingdom of heaven with an invitation extended to everyone without exception. Luke is writing for the Gentiles who are obviously included in this universal salvation.

Gospel of Prayer

In these limited introductory observations, we would like to make a few pertinent remarks about Luke's frequent mentions of prayer. In the twenty-four chapters, we find Jesus at prayer on many different occasions and using various methods of prayer. One approach to this theme of the Gospel is to observe the various ways in which Jesus prayed.

On one occasion Luke relates this scene of Jesus at prayer. "He was praying in a certain place, and when he had finished, one of his disciples said to him, 'Lord, teach us to pray . . . ' " (Lk 11:1). As we pursue our reflective reading and prayerful listening to the message of Luke's Gospel, we too would do well to approach the Gospel with the same request: "Lord, teach us to pray."

How Did Jesus Pray?

Jesus prayed always and everywhere. As we recall some of the methods Jesus used, it should bear fruit in our own life of prayer.

Liturgically: Jesus frequented the places of prayer and joined in the prayers and rituals of his own people.

Jesus went with Mary and Joseph to the temple to celebrate the feast of Passover. "Each year his parents went to Jerusalem for the feast of the Passover, and when he was twelve years old, they went up according to festival custom" (Lk 2:41-42).

Later in life Jesus made it a regular practice to pray with his people in the synagogue. "He came to Nazareth, where he had grown up, and went according to his custom into the synagogue on the sabbath day" (Lk 4:16ff).

Jesus urged us to pray liturgically when he instituted the Eucharist. His wish is quite imperative: "do this in memory of me" (Lk 22:19).

On Location: Jesus prayed before every important event in his life. When he was about to begin his mission of suffering he wanted his disciples to recognize him as the promised Savior. Jesus wanted to exact a profession of faith from them before he told them of his forthcoming suffering and death. First, Jesus took it to prayer: "Once when Jesus was praying in solitude, and his disciples were with him, he asked them . . ." (Lk 9:18ff).

Jesus even prayed from his deathbed on the Cross: "Father, forgive them, they know not what they do" (Lk 23:34).

With Others: Jesus had his own special prayer team. On three different recorded occasions, he invited Peter, John, and James to pray with him. When Jesus was asked to restore Jairus' daughter to life he took his prayer team with him. "When he arrived at the house he allowed no one to enter with him except Peter and John and James, and the child's father and mother . . ." (Lk 8:51ff).

At the time of the transfiguration when Jesus climbed the mountain to be with his Father in order to discern the Father's will, "he took Peter, John, and James and went up the mountain to pray . . ." (Lk 9:28). At that most crucial moment of life, when he struggled to say "yes" to the Father in the Garden of Gethsemane, Matthew tells us that he took his prayer team into the inner garden while the other disciples were stationed at the gate.

Contemplatively: Jesus entered into that deep form of prayer which we call the prayer of the heart. In this contemplative posture Jesus was in union with his Father. At the very outset of his public ministry Jesus turned to his Father in this quiet, listening prayer. "After all the people had been baptized and Jesus also had been baptized and was praying, heaven was opened and the Holy Spirit descended upon him in bodily form like a dove" (Lk 3:21-22).

After Jesus healed the leper, Luke commented: ". . . but he would withdraw to deserted places to pray" (Lk 5:16).

Before selecting the Twelve, Jesus prayed earnestly. As Luke described his prayer, it certainly indicated a contemplative prayer: "In those days he departed to the mountain to pray, and he spent the night in prayer to God" (Lk 6:12).

Jesus not only taught us the necessity and value of prayer, but he also gave us a sense of urgency by his own powerful example. Even though he had such a short time to evangelize the whole world and set up his kingdom, he set aside time regularly for long hours in prayer. His example is a compelling invitation for us to do likewise. May our prayerful listening to Luke's Gospel lead us into a deeper union with the Lord in prayer.

Our constant desire: "Lord, teach us to pray."

AUGUST 1

LUKE 1:1-38

Since many have undertaken to compile a narrative of the events that have been fulfilled among us, just as those who were eyewitnesses from the beginning and ministers of the word have handed them down to us, I too have decided, after investigating everything accurately anew, to write it down in an orderly sequence for you, most excellent Theophilus, so that you may realize the certainty of the teachings you have received.

In the days of Herod, King of Judea, there was a priest named Zechariah of the priestly division of Abijah; his wife was from the daughters of Aaron, and her name was Elizabeth. Both were righteous in the eyes of God, observing all the commandments and ordinances of the Lord blamelessly. But they had no child, because Elizabeth was barren and both were advanced in years. Once when he was serving as priest in his division's turn before God, according to the practice of the priestly service, he was chosen by lot to enter the sanctuary of the Lord to burn incense. Then, when the whole assembly of the people was praying outside at the hour of the incense offering, the angel of the Lord appeared to him, standing at the right of the altar of incense. Zechariah was troubled by what he saw, and fear came upon him. But the angel said to him, "Do not be afraid, Zechariah, because your prayer has been heard. Your wife Elizabeth will bear you a son, and you shall name him John. And you will have joy and gladness, and many will rejoice at his birth, for he will be great in the sight of [the] Lord. He will drink neither wine nor strong drink. He will be filled with the holy Spirit even from his mother's womb, and he will turn many of the children of Israel to the Lord their God. He will go before him in the spirit and power of Elijah to turn the hearts of fathers toward children and the disobedient to the understanding of the righteous, to prepare a people fit for the Lord." Then Zechariah said to the angel, "How shall I know this? For I am an old man, and my wife is advanced in years." And the angel said to him in reply, "I am Gabriel, who stand before God. I was sent to speak to you and to announce to you this good news. But now you will be speechless and unable to talk until the day these things take place, because you did not believe my words, which will be fulfilled at their proper time."

Meanwhile the people were waiting for Zechariah and were

amazed that he stayed so long in the sanctuary. But when he came out, he was unable to speak to them, and they realized that he had seen a vision in the sanctuary. He was gesturing to them but remained mute. Then, when his days of ministry were completed, he went home. After this time his wife Elizabeth conceived, and she went into seclusion for five months, saying, "So has the Lord done for me at a time when he has seen fit to take away my disgrace before others." ·

In the sixth month, the angel Gabriel was sent from God to a town of Galilee called Nazareth, to a virgin betrothed to a man named Joseph, of the house of David, and the virgin's name was Mary. And coming to her, he said, "Hail, favored one! The Lord is with you." But she was greatly troubled at what was said and pondered what sort of greeting this might be. Then the angel said to her, "Do not be afraid, Mary, for you have found favor with God. Behold, you will conceive in your womb and bear a son, and you shall name him Jesus. He will be great and will be called Son of the Most High, and the Lord God will give him the throne of David his father, and he will rule over the house of Jacob forever, and of his kingdom there will be no end." But Mary said to the angel, "How can this be, since I have no relations with a man?" And the angel said to her in reply, "The holy Spirit will come upon you, and the power of the Most High will overshadow you. Therefore the child to be born will be called holy, the Son of God. And behold, Elizabeth, your relative, has also conceived a son in her old age, and this is the sixth month for her who was called barren; for nothing will be impossible for God." Mary said, "Behold, I am the handmaid of the Lord. May it be done to me according to your word." Then the angel departed from her.

PSALM 89:1-9

A maskil of Ethan the Ezrahite.
The favors of the LORD I will sing
     forever;
  through all generations my
     mouth shall proclaim your
     faithfulness.
For you have said, "My kindness
     is established forever";
  in heaven you have confirmed
     your faithfulness:
"I have made a covenant with my
     chosen one,
  I have sworn to David my
     servant:
Forever will I confirm your
     posterity
  and establish your throne for
     all generations."
The heavens proclaim your
     wonders, O LORD,
  and your faithfulness, in the
     assembly of the holy ones.
For who in the skies can rank
     with the LORD?
  Who is like the LORD among
     the sons of God?
God is terrible in the council of
     the holy ones;
  he is great and awesome
     beyond all round about him.
O LORD, God of hosts, who is
     like you?
  Mighty are you, O LORD, and
     your faithfulness surrounds
     you.

The ear that hears, and the eye that sees—/ the LORD has made them both. / Love not sleep, lest you be reduced to poverty; / eyes wide open mean abundant food. / "Bad, bad!" says the buyer; / but once he has gone his way, he boasts. / Like gold or a wealth of corals, / wise lips are a precious ornament.

AUGUST 2

LUKE 1:39-80

During those days Mary set out and traveled to the hill country in haste to a town of Judah, where she entered the house of Zechariah and greeted Elizabeth. When Elizabeth heard Mary's greeting, the infant leaped in her womb, and Elizabeth, filled with the holy Spirit, cried out in a loud voice and said, "Most blessed are you among women, and blessed is the fruit of your womb. And how does this happen to me, that the mother of my Lord should come to me? For at the moment the sound of your greeting reached my ears, the infant in my womb leaped for joy. Blessed are you who believed that what was spoken to you by the Lord would be fulfilled."

And Mary said:

"My soul proclaims the
　　greatness of the Lord;
　　my spirit rejoices in God my
　　savior.
For he has looked upon his
　　handmaid's lowliness;
　　behold, from now on will all
　　ages call me blessed.
The Mighty One has done
　　great things for me,
　　and holy is his name.
His mercy is from age to age
　　to those who fear him.

He has shown might with his
　　arm,
　　dispersed the arrogant of
　　mind and heart.
He has thrown down the rulers
　　from their thrones
　　but lifted up the lowly.
The hungry he has filled with
　　good things;
　　the rich he has sent away
　　empty.
He has helped Israel his
　　servant,
　　remembering his mercy,
according to his promise to our
　　fathers,
　　to Abraham and to his
　　descendants forever."

Mary remained with her about three months and then returned to her home.

When the time arrived for Elizabeth to have her child she gave birth to a son. Her neighbors and relatives heard that the Lord had shown his great mercy toward her, and they rejoiced with her. When they came on the eighth day to circumcise the child, they were going to call him Zechariah after his father, but his mother said in reply, "No. He will be called John." But they answered her, "There is no one among your relatives who has this name." So they made signs, asking his father what he wished him to be called.

He asked for a tablet and wrote, "John is his name," and all were amazed. Immediately his mouth was opened, his tongue freed, and he spoke blessing God. Then fear came upon all their neighbors, and all these matters were discussed throughout the hill country of Judea. All who heard these things took them to heart, saying, "What, then, will this child be?" For surely the hand of the Lord was with him.

Then Zechariah his father, filled with the holy Spirit, prophesied, saying:

"Blessed be the Lord, the God of Israel,
  for he has visited and brought redemption to his people.
He has raised up a horn for our salvation
  within the house of David his servant,
even as he promised through the mouth of his holy prophets from of old:
  salvation from our enemies and from the hand of all who hate us,
to show mercy to our fathers and to be mindful of his holy covenant
and of the oath he swore to Abraham our father,
  and to grant us that, rescued from the hand of enemies,
without fear we might worship him in holiness and righteousness
  before him all our days.
And you, child, will be called prophet of the Most High,
  for you will go before the Lord to prepare his ways,
to give his people knowledge of salvation
  through the forgiveness of their sins,

because of the tender mercy of our God
  by which the daybreak from on high will visit us
to shine on those who sit in darkness and death's shadow,
  to guide our feet into the path of peace."

The child grew and became strong in spirit, and he was in the desert until the day of his manifestation to Israel.

PSALM 89:10-19

You rule over the surging of the sea;
  you still the swelling of its waves.
You have crushed Rahab with a mortal blow;
  with your strong arm you have scattered your enemies.
Yours are the heavens, and yours is the earth;
  the world and its fullness you have founded;
North and south you created;
  Tabor and Hermon rejoice at your name.
Yours is a mighty arm;
  strong is your hand, exalted your right hand.
Justice and judgment are the foundation of your throne;
  kindness and truth go before you.
Happy the people who know the joyful shout;
  in the light of your countenance, O LORD, they walk.
At your name they rejoice all the day,
  and through your justice they are exalted.
For you are the splendor of their strength,

and by your favor our horn is
    exalted.
For to the LORD belongs our
    shield,

and to the Holy One of Israel,
    our king.

PROVERBS 20:16-18

Take his garment who becomes surety for another, / and for strangers yield it up! / The bread of deceit is sweet to a man, / but afterward his mouth will be filled with gravel. / Plans made after advice succeed; / so with wise guidance wage your war.

AUGUST 3

LUKE 2:1-52

In those days a decree went out from Caesar Augustus that the whole world should be enrolled. This was the first enrollment, when Quirinius was governor of Syria. So all went to be enrolled, each to his own town. And Joseph too went up from Galilee from the town of Nazareth to Judea, to the city of David that is called Bethlehem, because he was of the house and family of David, to be enrolled with Mary, his betrothed, who was with child. While they were there, the time came for her to have her child, and she gave birth to her firstborn son. She wrapped him in swaddling clothes and laid him in a manger, because there was no room for them in the inn.

Now there were shepherds in that region living in the fields and keeping the night watch over their flock. The angel of the Lord appeared to them and the glory of the Lord shone around them, and they were struck with great fear. The angel said to them, "Do not be afraid; for behold, I proclaim to you good news of great joy that will be for all the people. For to-

day in the city of David a savior has been born for you who is Messiah and Lord. And this will be a sign for you: you will find an infant wrapped in swaddling clothes and lying in a manger." And suddenly there was a multitude of the heavenly host with the angel, praising God and saying:

"Glory to God in the highest
and on earth peace to those on
    whom his favor rests."

When the angels went away from them to heaven, the shepherds said to one another, "Let us go, then, to Bethlehem to see this thing that has taken place, which the Lord has made known to us." So they went in haste and found Mary and Joseph, and the infant lying in the manger. When they saw this, they made known the message that had been told them about this child. All who heard it were amazed by what had been told them by the shepherds. And Mary kept all these things, reflecting on them in her heart. Then the shepherds returned, glorifying and praising God for all they had heard and seen, just as it had been told to them.

When eight days were completed for his circumcision, he was named Jesus, the name given him by the angel before he was conceived in the womb.

When the days were completed for their purification according to the law of Moses, they took him up to Jerusalem to present him to the Lord, just as it is written in the law of the Lord, "Every male that opens the womb shall be consecrated to the Lord," and to offer the sacrifice of "a pair of turtledoves or two young pigeons," in accordance with the dictate in the law of the Lord.

Now there was a man in Jerusalem whose name was Simeon. This man was righteous and devout, awaiting the consolation of Israel, and the holy Spirit was upon him. It had been revealed to him by the holy Spirit that he should not see death before he had seen the Messiah of the Lord. He came in the Spirit into the temple; and when the parents brought in the child Jesus to perform the custom of the law in regard to him, he took him into his arms and blessed God, saying:

"Now, Master, you may let
  your servant go
  in peace, according to your
    word,
for my eyes have seen your
    salvation,
  which you prepared in sight
    of all the peoples,
a light for revelation to the
    Gentiles,
  and glory for your people
    Israel."

The child's father and mother were amazed at what was said about him; and Simeon blessed them and said to Mary his mother, "Behold, this child is destined for the fall and rise of many in Israel, and to be a sign that will be contradicted (and you yourself a sword will pierce) so that the thoughts of many hearts may be revealed." There was also a prophetess, Anna, the daughter of Phanuel, of the tribe of Asher. She was advanced in years, having lived seven years with her husband after her marriage, and then as a widow until she was eighty-four. She never left the temple, but worshiped night and day with fasting and prayer. And coming forward at that very time, she gave thanks to God and spoke about the child to all who were awaiting the redemption of Jerusalem.

When they had fulfilled all the prescriptions of the law of the Lord, they returned to Galilee, to their own town of Nazareth. The child grew and became strong, filled with wisdom; and the favor of God was upon him.

Each year his parents went to Jerusalem for the feast of Passover, and when he was twelve years old, they went up according to festival custom. After they had completed its days, as they were returning, the boy Jesus remained behind in Jerusalem, but his parents did not know it. Thinking that he was in the caravan, they journeyed for a day and looked for him among their relatives and acquaintances, but not finding him, they returned to Jerusalem to look for him. After three days they found him in the temple, sitting in the midst of the teachers, listening to them and asking them questions, and all who heard him were astounded at his understanding and his answers. When his parents saw him, they were astonished, and his mother said to him, "Son, why have you done this to us? Your father and I have been looking for you with great anxiety." And he said to them, "Why were you looking for me? Did you not know that I must be in my Father's house?" But they did not understand what he said to them. He went down with them and came to Nazareth, and was obedient to them; and his mother kept all these things in her heart. And Jesus advanced [in] wisdom and age and favor before God and man.

PSALM 89:20-30

Once you spoke in a vision,
and to your faithful ones you
said:
"On a champion I have placed a
crown;
over the people I have set a
youth.
I have found David, my servant;
with my holy oil I have
anointed him,
That my hand may be always
with him,
and that my arm may make
him strong.
"No enemy shall deceive him,
nor shall the wicked afflict him.
But I will crush his foes before
him
and those who hate him I will
smite.
My faithfulness and my kindness
shall be with him,
and through my name shall his
horn be exalted.
I will set his hand upon the sea,
his right hand upon the rivers.
He shall say of me, 'You are my
father,
my God, the Rock, my savior.'
And I will make him the firstborn,
highest of the kings of the
earth.
Forever I will maintain my
kindness toward him,
and my covenant with him
stands firm.
I will make his posterity endure
forever
and his throne as the days of
heaven."

PROVERBS 20:19

A newsmonger reveals secrets; / so have nothing to do with a babbler!

AUGUST 4

LUKE 3:1-38

In the fifteenth year of the reign of Tiberius Caesar, when Pontius Pilate was governor of Judea, and Herod was tetrarch of Galilee, and his brother Philip tetrarch of the region of Ituraea and Trachonitis, and Lysanias was tetrarch of Abilene, during the high priesthood of Annas and Caiaphas, the word of God came to John the son of Zechariah in the desert. He went throughout [the] whole region of the Jordan, proclaiming a baptism of repentance for the forgiveness of sins, as it is written in the book of the words of the prophet Isaiah:

"A voice of one crying out in
the desert:
'Prepare the way of the Lord,
make straight his paths.
Every valley shall be filled
and every mountain and hill
shall be made low.
The winding roads shall be
made straight,
and the rough ways made
smooth,
and all flesh shall see the
salvation of God.' "

He said to the crowds who came
out to be baptized by him, "You
brood of vipers! Who warned you
to flee from the coming wrath?
Produce good fruits as evidence of
your repentance; and do not begin to say to yourselves, 'We have
Abraham as our father,' for I tell
you, God can raise up children to
Abraham from these stones. Even
now the ax lies at the root of the
trees. Therefore every tree that
does not produce good fruit will
be cut down and thrown into the
fire."

And the crowds asked him,
"What then should we do?" He
said to them in reply, "Whoever
has two cloaks should share with
the person who has none. And
whoever has food should do likewise." Even tax collectors came to
be baptized and they said to him,
"Teacher, what should we do?"
He answered them, "Stop collect-
ing more than what is prescribed." Soldiers also asked him,
"And what is it that we should
do?" He told them, "Do not practice extortion, do not falsely accuse anyone, and be satisfied with
your wages."

Now the people were filled
with expectation, and all were asking in their hearts whether John
might be the Messiah. John answered them all, saying, "I am
baptizing you with water, but one
mightier than I is coming. I am
not worthy to loosen the thongs
of his sandals. He will baptize you
with the holy Spirit and fire. His
winnowing fan is in his hand to
clear his threshing floor and to
gather the wheat into his barn,
but the chaff he will burn with unquenchable fire." Exhorting them
in many other ways, he preached
good news to the people. Now
Herod the tetrarch, who had been
censured by him because of
Herodias, his brother's wife, and
because of all the evil deeds Herod had committed, added still another to these by [also] putting
John in prison.

After all the people had been
baptized and Jesus also had been
baptized and was praying,
heaven was opened and the holy
Spirit descended upon him in
bodily form like a dove. And a
voice came from heaven, "You are
my beloved Son; with you I am
well pleased."

When Jesus began his ministry
he was about thirty years of age.
He was the son, as was thought,
of Joseph, the son of Heli, the son
of Matthat, the son of Levi, the
son of Melchi, the son of Jannai,
the son of Joseph, the son of
Mattathias, the son of Amos, the
son of Nahum, the son of Esli, the
son of Naggai, the son of Maath,
the son of Mattathias, the son of
Semein, the son of Josech, the son
of Joda, the son of Joanan, the son
of Rhesa, the son of Zerubbabel,
the son of Shealtiel, the son of
Neri, the son of Melchi, the son of
Addi, the son of Cosam, the son
of Elmadam, the son of Er, the
son of Joshua, the son of Eliezer,
the son of Jorim, the son of
Matthat, the son of Levi, the son
of Simeon, the son of Judah, the
son of Joseph, the son of Jonam,

the son of Eliakim, the son of Melea, the son of Menna, the son of Mattatha, the son of Nathan, the son of David, the son of Jesse, the son of Obed, the son of Boaz, the son of Sala, the son of Nahshon, the son of Amminadab, the son of Admin, the son of Arni, the son of Hezron, the son of Perez, the son of Judah, the son of Jacob, the son of Isaac, the son of Abraham, the son of Terah, the son of Nahor, the son of Serug, the son of Reu, the son of Peleg, the son of Eber, the son of Shelah, the son of Cainan, the son of Arphaxad, the son of Shem, the son of Noah, the son of Lamech, the son of Methuselah, the son of Enoch, the son of Jared, the son of Mahalaleel, the son of Cainan, the son of Enos, the son of Seth, the son of Adam, the son of God.

and walk not according to my ordinances,
If they violate my statutes
and keep not my commands,
I will punish their crime with a rod
and their guilt with stripes.
Yet my kindness I will not take from him,
nor will I belie my faithfulness.
I will not violate my covenant;
the promise of my lips I will not alter.
Once, by my holiness, have I sworn;
I will not be false to David.
His posterity shall continue forever,
and his throne shall be like the sun before me;
Like the moon, which remains forever—
a faithful witness in the sky."

PSALM 89:31-38
"If his sons forsake my law

PROVERBS 20:20-21
If one curses his father or mother, / his lamp will go out at the coming of darkness. / Possessions gained hastily at the outset / will in the end not be blessed.

AUGUST 5

LUKE 4:1-44
Filled with the holy Spirit, Jesus returned from the Jordan and was led by the Spirit into the desert for forty days, to be tempted by the devil. He ate nothing during those days, and when they were over he was hungry. The devil said to him, "If you are the Son of God, command this stone to become bread." Jesus answered him, "It is written, 'One does not live by bread alone.' " Then he took him up and showed him all the kingdoms of the world in a single instant. The devil said to him, "I shall give to you all this power and their glory; for it has been handed over to me, and I may give it to whomever I wish. All this will be yours, if you worship

me." Jesus said to him in reply, "It is written:

'You shall worship the Lord, your God,
and him alone shall you serve.' "

Then he led him to Jerusalem, made him stand on the parapet of the temple, and said to him, "If you are the Son of God, throw yourself down from here, for it is written:

'He will command his angels concerning you,
to guard you,'

and:

'With their hands they will support you,
lest you dash your foot against a stone.' "

Jesus said to him in reply, "It also says, 'You shall not put the Lord, your God, to the test.' " When the devil had finished every temptation, he departed from him for a time.

Jesus returned to Galilee in the power of the Spirit, and news of him spread throughout the whole region. He taught in their synagogues and was praised by all.

He came to Nazareth, where he had grown up, and went according to his custom into the synagogue on the sabbath day. He stood up to read and was handed a scroll of the prophet Isaiah. He unrolled the scroll and found the passage where it was written:

"The Spirit of the Lord is upon me,
because he has anointed me
to bring glad tidings to the poor.
He has sent me to proclaim liberty to captives

and recovery of sight to the blind,
to let the oppressed go free,
and to proclaim a year acceptable to the Lord."

Rolling up the scroll, he handed it back to the attendant and sat down, and the eyes of all in the synagogue looked intently at him. He said to them, "Today this scripture passage is fulfilled in your hearing." And all spoke highly of him and were amazed at the gracious words that came from his mouth. They also asked, "Isn't this the son of Joseph?" He said to them, "Surely you will quote me this proverb, 'Physician, cure yourself,' and say, 'Do here in your native place the things that we heard were done in Capernaum.' " And he said, "Amen, I say to you, no prophet is accepted in his own native place. Indeed, I tell you, there were many widows in Israel in the days of Elijah when the sky was closed for three and a half years and a severe famine spread over the entire land. It was to none of these that Elijah was sent, but only to a widow in Zarephath in the land of Sidon. Again, there were many lepers in Israel during the time of Elisha the prophet; yet not one of them was cleansed, but only Naaman the Syrian." When the people in the synagogue heard this, they were all filled with fury. They rose up, drove him out of the town, and led him to the brow of the hill on which their town had been built, to hurl him down headlong. But he passed through the midst of them and went away.

Jesus then went down to Capernaum, a town of Galilee. He taught them on the sabbath, and they were astonished at his teaching because he spoke with authority. In the synagogue there was a man with the spirit of an unclean demon, and he cried out in a loud voice, "Ha! What have you to do with us, Jesus of Nazareth? Have you come to destroy us? I know who you are—the Holy One of God!" Jesus rebuked him and said, "Be quiet! Come out of him!" Then the demon threw the man down in front of them and came out of him without doing him any harm. They were all amazed and said to one another, "What is there about his word? For with authority and power he commands the unclean spirits, and they come out." And news of him spread everywhere in the surrounding region.

After he left the synagogue, he entered the house of Simon. Simon's mother-in-law was afflicted with a severe fever, and they interceded with him about her. He stood over her, rebuked the fever, and it left her. She got up immediately and waited on them.

At sunset, all who had people sick with various diseases brought them to him. He laid his hands on each of them and cured them. And demons also came out from many, shouting, "You are the Son of God." But he rebuked them and did not allow them to speak because they knew that he was the Messiah.

At daybreak, Jesus left and went to a deserted place. The crowds went looking for him, and when they came to him, they tried to prevent him from leaving them. But he said to them, "To the other towns also I must proclaim the good news of the kingdom of God, because for this purpose I have been sent." And he was preaching in the synagogues of Judea.

PSALM 89:39-46

Yet you have rejected and
 spurned
 and been enraged at your
 anointed.
You have renounced the
 covenant with your servant,
 and defiled his crown in the
 dust.
You have broken down all his
 walls;
 you have laid his strongholds
 in ruins.
All who pass by the way have
 plundered him;
 he is made the reproach of his
 neighbors.
You have exalted the right hands
 of his foes,
 you have gladdened all his
 enemies.
You have turned back his sharp
 sword
 and have not sustained him in
 battle.
You have deprived him of his
 luster
 and hurled his throne to the
 ground.
You have shortened the days of
 his youth;
 you have covered him with
 shame.

PROVERBS 20:22-23

Say not, "I will repay evil!" / Trust in the LORD and he will help you. / Varying weights are an abomination to the LORD, / and false scales are not good.

AUGUST 6

LUKE 5:1-39

While the crowd was pressing in on Jesus and listening to the word of God, he was standing by the Lake of Gennesaret. He saw two boats there alongside the lake; the fishermen had disembarked and were washing their nets. Getting into one of the boats, the one belonging to Simon, he asked him to put out a short distance from the shore. Then he sat down and taught the crowds from the boat. After he had finished speaking, he said to Simon, "Put out into deep water and lower your nets for a catch." Simon said in reply, "Master, we have worked hard all night and have caught nothing, but at your command I will lower the nets." When they had done this, they caught a great number of fish and their nets were tearing. They signaled to their partners in the other boat to come to help them. They came and filled both boats so that they were in danger of sinking. When Simon Peter saw this, he fell at the knees of Jesus and said, "Depart from me, Lord, for I am a sinful man." For astonishment at the catch of fish they had made seized him and all those with him, and likewise James and John, the sons of Zebedee, who were partners of Simon. Jesus said to Simon, "Do not be afraid; from now on you will be catching men." When they brought their boats to the shore, they left everything and followed him.

Now there was a man full of leprosy in one of the towns where he was; and when he saw Jesus, he fell prostrate, pleaded with him, and said, "Lord, if you wish, you can make me clean." Jesus stretched out his hand, touched him, and said, "I do will it. Be made clean." And the leprosy left him immediately. Then he ordered him not to tell anyone, but "Go, show yourself to the priest and offer for your cleansing what Moses prescribed; that will be proof for them." The report about him spread all the more, and great crowds assembled to listen to him and to be cured of their ailments, but he would withdraw to deserted places to pray.

One day as Jesus was teaching, Pharisees and teachers of the law were sitting there who had come from every village of Galilee and Judea and Jerusalem, and the power of the Lord was with him for healing. And some men brought on a stretcher a man who was paralyzed; they were trying to bring him in and set [him] in his presence. But not finding a way to bring him in because of the crowd, they went up on the roof and lowered him on the stretcher through the tiles into the middle in front of Jesus. When he saw their faith, he said, "As for you, your sins are forgiven." Then the scribes and Pharisees began to ask themselves, "Who is this who speaks blasphemies? Who but God alone can forgive sins?" Jesus knew their thoughts and said to them in reply, "What are you thinking in your hearts? Which is easier, to say, 'Your sins are forgiven,' or to say, 'Rise and walk'? But that you may know that the Son of Man has authority on earth to forgive sins"—he said to the man who was paralyzed, "I say to you, rise, pick up your stretcher, and go home." He stood up immediately before them, picked up what he had been lying on, and went home, glorifying God. Then astonishment seized them all and they glorified God, and, struck with awe, they said, "We have seen incredible things today."

After this he went out and saw a tax collector named Levi sitting at the customs post. He said to him, "Follow me." And leaving everything behind, he got up and followed him. Then Levi gave a great banquet for him in his house, and a large crowd of tax collectors and others were at table with them. The Pharisees and their scribes complained to his disciples, saying, "Why do you eat and drink with tax collectors and sinners?" Jesus said to them in reply, "Those who are healthy do not need a physician, but the sick do. I have not come to call the righteous to repentance but sinners."

And they said to him, "The disciples of John fast often and offer prayers, and the disciples of the Pharisees do the same; but yours eat and drink." Jesus answered them, "Can you make the wedding guests fast while the bridegroom is with them? But the days will come, and when the bridegroom is taken away from them, then they will fast in those days." And he also told them a parable. "No one tears a piece from a new cloak to patch an old one. Otherwise, he will tear the new and the piece from it will not match the old cloak. Likewise, no one pours new wine into old wineskins. Otherwise, the new wine will burst the skins, and it will be spilled, and the skins will be ruined. Rather, new wine must be poured into fresh wineskins. [And] no one who has been drinking old wine desires new, for he says, 'The old is good.' "

PSALM 89:47-53

How long, O LORD? Will you
    hide yourself forever?
  Will your wrath burn like fire?
Remember how short my life is;
  how frail you created all the
    children of men!
What man shall live, and not see
    death,
  but deliver himself from the
    power of the nether world?
Where are your ancient favors, O
    Lord,
  which you pledged to David by
    your faithfulness?
Remember, O Lord, the insults to
    your servants:
  I bear in my bosom all the
    accusations of the nations
With which your enemies have
    reviled, O LORD,
  with which they have reviled
    your anointed on his way!
Blessed be the LORD forever.
  Amen, and amen!

PROVERBS 20:24-25

Man's steps are from the LORD; / how, then, can a man understand his way? / Rashly to pledge a sacred gift is a trap for a man, / or to regret a vow once made.

AUGUST 7

LUKE 6:1-49

While he was going through a field of grain on a sabbath, his disciples were picking the heads of grain, rubbing them in their hands, aɳd eating them. Some Pharisees said, "Why are you doing what is unlawful on the sabbath?" Jesus said to them in reply, "Have you not read what David did when he and those [who were] with him were hungry? [How] he went in to the house of God, took the bread of offering, which only the priests could lawfully eat, ate of it, and shared it with his companions." Then he said to them, "The Son of Man is lord of the sabbath."

On another sabbath he went into the synagogue and taught, and there was a man there whose right hand was withered. The scribes and the Pharisees watched him closely to see if he would cure on the sabbath so that they might discover a reason to accuse him. But he realized their intentions and said to the man with the withered hand, "Come up and stand before us." And he rose and stood there. Then Jesus said to them, "I ask you, is it lawful to do good on the sabbath rather than to do evil, to save life rather than to destroy it?" Looking round at them all, he then said to him, "Stretch out your hand." He did so and his hand was restored. But they became enraged and discussed together what they might do to Jesus.

In those days he departed to the mountain to pray, and he spent the night in prayer to God. When day came, he called his disciples to himself, and from them he chose Twelve, whom he also named apostles: Simon, whom he named Peter, and his brother Andrew, James, John, Philip, Bartholomew, Matthew, Thomas, James the son of Alphaeus, Simon who was called a Zealot, and Judas the son of James, and Judas Iscariot, who became a traitor.

And he came down with them and stood on a stretch of level ground. A great crowd of his disciples and a large number of the people from all Judea and Jerusalem and the coastal region of Tyre and Sidon came to hear him and to be healed of their diseases; and even those who were tormented by unclean spirits were cured. Everyone in the crowd sought to touch him because power came forth from him and healed them all.

And raising his eyes toward his disciples he said:

"Blessed are you who are poor,
for the kingdom of God is yours.
Blessed are you who are now hungry,
for you will be satisfied.
Blessed are you who are now weeping,
for you will laugh.
Blessed are you when people hate you,
and when they exclude and insult you
and denounce your name as evil
on account of the Son of Man.

Rejoice and leap for joy on that day! Behold, your reward will be great in heaven. For their ancestors treated the prophets in the same way.

> But woe to you who are rich,
>> for you have received your consolation.
> But woe to you who are filled now,
>> for you will be hungry.
> Woe to you who laugh now,
>> for you will grieve and weep.
> Woe to you when all speak well of you,
>> for their ancestors treated the false prophets in this way.

"But to you who hear I say, love your enemies, do good to those who hate you, bless those who curse you, pray for those who mistreat you. To the person who strikes you on one cheek, offer the other one as well, and from the person who takes your cloak, do not withhold even your tunic. Give to everyone who asks of you, and from the one who takes what is yours do not demand it back. Do to others as you would have them do to you. For if you love those who love you, what credit is that to you? Even sinners love those who love them. And if you do good to those who do good to you, what credit is that to you? Even sinners do the same. If you lend money to those from whom you expect repayment, what credit [is] that to you? Even sinners lend to sinners, and get back the same amount. But rather, love your enemies and do good to them, and lend expecting nothing back; then your reward will be great and you will be children of the Most High, for he himself is kind to the ungrateful and the wicked. Be merciful, just as [also] your Father is merciful.

"Stop judging and you will not be judged. Stop condemning and you will not be condemned. Forgive and you will be forgiven. Give and gifts will be given to you; a good measure, packed together, shaken down, and overflowing, will be poured into your lap. For the measure with which you measure will in return be measured out to you." And he told them a parable, "Can a blind person guide a blind person? Will not both fall into a pit? No disciple is superior to the teacher; but when fully trained, every disciple will be like his teacher. Why do you notice the splinter in your brother's eye, but do not perceive the wooden beam in your own? How can you say to your brother, 'Brother, let me remove that splinter in your eye,' when you do not even notice the wooden beam in your own eye? You hypocrite! Remove the wooden beam from your eye first; then you will see clearly to remove the splinter in your brother's eye.

"A good tree does not bear rotten fruit, nor does a rotten tree bear good fruit. For every tree is known by its own fruit. For people do not pick figs from thornbushes, nor do they gather grapes from brambles. A good person out of the store of goodness in his heart produces good, but an evil person out of a store of evil produces evil; for from the fullness of the heart the mouth speaks.

"Why do you call me, 'Lord, Lord,' but not do what I command? I will show you what someone is like who comes to me, listens to my words, and acts on them. That one is like a person building a house, who dug deeply and laid the foundation on rock; when the flood came, the river burst against that house but could not shake it because it had been well built. But the one who listens and does not act is like a person who built a house on the ground without a foundation. When the river burst against it, it collapsed at once and was completely destroyed."

PSALM 90:1-6

A prayer of Moses, the man of God.
O Lord, you have been our refuge
   through all generations.
Before the mountains were begotten
   and the earth and the world
   were brought forth,
from everlasting to everlasting
   you are God.
You turn man back to dust,
   saying, "Return, O children of
   men."
For a thousand years in your sight
   are as yesterday, now that it is
   past,
   or as a watch of the night.
You make an end of them in their sleep;
   the next morning they are like
   the changing grass,
Which at dawn springs up anew,
   but by evening wilts and fades.

PROVERBS 20:26-27

A wise king winnows the wicked, / and threshes them under the cartwheel. / A lamp from the LORD is the breath of man; / it searches through all his inmost being.

AUGUST 8

LUKE 7:1-50

When he had finished all his words to the people, he entered Capernaum. A centurion there had a slave who was ill and about to die, and he was valuable to him. When he heard about Jesus, he sent elders of the Jews to him, asking him to come and save the life of his slave. They approached Jesus and strongly urged him to come, saying, "He deserves to have you do this for him, for he loves our nation and he built the synagogue for us." And Jesus went with them, but when he was only a short distance from the house, the centurion sent friends to tell him, "Lord, do not trouble yourself, for I am not worthy to have you enter under my roof. Therefore, I did not consider myself worthy to come to you; but say the word and let my servant be healed. For I too am a person subject to authority, with soldiers subject to me. And I say to one, 'Go,' and he goes; and to another, 'Come here,' and he comes; and to my slave, 'Do this,' and he does it." When Jesus heard this he was amazed at him and, turning, said to the crowd following him, "I tell you, not even in Israel have I found such faith." When the messengers returned to the house, they found the slave in good health.

Soon afterward he journeyed to a city called Nain, and his disciples and a large crowd accompanied him. As he drew near to the gate of the city, a man who had died was being carried out, the only son of his mother, and she was a widow. A large crowd from the city was with her. When the Lord saw her, he was moved with pity for her and said to her, "Do not weep." He stepped forward and touched the coffin; at this the bearers halted, and he said, "Young man, I tell you, arise!" The dead man sat up and began to speak, and Jesus gave him to his mother. Fear seized them all, and they glorified God, exclaiming, "A great prophet has arisen in our midst," and "God has visited his people." This report about him spread through the whole of Judea and in all the surrounding region.

The disciples of John told him about all these things. John summoned two of his disciples and sent them to the Lord to ask, "Are you the one who is to come, or should we look for another?" When the men came to him, they said, "John the Baptist has sent us to you to ask, 'Are you the one who is to come, or should we look for another?'" At that time he cured many of their diseases, sufferings, and evil spirits; he also granted sight to many who were blind. And he said to them in reply, "Go and tell John what you have seen and heard: the blind regain their sight, the lame walk, lepers are cleansed, the deaf hear, the dead are raised, the poor have the good news proclaimed to them. And blessed is the one who takes no offense at me."

When the messengers of John had left, Jesus began to speak to the crowds about John. "What did you go out to the desert to see—a reed swayed by the wind? Then what did you go out to see? Someone dressed in fine garments? Those who dress luxuriously and live sumptuously are found in royal palaces. Then what did you go out to see? A prophet? Yes, I tell you, and more than a prophet. This is the one about whom scripture says:

> 'Behold, I am sending my
>   messenger ahead of you,
> he will prepare your way
>   before you.'

I tell you, among those born of women, no one is greater than John; yet the least in the kingdom of God is greater than he." (All the people who listened, including the tax collectors, and who were baptized with the baptism of John, acknowledged the righteousness of God; but the Pharisees and scholars of the law, who were not baptized by him, rejected the plan of God for themselves.)

"Then to what shall I compare the people of this generation? What are they like? They are like children who sit in the marketplace and call to one another,

> 'We played the flute for you,
>   but you did not dance.
> We sang a dirge, but you did
>   not weep.'

For John the Baptist came neither eating food nor drinking wine, and you said, 'He is possessed by a demon.' The Son of Man came eating and drinking and you said, 'Look, he is a glutton and a drunkard, a friend of tax collectors and sinners.' But wisdom is vindicated by all her children."

A Pharisee invited him to dine with him, and he entered the Pharisee's house and reclined at table. Now there was a sinful woman in the city who learned that he was at table in the house of the Pharisee. Bringing an alabaster flask of ointment, she stood behind him at his feet weeping and began to bathe his feet with her tears. Then she wiped them with her hair, kissed them, and anointed them with the ointment. When the Pharisee who had invited him saw this he said to himself, "If this man were a prophet, he would know who and what sort of woman this is who is touching him, that she is a sinner." Jesus said to him in reply, "Simon, I have something to say to you." "Tell me, teacher," he said. "Two people were in debt to a certain creditor; one owed five hundred days' wages and the other owed fifty. Since they were unable to repay the debt, he forgave it for both. Which of them will love him more?" Simon said in reply, "the one, I suppose, whose larger debt was forgiven." He said to him, "You have judged rightly." Then he turned to the woman and said to Simon, "Do you see this woman? When I entered your house, you did not give me water for my feet, but she has bathed them with her tears and wiped them with her hair. You did not give me a kiss, but she has not ceased kissing my feet since the time I entered. You did not anoint my head with oil, but she anointed my feet with ointment. So I tell you, her many sins have been forgiven; hence, she has shown great love. But the one to whom little is forgiven, loves little." He said to her, "Your sins are forgiven." The others at table said to themselves, "Who is this who even forgives sins?" But he said to the woman, "Your faith has saved you; go in peace."

PSALM 90:7-11

Truly we are consumed by your anger,
   and by your wrath we are put to rout.
You have kept our iniquities before you,
   our hidden sins in the light of your scrutiny.
All our days have passed away in your indignation;
   we have spent our years like a sigh.
Seventy is the sum of our years, or eighty, if we are strong.
And most of them are fruitless toil,
   for they pass quickly and we drift away.
Who knows the fury of your anger
   or your indignation toward those who should fear you?

PROVERBS 20:28-30

Kindness and piety safeguard the king, / and he upholds his throne by justice. / The glory of young men is their strength, / and the dignity of old men is gray hair. / Evil is cleansed away by bloody lashes, / and a scourging to the inmost being.

AUGUST 9

LUKE 8:1-25

Afterward he journeyed from one town and village to another, preaching and proclaiming the good news of the kingdom of God. Accompanying him were the Twelve and some women who had been cured of evil spirits and infirmities, Mary, called Magdalene, from whom seven demons had gone out, Joanna, the wife of Herod's steward Chuza, Susanna, and many others who provided for them out of their resources.

When a large crowd gathered, with people from one town after another journeying to him, he spoke in a parable. "A sower went out to sow his seed. And as he sowed, some seed fell on the path and was trampled, and the birds of the sky ate it up. Some seed fell on rocky ground, and when it grew, it withered for lack of moisture. Some seed fell among thorns, and the thorns grew with it and choked it. And some seed fell on good soil, and when it grew, it produced fruit a hundredfold." After saying this, he called out, "Whoever has ears to hear ought to hear."

Then his disciples asked him what the meaning of this parable might be. He answered, "Knowledge of the mysteries of the kingdom of God has been granted to you; but to the rest, they are made known through parables so that 'they may look but not see, and hear but not understand.'

"This is the meaning of the parable. The seed is the word of God. Those on the path are the ones who have heard, but the devil comes and takes away the word from their hearts that they may not believe and be saved. Those on rocky ground are the ones who, when they hear, receive the word with joy, but they have no root; they believe only for a time and fall away in time of trial. As for the seed that fell among thorns, they are the ones who have heard, but as they go along, they are choked by the anxieties and riches and pleasures of life, and they fail to produce mature fruit. But as for the seed that fell on rich soil, they are the ones who, when they have heard the word, embrace it with a generous and good heart, and bear fruit through perseverance.

"No one who lights a lamp conceals it with a vessel or sets it under a bed; rather, he places it on a lampstand so that those who enter may see the light. For there is nothing hidden that will not become visible, and nothing secret that will not be known and come to light. Take care, then, how you hear. To anyone who has, more will be given, and from the one who has not, even what he seems to have will be taken away."

Then his mother and his brothers came to him but were unable to join him because of the crowd. He was told, "Your mother and your brothers are standing outside and they wish to see you." He said to them in reply, "My mother and my brothers are those who hear the word of God and act on it."

One day he got into a boat with his disciples and said to them, "Let us cross to the other side of the lake." So they set sail, and while they were sailing he fell asleep. A squall blew over the lake, and they were taking in water and were in danger. They came and woke him saying, "Master, master, we are perishing!" He awakened, rebuked the wind and the waves, and they subsided and there was a calm. Then he asked them, "Where is your faith?" But they were filled with awe and amazed and said to one another, "Who then is this, who commands even the winds and the sea, and they obey him?"

PSALM 90:12-17

Teach us to number our days aright,
  that we may gain wisdom of heart.
Return, O LORD! How long?
  Have pity on your servants!
  Fill us at daybreak with your kindness,
  that we may shout for joy and gladness all our days.
Make us glad, for the days when you afflicted us,
  for the years when we saw evil.
Let your work be seen by your servants
  and your glory by their children;
And may the gracious care of the Lord our God be ours;
  prosper the work of our hands for us!
  [Prosper the work of our hands!]

PROVERBS 21:1-2

Like a stream is the king's heart in the hand of the Lord; / wherever it pleases him, he directs it. / All the ways of a man may be right in his own eyes, / but it is the LORD who proves hearts.

AUGUST 10

LUKE 8:26-56

Then they sailed to the territory of the Gerasenes, which is opposite Galilee. When he came ashore a man from the town who was possessed by demons met him. For a long time he had not worn clothes; he did not live in a house, but lived among the tombs. When he saw Jesus, he cried out and fell down before him; in a loud voice he shouted, "What have you to do with me, Jesus, son of the Most High God? I beg you, do not torment me!" For he had ordered the unclean spirit to come out of the man. (It had taken hold of him many times, and he used to be bound with chains and shackles as a restraint, but he would break his bonds and be driven by the demon into deserted places.) Then Jesus asked him, "What is your name?" He replied, "Legion," because many demons had entered him. And they pleaded with him not to order them to depart to the abyss.

A herd of many swine was feeding there on the hillside, and they pleaded with him to allow them to enter those swine; and he let them. The demons came out of the man and entered the swine, and the herd rushed down the steep bank into the lake and was drowned. When the swineherds saw what had happened, they ran away and reported the incident in the town and throughout the countryside. People came out to see what had happened and, when they approached Jesus, they discovered the man from whom the demons had come out sitting at his feet. He was clothed and in his right mind, and they were seized with fear. Those who witnessed it told them how the possessed man had been saved. The entire population of the region of the Gerasenes asked Jesus to leave them because they were seized with great fear. So he got into a boat and returned. The man from whom the demons had come out begged to remain with him, but he sent him away, saying, "Return home and recount what God has done for you." The man went off and proclaimed throughout the whole town what Jesus had done for him.

When Jesus returned, the crowd welcomed him, for they were all waiting for him. And a man named Jairus, an official of the synagogue, came forward. He fell at the feet of Jesus and begged him to come to his house, because he had an only daughter, about twelve years old, and she was dying. As he went, the crowds almost crushed him. And a woman afflicted with hemorrhages for twelve years, who [had spent her whole livelihood on doctors and] was unable to be cured by anyone, came up behind him and touched the tassel on his cloak. Immediately her bleeding stopped. Jesus then asked, "Who touched me?" While all were denying it, Peter said, "Master, the crowds are pushing and pressing in upon you." But Jesus said, "Someone has touched me; for I know that power has gone out from me." When the woman realized that she had not escaped notice, she came forward trembling. Falling down before him, she explained in the presence of all the people why she had touched him and how she had been healed immediately. He said to her, "Daughter, your faith has saved you; go in peace."

While he was still speaking, someone from the synagogue official's house arrived and said, "Your daughter is dead; do not trouble the teacher any longer." On hearing this, Jesus answered him, "Do not be afraid; just have faith and she will be saved." When he arrived at the house he allowed no one to enter with him except Peter and John and James, and the child's father and mother. all were weeping and mourning for her, when he said, "Do not weep any longer, for she is not dead, but sleeping." And they ridiculed him, because they knew that she was dead. But he took her by the hand and called to her, "Child, arise!" Her breath returned and she immediately arose. He then directed that she should be given something to eat. Her parents were astounded, and he instructed them to tell no one what had happened.

PSALM 91:1-4

You who dwell in the shelter of
    the Most High,
      who abide in the shadow of the
      Almighty,
Say to the LORD, "My refuge and
    my fortress,
      my God, in whom I trust."
For he will rescue you from the
    snare of the fowler,
      from the destroying pestilence.

With his pinions he will cover
you,
and under his wings you shall
take refuge;

his faithfulness is a buckler and a
shield.

PROVERBS 21:3
To do what is right and just / is more acceptable to the LORD than sacrifice.

AUGUST 11

LUKE 9:1-27

He summoned the Twelve and gave them power and authority over all demons and to cure diseases, and he sent them to proclaim the kingdom of God and to heal [the sick]. He said to them, "Take nothing for the journey, neither walking stick, nor sack, nor food, nor money, and let no one take a second tunic. Whatever house you enter, stay there and leave from there. And as for those who do not welcome you, when you leave that town, shake the dust from your feet in testimony against them." Then they set out and went from village to village proclaiming the good news and curing diseases everywhere.

Herod the tetrarch heard about all that was happening, and he was greatly perplexed because some were saying, "John has been raised from the dead"; others were saying, "Elijah has appeared"; still others, "One of the ancient prophets has arisen." But Herod said, "John I beheaded. Who then is this about whom I hear such things?" And he kept trying to see him.

When the apostles returned, they explained to him what they had done. He took them and withdrew in private to a town called Bethsaida. The crowds, meanwhile, learned of this and followed him. He received them and spoke to them about the kingdom of God, and he healed those who needed to be cured. As the day was drawing to a close, the Twelve approached him and said, "Dismiss the crowd so that they can go to the surrounding villages and farms and find lodging and provisions; for we are in a deserted place here." He said to them, "Give them some food yourselves." They replied, "Five loaves and two fish are all we have, unless we ourselves go and buy food for all these people." Now the men there numbered about five thousand. Then he said to his disciples, "Have them sit down in groups of [about] fifty." They did so and made them all sit down. Then taking the five loaves and the two fish, and looking up to heaven, he said the blessing over them, broke them, and gave them to the disciples to set before the crowd. They all ate and were satisfied. And when the leftover fragments were picked up, they filled twelve wicker baskets.

Once when Jesus was praying in solitude, and the disciples were with him, he asked them, "Who do the crowds say that I am?"

They said in reply, "John the Baptist; others, Elijah; still others, 'One of the ancient prophets has arisen.' " Then he said to them, "But who do you say that I am?" Peter said in reply, "The Messiah of God." He rebuked them and directed them not to tell this to anyone.

He said, "The Son of Man must suffer greatly and be rejected by the elders, the chief priests, and the scribes, and be killed and on the third day be raised."

Then he said to all, "If anyone wishes to come after me, he must deny himself and take up his cross daily and follow me. For whoever wishes to save his life will lose it, but whoever loses his life for my sake will save it. What profit is there for one to gain the whole world yet lose or forfeit himself? Whoever is ashamed of me and of my words, the Son of Man will be ashamed of when he comes in his glory and in the glory of the Father and of the holy angels. Truly I say to you, there are some standing here who will not taste death until they see the kingdom of God."

PSALM 91:5-9

You shall not fear the terror of
the night
nor the arrow that flies by day:
Not the pestilence that roams in
darkness
nor the devastating plague at
noon.
Though a thousand fall at your
side,
ten thousand at your right
side,
near you it shall not come.
Rather with your eyes shall you
behold
and see the requital of the
wicked,
Because you have the LORD for
your refuge;
you have made the Most High
your stronghold.

PROVERBS 21:4

Haughty eyes and a proud heart—/ the tillage of the wicked is sin.

AUGUST 12

LUKE 9:28-62

About eight days after he said this, he took Peter, John, and James and went up the mountain to pray. While he was praying his face changed in appearance and his clothing became dazzling white. And behold, two men were conversing with him, Moses and Elijah, who appeared in glory and spoke of his exodus that he was going to accomplish in Jerusalem. Peter and his companions had been overcome by sleep, but becoming fully awake, they saw his glory and the two men standing with him. As they were about to part from him, Peter said to Jesus, "Master, it is good that we are here; let us make three tents, one for you, one for Moses, and one for Elijah." But he did not know what he was saying. While he was still speaking, a cloud came and cast a shadow over them, and they became frightened when they entered the cloud. Then from the cloud came a voice that said, "This is my chosen Son; listen to him." After the voice had spoken, Jesus was found alone. They fell silent and did not at that time tell anyone what they had seen.

On the next day, when they came down from the mountain, a large crowd met him. There was a man in the crowd who cried out, "Teacher, I beg you, look at my son; he is my only child. For a spirit seizes him and he suddenly screams and it convulses him until he foams at the mouth; it releases him only with difficulty, wearing him out. I begged your disciples to cast it out but they could not." Jesus said in reply, "O faithless and perverse generation, how long will I be with you and endure you? Bring your son here." As he was coming forward, the demon threw him to the ground in a convulsion; but Jesus rebuked the unclean spirit, healed the boy, and returned him to his father. And all were astonished by the majesty of God.

While they were all amazed at his every deed, he said to his disciples, "Pay attention to what I am telling you. The Son of Man is to be handed over to men." But they did not understand this saying; its meaning was hidden from them so that they should not understand it, and they were afraid to ask him about this saying.

An argument arose among the disciples about which of them was the greatest. Jesus realized the intention of their hearts and took a child and placed it by his side and said to them, "Whoever receives this child in my name receives me, and whoever receives me receives the one who sent me. For the one who is least among all of you is the one who is the greatest."

Then John said in reply, "Master, we saw someone casting out demons in your name and we tried to prevent him because he does not follow in our company." Jesus said to him, "Do not prevent him, for whoever is not against you is for you."

When the days for his being taken up were fulfilled, he resolutely determined to journey to Jerusalem, and he sent messengers ahead of him. On the way they entered a Samaritan village to prepare for his reception there, but they would not welcome him because the destination of his journey was Jerusalem. When the disciples James and John saw this they asked, "Lord, do you want us to call down fire from heaven to consume them?" Jesus turned and rebuked them, and they journeyed to another village.

As they were proceeding on their journey someone said to him, "I will follow you wherever you go." Jesus answered him, "Foxes have dens and birds of the sky have nests, but the Son of Man has nowhere to rest his head." And to another he said, "Follow me." But he replied, "[Lord,] let me go first and bury my father." But he answered him, "Let the dead bury their dead. But you, go and proclaim the kingdom of God." And another said, "I will follow you, Lord, but first let me say farewell to my family at home." [To him] Jesus said, "No one who sets a hand to the plow and looks to what was left behind is fit for the kingdom of God."

PSALM 91:10-16

No evil shall befall you,
   nor shall affliction come near
      your tent,
For to his angels he has given
      command about you,
   that they guard you in all your
      ways.
Upon their hands they shall bear
      you up,
   lest you dash your foot against
      a stone.
You shall tread upon the asp and
      the viper;
you shall trample down the
      lion and the dragon.
Because he clings to me, I will
      deliver him;
   I will set him on high because
      he acknowledges my name.
He shall call upon me, and I will
      answer him;
   I will be with him in distress;
I will deliver him and glorify him;
   with length of days I will
      gratify him
   and will show him my
      salvation.

PROVERBS 21:5-7

The plans of the diligent are sure of profit, / but all rash haste leads certainly to poverty. / He who makes a fortune by a lying tongue / is chasing a bubble over deadly snares. / The oppression of the wicked will sweep them away, / because they refuse to do what is right.

AUGUST 13

LUKE 10:1-42

After this the Lord appointed seventy[-two] others whom he sent ahead of him in pairs to every town and place he intended to visit. He said to them, "The harvest is abundant but the laborers are few; so ask the master of the harvest to send out laborers for his harvest. Go on your way; behold, I am sending you like lambs among wolves. Carry no money bag, no sack, no sandals; and greet no one along the way. Into whatever house you enter, first say, 'Peace to this household.' If a peaceful person lives there, your peace will rest on him; but if not, it will return to you. Stay in the same house and eat and drink what is offered to you, for the laborer deserves his payment. Do not move about from one house to another. Whatever town you enter and they welcome you, eat what is set before you, cure the sick in it and say to them, 'The kingdom of God is at hand for you.' Whatever town you enter and they do not receive you, go out into the streets and say, 'The dust of your town that clings to our feet, even that we shake off against you.' Yet know this: the kingdom of God is at hand. I tell you, it will be more tolerable for Sodom on that day than for that town.

"Woe to you, Chorazin! Woe to you, Bethsaida! For if the mighty deeds done in your midst had been done in Tyre and Sidon, they would long ago have repented, sitting in sackcloth and ashes. But it will be more tolerable for Tyre and Sidon at the judgment than for you. And as for you, Capernaum, 'Will you be exalted to heaven? You will go down to the netherworld.' " Whoever listens to you listens to me. Whoever rejects you rejects me. And whoever rejects me rejects the one who sent me."

The seventy[-two] returned rejoicing, and said, "Lord, even the demons are subject to us because of your name." Jesus said, "I have observed Satan fall like lightning from the sky. Behold, I have given you the power 'to tread upon serpents' and scorpions and upon the full force of the enemy and nothing will harm you. Nevertheless, do not rejoice because the spirits are subject to you, but rejoice because your names are written in heaven."

At that very moment he rejoiced [in] the holy Spirit and said, "I give you praise, Father, Lord of heaven and earth, for although you have hidden these things from the wise and the learned you have revealed them to the childlike. Yes, Father, such has been your gracious will. All things have been handed over to me by my Father. No one knows who the Son is except the Father, and who the Father is except the Son and anyone to whom the Son wishes to reveal him."

Turning to the disciples in private he said, "Blessed are the eyes that see what you see. For I say to you, many prophets and kings desired to see what you see, but did not see it, and to hear what you hear, but did not hear it."

There was a scholar of the law who stood up to test him and said, "Teacher, what must I do to inherit eternal life?" Jesus said to him, "What is written in the law?

How do you read it?" He said in reply, "You shall love the Lord, your God, with all your heart, with all your being, with all your strength, and with all your mind, and your neighbor as yourself." He replied to him, "You have answered correctly; do this and you will live."

But because he wished to justify himself, he said to Jesus, "And who is my neighbor?" Jesus replied, "A man fell victim to robbers as he went down from Jerusalem to Jericho. They stripped and beat him and went off leaving him half-dead. A priest happened to be going down that road, but when he saw him, he passed by on the opposite side. Likewise a Levite came to the place, and when he saw him, he passed by on the opposite side. But a Samaritan traveler who came upon him was moved with compassion at the sight. He approached the victim, poured oil and wine over his wounds and bandaged them. Then he lifted him up on his own animal, took him to an inn and cared for him. The next day he took out two silver coins and gave them to the innkeeper with the instruction, 'Take care of him. If you spend more than what I have given you, I shall repay you on my way back.' Which of these three, in your opinion, was neighbor to the robbers' victim?" He answered, "The one who treated him with mercy." Jesus said to him, "Go and do likewise."

As they continued their journey he entered a village where a woman whose name was Martha welcomed him. She had a sister named Mary [who] sat beside the Lord at his feet listening to him speak. Martha, burdened with much serving, came to him and said, "Lord, do you not care that my sister has left me by myself to do the serving? Tell her to help me." The Lord said to her in reply, "Martha, Martha, you are anxious and worried about many things. There is need of only one thing. Mary has chosen the better part and it will not be taken from her."

PSALM 92:1-9

A psalm; a song for the sabbath day.
It is good to give thanks to the LORD,
  to sing praise to your name, Most High,
To proclaim your kindness at dawn
  and your faithfulness throughout the night,
With ten-stringed instrument and lyre,
  with melody upon the harp.
For you make me glad, O LORD, by your deeds;
  at the works of your hands I rejoice.
How great are your works, O LORD!
  How very deep are your thoughts!
A senseless man knows not,
  nor does a fool understand this.
Though the wicked flourish like grass
  and all evildoers thrive,
They are destined for eternal destruction;
While you, O LORD, are the Most High forever.

PROVERBS: 21:8-10

The way of the culprit is crooked, / but the conduct of the innocent is right. / It is better to dwell in a corner of the housetop / than in a roomy house with a quarrelsome woman. / The soul of the wicked man desires evil; / his neighbor finds no pity in his eyes.

AUGUST 14

LUKE 11:1-54

He was praying in a certain place, and when he had finished, one of his disciples said to him, "Lord, teach us to pray just as John taught his disciples." He said to them, "When you pray, say:

Father, hallowed be your name,
  your kingdom come.
  Give us each day our daily bread
  and forgive us our sins
  for we ourselves forgive everyone in debt to us,
  and do not subject us to the final test."

And he said to them, "Suppose one of you has a friend to whom he goes at midnight and says, 'Friend, lend me three loaves of bread, for a friend of mine has arrived at my house from a journey and I have nothing to offer him,' and he says in reply from within, 'Do not bother me; the door has already been locked and my children and I are already in bed. I cannot get up to give you anything.' I tell you, if he does not get up to give him the loaves because of their friendship, he will get up to give him whatever he needs because of his persistence.

"And I tell you, ask and you will receive; seek and you will find; knock and the door will be opened to you. For everyone who asks, receives; and the one who seeks, finds; and to the one who knocks, the door will be opened. What father among you would hand his son a snake when he asks for a fish? Or hand him a scorpion when he asks for an egg? If you then, who are wicked, know how to give good gifts to your children, how much more will the Father in heaven give the holy Spirit to those who ask him?"

He was driving out a demon [that was] mute, and when the demon had gone out, the mute person spoke and the crowds were amazed. Some of them said, "By the power of Beelzebul, the prince of demons, he drives out demons." Others, to test him, asked him for a sign from heaven. But he knew their thoughts and said to them, "Every kingdom divided against itself will be laid waste and house will fall against house. And if Satan is divided against himself, how will his kingdom stand? For you say that it is by Beelzebul that I drive out demons. If I, then, drive out demons by Beelzebul, by whom do your own people drive them out? Therefore they will be your judges. But if it is by the finger of God that [I] drive out demons, then the kingdom of God has come upon you. When a strong man fully armed guards his palace, his possessions are safe. But when one stronger than he attacks and overcomes him, he takes away the armor on which he relied and distributes the spoils. Whoever is not with me is against me, and whoever does not gather with me scatters.

"When an unclean spirit goes out of someone, it roams through arid regions searching for rest but, finding none, it says, 'I shall return to my home from which I came.' But upon returning, it finds it swept clean and put in order. Then it goes and brings back seven other spirits more wicked than itself who move in and dwell there, and the last condition of that person is worse than the first."

While he was speaking, a woman from the crowd called out and said to him, "Blessed is the womb that carried you and the breasts at which you nursed." He replied, "Rather, blessed are those who hear the word of God and observe it."

While still more people gathered in the crowd, he said to them, "This generation is an evil generation; it seeks a sign, but no sign will be given it, except the sign of Jonah. Just as Jonah became a sign to the Ninevites, so will the Son of Man be to this generation. At the judgment the queen of the south will rise with the men of this generation and she will condemn them, because she came from the ends of the earth to hear the wisdom of Solomon, and there is something greater than Solomon here. At the judgment the men of Nineveh will arise with this generation and condemn it, because at the preaching of Jonah they repented, and there is something greater than Jonah here.

"No one who lights a lamp hides it away or places it [under a bushel basket], but on a lampstand so that those who enter might see the light. The lamp of the body is your eye. When your eye is sound, then your whole body is filled with light, but when it is bad, then your body is in darkness. Take care, then, that the light in you not become darkness. If your whole body is full of light, and no part of it is in darkness, then it will be as full of light as a lamp illuminating you with its brightness."

After he had spoken, a Pharisee invited him to dine at his home. He entered and reclined at table to eat. The Pharisee was amazed to see that he did not observe the prescribed washing before the meal. The Lord said to him, "Oh you Pharisees! Although you cleanse the outside of the cup and the dish, inside you are filled with plunder and evil. You fools! Did not the maker of the outside also make the inside? But as to what is within, give alms, and behold, everything will be clean for you. Woe to you Pharisees! You pay tithes of mint and of rue and of every garden herb, but you pay no attention to judgment and to love for God. These you should have done, without overlooking the others. Woe to you Pharisees! You love the seat of honor in synagogues and greetings in marketplaces. Woe to you! You are like unseen graves over which people unknowingly walk."

Then one of the scholars of the law said to him in reply, "Teacher, by saying this you are insulting us too." And he said, "Woe also to you scholars of the law! You impose on people burdens hard to carry, but you yourselves do not lift one finger to touch them. Woe to you! You build the memorials of the prophets whom your ancestors killed. Consequently, you bear witness and give consent to the deeds of your ancestors, for they killed them and you do the building. Therefore, the wisdom of God said, 'I will send to them prophets and apostles; some of them they will kill and persecute' in order that this generation might be charged with the blood of all the prophets shed since the foundation of the world, from the blood of Abel to the blood of Zechariah who died between the altar and the temple building. Yes, I tell you, this generation will be charged with their blood! Woe to you, scholars of the law! You have taken away the key of knowledge. You yourselves did not enter and you stopped those trying to enter." When he left, the scribes and Pharisees began to act with hostility toward him and to interrogate him about many things, for they were plotting to catch him at something he might say.

PSALM 92:10-16

For behold, your enemies, O LORD,
    for behold, your enemies shall perish;
    all evildoers shall be scattered.
You have exalted my horn like the wild bull's;
    you have anointed me with rich oil.
And my eye has looked down upon my foes,
    and my ears have heard of the fall of my wicked adversaries.
The just man shall flourish like the palm tree,
    like a cedar of Lebanon shall he grow.
They that are planted in the house of the LORD
    shall flourish in the courts of our God.

They shall bear fruit even in old
    age;
  vigorous and sturdy shall they
    be,

Declaring how just is the LORD,
  my Rock, in whom there is no
    wrong.

PROVERBS 21:11-12

When the arrogant man is punished, the simple are the wiser; / when the wise man is instructed, he gains knowledge. / The just man appraises the house of the wicked: / there is one who brings down the wicked to ruin.

AUGUST 15

LUKE 12:1-34

Meanwhile, so many people were crowding together that they were trampling one another underfoot. He began to speak, first to his disciples, "Beware of the leaven—that is, the hypocrisy—of the Pharisees.

"There is nothing concealed that will not be revealed, nor secret that will not be known. Therefore whatever you have said in the darkness will be heard in the light, and what you have whispered behind closed doors will be proclaimed on the housetops. I tell you, my friends, do not be afraid of those who kill the body but after that can do no more. I shall show you whom to fear. Be afraid of the one who after killing has the power to cast into Gehenna; yes, I tell you, be afraid of that one. Are not five sparrows sold for two small coins? Yet not one of them has escaped the notice of God. Even the hairs of your head have all been counted. Do not be afraid. You are worth more than many sparrows. I tell you, everyone who acknowledges me before others the Son of Man will acknowledge before the angels of God. But whoever denies me before others will be denied before the angels of God.

"Everyone who speaks a word against the Son of Man will be forgiven, but the one who blasphemes against the holy Spirit will not be forgiven. When they take you before synagogues and before rulers and authorities, do not worry about how or what your defense will be or about what you are to say. For the holy Spirit will teach you at that moment what you should say."

Someone in the crowd said to him, "Teacher, tell my brother to share the inheritance with me." He replied to him, "Friend, who appointed me as your judge and arbitrator?" Then he said to the crowd, "Take care to guard against all greed, for though one may be rich, one's life does not consist of possessions."

Then he told them a parable. "There was a rich man whose land produced a bountiful harvest. He asked himself, 'What shall I do, for I do not have space to store my harvest?' And he said, 'This is what I shall do: I shall tear down my barns and build larger ones. There I shall store all my grain and other goods and I shall say to myself, "Now as for you, you have so many good things stored up for many years, rest, eat, drink, be merry!" ' But God said to him, 'You fool, this night your life will be demanded of you; and the things you have prepared, to whom will they belong?' Thus will it be for the one who stores up treasure for himself but is not rich in what matters to God."

He said to [his] disciples, "Therefore I tell you, do not worry about your life and what you will eat, or about your body and what you will wear. For life is more than food and the body more than clothing. Notice the ravens: they do not sow or reap; they have neither storehouse nor barn, yet God feeds them. How much more important are you than birds! Can any of you by worrying add a moment to your lifespan? If even the smallest things are beyond your control, why are you anxious about the rest? Notice how the flowers grow. They do not toil or spin. But I tell you, not even Solomon in all his splendor was dressed like one of them. If God so clothes the grass in the field that grows today and is thrown into the oven tomorrow, will he not much more provide for you, O you of little faith? As for you, do not seek what you are to eat and what you are to drink, and do not worry anymore. All the nations of the world seek for these things, and your Father knows that you need them. Instead, seek his kingdom, and these other things will be given you besides. Do not be afraid any longer, little flock, for your Father is pleased to give you the kingdom. Sell your belongings and give alms. Provide money bags for yourselves that do not wear out, an inexhaustible treasure in heaven that no thief can reach nor moth destroy. For where your treasure is, there also will your heart be."

PSALM 93:1-5

The LORD is king, in splendor robed;
   robed is the LORD and girt about with strength;
And he has made the world firm, not to be moved.
Your throne stands firm from of old;
   from everlasting you are, O LORD.
The floods lift up, O LORD,
   the floods lift up their voice;
   the floods lift up their tumult.
More powerful than the roar of many waters,
   more powerful than the breakers of the sea—
   powerful on high is the LORD.
Your decrees are worthy of trust indeed:
   holiness befits your house,
   O LORD, for length of days.

PROVERBS 21:13

He who shuts his ear to the cry of the poor / will himself also call and not be heard.

AUGUST 16

LUKE 12:35-59

"Gird your loins and light your lamps and be like servants who await their master's return from a wedding, ready to open immediately when he comes and knocks. Blessed are those servants whom the master finds vigilant on his arrival. Amen, I say to you, he will gird himself, have them recline at table, and proceed to wait on them. And should he come in the second or third watch and find them prepared in this way, blessed are those servants. Be sure of this: if the master of the house had known the hour when the thief was coming, he would not have let his house be broken into. You also must be prepared, for at an hour you do not expect, the Son of Man will come."

Then Peter said, "Lord, is this parable meant for us or for everyone?" And the Lord replied, "Who, then, is the faithful and prudent steward whom the master will put in charge of his servants to distribute [the] food allowance at the proper time? Blessed is that servant whom his master on arrival finds doing so. Truly, I say to you, he will put him in charge of all his property. But if that servant says to himself, 'My master is delayed in coming,' and begins to beat the menservants and the maidservants, to eat and drink and get drunk, then that servant's master will come on an unexpected day and at an unknown hour and will punish him severely and assign him a place with the unfaithful. That servant who knew his master's will but did not make preparations nor act in accord with his will shall be beaten severely; and the servant who was ignorant of his master's will but acted in a way deserving of a severe beating shall be beaten only lightly. Much will be required of the person entrusted with much, and still more will be demanded of the person entrusted with more.

"I have come to set the earth on fire, and how I wish it were already blazing! There is a baptism with which I must be baptized, and how great is my anguish until it is accomplished! Do you think that I have come to establish peace on the earth? No, I tell you, but rather division. From now on a household of five will be divided, three against two and two against three; a father will be divided against his son and a son against his father, a mother against her daughter and a daughter against her mother, a mother-in-law against her daughter-in-law and a daughter-in-law against her mother-in-law."

He also said to the crowds, "When you see [a] cloud rising in the west you say immediately that it is going to rain—and so it does; and when you notice that the wind is blowing from the south you say that it is going to be hot—and so it is. You hypocrites! You know how to interpret the appearance of the earth and the sky; why do you not know how to interpret the present time?

"Why do you not judge for yourselves what is right? If you are to go with your opponent before a magistrate, make an effort to settle the matter on the way; otherwise your opponent will turn you over to the judge, and the judge hand you over to the constable, and the constable throw you into prison. I say to you, you will not be released until you have paid the last penny."

PSALM 94:1-7

God of vengeance, LORD,
    God of vengeance, show
        yourself.
Rise up, judge of the earth;
    render their deserts to the
        proud.

How long, O LORD, shall the
        wicked,
    how long shall the wicked
        glory,
Mouthing insolent speeches,
    boasting, all the evildoers?
Your people, O LORD, they
        trample down,
    your inheritance they afflict.
Widow and stranger they slay,
    the fatherless they murder,
And they say, "The LORD sees
        not;
    the God of Jacob perceives
        not."

PROVERBS 21:14-16

A secret gift allays anger, / and a concealed present, violent wrath. / To practice justice is a joy for the just, / but terror for evildoers. / The man who strays from the way of good sense / will abide in the assembly of the shades.

AUGUST 17

LUKE 13:1-35

At that time some people who were present there told him about the Galileans whose blood Pilate had mingled with the blood of their sacrifices. He said to them in reply, "Do you think that because these Galileans suffered in this way they were greater sinners than all other Galileans? By no means! But I tell you, if you do not repent, you will all perish as they did! Or those eighteen people who were killed when the tower at Siloam fell on them—do you think they were more guilty than everyone else who lived in Jerusalem? By no means! But I tell you, if you do not repent, you will all perish as they did!"

And he told them this parable: "There once was a person who had a fig tree planted in his or-chard, and when he came in search of fruit on it but found none, he said to the gardener, 'For three years now I have come in search of fruit on this fig tree but have found none. [So] cut it down. Why should it exhaust the soil?' He said to him in reply, 'Sir, leave it for this year also, and I shall cultivate the ground around it and fertilize it; it may bear fruit in the future. If not you can cut it down.' "

He was teaching in a synagogue on the sabbath. And a woman was there who for eighteen years had been crippled by a spirit; she was bent over, completely incapable of standing erect. When Jesus saw her, he called to her and said, "Woman, you are set free of your infirmity." He laid his hands on her, and she at once stood up straight and glorified God. But the leader of the synagogue, indignant that Jesus had cured on the sabbath, said to the crowd in reply, "There are six days when work should be done. Come on those days to be cured, not on the sabbath day." The Lord said to him in reply, "Hypocrites! Does not each one of you on the sabbath untie his ox or his ass from the manger and lead it out for watering? This daughter of Abraham, whom Satan has bound for eighteen years now, ought she not to have been set free on the sabbath day from this bondage?" When he said this, all his adversaries were humiliated; and the whole crowd rejoiced at all the splendid deeds done by him.

Then he said, "What is the kingdom of God like? To what can I compare it? It is like a mustard seed that a person took and planted in the garden. When it was fully grown, it became a large bush and 'the birds of the sky dwelt in its branches.' "

Again he said, "To what shall I compare the kingdom of God? It is like yeast that a woman took and mixed [in] with three measures of wheat flour until the whole batch of dough was leavened."

He passed through towns and villages, teaching as he went and making his way to Jerusalem. Someone asked him, "Lord, will only a few people be saved?" He answered them, "Strive to enter through the narrow gate, for many, I tell you, will attempt to enter but will not be strong enough. After the master of the house has arisen and locked the door, then will you stand outside knocking and saying, 'Lord, open the door for us.' He will say to you in reply, 'I do not know

where you are from.' And you will say, 'We ate and drank in your company and you taught in our streets.' Then he will say to you, 'I do not know where [you] are from. Depart from me, all you evildoers!' And there will be wailing and grinding of teeth when you see Abraham, Isaac, and Jacob and all the prophets in the kingdom of God and you yourselves cast out. And people will come from the east and the west and from the north and the south and will recline at table in the kingdom of God. For behold, some are last who will be first, and some are first who will be last."

At that time some Pharisees came to him and said, "Go away, leave this area because Herod wants to kill you." He replied, "Go and tell that fox, 'Behold, I cast out demons and I perform healings today and tomorrow, and on the third day I accomplish my purpose. Yet I must continue on my way today, tomorrow, and the following day, for it is impossible that a prophet should die outside of Jerusalem.'

"Jerusalem, Jerusalem, you who kill the prophets and stone those sent to you, how many times I yearned to gather your children together as a hen gathers her brood under her wings, but you were unwilling! Behold, your house will be abandoned. [But] I tell you, you will not see me until [the time comes when] you say, 'Blessed is he who comes in the name of the Lord.' "

PSALM 94:8-11

Understand, you senseless ones
   among the people;
   and, you fools, when will you
    be wise?

Shall he who shaped the ear not
    hear?
  or he who formed the eye not
    see?
Shall he who instructs nations
    not chastise,
he who teaches men
    knowledge?
The LORD knows the thoughts of
    men,
  and that they are vain.

PROVERBS 21:17-18

He who loves pleasure will suffer want; / he who loves wine and perfume will not be rich. / The wicked man serves as ransom for the just, / and the faithless man for the righteous.

AUGUST 18

LUKE 14:1-35

On a sabbath he went to dine at the home of one of the leading Pharisees, and the people there were observing him carefully. In front of him there was a man suffering from dropsy. Jesus spoke to the scholars of the law and Pharisees in reply, asking, "Is it lawful to cure on the sabbath or not?" But they kept silent; so he took the man and, after he had healed him, dismissed him. Then he said to them, "Who among you, if your son or ox falls into a cistern, would not immediately pull him out on the sabbath day?" But they were unable to answer his question.

He told a parable to those who had been invited, noticing how they were choosing the places of honor at the table. "When you are invited by someone to a wedding banquet, do not recline at table in the place of honor. A more distinguished guest than you may have been invited by him, and the host who invited both of you may approach you and say, 'Give your place to this man,' and then you would proceed with embarrass-ment to take the lowest place. Rather, when you are invited, go and take the lowest place so that when the host comes to you he may say, 'My friend, move up to a higher position.' Then you will enjoy the esteem of your companions at the table. For everyone who exalts himself will be humbled, but the one who humbles himself will be exalted." Then he said to the host who invited him, "When you hold a lunch or a dinner, do not invite your friends or your brothers or your relatives or your wealthy neighbors, in case they may invite you back and you have repayment. Rather, when you hold a banquet, invite the poor, the crippled, the lame, the blind; blessed indeed will you be because of their inability to repay you. For you will be repaid at the resurrection of the righteous."

One of his fellow guests on hearing this said to him, "Blessed is the one who will dine in the kingdom of God." He replied to him, "A man gave a great dinner to which he invited many. When the time for the dinner came, he dispatched his servant to say to those invited, 'Come, everything is now ready.' But one by one, they all began to excuse themselves. The first said to him, 'I have purchased a field and must go to examine it; I ask you, consider me excused.' And another said, 'I have purchased five yoke of oxen and am on my way to evaluate them; I ask you, consider me excused.' And another said, 'I have just married a woman, and therefore I cannot come.' The servant went and reported this to his master. Then the master of the house in a rage commanded his servant, 'Go out quickly into the streets and alleys of the town and bring in here the poor and the crippled, the blind and the lame.' The servant reported, 'Sir, your orders have been carried out and still there is room.' The master then ordered the servant, 'Go out to the highways and hedgerows and make people come in that my home may be filled. For, I tell you, none of those men who were invited will taste my dinner.' "

Great crowds were traveling with him, and he turned and addressed them, "If anyone comes to me without hating his father and mother, wife and children, brothers and sisters, and even his own life, he cannot be my disciple. Whoever does not carry his own cross and come after me cannot be my disciple. Which of you wishing to construct a tower does not first sit down and calculate the cost to see if there is enough for its completion? Otherwise, after laying the foundation and finding himself unable to finish the work the onlookers should laugh at him and say, 'This one began to build but did not have the resources to finish.' Or what king marching into battle would not first sit down and decide whether with ten thousand troops he can successfully oppose another king advancing upon him with twenty thousand troops? But if not, while he is still far away, he will send a delegation to ask for peace terms. In the same way, everyone of you who does not renounce all his possessions cannot be my disciple.

"Salt is good, but if salt itself loses its taste, with what can its flavor be restored? It is fit neither for the soil nor for the manure pile; it is thrown out. Whoever has ears to hear ought to hear."

PSALM 94:12-15

Happy the man whom you
  ˙instruct, O LORD,
  whom by your law you teach,
Giving him rest from evil days,
  till the pit be dug for the
  wicked.
For the LORD will not cast off his
  people,
  nor abandon his inheritance;
But judgment shall again be with
  justice,
  and all the upright of heart
  shall follow it.

PROVERBS 21:19-20

It is better to dwell in a wilderness / than with a quarrelsome and vexatious wife. / Precious treasure remains in the house of the wise, but the fool consumes it.

AUGUST 19

LUKE 15:1-32

The tax collectors and sinners were all drawing near to listen to him, but the Pharisees and scribes began to complain, saying, "This man welcomes sinners and eats with them." So to them he addressed this parable. "What man among you having a hundred sheep and losing one of them would not leave the ninety-nine in the desert and go after the lost one until he finds it? And when he does find it, he sets it on his shoulders with great joy and, upon his arrival home, he calls together his friends and neighbors and says to them, 'Rejoice with me because I have found my lost sheep.' I tell you, in just the same way there will be more joy in heaven over one sinner who repents than over ninety-nine righteous people who have no need of repentance.

"Or what woman having ten coins and losing one would not light a lamp and sweep the house, searching carefully until she finds it? And when she does find it, she calls together her friends and neighbors and says to them, 'Rejoice with me because I have found the coin that I lost.' In just the same way, I tell you, there will be rejoicing among the angels of God over one sinner who repents."

Then he said, "A man had two sons, and the younger son said to his father, 'Father, give me the share of your estate that should come to me.' So the father divided the property between them. After a few days, the younger son collected all his belongings and set off to a distant country where he squandered his inheritance on a life of dissipation. When he had freely spent everything, a severe famine struck that country, and he found himself in dire need. So he hired himself out to one of the local citizens who sent him to his farm to tend the swine. And he longed to eat his fill of the pods on which the swine fed, but nobody gave him any. Coming to his senses he thought, 'How many of my father's hired workers have more than enough food to eat, but here am I, dying from hunger. I shall get up and go to my father and I shall say to him, "Father, I have sinned against heaven and against you. I no longer deserve to be called your son; treat me as you would treat one of your hired workers."' So he got up and went back to his father. While he was still a long way off, his father caught sight of him, and was filled with compassion. He ran to his son, embraced him and kissed him. His son said to him, 'Father, I have sinned against heaven and against you; I no longer deserve to be called your son.' But his father ordered his servants, 'Quickly bring the finest robe and put it on him; put a ring on his finger and sandals on his feet. Take the fattened calf and slaughter it. Then let us celebrate with a feast, because this son of mine was dead, and has come to life again; he was lost, and has been found.' Then the celebration began. Now the older son had been out in the field, and on his way back, as he neared the house, he heard the sound of music and dancing. He called one of the servants and asked what this might mean. The servant said to him, 'Your brother has returned and your father has slaughtered the fattened calf because he has him back safe and sound.' He became angry, and when he refused to enter the house, his father came out and pleaded with him. He said to his father in reply, 'Look, all these years I served you and not once did I disobey your orders; yet you never gave me even a young goat to feast on with my friends. But when your son returns who swallowed up your property with prostitutes, for him you slaughter the fattened calf.' He said to him, 'My son, you are here with me always; everything I have is yours. But now we must celebrate and rejoice, because your brother was dead and has come to life again; he was lost and has been found.' "

PSALM 94:16-23

Who will rise up for me against the wicked?
Who will stand by me against the evildoers?
Were not the LORD my help,
I would soon swell in the silent grave.
When I say, "My foot is slipping,"
your kindness, O LORD, sustains me;
When cares abound within me,
your comfort gladdens my soul.
How could the tribunal of wickedness be leagued with you,
which creates burdens in the guise of law?
Though they attack the life of the just
and condemn innocent blood,
Yet the LORD is my stronghold,
and my God the rock of my refuge.
And he will requite them for their evildoing,
and for their wickedness he will destroy them;
the LORD, our God, will destroy them.

PROVERBS 21:21-22

He who pursues justice and kindness / will find life and honor. / The wise man storms a city of the mighty, / and overthrows the stronghold in which it trusts.

AUGUST 20

LUKE 16:1-31

Then he also said to his disciples, "A rich man had a steward who was reported to him for squandering his property. He summoned him and said, 'What is this I hear about you? Prepare a full account of your stewardship, because you can no longer be my steward.' The steward said to himself, 'What shall I do, now that my master is taking the position of steward away from me? I am not strong enough to dig and I am ashamed to beg. I know what I shall do so that, when I am removed from the stewardship, they may welcome me into their homes.' He called in his master's debtors one by one. To the first he said, 'How much do you owe my master?' He replied, 'One hundred measures of olive oil.' He said to him, 'Here is your promissory note. Sit down and quickly write one for fifty.' Then to another he said, 'And you, how much do you owe?' He replied, 'One hundred kors of wheat.' He said to him, 'Here is your promissory note; write one for eighty.' And the master commended that dishonest steward for acting prudently.

"For the children of this world are more prudent in dealing with their own generation than are the children of light. I tell you, make friends for yourselves with dishonest wealth, so that when it fails, you will be welcomed into eternal dwellings. The person who is trustworthy in very small matters is also trustworthy in great ones; and the person who is dishonest in very small matters is also dishonest in great ones. If, therefore, you are not trustworthy with dishonest wealth, who will trust you with true wealth? If you are not trustworthy with what belongs to another, who will give you what is yours? No servant can serve two masters. He will either hate one and love the other, or be devoted to one and despise the other. You cannot serve God and mammon."

The Pharisees, who loved money, heard all these things and sneered at him. And he said to them, "You justify yourselves in the sight of others, but God knows your hearts; for what is of human esteem is an abomination in the sight of God.

"The law and the prophets lasted until John; but from then on the kingdom of God is proclaimed, and everyone who enters does so with violence. It is eas-ier for heaven and earth to pass away than for the smallest part of a letter of the law to become invalid.

"Everyone who divorces his wife and marries another commits adultery, and the one who marries a woman divorced from her husband commits adultery.

"There was a rich man who dressed in purple garments and fine linen and dined sumptuously each day. And lying at his door was a poor man named Lazarus, covered with sores, who would gladly have eaten his fill of the scraps that fell from the rich man's table. Dogs even used to come and lick his sores. When the poor man died, he was carried away by angels to the bosom of Abraham. The rich man also died and was buried, and from the netherworld, where he was in torment, he raised his eyes and saw Abraham far off and Lazarus at his side. And he cried out, 'Father Abraham, have pity on me. Send Lazarus to dip the tip of his finger in water and cool my tongue, for I am suffering torment in these flames.' Abraham replied, 'My child, remember that you received what was good during your lifetime while Lazarus likewise received what was bad; but now he is comforted here, whereas you are tormented. Moreover, between us and you a great chasm is established to prevent anyone from crossing who might wish to go from our side to yours or from your side to ours.' He said, 'Then I beg you, father, send him to my father's house, for I have five brothers, so that he may warn them, lest they too come to this place of torment.' But Abraham replied, 'They have Moses and the prophets. Let them listen to them.' He said, 'Oh no, father

Abraham, but if someone from the dead goes to them, they will repent.' Then Abraham said, 'If they will not listen to Moses and the prophets, neither will they be persuaded if someone should rise from the dead.' "

PSALM 95:1-11

Come, let us sing joyfully to the LORD;
    let us acclaim the Rock of our salvation.
Let us greet him with thanksgiving;
    let us joyfully sing psalms to him.
For the LORD is a great God,
    and a great king above all gods;
In his hands are the depths of the earth,
    and the tops of the mountains are his.
His is the sea, for he has made it,
    and the dry land, which his hands have formed.
Come, let us bow down in worship;
    let us kneel before the LORD who made us.
For he is our God,
    and we are the people he shepherds, the flock he guides.
Oh, that today you would hear his voice:
    "Harden not your hearts as at Meribah,
    as in the day of Massah in the desert,
Where your fathers tempted me;
    they tested me though they had seen my works.
Forty years I loathed that generation,
    and I said: They are a people of erring heart,
    and they know not my ways.
Therefore I swore in my anger:
    They shall not enter into my rest."

PROVERBS 21:23-24

He who guards his mouth and his tongue / keeps himself from trouble. / Arrogant is the name for the man of overbearing pride / who acts with scornful effrontery.

AUGUST 21

LUKE 17:1-37

He said to his disciples, "Things that cause sin will inevitably occur, but woe to the person through whom they occur. It would be better for him if a millstone were put around his neck and he be thrown into the sea than for him to cause one of these little ones to sin. Be on your guard! If your brother sins, rebuke him; and if he repents, forgive him. And if he wrongs you seven times in one day and returns to you seven times saying, 'I am sorry,' you should forgive him."

And the apostles said to the Lord, "Increase our faith." The Lord replied, "If you have faith the size of a mustard seed, you would say to [this] mulberry tree,

'Be uprooted and planted in the sea,' and it would obey you.

"Who among you would say to your servant who has just come in from plowing or tending sheep in the field, 'Come here immediately and take your place at table'? Would he not rather say to him, 'Prepare something for me to eat. Put on your apron and wait on me while I eat and drink. You may eat and drink when I am finished'? Is he grateful to that servant because he did what was commanded? So should it be with you. When you have done all you have been commanded, say, 'We are unprofitable servants; we have done what we were obliged to do.' "

As he continued his journey to Jerusalem, he traveled through Samaria and Galilee. As he was entering a village, ten lepers met [him]. They stood at a distance from him and raised their voice, saying, "Jesus, Master! Have pity on us!" And when he saw them, he said, "Go show yourselves to the priests." As they were going they were cleansed. And one of them, realizing he had been healed, returned, glorifying God in a loud voice; and he fell at the feet of Jesus and thanked him. He was a Samaritan. Jesus said in reply, "Ten were cleansed, were they not? Where are the other nine? Has none but this foreigner returned to give thanks to God?" Then he said to him, "Stand up and go; your faith has saved you."

Asked by the Pharisees when the kingdom of God would come, he said in reply, "The coming of the kingdom of God cannot be observed, and no one will announce, 'Look, here it is,' or, 'There it is.' For behold, the kingdom of God is among you."

Then he said to his disciples, "The days will come when you will long to see one of the days of the Son of Man, but you will not see it. There will be those who will say to you, 'Look, there he is,' [or] 'Look, here he is.' Do not go off, do not run in pursuit. For just as lightning flashes and lights up the sky from one side to the other, so will the Son of Man be [in his day]. But first he must suffer greatly and be rejected by this generation. As it was in the days of Noah, so it will be in the days of the Son of Man; they were eating and drinking, marrying and giving in marriage up to the day that Noah entered the ark, and the flood came and destroyed them all. Similarly, as it was in the days of Lot: they were eating, drinking, buying, selling, planting, building; on the day when Lot left Sodom, fire and brimstone rained from the sky to destroy them all. So it will be on the day the Son of Man is revealed. On that day, a person who is on the housetop and whose belongings are in the house must not go down to get them, and likewise a person in the field must not return to what was left behind. Remember the wife of Lot. Whoever seeks to preserve his life will lose it, but whoever loses it will save it. I tell you, on that night there will be two people in one bed; one will be taken, the other left. And there will be two women grinding meal together; one will be taken, the other left." They said to him in reply, "Where, Lord?" He said to them, "Where the body is, there also the vultures will gather."

PSALM 96:1-13

Sing to the LORD a new song;
  sing to the LORD, all you lands.
Sing to the LORD, bless his name;

announce his salvation, day
after day.
Tell his glory among the nations;
among all peoples, his
wondrous deeds.
For great is the LORD and highly
to be praised;
awesome is he, beyond all
gods.
For all the gods' of the nations are
things of nought,
but the LORD made the
heavens.
Splendor and majesty go before
him;
praise and grandeur are in his
sanctuary.
Give to the LORD, you families of
nations,
give to the LORD glory and
praise;
give to the LORD the glory due
his name!
Bring gifts, and enter his courts;

worship the LORD in holy
attire.
Tremble before him, all the earth;
say among the nations: The
LORD is king.
He has made the world firm, not
to be moved;
he governs the peoples with
equity.
Let the heavens be glad and the
earth rejoice;
let the sea and what fills it
resound;
let the plains be joyful and all
that is in them!
Then shall all the trees of the
forest exult
before the LORD, for he comes;
for he comes to rule the earth.
He shall rule the world with
justice
and the peoples with his
constancy.

PROVERBS 21:25-26

The sluggard's propensity slays him, / for his hands refuse to work. / Some are
consumed with avarice all the day, / but the just man gives unsparingly.

AUGUST 22

LUKE 18:1-43

Then he told them a parable
about the necessity for them to
pray always without becoming
weary. He said, "There was a
judge in a certain town who neither feared God nor respected any
human being. And a widow in
that town used to come to him
and say, 'Render a just decision
for me against my adversary.' For
a long time the judge was unwilling, but eventually he thought,
'While it is true that I neither fear
God or respect any human being,

because this widow keeps bother-
ing me I shall deliver a just decision for her lest she finally come
and strike me.' " The Lord said,
"Pay attention to what the dishonest judge says. Will not God then
secure the rights of his chosen
ones who call out to him day and
night? Will he be slow to answer
them? I tell you, he will see to it
that justice is done for them speed-
ily. But when the Son of Man
comes, will he find faith on
earth?"

He then addressed this parable

to those who were convinced of their own righteousness and despised everyone else. "Two people went up to the temple area to pray; one was a Pharisee and the other was a tax collector. The Pharisee took up his position and spoke this prayer to himself, 'O God, I thank you that I am not like the rest of humanity—greedy, dishonest, adulterous or even like this tax collector. I fast twice a week, and I pay tithes on my whole income.' But the tax collector stood off at a distance and would not even raise his eyes to heaven but beat his breast and prayed, 'O God, be merciful to me a sinner.' I tell you, the latter went home justified, not the former; for everyone who exalts himself will be humbled, and the one who humbles himself will be exalted."

People were bringing even infants to him that he might touch them, and when the disciples saw this, they rebuked them. Jesus, however, called the children to himself and said, "Let the children come to me and do not prevent them; for the kingdom of God belongs to such as these. Amen, I say to you, whoever does not accept the kingdom of God like a child will not enter it."

An official asked him this question, "Good teacher, what must I do to inherit eternal life?" Jesus answered him, "Why do you call me good? No one is good but God alone. You know the commandments, 'You shall not commit adultery; you shall not kill; you shall not steal; you shall not bear false witness; honor your father and your mother.' " And he replied, "All of these I have observed from my youth." When Jesus heard this he said to him, "There is still one thing left for you: sell all that you have and distribute it to the poor, and you will have a treasure in heaven. Then come, follow me." But when he heard this he became quite sad, for he was very rich.

Jesus looked at him [now sad] and said, "How hard it is for those who have wealth to enter the kingdom of God! For it is easier for a camel to pass through the eye of a needle than for a rich person to enter the kingdom of God." Those who heard this said, "Then who can be saved?" And he said, "What is impossible for human beings is possible for God." Then Peter said, "We have given up our possessions and followed you." He said to them, "Amen, I say to you, there is no one who has given up house or wife or brothers or parents or children for the sake of the kingdom of God who will not receive [back] an overabundant return in this present age and eternal life in the age to come."

Then he took the Twelve aside and said to them, "Behold, we are going up to Jerusalem and everything written by the prophets about the Son of Man will be fulfilled. He will be handed over to the Gentiles and he will be mocked and insulted and spat upon; and after they have scourged him they will kill him, but on the third day he will rise." But they understood nothing of this; the word remained hidden from them and they failed to comprehend what he said.

Now as he approached Jericho a blind man was sitting by the roadside begging, and hearing a crowd going by, he inquired what was happening. They told him, "Jesus of Nazareth is passing by." He shouted, "Jesus, Son of David, have pity on me!" Then Jesus stopped and ordered that he be brought to him; and when he came near, Jesus asked him, "What do you want me to do for you?" He replied, "Lord, please let me see." Jesus told him, "Have sight; your faith has saved you." He immediately received his sight and followed him, giving glory to God. When they saw this, all the people gave praise to God.

PSALM 97:1-6

The LORD is king; let the earth rejoice;
let the many isles be glad.
Clouds and darkness are round about him,
   justice and judgment are the foundation of his throne.
Fire goes before him
   and consumes his foes round about.
His lightnings illumine the world;
   the earth sees and trembles.
The mountains melt like wax before the LORD,
   before the Lord of all the earth.
The heavens proclaim his justice,
   and all peoples see his glory.

PROVERBS 21:27

The sacrifice of the wicked is an abomination, / the more so when they offer it with a bad intention.

AUGUST 23

LUKE 19:1-48

He came to Jericho and intended to pass through the town. Now a man there named Zacchaeus, who was a chief tax collector and also a wealthy man, was seeking to see who Jesus was; but he could not see him because of the crowd, for he was short in stature. So he ran ahead and climbed a sycamore tree in order to see Jesus, who was about to pass that way. When he reached the place, Jesus looked up and said to him, "Zacchaeus, come down quickly, for today I must stay at your house." And he came down quickly and received him with joy. When they all saw this, they began to grumble, saying, "He has gone to stay at the house of a sinner." But Zacchaeus stood there and said to the Lord, "Behold, half of my possessions, Lord, I shall give to the poor, and if I have extorted anything from anyone I shall repay it four times over." And Jesus said to him, "Today salvation has come to this house because this man too is a descendant of Abraham. For the Son of Man has come to seek and to save what was lost."

While they were listening to him speak, he proceeded to tell a parable because he was near Jerusalem and they thought that the kingdom of God would appear there immediately. So he said, "A nobleman went off to a distant country to obtain the kingship for himself and then to return. He called ten of his servants and gave them ten gold coins and told them, 'Engage in trade with these until I return.' His fellow citizens, however, despised him and sent a delegation after him to announce,

'We do not want this man to be our king.' But when he returned after obtaining the kingship, he had the servants called, to whom he had given the money, to learn what they had gained by trading. The first came forward and said, 'Sir, your gold coin has earned ten additional ones.' He replied, 'Well done, good servant! You have been faithful in this very small matter; take charge of ten cities.' Then the second came and reported, 'Your gold coin, sir, has earned five more.' And to this servant too he said, 'You, take charge of five cities.' Then the other servant came and said, 'Sir, here is your gold coin; I kept it stored away in a handkerchief, for I was afraid of you, because you are a demanding person; you take up what you did not lay down and you harvest what you did not plant.' He said to him, 'With your own words I shall condemn you, you wicked servant. You knew I was a demanding person, taking up what I did not lay down and harvesting what I did not plant; why did you not put my money in a bank? Then on my return I would have collected it with interest.' And to those standing by he said, 'Take the gold coin from him and give it to the servant who has ten.' But they said to him, 'Sir, he has ten gold coins.' 'I tell you, to everyone who has, more will be given, but from the one who has not, even what he has will be taken away. Now as for those enemies of mine who did not want me as their king, bring them here and slay them before me.' "

After he had said this, he proceeded on his journey up to Jerusalem. As he drew near to Bethphage and Bethany at the place called the Mount of Olives, he sent two of his disciples. He said, "Go into the village opposite you, and as you enter it you will find a colt tethered on which no one has ever sat. Untie it and bring it here. And if anyone should ask you, 'Why are you untying it?' you will answer, 'The Master has need of it.' " So those who had been sent went off and found everything just as he had told them. And as they were untying the colt, its owners said to them, "Why are you untying this colt?" They answered, "The Master has need of it." So they brought it to Jesus, threw their cloaks over the colt, and helped Jesus to mount. As he rode along, the people were spreading their cloaks on the road; and now as he was approaching the slope of the Mount of Olives, the whole multitude of his disciples began to praise God aloud with joy for all the mighty deeds they had seen. They proclaimed:

"Blessed is the king who comes
    in the name of the Lord.
Peace in heaven
    and glory in the highest."

Some of the Pharisees in the crowd said to him, "Teacher, rebuke your disciples." He said in reply, "I tell you, if they keep silent, the stones will cry out!"

As he drew near, he saw the city and wept over it, saying, "If this day you only knew what makes for peace—but now it is hidden from your eyes. For the days are coming upon you when your enemies will raise a palisade against you; they will encircle you and hem you in on all sides. They will smash you to the ground and your children within you, and they will not leave one stone upon another within you because you did not recognize the time of your visitation."

Then Jesus entered the temple area and proceeded to drive out those who were selling things, saying to them, "It is written, 'My house shall be a house of prayer, but you have made it a den of thieves.' " And every day he was teaching in the temple area. The chief priests, the scribes, and the leaders of the people, meanwhile, were seeking to put him to death, but they could find no way to accomplish their purpose because all the people were hanging on his words.

PSALM 97:7-12

All who worship graven things
    are put to shame,
who glory in the things of
    nought;
all gods are prostrate before
    him.
Zion hears and is glad,
    and the cities of Judah rejoice
    because of your judgments, O
    LORD.
Because you, O LORD, are the
    Most High over all the earth,
    exalted far above all gods.
The LORD loves those that hate
    evil;
    he guards the lives of his
    faithful ones;
    from the hand of the wicked he
    delivers them.
Light dawns for the just;
    and gladness, for the upright of
    heart.
Be glad in the LORD, you just,
    and give thanks to his holy
    name.

PROVERBS 21:28-29

The false witness will perish, / but he who listens will finally have his say. / The wicked man is brazenfaced, / but the upright man pays heed to his ways.

AUGUST 24

LUKE 20:1-47

One day as he was teaching the people in the temple area and proclaiming the good news, the chief priests and scribes, together with the elders, approached him and said to him, "Tell us, by what authority are you doing these things? Or who is the one who gave you this authority?" He said to them in reply, "I shall ask you a question. Tell me, was John's baptism of heavenly or of human origin?" They discussed this among themselves, and said, "If we say, 'Of heavenly origin,' he will say, 'Why did you not believe him?' But if we say, 'Of human origin,' then all the people will stone us, for they are convinced that John was a prophet." So they answered that they did not know from where it came. Then Jesus said to them, "Neither shall I tell you by what authority I do these things."

Then he proceeded to tell the people this parable. "[A] man planted a vineyard, leased it to tenant farmers, and then went on a journey for a long time. At harvest time he sent a servant to the tenant farmers to receive some of the produce of the vineyard. But they beat the servant and sent him away empty-handed. So he proceeded to send another servant, but him also they beat and insulted and sent away empty-handed. Then he proceeded to send a third, but this one too they wounded and threw out. The owner of the vineyard said, 'What shall I do? I shall send my beloved son; maybe they will respect him.' But when the tenant farmers saw him they said to one another, 'This is the heir. Let us kill him that the inheritance may become ours.' So they threw him out of the vineyard and killed him. What will the owner of the vineyard do to them? He will come and put those tenant farmers to death and turn over the vineyard to others." When the people heard this, they exclaimed, "Let it not be so!" But he looked at them and asked, "What then does this scripture passage mean:

'The stone which the builders
  rejected
  has become the cornerstone'?

Everyone who falls on that stone will be dashed to pieces; and it will crush anyone on whom it falls." The scribes and chief priests sought to lay their hands on him at that very hour, but they feared the people, for they knew that he had addressed this parable to them.

They watched him closely and sent agents pretending to be righteous who were to trap him in speech, in order to hand him over to the authority and power of the governor. They posed this question to him, "Teacher, we know that what you say and teach is correct, and you show no partiality, but teach the way of God in accordance with the truth. Is it lawful for us to pay tribute to Caesar or not?" Recognizing their craftiness he said to them, "Show me a denarius; whose image and name does it bear?" They replied, "Caesar's." So he said to them, "Then repay to Caesar what belongs to Caesar and to God what belongs to God." They were unable to trap him by something he might say before the people, and so amazed were they at his reply that they fell silent.

Some Sadducees, those who deny that there is a resurrection, came forward and put this question to him, saying, "Teacher, Moses wrote for us, 'If someone's brother dies leaving a wife but no child, his brother must take the wife and raise up descendants for his brother.' Now there were seven brothers; the first married a woman but died childless. Then the second and the third married her, and likewise all the seven died childless. Finally the woman also died. Now at the resurrection whose wife will that woman be? For all seven had been married to her." Jesus said to them, "The children of this age marry and remarry; but those who are deemed worthy to attain to the coming age and to the resurrection of the dead neither marry nor are given in marriage. They can no longer die, for they are like angels; and they are the children of God because they are the ones who will rise. That the dead will rise even Moses made known in the passage about the bush, when he called 'Lord' the God of Abraham, the God of Isaac, and the God of Jacob; and he is not God of the dead, but of the living, for to him all are alive." Some of the scribes said in reply, "Teacher, you have answered well." And they no longer dared to ask him anything.

Then he said to them, "How do they claim that the Messiah is the Son of David? For David himself in the Book of Psalms says:

'The Lord said to my lord,
"Sit at my right hand
till I make your enemies your footstool." '

Now if David calls him 'lord,' how can he be his son?"

Then, within the hearing of all the people, he said to [his] disciples, "Be on guard against the scribes, who like to go around in long robes and love greetings in marketplaces, seats of honor in synagogues, and places of honor at banquets. They devour the houses of widows and, as a pretext, recite lengthy prayers. They will receive a very severe condemnation."

PSALM 98:1-9

A psalm.
Sing to the LORD a new song,
for he has done wondrous deeds;
His right hand has won victory for him,

his holy arm.
The LORD has made his salvation known:
in the sight of the nations he has revealed his justice.
He has remembered his kindness and his faithfulness
toward the house of Israel.
All the ends of the earth have seen
the salvation by our God.
Sing joyfully to the LORD, all you lands;
break into song; sing praise.
Sing praise to the LORD with the harp,
with the harp and melodious song.
With trumpets and the sound of the horn
sing joyfully before the King, the LORD.
Let the sea and what fills it resound,
the world and those who dwell in it;
Let the rivers clap their hands,
the mountains shout with them for joy
Before the LORD, for he comes,
for he comes to rule the earth;
He will rule the world with justice
and the peoples with equity.

PROVERBS 21:30-31

There is no wisdom, no understanding, / no counsel, against the LORD. / The horse is equipped for the day of battle, / but victory is the LORD's.

AUGUST 25

LUKE 21:1-38

When he looked up he saw some wealthy people putting their offerings into the treasury and he noticed a poor widow putting in two small coins. He said, "I tell you truly, this poor widow put in more than all the rest; for those others have all made offerings from their surplus wealth, but she, from her poverty, has offered her whole livelihood."

While some people were speaking about how the temple was adorned with costly stones and votive offerings, he said, "All that you see here—the days will come when there will not be left a stone upon another stone that will not be thrown down."

Then they asked him, "Teacher, when will this happen? And what sign will there be when all these things are about to happen?" He answered, "See that you not be deceived, for many will come in my name, saying, 'I am he,' and 'The time has come.' Do not follow them! When you hear of wars and insurrections, do not be terrified; for such things must happen first, but it will not immediately be the end." Then he said to them, "Nation will rise against nation, and kingdom against kingdom. There will be powerful earthquakes, famines, and plagues from place to place; and awesome sights and mighty signs will come from the sky.

"Before all this happens, however, they will seize and persecute you, they will hand you over to the synagogues and to prisons, and they will have you led before kings and governors because of my name. It will lead to your giving testimony. Remember, you are not to prepare your defense beforehand, for I myself shall give you a wisdom in speaking that all your adversaries will be powerless to resist or refute. You will even be handed over by parents, brothers, relatives, and friends, and they will put some of you to death. You will be hated by all because of my name, but not a hair on your head will be destroyed.

By your perseverance you will secure your lives.

"When you see Jerusalem surrounded by armies, know that its desolation is at hand. Then those in Judea must flee to the mountains. Let those within the city escape from it, and let those in the countryside not enter the city, for these days are the time of punishment when all the scriptures are fulfilled. Woe to pregnant women and nursing mothers in those days, for a terrible calamity will come upon the earth and a wrathful judgment upon this people. They will fall by the edge of the sword and be taken as captives to all the Gentiles; and Jerusalem will be trampled underfoot by the Gentiles until the times of the Gentiles are fulfilled.

"There will be signs in the sun, the moon, and the stars, and on earth nations will be in dismay, perplexed by the roaring of the sea and the waves. People will die of fright in anticipation of what is coming upon the world, for the powers of the heavens will be shaken. And then they will see the Son of Man coming in a cloud with power and great glory. But when these signs begin to happen, stand erect and raise your heads because your redemption is at hand."

He taught them a lesson. "Consider the fig tree and all the other trees. When their buds burst open, you see for yourselves and know that summer is now near; in the same way, when you see these things happening, know that the kingdom of God is near. Amen, I say to you, this generation will not pass away until all these things have taken place. Heaven and earth will pass away, but my words will not pass away.

"Beware that your hearts do not

become drowsy from carousing and drunkenness and the anxieties of daily life, and that day catch you by surprise like a trap. For that day will assault everyone who lives on the face of the earth. Be vigilant at all times and pray that you have the strength to escape the tribulations that are imminent and to stand before the Son of Man."

During the day, Jesus was teaching in the temple area, but at night he would leave and stay at the place called the Mount of Olives. And all the people would get up early each morning to listen to him in the temple area.

PSALM 99:1-9

The LORD is king; the peoples tremble;
　he is throned upon the cherubim; the earth quakes.
The LORD in Zion is great,
　he is high above all the people.
Let them praise your great and awesome name;
　holy is he!
The King in his might loves justice;
　you have established equity;
　justice and judgment in Jacob you have wrought.
Extol the LORD, our God,
and worship at his footstool;
holy is he!
Moses and Aaron were among his priests,
　and Samuel, among those who called upon his name;
　they called upon the LORD, and he answered them.
From the pillar of cloud he spoke to them;
　they heard his decrees and the law he gave them.
O LORD, our God, you answered them;
　a forgiving God you were to them,
　though requiting their misdeeds.
Extol the LORD, our God,
and worship at his holy mountain;
for holy is the LORD, our God.

PROVERBS 22:1

A good name is more desirable than great riches, / and high esteem, than gold and silver.

AUGUST 26

LUKE 22:1-23

Now the feast of Unleavened Bread, called the Passover, was drawing near, and the chief priests and the scribes were seeking a way to put him to death, for they were afraid of the people. Then Satan entered into Judas, the one surnamed Iscariot, who was counted among the Twelve, and he went to the chief priests and temple guards to discuss a plan for handing him over to them. They were pleased and agreed to pay him money. He accepted their offer and sought a favorable opportunity to hand him over to them in the absence of a crowd.

When the day of the feast of Unleavened Bread arrived, the day for sacrificing the Passover lamb, he sent out Peter and John, instructing them, "Go and make preparations for us to eat the Passover." They asked him, "Where do you want us to make the preparations?" And he answered them, "When you go into the city, a man will meet you carrying a jar of water. Follow him into the house that he enters and say to the master of the house, 'The teacher says to you, "Where is the guest room where I may eat the Passover with my disciples?" ' He will show you a large upper room that is furnished. Make the preparations there." Then they went off and found everything exactly as he had told them, and there they prepared the Passover.

When the hour came, he took his place at table with the apostles. He said to them, "I have eagerly desired to eat this Passover with you before I suffer, for, I tell you, I shall not eat it [again] until there is fulfillment in the kingdom of God." Then he took a cup, gave thanks, and said, "Take this and share it among yourselves; for I tell you [that] from this time on I shall not drink of the fruit of the vine until the kingdom of God comes." Then he took the bread, said the blessing, broke it, and gave it to them, saying, "This is my body, which will be given for you; do this in memory of me." And likewise the cup after they had eaten, saying, "This cup is the new covenant in my blood, which will be shed for you.

"And yet behold, the hand of the one who is to betray me is with me on the table; for the Son of Man indeed goes as it has been determined; but woe to that man by whom he is betrayed." And they began to debate among themselves who among them would do such a deed.

PSALM 100:1-5

A psalm of thanksgiving.
Sing joyfully to the LORD, all you
     lands;
   serve the LORD with gladness;
   come before him with joyful
     song.
Know that the LORD is God;
   he made us, his we are;
   his people, the flock he tends.
Enter his gates with
     thanksgiving,
   his courts with praise;
Give thanks to him; bless his
     name, for he is good:
   the LORD, whose kindness
     endures forever,
   and his faithfulness, to all
     generations.

PROVERBS 22:2-4

Rich and poor have a common bond: / the LORD is the maker of them all. / The shrewd man perceives evil and hides, / while simpletons continue on and suffer the penalty. / The reward of humility and fear of the LORD / is riches, honor and life.

AUGUST 27

LUKE 22:24-53

Then an argument broke out among them about which of them should be regarded as the greatest. He said to them, "The kings of the Gentiles lord it over them and those in authority over them are addressed as 'Benefactors'; but among you it shall not be so. Rather, let the greatest among you be as the youngest, and the leader as the servant. For who is greater: the one seated at table or the one who serves? Is it not the one seated at table? I am among you as the one who serves. It is you who have stood by me in my trials; and I confer a kingdom on you, just as my Father has conferred one on me, that you may eat and drink at my table in my kingdom; and you will sit on thrones judging the twelve tribes of Israel.

"Simon, Simon, behold Satan has demanded to sift all of you like wheat, but I have prayed that your own faith may not fail; and once you have turned back, you must strengthen your brothers." He said to him, "Lord, I am prepared to go to prison and to die with you." But he replied, "I tell you, Peter, before the cock crows this day, you will deny three times that you know me."

He said to them, "When I sent you forth without a money bag or a sack or sandals, were you in need of anything?" "No, nothing," they replied. He said to them, "But now one who has a money bag should take it, and likewise a sack, and one who does not have a sword should sell his cloak and buy one. For I tell you that this scripture must be fulfilled in me, namely, 'He was counted among the wicked'; and indeed what is written about me is coming to fulfillment." Then they said, "Lord, look, there are two swords here." But he replied, "It is enough!"

Then going out he went, as was his custom, to the Mount of Olives, and the disciples followed him. When he arrived at the place he said to them, "Pray that you may not undergo the test." After withdrawing about a stone's throw from them and kneeling, he prayed, saying, "Father, if you are willing, take this cup away from me; still, not my will but yours be done." [And to strengthen him an angel from heaven appeared to him. He was in such agony and he prayed so fervently that his sweat became like drops of blood falling on the ground.] When he rose from prayer and returned to his disciples, he found them sleeping from grief. He said to them, "Why are you sleeping? Get up and pray that you may not undergo the test."

While he was still speaking, a crowd approached and in front was one of the Twelve, a man named Judas. He went up to Jesus to kiss him. Jesus said to him, "Judas, are you betraying the Son of Man with a kiss?" His disciples realized what was about to happen, and they asked, "Lord, shall we strike with a sword?" And one of them struck the high priest's servant and cut off his right ear. But Jesus said in reply, "Stop, no more of this!" Then he touched the servant's ear and healed him. And Jesus said to the chief priests and temple guards and elders who had come for him, "Have you come out as against a robber, with swords and clubs? Day after day I was with you in the temple area, and you did not seize me; but this is your hour, the time for the power of darkness."

PSALM 101:1-8

A psalm of David.

Of kindness and judgment I will
     sing;
  to you, O LORD, I will sing
     praise.
I will persevere in the way of
     integrity;
  when will you come to me?
I will walk in the integrity of my
     heart,
  within my house;
I will not set before my eyes
  any base thing.
I hate him who does perversely;
  he shall not remain with me.

A crooked heart shall be far from
     me;
  evil I will not know.
Whoever slanders his neighbor in
     secret,
  him will I destroy.
The man of haughty eyes and
     puffed-up heart
  I will not endure.
My eyes are upon the faithful of
     the land,
  that they may dwell with me.
He who walks in the way of
     integrity
  shall be in my service.
He shall not dwell within my
     house
  who practices deceit.
He who speaks falsehood shall
     not stand
  before my eyes.
Each morning I will destroy
  all the wicked of the land,
And uproot from the city of the
     LORD
  all evildoers.

PROVERBS 22:5-6

Thorns and snares are on the paths of the crooked; / he who would safeguard his life will shun them. / Train a boy in the way he should go; / even when he is old, he will not swerve from it.

AUGUST 28

LUKE 22:54-71

After arresting him they led him away and took him into the house of the high priest; Peter was following at a distance. They lit a fire in the middle of the courtyard and sat around it, and Peter sat down with them. When a maid saw him seated in the light, she looked intently at him and said, "This man too was with him." But he denied it saying, "Woman, I do not know him." A short while later someone else saw him and said, "You too are one of them"; but Peter answered, "My friend, I am not." About an hour later, still another insisted, "Assuredly, this man too was with him, for he also is a Galilean." But Peter said, "My friend, I do not know what you are talking about." Just as he was saying this, the cock crowed, and the

Lord turned and looked at Peter; and Peter remembered the word of the Lord, how he had said to him, "Before the cock crows today, you will deny me three times." He went out and began to weep bitterly. The men who held Jesus in custody were ridiculing and beating him. They blindfolded him and questioned him, saying, "Prophesy! Who is it that struck you?" And they reviled him in saying many other things against him.

When day came the council of elders of the people met, both chief priests and scribes, and they brought him before their Sanhedrin. They said, "If you are the Messiah, tell us," but he replied to them, "If I tell you, you will not believe, and if I question, you will not respond. But from this time on the Son of Man will be seated at the right hand of the power of God." They all asked, "Are you then the Son of God?" He replied to them, "You say that

I am." Then they said, "What further need have we for testimony? We have heard it from his own mouth."

PSALM 102:1-7

The prayer of an afflicted one when he is faint and pours out his anguish before the LORD.
O LORD, hear my prayer,
    and let my cry come to you.
Hide not your face from me in
    the day of my distress.
Incline your ear to me;
    in the day when I call, answer
    me speedily.
For my days vanish like smoke,
    and my bones burn like fire.
Withered and dried up like grass
    is my heart;
    I forget to eat my bread.
Because of my insistent sighing
    I am reduced to skin and bone.
I am like a desert owl;
    I have become like an owl
    among the ruins.

PROVERBS 22:7

The rich rule over the poor, / and the borrower is the slave of the lender.

AUGUST 29

LUKE 23:1-25

Then the whole assembly of them arose and brought him before Pilate. They brought charges against him, saying, "We found this man misleading our people; he opposes the payment of taxes to Caesar and maintains that he is the Messiah, a king." Pilate asked him, "Are you the king of the Jews?" He said to him in reply, "You say so." Pilate then ad-

dressed the chief priests and the crowds, "I find this man not guilty." But they were adamant and said, "He is inciting the people with his teaching throughout all Judea, from Galilee where he began even to here."

On hearing this Pilate asked if the man was a Galilean; and upon learning that he was under Herod's jurisdiction, he sent him to Herod who was in Jerusalem at that time. Herod was very glad to see Jesus; he had been wanting to see him for a long time, for he had heard about him and had been hoping to see him perform some sign. He questioned him at length, but he gave him no answer. The chief priests and scribes, meanwhile, stood by accusing him harshly. [Even] Herod and his soldiers treated him contemptuously and mocked him, and after clothing him in resplendent garb, he sent him back to Pilate. Herod and Pilate became friends that very day, even though they had been enemies formerly. Pilate then summoned the chief priests, the rulers, and the people and said to them, "You brought this man to me and accused him of inciting the people to revolt. I have conducted my investigation in your presence and have not found this man guilty of the charges you have brought against him, nor did Herod, for he sent him back to us. So no capital crime has been committed by him. Therefore I shall have him flogged and then release him."

But all together they shouted out, "Away with this man! Release Barabbas to us." (Now Barabbas had been imprisoned for a rebellion that had taken place in the city and for murder.) Again Pilate addressed them, still wishing to release Jesus, but they continued their shouting, "Crucify him! Crucify him!" Pilate addressed them a third time, "What evil has this man done? I found him guilty of no capital crime. Therefore I shall have him flogged and then release him." With loud shouts, however, they persisted in calling for his crucifixion, and their voices prevailed. The verdict of Pilate was that their demand should be granted. So he released the man who had been imprisoned for rebellion and murder, for whom they asked, and he handed Jesus over to them to deal with as they wished.

PSALM 102:8-12

I am sleepless, and I moan;
   I am like a sparrow alone on
      the housetop.
All the day my enemies revile
      me;
   in their rage against me they
      make a curse of me.
For I eat ashes like bread
   and mingle my drink with
      tears,
Because of your fury and your
      wrath;
   for you lifted me up only to
      cast me down.
My days are like a lengthening
      shadow,
   and I wither like grass.

PROVERBS 22:8-9

He who sows iniquity reaps calamity, / and the rod destroys his labors. / The kindly man will be blessed, / for he gives of his sustenance to the poor.

LUKE 23:26-56

As they led him away they took hold of a certain Simon, a Cyrenian, who was coming in from the country; and after laying the cross on him, they made him carry it behind Jesus. A large crowd of people followed Jesus, including many women who mourned and lamented him. Jesus turned to them and said, "Daughters of Jerusalem, do not weep for me; weep instead for yourselves and for your children, for indeed, the days are coming when people will say, 'Blessed are the barren, the wombs that never bore and the breasts that never nursed.' At that time people will say to the mountains, 'Fall upon us!' and to the hills, 'Cover us!' for if these things are done when the wood is green what will happen when it is dry?" Now two others, both criminals, were led away with him to be executed.

When they came to the place called the Skull, they crucified him and the criminals there, one on his right, the other on his left. [Then Jesus said, "Father, forgive them, they know not what they do."] They divided his garments by casting lots. The people stood by and watched; the rulers, meanwhile, sneered at him and said, "He saved others, let him save himself if he is the chosen one, the Messiah of God." Even the soldiers jeered at him. As they approached to offer him wine they called out, "If you are King of the Jews, save yourself." Above him there was an inscription that read, "This is the King of the Jews."

Now one of the criminals hanging there reviled Jesus, saying, "Are you not the Messiah? Save yourself and us." The other, however, rebuking him, said in reply, "Have you no fear of God, for you are subject to the same condemnation? And indeed, we have been condemned justly, for the sentence we received corresponds to our crimes, but this man has done nothing criminal." Then he said, "Jesus, remember me when you come into your kingdom." He replied to him, "Amen, I say to you, today you will be with me in Paradise."

It was now about noon and darkness came over the whole land until three in the afternoon because of an eclipse of the sun. Then the veil of the temple was torn down the middle. Jesus cried out in a loud voice, "Father, into your hands I commend my spirit"; and when he had said this he breathed his last. The centurion who witnessed what had happened glorified God and said, "This man was innocent beyond doubt." When all the people who had gathered for this spectacle saw what had happened, they returned home beating their breasts; but all his acquaintances stood at a distance, including the women who had followed him from Galilee and saw these events.

Now there was a virtuous and righteous man named Joseph who, though he was a member of the council, had not consented to their plan of action. He came from the Jewish town of Arimathea and was awaiting the kingdom of God. He went to Pilate and asked for the body of Jesus. After he had taken the body down, he wrapped it in a linen cloth and laid him in a rock-hewn tomb in which no one had yet been buried. It was the day of preparation, and the sabbath was about to begin. The women who had come from Galilee with him followed behind, and when they had seen the tomb and the way in which his body was laid in it, they returned and prepared spices and perfumed oils. Then they rested on the sabbath according to the commandment.

PSALM 102:13-18

But you, O LORD, abide forever,
and your name through all
generations.

You will arise and have mercy on
Zion,
for it is time to pity her,
for the appointed time has
come.
For her stones are dear to your
servants,
and her dust moves them to
pity.
And the nations shall revere your
name, O LORD,
and all the kings of the earth
your glory,
When the LORD has rebuilt Zion
and appeared in his glory;
When he has regarded the prayer
of the destitute,
and not despised their prayer.

PROVERBS 22:10-12

Expel the arrogant man and discord goes out; / strife and insult cease. / The LORD loves the pure of heart; / the man of winning speech has the king for his friend. / The eyes of the LORD safeguard knowledge, / but he defeats the projects of the faithless.

AUGUST 31

LUKE 24:1-53

But at daybreak on the first day of the week they took the spices they had prepared and went to the tomb. They found the stone rolled away from the tomb; but when they entered, they did not find the body of the Lord Jesus. While they were puzzling over this, behold, two men in dazzling garments appeared to them. They were terrified and bowed their faces to the ground. They said to them, "Why do you seek the living one among the dead? He is not here, but he has been raised. Remember what he said to you while he was still in Galilee, that the Son of Man must be handed over to sinners and be crucified, and rise on the third day." And they remembered his words. Then they returned from the tomb and announced all these things to the eleven and to all the others. The women were Mary Magdalene, Joanna, and Mary the mother of James; the others who accompanied them also told this to the apostles, but their story seemed like nonsense and they did not believe them. But Peter got up and ran to the tomb, bent down, and saw the burial cloths alone; then he went home amazed at what had happened.

Now that very day two of them were going to a village seven miles from Jerusalem called Emmaus, and they were conversing about all the things that had occurred. And it happened that while they were conversing and debating, Jesus himself drew near and walked with them, but their eyes were prevented from recognizing him. He asked them, "What are you discussing as you walk along?" They stopped, looking downcast. One of them, named Cleopas, said to him in reply, "Are you the only visitor to Jerusalem who does not know of the things that have taken place there in these days?" And he replied to them, "What sort of things?" They said to him, "The things that happened to Jesus the Nazarene, who was a prophet mighty in deed and word before God and all the people, how our chief priests and rulers both handed him over to a sentence of death and crucified him. But we were hoping that he would be the one to redeem Israel; and besides all this, it is now the third day since this took place. Some women from our group, however, have astounded us: they were at the tomb early in the morning and did not find his body; they came back and reported that they had indeed seen a vision of angels who announced that he was alive. Then some of those with us went to the tomb and found things just as the women had described, but him they did not see." And he said to them, "Oh how foolish you are! How slow of heart to believe all that the prophets spoke! Was it not necessary that the Messiah should suffer these things and en-

ter into his glory?" Then beginning with Moses and all the prophets, he interpreted to them what referred to him in all the scriptures. As they approached the village to which they were going, he gave the impression that he was going on farther. But they urged him, "Stay with us, for it is nearly evening and the day is almost over." So he went in to stay with them. And it happened that, while he was with them at table, he took bread, said the blessing, broke it, and gave it to them. With that their eyes were opened and they recognized him, but he vanished from their sight. Then they said to each other, "Were not our hearts burning [within us] while he spoke to us on the way and opened the scriptures to us?" So they set out at once and returned to Jerusalem where they found gathered together the eleven and those with them who were saying, "The Lord has truly been raised and has appeared to Simon!" Then the two recounted what had taken place on the way and how he was made known to them in the breaking of the bread.

While they were still speaking about this, he stood in their midst and said to them, "Peace be with you." But they were startled and terrified and thought that they were seeing a ghost. Then he said to them, "Why are you troubled? And why do questions arise in your hearts? Look at my hands and my feet, that it is I myself. Touch me and see, because a ghost does not have flesh and bones as you can see I have." And as he said this, he showed them his hands and his feet. While they were still incredulous for joy and were amazed, he asked them, "Have you anything here to eat?"

They gave him a piece of baked fish; he took it and ate it in front of them.

He said to them, "These are my words that I spoke to you while I was still with you, that everything written about me in the law of Moses and in the prophets and psalms must be fulfilled." Then he opened their minds to understand the scriptures. And he said to them, "Thus it is written that the Messiah would suffer and rise from the dead on the third day and that repentance, for the forgiveness of sins, would be preached in his name to all the nations, beginning from Jerusalem. You are witnesses of these things. And [behold] I am sending the promise of my Father upon you; but stay in the city until you are clothed with power from on high."

Then he led them [out] as far as Bethany, raised his hands, and blessed them. As he blessed them he parted from them and was taken up to heaven. They did him homage and then returned to Jerusalem with great joy, and they were continually in the temple praising God.

PSALM 102:19-23

Let this be written for the
    generation to come,
  and let his future creatures
    praise the Lord:
"The LORD looked down from his
    holy height,
  from heaven he beheld the
    earth,
To hear the groaning of the
    prisoners,
  to release those doomed to
    die"—
That the name of the LORD may
    be declared in Zion;
  and his praise, in Jerusalem,
When the peoples gather
    together,
  and the kingdoms, to serve the
    LORD.

PROVERBS 22:13

The sluggard says, "A lion is outside; / in the streets I might be slain."

SEPTEMBER

Proverbs 1

"**T**HE FEAR OF THE LORD is the beginning of knowledge." (Prv 1:7)

In our high-velocity society we are always anxious to discover short, snappy ways to accomplish a task. We want only a short indoctrination into some subject or only a brief orientation into some practice rather than going at a more relaxed, slower pace. We desire "instant" everything.

Our attitudes and our mode of conduct are often formed by some slogan or pithy saying which, wittingly or unwittingly, has become a rule of life for some of us. In the media, advertising capitalizes on this type of jargon to help us remember a product or brand when we go shopping.

For our spiritual growth, many of us have adopted certain expressions which remind us of God's goodness and his loving concern for us. By way of example: "If God seems far away, who do you think moved?" or "God is good and he is getting better every day." These sayings will automatically encourage us and help us become more aware of the Lord's abiding presence in us.

Jesus gave us similar expressions as norms for our spiritual growth. "Be merciful, just as [also] your Father is merciful" (Lk 6:36). Another one has become the Golden Rule: "Do to others whatever you would have them do to you" (Mt 7:12). It is easier for us to remember these one-liners. They do have the potential to mold and shape our habits.

We find a whole treasury of these sayings in the Book of Proverbs, one of the Wisdom Books of the Old Testament. Proverbs is a rich anthology of poetic expressions whose purpose is to impart a wisdom which will mold and influence our attitudes and actions. This collection covers a whole range of subjects, from the mundane and common activities of life to lofty moral ideals and deep religious truths.

These Proverbs remind us of the power and providence of God as well as his goodness and fidelity to his promises. If we live according to their dictates, they will become a source of much peace and joy for us. We will likewise find them a source of strength and encouragement in time of need.

The Book of Proverbs is not a literary collection which is to be scanned or read hurriedly. Each proverb requires our quiet meditative reflection. After we have absorbed the lesson which is contained in it, we will naturally want to respond to our gracious God with an affective prayer of love and gratitude. To appreciate this rich gold mine, we need to read and reread, to ponder and reflect, and finally to respond from the depth of our being.

Occasionally as we reflect on some of these admonitions, we may be struck, or even a bit surprised, by the common sense nature of some of the advice propounded by them. We may be shocked by the self-interest and personal concerns which seem to warrant and justify a mode of conduct which does not coincide with our Christian ethic. One such instance is the attitude toward helping the poor. The sages of the Old Testament maintain that poverty is a punishment from God for the wicked. According to their belief, no good person will ever be poor.

In order for us to understand this kind of teaching, we need to recall that their understanding of theology and morality was far from the revealed tenets of Christianity. The teachers in Israel at that time were the priests, prophets, and wise men who believed that God would apportion justice by granting prosperity to the good and suffering to the wicked.

We must also remember that the teachers of that day had little clear vision of life after death. Since they had faith in God's justice, they had to find a way to explain how God would reward the upright and just person. These wise men were firmly convinced that God would reward the good person with wealth, honor, family, and a long life. These blessings would be granted to a person who was humble and who feared the Lord. "The reward of humility and fear of the Lord is riches, honor and life" (Prv 22:4).

Jesus completed this teaching by explaining that a treasure in this world was not the source of true happiness, but a treasure in heaven is. "But store up treasures in heaven, where neither moth nor decay destroys, nor thieves break in and steal. For where your treasure is, there also will your heart be" (Mt 6:20-21).

These observations are intended to help us appreciate the fullness of revelation which we have. Jesus used many of these proverbs in his own teaching, but he added a more developed dimension to them. For example: The Beatitudes are a further development of the Decalogue. The Beatitudes lead us far beyond the directives and incentives of the Commandments.

Here is a brief insight on how Jesus developed the wisdom and counsel of the Proverbs: "The rich man's wealth is his strong city; the ruination of the lowly is their poverty" (Prv 10:15).

But Jesus teaches: "Blessed are the poor in spirit, for theirs is the kingdom of heaven" (Mt 5:3).

Also: "The sacrifice of the wicked is an abomination to the Lord, but the prayer of the upright is his delight" (Prv 15:8). To confirm this lesson Jesus told us the story of the Pharisee and the tax collector who went up to the temple to pray. The tax collector was a humble man and Jesus said of him: "I tell you, the latter went home justified, not the former" (Lk 18:14).

When a proverb catches your fancy and touches your heart and you have an inclination to put it into practice in your life, by all means do so. You will find it profitable to jot it down in your prayer journal, thus permitting it to make a deeper impression on you. In this way it will soon become a norm for your Christian living and another step toward greater happiness in your life.

"He who keeps the precept keeps his life, but the despiser of the word will die" (Prv 19:16).

SEPTEMBER 1

TITUS 1:1-16

Paul, a slave of God and apostle of Jesus Christ for the sake of the faith of God's chosen ones and the recognition of religious truth, in the hope of eternal life that God, who does not lie, promised before time began, who indeed at the proper time revealed his word in the proclamation with which I was entrusted by the command of God our savior, to Titus, my true child in our common faith: grace and peace from God the Father and Christ Jesus our savior.

For this reason I left you in Crete so that you might set right what remains to be done and appoint presbyters in every town, as I directed you, on condition that a man be blameless, married only once, with believing children who are not accused of licentiousness or rebellious. For a bishop as God's steward must be blameless, not arrogant, not irritable, not a drunkard, not aggressive, not greedy for sordid gain, but hospitable, a lover of goodness, temperate, just, holy, and self-controlled, holding fast to the true message as taught so that he will be able both to exhort with sound doctrine and to refute opponents. For there are also many rebels, idle talkers and deceivers, especially the Jewish Christians. It is imperative to silence them, as they are upsetting whole families by teaching for sordid gain what they should not. One of them, a prophet of their own, once said, "Cretans have always been liars, vicious beasts, and lazy gluttons." That testimony is true. Therefore, admonish them sharply, so that they may be sound in the faith, instead of paying attention to Jewish myths and regulations of people who have repudiated the truth. To the clean all things are clean, but to those who are defiled and unbelieving nothing is clean; in fact, both their minds and their consciences are tainted. They claim to know God, but by their deeds they deny him. They are vile and disobedient and unqualified for any good deed.

PSALM 102:24-29

He has broken down my strength
    in the way;
    he has cut short my days. I say:
    O my God,
Take me not hence in the midst
    of my days;
    through all generations your
    years endure.
Of old you established the earth,
    and the heavens are the work
    of your hands.
They shall perish, but you remain
    though all of them grow old
    like a garment.

Like clothing you change them,
and they are changed,
but you are the same, and your
years have no end.

The children of your servants
shall abide,
and their posterity shall
continue in your presence.

PROVERBS 22:14

The mouth of the adulteress is a deep pit; / he with whom the LORD is angry will fall into it.

SEPTEMBER 2

TITUS 2:1-15

As for yourself, you must say what is consistent with sound doctrine, namely, that older men should be temperate, dignified, self-controlled, sound in faith, love, and endurance. Similarly, older women should be reverent in their behavior, not slanderers, not addicted to drink, teaching what is good, so that they may train younger women to love their husbands and children, to be self-controlled, chaste, good homemakers, under the control of their husbands, so that the word of God may not be discredited.

Urge the younger men, similarly, to control themselves, showing yourself as a model of good deeds in every respect, with integrity in your teaching, dignity, and sound speech that cannot be criticized, so that the opponent will be put to shame without anything bad to say about us.

Slaves are to be under the control of their masters in all respects, giving them satisfaction, not talking back to them or stealing from them, but exhibiting complete good faith, so as to adorn the doctrine of God our savior in every way.

For the grace of God has appeared, saving all and training us to reject godless ways and worldly desires and to live temperately, justly, and devoutly in this age, as we await the blessed hope, the appearance of the glory of the great God and of our savior Jesus Christ, who gave himself for us to deliver us from all lawlessness and to cleanse for himself a people as his own, eager to do what is good.

Say these things. Exhort and correct with all authority. Let no one look down on you.

PSALM 103:1-5

Of David.
Bless the LORD, O my soul;
and all my being, bless his holy
name.
Bless the LORD, O my soul,
and forget not all his benefits;
He pardons all your iniquities,
he heals all your ills.
He redeems your life from
destruction,
he crowns you with kindness
and compassion,
He fills your lifetime with good;
your youth is renewed like the
eagle's.

PROVERBS 22:15

Folly is close to the heart of a child, / but the rod of discipline will drive it far from him.

SEPTEMBER 3

TITUS 3:1-15

Remind them to be under the control of magistrates and authorities, to be obedient, to be open to every good enterprise. They are to slander no one, to be peaceable, considerate, exercising all graciousness toward everyone. For we ourselves were once foolish, disobedient, deluded, slaves to various desires and pleasures, living in malice and envy, hateful ourselves and hating one another.

But when the kindness and
    generous love
of God our savior appeared,
not because of any righteous
    deeds we had done
but because of his mercy,
he saved us through the bath
    of rebirth
    and renewal by the holy
    Spirit,
whom he richly poured out on
    us
    through Jesus Christ our
    savior,
so that we might be justified by
    his grace
and become heirs in hope of
    eternal life.

This saying is trustworthy.

I want you to insist on these points, that those who have believed in God be careful to devote themselves to good works; these are excellent and beneficial to others. Avoid foolish arguments, genealogies, rivalries, and quarrels about the law, for they are useless and futile. After a first and second warning, break off contact with a heretic, realizing that such a person is perverted and sinful and stands self-condemned.

When I send Artemas to you, or Tychicus, try to join me at Nicopolis, where I have decided to spend the winter. Send Zenas the lawyer and Apollos on their journey soon, and see to it that they have everything they need. But let our people, too, learn to devote themselves to good works to supply urgent needs, so that they may not be unproductive.

All who are with me send you greetings. Greet those who love us in the faith.

Grace be with all of you.

PSALM 103:6-10

The LORD secures justice
    and the rights of all the
    oppressed.
He has made known his ways to
    Moses,
    and his deeds to the children of
    Israel.
Merciful and gracious is the
    LORD,
    slow to anger and abounding
    in kindness.
He will not always chide,

nor does he keep his wrath
  forever.
Not according to our sins does he
  deal with us,

nor does he requite us
  according to our crimes.

PROVERBS 22:16

He who oppresses the poor to enrich himself / will yield up his gains to the rich as sheer loss.

SEPTEMBER 4

PHILEMON 1:1-25

Paul, a prisoner for Christ Jesus, and Timothy our brother, to Philemon, our beloved and our co-worker, to Apphia our sister, to Archippus our fellow soldier, and to the church at your house. Grace to you and peace from God our Father and the Lord Jesus Christ.

I give thanks to my God always, remembering you in my prayers, as I hear of the love and the faith you have in the Lord Jesus and for all the holy ones, so that your partnership in the faith may become effective in recognizing every good there is in us that leads to Christ.

For I have experienced much joy and encouragement from your love, because the hearts of the holy ones have been refreshed by you, brother. Therefore, although I have the full right in Christ to order you to do what is proper, I rather urge you out of love, being as I am, Paul, an old man, and now also a prisoner for Christ Jesus. I urge you on behalf of my child Onesimus, whose father I have become in my imprisonment, who was once useless to you but is now useful to [both] you and me. I am sending him, that is, my own heart, back to you. I should have liked to retain him for myself, so that he might serve me on your behalf in my imprisonment for the gospel, but I did not want to do anything without your consent, so that the good you do might not be forced but voluntary. Perhaps this is why he was away from you for a while, that you might have him back forever, no longer as a slave but more than a slave, a brother, beloved especially to me, but even more so to you, as a man and in the Lord. So if you regard me as a partner, welcome him as you would me. And if he has done you any injustice or owes you anything, charge it to me. I, Paul, write this in my own hand: I will pay. May I not tell you that you owe me your very self. Yes, brother, may I profit from you in the Lord. Refresh my heart in Christ.

With trust in your compliance I write to you, knowing that you will do even more than I say. At the same time prepare a guest room for me, for I hope to be granted to you through your prayers.

Epaphras, my fellow prisoner in Christ Jesus, greets you, as well as Mark, Aristarchus, Demas, and Luke, my co-workers. The grace of the Lord Jesus Christ be with your spirit.

PSALM 103:11-18

For as the heavens are high
  above the earth,
    so surpassing is his kindness
    toward those who fear him.
As far as the east is from the
  west,
    so far has he put our
    transgressions from us.
As a father has compassion on
  his children,
    so the LORD has compassion on
    those who fear him,
For he knows how we are
  formed;
    he remembers that we are
    dust.
Man's days are like those of
  grass;
like a flower of the field he
  blooms;
The wind sweeps over him and
  he is gone,
    and his place knows him no
    more.
But the kindness of the LORD is
  from eternity
    to eternity toward those who
    fear him,
And his justice toward children's
  children
    among those who keep his
    covenant
    and remember to fulfill his
    precepts.

PROVERBS 22:17-19

The sayings of the wise: / Incline your ear, and hear my words, / and apply your heart to my doctrine; / For it will be well if you keep them in your bosom, / if they all are ready on your lips. / That your trust may be in the LORD, / I make known to you the words of Amen-em-Ope.

SEPTEMBER 5

HEBREWS 1:1-14

In times past, God spoke in partial and various ways to our ancestors through the prophets; in these last days, he spoke to us through a son, whom he made heir of all things and through whom he created the universe,
  who is the refulgence of his
    glory,
    the very imprint of his being,
  and who sustains all things by
    his mighty word.
When he had accomplished
  purification from sins,
he took his seat at the right
  hand of the Majesty on
  high,
as far superior to the angels
as the name he has inherited is
  more excellent than theirs.

For to which of the angels did
God ever say:

"You are my son; this day I
  have begotten you"?

Or again:

"I will be a father to him, and
  he shall be a son to me"?

And again, when he leads the first-born into the world, he says:

"Let all the angels of God worship him."

Of the angels he says:

"He makes his angels winds and his ministers a fiery flame";

but of the Son:

"Your throne, O God, stands forever and ever;
and a righteous scepter is the scepter of your kingdom.
You loved justice and hated wickedness;
therefore God, your God, anointed you
with the oil of gladness above your companions";

and:

"At the beginning, O Lord, you established the earth,
and the heavens are the works of your hands.
They will perish, but you remain;
and they will all grow old like a garment.
You will roll them up like a cloak,
and like a garment they will be changed.
But you are the same, and your years will have no end."

But to which of the angels has he ever said:

"Sit at my right hand
until I make your enemies your footstool"?

Are they not all ministering spirits sent to serve, for the sake of those who are to inherit salvation?

PSALM 103:19-22

The LORD has established his throne in heaven,
and his kingdom rules over all.
Bless the LORD, all you his angels,
you mighty in strength, who do his bidding,
obeying his spoken word.
Bless the LORD, all you his hosts,
his ministers, who do his will.
Bless the LORD, all his works,
everywhere in his domain.
Bless the LORD, O my soul!

PROVERBS 22:20-21

Have I not written for you the "Thirty," / with counsels and knowledge, / To teach you truly / how to give a dependable report to one who sends you?

SEPTEMBER 6

HEBREWS 2:1-18

Therefore, we must attend all the more to what we have heard, so that we may not be carried away. For if the word announced through angels proved firm, and every transgression and disobedience received its just recompense, how shall we escape if we ignore so great a salvation? Announced originally through the Lord, it was confirmed for us by those who had heard. God added his testimony by signs, wonders, various acts of power, and distribution of the gifts of the holy Spirit according to his will.

For it was not to angels that he subjected the world to come, of which we are speaking. Instead, someone has testified somewhere:

"What is man that you are
    mindful of him,
  or the son of man that you
    care for him?
You made him for a little while
    lower than the angels;
  you crowned him with glory
    and honor,
  subjecting all things under
    his feet."

In "subjecting" all things [to him], he left nothing not "subject to him." Yet at present we do not see "all things subject to him," but we do see Jesus "crowned with glory and honor" because he suffered death, he who "for a little while" was made "lower than the angels," that by the grace of God he might taste death for everyone.

For it was fitting that he, for whom and through whom all things exist, in bringing many children to glory, should make the leader to their salvation perfect through suffering. He who consecrates and those who are being consecrated all have one origin. Therefore, he is not ashamed to call them "brothers," saying:

"I will proclaim your name to
    my brothers,

in the midst of the assembly I
    will praise you";

and again:

"I will put my trust in him";

and again;

"Behold, I and the children
    God has given me."

Now since the children share in blood and flesh, he likewise shared in them, that through death he might destroy the one who has the power of death, that is, the devil, and free those who through fear of death had been subject to slavery all their life. Surely he did not help angels but rather the descendants of Abraham; therefore, he had to become like his brothers in every way, that he might be a merciful and faithful high priest before God to expiate the sins of the people. Because he himself was tested through what he suffered, he is able to help those who are being tested.

PSALMS 104:1-4

Bless the LORD, O my soul!
  O LORD, my God, you are great
    indeed!
You are clothed with majesty and
    glory,
  robed in light as with a cloak.
You have spread out the heavens
    like a tent-cloth;
  you have constructed your
    palace upon the waters.
You make the clouds your
    chariot;
  you travel on the wings of the
    wind.
You make the winds your
    messengers,
  and flaming fire your ministers.

PROVERBS 22:22-23

Injure not the poor because they are poor, / nor crush the needy at the gate; / For the LORD will defend their cause, / and will plunder the lives of those who plunder them.

SEPTEMBER 7

HEBREWS 3:1-19

Therefore, holy "brothers," sharing in a heavenly calling, reflect on Jesus, the apostle and high priest of our confession, who was faithful to the one who appointed him, just as Moses was "faithful in [all] his house." But he is worthy of more "glory" than Moses, as the founder of a house has more "honor" than the house itself. Every house is founded by someone, but the founder of all is God. Moses was "faithful in all his house" as a "servant" to testify to what would be spoken, but Christ was faithful as a son placed over his house. We are his house, if [only] we hold fast to our confidence and pride in our hope.

Therefore, as the holy Spirit says:

"Oh, that today you would
hear his voice,
'Harden not your hearts as at
the rebellion
in the day of testing in the
desert,
where your ancestors tested
and tried me
and saw my works for forty
years.
Because of this I was provoked
with that generation
and I said, "They have
always been of erring
heart,

and they do not know my
ways."
As I swore in my wrath,
"They shall not enter into my
rest." ' "

Take care, brothers, that none of you may have an evil and unfaithful heart, so as to forsake the living God. Encourage yourselves daily while it is still "today," so that none of you may grow hardened by the deceit of sin. We have become partners of Christ if only we hold the beginning of the reality firm until the end, for it is said:

"Oh, that today you would
hear his voice:
'Harden not your hearts as at
the rebellion.' "

Who were those who rebelled when they heard? Was it not all those who came out of Egypt under Moses? With whom was he "provoked for forty years"? Was it not those who had sinned, whose corpses fell in the desert? And to whom did he "swear that they should not enter into his rest," if not to those who were disobedient? And we see that they could not enter for lack of faith.

PSALM 104:5-9

You fixed the earth upon its
foundation,
not to be moved forever;

With the ocean, as with a
    garment, you covered it;
  above the mountains the
    waters stood.
At your rebuke they fled,
  at the sound of your thunder
    they took to flight;

As the mountains rose, they went
    down the valleys
  to the place you had fixed for
    them.
You set a limit they may not pass,
  nor shall they cover the earth
    again.

PROVERBS 22:24-25

*Be not friendly with a hotheaded man, / nor the companion of a wrathful man, /
Lest you learn his ways, / and get yourself into a snare.*

SEPTEMBER 8

HEBREWS 4:1-16

Therefore, let us be on our guard while the promise of entering into his rest remains, that none of you seem to have failed. For in fact we have received the good news just as they did. But the word that they heard did not profit them, for they were not united in faith with those who listened. For we who believed enter into [that] rest, just as he has said:

"As I swore in my wrath,
  'They shall not enter into my
    rest,' "

and yet his works were accomplished at the foundation of the world. For he has spoken somewhere about the seventh day in this manner, "And God rested on the seventh day from all his works"; and again, in the previously mentioned place, "They shall not enter into my rest." Therefore, since it remains that some will enter into it, and those who formerly received the good news did not enter because of disobedience, he once more set a

day, "today," when long afterwards he spoke through David, as already quoted:

"Oh, that today you would
  hear his voice:
  'Harden not your hearts.' "

Now if Joshua had given them rest, he would not have spoken afterwards of another day. Therefore, a sabbath rest still remains for the people of God. And whoever enters into God's rest, rests from his own works as God did from his. Therefore, let us strive to enter into that rest, so that no one may fall after the same example of disobedience.

Indeed, the word of God is living and effective, sharper than any two-edged sword, penetrating even between soul and spirit, joints and marrow, and able to discern reflections and thoughts of the heart. No creature is concealed from him, but everything is naked and exposed to the eyes of him to whom we must render an account.

Therefore, since we have a

great high priest who has passed through the heavens, Jesus, the Son of God, let us hold fast to our confession. For we do not have a high priest who is unable to sympathize with our weaknesses, but one who has similarly been tested in every way, yet without sin. So let us confidently approach the throne of grace to receive mercy and to find grace for timely help.

PSALM 104:10-13

You send forth springs into the watercourses
that wind among the mountains,
And give drink to every beast of the field,
till the wild asses quench their thirst.
Beside them the birds of heaven dwell;
from among the branches they send forth their song.
You water the mountains from your palace;
the earth is replete with the fruit of your works.

PROVERBS 22:26-27

Be not one of those who give their hand in pledge, / of those who become surety for debts; / For if you have not the means to pay, / your bed will be taken from under you.

SEPTEMBER 9

HEBREWS 5:1-14

Every high priest is taken from among men and made their representative before God, to offer gifts and sacrifices for sins. He is able to deal patiently with the ignorant and erring, for he himself is beset by weakness and so, for this reason, must make sin offerings for himself as well as for the people. No one takes this honor upon himself but only when called by God, just as Aaron was. In the same way, it was not Christ who glorified himself in becoming high priest, but rather the one who said to him:

"You are my son;
this day I have begotten you";

just as he says in another place:

"You are a priest forever
according to the order of Melchizedek."

In the days when he was in the flesh, he offered prayers and supplications with loud cries and tears to the one who was able to save him from death, and he was heard because of his reverence. Son though he was, he learned obedience from what he suffered; and when he was made perfect, he became the source of eternal salvation for all who obey him, declared by God high priest according to the order of Melchizedek.

About this we have much to say, and it is difficult to explain, for you have become sluggish in hearing. Although you should be teachers by this time, you need to have someone teach you again the basic elements of the utterances of God. You need milk, [and] not solid food. Everyone who lives on milk lacks experience of the word of righteousness, for he is a child. But solid food is for the mature, for those whose faculties are trained by practice to discern good and evil.

PSALM 104:14-18

You raise grass for the cattle,
  and vegetation for men's use,
Producing bread from the earth,
  and wine to gladden men's
    hearts,
So that their faces gleam with oil,
  and bread fortifies the hearts of
    men.
Well watered are the trees of the
    LORD,
  the cedars of Lebanon, which
    he planted;
In them the birds build their
    nests;
  fir trees are the home of the
    stork.
The high mountains are for wild
    goats;
  the cliffs are a refuge for
    rockbadgers.

PROVERBS 22:28

Remove not the ancient landmark / which your fathers set up.

SEPTEMBER 10

HEBREWS 6:1-20

Therefore, let us leave behind the basic teaching about Christ and advance to maturity, without laying the foundation all over again: repentance from dead works and faith in God, instruction about baptisms and laying on of hands, resurrection of the dead and eternal judgment. And we shall do this, if only God permits. For it is impossible in the case of those who have once been enlightened and tasted the heavenly gift and shared in the holy Spirit and tasted the good word of God and the powers of the age to come, and then have fallen away, to bring them to repentance again, since they are recrucifying the Son of God for themselves and holding him up to contempt. Ground that has absorbed the rain falling upon it repeatedly and brings forth crops useful to those for whom it is cultivated receives a blessing from God. But if it produces thorns and thistles, it is rejected; it will soon be cursed and finally burned.

But we are sure in your regard, beloved, of better things related to salvation, even though we speak in this way. For God is not unjust so as to overlook your work and the love you have demonstrated for his name by having served and continuing to serve the holy ones. We earnestly desire each of you to demonstrate the same eagerness for the fulfillment of hope until the end, so that you may not become sluggish, but imitators of those who, through faith and patience, are inheriting the promises.

When God made the promise to Abraham, since he had no one greater by whom to swear, "he swore by himself," and said, "I will indeed bless you and multiply" you. And so, after patient waiting, he obtained the promise. Human beings swear by someone greater than themselves; for them an oath serves as a guarantee and puts an end to all argument. So when God wanted to give the heirs of his promise an even clearer demonstration of the immutability of his purpose, he intervened with an oath, so that by two immutable things, in which it was impossible for God to lie, we who have taken refuge might be strongly encouraged to hold fast to the hope that lies before us. This we have as an anchor of the soul, sure and firm, which reaches into the interior behind the veil, where Jesus has entered on our behalf as forerunner, becoming high priest forever according to the order of Melchizedek.

PSALM 104:19-23

You made the moon to mark the seasons;
   the sun knows the hour of its setting.
You bring darkness, and it is night;
   then all the beasts of the forest roam about;
Young lions roar for the prey
   and seek their food from God.
When the sun rises, they withdraw
   and couch in their dens.
Man goes forth to his work
   and to his tillage till the evening.

PROVERBS 22:29

You see a man skilled at his work? / He will stand in the presence of kings; / he will not stand in the presence of obscure men.

SEPTEMBER 11

HEBREWS 7:1-10

This "Melchizedek, king of Salem and priest of God Most High," "met Abraham as he returned from his defeat of the kings" and "blessed him." And Abraham apportioned to him "a tenth of everything." His name first means righteous king, and he was also "king of Salem," that is, king of peace. Without father, mother, or ancestry, without beginning of days or end of life, thus made to resemble the Son of God, he remains a priest forever.

See how great he is to whom the patriarch "Abraham [indeed] gave a tenth" of his spoils. The descendants of Levi who receive the office of priesthood have a commandment according to the law to exact tithes from the people, that is, from their brothers, although they also have come from the loins of Abraham. But he who was not of their ancestry received tithes from Abraham and blessed him who had received the promises. Unquestionably, a lesser person is blessed by a greater. In the one case, mortal men receive tithes; in the other, a man of whom it is testified that he lives on. One might even say that Levi himself, who receives tithes, was tithed through Abraham, for he was still in his father's loins when Melchizedek met him.

PSALM 104:24-30

How manifold are your works, O LORD!
  In wisdom you have wrought them all—
  the earth is full of your creatures;
The sea also, great and wide,
  in which are schools without number
of living things both small and great,
And where ships move about with Leviathan, which you formed to make sport of it.
They all look to you
  to give them food in due time.
When you give it to them, they gather it;
  when you open your hand, they are filled with good things.
If you hide your face, they are dismayed;
  if you take away their breath, they perish
  and return to their dust.
When you send forth your spirit, they are created,
  and you renew the face of the earth.

PROVERBS 23:1-3

When you sit down to dine with a ruler, / keep in mind who is before you; / And put a knife to your throat / if you have a ravenous appetite. / Do not desire his delicacies; / they are deceitful food.

SEPTEMBER 12

HEBREWS 7:11-28

If, then, perfection came through the levitical priesthood, on the basis of which the people received the law, what need would there still have been for another priest to arise according to the order of Melchizedek, and not reckoned according to the order of Aaron? When there is a change of priesthood, there is necessarily a change of law as well. Now he of whom these things are said belonged to a different tribe, of which no member ever officiated at the altar. It is clear that our Lord arose from Judah, and in regard to that tribe Moses said nothing about priests. It is even more obvious if another priest is raised up after the likeness of Melchizedek, who has become so, not by a law expressed in a commandment concerning physical descent but by the power of a life that cannot be destroyed. For it is testified:

"You are a priest forever

according to the order of Melchizedek."

On the one hand, a former commandment is annulled because of its weakness and uselessness, for the law brought nothing to perfection; on the other hand, a better hope is introduced, through which we draw near to God. And to the degree that this happened not without the taking of an oath—for others became priests without an oath, but he with an oath, through the one who said to him:

"The Lord has sworn, and he will not repent:
'You are a priest forever' "—

to that same degree has Jesus [also] become the guarantee of an [even] better covenant. Those priests were many because they were prevented by death from remaining in office, but he, because he remains forever, has a priesthood that does not pass away. Therefore, he is always able to save those who approach God through him, since he lives forever to make intercession for them.

It was fitting that we should have such a high priest: holy, innocent, undefiled, separated from sinners, higher than the heavens. He has no need, as did the high priests, to offer sacrifice day after day, first for his own sins and then for those of the people; he did that once for all when he offered himself. For the law appoints men subject to weakness to be high priests, but the word of the oath, which was taken after the law, appoints a son, who has been made perfect forever.

PSALM 104:31-35

May the glory of the LORD endure forever;
  may the LORD be glad in his works!
He who looks upon the earth, and it trembles;
  who touches the mountains, and they smoke!
I will sing to the LORD all my life;
  I will sing praise to my God while I live.
Pleasing to him be my theme;
  I will be glad in the LORD.
May sinners cease from the earth, and may the wicked be no more.
  Bless the LORD, O my soul!
  Alleluia.

PROVERBS 23:4-5

Toil not to gain wealth, / cease to be concerned about it; / While your glance flits to it, it is gone! / for assuredly it grows wings, / like the eagle that flies toward heaven.

SEPTEMBER 13

HEBREWS 8:1-13

The main point of what has been said is this: we have such a high priest, who has taken his seat at the right hand of the throne of the Majesty in heaven, a minister of the sanctuary and of the true tabernacle that the Lord, not man, set up. Now every high priest is appointed to offer gifts and sacrifices; thus the necessity for this one also to have something to offer. If then he were on earth, he would not be a priest, since there are those who offer gifts according to the law. They worship in a copy and shadow of the heavenly sanctuary, as Moses was warned when he was about to erect the tabernacle. For he says, "See that you make everything according to the pattern shown you on the mountain." Now he has obtained so much more excellent a ministry as he is mediator of a better covenant, enacted on better promises.

For if that first covenant had been faultless, no place would have been sought for a second one. But he finds fault with them and says:

"Behold, the days are coming, says the Lord,
when I will conclude a new covenant
    with the house of Israel and the house of Judah.
It will not be like the covenant I made with their fathers
    the day I took them by the hand to
    lead them forth from the land of Egypt;
for they did not stand by my covenant
    and I ignored them, says the Lord.
But this is the covenant I will establish with the house of Israel

after those days, says the Lord:
I will put my laws in their minds
    and I will write them upon their hearts.
I will be their God,
    and they shall be my people.
And they shall not teach, each one his fellow citizen
    and kinsman, saying, 'Know the Lord,'
for all shall know me,
    from least to greatest.
For I will forgive their evildoing
    and remember their sins no more."

When he speaks of a "new" covenant, he declares the first one obsolete. And what has become obsolete and has grown old is close to disappearing.

PSALM 105:1-6

Give thanks to the LORD, invoke his name;
    make known among the nations his deeds.
Sing to him, sing his praise,
    proclaim all his wondrous deeds.
Glory in his holy name;
    rejoice, O hearts that seek the LORD!
Look to the LORD in his strength;
    seek to serve him constantly.
Recall the wondrous deeds that he has wrought,
    his portents, and the judgments he has uttered,
You descendants of Abraham, his servants,
    sons of Jacob, his chosen ones!

PROVERBS 23:6-8

Do not take food with a grudging man, / and do not desire his dainties; / For in his greed he is like a storm. / "Eat and drink," he says to you, / though his heart is not with you; / The little you have eaten you will vomit up, / and you will have wasted your agreeable words.

SEPTEMBER 14

HEBREWS 9:1-14

Now [even] the first covenant had regulations for worship and an earthly sanctuary. For a tabernacle was constructed, the outer one, in which were the lampstand, the table, and the bread of offering; this is called the Holy Place. Behind the second veil was the tabernacle called the Holy of Holies, in which were the gold altar of incense and the ark of the covenant entirely covered with gold. In it were the gold jar containing the manna, the staff of Aaron that had sprouted, and the tablets of the covenant. Above it were the cherubim of glory overshadowing the place of expiation. Now is not the time to speak of these in detail.

With these arrangements for worship, the priests, in performing their service, go into the outer tabernacle repeatedly, but the high priest alone goes into the inner one once a year, not without blood that he offers for himself and for the sins of the people. In this way the holy Spirit shows that the way into the sanctuary had not yet been revealed while the outer tabernacle still had its place. This is a symbol of the present time, in which gifts and sacrifices are offered that cannot perfect the worshiper in conscience but only in matters of food and drink and various ritual washings: regulations concerning the flesh, imposed until the time of the new order.

But when Christ came as high priest of the good things that have come to be, passing through the greater and more perfect tabernacle not made by hands, that is, not belonging to this creation, he entered once for all into the sanctuary, not with the blood of goats and calves but with his own blood, thus obtaining eternal redemption. For if the blood of goats and bulls and the sprinkling of a heifer's ashes can sanctify those who are defiled so that their flesh is cleansed, how much more will the blood of Christ, who through the eternal spirit offered himself unblemished to God, cleanse our consciences from dead works to worship the living God.

PSALM 105:7-15

He, the LORD, is our God;
   throughout the earth his
   judgments prevail.
He remembers forever his
   covenant
  which he made binding for a
   thousand generations—
Which he entered into with
   Abraham
  and by his oath to Isaac;
Which he established for Jacob by
   statute,
  for Israel as an everlasting
   covenant,
Saying, "To you will I give the
   land of Canaan
  as your allotted inheritance."
When they were few in number,

a handful, and strangers there,
Wandering from nation to nation
  and from one kingdom to
  another people,
He let no man oppress them,
and for their sake he rebuked
  kings:
"Touch not my anointed,
  and to my prophets do no
  harm."

PROVERBS 23:9-11

Speak not for the fool's hearing; / he will despise the wisdom of your words. / Remove not the ancient landmark, / nor invade the fields of orphans; / For their redeemer is strong; / he will defend their cause against you.

SEPTEMBER 15

HEBREWS 9:15-28

For this reason he is mediator of a new covenant: since a death has taken place for deliverance from transgressions under the first covenant, those who are called may receive the promised eternal inheritance. Now where there is a will, the death of the testator must be established. For a will takes effect only at death; it has no force while the testator is alive. Thus not even the first covenant was inaugurated without blood. When every commandment had been proclaimed by Moses to all the people according to the law, he took the blood of calves [and goats], together with water and crimson wool and hyssop, and sprinkled both the book itself and all the people, saying, "This is 'the blood of the covenant which God has enjoined upon you.'" In the same way, he sprinkled also the tabernacle and all the vessels of worship with blood. According to the law almost everything is purified by blood, and without the shedding of blood there is no forgiveness.

Therefore, it was necessary for the copies of the heavenly things to be purified by these rites, but the heavenly things themselves by better sacrifices than these. For Christ did not enter into a sanctuary made by hands, a copy of the true one, but heaven itself, that he might now appear before God on our behalf. Not that he might offer himself repeatedly, as the high priest enters each year into the sanctuary with blood that is not his own; if that were so, he would have had to suffer repeatedly from the foundation of the world. But now once for all he has appeared at the end of the ages to take away sin by his sacrifice. Just as it is appointed that human beings die once, and after this the judgment, so also Christ, offered once to take away the sins of many, will appear a second time, not to take away sin but to bring salvation to those who eagerly await him.

PSALM 105:16-27

When he called down a famine
  on the land
  and ruined the crop that
  sustained them,
He sent a man before them,

Joseph, sold as a slave;
They had weighed him down
    with fetters,
  and he was bound with chains,
Till his prediction came to pass
  and the word of the LORD
    proved him true.
The king sent and released him,
  the ruler of the peoples set him
    free.
He made him lord of his house
  and ruler of all his possessions,
That he might train his princes to
    be like him
  and teach his elders wisdom.
Then Israel came to Egypt,

and Jacob sojourned in the land
    of Ham.
He greatly increased his people
  and made them stronger than
    their foes,
Whose hearts he changed, so that
    they hated his people,
  and dealt deceitfully with his
    servants.
He sent Moses his servant;
  Aaron, whom he had chosen.
They wrought his signs among
    them,
  and wonders in the land of
    Ham.

PROVERBS 23:12

Apply your heart to instruction, / and your ears to words of knowledge.

SEPTEMBER 16

HEBREWS 10:1-18

Since the law has only a shadow of the good things to come, and not the very image of them, it can never make perfect those who come to worship by the same sacrifices that they offer continually each year. Otherwise, would not the sacrifices have ceased to be offered, since the worshipers, once cleansed, would no longer have had any consciousness of sins? But in those sacrifices there is only a yearly remembrance of sins, for it is impossible that the blood of bulls and goats take away sins. For this reason, when he came into the world, he said:

  "Sacrifice and offering you did
    not desire,
    but a body you prepared for
      me;

holocausts and sin offerings
    you took no delight in.
Then I said, 'As is written of
    me in the scroll,
Behold, I come to do your will,
    O God.' "

First he says, "Sacrifices and offerings, holocausts and sin offerings, you neither desired nor delighted in." These are offered according to the law. Then he says, "Behold, I come to do your will." He takes away the first to establish the second. By this "will," we have been consecrated through the offering of the body of Jesus Christ once for all.

Every priest stands daily at his ministry, offering frequently those same sacrifices that can never take away sins. But this one offered one sacrifice for sins, and took his seat forever at the right hand of God; now he waits until his enemies are made his footstool. For by one offering he has made perfect forever those who are being consecrated. The holy Spirit also testifies to us, for after saying:

"This is the covenant I will
    establish
  with them after those days,
    says the Lord:
'I will put my laws in their
    hearts,
  and I will write them upon
    their minds,' "

he also says:

"Their sins and their evildoing
  I will remember no more."

Where there is forgiveness of these, there is no longer offering for sin.

PSALM 105:28-38

He sent the darkness; it grew
    dark,
  but they rebelled against his
    words.
He turned their waters into blood
and killed their fish.
Their land swarmed with frogs,
  even in the chambers of their
    kings.
He spoke, and there came
    swarms of flies;
  gnats, throughout all their
    borders.
For rain he gave them hail,
  with flashing fires throughout
    their land.
He struck down their vines and
    their fig trees
  and shattered the trees
    throughout their borders.
He spoke, and there came locusts
    and grasshoppers without
    number;
And they devoured every plant
    throughout the land,
  they devoured the fruit of their
    soil.
Then he struck every first-born
    throughout their land,
  the first fruits of all their
    manhood.
And he led them forth laden with
    silver and gold,
  with not a weakling among
    their tribes.
Egypt rejoiced at their going,
  for the dread of them had
    fallen upon it.

PROVERBS 23:13-16

Withhold not chastisement from a boy; / if you beat him with the rod, he will not die. / Beat him with the rod, / and you will save him from the nether world. / My son, if your heart be wise, / my own heart also will rejoice; / And my inmost being will exult, / when your lips speak what is right.

SEPTEMBER 17

HEBREWS 10:19-39

Therefore, brothers, since through the blood of Jesus we have confidence of entrance into the sanctuary by the new and living way he opened for us through the veil, that is, his flesh, and since we have "a great priest over the house of God," let us approach with a sincere heart and in absolute trust, with our hearts sprinkled clean from an evil conscience and our bodies washed in pure water. Let us hold unwaveringly to our confession that gives us hope, for he who made the promise is trustworthy. We must consider how to rouse one another to love and good works. We should not stay away from our assembly, as is the custom of some, but encourage one another, and this all the more as you see the day drawing near.

If we sin deliberately after receiving knowledge of the truth, there no longer remains sacrifice for sins but a fearful prospect of judgment and a flaming fire that is going to consume the adversaries. Anyone who rejects the law of Moses is put to death without pity on the testimony of two or three witnesses. Do you not think that a much worse punishment is due the one who has contempt for the Son of God, considers unclean the covenant-blood by which he was consecrated, and insults the spirit of grace? We know the one who said:

"Vengeance is mine; I will repay,"

and again:

"The Lord will judge his people."

It is a fearful thing to fall into the hands of the living God.

Remember the days past when, after you had been enlightened, you endured a great contest of suffering. At times you were publicly exposed to abuse and affliction; at other times you associated yourselves with those so treated. You even joined in the sufferings of those in prison and joyfully accepted the confiscation of your property, knowing that you had a better and lasting possession. Therefore, do not throw away your confidence; it will have great recompense. You need endurance to do the will of God and receive what he has promised.

"For, after just a brief moment,
    he who is to come shall
        come;
    he shall not delay.
But my just one shall live by
    faith,
    and if he draws back I take
        no pleasure in him."

We are not among those who draw back and perish, but among those who have faith and will possess life.

PSALM 105:39-45

He spread a cloud to cover them
    and fire to give them light by
        night.
They asked, and he brought them
    quail,
    and with bread from heaven he
        satisfied them.
He cleft the rock, and the water
    gushed forth;
    it flowed through the dry lands
        like a stream,
For he remembered his holy
    word
    to his servant Abraham.
And he led forth his people with
    joy;
    with shouts of joy, his chosen
        ones.
And he gave them the lands of
    the nations,
    and they took what the peoples
        had toiled for,
That they might keep his statutes
    and observe his laws. Alleluia.

PROVERBS 23:17-18

Let not your heart emulate sinners, / but be zealous for the fear of the LORD always; / For you will surely have a future, / and your hope will not be cut off.

SEPTEMBER 18

HEBREWS 11:1-16

Faith is the realization of what is hoped for and evidence of things not seen. Because of it the ancients were well attested. By faith we understand that the universe was ordered by the word of God, so that what is visible came into being through the invisible. By faith Abel offered to God a sacrifice greater than Cain's. Through this he was attested to be righteous, God bearing witness to his gifts, and through this, though dead, he still speaks. By faith Enoch was taken up so that he should not see death, and "he was found no more because God had taken him." Before he was taken up, he was attested to have pleased God. But without faith it is impossible to please him, for anyone who approaches God must believe that he exists and that he rewards those who seek him. By faith Noah, warned about what was not yet seen, with reverence built an ark for the salvation of his household. Through this he condemned the world and inherited the righteousness that comes through faith.

By faith Abraham obeyed when he was called to go out to a place that he was to receive as an inheritance; he went out, not knowing where he was to go. By faith he sojourned in the promised land as in a foreign country, dwelling in tents with Isaac and Jacob, heirs of the same promise; for he was looking forward to the city with foundations, whose architect and maker is God. By faith he received power to generate, even though he was past the normal age—and Sarah herself was sterile—for he thought that the one who had made the promise was trustworthy. So it was that there came forth from one man, himself as good as dead, descendants as numerous as the stars in the sky and as countless as the sands on the seashore.

All these died in faith. They did not receive what had been promised but saw it and greeted it from afar and acknowledged themselves to be strangers and aliens on earth, for those who speak thus show that they are seeking a homeland. If they had been thinking of the land from which they had come, they would have had opportunity to return. But now they desire a better homeland, a heavenly one. Therefore, God is not ashamed to be called their God, for he has prepared a city for them.

PSALM 106:1-5

Alleluia.

Give thanks to the LORD, for he is good,
　for his kindness endures
　forever.

Who can tell the mighty deeds of
 the LORD,
  or proclaim all his praises?
Happy are they who observe
  what is right,
  who do always what is just.
Remember me, O LORD, as you
  favor your people;

visit me with your saving help,
That I may see the prosperity of
  your chosen ones,
  rejoice in the joy of your
  people,
  and glory with your
  inheritance.

PROVERBS 23:19-21

Hear, my son, and be wise, / and guide your heart in the right way. / Consort not with winebibbers, / nor with those who eat meat to excess; / For the drunkard and the glutton come to poverty, / and torpor clothes a man in rags.

SEPTEMBER 19

HEBREWS 11:17-40

By faith Abraham, when put to the test, offered up Isaac, and he who had received the promises was ready to offer his only son, of whom it was said, "Through Isaac descendants shall bear your name." He reasoned that God was able to raise even from the dead, and he received Isaac back as a symbol. By faith regarding things still to come Isaac blessed Jacob and Esau. By faith Jacob, when dying, blessed each of the sons of Joseph and "bowed in worship, leaning on the top of his staff." By faith Joseph, near the end of his life, spoke of the Exodus of the Israelites and gave instructions about his bones.

By faith Moses was hidden by his parents for three months after his birth, because they saw that he was a beautiful child, and they were not afraid of the king's edict. By faith Moses, when he had grown up, refused to be known as the son of Pharaoh's daughter; he chose to be ill-treated along with the people of God rather than enjoy the fleeting pleasure of sin. He considered the reproach of the Anointed greater wealth than the treasures of Egypt, for he was looking to the recompense. By faith he left Egypt, not fearing the king's fury, for he persevered as if seeing the one who is invisible. By faith he kept the Passover and sprinkled the blood, that the Destroyer of the firstborn might not touch them. By faith they crossed the Red Sea as if it were dry land, but when the Egyptians attempted it they were drowned. By faith the walls of Jericho fell after being encircled for seven days. By faith Rahab the harlot did not perish with the disobedient, for she had received the spies in peace.

What more shall I say? I have not time to tell of Gideon, Barak, Samson, Jephthah, of David and Samuel and the prophets, who by faith conquered kingdoms, did what was righteous, obtained the promises; they closed the mouths of lions, put out raging fires, escaped the devouring sword; out of weakness they were made powerful, became strong in battle, and turned back foreign invaders. Women received back their dead through resurrection. Some were tortured and would not accept deliverance, in order to obtain a better resurrection. Others endured mockery, scourging, even chains and imprisonment. They were stoned, sawed in two, put to death at sword's point; they went about in skins of sheep or goats, needy, afflicted, tormented. The world was not worthy of them. They wandered about in deserts and on mountains, in caves and in crevices in the earth.

Yet all these, though approved because of their faith, did not receive what had been promised. God had foreseen something better for us, so that without us they should not be made perfect.

PSALM 106:6-15

We have sinned, we and our fathers;
  we have committed crimes; we have done wrong.

Our fathers in Egypt
  considered not your wonders;
They remembered not your
    abundant kindness,
  but rebelled against the Most
    High at the Red Sea.
Yet he saved them for his name's
    sake,
  to make known his power.
He rebuked the Red Sea, and it
    was dried up,
  and he led them through the
    deep as through a desert.
He saved them from hostile
    hands
  and freed them from the hands
    of the enemy.
The waters covered their foes;
  not one of them was left.
Then they believed his words
  and sang his praises.
But soon they forgot his works;
  they waited not for his counsel.
They gave way to craving in the
    desert
  and tempted God in the
    wilderness.
He gave them what they asked
  but sent a wasting disease
    against them.

PROVERBS 23:22

Listen to your father who begot you, / and despise not your mother when she is old.

SEPTEMBER 20

HEBREWS 12:1-13

Therefore, since we are surrounded by so great a cloud of witnesses, let us rid ourselves of every burden and sin that clings to us and persevere in running the race that lies before us while keeping our eyes fixed on Jesus, the leader and perfecter of faith. For the sake of the joy that lay before him he endured the cross, despising its shame, and has taken his seat at the right of the throne of God. Consider how he endured such opposition from sinners, in order that you may not grow weary and lose heart. In your struggle against sin you have not yet resisted to the point of shedding blood. You have also forgotten the exhortation addressed to you as sons:

> "My son, do not disdain the
> discipline of the Lord
> or lose heart when reproved
> by him;
> for whom the Lord loves, he
> disciplines;
> he scourges every son he
> acknowledges."

Endure your trials as "discipline"; God treats you as sons. For what "son" is there whom his father does not discipline? If you are without discipline, in which all have shared, you are not sons but bastards. Besides this, we have had our earthly fathers to discipline us, and we respected them. Should we not [then] submit all the more to the Father of spirits and live? They disciplined us for a short time as seemed right to them, but he does so for our benefit, in order that we may share his holiness. At the time, all discipline seems a cause not for joy but for pain, yet later it brings the peaceful fruit of righteousness to those who are trained by it.

So strengthen your drooping hands and your weak knees. Make straight paths for your feet, that what is lame may not be dislocated but healed.

The earth opened and swallowed
up Dathan,
and covered the faction of
Abiram.
Fire broke out against their
faction;
a flame consumed the wicked.
They made a calf in Horeb
and adored a molten image;
They exchanged their glory
for the image of a grass-eating
bullock.
They forgot the God who had
saved them,
who had done great deeds in
Egypt,
Wondrous deeds in the land of
Ham,
terrible things at the Red Sea.
Then he spoke of exterminating
them,
but Moses, his chosen one,
Withstood him in the breach
to turn back his destructive
wrath.
Yet they despised the desirable
land;
they believed not his word.
They murmured in their tents,
and obeyed not the voice of the
LORD.
Then with raised hand he swore
against them
to let them perish in the desert,
To scatter their descendants
among the nations,
and to disperse them over the
lands.

PSALM 106:16–27

They envied Moses in the camp,
and Aaron, the holy one of the
LORD.

PROVERBS 23:23

Get the truth, and sell it not—/ wisdom, instruction and understanding.

HEBREWS 12:14-29

Strive for peace with everyone, and for that holiness without which no one will see the Lord. See to it that no one be deprived of the grace of God, that no bitter root spring up and cause trouble, through which many may become defiled, that no one be an immoral or profane person like Esau, who sold his birthright for a single meal. For you know that later, when he wanted to inherit his father's blessing, he was rejected because he found no opportunity to change his mind, even though he sought the blessing with tears.

You have not approached that which could not be touched and a blazing fire and gloomy darkness and storm and a trumpet blast and a voice speaking words such that those who heard begged that no message be further addressed to them, for they could not bear to hear the command: "If even an animal touches the mountain, it shall be stoned." Indeed, so fearful was the spectacle that Moses said, "I am terrified and trembling." No, you have approached Mount Zion and the city of the living God, the heavenly Jerusalem, and countless angels in festal gathering, and the assembly of the firstborn enrolled in heaven, and God the judge of all, and the spirits of the just made perfect, and Jesus, the mediator of a new covenant, and the sprinkled blood that speaks more eloquently than that of Abel.

See that you do not reject the one who speaks. For if they did not escape when they refused the one who warned them on earth, how much more in our case if we turn away from the one who warns from heaven. His voice shook the earth at that time, but now he has promised, "I will once more shake not only earth but heaven." That phrase, "once more," points to [the] removal of shaken, created things, so that what is unshaken may remain. Therefore, we who are receiving the unshakable kingdom should have gratitude, with which we should offer worship pleasing to God in reverence and awe. For our God is a consuming fire.

PSALM 106:28-33

And they submitted to the rites
of Baal of Peor
and ate the sacrifices of dead
gods.
They provoked him by their
deeds,
and a plague attacked them.
Then Phinehas stood forth in
judgment
and the plague was checked;
And it was imputed to him for
merit
through all generations forever.
They angered him at the waters
of Meribah,
and Moses fared ill on their
account,
For they embittered his spirit,
and the rash utterance passed
his lips.

PROVERBS 23:24-25

The father of a just man will exult with glee; / he who begets a wise son will have joy in him. / Let your father and mother have joy; / let her who bore you exult.

SEPTEMBER 22

HEBREWS 13:1-25

Let mutual love continue. Do not neglect hospitality, for through it some have unknowingly entertained angels. Be mindful of prisoners as if sharing their imprisonment, and of the ill-treated as of yourselves, for you also are in the body. Let marriage be honored among all and the marriage bed be kept undefiled, for God will judge the immoral and adulterers. Let your life be free from love of money but be content with what you have, for he has said, "I will never forsake you or abandon you." Thus we may say with confidence:

"The Lord is my helper,
[and] I will not be afraid.
What can anyone do to me?"

Remember your leaders who spoke the word of God to you. Consider the outcome of their way of life and imitate their faith. Jesus Christ is the same yesterday, today, and forever.

Do not be carried away by all kinds of strange teaching. It is good to have our hearts strengthened by grace and not by foods, which do not benefit those who live by them. We have an altar from which those who serve the tabernacle have no right to eat. The bodies of the animals whose blood the high priest brings into the sanctuary as a sin offering are burned outside the camp. Therefore, Jesus also suffered outside the gate, to consecrate the people by his own blood. Let us then go to him outside the camp, bearing the reproach that he bore. For here we have no lasting city, but we seek the one that is to come. Through him [then] let us continually offer God a sacrifice of praise, that is, the fruit of lips that confess his name. Do not neglect to do good and to share what you have; God is pleased by sacrifices of that kind.

Obey your leaders and defer to them, for they keep watch over you and will have to give an account, that they may fulfill their task with joy and not with sorrow, for that would be of no advantage to you.

Pray for us, for we are confident that we have a clear conscience, wishing to act rightly in every respect. I especially ask for your prayers that I may be restored to you very soon.

May the God of peace, who brought up from the dead the great shepherd of the sheep by the blood of the eternal covenant, Jesus our Lord, furnish you with all that is good, that you may do his will. May he carry out in you what is pleasing to him through Jesus Christ, to whom be glory forever [and ever]. Amen.

Brothers, I ask you to bear with this message of encouragement, for I have written to you rather briefly. I must let you know that our brother Timothy has been set free. If he comes soon, I shall see you together with him. Greetings to all your leaders and to all the holy ones. Those from Italy send you greetings. Grace be with all of you.

PSALM 106:34-39

They did not exterminate the peoples,
  as the LORD had commanded them,
But mingled with the nations and learned their works.
They served their idols,
  which became a snare for them.
They sacrificed their sons
  and their daughters to demons,
And they shed innocent blood,
  the blood of their sons and their daughters,
Whom they sacrificed to the idols of Canaan,
  desecrating the land with bloodshed;
They became defiled by their works,
  and wanton in their crimes.

PROVERBS 23:26-28

My son, give me your heart, / and let your eyes keep to my ways. / For the harlot is a deep ditch, / and the adulteress a narrow pit; / Yes, she lies in wait like a robber, / and increases the faithless among men.

SEPTEMBER 23

JAMES 1:1-18

James, a slave of God and of the Lord Jesus Christ, to the twelve tribes in the dispersion, greetings.

Consider it all joy, my brothers, when you encounter various trials, for you know that the testing of your faith produces perseverance. And let perseverance be perfect, so that you may be perfect and complete, lacking in nothing. But if any of you lacks wisdom, he should ask God who gives to all generously and ungrudgingly, and he will be given it. But he should ask in faith, not doubting, for the one who doubts is like a wave of the sea that is driven and tossed about by the wind. For that person must not suppose that he will receive anything from the Lord, since he is a man of two minds, unstable in all his ways.

The brother in lowly circumstances should take pride in his high standing, and the rich one in his lowliness, for he will pass away "like the flower of the field." For the sun comes up with its scorching heat and dries up the grass, its flower droops, and the beauty of its appearance vanishes. So will the rich person fade away in the midst of his pursuits.

Blessed is the man who perseveres in temptation, for when he has been proved he will receive the crown of life that he promised to those who love him. No one experiencing temptation should say, "I am being tempted by God"; for God is not subject to temptation to evil, and he himself tempts no one. Rather, each person is tempted when he is lured and enticed by his own desire. Then desire conceives and brings forth sin, and when sin reaches maturity it gives birth to death.

Do not be deceived, my beloved brothers: all good giving and every perfect gift is from above, coming down from the Father of lights, with whom there is no alteration or shadow caused by change. He willed to give us birth by the word of truth that we may be a kind of firstfruits of his creatures.

PSALM 106:40-48

And the LORD grew angry with
    his people,
  and abhorred his inheritance;
He gave them over into the
    hands of the nations,
  and their foes ruled over them.
Their enemies oppressed them,
and they were humbled under
    their power.
Many times did he rescue them,
  but they embittered him with
    their counsels
  and were brought low by their
    guilt.
Yet he had regard for their
    affliction
  when he heard their cry;
And for their sake he was
    mindful of his covenant
  and relented, in his abundant
    kindness,
And he won for them
    compassion
  from all who held them
    captive.
Save us, O LORD, our God,
  and gather us from among the
    nations,
That we may give thanks to your
    holy name
  and glory in praising you.
Blessed be the LORD, the God of
    Israel, through all eternity!
  Let all the people say, Amen!
  Alleluia.

PROVERBS 23:29-35

Who scream? Who shriek? / Who have strife? Who have anxiety? / Who have wounds for nothing? / Who have black eyes? / Those who linger long over wine, / those who engage in trials of blended wine. / Look not on the wine when it is red, / when it sparkles in the glass. / It goes down smoothly; / but in the end it bites like a serpent, / or like a poisonous adder. / Your eyes behold strange sights, / and your heart utters disordered thoughts; / You are like one now lying in the depths of the sea, / now sprawled at the top of the mast. / "They struck me, but it pained me not; / they beat me, but I felt it not; / When shall I awake / to seek wine once again?"

SEPTEMBER 24

JAMES 1:19-27

Know this, my dear brothers: everyone should be quick to hear, slow to speak, slow to wrath, for the wrath of a man does not accomplish the righteousness of God. Therefore, put away all filth and evil excess and humbly welcome the word that has been planted in you and is able to save your souls.

Be doers of the word and not hearers only, deluding yourselves. For if anyone is a hearer of the word and not a doer, he is like a man who looks at his own face in a mirror. He sees himself, then goes off and promptly forgets what he looked like. But the one who peers into the perfect law of freedom and perseveres, and is not a hearer who forgets but a doer who acts, such a one shall be blessed in what he does.

If anyone thinks he is religious and does not bridle his tongue but deceives his heart, his religion is vain. Religion that is pure and undefiled before God and the Father is this: to care for orphans and widows in their affliction and to keep oneself unstained by the world.

PSALM 107:1-9

"Give thanks to the LORD, for he is good,

for his kindness endures forever!"
Thus let the redeemed of the LORD say,
those whom he has redeemed from the hand of the foe
And gathered from the lands, from the east and the west, from the north and the south.
They went astray in the desert wilderness;
the way to an inhabited city they did not find.
Hungry and thirsty,
their life was wasting away within them.
They cried to the LORD in their distress;
from their straits he rescued them.
And he led them by a direct way to reach an inhabited city.
Let them give thanks to the LORD for his kindness
and his wondrous deeds to the children of men,
Because he satisfied the longing soul
and filled the hungry soul with good things.

PROVERBS 24:1-2

Be not emulous of evil men, / and desire not to be with them; / For their hearts plot violence, / and their lips speak of foul play.

SEPTEMBER 25

JAMES 2:1-13

My brothers, show no partiality as you adhere to the faith in our glorious Lord Jesus Christ. For if a man with gold rings on his fingers and in fine clothes comes into your assembly, and a poor person in shabby clothes also comes in, and you pay attention to the one wearing the fine clothes and say, "Sit here, please," while you say to the poor one, "Stand there," or "Sit at my feet," have you not made distinctions among yourselves and become judges with evil designs?

Listen, my beloved brothers. Did not God choose those who are poor in the world to be rich in faith and heirs of the kingdom that he promised to those who love him? But you dishonored the poor person. Are not the rich oppressing you? And do they themselves not haul you off to court? Is it not they who blaspheme the noble name that was invoked over you? However, if you fulfill the royal law according to the scripture, "You shall love your neighbor as yourself," you are doing well. But if you show partiality, you commit sin, and are convicted by the law as transgressors. For whoever keeps the whole law, but falls short in one particular, has become guilty in respect to all of it. For he who said, "You shall not commit adultery," also said, "You shall not kill." Even if you do not commit adultery but kill, you have become a transgressor of the law. So speak and so act as people who will be judged by the law of freedom. For the judgment is merciless to one who has not shown mercy; mercy triumphs over judgment.

PSALM 107:10-16

They dwelt in darkness and
    gloom,
  bondsmen in want and in
    chains,
Because they had rebelled against
    the words of God
  and scorned the counsel of the
    Most High.
And he humbled their hearts
    with trouble;
  when they stumbled, there was
    no one to help them.
They cried to the LORD in their
    distress;
  from their straits he rescued
    them.
And he led them forth from
    darkness and gloom
  and broke their bonds asunder.
Let them give thanks to the LORD
    for his kindness
  and his wondrous deeds to the
    children of men,
Because he shattered the gates of
    brass
  and burst the bars of iron.

PROVERBS 24:3-4

By wisdom is a house built, / by understanding is it made firm; / And by knowledge are its rooms filled / with every precious and pleasing possession.

SEPTEMBER 26

JAMES 2:14-26

What good is it, my brothers, if someone says he has faith but does not have works? Can that faith save him? If a brother or sister has nothing to wear and has no food for the day, and one of you says to them, "Go in peace, keep warm, and eat well," but you do not give them the necessities of the body, what good is it? So also faith of itself, if it does not have works, is dead.

Indeed someone might say,

"You have faith and I have works." Demonstrate your faith to me without works, and I will demonstrate my faith to you from my works. You believe that God is one. You do well. Even the demons believe that and tremble. Do you want proof, you ignoramus, that faith without works is useless? Was not Abraham our father justified by works when he offered his son Isaac upon the altar? You see that faith was active along with his works, and faith was completed by the works. Thus the scripture was fulfilled that says, "Abraham believed God, and it was credited to him as righteousness," and he was called "the friend of God." See how a person is justified by works and not by faith alone. And in the same way, was not Rahab the harlot also justified by works when she welcomed the messengers and sent them out by a different route? For just as a body without a spirit is dead, so also faith without works is dead.

PSALM 107:17-22

Stricken because of their wicked ways
  and afflicted because of their sins,
They loathed all manner of food,
  so that they were near the gates of death.
They cried to the LORD in their distress;
  from their straits he rescued them.
He sent forth his word to heal them
  and to snatch them from destruction.
Let them give thanks to the LORD for his kindness
  and his wondrous deeds to the children of men.
Let them make thank offerings
  and declare his works with shouts of joy.

PROVERBS 24:5-6

A wise man is more powerful than a strong man, / and a man of knowledge than a man of might; / For it is by wise guidance that you wage your war, / and the victory is due to a wealth of counselors.

SEPTEMBER 27

JAMES 3:1-18

Not many of you should become teachers, my brothers, for you realize that we will be judged more strictly, for we all fall short in many respects. If anyone does not fall short in speech, he is a perfect man, able to bridle his whole body also. If we put bits into the mouths of horses to make them obey us, we also guide their whole bodies. It is the same with ships: even though they are so large and driven by fierce winds, they are steered by a very small rudder wherever the pilot's inclination wishes. In the same way the tongue is a small member and yet has great pretensions.

Consider how small a fire can set a huge forest ablaze. The tongue is also a fire. It exists among our members as a world of malice, defiling the whole body and setting the entire course of our lives on fire, itself set on fire by Gehenna. For every kind of beast and bird, of reptile and sea creature, can be tamed and has been tamed by the human species, but no human being can tame the tongue. It is a restless evil, full of deadly poison. With it we bless the Lord and Father, and with it we curse human beings who are made in the likeness of God. From the same mouth come blessing and cursing. This need not be so, ˙my brothers. Does a spring gush forth from the same opening both pure and brackish water? Can a fig tree, my brothers, produce olives, or a grapevine figs? Neither can salt water yield fresh.

Who among you is wise and understanding? Let him show his works by a good life in the humility that comes from wisdom. But if you have bitter jealousy and selfish ambition in your hearts, do not boast and be false to the truth. Wisdom of this kind does not come down from above but is earthly, unspiritual, demonic. For where jealousy and selfish ambition exist, there is disorder and every foul practice. But the wisdom from above is first of all pure, then peaceable, gentle, compliant, full of mercy and good fruits, without inconstancy or insincerity. And the fruit of righteousness is sown in peace for those who cultivate peace.

PSALM 107:23-32

They who sailed the sea in ships,
    trading on the deep waters,
These saw the works of the Lord
    and his wonders in the abyss.
His command raised up a storm wind
      which tossed its waves on high.
They mounted up to heaven;
      they sank to the depths;
      their hearts melted away in their plight.
They reeled and staggered like drunken men,
    and all their skill was swallowed up.
They cried to the Lord in their distress;
    from their straits he rescued them.
He hushed the storm to a gentle breeze,
    and the billows of the sea were stilled;
They rejoiced that they were calmed,
    and he brought them to their desired haven.
Let them give thanks to the Lord for his kindness
    and his wondrous deeds to the children of men.
Let them extol him in the assembly of the people
    and praise him in the council of the elders.

PROVERBS 24:7

For a fool, to be silent is wisdom; / not to open his mouth at the gate.

JAMES 4:1-17

Where do the wars and where do the conflicts among you come from? Is it not from your passions that make war within your members? You covet but do not possess. You kill and envy but you cannot obtain; you fight and wage war. You do not possess because you do not ask. You ask but do not receive, because you ask wrongly, to spend it on your passions. Adulterers! Do you not know that to be a lover of the world means enmity with God? Therefore, whoever wants to be a lover of the world makes himself an enemy of God. Or do you suppose that the scripture speaks without meaning when it says, "The spirit that he has made to dwell in us tends toward jealousy"? But he bestows a greater grace; therefore, it says:

"God resists the proud,
but gives grace to the
humble."

So submit yourselves to God. Resist the devil, and he will flee from you. Draw near to God, and he will draw near to you. Cleanse your hands, you sinners, and purify your hearts, you of two minds. Begin to lament, to mourn, to weep. Let your laughter be turned into mourning and your joy into dejection. Humble yourselves before the Lord and he will exalt you.

Do not speak evil of one another, brothers. Whoever speaks evil of a brother or judges his brother speaks evil of the law and judges the law. If you judge the law, you are not a doer of the law but a judge. There is one lawgiver and judge who is able to save or to destroy. Who then are you to judge your neighbor?

Come now, you who say, "Today or tomorrow we shall go into such and such a town, spend a year there doing business, and make a profit,"—you have no idea what your life will be like tomorrow. You are a puff of smoke that appears briefly and then disappears. Instead you should say, "If the Lord wills it, we shall live to do this or that." But now you are boasting in your arrogance. All such boasting is evil. So for one who knows the right thing to do and does not do it, it is a sin.

PSALM 107:33-43

He changed rivers into desert,
    water springs into thirsty
        ground,
Fruitful land into salt marsh,
    because of the wickedness of
        its inhabitants.
He changed the desert into pools
        of water,
    waterless land into water
        springs.
And there he settled the hungry,
    and they built a city to dwell
        in.
They sowed fields and planted
        vineyards,
    and they obtained a fruitful
        yield.
He blessed them, and they
        became very many;
    nor did he suffer their cattle to
        decrease.
And they dwindled and were
        brought low
    through oppression, affliction
        and sorrow.

But he who pours out contempt
    upon princes,
  and sends them astray through
    a trackless waste,
Lifted up the needy out of misery
  and made the families
    numerous like flocks.

The upright see this and rejoice,
  and all wickedness closes its
    mouth.
Who is wise enough to observe
  these things
  and to understand the favors of
    the LORD?

PROVERBS 24:8-9

He who plots evil doing—/ men call him an intriguer. / Beyond intrigue and folly and sin, / it is arrogance that men find abominable.

SEPTEMBER 29

JAMES 5:1-12

Come now, you rich, weep and wail over your impending miseries. Your wealth has rotted away, your clothes have become moth-eaten, your gold and silver have corroded, and that corrosion will be a testimony against you; it will devour your flesh like a fire. You have stored up treasure for the last days. Behold, the wages you withheld from the workers who harvested your fields are crying aloud, and the cries of the harvesters have reached the ears of the Lord of hosts. You have lived on earth in luxury and pleasure; you have fattened your hearts for the day of slaughter. You have condemned; you have murdered the righteous one; he offers you no resistance.

Be patient, therefore, brothers, until the coming of the Lord. See how the farmer waits for the precious fruit of the earth, being patient with it until it receives the early and the late rains. You too must be patient. Make your hearts firm, because the coming of the Lord is at hand. Do not complain, brothers, about one another, that you may not be judged. Behold, the Judge is standing before the gates. Take as an example of hardship and patience, brothers, the prophets who spoke in the name of the Lord. Indeed we call blessed those who have persevered. You have heard of the perseverance of Job, and you have seen the purpose of the Lord, because "the Lord is compassionate and merciful."

But above all, my brothers, do not swear, either by heaven or by earth or with any other oath, but let your "Yes" mean "Yes" and your "No" mean "No," that you may not incur condemnation.

PSALM 108:1-14

A song; a psalm of David.
My heart is steadfast, O God; my
    heart is steadfast;
  I will sing and chant praise.
Awake, O my soul; awake, lyre
    and harp;
  I will wake the dawn.
I will give thanks to you among
    the peoples, O LORD;
  I will chant your praise among
    the nations,

For your kindness towers to the
heavens,
and your faithfulness to the
skies.
Be exalted above the heavens, O
God;
over all the earth be your glory!
That your loved ones may
escape,
help us by your right hand,
and answer us.
God promised in his sanctuary:
"Exultantly I will apportion
Shechem,
and measure off the valley of
Succoth;
Mine is Gilead, and mine
Manasseh,

Ephraim is the helmet for my
head; Judah, my scepter;
Moab shall serve as my
washbowl;
upon Edom I will set my shoe;
I will triumph over Philistia."
Who will bring me into the
fortified city?
Who will lead me into Edom?
Have not you, O God, rejected
us,
so that you go not forth, O
God, with our armies?
Give us aid against the foe,
for worthless is the help of
men.
Under God we shall do valiantly;
it is he who will tread down
our foes.

PROVERBS 24:10

If you remain indifferent in time of adversity, / your strength will depart from you.

SEPTEMBER 30

JAMES 5:13-20

Is anyone among you suffering? He should pray. Is anyone in good spirits? He should sing praise. Is anyone among you sick? He should summon the presbyters of the church, and they should pray over him and anoint [him] with oil in the name of the Lord, and the prayer of faith will save the sick person, and the Lord will raise him up. If he has committed any sins, he will be forgiven.

Therefore, confess your sins to one another and pray for one another, that you may be healed. The fervent prayer of a righteous person is very powerful. Elijah was a human being like us; yet he prayed earnestly that it might not rain, and for three years and six months it did not rain upon the land. Then he prayed again, and the sky gave rain and the earth produced its fruit.

My brothers, if anyone among you should stray from the truth and someone bring him back, he should know that whoever brings back a sinner from the error of his way will save his soul from death and will cover a multitude of sins.

PSALM 109:1-5

For the leader. A psalm of David.
O God, whom I praise, be not
silent,

for they have opened wicked
and treacherous mouths
against me.
They have spoken to me with
lying tongues,
and with words of hatred they
have encompassed me
and attacked me without
cause.
In return for my love they
slandered me,
but I prayed.
They repaid me evil for good
and hatred for my love.

PROVERBS 24:11-12

Rescue those. who are being dragged to death, / and from those tottering to execution withdraw not. / If you say, "I know not this man!" / does not he who tests hearts perceive it? / He who guards your life knows it, / and he will repay each one according to his deeds.

OCTOBER

Love Letter

WHAT WOULD YOU SUGGEST as the greatest longing of every human heart? What is the one single desire of every man, woman, and child? In spite of all the diversities of our human personalities, there is one characteristic common to all of us. There is in every human heart a desire to love and to be loved.

This longing to love and to be loved is God's special gift to each one of us. In his first letter, John, the disciple whom Jesus loved, gives us a most concise definition of God. He says simply: "God is love" (1 Jn 4:16). God created us not only as an expression of his love but he also gave us a partial share in his divine nature. We are created in the image and likeness of God. Since God is love, and since he wants to be loved by us, he implanted that same desire in our human nature.

This desire to love and to be loved can also be the crux of our spiritual growth and maturation. Most of us live with a feeling of insecurity. We are not convinced deep within ourselves that we are loved or even lovable. We look at ourselves and see all the unlovable traits about us. We readily recognize our self-centeredness, the ulterior motives which prompt us into action. We are baffled by all that is undesirable within us.

This creates in our hearts a fear of rejection. Our self-image suffers. Our profile sinks, sometimes not only down to the carpet but even under the carpet. When we feel that we are not very lovable, our self-image deteriorates.

A natural conclusion follows. If we are convinced that other human beings would not love us if they really knew us as we are, then how can God love us for he knows our faults and failures better than anyone else? He knows our selfishness and our willful neglect to respond to his love.

Reasons Aplenty

In our mind we could list a whole series of reasons to prove God's love for us. However, these are all intellectual reasons, and we do not live by our intellect but by our heart. We must know with our heart that God loves us just as we are. We need to hear God tell us that he does not care who we are or what we have done—he loves us anyway. Only then can we be convinced of God's love for us.

There is another hurdle we must overcome. We are greatly influenced by the culture in which we live. It is a materialistic culture which centers on productivity. This attitude has imbued us with the conviction that we must earn God's love. We must perform a long list of good works in order to merit God's love. We are left with a feeling of failure and frustration because our record is not all that creditable.

Listen to Love

Let us look at the other side of the ledger and listen to God himself tell us about his love for us in his inspired Word. John, the great apostle of love, under the inspiration of the Holy Spirit, assures us that this popular idea of deserving God's love is erroneous. How simply John speaks of this profound mystery in these words: "In this is love: not that we have loved God, but that he loved us and sent his Son as expiation for our sins" (1 Jn 4:10).

The truth of this statement is impressed upon us when we realize that were it not for God's love for us personally, we would not even be in existence.

Already in his Gospel, John recalls the love of the Father for each one of us: "For God so loved the world [you and me] that he gave his only Son, so that everyone who believes in him might not perish but might have eternal life" (Jn 3:16).

John is eloquent about God's unconditional and enduring love for us. We need to hear this truth many times over to be convinced that we are loved and lovable. Let the inspired words really touch our hearts and transform our whole attitude: "God is love, and whoever remains in love remains in God and God in him" (1 Jn 4:16).

If we know with our heart that God loves us just as we are, then we are not concerned about how others may feel toward us. If God loves us, we know that we are loved and lovable. John tells us that fear has no place in our relationship with our compassionate Father, nor in our relationship with our brothers and sisters. His words go right to the point: "There is no fear in love, but perfect love drives out fear . . ." (1 Jn 4:18).

In his apocalyptic vision recorded in the Book of Revelation, John emphasizes the caring, concerned love of God for us. Even in the letters to the various churches, his warnings reflect a loving concern.

John's vision concludes with the divine promise of a new heaven and a new earth where love will reign supreme. Again the Lord reiterates in the closing chapter that he will be our compassionate Father and we will be his children.

An avid reading of God's Word to satisfy our curiosity will not empower that Word to transform and mold us. We need to rest quietly and attentively, pondering his Word, to behold the over-whelming love of God, like rays of the setting sun which warm, nourish, and delight us. Then we shall know that we are loved and lovable: "But you, beloved, build yourselves up in your most holy faith. Pray in the Holy Spirit. Keep yourselves in the love of God and wait for the mercy of the Lord Jesus Christ that leads to eternal life" (Jude 20-21).

OCTOBER 1

1 PETER 1:1-12

Peter, an apostle of Jesus Christ, to the chosen sojourners of the dispersion in Pontus, Galatia, Cappadocia, Asia, and Bithynia, in the foreknowledge of God the Father, through sanctification by the Spirit, for obedience and sprinkling with the blood of Jesus Christ: may grace and peace be yours in abundance.

Blessed be the God and Father of our Lord Jesus Christ, who in his great mercy gave us a new birth to a living hope through the resurrection of Jesus Christ from the dead, to an inheritance that is imperishable, undefiled, and unfading, kept in heaven for you who by the power of God are safeguarded through faith, to a salvation that is ready to be revealed in the final time. In this you rejoice, although now for a little while you may have to suffer through various trials, so that the genuineness of your faith, more precious than gold that is perishable even though tested by fire, may prove to be for praise, glory, and honor at the revelation of Jesus Christ. Although you have not seen him you love him; even though you do not see him now yet believe in him, you rejoice with an indescribable and glorious joy, as you attain the goal of [your] faith, the salvation of your soul.

Concerning this salvation, prophets who prophesied about the grace that was to be yours searched and investigated it, investigating the time and circumstances that the Spirit of Christ within them indicated when it testified in advance to the sufferings destined for Christ and the glories to follow them. It was revealed to them that they were serving not themselves but you with regard to the things that have now been announced to you by those who preached the good news to you [through] the holy Spirit sent from heaven, things into which angels longed to look.

PSALM 109:6-19

Raise up a wicked man against him,
> and let the accuser stand at his right hand.
When he is judged, let him go forth condemned,
> and may his plea be in vain.
May his days be few;
> may another take his office.
May his children be fatherless,
> and his wife a widow.
May his children be roaming vagrants and beggars;
> may they be cast out of the ruins of their homes.
May the usurer ensnare all his belongings,

and strangers plunder the fruit
of his labors.
May there be no one to do him a
kindness,
nor anyone to pity his orphans.
May his posterity meet with
destruction;
in the next generation may
their name be blotted out.
May the guilt of his fathers be
remembered by the Lord;
let not his mother's sin be
blotted out;
May they be continually before
the LORD,
till he banish the memory of
these parents from the earth,
Because he remembered not to
show kindness,

but persecuted the wretched
and poor
and the brokenhearted, to do
them to death.
He loved cursing; may it come
upon him;
he took no delight in blessing;
may it be far from him.
And may he be clothed with
cursing as with a robe;
may it penetrate into his
entrails like water
and like oil into his bones;
May it be for him like a garment
which covers him,
like a girdle which is always
about him.

PROVERBS 24:13-14

If you eat honey, my son, because it is good, / if virgin honey is sweet to your taste; / Such, you must know, is wisdom to your soul. / If you find it, you will have a future, / and your hope will not be cut off.

OCTOBER 2

1 PETER 1:13-25

Therefore, gird up the loins of your mind, live soberly, and set your hopes completely on the grace to be brought to you at the revelation of Jesus Christ. Like obedient children, do not act in compliance with the desires of your former ignorance but, as he who called you is holy, be holy yourselves in every aspect of your conduct, for it is written, "Be holy because I [am] holy."

Now if you invoke as Father him who judges impartially according to each one's works, conduct yourselves with reverence during the time of your sojourning, realizing that you were ran-

somed from your futile conduct, handed on by your ancestors, not with perishable things like silver or gold but with the precious blood of Christ as of a spotless unblemished lamb. He was known before the foundation of the world but revealed in the final time for you, who through him believe in God who raised him from the dead and gave him glory, so that your faith and hope are in God.

Since you have purified yourselves by obedience to the truth for sincere mutual love, love one another intensely from a [pure] heart. You have been born anew, not from perishable but from imperishable seed, through the living and abiding word of God, for:

"All flesh is like grass,
    and all its glory like the
        flower of the field;
the grass withers,
    and the flower wilts;
but the word of the Lord
    remains forever."

This is the word that has been proclaimed to you.

PSALM 109:20-31

May this be the recompense from
    the LORD upon my accusers
    and upon those who speak evil
        against me.
But do you, O GOD, my Lord,
    deal kindly with me for your
        name's sake;
    in your generous kindness
        rescue me;
For I am wretched and poor,
    and my heart is pierced within
        me.
Like a lengthening shadow I pass
    away;

I am swept away like the
    locust.
My knees totter from my fasting,
    and my flesh is wasted of its
        substance.
And I am become a mockery to
    them;
    when they see me, they shake
        their heads.
Help me, O LORD, my God;
    save me, in your kindness,
And let them know that this is
    your hand,
    that you, O LORD, have done
        this.
Let them curse, but do you bless;
    may my adversaries be put to
        shame,
    but let your servant rejoice.
Let my accusers be clothed with
    disgrace
    and let them wear their shame
        like a mantle.
I will speak my thanks earnestly
    to the LORD,
    and in the midst of the throng I
        will praise him,
For he stood at the right hand of
    the poor man,
    to save him from those who
        would condemn him.

PROVERBS 24:15-16

*Lie not in wait against the home of the just man, / ravage not his dwelling place; /
For the just man falls seven times and rises again, / but the wicked stumble to
ruin.*

OCTOBER 3

1 PETER 2:1-12

Rid yourselves of all malice and all deceit, insincerity, envy, and all slander; like newborn infants, long for pure spiritual milk so that through it you may grow into salvation, for you have tasted that the Lord is good. Come to him, a living stone, rejected by human beings but chosen and precious in the sight of God, and, like living stones, let yourselves be built into a spiritual house to be a holy priesthood to offer spiritual sacrifices acceptable to God through Jesus Christ. For it says in scripture:

"Behold, I am laying a stone in Zion,
a cornerstone, chosen and precious,
and whoever believes in it shall not be put to shame."

Therefore, its value is for you who have faith, but for those without faith:

"The stone which the builders rejected
has become the cornerstone,"

and

"A stone that will make people stumble,
and a rock that will make them fall."

They stumble by disobeying the word, as is their destiny.

But you are "a chosen race, a royal priesthood, a holy nation, a people of his own, so that you may announce the praises" of him who called you out of darkness into his wonderful light.

Once you were "no people"
but now you are God's people;
you "had not received mercy"
but now you have received mercy.

Beloved, I urge you as aliens and sojourners to keep away from worldly desires that wage war against the soul. Maintain good conduct among the Gentiles, so that if they speak of you as evildoers, they may observe your good works and glorify God on the day of visitation.

PSALM 110:1-7

A psalm of David.
The LORD said to my Lord: "Sit at my right hand
till I make your enemies your footstool."
The scepter of your power the LORD will stretch forth from Zion:
"Rule in the midst of your enemies.
Yours is princely power in the day of your birth, in holy splendor;
before the daystar, like the dew, I have begotten you."
The LORD has sworn, and he will not repent:
"You are a priest forever, according to the order of Melchizedek."
The LORD is at your right hand;
he will crush kings on the day of his wrath.
He will do judgment on the nations, heaping up corpses;
he will crush heads over the wide earth.
From the brook by the wayside he will drink;
therefore will he lift up his head.

PROVERBS 24:17-20

Rejoice not when your enemy falls, / and when he stumbles, let not your heart exult, / Lest the LORD see it, be displeased with you, / and withdraw his wrath from your enemy. / Be not provoked with evildoers, / nor envious of the wicked; / For the evil man has no future, / the lamp of the wicked will be put out.

OCTOBER 4

1 PETER 2:13-25

Be subject to every human institution for the Lord's sake, whether it be to the king as supreme or to governors as sent by him for the punishment of evildoers and the approval of those who do good. For it is the will of God that by doing good you may silence the ignorance of foolish people. Be free, yet without using freedom as a pretext for evil, but as slaves of God. Give honor to all, love the community, fear God, honor the king.

Slaves, be subject to your masters with all reverence, not only to those who are good and equitable but also to those who are perverse. For whenever anyone bears the pain of unjust suffering because of consciousness of God, that is a grace. But what credit is there if you are patient when beaten for doing wrong? But if you are patient when you suffer for doing what is good, this is a grace before God. For to this you have been called, because Christ also suffered for you, leaving you an example that you should follow in his footsteps.

"He committed no sin,
and no deceit was found in
his mouth."

When he was insulted, he returned no insult; when he suffered, he did not threaten; instead, he handed himself over to the one who judges justly. He himself bore our sins in his body upon the cross, so that, free from sin, we might live for righteousness. By his wounds you have been healed. For you had gone astray like sheep, but you have now returned to the shepherd and guardian of your souls.

PSALM 111:1-10

Alleluia.
I will give thanks to the LORD
with all my heart
in the company and assembly
of the just.
Great are the works of the LORD,
exquisite in all their delights.
Majesty and glory are his work,
and his justice endures forever.
He has won renown for his
wondrous deeds;
gracious and merciful is the
LORD.
He has given food to those who
fear him;
he will forever be mindful of
his covenant.
He has made known to his
people the power of his
works,
giving them the inheritance of
the nations.
The works of his hands are
faithful and just;
sure are all his precepts,
Reliable forever and ever,
wrought in truth and equity.
He has sent deliverance to his
people;
he has ratified his covenant
forever;
holy and awesome is his name.
The fear of the LORD is the
beginning of wisdom;
prudent are all who live by it.
His praise endures forever.

PROVERBS 24:21-22

My son, fear the LORD and the king; / have nothing to do with those who rebel against them; / For suddenly arises the destruction they send, / and the ruin from either one, who can measure?

OCTOBER 5

1 PETER 3:1-22

Likewise, you wives should be subordinate to your husbands so that, even if some disobey the word, they may be won over without a word by their wives' conduct when they observe your reverent and chaste behavior. Your adornment should not be an external one: braiding the hair, wearing gold jewelry, or dressing in fine clothes, but rather the hidden character of the heart, expressed in the imperishable beauty of a gentle and calm disposition, which is precious in the sight of God. For this is also how the holy women who hoped in God once used to adorn themselves and were subordinate to their husbands; thus Sarah obeyed Abraham, calling him "lord." You are her children when you do what is good and fear no intimidation.

Likewise, you husbands should live with your wives in understanding, showing honor to the weaker female sex, since we are joint heirs of the gift of life, so that your prayers may not be hindered.

Finally, all of you, be of one mind, sympathetic, loving toward one another, compassionate, humble. Do not return evil for evil, or insult for insult; but, on the contrary, a blessing, because to this you were called, that you might inherit a blessing. For:

"Whoever would love life
and see good days
must keep the tongue from evil
and the lips from speaking
deceit,
must turn from evil and do
good,
seek peace and follow after
it.
For the eyes of the Lord are on
the righteous
and his ears turned to their
prayer,
but the face of the Lord is
against evildoers."

Now who is going to harm you if you are enthusiastic for what is good? But even if you should suffer because of righteousness, blessed are you. Do not be afraid or terrified with fear of them, but sanctify Christ as Lord in your hearts. Always be ready to give an explanation to anyone who asks you for a reason for your hope, but do it with gentleness and reverence, keeping your conscience clear, so that, when you are maligned, those who defame your good conduct in Christ may themselves be put to shame. For it is better to suffer for doing good, if that be the will of God, than for doing evil.

For Christ also suffered for sins once, the righteous for the sake of the unrighteous, that he might lead you to God. Put to death in the flesh, he was brought to life in the spirit. In it he also went to preach to the spirits in prison, who had once been disobedient while God patiently waited in the days of Noah during the building of the ark, in which a few persons, eight in all, were saved through water. This prefigured baptism, which saves you now. It is not a removal of dirt from the body but an appeal to God for a clear conscience, through the resurrection of Jesus Christ, who has gone into heaven and is at the right hand of God, with angels, authorities, and powers subject to him.

PSALM 112:1-10

Alleluia.
Happy the man who fears the
    LORD,
  who greatly delights in his
    commands.
His posterity shall be mighty
    upon the earth;
  the upright generation shall be
    blessed.
Wealth and riches shall be in his
    house;

his generosity shall endure
    forever.
He dawns through the darkness,
    a light for the upright;
  he is gracious and merciful and
    just.
Well for the man who is gracious
    and lends,
  who conducts his affairs with
    justice;
He shall never be moved;
  the just man shall be in
    everlasting remembrance.
An evil report he shall not fear;
  his heart is firm, trusting in the
    LORD.
His heart is steadfast; he shall not
    fear
  till he looks down upon his
    foes.
Lavishly he gives to the poor;
  his generosity shall endure
    forever;
  his horn shall be exalted in
    glory.
The wicked man shall see it and
    be vexed;
  he shall gnash his teeth and
    pine away;
  the desire of the wicked shall
    perish.

PROVERBS 24:23-25

These also are sayings of the wise: / To show partiality in judgment is not good. / He who says to the wicked man, "You are just"— / men will curse him, people will denounce him; / But those who convict the evildoer will fare well, / and on them will come the blessing of prosperity.

OCTOBER 6

1 PETER 4:1-19

Therefore, since Christ suffered in the flesh, arm yourselves also with the same attitude (for whoever suffers in the flesh has bro-

ken with sin), so as not to spend what remains of one's life in the flesh on human desires, but on the will of God. For the time that has passed is sufficient for doing what the Gentiles like to do: living in debauchery, evil desires, drunkenness, orgies, carousing, and wanton idolatry. They are surprised that you do not plunge into the same swamp of profligacy, and they vilify you; but they will give an account to him who stands ready to judge the living and the dead. For this is why the gospel was preached even to the dead that, though condemned in the flesh in human estimation, they might live in the spirit in the estimation of God.

The end of all things is at hand. Therefore, be serious and sober for prayers. Above all, let your love for one another be intense, because love covers a multitude of sins. Be hospitable to one another without complaining. As each one has received a gift, use it to serve one another as good stewards of God's varied grace. Whoever preaches, let it be with the words of God; whoever serves, let it be with the strength that God supplies, so that in all things God may be glorified through Jesus Christ, to whom belong glory and dominion forever and ever. Amen.

Beloved, do not be surprised that a trial by fire is occurring among you, as if something strange were happening to you. But rejoice to the extent that you share in the sufferings of Christ, so that when his glory is revealed you may also rejoice exultantly. If you are insulted for the name of Christ, blessed are you, for the Spirit of glory and of God rests upon you. But let no one among you be made to suffer as a murderer, a thief, an evildoer, or as an intriguer. But whoever is made to suffer as a Christian should not be ashamed but glorify God because of the name. For it is time for the judgment to begin with the household of God; if it begins with us, how will it end for those who fail to obey the gospel of God?

"And if the righteous one is
     barely saved,
   where will the godless and
      the sinner appear?"

As a result, those who suffer in accord with God's will hand their souls over to a faithful creator as they do good.

PSALM 113:1-9

Alleluia.
Praise, you servants of the LORD,
   praise the name of the LORD.
Blessed be the name of the LORD
   both now and forever.
From the rising to the setting of
      the sun
   is the name of the LORD to be
      praised.
High above all nations is the
      LORD,
   above the heavens is his glory.
Who is like the LORD, our God,
      who is enthroned on high
   and looks upon the heavens
      and the earth below?
He raises up the lowly from the
      dust;
   from the dunghill he lifts up
      the poor
To seat them with princes,
   with the princes of his own
      people.
He establishes in her home the
      barren wife
   as the joyful mother of
      children.

He gives a kiss on the lips / who makes an honest reply.

OCTOBER 7

1 PETER 5:1-14

So I exhort the presbyters among you, as a fellow presbyter and witness .to the sufferings of Christ and one who has a share in the glory to be revealed. Tend the flock of God in your midst, [overseeing] not by constraint but willingly, as God would have it, not for shameful profit but eagerly. Do not lord it over those assigned to you, but be examples to the flock. And when the chief Shepherd is revealed, you will receive the unfading crown of glory.

Likewise, you younger members, be subject to the presbyters. And all of you, clothe yourselves with humility in your dealings with one another, for:

"God opposes the proud
but bestows favor on the
humble."

So humble yourselves under the mighty hand of God, that he may exalt you in due time. Cast all your worries upon him because he cares for you.

Be sober and vigilant. Your opponent the devil is prowling around like a roaring lion looking for [someone] to devour. Resist him, steadfast in faith, knowing that your fellow believers throughout the world undergo the same sufferings. The God of all grace who called you to his eternal glory through Christ [Jesus] will himself restore, confirm, strengthen, and establish you after you have suffered a little. To him be dominion forever. Amen.

I write you this briefly through Silvanus, whom I consider a faithful brother, exhorting you and testifying that this is the true grace of God. Remain firm in it. The chosen one at Babylon sends you greeting, as does Mark, my son. Greet one another with a loving kiss. Peace to all of you who are in Christ.

PSALM 114:1-8

Alleluia.

When Israel came forth from
    Egypt,
  the house of Jacob from a
    people of alien tongue,
Judah became his sanctuary,
  Israel his domain.
The sea beheld and fled;
  Jordan turned back.
The mountains skipped like
    rams,
  the hills like the lambs of the
    flock.
Why is it, O sea, that you flee?
  O Jordan, that you turn back?
You mountains, that you skip
    like rams?
  You hills, like the lambs of the
    flock?
Before the face of the Lord,
    tremble, O earth,
  before the face of the God of
    Jacob,
Who turned the rock into pools of
    water,
  the flint into flowing springs.

OCTOBER 8

2 PETER 1:1-21

Symeon Peter, a slave and apostle of Jesus Christ, to those who have received a faith of equal value to ours through the righteousness of our God and savior Jesus Christ: may grace and peace be yours in abundance through knowledge of God and of Jesus our Lord.

His divine power has bestowed on us everything that makes for life and devotion, through the knowledge of him who called us by his own glory and power. Through these, he has bestowed on us the precious and very great promises, so that through them you may come to share in the divine nature, after escaping from the corruption that is in the world because of evil desire. For this very reason, make every effort to supplement your faith with virtue, virtue with knowledge, knowledge with self-control, self-control with endurance, endurance with devotion, devotion with mutual affection, mutual affection with love. If these are yours and increase in abundance, they will keep you from being idle or unfruitful in the knowledge of our Lord Jesus Christ. Anyone who lacks them is blind and shortsighted, forgetful of the cleansing of his past sins. Therefore, broth-

ers, be all the more eager to make your call and election firm, for, in doing so, you will never stumble. For, in this way, entry into the eternal kingdom of our Lord and savior Jesus Christ will be richly provided for you.

Therefore, I will always remind you of these things, even though you already know them and are established in the truth you have. I think it right, as long as I am in this "tent," to stir you up by a reminder, since I know that I will soon have to put it aside, as indeed our Lord Jesus Christ has shown me. I shall also make every effort to enable you always to remember these things after my departure.

We did not follow cleverly devised myths when we made known to you the power and coming of our Lord Jesus Christ, but we had been eyewitnesses of his majesty. For he received honor and glory from God the Father when that unique declaration came to him from the majestic glory, "This is my Son, my beloved, with whom I am well pleased." We ourselves heard this voice come from heaven while we were with him on the holy mountain. Moreover, we possess the prophetic message that is altogether reliable. You will do well to be attentive to it, as to a lamp shining in a dark place, until day dawns and the morning star rises in your hearts. Know this first of all, that there is no prophecy of scripture that is a matter of personal interpretation, for no prophecy ever came through human will; but rather human beings moved by the holy Spirit spoke under the influence of God.

PSALM 115:1-8

Not to us, O LORD, not to us
but to your name give glory
because of your kindness,
because of your truth.

Why should the pagans say,
"Where is their God?"
Our God is in heaven;
whatever he wills, he does.
Their idols are silver and gold,
the handiwork of men.
They have mouths but speak not;
they have eyes but see not;
They have ears but hear not;
They have noses but smell not;
They have hands but feel not;
they have feet but walk not;
they utter no sound from their
throat.
Their makers shall be like them,
everyone that trusts in them.

PROVERBS 24:28-29

Be not a witness against your neighbor without just cause, / thus committing folly with your lips. / Say not, "As he did to me, so will I do to him; / I will repay the man according to his deeds."

OCTOBER 9

---

2 PETER 2:1-22

There were also false prophets among the people, just as there will be false teachers among you, who will introduce destructive heresies and even deny the Master who ransomed them, bringing swift destruction on themselves. Many will follow their licentious ways, and because of them the way of truth will be reviled. In their greed they will exploit you with fabrications, but from of old their condemnation has not been idle and their destruction does not sleep.

For if God did not spare the angels when they sinned, but condemned them to the chains of Tartarus and handed them over to be kept for judgment; and if he did not spare the ancient world, even though he preserved Noah, a herald of righteousness, together with seven others, when he brought a flood upon the godless world; and if he condemned the cities of Sodom and Gommorah [to destruction], reducing them to ashes, making them an example for the godless [people] of what is coming; and if he rescued Lot, a righteous man oppressed by the licentious conduct of unprincipled people (for day after day that righteous man living among them was tormented in his righteous soul at the lawless deeds that he saw and heard), then the Lord knows how to rescue the devout from trial and to keep the unrighteous under punishment for the day of judgment, and especially those who follow the flesh with its depraved desire and show contempt for lordship.

Bold and arrogant, they are not afraid to revile glorious beings, whereas angels, despite their superior strength and power, do not bring a reviling judgment against them from the Lord. But these people, like irrational animals born by nature for capture and destruction, revile things that they do not understand, and in their destruction they will also be destroyed, suffering wrong as payment for wrongdoing. Thinking daytime revelry a delight, they are stains and defilements as they revel in their deceits while carousing with you. Their eyes are full of adultery and insatiable for sin. They seduce unstable people, and their hearts are trained in greed. Accursed children! Abandoning the straight road, they have gone astray, following the road of Balaam, the son of Bosor, who loved payment for wrongdoing, but he received a rebuke for his own crime: a mute beast spoke with a human voice and restrained the prophet's madness.

These people are waterless springs and mists driven by a gale; for them the gloom of darkness has been reserved. For, talking empty bombast, they seduce with licentious desires of the flesh those who have barely escaped from people who live in error. They promise them freedom, though they themselves are slaves of corruption, for a person is a slave of whatever overcomes him. For if they, having escaped the defilements of the world through the knowledge of [our] Lord and savior Jesus Christ, again become entangled and overcome by them, their last condition is worse than their first. For it would have been better for them not to have known the way of righteousness than after knowing it to turn back from the holy commandment handed down to them. What is expressed in the true proverb has happened to them, "The dog returns to its own vomit," and "A bathed sow returns to wallowing in the mire."

PSALM 115:9-18

The house of Israel trusts in the
    LORD;
  he is their help and their
    shield.
The house of Aaron trusts in the
    LORD;
  he is their help and their
    shield.
Those who fear the LORD trust in
    the LORD;
  he is their help and their
    shield.
The LORD remembers us and will
    bless us:
  he will bless the house of
    Israel;
  he will bless the house of
    Aaron;
He will bless those who fear the
    LORD,
  both the small and the great.
May the LORD bless you more
    and more,
  both you and your children.
May you be blessed by the LORD,
  who made heaven and earth.
Heaven is the heaven of the
    LORD,
  but the earth he has given to
    the children of men.
It is not the dead who praise the
    LORD,
  nor those who go down into
    silence;
But we bless the LORD,
  both now and forever.

I passed by the field of the sluggard, / by the vineyard of the man without sense; / And behold! it was all overgrown with thistles; / its surface was covered with nettles, / and its stone wall broken down. / And as I gazed at it, I reflected; / I saw and learned the lesson: / A little sleep, a little slumber, / a little folding of the arms to rest—/ Then will poverty come upon you like a highwayman, / and want like an armed man.

OCTOBER 10

2 PETER 3:1-18

This is now, beloved, the second letter I am writing to you; through them by way of reminder I am trying to stir up your sincere disposition, to recall the words previously spoken by the holy prophets and the commandment of the Lord and savior through your apostles. Know this first of all, that in the last days scoffers will come [to] scoff, living according to their own desires and saying, "Where is the promise of his coming? From the time when our ancestors fell asleep, everything has remained as it was from the beginning of creation." They deliberately ignore the fact that the heavens existed of old and earth was formed out of water and through water by the word of God; through these the world that then existed was destroyed, deluged with water. The present heavens and earth have been reserved by the same word for fire, kept for the day of judgment and of destruction of the godless.

But do not ignore this one fact, beloved, that with the Lord one day is like a thousand years and a thousand years like one day. The Lord does not delay his promise, as some regard "delay," but he is patient with you, not wishing that any should perish but that all should come to repentance. But the day of the Lord will come like a thief, and then the heavens will pass away with a mighty roar and the elements will be dissolved by fire, and the earth and everything done on it will be found out.

Since everything is to be dissolved in this way, what sort of persons ought [you] to be, conducting yourselves in holiness and devotion, waiting for and hastening the coming of the day of God, because of which the heavens will be dissolved in flames and the elements melted by fire. But according to his promise we await new heavens and a new earth in which righteousness dwells.

Therefore, beloved, since you await these things, be eager to be found without spot or blemish before him, at peace. And consider the patience of our Lord as salvation, as our beloved brother Paul, according to the wisdom given to him, also wrote to you, speaking of these things as he does in all his letters. In them there are some things hard to understand that the ignorant and unstable distort to their own destruction, just as they do the other scriptures. Therefore, beloved, since you are forewarned, be on your guard not to be led into the error of the unprincipled and to fall from your own stability. But grow in grace and in the knowledge of our Lord and savior Jesus Christ. To him be glory now and to the day of eternity. [Amen.]

PSALM 116:1-9

Alleluia.

I love the LORD because he has heard
  my voice in supplication,
Because he has inclined his ear to me
  the day I called.
The cords of death encompassed me;

the snares of the nether world
  seized upon me;
I fell into distress and sorrow,
And I called upon the name of the LORD,
  "O LORD, save my life!"
Gracious is the LORD and just;
  yes, our God is merciful.
The LORD keeps the little ones;
  I was brought low, and he saved me.
Return, O my soul, to your tranquillity,
  for the LORD has been good to you.
For he has freed my soul from death,
  my eyes from tears, my feet from stumbling.
I shall walk before the LORD
  in the lands of the living.

PROVERBS 25:1-5

These also are proverbs of Solomon. / The men of Hezekiah, king of Judah, transmitted them. / God has glory in what he conceals, / kings have glory in what they fathom. / As the heavens in height, and the earth in depth, / the heart of kings is unfathomable. / Remove the dross from silver, / and it comes forth perfectly purified; / Remove the wicked from the presence of the king, / and his throne is made firm through righteousness.

OCTOBER 11

1 JOHN 1:1-10

What was from the beginning,
what we have heard,
what we have seen with our eyes,
what we looked upon
and touched with our hands
concerns the Word of life—
for the life was made visible;
we have seen it and testify to it
and proclaim to you the eternal life
that was with the Father and was made visible to us—

what we have seen and heard
we proclaim now to you,
so that you too may have fellowship with us;
for our fellowship is with the Father
and with his Son, Jesus Christ.
We are writing this so that our joy may be complete.

Now this is the message that we have heard from him and proclaim to you: God is light, and in him there is no darkness at all. If we say, "We have fellowship with him," while we continue to walk in darkness, we lie and do not act in truth. But if we walk in the light as he is in the light, then we have fellowship with one another, and the blood of his Son Jesus cleanses us from all sin. If we say, "We are without sin," we deceive ourselves, and the truth is not in us. If we acknowledge our sins, he is faithful and just and will forgive our sins and cleanse us from every wrongdoing. If we say, "We have not sinned," we make him a liar, and his word is not in us.

PSALM 116:10-19

I believed, even when I said,
  "I am greatly afflicted";
I said in my alarm,
  "No man is dependable."
How shall I make a return to the
  LORD

for all the good he has done for
  me?
The cup of salvation I will take
  up,
  and I will call upon the name of
  the LORD;
My vows to the LORD I will pay
  in the presence of all his
  people.
Precious in the eyes of the LORD
  is the death of his faithful ones.
O LORD, I am your servant;
  I am your servant, the son of
  your handmaid;
  you have loosed my bonds.
To you will I offer sacrifice of
  thanksgiving,
  and I will call upon the name of
  the LORD.
My vows to the LORD I will pay
  in the presence of all his
  people,
In the courts of the house of the
  LORD,
  in your midst, O Jerusalem.

PROVERBS 25:6-7

Claim no honor in the king's presence, / nor occupy the place of great men; / For it is better that you be told, "Come up closer!" / than that you be humbled before the prince.

OCTOBER 12

1 JOHN 2:1-11

My children, I am writing this to you so that you may not commit sin. But if anyone does sin, we have an Advocate with the Father, Jesus Christ the righteous one. He is expiation for our sins, and not for our sins only but for those of the whole world. The way we may be sure that we know him is to keep his commandments. Whoever says, "I know him," but does not keep his com-

mandments is a liar, and the truth is not in him. But whoever keeps his word, the love of God is truly perfected in him. This is the way we may know that we are in union with him: whoever claims to abide in him ought to live [just] as he lived.

Beloved, I am writing no new commandment to you but an old commandment that you had from the beginning. The old commandment is the word that you have heard. And yet I do write a new commandment to you, which holds true in him and among you, for the darkness is passing away, and the true light is already shining. Whoever says he is in the light, yet hates his brother, is still in the darkness. Whoever loves his brother remains in the light, and there is nothing in him to cause a fall. Whoever hates his brother is in darkness; he walks in darkness and does not know where he is going because the darkness has blinded his eyes.

PSALM 117:1-2

Alleluia.
Praise the LORD, all you nations;
    glorify him, all you peoples!
For steadfast is his kindness
    toward us,
    and the fidelity of the LORD
    endures forever.

PROVERBS 25:8-10

What your eyes have seen / bring not forth hastily against an opponent; / For what will you do later on / when your neighbor puts you to shame? / Discuss your case with your neighbor, / but another man's secret do not disclose; / Lest, hearing it, he reproach you, / and your ill repute cease not.

OCTOBER 13

1 JOHN 2:12-29

I am writing to you, children, because your sins have been forgiven for his name's sake.

I am writing to you, fathers, because you know him who is from the beginning.

I am writing to you, young men, because you have conquered the evil one.

I write to you, children, because you know the Father.

I write to you, fathers, because you know him who is from the beginning.

I write to you, young men, because you are strong and the word of God remains in you, and you have conquered the evil one.

Do not love the world or the things of the world. If anyone loves the world, the love of the Father is not in him. For all that is in the world, sensual lust, entice-ment for the eyes, and a pretentious life, is not from the Father but is from the world. Yet the world and its enticement are passing away. But whoever does the will of God remains forever.

Children, it is the last hour; and just as you heard that the antichrist was coming, so now many antichrists have appeared. Thus we know this is the last hour. They went out from us, but they were not really of our number; if they had been, they would have remained with us. Their desertion shows that none of them was of our number. But you have the anointing that comes from the holy one, and you all have knowledge. I write to you not because you do not know the truth but because you do, and because every lie is alien to the truth. Who is the liar? Whoever denies that Jesus is the Christ. Whoever denies the Father and the Son, this is the antichrist. No one who denies the Son has the Father, but whoever confesses the Son has the Father as well.

Let what you heard from the beginning remain in you. If what you heard from the beginning remains in you, then you will remain in the Son and in the Father. And this is the promise that he made us: eternal life. I write you these things about those who would deceive you. As for you, the anointing that you received from him remains in you, so that you do not need anyone to teach you. But his anointing teaches you about everything and is true and not false; just as it taught you, remain in him.

And now, children, remain in him, so that when he appears we may have confidence and not be put to shame by him at his coming. If you consider that he is righteous, you also know that everyone who acts in righteousness is begotten by him.

PSALM 118:1-9

Alleluia.

Give thanks to the LORD, for he is good,
    for his mercy endures forever.
Let the house of Israel say,
    "His mercy endures forever."
Let the house of Aaron say,
    "His mercy endures forever."
Let those who fear the LORD say,
    "His mercy endures forever."
In my straits I called upon the LORD;
    the LORD answered me and set me free.
The LORD is with me; I fear not;
    what can man do against me?
The LORD is with me to help me,
    and I shall look down upon my foes.
It is better to take refuge in the LORD
    than to trust in man.
It is better to take refuge in the LORD
    than to trust in princes.

PROVERBS 25:11-14

Like golden apples in silver settings / are words spoken at the proper time. / Like a golden earring, or a necklace of fine gold, / is a wise reprover to an obedient ear. / Like the coolness of snow in the heat of the harvest / is a faithful messenger for the one who sends him. / [He refreshes the soul of his master.] / Like clouds and wind when no rain follows / is the man who boastfully promises what he never gives.

OCTOBER 14

1 JOHN 3:1-10

See what love the Father has bestowed on us that we may be called the children of God. Yet so we are. The reason the world does not know us is that it did not know him. Beloved, we are God's children now; what we shall be has not yet been revealed. We do know that when it is revealed we shall be like him, for we shall see him as he is. Everyone who has this hope based on him makes himself pure, as he is pure.

Everyone who commits sin commits lawlessness, for sin is lawlessness. You know that he was revealed to take away sins, and in him there is no sin. No one who remains in him sins; no one who sins has seen him or known him. Children, let no one deceive you. The person who acts in righteousness is righteous, just as he is righteous. Whoever sins belongs to the devil, because the devil has sinned from the beginning. Indeed, the Son of God was revealed to destroy the works of the devil. No one who is begotten by God commits sin, because God's seed remains in him; he cannot sin because he is begotten by God. In this way, the children of God and the children of the devil are made plain; no one who fails to act in righteousness belongs to God, nor anyone who does not love his brother.

PSALM 118:10-14

All the nations encompassed me;
  in the name of the LORD I
    crushed them.
They encompassed me on every
    side;
  in the name of the LORD I
    crushed them.
They encompassed me like bees,
  they flared up like fire among
    thorns;
  in the name of the LORD I
    crushed them.
I was hard pressed and was
    falling,
  but the LORD helped me.
My strength and my courage is
    the LORD,
  and he has been my savior.

PROVERBS 25:15

By patience is a ruler persuaded, / and a soft tongue will break a bone.

OCTOBER 15

1 JOHN 3:11-24

For this is the message you have heard from the beginning: we should love one another, unlike Cain who belonged to the evil one and slaughtered his brother. Why did he slaughter him? Because his own works were evil, and those of his brother righteous. Do not be amazed, [then,] brothers, if the world hates you. We know that we have passed from death to life because we love our brothers. Whoever does not love remains in death. Everyone who hates his brother is a murderer, and you know that no murderer has eternal life remaining in him. The way we came to know love was that he laid down his life for us; so we ought to lay down our lives for our brothers. If someone who has worldly means sees a brother in need and refuses him compassion, how can the love of God remain in him? Children, let us love not in word or speech but in deed and truth.

[Now] this is how we shall know that we belong to the truth

and reassure our hearts before him in whatever our hearts condemn, for God is greater than our hearts and knows everything. Beloved, if [our] hearts do not condemn us, we have confidence in God and receive from him whatever we ask, because we keep his commandments and do what pleases him. And his commandment is this: we should believe in the name of his Son, Jesus Christ, and love one another just as he commanded us. Those who keep his commandments remain in him, and he in them, and the way we know that he remains in us is from the Spirit that he gave us.

PSALM 118:15-18

The joyful shout of victory
  in the tents of the just:
  "The right hand of the LORD
    has struck with power:
  the right hand of the LORD is
    exalted;
  the right hand of the LORD has
    struck with power."
I shall not die, but live,
  and declare the works of the
    LORD.
Though the LORD has indeed
    chastised me,
  yet he has not delivered me to
    death.

PROVERBS 25:16

If you find honey, eat only what you need, / lest you become glutted with it and vomit it up.

OCTOBER 16

1 JOHN 4:1-21

Beloved, do not trust every spirit but test the spirits to see whether they belong to God, because many false prophets have gone out into the world. This is how you can know the Spirit of God: every spirit that acknowledges Jesus Christ come in the flesh belongs to God, and every spirit that does not acknowledge Jesus does not belong to God. This is the spirit of the antichrist that, as you heard, is to come, but in fact is already in the world. You belong to God, children, and you have conquered them, for the one who is in you is greater than the one who is in the world. They belong to the world; accordingly, their teaching belongs to the world, and the world listens to them. We belong to God, and anyone who knows God listens to us, while anyone who does not belong to God refuses to hear us. This is how we know the spirit of truth and the spirit of deceit.

Beloved, let us love one another, because love is of God; everyone who loves is begotten by God and knows God. Whoever is without love does not know God, for God is love. In this way the love of God was revealed to us: God sent his only Son into the world so that we might have life through him. In this is love: not that we have loved God, but that he loved us and sent his Son as expiation for our sins. Beloved, if God so loved us, we also must love one another. No one has ever seen God. Yet, if we love one another, God remains in us, and his love is brought to perfection in us.

This is how we know that we remain in him and he in us, that he has given us of his Spirit. Moreover, we have seen and testify that the Father sent his Son as savior of the world. Whoever acknowledges that Jesus is the Son of God, God remains in him and he in God. We have come to know and to believe in the love God has for us.

God is love, and whoever remains in love remains in God and God in him. In this is love brought to perfection among us, that we have confidence on the day of judgment because as he is, so are we in this world. There is no fear in love, but perfect love drives out fear because fear has to do with punishment, and so one who fears is not yet perfect in love. We love because he first loved us. If anyone says, "I love God," but hates his brother, he is a liar; for whoever does not love a brother whom he has seen cannot love God whom he has not seen. This is the commandment we have from him: whoever loves God must also love his brother.

PSALM 118:19-29

Open to me the gates of justice;
   I will enter them and give
      thanks to the LORD.
This gate is the LORD's;
   the just shall enter it.
I will give thanks to you, for you
     have answered me
   and have been my savior.
The stone which the builders
     rejected
   has become the cornerstone.
By the LORD has this been done;
   it is wonderful in our eyes.
This is the day the LORD has
     made;
   let us be glad and rejoice in it.
O LORD, grant salvation!
   O LORD, grant prosperity!
Blessed is he who comes in the
     name of the LORD;
   we bless you from the house of
     the LORD.
   The LORD is God, and he has
     given us light.
Join in procession with leafy
     boughs
   up to the horns of the altar.
You are my God, and I give
     thanks to you;
   O my God, I extol you.
Give thanks to the LORD, for he is
     good;
   for his kindness endures
     forever.

PROVERBS 25:17

Let your foot be seldom in your neighbor's house, / lest he have more than enough of you, and hate you.

1 JOHN 5:1-12

Everyone who believes that Jesus is the Christ is begotten by God, and everyone who loves the father loves [also] the one begotten by him. In this way we know that we love the children of God when we love God and obey his commandments. For the love of God is this, that we keep his commandments. And his commandments are not burdensome, for whoever is begotten by God conquers the world. And the victory that conquers the world is our faith. Who [indeed] is the victor over the world but the one who believes that Jesus is the Son of God?

This is the one who came through water and blood, Jesus Christ, not by water alone, but by water and blood. The Spirit is the one that testifies, and the Spirit is truth. So there are three that testify, the Spirit, the water, and the blood, and the three are of one accord. If we accept human testimony, the testimony of God is surely greater. Now the testimony of God is this, that he has testified on behalf of his Son. Whoever believes in the Son of God has this testimony within himself. Whoever does not believe God has made him a liar by not believing the testimony God has given about his Son. And this is the testimony: God gave us eternal life, and this life is in his Son. Whoever possesses the Son has life; whoever does not possess the Son of God does not have life.

PSALM 119:1-8

Happy are they whose way is blameless,
  who walk in the law of the LORD.
Happy are they who observe his decrees,
  who seek him with all their heart,
And do no wrong,
  but walk in his ways.
You have commanded that your precepts
  be diligently kept.
Oh, that I might be firm in the ways
  of keeping your statutes!
Then should I not be put to shame
  when I beheld all your commands.
I will give you thanks with an upright heart,
  when I have learned your just ordinances.
I will keep your statutes;
  do not utterly forsake me.

PROVERBS 25:18-19

Like a club, or a sword, or a sharp arrow, / is the man who bears false witness against his neighbor. / Like an infected tooth or an unsteady foot / is [dependence on] a faithless man in time of trouble.

OCTOBER 18

1 JOHN 5:13-21

I write these things to you so that you may know that you have eternal life, you who believe in the name of the Son of God. And we have this confidence in him, that if we ask anything according to his will, he hears us. And if we know that he hears us in regard to whatever we ask, we know that what we have asked him for is ours. If anyone sees his brother sinning, if the sin is not deadly, he should pray to God and he will give him life. This is only for those whose sin is not deadly. There is such a thing as deadly sin, about which I do not say that you should pray. All wrongdoing is sin, but there is sin that is not deadly.

We know that no one begotten by God sins; but the one begotten by God he protects, and the evil one cannot touch him. We know that we belong to God, and the whole world is under the power of the evil one. We also know that the Son of God has come and has given us discernment to know the one who is true. And we are in the one who is true, in his Son Jesus Christ. He is the true God and eternal life. Children, be on your guard against idols.

PSALM 119:9-16

How shall a young man be
    faultless in his way?
  By keeping to your words.
With all my heart I seek you;
  let me not stray from your
    commands.
Within my heart I treasure your
    promise,
  that I may not sin against you.
Blessed are you, O LORD;
  teach me your statutes.
With my lips I declare
  all the ordinances of your
    mouth.
In the way of your decrees I
    rejoice,
  as much as in all riches.
I will meditate on your precepts
  and consider your ways.
In your statutes I will delight;
  I will not forget your words.

PROVERBS 25:20-22

Like a moth in clothing, or a maggot in wood, / sorrow gnaws at the human heart. / If your enemy be hungry, give him food to eat, / if he be thirsty, give him to drink; / For live coals you will heap on his head, and the LORD will vindicate you.

OCTOBER 19

2 JOHN 1-13

The Presbyter to the chosen Lady and to her children whom I love in truth—and not only I but also all who know the truth—because of the truth that dwells in us and will be with us forever. Grace, mercy, and peace will be with us from God the Father and from Jesus Christ the Father's Son in truth and love.

I rejoiced greatly to find some of your children walking in the truth just as we were commanded by the Father. But now, Lady, I ask you, not as though I were writing a new commandment but the one we have had from the beginning: let us love one another. For this is love, that we walk according to his commandments; this is the commandment, as you heard from the beginning, in which you should walk.

Many deceivers have gone out into the world, those who do not acknowledge Jesus Christ as coming in the flesh; such is the deceitful one and the antichrist. Look to yourselves that you do not lose what we worked for but may receive a full recompense. Anyone who is so "progressive" as not to remain in the teaching of the Christ does not have God; whoever remains in the teaching has the Father and the Son. If anyone comes to you and does not bring this doctrine, do not receive him in your house or even greet him; for whoever greets him shares in his evil works.

Although I have much to write to you, I do not intend to use paper and ink. Instead, I hope to visit you and to speak face to face so that our joy may be complete. The children of your chosen sister send you greetings.

PSALM 119:17-24

Be good to your servant, that I
    may live
    and keep your words.
Open my eyes, that I may
    consider
    the wonders of your law.
I am a wayfarer of earth;
    hide not your commands from
    me.
My soul is consumed with
    longing
    for your ordinances at all
    times.
You rebuke the accursed proud,
    who turn away from your
    commands.
Take away from me reproach and
    contempt,
    for I observe your decrees.
Though princes meet and talk
    against me,
    your servant meditates on your
    statutes.
Yes, your decrees are my delight;
    they are my counselors.

PROVERBS 25:23-24

*The north wind brings rain, / and a backbiting tongue an angry countenance. /
It is better to dwell in a corner of the housetop / than in a roomy house with a
quarrelsome woman.*

OCTOBER 20

3 JOHN 1-14

The Presbyter to the beloved Gaius whom I love in truth.

Beloved, I hope you are prospering in every respect and are in good health, just as your soul is prospering. I rejoiced greatly when some of the brothers came and testified to how truly you walk in the truth. Nothing gives me greater joy than to hear that my children are walking in the truth.

Beloved, you are faithful in all you do for the brothers, especially for strangers; they have testified to your love before the church. Please help them in a way worthy of God to continue their journey. For they have set out for the sake of the Name and are accepting nothing from the pagans. Therefore, we ought to support such persons, so that we may be co-workers in the truth.

I wrote to the church, but Diotrephes, who loves to dominate, does not acknowledge us. Therefore, if I come, I will draw attention to what he is doing, spreading evil nonsense about us. And not content with that, he will not receive the brothers, hindering those who wish to do so and expelling them from the church.

Beloved, do not imitate evil but imitate good. Whoever does what is good is of God; whoever does what is evil has never seen God. Demetrius receives a good report from all, even from the truth itself. We give our testimonial as well, and you know our testimony is true.

I have much to write to you, but I do not wish to write with pen and ink. Instead, I hope to see you soon, when we can talk face to face. Peace be with you. The friends greet you; greet the friends there each by name.

PSALM 119:25-32

I lie prostrate in the dust;
   give me life according to your
      word.
I declared my ways, and you
      answered me;
   teach me your statutes.
Make me understand the way of
      your precepts,
   and I will meditate on your
      wondrous deeds.
My soul weeps for sorrow;
   strengthen me according to
      your words.
Remove from me the way of
      falsehood,
   and favor me with your law.
The way of truth I have chosen;
   I have set your ordinances
      before me.
I cling to your decrees;
   O Lord, let me not be put to
      shame.
I will run the way of your
      commands
   when you give me a docile
      heart.

PROVERBS 25:25-27

Like a cool water to one faint from thirst / is good news from a far country. / Like a troubled fountain or a polluted spring / is a just man who gives way before the wicked. / To eat too much honey is not good; / nor to seek honor after honor.

JUDE 1-16

Jude, a slave of Jesus Christ and brother of James, to those who are called, beloved in God the Father and kept safe for Jesus Christ: may mercy, peace, and love be yours in abundance.

Beloved, although I was making every effort to write to you about our common salvation, I now feel a need to write to encourage you to contend for the faith that was once for all handed down to the holy ones. For there have been some intruders, who long ago were designated for this condemnation, godless persons, who pervert the grace of our God into licentiousness and who deny our only Master and Lord, Jesus Christ.

I wish to remind you, although you know all things, that [the] Lord who once saved a people from the land of Egypt later destroyed those who did not believe. The angels too, who did not keep to their own domain but deserted their proper dwelling, he has kept in eternal chains, in gloom, for the judgment of the great day. Likewise, Sodom, Gomorrah, and the surrounding towns, which, in the same manner as they, indulged in sexual promiscuity and practiced unnatural vice, serve as an example by undergoing a punishment of eternal fire.

Similarly, these dreamers nevertheless also defile the flesh, scorn lordship, and revile glorious beings. Yet the archangel Michael, when he argued with the devil in a dispute over the body of Moses, did not venture to pronounce a reviling judgment upon him but said, "May the Lord rebuke you!" But these people revile what they do not understand and are destroyed by what they know by nature like irrational animals. Woe to them! They followed the way of Cain, abandoned themselves to Balaam's error for the sake of gain, and perished in the rebellion of Korah. These are blemishes on your love feasts, as they carouse fearlessly and look after themselves. They are waterless clouds blown about by winds, fruitless trees in late autumn, twice dead and uprooted. They are like wild waves of the sea, foaming up their shameless deeds, wandering stars for whom the gloom of darkness has been reserved forever.

Enoch, of the seventh generation from Adam, prophesied also about them when he said, "Behold, the Lord has come with his countless holy ones to execute judgment on all and to convict everyone for all the godless deeds that they committed and for all the harsh words godless sinners have uttered against him." These people are complainers, disgruntled ones who live by their desires; their mouths utter bombast as they fawn over people to gain advantage.

PSALM 119:33-40

Instruct me, O LORD, in the way
    of your statutes,
  that I may exactly observe
    them.
Give me discernment, that I may
    observe your law
  and keep it with all my heart.
Lead me in the path of your
    commands,

for in it I delight.
Incline my heart to your decrees
and not to gain.
Turn away my eyes from seeing
what is vain;
by your way give me life.
Fulfill for your servant

your promise to those who fear
you.
Turn away from me the reproach
which I dread,
for your ordinances are good.
Behold, I long for your precepts;
in your justice give me life.

PROVERBS 25:28

Like an open city with no defenses / is the man with no check on his feelings.

OCTOBER 22

JUDE 17-25

But you, beloved, remember the words spoken beforehand by the apostles of our Lord Jesus Christ, for they told you, "In [the] last time there will be scoffers who will live according to their own godless desires." These are the ones who cause divisions; they live on the natural plane, devoid of the Spirit. But you, beloved, build yourselves up in your most holy faith; pray in the holy Spirit. Keep yourselves in the love of God and wait for the mercy of our Lord Jesus Christ that leads to eternal life. On those who waver, have mercy; save others by snatching them out of the fire; on others have mercy with fear, abhorring even the outer garment stained by the flesh.

To the one who is able to keep you from stumbling and to present you unblemished and exultant, in the presence of his glory, to the only God, our savior, through Jesus Christ our Lord be glory, majesty, power, and authority from ages past, now, and for ages to come. Amen.

PSALM 119:41-48

Let your kindness come to me, O
LORD,
your salvation according to
your promise.
So shall I have an answer for
those who reproach me,
for I trust in your words.
Take not the word of truth from
my mouth,
for in your ordinances is my
hope;
And I will keep your law
continually,
forever and ever.
And I will walk at liberty,
because I seek your precepts.
I will speak of your decrees
before kings
without being ashamed.
And I will delight in your
commands,
which I love.
And I will lift up my hands to
your commands
and meditate on your statutes.

PROVERBS 26:1-2

Like snow in summer, or rain in harvest, / honor for a fool is out of place. / Like the sparrow in its flitting, like the swallow in its flight, / a curse uncalled-for arrives nowhere.

OCTOBER 23

REVELATION 1:1-8

The revelation of Jesus Christ, which God gave to him, to show his servants what must happen soon. He made it known by sending his angel to his servant John, who gives witness to the word of God and to the testimony of Jesus Christ by reporting what he saw. Blessed is the one who reads aloud and blessed are those who listen to this prophetic message and heed what is written in it, for the appointed time is near.

John, to the seven churches in Asia: grace to you and peace from him who is and who was and who is to come, and from the seven spirits before his throne, and from Jesus Christ, the faithful witness, the firstborn of the dead and ruler of the kings of the earth. To him who loves us and has freed us from our sins by his blood, who has made us into a kingdom, priests for his God and Father, to him be glory and power forever [and ever]. Amen.

Behold, he is coming amid the clouds,
  and every eye will see him,
  even those who pierced him.

All the peoples of the earth will lament him.
  Yes. Amen.

"I am the Alpha and the Omega," says the Lord God, "the one who is and who was and who is to come, the almighty."

PSALM 119:49-56

Remember your word to your servant
  since you have given me hope.
My comfort in my affliction is
  that your promise gives me life.
Though the proud scoff bitterly at me,
  I turn not away from your law.
I remember your ordinances of old, O LORD,
  and I am comforted.
Indignation seizes me because of the wicked
  who forsake your law.
Your statutes are the theme of my song
  in the place of my exile.
By night I remember your name, O LORD,
  and I will keep your law.
This I have had,
  that I have observed your precepts.

PROVERBS 26:3-5

The whip for the horse, the bridle for the ass, / and the rod for the back of fools. / Answer not the fool according to his folly, / lest you too become like him. / Answer the fool according to his folly, / lest he become wise in his own eyes.

OCTOBER 24

REVELATION 1:9-20

I, John, your brother, who share with you the distress, the kingdom, and the endurance we have in Jesus, found myself on the island called Patmos because I proclaimed God's word and gave testimony to Jesus. I was caught up in spirit on the Lord's day and heard behind me a voice as loud as a trumpet, which said, "Write on a scroll what you see and send it to the seven churches: to Ephesus, Smyrna, Pergamum, Thyatira, Sardis, Philadelphia, and Laodicea." Then I turned to see whose voice it was that spoke to me, and when I turned, I saw seven gold lampstands and in the midst of the lampstands one like a son of man, wearing an ankle-length robe, with a gold sash around his chest. The hair of his head was as white as white wool or as snow, and his eyes were like a fiery flame. His feet were like polished brass refined in a furnace, and his voice was like the sound of rushing water. In his right hand he held seven stars. A sharp two-edged sword came out of his mouth, and his face shone like the sun at its brightest.

When I caught sight of him, I fell down at his feet as though dead. He touched me with his right hand and said, "Do not be afraid. I am the first and the last, the one who lives. Once I was dead, but now I am alive forever and ever. I hold the keys to death and the netherworld. Write down, therefore, what you have seen, and what is happening, and what will happen afterwards. This is the secret meaning of the seven stars you saw in my right hand, and of the seven gold lampstands: the seven stars are the angels of the seven churches, and the seven lampstands are the seven churches."

PSALM 119:57-64

I have said, O LORD, that my part
    is to keep your words.
I entreat you with all my heart,
    have pity on me according to
      your promise.
I considered my ways
    and turned my feet to your
      decrees.
I was prompt and did not hesitate
    in keeping your commands.
Though the snares of the wicked
    are twined about me
    your law I have not forgotten.
At midnight I rise to give you
    thanks
    because of your just
      ordinances.
I am the companion of all who
    fear you
    and keep your precepts.
Of your kindness, O LORD, the
    earth is full;
    teach me your statutes.

PROVERBS 26:6-8

He cuts off his feet, he drinks down violence, / who sends messages by a fool. / A proverb in the mouth of a fool / hangs limp, like crippled legs. / Like one who entangles the stone in the sling / is he who gives honor to a fool.

OCTOBER 25

REVELATION 2:1-7

"To the angel of the church in Ephesus, write this: 'The one who holds the seven stars in his right hand and walks in the midst of the seven gold lampstands says this: "I know your works, your labor, and your endurance, and that you cannot tolerate the wicked; you have tested those who call themselves apostles but are not, and discovered that they are impostors. Moreover, you have endurance and have suffered for my name, and you have not grown weary. Yet I hold this against you: you have lost the love you had at first. Realize how far you have fallen. Repent, and do the works you did at first. Otherwise, I will come to you and remove your lampstand from its place, unless you repent. But you have this in your favor: you hate the works of the Nicolaitans, which I also hate.

" ' "Whoever has ears ought to hear what the Spirit says to the churches. To the victor I will give the right to eat from the tree of life that is in the garden of God." ' "

PSALM 119:65-72

You have done good to your
    servant,
  O LORD, according to your
    word.
Teach me wisdom and
    knowledge,
  for in your commands I trust.
Before I was afflicted I went
    astray,
  but now I hold to your
    promise.
You are good and bountiful;
  teach me your statutes.
Though the proud forge lies
    against me,
  with all my heart I will observe
    your precepts.
Their heart has become gross and
    fat;
  as for me, your law is my
    delight.
It is good for me that I have been
    afflicted,
  that I may learn your statutes.
The law of your mouth is to me
    more precious
  than thousands of gold and
    silver pieces.

PROVERBS 26:9-12

Like a thorn stick brandished by the hand of a drunkard / is a proverb in the mouth of fools. / Like an archer wounding all who pass by / is he who hires a drunken fool. / As the dog returns to his vomit, / so the fool repeats his folly. / You see a man wise in his own eyes? / There is more hope for a fool than for him.

OCTOBER 26

REVELATION 2:8-11

"To the angel of the church in Smyrna, write this: 'The first and the last, who once died but came to life, says this: "I know your tribulation and poverty, but you are rich. I know the slander of those who claim to be Jews and are not, but rather are members of the assembly of Satan. Do not be afraid of anything that you are going to suffer. Indeed, the devil will throw some of you into prison, that you may be tested, and you will face an ordeal for ten days. Remain faithful until death, and I will give you the crown of life.

" ' "Whoever has ears ought to hear what the Spirit says to the churches. The victor shall not be harmed by the second death." ' "

PSALM 119:73-80

Your hands have made me and
   fashioned me;
give me discernment that I may
   learn your commands.
Those who fear you shall see me
   and be glad,
   because I hope in your word.
I know, O LORD, that your
   ordinances are just,
   and in your faithfulness you
      have afflicted me.
Let your kindness comfort me
   according to your promise to
      your servants.
Let your compassion come to me
   that I may live,
   for your law is my delight.
Let the proud be put to shame for
   oppressing me unjustly;
   I will meditate on your
      precepts.
Let those turn to me who fear
   you
   and acknowledge your decrees.
Let my heart be perfect in your
   statutes,
   that I be not put to shame.

PROVERBS 26:13-16

The sluggard says, "There is a lion in the street, / a lion in the middle of the square!" / The door turns on its hinges, / the sluggard, on his bed! / The sluggard loses his hand in the dish; / he is too weary to lift it to his mouth. / The sluggard imagines himself wiser / than seven men who answer with good sense.

OCTOBER 27

REVELATION 2:12-17

"To the angel of the church in Pergamum, write this: 'The one with the sharp two-edged sword says this: "I know that you live where Satan's throne is, and yet you hold fast to my name and have not denied your faith in me, not even in the days of Antipas, my faithful witness, who was martyred among you, where Satan lives. Yet I have a few things against you. You have some people there who hold to the teaching of Balaam, who instructed Balak to put a stumbling block before the Israelites: to eat food sacrificed to idols and to play the harlot. Likewise, you also have some people who hold to the teaching of [the] Nicolaitans. Therefore, repent. Otherwise, I will come to you quickly and wage war against them with the sword of my mouth.

" ' "Whoever has ears ought to hear what the Spirit says to the churches. To the victor I shall give some of the hidden manna; I shall also give a white amulet upon which is inscribed a new name, which no one knows except the one who receives it." ' "

PSALM 119:81-88

My soul pines for your salvation;
I hope in your word.
My eyes strain after your
  promise;
  when will you comfort me?
Though I am shriveled like a
  leathern flask in the smoke,
  I have not forgotten your
  statutes.
How many are the days of your
  servant?
  When will you do judgment on
  my persecutors?
The proud have dug pits for me;
  this is against your law.
All your commands are steadfast;
  they persecute me wrongfully;
  help me!
They have all but put an end to
  me on the earth,
  but I have not forsaken your
  precepts.
In your kindness give me life,
  that I may keep the decrees of
  your mouth.

PROVERBS 26:17

Like the man who seizes a passing dog by the ears / is he who meddles in a quarrel not his own.

OCTOBER 28

REVELATION 2:18-29

"To the angel of the church in Thyatira, write this: 'The Son of God, whose eyes are like a fiery flame and whose feet are like polished brass, says this: "I know your works, your love, faith, service, and endurance, and that your last works are greater than the first. Yet I hold this against you, that you tolerate the woman Jezebel, who calls herself a prophetess, who teaches and misleads my servants to play the harlot and to eat food sacrificed to idols. I have given her time to repent, but she refuses to repent of her harlotry. So I will cast her on a sickbed and plunge those who commit adultery with her into intense suffering unless they repent of her works. I will also put her children to death. Thus shall all the churches come to know that I am the searcher of hearts and minds and that I will give each of you what your works deserve. But I say to the rest of you in Thyatira, who do not uphold this teaching and know nothing of the so-called deep secrets of Satan: on you I will place no further burden, except that you must hold fast to what you have until I come.

" ' "To the victor, who keeps to
    my ways until the end,
I will give authority over the
    nations.
He will rule them with an iron
    rod.
    Like clay vessels will they be
        smashed,

just as I received authority from my Father. And to him I will give the morning star.
    " ' "Whoever has ears ought to hear what the Spirit says to the churches." ' "

PSALM 119:89-96

Your word, O LORD, endures
    forever;
it is firm as the heavens.
Through all generations your
    truth endures;
    you have established the earth,
        and it stands firm:
According to your ordinances
    they still stand firm;
all things serve you.
Had not your law been my
    delight,
    I should have perished in my
        affliction.
Never will I forget your precepts,
    for through them you give me
        life.
I am yours; save me,
    for I have sought your
        precepts.
Sinners wait to destroy me,
    but I pay heed to your decrees.
I see that all fulfillment has its
    limits;
    broad indeed is your
        command.

PROVERBS 26:18-19

Like a crazed archer / scattering firebrands and deadly arrows / Is the man who deceives his neighbor, / and then says, "I was only joking."

OCTOBER 29

REVELATION 3:1-6

"To the angel of the church in Sardis, write this: 'The one who has the seven spirits of God and the seven stars says this: "I know your works, that you have the reputation of being alive, but you are dead. Be watchful and strengthen what is left, which is going to die, for I have not found your works complete in the sight of my God. Remember then how you accepted and heard; keep it, and repent. If you are not watchful, I will come like a thief, and you will never know at what hour I will come upon you. However, you have a few people in Sardis who have not soiled their garments; they will walk with me dressed in white, because they are worthy.
    " ' "The victor will thus be dressed in white, and I will never

erase his name from the book of life but will acknowledge his name in the presence of my Father and of his angels.

" ' "Whoever has ears ought to hear what the Spirit says to the churches." ' "

PSALM 119:97-104

How I love your law, O LORD!
  It is my meditation all the day.
Your command has made me
    wiser than my enemies,
  for it is ever with me.
I have more understanding than
    all my teachers
  when your decrees are my
    meditation.
I have more discernment than the
    elders,
  because I observe your
    precepts.
From every evil way I withhold
    my feet,
  that I may keep your words.
From your ordinances I turn not
    away,
  for you have instructed me.
How sweet to my palate are your
    promises,
  sweeter than honey to my
    mouth!
Through your precepts I gain
    discernment;
  therefore I hate every false
    way.

PROVERBS 26:20-22

For lack of wood, the fire dies out; / and when there is no talebearer, strife subsides. / What a bellows is to live coals, what wood is to fire, / such is a contentious man in enkindling strife. / The words of a talebearer are like dainty morsels / that sink into one's inmost being.

OCTOBER 30

REVELATION 3:7-13

"To the angel of the church in Philadelphia, write this:

'The holy one, the true,
who holds the key of David,
who opens and no one shall
    close,
who closes and no one shall
    open,

says this:
" ' "I know your works (behold, I have left an open door before you, which no one can close). You have limited strength, and yet you have kept my word and have not denied my name. Behold, I will make those of the assembly of Satan who claim to be Jews and are not, but are lying, behold I will make them come and fall prostrate at your feet, and they will realize that I love you. Because you have kept my message of endurance, I will keep you safe in the time of trial that is going to come to the whole world to test the inhabitants of the earth. I am coming quickly. Hold fast to what you have, so that no one may take your crown.

" ' "The victor I will make into a pillar in the temple of my God, and he will never leave it again. On him I will inscribe the name of my God and the name of the city of my God, the new Jerusalem, which comes down out of heaven from my God, as well as my new name.

" ' "Whoever has ears ought to hear what the Spirit says to the churches." ' "

PSALM 119:105-112

A lamp to my feet is your word,
  a light to my path.
I resolve and swear
  to keep your just ordinances.
I am very much afflicted;
  O LORD, give me life according
  to your word.

Accept, O LORD, the free homage
  of my mouth,
  and teach me your decrees.
Though constantly I take my life
  in my hands,
  yet I forget not your law.
The wicked have laid a snare for
  me,
  but from your precepts I have
  not strayed.
Your decrees are my inheritance
  forever;
  the joy of my heart they are.
I intend in my heart to fulfill your
  statutes
  always, to the letter.

PROVERBS 26:23

Like a glazed finish on earthenware / are smooth lips with a wicked heart.

OCTOBER 31

REVELATION 3:14-22

"To the angel of the church in Laodicea, write this: 'The Amen, the faithful and true witness, the source of God's creation, says this: "I know your works; I know that you are neither cold nor hot. I wish you were either cold or hot. So, because you are lukewarm, neither hot nor cold, I will spit you out of my mouth. For you say, 'I am rich and affluent and have no need of anything,' and yet do not realize that you are wretched, pitiable, poor, blind, and naked. I advise you to buy from me gold refined by fire so that you may be rich, and white garments to put on so that your shameful nakedness may not be exposed, and buy ointment to smear on your eyes so that you may see. Those whom I love, I reprove and chastise. Be earnest, therefore, and repent.

" ' "Behold, I stand at the door and knock. If anyone hears my voice and opens the door, [then] I will enter his house and dine with him, and he with me. I will give the victor the right to sit with me on my throne, as I myself first won the victory and sit with my Father on his throne.

" ' "Whoever has ears ought to hear what the Spirit says to the churches." ' "

PSALM 119:113-120

I hate men of divided heart,
  but I love your law.
You are my refuge and my shield;
  in your word I hope.

Depart from me, you
wrongdoers,
and I will observe the
commands of my God.
Sustain me as you have
promised, that I may live;
disappoint me not in my hope.
Help me, that I may be safe
and ever delight in your
statutes.

You despise all who stray from
your statutes,
for their deceitfulness is in
vain.
You account all the wicked of the
earth as dross;
therefore I love your decrees.
My flesh shudders with dread of
you,
and I fear your ordinances.

PROVERBS 26:24-26

*With his lips an enemy pretends, / but in his inmost being he maintains deceit; /
When he speaks graciously, trust him not, / for seven abominations are in his
heart. / A man may conceal hatred under dissimulation, / but his malice will be
revealed in the assembly.*

NOVEMBER

Book for Troubled Times

THERE HAS BEEN A GREAT CHANGE in our modern day attitude toward the Book of Revelation. At one time, it was considered too difficult to understand. Its symbolism was, and still remains, a mystery. For this reason interest in its message lagged, and it was seldom read.

In our times, however, a great interest has been enkindled in this book. It is natural for us to turn to apocalyptic literature in times of crisis. We are living in troubled times, and fear and anxiety dominate much of our thinking. In times of crisis, apocalyptic literature enjoys great popularity, but not always for the right reason. We are living in a great transition period, and perhaps such critical times are rare in the history of the world.

Other "crisis" or "apocalyptic" literature is being avidly read in this critical era. Throughout Scripture we find such writings in Daniel, Ezekiel, Matthew 24, Luke 21, and Mark 13.

Unfortunately, a mistaken notion has arisen about the Book of Revelation. Many are accepting it primarily as a book of prophecy. They interpret these prophecies as detailing what is supposed to happen here and now. They even attempt to explain the mysterious symbolism in Revelation. When we look for modern applications, we miss the original purpose of the Book of Revelation. Only about five percent of the book is prophetic. The rest of the book is apocalyptic. This kind of literature has always appeared throughout biblical history in times of grave crisis. Its purpose is to generate trust and confidence in a loving God even though he may seem to be far removed. The Book of Revelation was written in the first century to encourage and support people in their struggles and sufferings in times of transition and persecution.

Prayer of Praise

This inspired book of the New Testament is rich in many other aspects. It offers great incentive for our devotional life. In chapters four and five, we find magnificent prayers of praise and glory to God. Here is just one example:

"Worthy are you, Lord our God,
to receive glory and honor and power,
For you created all things;
because of your will they came to be and were created."
(Rv 4:11)

These prayers should lead us into deeper and more frequent prayers of praise for our almighty Father. As you are aware, prayers of pure praise are not all that common in our devotional life.

Beatitudes

As we pray with the Book of Revelation, we discover six beatitudes. They remind us that we will be happy if our attitudes and lifestyle conform to certain standards. Like the Beatitudes in Matthew 5:3-12, they encourage us to a more perfect way of living. In them we can find much inspiration and motivation for our daily routine duties. John tells us that happy are they:

who hear and heed the word (1:3);
who die in the Lord (14:13);
who stay wide awake (16:15);
who have been invited to the wedding feast (19:9);
who share in the resurrection (20:6);
who wash their robes (22:14).

As we ponder and listen to what the Spirit is telling us, we will find a way of life not only pleasing to the Lord but also conducive to genuine happiness for ourselves.

By Post

An extremely important contribution to our spiritual growth are the seven letters addressed to the seven churches in that part of the world. These missives are addressed to the "presiding spirit," but they are very personal for each one of us. The Holy Spirit commends each one of the presiding spirits for the good accomplished, but also points out some of the faults and failures which should be corrected.

Each letter ends with the same refrain: "Whoever has ears

ought to hear what the Spirit says to the churches." By heeding the word of the Lord, a conversion should take place.

These letters form an ideal and necessary review of life for each one of us. While we are intent upon serving the Lord we can easily become careless or neglectful in some areas of our spiritual growth. The Holy Spirit emphasizes and repeats the admonition to listen. This kind of listening means being very open and receptive to what the Lord is trying to tell us. It means putting ourselves totally at the disposal of the Lord, thus permitting him to transform us and mold us according to his mind and heart.

The purpose of apocalyptic literature is to instill within us a trust and confidence in God and his designs for each one of us. As the love for the Lord increases within us, our own confidence and trust will be greatly increased and strengthened. This "crisis literature" is a source of hope and encouragement to all of us.

Speaking through the inspired writer, the Lord assures us that he is creating a new heaven and a new earth. What faith, hope, and love, what peace and joy we find in that new creation! "Behold, God's dwelling is with the human race. He will dwell with them and they will be his people and God himself will always be with them [as their God]" (Rv 21:3). Jesus gives us much hope and reassurance of his loving concern: "Behold, I stand at the door and knock" (Rv 3:20).

NOVEMBER 1

REVELATION 4:1-11

After this I had a vision of an open door to heaven, and I heard the trumpetlike voice that had spoken to me before, saying, "Come up here and I will show you what must happen afterwards." At once I was caught up in spirit. A throne was there in heaven, and on the throne sat one whose appearance sparkled like jasper and carnelian. Around the throne was a halo as brilliant as an emerald. Surrounding the throne I saw twenty-four other thrones on which twenty-four elders sat, dressed in white garments and with gold crowns on their heads. From the throne came flashes of lightning, rumblings, and peals of thunder. Seven flaming torches burned in front of the throne, which are the seven spirits of God. In front of the throne was something that resembled a sea of glass like crystal.

In the center and around the throne, there were four living creatures covered with eyes in front and in back. The first creature resembled a lion, the second was like a calf, the third had a face like that of a human being, and the fourth looked like an eagle in flight. The four living creatures, each of them with six wings, were covered with eyes inside and out.

Day and night they do not stop exclaiming:

"Holy, holy, holy is the Lord
    God almighty,
  who was, and who is, and
    who is to come."

Whenever the living creatures give glory and honor and thanks to the one who sits on the throne, who lives forever and ever, the twenty-four elders fall down before the one who sits on the throne and worship him, who lives forever and ever. They throw down their crowns before the throne, exclaiming:

"Worthy are you, Lord our
    God,
  to receive glory and honor
    and power,
  for you created all things;
    because of your will they
      came to be and were
      created."

PSALM 119:121-128

I have fulfilled just ordinances;
  leave me not to my oppressors.
Be surety for the welfare of your
    servant;
  let not the proud oppress me.
My eyes strain after your
    salvation

and your just promise.
Deal with your servant according
    to your kindness,
    and teach me your statutes.
I am your servant; give me
    discernment
    that I may know your decrees.

It is time for the LORD to act:
    they have broken your law.
For I love your command
    more than gold, however fine.
For in all your precepts I go
    forward;
    every false way I hate.

PROVERBS 26:27

He who digs a pit falls into it; / and a stone comes back upon him who rolls it.

NOVEMBER 2

REVELATION 5:1-14

I saw a scroll in the right hand of the one who sat on the throne. It had writing on both sides and was sealed with seven seals. Then I saw a mighty angel who proclaimed in a loud voice, "Who is worthy to open the scroll and break its seals?" But no one in heaven or on earth or under the earth was able to open the scroll or to examine it. I shed many tears because no one was found worthy to open the scroll or to examine it. One of the elders said to me, "Do not weep. The lion of the tribe of Judah, the root of David, has triumphed, enabling him to open the scroll with its seven seals."

Then I saw standing between the throne, surrounded by the four living creatures and the elders, a Lamb that seemed to have been slain. He had seven horns and seven eyes; these are the [seven] spirits of God sent out into the whole world. He came and received the scroll from the right hand of the one who sat on the throne. When he took it, the four living creatures and the twenty-four elders fell down be-

fore the Lamb. Each of the elders held a harp and gold bowls filled with incense, which are the prayers of the holy ones. They sang a new hymn:

"Worthy are you to receive the
    scroll
    and to break open its seals,
    for you were slain and with
        your blood you purchased
        for God
    those from every tribe and
        tongue, people and nation.
You made them a kingdom and
    priests for our God,
    and they will reign on
        earth."

I looked again and heard the voices of many angels who surrounded the throne and the living creatures and the elders. They were countless in number, and they cried out in a loud voice:

"Worthy is the Lamb that was
    slain
    to receive power and riches,
        wisdom and strength,
    honor and glory and
        blessing."

Then I heard every creature in heaven and on earth and under the earth and in the sea, everything in the universe, cry out:

"To the one who sits on the throne and to the Lamb be blessing and honor, glory and might, forever and ever."

The four living creatures answered, "Amen," and the elders fell down and worshiped.

PSALM 119:129-136

Wonderful are your decrees;
 therefore I observe them.
The revelation of your words
 sheds light,
 giving understanding to the
 simple.
I gasp with open mouth
 in my yearning for your
 commands.
Turn to me in pity
 as you turn to those who love
 your name.
Steady my footsteps according to
 your promise,
 and let no iniquity rule over
 me.
Redeem me from the oppression
 of men,
 that I may keep your precepts.
Let your countenance shine upon
 your servant,
 and teach me your statutes.
My eyes shed streams of tears
 because your law has not been
 kept.

PROVERBS 26:28

The lying tongue is its owner's enemy, / and the flattering mouth works ruin.

NOVEMBER 3

REVELATION 6:1-11

Then I watched while the Lamb broke open the first of the seven seals, and I heard one of the four living creatures cry out in a voice like thunder, "Come forward." I looked, and there was a white horse, and its rider had a bow. He was given a crown, and he rode forth victorious to further his victories.

When he broke open the second seal, I heard the second living creature cry out, "Come forward." Another horse came out, a red one. Its rider was given power to take peace away from the earth, so that people would slaughter one another. And he was given a huge sword.

When he broke open the third seal, I heard the third living creature cry out, "Come forward." I looked, and there was a black horse, and its rider held a scale in his hand. I heard what seemed to be a voice in the midst of the four living creatures. It said, "A ration of wheat costs a day's pay, and three rations of barley cost a day's pay. But do not damage the olive oil or the wine."

When he broke open the fourth seal, I heard the voice of the fourth living creature cry out, "Come forward." I looked, and there was a pale green horse. Its rider was named Death, and Hades accompanied him. They were given authority over a quarter of the earth, to kill with sword, famine, and plague, and by means of the beasts of the earth.

When he broke open the fifth seal, I saw underneath the altar the souls of those who had been slaughtered because of the witness they bore to the word of God. They cried out in a loud voice, "How long will it be, holy and true master, before you sit in judgment and avenge our blood on the inhabitants of the earth?" Each of them was given a white robe, and they were told to be patient a little while longer until the number was filled of their fellow servants and brothers who were going to be killed as they had been.

PSALM 119:137-144

You are just, O LORD,
  and your ordinance is right.
You have pronounced your
    decrees in justice
  and in perfect faithfulness.
My zeal consumes me,
  because my foes forget your
    words.
Your promise is very sure,
  and your servant loves it.
I am mean and contemptible,
  but your precepts I have not
    forgotten.
Your justice is everlasting justice,
  and your law is permanent.
Though distress and anguish
    have come upon me,
  your commands are my
    delight.
Your decrees are forever just;
  give me discernment that I may
    live.

PROVERBS 27:1

Boast not of tomorrow, / for you know not what any day may bring forth.

NOVEMBER 4

REVELATION 6:12-17

Then I watched while he broke open the sixth seal, and there was a great earthquake; the sun turned as black as dark sackcloth and the whole moon became like blood. The stars in the sky fell to the earth like unripe figs shaken loose from the tree in a strong wind. Then the sky was divided like a torn scroll curling up, and every mountain and island was moved from its place. The kings of the earth, the nobles, the military officers, the rich, the powerful, and every slave and free person hid themselves in caves and among mountain crags. They cried out to the mountains and the rocks, "Fall on us and hide us from the face of the one who sits on the throne and from the wrath of the Lamb, because the great day of their wrath has come and who can withstand it?"

PSALM 119:145-152

I call out with all my heart;
    answer me, O LORD;
  I will observe your statutes.
I call upon you; save me,
  and I will keep your decrees.
Before dawn I come and cry out;
  I hope in your words.
My eyes greet the night watches
  in meditation on your promise.
Hear my voice according to your
  kindness, O LORD;
according to your ordinance
  give me life.
I am attacked by malicious
  persecutors
who are far from your law.
You, O LORD, are near,
  and all your commands are
    permanent.
Of old I know from your decrees,
  that you have established them
    forever.

PROVERBS 27:2

Let another praise you—not your own mouth; / someone else—not your own lips.

NOVEMBER 5

REVELATION 7:1-8

After this I saw four angels standing at the four corners of the earth, holding back the four winds of the earth so that no wind could blow on land or sea or against any tree. Then I saw another angel come up from the East, holding the seal of the living God. He cried out in a loud voice to the four angels who were given power to damage the land and the sea, "Do not damage the land or the sea or the trees until we put the seal on the foreheads of the servants of our God." I heard the number of those who had been marked with the seal, one hundred and forty-four thousand marked from every tribe of the Israelites: twelve thousand were marked from the tribe of Judah, twelve thousand from the tribe of Reuben, twelve thousand from the tribe of Gad, twelve thousand from the tribe of Asher, twelve thousand from the tribe of Naphtali, twelve thousand from the tribe of Manasseh, twelve thousand from the tribe of Simeon, twelve thousand from the tribe of Levi, twelve thousand from the tribe of Issachar, twelve thousand from the tribe of Zebulun, twelve thousand from the tribe of Joseph, and twelve thousand were marked from the tribe of Benjamin.

PSALM 119:153-160

Behold my affliction, and rescue
  me,
    for I have not forgotten your
      law.
Plead my cause, and redeem me;
  for the sake of your promise
    give me life.
Far from sinners is salvation,
  because they seek not your
    statutes.

Your compassion is great, O
LORD;
according to your ordinances
give me life.
Though my persecutors and my
foes are many,
I turn not away from your
decrees.
I beheld the apostates with
loathing,
because they kept not to your
promise.
See how I love your precepts, O
LORD;
in your kindness give me life.
Permanence is your word's chief
trait;
each of your just ordinances is
everlasting.

PROVERBS 27:3

Stone is heavy, and sand a burden, / but a fool's provocation is heavier than both.

NOVEMBER 6

REVELATION 7:9-17

After this I had a vision of a great multitude, which no one could count, from every nation, race, people, and tongue. They stood before the throne and before the Lamb, wearing white robes and holding palm branches in their hands. They cried out in a loud voice:

"Salvation comes from our
God, who is seated on the
throne,
and from the Lamb."

All the angels stood around the throne and around the elders and the four living creatures. They prostrated themselves before the throne, worshiped God, and exclaimed:

"Amen. Blessing and glory,
wisdom and thanksgiving,
honor, power, and might
be to our God forever and
ever. Amen."

Then one of the elders spoke up and said to me, "Who are these wearing white robes, and where did they come from?" I said to him, "My lord, you are the one who knows." He said to me, "These are the ones who have survived the time of great distress; they have washed their robes and made them white in the blood of the Lamb.

"For this reason they stand
before God's throne
and worship him day and
night in his temple.
The one who sits on the throne
will shelter them.
They will not hunger or thirst
anymore,
nor will the sun or any heat
strike them.
For the Lamb who is in the
center of the throne will
shepherd them
and lead them to springs of
life-giving water,

and God will wipe away
every tear from their
eyes."

PSALM 119:161-168

Princes persecute me without
cause
but my heart stands in awe of
your word.
I rejoice at your promise,
as one who has found rich
spoil.
Falsehood I hate and abhor;
your law I love.
Seven times a day I praise you
for your just ordinances.
Those who love your law have
great peace,
and for them there is no
stumbling block.
I wait for your salvation, O LORD,
and your commands I fulfill.
I keep your decrees
and love them deeply.
I keep your precepts and your
decrees,
for all my ways are before you.

PROVERBS 27:4-6

*Anger is relentless, and wrath overwhelming—/ but before jealousy who can
stand? / Better is an open rebuke / than a love that remains hidden. / Wounds
from a friend may be accepted as well meant, / but the greetings of an enemy one
prays against.*

NOVEMBER 7

REVELATION 8:1-13

When he broke open the seventh seal, there was silence in heaven for about half an hour. And I saw that the seven angels who stood before God were given seven trumpets.

Another angel came and stood at the altar, holding a gold censer. He was given a great quantity of incense to offer, along with the prayers of all the holy ones, on the gold altar that was before the throne. The smoke of the incense along with the prayers of the holy ones went up before God from the hand of the angel. Then the angel took the censer, filled it with burning coals from the altar, and hurled it down to the earth. There were peals of thunder, rumblings, flashes of lightning, and an earthquake.

The seven angels who were holding the seven trumpets prepared to blow them.

When the first one blew his trumpet, there came hail and fire mixed with blood, which was hurled down to the earth. A third of the land was burned up, along with a third of the trees and all green grass.

When the second angel blew his trumpet, something like a large burning mountain was hurled into the sea. A third of the sea turned to blood, a third of the creatures living in the sea died, and a third of the ships were wrecked.

When the third angel blew his trumpet, a large star burning like a torch fell from the sky. It fell on a third of the rivers and on the springs of water. The star was called "Wormwood," and a third of all the water turned to wormwood. Many people died from this water, because it was made bitter.

When the fourth angel blew his trumpet, a third of the sun, a third of the moon, and a third of the stars were struck, so that a third of them became dark. The day lost its light for a third of the time, as did the night.

Then I looked again and heard an eagle flying high overhead cry out in a loud voice, "Woe! Woe! Woe to the inhabitants of the earth from the rest of the trumpet blasts that the three angels are about to blow!"

PSALM 119:169-176

Let my cry come before you, O
    LORD;
in keeping with your word,
    give me discernment.
Let my supplication reach you;
    rescue me according to your
    promise.
My lips pour forth your praise,
    because you teach me your
    statutes.
May my tongue sing of your
    promise,
    for all your commands are just.
Let your hand be ready to help
    me,
    for I have chosen your
    precepts.
I long for your salvation, O LORD,
    and your law is my delight.
Let my soul live to praise you,
    and may your ordinances help
    me.
I have gone astray [like a lost
    sheep]; seek your servant,
    because your commands I do
    not forget.

PROVERBS 27:7-9

One who is full, tramples on virgin honey; / but to the man who is hungry, any bitter thing is sweet. / Like a bird that is far from its nest / is a man who is far from his home. / Perfume and incense gladden the heart, / but by grief the soul is torn asunder.

NOVEMBER 8

REVELATION 9:1-12

Then the fifth angel blew his trumpet, and I saw a star that had fallen from the sky to the earth. It was given the key for the passage to the abyss. It opened the passage to the abyss, and smoke came up out of the passage like smoke from a huge furnace. The sun and the air were darkened by the smoke from the passage. Locusts came out of the smoke onto the land, and they were given the same power as scorpions of the earth. They were told not to harm the grass of the earth or any plant or any tree, but only those people who did not have the seal of God on their foreheads. They were not allowed to kill them but only to torment them for five months; the torment they inflicted was like that of a scorpion when it stings a person. During that time these people will seek death but will not find it, and they will long to die but death will escape them.

The appearance of the locusts was like that of horses ready for battle. On their heads they wore what looked like crowns of gold; their faces were like human faces, and they had hair like women's hair. Their teeth were like lions' teeth, and they had chests like iron breastplates. The sound of their wings was like the sound of many horse-drawn chariots racing into battle. They had tails like scorpions, with stingers; with their tails they had power to harm people for five months. They had as their king the angel of the abyss, whose name in Hebrew is Abaddon and in Greek Apollyon.

The first woe has passed, but there are two more to come.

PSALM 120:1-7

A song of ascents.
In my distress I called to the
 LORD,
 and he answered me.
O LORD, deliver me from lying
 lip,
 from treacherous tongue.
What will he inflict on you, with
 more besides,
 O treacherous tongue?
Sharp arrows of a warrior
 with fiery coals of brushwood.
Woe is me that I sojourn in
 Meshech,
 that I dwell amid the tents of
 Kedar!
All too long have I dwelt
 with those who hate peace.
When I speak of peace,
 they are ready for war.

PROVERBS 27:10

Your own friend and your father's friend forsake not; / but if ruin befalls you, enter not a kinsman's house. / Better is a neighbor near at hand / than a brother far away.

NOVEMBER 9

REVELATION 9:13-21

Then the sixth angel blew his trumpet, and I heard a voice coming from the [four] horns of the gold altar before God, telling the sixth angel who held the trumpet, "Release the four angels who are bound at the banks of the great river Euphrates." So the four angels were released, who were prepared for this hour, day, month, and year to kill a third of the human race. The number of cavalry troops was two hundred million; I heard their number. Now in my vision this is how I saw the horses and their riders. They wore red, blue, and yellow breastplates, and the horses' heads were like heads of lions, and out of their mouths came fire, smoke, and sulfur. By these three plagues of fire, smoke, and sulfur that came out of their mouths a third of the human race was killed. For the power of the horses is in their mouths and in their tails; for their tails are like snakes, with heads that inflict harm.

The rest of the human race, who were not killed by these plagues, did not repent of the works of their hands, to give up the worship of demons and idols made from gold, silver, bronze, stone, and wood, which cannot see or hear or walk. Nor did they repent of their murders, their magic potions, their unchastity, or their robberies.

PSALM 121:1-8

A song of ascents.
I lift up my eyes toward the
 mountains;
 whence shall help come to me?
My help is from the LORD,
 who made heaven and earth.
May he not suffer your foot to
 slip;
 may he slumber not who
 guards you:
Indeed he neither slumbers nor
 sleeps,
 the guardian of Israel.
The LORD is your guardian; the
 LORD is your shade;
 he is beside you at your right
 hand.
The sun shall not harm you by
 day,
 nor the moon by night.
The LORD will guard you from all
 evil;
 he will guard your life.
The LORD will guard your coming
 and your going,
 both now and forever.

PROVERBS 27:11

If you are wise, my son, you will gladden my heart, / and I will be able to rebut him who taunts me.

NOVEMBER 10

REVELATION 10:1-11

Then I saw another mighty angel come down from heaven wrapped in a cloud, with a halo around his head; his face was like the sun and his feet were like pillars of fire. In his hand he held a small scroll that had been opened. He placed his right foot on the sea and his left foot on the land, and then he cried out in a loud voice as a lion roars. When he cried out, the seven thunders raised their voices, too. When the seven thunders had spoken, I was about to write it down; but I heard a voice from heaven say, "Seal up what the seven thunders have spoken, but do not write it down." Then the angel I saw standing on the sea and on the land raised his right hand to heaven and swore by the one who lives forever and ever, who created heaven and earth and sea and all that is in them, "There shall be no more delay. At the time when you hear the seventh angel blow his trumpet, the mysterious plan of God shall be fulfilled, as he promised to his servants the prophets."

Then the voice that I had heard

from heaven spoke to me again and said, "Go, take the scroll that lies open in the hand of the angel who is standing on the sea and on the land." So I went up to the angel and told him to give me the small scroll. He said to me, "Take and swallow it. It will turn your stomach sour, but in your mouth it will taste as sweet as honey." I took the small scroll from the angel's hand and swallowed it. In my mouth it was like sweet honey, but when I had eaten it, my stomach turned sour. Then someone said to me, "You must prophesy again about many peoples, nations, tongues, and kings."

PSALM 122:1-5

A song of ascents. Of David.
I rejoiced because they said to me,
    "We will go up to the house of the LORD."
And now we have set foot
    within your gates, O Jerusalem—
Jerusalem, built as a city
    with compact unity.
To it the tribes go up,
    the tribes of the LORD,
According to the decree for Israel,
    to give thanks to the name of the LORD.
In it are set up judgment seats,
    seats for the house of David.

PROVERBS 27:12

The shrewd man perceives evil and hides; / simpletons continue on and suffer the penalty.

NOVEMBER 11

REVELATION 11:1-19

Then I was given a measuring rod like a staff and I was told, "Come and measure the temple of God and the altar, and count those who are worshiping in it. But exclude the outer court of the temple; do not measure it, for it has been handed over to the Gentiles, who will trample the holy city for forty-two months. I will commission my two witnesses to prophesy for those twelve hundred and sixty days, wearing sackcloth." These are the two olive trees and the two lampstands that stand before the Lord of the earth. If anyone wants to harm them, fire comes out of their mouths and devours their enemies. In this way, anyone wanting to harm them is sure to be slain. They have the power to close up the sky so that no rain can fall during the time of their prophesying. They also have power to turn water into blood and to afflict the earth with any plague as often as they wish.

When they have finished their testimony, the beast that comes up from the abyss will wage war against them and conquer them and kill them. Their corpses will lie in the main street of the great city, which has the symbolic names "Sodom" and "Egypt," where indeed their Lord was crucified. Those from every people, tribe, tongue, and nation will gaze on their corpses for three and a half days, and they will not allow their corpses to be buried. The inhabitants of the earth will gloat over them and be glad and exchange gifts because these two prophets tormented the inhabitants of the earth. But after the three and a half days, a breath of life from God entered them. When they stood on their feet, great fear fell on those who saw them. Then they heard a loud voice from heaven say to them, "Come up here." So they went up to heaven in a cloud as their enemies looked on. At that moment there was a great earthquake, and a tenth of the city fell in ruins. Seven thousand people were killed during the earthquake; the rest were terrified and gave glory to the God of heaven.

The second woe has passed, but the third is coming soon.

Then the seventh angel blew his trumpet. There were loud voices in heaven, saying, "The kingdom of the world now belongs to our Lord and to his Anointed, and he will reign forever and ever." The twenty-four elders who sat on their thrones before God prostrated themselves and worshiped God and said:

"We give thanks to you, Lord
   God almighty,
   who are and who were.
For you have assumed your
      great power
   and have established your
      reign.
The nations raged,
   but your wrath has come,
   and the time for the dead to
      be judged,
and to recompense your
      servants, the prophets,
   and the holy ones and those
      who fear your name,
   the small and the great alike,
and to destroy those who
      destroy the earth."

Then God's temple in heaven was opened, and the ark of his covenant could be seen in the temple. There were flashes of lightning, rumblings, and peals of thunder, an earthquake, and a violent hailstorm.

PSALM 122:6-9

Pray for the peace of Jerusalem!
   May those who love you
      prosper!
May peace be within your walls,
   prosperity in your buildings.
Because of my relatives and
      friends
   I will say, "Peace be within
      you!"
Because of the house of the LORD,
      our God,
   I will pray for your good.

PROVERBS 27:13

Take his garment who becomes surety for another, / and for the sake of a stranger, yield it up!

NOVEMBER 12

REVELATION 12:1-6

A great sign appeared in the sky, a woman clothed with the sun, with the moon under her feet, and on her head a crown of twelve stars. She was with child and wailed aloud in pain as she labored to give birth. Then another sign appeared in the sky; it was a huge red dragon, with seven heads and ten horns, and on its heads were seven diadems. Its tail swept away a third of the stars in the sky and hurled them down to the earth. Then the dragon stood before the woman about to give birth, to devour her child when she gave birth. She gave birth to a son, a male child, destined to rule all the nations with an iron rod. Her child was caught up to God and his throne. The woman herself fled into the desert where she had a place prepared by God, that there she might be taken care of for twelve hundred and sixty days.

PSALM 123:1-4

A song of ascents.
To you I lift up my eyes
　who are enthroned in heaven.
Behold, as the eyes of servants
　are on the hands of their
　　masters,
As the eyes of a maid
　are on the hands of her
　　mistress,
So are our eyes on the LORD, our
　　God,
　till he have pity on us.
Have pity on us, O LORD, have
　　pity on us,
　for we are more than sated
　　with contempt;
Our souls are more than sated
　with the mockery of the
　　arrogant,
　with the contempt of the
　　proud.

PROVERBS 27:14

When one greets his neighbor with a loud voice in the early morning, / a curse can be laid to his charge.

NOVEMBER 13

REVELATION 12:7-18

Then war broke out in heaven; Michael and his angels battled against the dragon. The dragon and its angels fought back, but they did not prevail and there was no longer any place for them in heaven. The huge dragon, the ancient serpent, who is called the Devil and Satan, who deceived the whole world, was thrown down to earth, and its angels were thrown down with it.

Then I heard a loud voice in heaven say:

"Now have salvation and
power come,
and the kingdom of our God
and the authority of his
Anointed.
For the accuser of our brothers
is cast out,
who accuses them before our
God day and night.
They conquered him by the
blood of the Lamb
and by the word of their
testimony;
love for life did not deter
them from death.
Therefore, rejoice, you
heavens,
and you who dwell in them.
But woe to you, earth and sea,
for the Devil has come down
to you in great fury,
for he knows he has but a
short time."

When the dragon saw that it had been thrown down to the earth, it pursued the woman who had given birth to the male child. But the woman was given the two wings of the great eagle, so that she could fly to her place in the desert, where, far from the serpent, she was taken care of for a year, two years, and a half-year. The serpent, however, spewed a torrent of water out of his mouth after the woman to sweep her away with the current. But the earth helped the woman and opened its mouth and swallowed the flood that the dragon spewed out of its mouth. Then the dragon became angry with the woman and went off to wage war against the rest of her offspring, those who keep God's commandments and bear witness to Jesus. It took its position on the sand of the sea.

PSALM 124:1-8

A song of ascents. Of David.
Had not the LORD been with us,
let Israel say,
had not the LORD been with
us—
When men rose up against us,
then would they have
swallowed us alive.
When their fury was inflamed
against us,
then would the waters have
overwhelmed us;
The torrent would have swept
over us;
over us then would have swept
the raging waters.
Blessed be the LORD, who did not
leave us
a prey to their teeth.
We were rescued like a bird
from the fowlers' snare;
Broken was the snare,
and we were freed.
Our help is in the name of the
LORD,
who made heaven and earth.

PROVERBS 27:15-16

For a persistent leak on a rainy day / the match is a quarrelsome woman. / He who keeps her stores up a stormwind; / he cannot tell north from south.

NOVEMBER 14

REVELATION 13:1-10

Then I saw a beast come out of the sea with ten horns and seven heads; on its horns were ten diadems, and on its heads blasphemous name[s]. The beast I saw was like a leopard, but it had feet like a bear's, and its mouth was like the mouth of a lion. To it the dragon gave its own power and throne, along with great authority. I saw that one of its heads seemed to have been mortally wounded, but this mortal wound was healed. Fascinated, the whole world followed after the beast. They worshiped the dragon because it gave its authority to the beast; they also worshiped the beast and said, "Who can compare with the beast or who can fight against it?"

The beast was given a mouth uttering proud boasts and blaphemies, and it was given authority to act for forty-two months. It opened its mouth to utter blasphemies against God, blaspheming his name and his dwelling and those who dwell in heaven. It was also allowed to wage war against the holy ones and conquer them, and it was granted authority over every tribe, people, tongue, and nation. All the inhabitants of the earth will worship it, all whose names were not written from the foundation of the world in the book of life, which belongs to the Lamb who was slain.

> Whoever has ears ought to
>   hear these words.
> Anyone destined for captivity
>   goes into captivity.
> Anyone destined to be slain by
>   the
>   sword shall be slain by the
>   sword.

Such is the faithful endurance of the holy ones.

PSALM 125:1-5

A song of ascents.
They who trust in the LORD are
    like Mount Zion,
  which is immovable; which
    forever stands.
Mountains are round about
    Jerusalem;
  so the LORD is round about his
    people,
  both now and forever.
For the scepter of the wicked
    shall not remain
  upon the territory of the just,
Lest the just put forth
  to wickedness their hands.
Do good, O LORD, to the good
  and to the upright of heart.
But such as turn aside to crooked
    ways
  may the LORD lead away with
    the evildoers!
  Peace be upon Israel!

PROVERBS 27:17

As iron sharpens iron, / so man sharpens his fellow man.

NOVEMBER 15

REVELATION 13:11-18

Then I saw another beast come up out of the earth; it had two horns like a lamb's but spoke like a dragon. It wielded all the authority of the first beast in its sight and made the earth and its inhabitants worship the first beast, whose mortal wound had been healed. It performed great signs, even making fire come down from heaven to earth in the sight of everyone. It deceived the inhabitants of the earth with the signs it was allowed to perform in the sight of the first beast, telling them to make an image for the beast who had been wounded by the sword and revived. It was then permitted to breathe life into the beast's image, so that the beast's image could speak and [could] have anyone who did not worship it put to death. It forced all the people, small and great, rich and poor, free and slave, to be given a stamped image on their right hands or their foreheads, so that no one could buy or sell except one who had the stamped image of the beast's name or the number that stood for its name.

Wisdom is needed here; one who understands can calculate the number of the beast, for it is a number that stands for a person. His number is six hundred and sixty-six.

PSALM 126:1-6

A song of ascents.
When the LORD brought back the
    captives of Zion,
  we were like men dreaming.
Then our mouth was filled with
    laughter,
  and our tongue with rejoicing.
Then they said among the
    nations,
  "The LORD has done great
    things for them."
  The LORD has done great
    things for us;
  we are glad indeed.
Restore our fortunes, O LORD,
  like the torrents in the southern
    desert.
Those that sow in tears
  shall reap rejoicing.
Although they go forth weeping,
  carrying the seed to be sown,
They shall come back rejoicing,
  carrying their sheaves.

PROVERBS 27:18-20

He who tends a fig tree eats its fruit, / and he who is attentive to his master will be enriched. / As one face differs from another, / so does one human heart from another. / The nether world and the abyss are never satisfied; / so too the eyes of men.

NOVEMBER 16

REVELATION 14:1-7

Then I looked and there was the Lamb standing on Mount Zion, and with him a hundred and forty-four thousand who had his name and his Father's name written on their foreheads. I heard a sound from heaven like the sound of rushing water or a loud peal of thunder. The sound I heard was like that of harpists playing their harps. They were singing [what seemed to be] a new hymn before the throne, before the four living creatures and the elders. No one could learn this hymn except the hundred and forty-four thousand who had been ransomed from the earth. These are they who were not defiled with women; they are virgins and these are the ones who follow the Lamb wherever he goes. They have been ransomed as the firstfruits of the human race for God and the Lamb. On their lips no deceit has been found; they are unblemished.

Then I saw another angel flying high overhead, with everlasting good news to announce to those who dwell on earth, to every nation, tribe, tongue, and people.

He said in a loud voice, "Fear God and give him glory, for his time has come to sit in judgment. Worship him who made heaven and earth and sea and springs of water."

PSALM 127:1-5

A song of ascents. Of Solomon.

Unless the LORD build the house,
    they labor in vain who build it.
Unless the LORD guard the city,
    in vain does the guard keep
        vigil.
It is vain for you to rise early,
    or put off your rest,
You that eat hard-earned bread,
    for he gives to his beloved in
        sleep.
Behold, sons are a gift from the
        LORD;
    the fruit of the womb is a
        reward.
Like arrows in the hand of a
        warrior
    are the sons of one's youth.
Happy the man whose quiver is
        filled with them;
    they shall not be put to shame
        when they contend
    with enemies at the gate.

PROVERBS 27:21-22

As the crucible tests silver and the furnace gold, / so a man is tested by the praise he receives. / Though you should pound the fool to bits / with the pestle, amid the grits in a mortar, / his folly would not go out of him.

NOVEMBER 17

REVELATION 14:8-13

A second angel followed,
    saying:
"Fallen, fallen is Babylon the
    great,
    that made all the nations
        drink
    the wine of her licentious
        passion."

A third angel followed them and said in a loud voice, "Anyone who worships the beast or its image, or accepts its mark on forehead or hand, will also drink the wine of God's fury, poured full strength into the cup of his wrath, and will be tormented in burning sulfur before the holy angels and before the Lamb. The smoke of the fire that torments them will rise forever and ever, and there will be no relief day or night for those who worship the beast or its image or accept the mark of its name." Here is what sustains the holy ones who keep God's commandments and their faith in Jesus.

I heard a voice from heaven say, "Write this: Blessed are the dead who die in the Lord from now on." "Yes," said the Spirit, "Let them find rest from their labors, for their works accompany them."

PSALM 128:1-6

A song of ascents.
Happy are you who fear the
    LORD,
    who walk in his ways!
For you shall eat the fruit of your
        handiwork;
    happy shall you be, and
        favored.
Your wife shall be like a fruitful
        vine
    in the recesses of your home;
Your children like olive plants
    around your table.
Behold, thus is the man blessed
    who fears the LORD.
The LORD bless you from Zion:
    may you see the prosperity of
        Jerusalem
    all the days of your life;
May you see your children's
        children.
    Peace be upon Israel!

PROVERBS 27:23-27

Take good care of your flocks, / give careful attention to your herds; / For wealth lasts not forever, / nor even a crown from age to age. / When the grass is taken away and the aftergrowth appears, / and the mountain greens are gathered in, / The lambs will provide you with clothing, / and the goats will bring the price of a field, / And there will be ample goat's milk to supply you, / to supply your household, / and maintenance for your maidens.

NOVEMBER 18

REVELATION 14:14-20

Then I looked and there was a white cloud, and sitting on the cloud one who looked like a son of man, with a gold crown on his head and a sharp sickle in his hand. Another angel came out of the temple, crying out in a loud voice to the one sitting on the cloud, "Use your sickle and reap the harvest, for the time to reap has come, because the earth's harvest is fully ripe." So the one who was sitting on the cloud swung his sickle over the earth, and the earth was harvested.

Then another angel came out of the temple in heaven who also had a sharp sickle. Then another angel [came] from the altar, [who] was in charge of the fire, and cried out in a loud voice to the one who had the sharp sickle, "Use your sharp sickle and cut the clusters from the earth's vines, for its grapes are ripe." So the angel swung his sickle over the earth and cut the earth's vintage. He threw it into the great wine press of God's fury. The wine press was trodden outside the city and blood poured out of the wine press to the height of a horse's bridle for two hundred miles.

PSALM 129:1-8

A song of ascents.
Much have they oppressed me
    from my youth,
    let Israel say,
Much have they oppressed me
    from my youth;
    yet they have not prevailed
    against me.
Upon my back the plowers
    plowed;
    long did they make their
    furrows
But the just LORD has severed
    the cords of the wicked.
May all be put to shame and fall
    back that hate Zion.
May they be like grass on the
    housetops,
    which withers before it is
    plucked;
With which the reaper fills not
    his hand,
    nor the gatherer of sheaves his
    arms;
And those that pass by say not,
    "The blessing of the LORD be
    upon you!
    We bless you in the name of
    the LORD!"

PROVERBS 28:1

The wicked man flees although no one pursues him; / but the just man, like a lion, feels sure of himself.

NOVEMBER 19

REVELATION 15:1-8

Then I saw in heaven another sign, great and awe-inspiring: seven angels with the seven last plagues, for through them God's fury is accomplished.

Then I saw something like a sea of glass mingled with fire. On the sea of glass were standing those who had won the victory over the beast and its image and the number that signified its name. They were holding God's harps, and they sang the song of Moses, the servant of God, and the song of the Lamb:

"Great and wonderful are your works,
 Lord God almighty.
Just and true are your ways,
 O king of the nations.
Who will not fear you, Lord,
 or glorify your name?
For you alone are holy.
 All the nations will come
 and worship before you,
 for your righteous acts have
 been revealed."

After this I had another vision. The temple that is the heavenly tent of testimony opened, and the seven angels with the seven plagues came out of the temple. They were dressed in clean white linen, with a gold sash around their chests. One of the four living creatures gave the seven angels seven gold bowls filled with the fury of God, who lives forever and ever. Then the temple became so filled with the smoke from God's glory and might that no one could enter it until the seven plagues of the seven angels had been accomplished.

PSALM 130:1-4

A song of ascents.
Out of the depths I cry to you, O
 LORD;
 LORD, hear my voice!
Let your ears be attentive
 to my voice in supplication:
If you, O LORD, mark iniquities,
 LORD, who can stand?
But with you is forgiveness,
 that you may be revered.

PROVERBS 28:2

If a land is rebellious, its princes will be many; / but with a prudent man it knows security.

NOVEMBER 20

REVELATION 16:1-11

I heard a loud voice speaking from the temple to the seven angels, "Go and pour out the seven bowls of God's fury upon the earth."

The first angel went and poured out his bowl on the earth. Festering and ugly sores broke out on those who had the mark of the beast or worshiped its image.

The second angel poured out his bowl on the sea. The sea turned to blood like that from a corpse; every creature living in the sea died.

The third angel poured out his bowl on the rivers and springs of water. These also turned to blood. Then I heard the angel in charge of the waters say:

"You are just, O Holy One,
    who are and who were,
    in passing this sentence.
For they have shed the blood
    of the holy ones and the
    prophets,
    and you [have] given them
    blood to drink;
    it is what they deserve."

Then I heard the altar cry out,

"Yes, Lord God almighty,
    your judgments are true and
    just."

The fourth angel poured out his bowl on the sun. It was given the power to burn people with fire. People were burned by the scorching heat and blasphemed the name of God who had power over these plagues, but they did not repent or give him glory.

The fifth angel poured out his bowl on the throne of the beast. Its kingdom was plunged into darkness, and people bit their tongues in pain and blasphemed the God of heaven because of their pains and sores. But they did not repent of their works.

PSALM 130:5-8

I trust in the LORD;
    my soul trusts in his word.
My soul waits for the LORD
    more than sentinels wait for
    the dawn.
More than sentinels wait for the
    dawn,
    let Israel wait for the LORD,
For with the LORD is kindness
    and with him is plenteous
    redemption;
And he will redeem Israel
    from all their iniquities.

PROVERBS 28:3-5

A rich man who oppresses the poor / is like a devastating rain that leaves no food. / Those who abandon the law praise the wicked man, / but those who keep the law war against him. / Evil men understand nothing of justice, / but those who seek the LORD understand all.

NOVEMBER 21

REVELATION 16:12-21

The sixth angel emptied his bowl on the great river Euphrates. Its water was dried up to prepare the way for the kings of the East. I saw three unclean spirits like frogs come from the mouth of the dragon, from the mouth of the beast, and from the mouth of the false prophet. These were demonic spirits who performed signs. They went out to the kings of the whole world to assemble them for the battle on the great day of God the almighty. ("Behold, I am coming like a thief." Blessed is the one who watches and keeps his clothes ready, so that he may not go naked and people see him exposed.) They then assembled the kings in the place that is named Armageddon in Hebrew.

The seventh angel poured out his bowl into the air. A loud voice came out of the temple from the throne, saying, "It is done." Then there were lightning flashes, rumblings, and peals of thunder, and a great earthquake. It was such a violent earthquake that there has never been one like it since the human race began on earth. The great city was split into three parts, and the gentile cities fell. But God remembered great Babylon, giving it the cup filled with the wine of his fury and wrath.

Every island fled, and mountains disappeared. Large hailstones like huge weights came down from the sky on people, and they blasphemed God for the plague of hail because this plague was so severe.

PSALM 131:1-3

A song of ascents. Of David.
O LORD, my heart is not proud,
  nor are my eyes haughty;
I busy not myself with great
    things,
  nor with things too sublime for
    me.
Nay rather, I have stilled and
    quieted
  my soul like a weaned child.
Like a weaned child on its
    mother's lap,
  [so is my soul within me.]
  O Israel, hope in the LORD,
  both now and forever.

PROVERBS 28:6-7

Better a poor man who walks in his integrity / than he who is crooked in his ways and rich. / He who keeps the law is a wise son, / but the gluttons' companion disgraces his father.

NOVEMBER 22

REVELATION 17:1-18

Then one of the seven angels who were holding the seven bowls came and said to me, "Come here. I will show you the judgment on the great harlot who lives near the many waters. The kings of the earth have had intercourse with her, and the inhabitants of the earth became drunk on the wine of her harlotry." Then he carried me away in spirit to a de-

serted place where I saw a woman seated on a scarlet beast that was covered with blasphemous names, with seven heads and ten horns. The woman was wearing purple and scarlet and adorned with gold, precious stones, and pearls. She held in her hand a gold cup that was filled with the abominable and sordid deeds of her harlotry. On her forehead was written a name, which is a mystery, "Babylon the great, the mother of harlots and of the abominations of the earth." I saw that the woman was drunk on the blood of the holy ones and on the blood of the witnesses to Jesus.

When I saw her I was greatly amazed. The angel said to me, "Why are you amazed? I will explain to you the mystery of the woman and of the beast that carries her, the beast with the seven heads and the ten horns. The beast that you saw existed once but now exists no longer. It will come up from the abyss and is headed for destruction. The inhabitants of the earth whose names have not been written in the book of life from the foundation of the world shall be amazed when they see the beast, because it existed once but exists no longer, and yet it will come again. Here is a clue for one who has wisdom. The seven heads represent seven hills upon which the woman sits. They also represent seven kings: five have already fallen, one still lives, and the last has not yet come, and when he comes he must remain only a short while. The beast that existed once but exists no longer is an eighth king, but really belongs to the seven and is headed for destruction. The ten horns that you saw represent ten kings who have not yet been crowned; they will receive royal authority along with the beast for one hour. They are of one mind and will give their power and authority to the beast. They will fight with the Lamb, but the Lamb will conquer them, for he is Lord of lords and King of kings, and those with him are called, chosen, and faithful."

Then he said to me, "The waters that you saw where the harlot lives represent large numbers of peoples, nations, and tongues. The ten horns that you saw and the beast will hate the harlot; they will leave her desolate and naked; they will eat her flesh and consume her with fire. For God has put it into their minds to carry out his purpose and to make them come to an agreement to give their kingdom to the beast until the words of God are accomplished. The woman whom you saw represents the great city that has sovereignty over the kings of the earth."

PSALM 132:1-10

A song of ascents.
Remember, O LORD, for David
    all his anxious care:
How he swore to the LORD,
    vowed to the Mighty One of
      Jacob:
"I will not enter the house I live
    in,
    nor lie on the couch where I
      sleep;
I will give my eyes no sleep,
    my eyelids no rest,
Till I find a place for the LORD,
    a dwelling for the Mighty One
      of Jacob."
Behold, we heard of it in
    Ephrathah;
    we found it in the fields of Jaar.
Let us enter into his dwelling,
    let us worship at his footstool.
Advance, O LORD, to your resting
    place,
    you and the ark of your
      majesty.
May your priests be clothed with
    justice;
    let your faithful ones shout
      merrily for joy.
For the sake of David your
    servant,
    reject not the plea of your
      anointed.

PROVERBS 28:8-10

He who increases his wealth by interest and overcharge / gathers it for him who is kind to the poor. / When one turns away his ear from hearing the law, / even his prayer is an abomination. / He who seduces the upright into an evil way / will himself fall into his own pit. / [And blameless men will gain prosperity.]

NOVEMBER 23

REVELATION 18:1-24

After this I saw another angel coming down from heaven, having great authority, and the earth became illumined by his splendor. He cried out in a mighty voice:

"Fallen, fallen is Babylon the great.
She has become a haunt for demons.
She is a cage for every unclean spirit,
a cage for every unclean bird,
[a cage for every unclean]
and disgusting [beast].
For all the nations have drunk the wine of her licentious passion.
The kings of the earth had intercourse with her,
and the merchants of the earth grew
rich from her drive for luxury."

Then I heard another voice from heaven say:

"Depart from her, my people, so as not to take part in her sins
and receive a share in her plagues,
for her sins are piled up to the sky,

and God remembers her crimes.
Pay her back as she has paid others.
Pay her back double for her deeds.
Into her cup pour double what she poured.
To the measure of her boasting and wantonness
repay her in torment and grief;
for she said to herself,
'I sit enthroned as queen;
I am no widow,
and I will never know grief.'
Therefore, her plagues will come in one day,
pestilence, grief, and famine;
she will be consumed by fire.
For mighty is the Lord God who judges her."

The kings of the earth who had intercourse with her in their wantonness will weep and mourn over her when they see the smoke of her pyre. They will keep their distance for fear of the torment inflicted on her, and they will say:

"Alas, alas, great city,
Babylon, mighty city.
In one hour your judgment has come."

The merchants of the earth will weep and mourn for her, because there will be no more markets for their cargo: their cargo of gold, silver, precious stones, and pearls; fine linen, purple silk, and scarlet cloth; fragrant wood of every kind, all articles of ivory and all articles of the most expensive wood, bronze, iron, and marble; cinnamon, spice, incense, myrrh, and frankincense; wine, olive oil, fine flour, and wheat; cattle and sheep, horses and chariots, and slaves, that is, human beings.

> "The fruit you craved
> has left you.
> All your luxury and splendor
> are gone,
> never again will one find
> them."

The merchants who deal in these goods, who grew rich from her, will keep their distance for fear of the torment inflicted on her. Weeping and mourning, they cry out:

> "Alas, alas, great city,
> wearing fine linen, purple
> and scarlet,
> adorned [in] gold, precious
> stones, and pearls.
> In one hour this great wealth
> has been ruined."

Every captain of a ship, every traveler at sea, sailors, and seafaring merchants stood at a distance and cried out when they saw the smoke of her pyre, "What city could compare with the great city?" They threw dust on their heads and cried out, weeping and mourning:

> "Alas, alas, great city,
> in which all who had ships at
> sea
> grew rich from her wealth.

> In one hour she has been
> ruined.
> Rejoice over her, heaven,
> you holy ones, apostles, and
> prophets.
> For God has judged your case
> against her."

A mighty angel picked up a stone like a huge millstone and threw it into the sea and said:

> "With such force will Babylon
> the great city be thrown
> down,
> and will never be found
> again.
> No melodies of harpists and
> musicians,
> flutists and trumpeters,
> will ever be heard in you
> again.
> No craftsmen in any trade
> will ever be found in you
> again.
> No sound of the millstone
> will ever be heard in you
> again.
> No light from a lamp
> will ever be seen in you
> again.
> No voices of bride and groom
> will ever be heard in you
> again.
> Because your merchants were
> the great ones of the
> world,
> all nations were led astray by
> your magic potion.
> In her was found the blood of
> prophets and holy ones
> and all who have been slain
> on the earth."

PSALM 132:11-18

The LORD swore to David
a firm promise from which he
will not withdraw:
"Your own offspring
I will set upon your throne;

If your sons keep my covenant
  and the decrees which I shall
    teach them,
Their sons, too, forever
  shall sit upon your throne."
For the LORD has chosen Zion;
  he prefers her for his dwelling.
"Zion is my resting place forever;
  in her will I dwell, for I prefer
    her.
I will bless her with abundant
    provision,
  her poor I will fill with bread.

Her priests I will clothe with
    salvation,
  and her faithful ones shall
    shout merrily for joy.
In her will I make a horn to
    sprout forth for David;
  I will place a lamp for my
    anointed.
His enemies I will clothe with
    shame,
  but upon him my crown shall
    shine."

PROVERBS 28:11

The rich man is wise in his own eyes, / but a poor man who is intelligent sees through him.

NOVEMBER 24

REVELATION 19:1-10

After this I heard what sounded like the loud voice of a great multitude in heaven, saying:

"Alleluia!
Salvation, glory, and might
    belong to our God,
  for true and just are his
    judgments.
He has condemned the great
    harlot
  who corrupted the earth
    with her harlotry.
He has avenged on her the
    blood of his servants."

They said a second time:

"Alleluia! Smoke will rise from
    her forever and ever."

The twenty-four elders and the four living creatures fell down and worshiped God who sat on the throne, saying, "Amen. Alleuia."

A voice coming from the throne said:

"Praise our God, all you his
    servants,
  [and] you who revere him,
    small and great."

Then I heard something like the sound of a great multitude or the sound of rushing water or mighty peals of thunder, as they said:

"Alleluia!
The Lord has established his
    reign,
  [our] God, the almighty.
Let us rejoice and be glad
  and give him glory.
For the wedding day of the
    Lamb has come,
  his bride has made herself
    ready.

She was allowed to wear
a bright, clean linen
garment."

(The linen represents the righteous deeds of the holy ones.)

Then the angel said to me, "Write this: Blessed are those who have been called to the wedding feast of the Lamb." And he said to me, "These words are true; they come from God." I fell at his feet to worship him. But he said to me, "Don't! I am a fellow servant of yours and of your brothers who bear witness to Jesus. Worship God. Witness to Jesus is the spirit of prophecy."

PSALM 133:1-3

A song of ascents. Of David.
Behold, how good it is, and how
    pleasant,
  where brethren dwell at one!
It is as when the precious
    ointment upon the head
runs down over the beard, the
    beard of Aaron,
  till it runs down upon the collar
    of his robe.
It is a dew like that of Hermon,
  which comes down upon the
    mountains of Zion;
For there the LORD has
  pronounced his blessing,
life forever.

PROVERBS 28:12-13

When the just are triumphant, there is great jubilation; / but when the wicked gain pre-eminence, people hide. / He who conceals his sins prospers not, / but he who confesses and forsakes them obtains mercy.

NOVEMBER 25

REVELATION 19:11-21

Then I saw the heavens opened, and there was a white horse; its rider was [called] "Faithful and True." He judges and wages war in righteousness. His eyes were [like] a fiery flame, and on his head were many diadems. He had a name inscribed that no one knows except himself. He wore a cloak that had been dipped in blood, and his name was called the Word of God. The armies of heaven followed him, mounted on white horses and wearing clean white linen. Out of his mouth came a sharp sword to strike the nations. He will rule them with an iron rod, and he himself will tread out in the wine press the wine of the fury and wrath of God the almighty. He has a name written on his cloak and on his thigh, "King of kings and Lord of lords."

Then I saw an angel standing on the sun. He cried out [in] a loud voice to all the birds flying high overhead, "Come here. Gather for God's great feast, to eat the flesh of kings, the flesh of military officers, and the flesh of warriors, the flesh of horses and of their riders, and the flesh of all, free and slave, small and great." Then I saw the beast and the kings of the earth and their armies gathered to fight against the one riding the horse and against his army. The beast was caught and with it the false prophet who had performed in its sight the signs by which he led astray those who had accepted the mark of the beast and those who had worshiped its image. The two were thrown alive into the fiery pool burning with sulfur. The rest were killed by the sword that came out of the mouth of the one riding the horse, and all the birds gorged themselves on their flesh.

PSALM 134:1-3

A song of ascents.
Come, bless the LORD,
    all you servants of the LORD
Who stand in the house of the
    LORD
    during the hours of night.
Lift up your hands toward the
    sanctuary,
    and bless the LORD.
May the LORD bless you from
    Zion,
    the maker of heaven and earth.

PROVERBS 28:14

Happy the man who is always on his guard; / but he who hardens his heart will fall into evil.

NOVEMBER 26

REVELATION 20:1-15

Then I saw an angel come down from heaven, holding in his hand the key to the abyss and a heavy chain. He seized the dragon, the ancient serpent, which is the Devil or Satan, and tied it up for a thousand years and threw it into the abyss, which he locked over it and sealed, so that it could no longer lead the nations astray until the thousand years are completed. After this, it is to be released for a short time.

Then I saw thrones; those who sat on them were entrusted with judgment. I also saw the souls of those who had been beheaded for their witness to Jesus and for the word of God, and who had not worshiped the beast or its image nor had accepted its mark on their foreheads or hands. They came to life and they reigned with Christ for a thousand years. The rest of the dead did not come to life until the thousand years were over. This is the first resurrection. Blessed and holy is the one who shares in the first resurrection. The second death has no power over these; they will be priests of God and of Christ, and they will reign with him for [the] thousand years.

When the thousand years are completed, Satan will be released from his prison. He will go out to deceive the nations at the four corners of the earth, Gog and Magog, to gather them for battle; their number is like the sand of the sea. They invaded the breadth of the earth and surrounded the camp of the holy ones and the beloved city. But fire came down from heaven and consumed them. The Devil who had led them astray was thrown into the pool of fire and sulfur, where the beast and the false prophet were. There they will be tormented day and night forever and ever.

Next I saw a large white throne and the one who was sitting on it. The earth and the sky fled from his presence and there was no place for them. I saw the dead, the great and the lowly, standing before the throne, and scrolls were opened. Then another scroll was opened, the book of life. The dead were judged according to their deeds, by what was written in the scrolls. The sea gave up its dead; then Death and Hades gave up their dead. All the dead were judged according to their deeds. Then Death and Hades were thrown into the pool of fire. (This pool of fire is the second death.) Anyone whose name was not found written in the book of life was thrown into the pool of fire.

PSALM 135:1-4

Alleluia.

Praise the name of the LORD;
　Praise, you servants of the
　　LORD
Who stand in the house of the
　LORD,
　in the courts of the house of
　　our God.
Praise the LORD, for the LORD is
　good;
　sing praise to his name, which
　we love;
For the LORD has chosen Jacob
　for himself,
　Israel for his own possession.

PROVERBS 28:15-16

Like a roaring lion or a ravenous bear / is a wicked ruler over a poor people. / The less prudent the prince, the more his deeds oppress. / He who hates ill-gotten gain prolongs his days.

NOVEMBER 27

REVELATION 21:1-8

Then I saw a new heaven and a new earth. The former heaven and the former earth had passed away, and the sea was no more. I also saw the holy city, a new Jerusalem, coming down out of heaven from God, prepared as a bride adorned for her husband. I heard a loud voice from the throne saying, "Behold, God's dwelling is with the human race. He will dwell with them and they will be his people and God himself will always be with them [as their God]. He will wipe every tear from their eyes, and there shall be no more death or mourning, wailing or pain, [for] the old order has passed away."

The one who sat on the throne said, "Behold, I make all things new." Then he said, "Write these words down, for they are trustworthy and true." He said to me, "They are accomplished. I [am] the Alpha and the Omega, the beginning and the end. To the thirsty I will give a gift from the spring of life-giving water. The victor will inherit these gifts, and I shall be his God, and he will be my son. But as for cowards, the unfaithful, the depraved, murderers, the unchaste, sorcerers, idol-worshipers, and deceivers of every sort, their lot is in the burning pool of fire and sulfur, which is the second death."

PSALM 135:5-7

For I know that the LORD is great;
our LORD is greater than all
    gods.
All that the LORD wills he does
    in heaven and on earth,
    in the seas and in all the deeps.
He raises storm clouds from the
    end of the earth;
    with the lightning he makes
      the rain;
    he brings forth the winds from
      his storehouse.

PROVERBS 28:17-18

Though a man burdened with human blood / were to flee to the grave, none should support him. / He who walks uprightly is safe, / but he whose ways are crooked falls into the pit.

NOVEMBER 28

REVELATION 21:9-27

One of the seven angels who held the seven bowls filled with the seven last plagues came and said to me, "Come here. I will show you the bride, the wife of the Lamb." He took me in spirit to a great, high mountain and showed me the holy city Jerusalem coming down out of heaven from God. It gleamed with the splendor of God. Its radiance was like that of a precious stone, like jasper, clear as crystal. It had a massive, high wall, with twelve gates where twelve angels were stationed and on which names were inscribed, [the names] of the twelve tribes of the Israelites. There were three gates facing east, three north, three south, and three west. The wall of the city had twelve courses of stones as its foundation, on which were inscribed the twelve names of the twelve apostles of the Lamb.

The one who spoke to me held a gold measuring rod to measure the city, its gates, and its wall. The city was square, its length the same as [also] its width. He measured the city with the rod and found it fifteen hundred miles in length and width and height. He also measured its wall: one hundred and forty-four cubits according to the standard unit of measurement the angel used. The wall was constructed of jasper, while the city was pure gold, clear as glass. The foundations of the city wall were decorated with every precious stone; the first course of stones was jasper, the second sapphire, the third chalcedony, the fourth emerald, the fifth sardonyx, the sixth carnelian, the seventh chrysolite, the eighth beryl, the ninth topaz, the tenth chrysoprase, the eleventh hyacinth, and the twelfth amethyst. The twelve gates were twelve pearls, each of the gates made from a single pearl; and the street of the city was of pure gold, transparent as glass.

I saw no temple in the city, for its temple is the Lord God almighty and the Lamb. The city had no need of sun or moon to shine on it, for the glory of God gave it light, and its lamp was the Lamb. The nations will walk by its light, and to it the kings of the earth will bring their treasure. During the day its gates will never be shut, and there will be no night there. The treasure and wealth of the nations will be brought there, but nothing unclean will enter it, nor any[one] who does abominable things or tells lies. Only those will enter whose names are written in the Lamb's book of life.

PSALM 135:8-21

He smote the first born in Egypt,
    both of man and of beast.
He sent signs and wonders
    into your midst, O Egypt,
    against Pharaoh and against all
        his servants.

He smote many nations
    and slew mighty kings:
Sihon, king of the Amorites,
    and Og, king of Bashan,
    and all the kings of Canaan;
And he made their land a
        heritage,
    the heritage of Israel his
        people.
Your name, O LORD, endures
        forever;
    LORD is your title through all
        generations,
For the LORD defends his people,
    and is merciful to his servants.
The idols of the nations are silver
        and gold,
    the handiwork of men.
They have mouths but speak not;
    they have eyes but see not;
They have ears but hear not;
    nor is there breath in their
        mouths.
Their makers shall be like them,
    everyone that trusts in them.
House of Israel, bless the LORD,
    house of Aaron, bless the
        LORD,
House of Levi, bless the LORD;
    you who fear the LORD, bless
        the LORD.
Blessed from Zion be the LORD,
    who dwells in Jerusalem.

PROVERBS 28:19-20

He who cultivates his land will have plenty of food, / but from idle pursuits a man has his fill of poverty. / The trustworthy man will be richly blessed; / he who is in haste to grow rich will not go unpunished.

NOVEMBER 29

REVELATION 22:1-15

Then the angel showed me the river of life-giving water, sparkling like crystal, flowing from the throne of God and of the Lamb down the middle of its street. On either side of the river grew the tree of life that produces fruit twelve times a year, once each month; the leaves of the trees serve as medicine for the nations. Nothing accursed will be found there anymore. The throne of God and of the Lamb will be in it, and his servants will worship him. They will look upon his face, and his name will be on their foreheads. Night will be no more, nor will they need light from lamp or sun, for the Lord God shall give them light, and they shall reign forever and ever.

And he said to me, "These words are trustworthy and true, and the Lord, the God of prophetic spirits, sent his angel to show his servants what must happen soon." "Behold, I am coming soon." Blessed is the one who keeps the prophetic message of this book.

It is I, John, who heard and saw these things, and when I heard and saw them I fell down to worship at the feet of the angel who showed them to me. But he said to me, "Don't! I am a fellow servant of yours and of your brothers the prophets and of those who keep the message of this book. Worship God."

Then he said to me, "Do not seal up the prophetic words of this book, for the appointed time is near. Let the wicked still act wickedly, and the filthy still be filthy. The righteous must still do right, and the holy still be holy."

"Behold, I am coming soon. I bring with me the recompense I will give to each according to his deeds. I am the Alpha and the Omega, the first and the last, the beginning and the end."

Blessed are they who wash their robes so as to have the right to the tree of life and enter the city through its gates. Outside are the dogs, the sorcerers, the unchaste, the murderers, the idol-worshipers, and all who love and practice deceit.

PSALM 136:1-9

Alleluia.
Give thanks to the LORD, for he is
    good,
    for his mercy endures forever;
Give thanks to the God of gods,
    for his mercy endures forever;
Give thanks to the Lord of lords,
    for his mercy endures forever;
Who alone does great wonders,
    for his mercy endures forever;
Who made the heavens in
    wisdom,
    for his mercy endures forever;
Who spread out the earth upon
    the waters,
    for his mercy endures forever;
Who made the great lights,
    for his mercy endures forever;
The sun to rule over the day,
    for his mercy endures forever;
The moon and the stars to rule
    over the night,
    for his mercy endures forever.

PROVERBS 28:21-22

To show partiality is never good: / for even a morsel of bread a man may do wrong. / The avaricious man is perturbed about his wealth, / and he knows not when want will come upon him.

NOVEMBER 30

REVELATION 22:16-21

"I, Jesus, sent my angel to give you this testimony for the churches. I am the root and off-spring of David, the bright morning star."

The Spirit and the bride say, "Come." Let the hearer say, "Come." Let the one who thirsts come forward, and the one who wants it receive the gift of life-giving water.

I warn everyone who hears the prophetic words in this book: if anyone adds to them, God will add to him the plagues described in this book, and if anyone takes away from the words in this prophetic book, God will take away his share in the tree of life and in the holy city described in this book.

The one who gives this testimony says, "Yes, I am coming soon." Amen! Come, Lord Jesus!

The grace of the Lord Jesus be with all.

PSALM 136:10-22

Who smote the Egyptians in their firstborn,
for his mercy endures forever;
And brought out Israel from their midst,
for his mercy endures forever;
With a mighty hand and an outstretched arm,
for his mercy endures forever;
Who split the Red Sea in twain,
for his mercy endures forever;
And led Israel through its midst,
for his mercy endures forever;
But swept Pharaoh and his army into the Red Sea,
for his mercy endures forever;
Who led his people through the wilderness,
for his mercy endures forever;
Who smote great kings,
for his mercy endures forever;
And slew powerful kings,
for his mercy endures forever;
Sihon, king of the Amorites,
for his mercy endures forever;
And Og, king of Bashan,
for his mercy endures forever;
And made their land a heritage,
for his mercy endures forever;
The heritage of Israel his servant,
for his mercy endures forever.

PROVERBS 28:23-24

He who rebukes a man gets more thanks in the end / than one with a flattering tongue. / He who defrauds father or mother and calls it no sin, / is a partner of the brigand.

DECEMBER

John and the Word

THE GOSPEL OF JOHN focuses on the Word of God. This key word surfaces frequently throughout the Gospel. John introduces Jesus as the definitive Word of God. "In the beginning was the Word . . . and the Word was God. . . . And the Word became flesh and made his dwelling among us. . . ." (Jn 1:1ff).

Jesus Proclaimed the Word

On every possible occasion, Jesus proclaimed the Word of God. He taught, preached, explained, and shared the Word of the Lord. Jesus' Word is the way of life. In his Word, Jesus showed us the way to the Father: "No one comes to the Father except through me" (Jn 14:6).

In those days, the rabbis' teachings were rather confusing. If someone asked for a clarification of the law, the rabbis responded by quoting a number of different opinions of famous teachers in Israel without drawing any conclusion. This left inquirers rather perplexed and their question unanswered. On the other hand, Jesus taught with authority. His teaching was clear, direct, and understandable even to the ordinary people.

As Jesus set forth the Word of God, it brought hope and reassurance, trust and confidence, peace and joy to his hearers. Above all, Jesus assured them and us of the Father's unconditional love for us and his own redemptive love for each one of us. If we listen with our whole being, the impact of his words will not escape us: "As the Father loves me, so I also love you. Remain in my love" (Jn 15:9).

Jesus Lived the Word

There is only one way to teach a spiritual truth effectively and that is by witnessing to it by our own lifestyle. Jesus lived what he taught. His will was always in tune with the Father's will. He was most solicitous about doing exactly what the Father asked of him. He invites us to be single-hearted as he was. Jesus could say of himself: "My food is to do the will of the one who sent me and to finish his work" (Jn 4:34). Little wonder that the psalmist could quote the Messiah as saying: "To do your will, O my God, is my delight" (Ps 40:9).

Jesus not only taught us by his way of life but also he urgently encouraged us to follow his example. His words are quite explicit: "I have given you a model to follow, so that as I have done for you, you should also do. . . . I give you a new commandment: love one another. As I have loved you, so you also should love one another" (Jn 13:15, 34).

Jesus lived his Word to the utmost. At the Last Supper he said: "No one has greater love than this, to lay down one's life for one's friends" (Jn 15:13). The very next day he lived out that love by laying down his life for us.

How simply yet how powerfully Jesus challenged his enemies when they maligned him by alleging that he was not living the Word of God: "Can any of you charge me with sin?" (Jn 8:46).

In like manner, Jesus challenges us, his followers, to live the Word of God by adopting his lifestyle of total dedication. We cannot live the Word unless we know and understand his Word. To know the Word with heart knowledge, we must pray with his Word in quiet solitude so that it may find a home in our heart. There it will mold and transform our mind, heart, and attitudes, so that we too will become "gentle and humble of heart." As we listen with our whole being, we will begin to live his Word.

Jesus Fulfills the Word

Many of the Old Testament prophecies point to Jesus as Savior and Redeemer. The Psalms abound in prophetic utterances and images of the Messiah and the kingdom which he would establish. We discover the fulfillment of these prophecies in the pages of the New Testament. In his teaching, Jesus confirms that he is fulfilling the prophecies and promises made to the ancients.

Jesus fulfilled the Word of God in another manner. Many of the axioms in the Book of Proverbs and also in the Psalter are simply pragmatic. Jesus enriched and expanded many of these maxims and truths with his teaching on the love of God, of self, and of neighbor. He added a deeper spiritual dimension to them, thus enabling us to adopt them as axioms for our own daily living. In many other ways, Jesus fulfilled the teachings of the Hebrew Testament, updating them in the light of the Word he was proclaiming.

When we listen to the Word of God proclaimed in the readings of the Old Testament and discover them reiterated and explained by Jesus and recorded by the inspired writers of the New Testament, we begin to appreciate its power to transform our lives.

Jesus frequently reminds us of the necessity of listening to his Word and permitting it to become a way of life for us. He says: "Amen, amen, I say to you, whoever hears my word and believes in the one who sent me has eternal life" (Jn 5:24). On another occasion he said very explicitly: "Whoever belongs to God hears the words of God" (Jn 8:47).

Jesus informed us that a marvelous blessing is in store for those who keep his Word: "Whoever loves me will keep my word, and my Father will love him, and we will come to him and make our dwelling with him" (Jn 14:23). This divine presence is the source of genuine happiness.

Can there be any doubt that John's Gospel is the Gospel of the Word! "Rather, blessed are those who hear the word of God and observe it" (Lk 11:28).

DECEMBER 1

JOHN 1:1-28

In the beginning was the
Word,
and the Word was with God,
and the Word was God.
He was in the beginning with
God.
All things came to be through
him,
and without him nothing
came to be.
What came to be through him
was life,
and this life was the light of
the human race;
the light shines in the
darkness,
and the darkness has not
overcome it.

A man named John was sent
from God. He came for testimony,
to testify to the light, so that all
might believe through him. He
was not the light, but came to testify to the light. The true light,
which enlightens everyone, was
coming into the world.

He was in the world,
and the world came to be
through him,
but the world did not know
him.
He came to what was his own,
but his own people did not
accept him.

But to those who did accept him
he gave power to become children
of God, to those who believe in
his name, who were born not by
natural generation nor by human
choice nor by a man's decision but
of God.

And the Word became flesh
and made his dwelling
among us,
and we saw his glory,
the glory as of the Father's
only Son,
full of grace and truth.

John testified to him and cried
out, saying, "This was he of
whom I said, 'The one who is coming after me ranks ahead of me
because he existed before me.' "
From his fullness we have all received, grace in place of grace. Because while the law was given
through Moses, grace and truth
came through Jesus Christ. No
one has ever seen God. The only
Son, God, who is at the Father's
side, has revealed him.

And this is the testimony of
John. When the Jews from Jerusalem sent priests and Levites [to
him] to ask him, "Who are you?"
he admitted and did not deny it,
but admitted, "I am not the Messiah." So they asked him, "What
are you then? Are you Elijah?"
And he said, "I am not." "Are you

the Prophet?" He answered, "No." So they said to him, "Who are you, so we can give an answer to those who sent us? What do you have to say for yourself?" He said:

"I am 'the voice of one crying out in the desert,
"Make straight the way of the Lord," '

as Isaiah the prophet said." Some Pharisees were also sent. They asked him, "Why then do you baptize if you are not the Messiah or Elijah or the Prophet?" John answered them, "I baptize with water; but there is one among you whom you do not recognize, the one who is coming after me, whose sandal strap I am not worthy to untie." This happened in Bethany across the Jordan, where John was baptizing.

PSALM 136:23-26

Who remembered us in our abjection,
for his mercy endures forever;
and freed us from our foes,
for his mercy endures forever;
Who gives food to all flesh,
for his mercy endures forever.
Give thanks to the God of heaven,
for his mercy endures forever.

PROVERBS 28:25-26

The greedy man stirs up disputes, / but he who trusts in the LORD will prosper. / He who trusts in himself is a fool, / but he who walks in wisdom is safe.

DECEMBER 2

JOHN 1:29-51

The next day he saw Jesus coming toward him and said, "Behold, the Lamb of God, who takes away the sin of the world. He is the one of whom I said, 'A man is coming after me who ranks ahead of me because he existed before me.' I did not know him, but the reason why I came baptizing with water was that he might be made known to Israel." John testified further, saying, "I saw the Spirit come down like a dove from the sky and remain upon him. I did not know him, but the one who sent me to baptize with water told me, 'On whomever you see the Spirit come down and remain, he is the one who will baptize with the holy Spirit.' Now I have seen and testified that he is the Son of God."

The next day John was there again with two of his disciples, and as he watched Jesus walk by, he said, "Behold, the Lamb of God." The two disciples heard what he said and followed Jesus. Jesus turned and saw them following him and said to them, "What are you looking for?" They said to him, "Rabbi" (which translated means Teacher), "where are you staying?" He said to them, "Come, and you will see." So they went and saw where he was staying, and they stayed with him that day. It was about four in the afternoon. Andrew, the brother of

Simon Peter, was one of the two who heard John and followed Jesus. He first found his own brother Simon and told him, "We have found the Messiah" (which is translated Anointed). Then he brought him to Jesus. Jesus looked at him and said, "You are Simon the son of John; you will be called Kephas" (which is translated Peter).

The next day he decided to go to Galilee, and he found Philip. And Jesus said to him, "Follow me." Now Philip was from Bethsaida, the town of Andrew and Peter. Philip found Nathanael and told him, "We have found the one about whom Moses wrote in the law, and also the prophets, Jesus, son of Joseph, from Nazareth." But Nathanael said to him, "Can anything good come from Nazareth?" Philip said to him, "Come and see." Jesus saw Nathanael coming toward him and said of him, "Here is a true Israelite. There is no duplicity in him."

Nathanael said to him, "How do you know me?" Jesus answered and said to him, "Before Philip called you, I saw you under the fig tree." Nathanael answered him, "Rabbi, you are the Son of God; you are the King of Israel." Jesus answered and said to him, "Do you believe because I told you that I saw you under the fig tree? You will see greater things than this." And he said to him, "Amen, amen, I say to you, you will see the sky opened and the angels of God ascending and descending on the Son of Man."

PSALM 137:1-9

By the streams of Babylon
    we sat and wept
    when we remembered Zion.
On the aspens of that land
    we hung up our harps,
Though there our captors asked
    of us
    the lyrics of our songs,
And our despoilers urged us to
    be joyous:
    "Sing for us the songs of Zion!"
How could we sing a song of the
    LORD
    in a foreign land?
If I forget you, Jerusalem,
    may my right hand be
    forgotten!
May my tongue cleave to my
    palate
    if I remember you not,
If I place not Jerusalem
    ahead of my joy.
Remember, O LORD, against the
    children of Edom,
    the day of Jerusalem,
When they said, "Raze it, raze it
    down to its foundations!"
O daughter of Babylon, you
    destroyer,
    happy the man who shall
    repay you
    the evil you have done us!
Happy the man who shall seize
    and smash
    your little ones against the
    rock!

PROVERBS 28:27-28

He who gives to the poor suffers no want, / but he who ignores them gets many a curse. / When the wicked gain pre-eminence, other men hide; / but at their fall the just flourish.

DECEMBER 3

JOHN 2:1-25

On the third day there was a wedding in Cana in Galilee, and the mother of Jesus was there. Jesus and his disciples were also invited to the wedding. When the wine ran short, the mother of Jesus said to him, "They have no wine." [And] Jesus said to her, "Woman, how does your concern affect me? My hour has not yet come." His mother said to the servers, "Do whatever he tells you." Now there were six stone water jars there for Jewish ceremonial washings, each holding twenty to thirty gallons. Jesus told them, "Fill the jars with water." So they filled them to the brim. Then he told them, "Draw some out now and take it to the headwaiter." So they took it. And when the headwaiter tasted the water that had become wine, without knowing where it came from (although the servers who had drawn the water knew), the headwaiter called the bridegroom and said to him, "Everyone serves good wine first, and then when people have drunk freely, an inferior one; but you have kept the good wine until now." Jesus did this as the beginning of his signs in Cana in Galilee and so revealed his glory, and his disciples began to believe in him.

After this, he and his mother, [his] brothers, and his disciples went down to Capernaum and stayed there only a few days.

Since the Passover of the Jews was near, Jesus went up to Jerusalem. He found in the temple area those who sold oxen, sheep, and doves, as well as the money-changers seated there. He made a whip out of cords and drove them all out of the temple area, with the sheep and oxen, and spilled the coins of the money-changers and overturned their tables, and to those who sold doves he said, "Take these out of here, and stop making my Father's house a marketplace." His disciples recalled the words of scripture, "Zeal for your house will consume me." At this the Jews answered and said to him, "What sign can you show us for doing this?" Jesus answered and said to them, "Destroy this temple and in three days I will raise it up." The Jews said, "This temple has been under construction for forty-six years, and you will raise it up in three days?" But he was speaking about the temple of his body. Therefore, when he was raised from the dead, his disciples remembered that he had said this, and they came to believe the scripture and the word Jesus had spoken.

While he was in Jerusalem for the feast of Passover, many began to believe in his name when they saw the signs he was doing. But Jesus would not trust himself to them because he knew them all, and did not need anyone to testify about human nature. He himself understood it well.

PSALM 138:1-8

Of David.

I will give thanks to you, O
　　LORD, with all my heart,
　　[for you have heard the words
　　　　of my mouth;]
　　in the presence of the angels I
　　　　will sing your praise;

I will worship at your holy
   temple
   and give thanks to your name,
Because of your kindness and
   your truth;
   for you have made great above
   all things
   your name and your promise.
When I called, you answered me;
   you built up strength within
   me.
All the kings of the earth shall
   give
   thanks to you, O LORD,
   when they hear the words of
   your mouth;
And they shall sing of the ways
   of the LORD:

"Great is the glory of the
   LORD."
The LORD is exalted, yet the lowly
   he sees,
   and the proud he knows from
   afar.
Though I walk amid distress, you
   preserve me;
   against the anger of my
   enemies you raise your hand;
   your right hand saves me.
The LORD will complete what he
   has done for me;
   your kindness, O LORD,
   endures forever;
   forsake not the work of your
   hands.

PROVERBS 29:1

*The man who remains stiff-necked and hates rebuke / will be crushed suddenly
beyond cure.*

DECEMBER 4

JOHN 3:1-36

Now there was a Pharisee
named Nicodemus, a ruler of the
Jews. He came to Jesus at night
and said to him, "Rabbi, we know
that you are a teacher who has
come from God, for no one can do
these signs that you are doing unless God is with him." Jesus answered and said to him, "Amen,
amen, I say to you, no one can see
the kingdom of God without being born from above." Nicodemus
said to him, "How can a person
once grown old be born again?
Surely he cannot reenter his mother's womb and be born again, can
he?" Jesus answered, "Amen,
amen, I say to you, no one can
enter the kingdom of God without
being born of water and Spirit.

What is born of flesh is flesh and
what is born of spirit is spirit. Do
not be amazed that I told you,
'You must be born from above.'
The wind blows where it wills,
and you can hear the sound it
makes, but you do not know
where it comes from or where it
goes; so it is with everyone who is
born of the Spirit." Nicodemus answered and said to him, "How
can this happen?" Jesus answered
and said to him, "You are the
teacher of Israel and you do not
understand this? Amen, amen, I
say to you, we speak of what we
know and we testify to what we
have seen, but you people do not
accept our testimony. If I tell you
about earthly things and you do
not believe, how will you believe

if I tell you about heavenly things? No one has gone up to heaven except the one who has come down from heaven, the Son of Man. And just as Moses lifted up the serpent in the desert, so must the Son of Man be lifted up, so that everyone who believes in him may have eternal life."

For God so loved the world that he gave his only Son, so that everyone who believes in him might not perish but might have eternal life. For God did not send his Son into the world to condemn the world, but that the world might be saved through him. Whoever believes in him will not be condemned, but whoever does not believe has already been condemned, because he has not believed in the name of the only Son of God. And this is the verdict, that the light came into the world, but people preferred darkness to light, because their works were evil. For everyone who does wicked things hates the light and does not come toward the light, so that his works might not be exposed. But whoever lives the truth comes to the light, so that his works may be clearly seen as done in God.

After this, Jesus and his disciples went into the region of Judea, where he spent some time with them baptizing. John was also baptizing in Aenon near Salim, because there was an abundance of water there, and people came to be baptized, for John had not yet been imprisoned. Now a dispute arose between the disciples of John and a Jew about ceremonial washings. So they came to John and said to him, "Rabbi, the one who was with you across the Jordan, to whom you testified, here he is baptizing and everyone is coming to him." John answered and said, "No one can receive anything except what has been given him from heaven. You yourselves can testify that I said [that] I am not the Messiah, but that I was sent before him. The one who has the bride is the bridegroom; the best man, who stands and listens for him, rejoices greatly at the bridegroom's voice. So this joy of mine has been made complete. He must increase; I must decrease."

The one who comes from above is above all. The one who is of the earth is earthly and speaks of earthly things. But the one who comes from heaven [is above all]. He testifies to what he has seen and heard, but no one accepts his testimony. Whoever does accept his testimony certifies that God is trustworthy. For the one whom God sent speaks the words of God. He does not ration his gift of the Spirit. The Father loves the Son and has given everything over to him. Whoever believes in the Son has eternal life, but whoever disobeys the Son will not see life, but the wrath of God remains upon him.

PSALM 139:1-6

For the leader. A psalm of David.
O Lord, you have probed me
    and you know me;
  you know when I sit and when
    I stand;
  you understand my thoughts
    from afar.
My journeys and my rest you
    scrutinize,
  with all my ways you are
    familiar.
Even before a word is on my
    tongue,
  behold, O Lord, you know the
    whole of it.

Behind me and before, you hem
me in
and rest your hand upon me.

Such knowledge is too wonderful
for me;
too lofty for me to attain.

PROVERBS 29:2-4

When the just prevail, the people rejoice; / but when the wicked rule, the people groan. / He who loves wisdom makes his father glad, / but he who consorts with harlots squanders his wealth. / By justice a king gives stability to the land; / but he who imposes heavy taxes ruins it.

DECEMBER 5

JOHN 4:1-42

Now when Jesus learned that the Pharisees had heard that Jesus was making and baptizing more disciples than John (although Jesus himself was not baptizing, just his disciples), he left Judea and returned to Galilee.

He had to pass through Samaria. So he came to a town of Samaria called Sychar, near the plot of land that Jacob had given to his son Joseph. Jacob's well was there. Jesus, tired from his journey, sat down there at the well. It was about noon.

A woman of Samaria came to draw water. Jesus said to her, "Give me a drink." His disciples had gone into the town to buy food. The Samaritan woman said to him, "How can you, a Jew, ask me, a Samaritan woman, for a drink?" (For Jews use nothing in common with Samaritans.) Jesus answered and said to her, "If you knew the gift of God and who is saying to you, 'Give me a drink,' you would have asked him and he would have given you living water." [The woman] said to him, "Sir, you do not even have a bucket and the cistern is deep; where then can you get this living water? Are you greater than our father Jacob, who gave us this cistern and drank from it himself with his children and his flocks?" Jesus answered and said to her, "Everyone who drinks this water will be thirsty again; but whoever drinks the water I shall give will never thirst; the water I shall give will become in him a spring of water welling up to eternal life." The woman said to him, "Sir, give me this water, so that I may not be thirsty or have to keep coming here to draw water."

Jesus said to her, "Go call your husband and come back." The woman answered and said to him, "I do not have a husband." Jesus answered her, "You are right in saying, 'I do not have a husband.' For you have had five husbands, and the one you have now is not your husband. What you have said is true." The woman said to him, "Sir, I can see that you are a prophet. Our ancestors worshiped on this mountain; but you people say that the place to worship is in Jerusalem." Jesus said to her, "Believe me, woman, the hour is coming when you will worship the Father neither on this mountain nor in Jerusalem. You people worship what you do not understand; we worship what we understand, because salvation is from the Jews. But the hour is coming, and is now here, when true worshipers will worship the Father in Spirit and truth; and indeed the Father seeks such people to worship him. God is Spirit, and those who worship him must worship in Spirit and truth." The woman said to him, "I know that the Messiah is coming, the one called the Anointed; when he comes, he will tell us everything." Jesus said to her, "I am he, the one who is speaking with you."

At that moment his disciples returned, and were amazed that he was talking with a woman, but still no one said, "What are you looking for?" or "Why are you talking with her?" The woman left her water jar and went into the town and said to the people, "Come see a man who told me everything I have done. Could he possibly be the Messiah?" They went out of the town and came to him. Meanwhile, the disciples urged him, "Rabbi, eat." But he said to them, "I have food to eat of which you do not know." So the disciples said to one another, "Could someone have brought him something to eat?" Jesus said to them, "My food is to do the will of the one who sent me and to finish his work. Do you not say, 'In four months the harvest will be here'? I tell you, look up and see the fields ripe for the harvest. The reaper is already receiving his payment and gathering crops for eternal life, so that the sower and reaper can rejoice together. For here the saying is verified that 'One sows and another reaps.' I sent you to reap what you have not worked for; others have done the work, and you are sharing the fruits of their work."

Many of the Samaritans of that town began to believe in him because of the word of the woman who testified, "He told me everything I have done." When the Samaritans came to him, they invited him to stay with them; and he stayed there two days. Many more began to believe in him because of his word, and they said to the woman, "We no longer believe because of your word; for we have heard for ourselves, and we know that this is truly the savior of the world."

PSALM 139:7-12

Where can I go from your spirit?
    from your presence where can I flee?
If I go up to the heavens, you are there;
    if I sink to the nether world, you are present there.
If I take the wings of the dawn,
    if I settle at the farthest limits of the sea,
Even there your hand shall guide me,
    and your right hand hold me fast.
If I say, "Surely the darkness shall hide me,
    and night shall be my light"—
For you darkness itself is not dark,
    and night shines as the day.
    [Darkness and light are the same.]

PROVERBS 29:5-8

The man who flatters his neighbor / is spreading a net under his feet. / The wicked man steps into a snare, / but the just man runs on joyfully. / The just man has a care for the rights of the poor; / the wicked man has no such concern. / Arrogant men set the city ablaze, / but wise men calm the fury.

DECEMBER 6

JOHN 4:43-54

After the two days, he left there for Galilee. For Jesus himself testified that a prophet has no honor in his native place. When he came into Galilee, the Galileans welcomed him, since they had seen all he had done in Jerusalem at the feast; for they themselves had gone to the feast.

Then he returned to Cana in Galilee, where he had made the water wine. Now there was a royal official whose son was ill in Capernaum. When he heard that Jesus had arrived in Galilee from Judea, he went to him and asked him to come down and heal his son, who was near death. Jesus said to him, "Unless you people see signs and wonders, you will not believe." The royal official said to him, "Sir, come down before my child dies." Jesus said to him, "You may go; your son will live." The man believed what Jesus said to him and left. While he was on his way back, his slaves met him and told him that his boy would live. He asked them when he began to recover. They told him, "The fever left him yesterday, about one in the afternoon." The father realized that just at that time Jesus had said to him, "Your son will live," and he and his whole household came to believe. [Now] this was the second sign Jesus did when he came to Galilee from Judea.

PSALM 139:13-18

Truly you have formed my
    inmost being;
  you knit me in my mother's
    womb.
I give you thanks that I am
    fearfully, wonderfully made;
  wonderful are your works.
My soul also you knew full well;
  nor was my frame unknown to
    you
When I was made in secret,
  when I was fashioned in the
    depths of the earth.
Your eyes have seen my actions;
  in your book they are all
    written;
  my days were limited before
    one of them existed.
How weighty are your designs,
  O God;
  how vast the sum of them!
Were I to recount them, they
    would outnumber the sands;
  did I reach the end of them, I
    should still be with you.

PROVERBS 29:9-11

If a wise man disputes with a fool, / he may rage or laugh but can have no peace. / Bloodthirsty men hate the honest man, / but the upright show concern for his life. / The fool gives vent to all his anger; / but by biding his time, the wise man calms it.

DECEMBER 7

JOHN 5:1-18

After this, there was a feast of the Jews, and Jesus went up to Jerusalem. Now there is in Jerusalem at the Sheep [Gate] a pool called in Hebrew Bethesda, with five porticoes. In these lay a large number of ill, blind, lame, and crippled. One man was there who had been ill for thirty-eight years. When Jesus saw him lying there and knew that he had been ill for a long time, he said to him, "Do you want to be well?" The sick man answered him, "Sir, I have no one to put me into the pool when the water is stirred up; while I am on my way, someone else gets down there before me." Jesus said to him, "Rise, take up your mat, and walk." Immediately the man became well, took up his mat, and walked.

Now that day was a sabbath. So the Jews said to the man who was cured, "It is the sabbath, and it is not lawful for you to carry your mat." He answered them, "The man who made me well told me, 'Take up your mat and walk.' " They asked him, "Who is the man who told you, 'Take it up and walk'?" The man who was healed did not know who it was, for Jesus had slipped away, since there was a crowd there. After this Jesus found him in the temple area and said to him, "Look, you are well; do not sin any more, so that nothing worse may happen to you." The man went and told the Jews that Jesus was the one who had made him well. Therefore, the Jews began to persecute Jesus because he did this on a sabbath. But Jesus answered them, "My Father is at work until now, so I am at work." For this reason the Jews tried all the more to kill him, because he not only broke the sabbath but he also called God his own father, making himself equal to God.

PSALM 139:19-24

If only you would destroy the
    wicked, O God,
  and the men of blood were to
    depart from me!
Wickedly they invoke your name;
  your foes swear faithless oaths.
Do I not hate, O LORD, those who
    hate you?
  Those who rise up against you
    do I not loathe?
With a deadly hatred I hate them;
  they are my enemies.
Probe me, O God, and know my
    heart;
  try me, and know my
    thoughts;
See if my way is crooked,
  and lead me in the way of old.

PROVERBS 29:12-14

If a ruler listens to lying words, / his servants all become wicked. / The poor and the oppressor have a common bond: / the Lord gives light to the eyes of both. / If a king is zealous for the rights of the poor, / his throne stands firm forever.

DECEMBER 8

JOHN 5:19-47

Jesus answered and said to them, "Amen, amen, I say to you, a son cannot do anything on his own, but only what he sees his father doing; for what he does, his son will do also. For the Father loves his Son and shows him everything that he himself does, and he will show him greater works than these, so that you may be amazed. For just as the Father raises the dead and gives life, so also does the Son give life to whomever he wishes. Nor does the Father judge anyone, but he has given all judgment to his Son, so that all may honor the Son just as they honor the Father. Whoever does not honor the Son does not honor the Father who sent him. Amen, amen, I say to you, whoever hears my word and believes in the one who sent me has eternal life and will not come to condemnation, but has passed from death to life. Amen, amen, I say to you, the hour is coming and is now here when the dead will hear the voice of the Son of God, and those who hear will live. For just as the Father has life in himself, so also he gave to his Son the possession of life in himself. And he gave him power to exercise judgment, because he is the Son of Man. Do not be amazed at this, because the hour is coming in which all who are in the tombs will hear his voice and will come out, those who have done good deeds to the resurrection of life, but those who have done wicked deeds to the resurrection of condemnation.

"I cannot do anything on my own; I judge as I hear, and my judgment is just, because I do not seek my own will but the will of the one who sent me.

"If I testify on my own behalf, my testimony cannot be verified. But there is another who testifies on my behalf, and I know that the testimony he gives on my behalf is true. You sent emissaries to John, and he testified to the truth. I do not accept testimony from a human being, but I say this so that you may be saved. He was a burning and shining lamp, and for a while you were content to rejoice in his light. But I have testimony greater than John's. The works that the Father gave me to accomplish, these works that I perform testify on my behalf that the Father has sent me. Moreover, the Father who sent me has testified on my behalf. But you have never heard his voice nor seen his form, and you do not have his word remaining in you, because you do not believe in the one whom he has sent. You search the scriptures, because you think you have eternal life through them; even they testify on my behalf. But you do not want to come to me to have life.

"I do not accept human praise; moreover, I know that you do not have the love of God in you. I came in the name of my Father, but you do not accept me; yet if another comes in his own name, you will accept him. How can you believe, when you accept praise from one another and do not seek the praise that comes from the only God? Do not think that I will accuse you before the Father: the one who will accuse you is Moses, in whom you have placed your hope. For if you had believed Moses, you would have believed me, because he wrote about me. But if you do not believe his writings, how will you believe my words?"

PSALM 140:1-8

For the leader. A psalm of David.
Deliver me, O LORD, from evil men;
  preserve me from violent men,
From those who devise evil in their hearts,
  and stir up wars every day.
They make their tongues sharp as those of serpents;
  the venom of asps is under their lips.

Save me, O LORD, from the hands of the wicked;
  preserve me from violent men
Who plan to trip up my feet—
  the proud who have hidden a trap for me;
They have spread cords for a net;
  by the wayside they have laid snares for me.
I say to the LORD, you are my God;
  hearken, O LORD, to my voice in supplication.
O God, my Lord, my strength and my salvation;
  you are my helmet in the day of battle!

PROVERBS 29:15-17

The rod of correction gives wisdom, / but a boy left to his whims disgraces his mother. / When the wicked prevail, crime increases; / but their downfall the just will behold. / Correct your son, and he will bring you comfort, / and give delight to your soul.

DECEMBER 9

JOHN 6:1-21

After this, Jesus went across the Sea of Galilee [of Tiberias]. A large crowd followed him, because they saw the signs he was performing on the sick. Jesus went up on the mountain, and there he sat down with his disciples. The Jewish feast of Passover was near. When Jesus raised his eyes and saw that a large crowd was coming to him, he said to Philip, "Where can we buy enough food for them to eat?" He said this to test him, because he himself knew what he was going to do. Philip answered him, "Two hundred days' wages worth of food would not be enough for each of them to have a little [bit]." One of his disciples, Andrew, the brother of Simon Peter, said to him, "There is a boy here who has five barley loaves and two fish; but what good are these for so many?" Jesus said, "Have the people recline." Now there was a great deal of grass in that place. So the men reclined, about five thousand in number. Then Jesus took the loaves, gave thanks, and distributed them to those who were reclining, and also as much of the fish as they wanted. When they had had their fill, he said to his disciples, "Gather the fragments left over, so that nothing will be wasted." So they collected them, and filled twelve wicker baskets with fragments from the five barley loaves that had been more than they could eat. When the people saw the sign he had done, they said, "This is truly the Prophet, the one who is to come into the world." Since Jesus knew that they were going to come and carry him off to make him king, he withdrew again to the mountain alone.

When it was evening, his disciples went down to the sea, embarked in a boat, and went across the sea to Capernaum. It had already grown dark, and Jesus had not yet come to them. The sea was stirred up because a strong wind was blowing. When they had rowed about three or four miles, they saw Jesus walking on the sea and coming near the boat, and they began to be afraid. But he said to them, "It is I. Do not be afraid." They wanted to take him into the boat, but the boat immediately arrived at the shore to which they were heading.

PSALM 140:9-14

Grant not, O LORD, the desires of
    the wicked;
  further not their plans.
Those who surround me lift up
    their heads;
  may the mischief which they
    threaten overwhelm them.
May he rain burning coals upon
    them;
  may he cast them into the
    depths, never to rise.
A man of wicked tongue shall not
    abide in the land;
  evil shall abruptly entrap the
    violent man.
I know that the LORD renders
    justice to the afflicted,
    judgment to the poor.
Surely the just shall give thanks
    to your name;
  the upright shall dwell in your
    presence.

PROVERBS 29:18

Without prophecy the people become demoralized; / but happy is he who keeps the law.

DECEMBER 10

JOHN 6:22-40

The next day, the crowd that remained across the sea saw that there had been only one boat there, and that Jesus had not gone along with his disciples in the boat, but only his disciples had left. Other boats came from Tiberias near the place where they had eaten the bread when the Lord gave thanks. When the crowd saw that neither Jesus nor his disciples were there, they themselves got into boats and came to Capernaum looking for Jesus. And when they found him across the sea they said to him, "Rabbi, when did you get here?" Jesus answered them and said, "Amen, amen, I say to you, you are looking for me not because you saw signs but because you ate the loaves and were filled. Do not work for food that perishes but for the food that endures for eternal life, which the Son of Man will give you. For on him the Father, God, has set his seal." So they said to him, "What can we do to accomplish the works of God?" Jesus answered and said to them, "This is the work of God, that you believe in the one he sent." So they said to him, "What sign can you do, that we may see and believe in you? What can you do? Our ancestors ate manna in the desert, as it is written:

> 'He gave them bread from
> heaven to eat.' "

So Jesus said to them, "Amen, amen, I say to you, it was not Moses who gave the bread from heaven; my Father gives you the true bread from heaven. For the bread of God is that which comes down from heaven and gives life to the world."

So they said to him, "Sir, give us this bread always." Jesus said to them, "I am the bread of life; whoever comes to me will never hunger, and whoever believes in me will never thirst. But I told you that although you have seen [me], you do not believe. Everything that the Father gives me will come to me, and I will not reject anyone who comes to me, because I came down from heaven not to do my own will but the will of the one who sent me. And this is the will of the one who sent me, that I should not lose anything of what

he gave me, but that I should raise it [on] the last day. For this is the will of my Father, that everyone who sees the Son and believes in him may have eternal life, and I shall raise him [on] the last day."

PSALM 141:1-7

A psalm of David.
O LORD, to you I call; hasten to
    me;
    hearken to my voice when I call
        upon you.
Let my prayer come like incense
    before you;
    the lifting up of my hands like
        the evening sacrifice.
O LORD, set a watch before my
    mouth,
    a guard at the door of my lips.
Let not my heart incline to the
    evil
    of engaging in deeds of
        wickedness
With men who are evildoers;
    and let me not partake of their
        dainties.
Let the just man strike me; that is
    kindness;
    let him reprove me; it is oil for
        the head,
Which my head shall not refuse,
    but I will still pray under these
        afflictions.
Their judges were cast down over
    the crag,
    and they heard how pleasant
        were my words.
As when a plowman breaks
    furrows in the field,
    so their bones are strewn by
        the edge of the nether world.

PROVERBS 29:19-20

By words no servant can be trained; / for he understands what is said, but obeys not. / Do you see a man hasty in his words? / More can be hoped for from a fool!

JOHN 6:41-71

The Jews murmured about him because he said, "I am the bread that came down from heaven," and they said, "Is this not Jesus, the son of Joseph? Do we not know his father and mother? Then how can he say, 'I have come down from heaven'?" Jesus answered and said to them, "Stop murmuring among yourselves. No one can come to me unless the Father who sent me draw him, and I will raise him on the last day. It is written in the prophets:

'They shall all be taught by God.'

Everyone who listens to my Father and learns from him comes to me. Not that anyone has seen the Father except the one who is from God; he has seen the Father. Amen, amen, I say to you, whoever believes has eternal life. I am the bread of life. Your ancestors ate the manna in the desert, but they died; this is the bread that comes down from heaven so that one may eat it and not die. I am the living bread that came down from heaven; whoever eats this bread will live forever; and the bread that I will give is my flesh for the life of the world."

The Jews quarreled among themselves, saying, "How can this man give us [his] flesh to eat?" Jesus said to them, "Amen, amen, I say to you, unless you eat the flesh of the Son of Man and drink his blood, you do not have life within you. Whoever eats my flesh and drinks my blood has eternal life, and I will raise him on the last day. For my flesh is true food, and my blood is true drink. Whoever eats my flesh and drinks my blood remains in me and I in him. Just as the living Father sent me and I have life because of the Father, so also the one who feeds on me will have life because of me. This is the bread that came down from heaven. Unlike your ancestors who ate and still died, whoever eats this bread will live forever." These things he said while teaching in the synagogue in Capernaum.

Then many of his disciples who were listening said, "This saying is hard; who can accept it?" Since Jesus knew that his disciples were murmuring about this, he said to them, "Does this shock you? What if you were to see the Son of Man ascending to where he was before? It is the spirit that gives life, while the flesh is of no avail. The words I have spoken to you are spirit and life. But there are some of you who do not believe." Jesus knew from the beginning the ones who would not believe and the one who would betray him. And he said, "For this reason I have told you that no one can come to me unless it is granted him by my Father."

As a result of this, many [of] his disciples returned to their former way of life and no longer accompanied him. Jesus then said to the Twelve, "Do you also want to leave?" Simon Peter answered him, "Master, to whom shall we go? You have the words of eternal life. We have come to believe and are convinced that you are the Holy One of God." Jesus answered them, "Did I not choose you twelve? Yet is not one of you a devil?" He was referring to Judas, son of Simon the Iscariot; it was he who would betray him, one of the Twelve.

PSALM 141:8-10

For toward you, O GOD, my
Lord, my eyes are turned;
in you I take refuge; strip me
not of life.
Keep me from the trap they have
set for me,
and from the snares of
evildoers.
Let all the wicked fall, each into
his own net,
while I escape.

PROVERBS 29:21-22

If a man pampers his servant from childhood, / he will turn out to be stubborn. / An ill-tempered man stirs up disputes, / and a hotheaded man is the cause of many sins.

DECEMBER 12

JOHN 7:1-24

After this, Jesus moved about within Galilee; but he did not wish to travel in Judea, because the Jews were trying to kill him. But the Jewish feast of Tabernacles was near. So his brothers said to him, "Leave here and go to Judea, so that your disciples also may see the works you are doing. No one works in secret if he wants to be known publicly. If you do these things, manifest yourself to the world." For his brothers did not believe in him. So Jesus said to them, "My time is not yet here, but the time is always right for you. The world cannot hate you, but it hates me, because I testify to it that its works are evil. You go up to the feast. I am not going up to this feast, because my time has not yet been fulfilled." After he had said this, he stayed on in Galilee.

But when his brothers had gone up to the feast, he himself also went up, not openly but [as it were] in secret. The Jews were looking for him at the feast and saying, "Where is he?" And there was considerable murmuring about him in the crowds. Some said, "He is a good man," [while] others said, "No; on the contrary, he misleads the crowd." Still, no one spoke openly about him because they were afraid of the Jews.

When the feast was already half over, Jesus went up into the temple area and began to teach. The Jews were amazed and said, "How does he know scripture without having studied?" Jesus answered them and said, "My teaching is not my own but is from the one who sent me. Whoever chooses to do his will shall know whether my teaching is from God or whether I speak on my own. Whoever speaks on his own seeks his own glory, but whoever seeks the glory of the one who sent him is truthful, and there is no wrong in him. Did not Moses give you the law? Yet none of you keeps the law. Why are you trying to kill me?" The crowd answered, "You are possessed! Who is trying to kill you?" Jesus answered and said to them, "I performed one work and all of you are amazed because of it. Moses gave you circumcision—not that it came from Moses but rather from the patriarchs—and you circumcise a man on the sabbath. If a man can receive circumcision on a sabbath so that the law of Moses may not be broken, are you angry with me because I made a whole person well on a sabbath? Stop judging by appearances, but judge justly."

PSALM 142:1-8

A maskil of David. A prayer when he
was in the cave.

With a loud voice I cry out to the
LORD;
  with a loud voice I beseech the
LORD.
My complaint I pour out before
him;

before him I lay bare my
distress.
When my spirit is faint within
me,
  you know my path.
In the way along which I walk
  they have hid a trap for me.
I look to the right to see,
  but there is no one who pays
me heed.
I have lost all means of escape;
  there is no one who cares for
my life.
I cry out to you, O LORD;
  I say, "You are my refuge,
my portion in the land of the
living."
Attend to my cry,
  for I am brought low indeed.
Rescue me from my persecutors,
  for they are too strong for me.
Lead me forth from prison,
  that I may give thanks to your
name.
The just shall gather around me
  when you have been good to
me.

PROVERBS 29:23

Man's pride causes his humiliation, / but he who is humble of spirit obtains
honor.

DECEMBER 13

JOHN 7:25-53

So some of the inhabitants of Jerusalem said, "Is he not the one they are trying to kill? And look, he is speaking openly and they say nothing to him. Could the authorities have realized that he is the Messiah? But we know where he is from. When the Messiah comes, no one will know where he is from." So Jesus cried out in the temple area as he was teaching and said, "You know me and also know where I am from. Yet I did not come on my own, but the one who sent me, whom you do not know, is true. I know him, because I am from him, and he sent me." So they tried to arrest him, but no one laid a hand upon him, because his hour had not yet come. But many of the crowd began to believe in him, and said, "When the Messiah comes, will he perform more signs than this man has done?"

The Pharisees heard the crowd murmuring about him to this effect, and the chief priests and the Pharisees sent guards to arrest him. So Jesus said, "I will be with you only a little while longer, and then I will go to the one who sent me. You will look for me but not find [me], and where I am you cannot come." So the Jews said to one another, "Where is he going that we will not find him? Surely he is not going to the dispersion among the Greeks to teach the Greeks, is he? What is the meaning of his saying, 'You will look for me and not find [me], and where I am you cannot come'?"

On the last and greatest day of the feast, Jesus stood up and exclaimed, "Let anyone who thirsts come to me and drink. Whoever believes in me, as scripture says:

'Rivers of living water will flow from within him.' "

He said this in reference to the Spirit that those who came to believe in him were to receive. There was, of course, no Spirit yet, because Jesus had not yet been glorified.

Some in the crowd who heard these words said, "This is truly the Prophet." Others said, "This is the Messiah." But others said, "The Messiah will not come from Galilee, will he? Does not scripture say that the Messiah will be of David's family and come from Bethlehem, the village where David lived?" So a division occurred in the crowd because of him. Some of them even wanted to arrest him, but no one laid hands on him.

So the guards went to the chief priests and Pharisees, who asked them, "Why did you not bring him?" The guards answered, "Never before has anyone spoken like this one." So the Pharisees answered them, "Have you also been deceived? Have any of the authorities or the Pharisees believed in him? But this crowd, which does not know the law, is accursed." Nicodemus, one of their members who had come to him earlier, said to them, "Does our law condemn a person before it first hears him and finds out what he is doing?" They answered and said to him, "You are not from Galilee also, are you? Look and see that no prophet arises from Galilee."

PSALM 143:1-6

A psalm of David.
O LORD, hear my prayer;
   hearken to my pleading in your
      faithfulness;
   in your justice answer me.
And enter not into judgment
      with your servant,
   for before you no living man is
      just.
For the enemy pursues me;
   he has crushed my life to the
      ground;
   he has left me dwelling in the
      dark, like those long dead.
And my spirit is faint within me,
   my heart within me is
      appalled.
I remember the days of old;
   I meditate on all your doings,
      the works of your hand I
      ponder.
I stretch out my hands to you;
   my soul thirsts for you like
      parched land.

The accomplice of a thief is his own enemy: / he hears himself put under a curse, / yet discloses nothing. / The fear of man brings a snare, / but he who trusts in the LORD is safe.

DECEMBER 14

JOHN 8:1-30

[Then each went to his own house, while Jesus went to the Mount of Olives. But early in the morning he arrived again in the temple area, and all the people started coming to him, and he sat down and taught them. Then the scribes and the Pharisees brought a woman who had been caught in adultery and made her stand in the middle. They said to him, "Teacher, this woman was caught in the very act of committing adultery. Now in the law, Moses commanded us to stone such women. So what do you say?" They said this to test him, so that they could have some charge to bring against him. Jesus bent down and began to write on the ground with his finger. But when they continued asking him, he straightened up and said to them, "Let the one among you who is without sin be the first to throw a stone at her." Again he bent down and wrote on the ground. And in response, they went away one by one, beginning with the elders. So he was left alone with the woman before him. Then Jesus straightened up and said to her, "Woman, where are they? Has no one condemned you?" She replied, "No one, sir." Then Jesus said, "Neither do I condemn you. Go, [and] from now on do not sin any more."]

Jesus spoke to them again, saying, "I am the light of the world. Whoever follows me will not walk in darkness, but will have the light of life." So the Pharisees said to him, "You testify on your own behalf, so your testimony cannot be verified." Jesus answered and said to them, "Even if I do testify on my own behalf, my testimony can be verified, because I know where I came from and where I am going. But you do not know where I come from or where I am going. You judge by appearances, but I do not judge anyone. And even if I should judge, my judgment is valid, because I am not alone, but it is I and the Father who sent me. Even in your law it is written that the testimony of two men can be verified. I testify on my behalf and so does the Father who sent me." So they said to him, "Where is your father?" Jesus answered, "You know neither me nor my Father. If you knew me, you would know my Father also." He spoke these words while teaching in the treasury in the temple area. But no one arrested him, because his hour had not yet come.

He said to them again, "I am going away and you will look for me, but you will die in your sin. Where I am going you cannot come." So the Jews said, "He is not going to kill himself, is he, because he said, 'Where I am going you cannot come'?" He said to them, "You belong to what is below, I belong to what is above. You belong to this world, but I do not belong to this world. That is why I told you that you will die in your sins. For if you do not believe that I AM, you will die in your sins." So they said to him, "Who are you?" Jesus said to them, "What I told you from the beginning. I have much to say about you in condemnation. But the one who sent me is true, and what I heard from him I tell the world." They did not realize that he was speaking to them of the Father. So Jesus said [to them], "When you lift up the Son of Man, then you will realize that I AM, and that I do nothing on my own, but I say only what the Father taught me. The one who sent me is with me. He has not left me alone, because I always do what is pleasing to him." Because he spoke this way, many came to believe in him.

lest I become like those who go
    down into the pit.
At dawn let me hear of your
    kindness,
  for in you I trust.
Show me the way in which I
    should walk,
  for to you I lift up my soul.
Rescue me from my enemies, O
    LORD,
  for in you I hope.
Teach me to do your will,
  for you are my God.
May your good spirit guide me
  on level ground.
For your name's sake, O LORD,
    preserve me;
  in your justice free me from
    distress,
And in your kindness destroy my
    enemies;
  bring to nought all my foes,
  for I am your servant.

PSALM 143:7-12

Hasten to answer me, O LORD,
  for my spirit fails me.
Hide not your face from me

PROVERBS 29:26-27

Many curry favor with the ruler, / but the rights of each are from the LORD. / The evildoer is an abomination to the just, / and he who walks uprightly is an abomination to the wicked.

DECEMBER 15

JOHN 8:31-59

Jesus then said to those Jews who believed in him, "If you remain in my word, you will truly be my disciples, and you will know the truth, and the truth will set you free." They answered him, "We are descendants of Abraham and have never been enslaved to anyone. How can you say, 'You will become free'?" Jesus answered them, "Amen,

amen, I say to you, everyone who commits sin is a slave of sin. A slave does not remain in a household forever, but a son always remains. So if a son frees you, then you will truly be free. I know that you are descendants of Abraham. But you are trying to kill me, because my word has no room among you. I tell you what I have seen in the Father's presence; then do what you have heard from the Father."

They answered and said to him, "Our father is Abraham." Jesus said to them, "If you were Abraham's children, you would be doing the works of Abraham. But now you are trying to kill me, a man who has told you the truth that I heard from God; Abraham did not do this. You are doing the works of your father!" [So] they said to him, "We are not illegitimate. We have one Father, God." Jesus said to them, "If God were your Father, you would love me, for I came from God and am here; I did not come on my own, but he sent me. Why do you not understand what I am saying? Because you cannot bear to hear my word. You belong to your father the devil and you willingly carry out your father's desires. He was a murderer from the beginning and does not stand in truth, because there is no truth in him. When he tells a lie, he speaks in character, because he is a liar and the father of lies. But because I speak the truth, you do not believe me. Can any of you charge me with sin? If I am telling the truth, why do you not believe me? Whoever belongs to God hears the words of God; for this reason you do not listen, because you do not belong to God."

The Jews answered and said to him, "Are we not right in saying that you are a Samaritan and are possessed?" Jesus answered, "I am not possessed; I honor my Father, but you dishonor me. I do not seek my own glory; there is one who seeks it and he is the one who judges. Amen, amen, I say to you, whoever keeps my word will never see death." [So] the Jews said to him, "Now we are sure that you are possessed. Abraham died, as did the prophets, yet you say, 'Whoever keeps my word will never taste death.' Are you greater than our father Abraham, who died? Or the prophets, who died? Who do you make yourself out to be?" Jesus answered, "If I glorify myself, my glory is worth nothing; but it is my Father who glorifies me, of whom you say, 'He is our God.' You do not know him, but I know him. And if I should say that I do not know him, I would be a liar like you. But I do know him and I keep his word. Abraham your father rejoiced to see my day; he saw it and was glad." So the Jews said to him, "You are not yet fifty years old and you have seen Abraham?" Jesus said to them, "Amen, amen, I say to you, before Abraham came to be, I AM." So they picked up stones to throw at him; but Jesus hid and went out of the temple area.

PSALM 144:1-2

Of David.
Blessed be the LORD, my rock,
    who trains my hands for battle,
        my fingers for war;
My refuge and my fortress,
    my stronghold, my deliverer,
My shield, in whom I trust,
    who subdues peoples under
        me.

PROVERBS 30:1-4

The words of Agur, son of Jakeh the Massaite: / The pronouncement of mortal man: "I am not God; / I am not God, that I should prevail. / Why, I am the most stupid of men, / and have not even human intelligence; / Neither have I learned wisdom, / nor have I the knowledge of the Holy One. / Who has gone up to heaven and come down again—/ who has cupped the wind in his hands? / Who has bound up the waters in a cloak—/ who has marked out all the ends of the earth? / What is his name, what is his son's name, / if you know it?"

DECEMBER 16

JOHN 9:1-41

As he passed by he saw a man blind from birth. His disciples asked him, "Rabbi, who sinned, this man or his parents, that he was born blind?" Jesus answered, "Neither he nor his parents sinned; it is so that the works of God might be made visible through him. We have to do the works of the one who sent me while it is day. Night is coming when no one can work. While I am in the world, I am the light of the world." When he had said this, he spat on the ground and made clay with the saliva, and smeared the clay on his eyes, and said to him, "Go wash in the Pool of Siloam" (which means Sent). So he went and washed, and came back able to see.

His neighbors and those who had seen him earlier as a beggar said, "Isn't this the one who used to sit and beg?" Some said, "It is," but others said, "No, he just looks like him." He said, "I am." So they said to him, "[So] how were your eyes opened?" He replied, "The man called Jesus made clay and anointed my eyes and told me, 'Go to Siloam and wash.' So I went there and washed and was able to see." And they said to

him, "Where is he?" He said, "I don't know."

They brought the one who was once blind to the Pharisees. Now Jesus had made clay and opened his eyes on a sabbath. So then the Pharisees also asked him how he was able to see. He said to them, "He put clay on my eyes, and I washed, and now I can see." So some of the Pharisees said, "This man is not from God, because he does not keep the sabbath." [But] others said, "How can a sinful man do such signs?" And there was a division among them. So they said to the blind man again, "What do you have to say about him, since he opened your eyes?" He said, "He is a prophet."

Now the Jews did not believe that he had been blind and gained his sight until they summoned the parents of the one who had gained his sight. They asked them, "Is this your son, who you say was born blind? How does he now see?" His parents answered and said, "We know that this is our son and that he was born blind. We do not know how he sees now, nor do we know who opened his eyes. Ask him, he is of age; he can speak for himself." His parents said this because they were afraid of the Jews, for the Jews had already agreed that if anyone acknowledged him as the Messiah, he would be expelled from the synagogue. For this reason his parents said, "He is of age; question him."

So a second time they called the man who had been blind and said to him, "Give God the praise! We know that this man is a sinner." He replied, "If he is a sinner, I do not know. One thing I do know is that I was blind and now I see." So they said to him, "What did he do to you? How did he open your eyes?" He answered them, "I told you already and you did not listen. Why do you want to hear it again? Do you want to become his disciples, too?" They ridiculed him and said, "You are that man's disciple; we are disciples of Moses! We know that God spoke to Moses, but we do not know where this one is from." The man answered and said to them, "This is what is so amazing, that you do not know where he is from, yet he opened my eyes. We know that God does not listen to sinners, but if one is devout and does his will, he listens to him. It is unheard of that anyone ever opened the eyes of a person born blind. If this man were not from God, he would not be able to do anything." They answered and said to him, "You were born totally in sin, and are you trying to teach us?" Then they threw him out.

When Jesus heard that they had thrown him out, he found him and said, "Do you believe in the Son of Man?" He answered and said, "Who is he, sir, that I may believe in him?" Jesus said to him, "You have seen him and the one speaking with you is he." He said, "I do believe, Lord," and he worshiped him. Then Jesus said, "I came into this world for judgment, so that those who do not see might see, and those who do see might become blind."

Some of the Pharisees who were with him heard this and said to him, "Surely we are not also blind, are we?" Jesus said to them, "If you were blind, you would have no sin; but now you are saying, 'We see,' so your sin remains."

PSALM 144:3-8

LORD, what is man, that you notice him;
　the son of man, that you take thought of him?
Man is like a breath;
　his days, like a passing shadow.
Incline your heavens, O LORD, and come down;
　touch the mountains, and they shall smoke;
Flash forth lightning, and put them to flight,
　shoot your arrows, and rout them;
Reach out your hand from on high—
　Deliver me and rescue me from many waters,
　from the hands of aliens,
　Whose mouths swear false promises
　while their right hands are raised in perjury.

PROVERBS 30:5-6

Every word of God is tested; / he is a shield to those who take refuge in him. / Add nothing to his words, / lest he reprove you, and you be exposed as a deceiver.

DECEMBER 17

JOHN 10:1-42

"Amen, amen, I say to you, whoever does not enter a sheepfold through the gate but climbs over elsewhere is a thief and a robber. But whoever enters through the gate is the shepherd of the sheep. The gatekeeper opens it for him, and the sheep hear his voice, as he calls his own sheep by name and leads them out. When he has driven out all his own, he walks ahead of them, and the sheep follow him, because they recognize his voice. But they will not follow a stranger; they will run away from him, because they do not recognize the voice of strangers." Although Jesus used this figure of speech, they did not realize what he was trying to tell them.

So Jesus said again, "Amen, amen, I say to you, I am the gate for the sheep. All who came [before me] are thieves and robbers, but the sheep did not listen to them. I am the gate. Whoever enters through me will be saved, and will come in and go out and find pasture. A thief comes only to steal and slaughter and destroy; I came so that they might have life and have it more abundantly. I am the good shepherd. A good shepherd lays down his life for the sheep. A hired man, who is not a shepherd and whose sheep are not his own, sees a wolf coming and leaves the sheep and runs away, and the wolf catches and scatters them. This is because he works for pay and has no concern for the sheep. I am the good shepherd, and I know mine and mine know me, just as the Father knows me and I know the Father;

and I will lay down my life for the sheep. I have other sheep that do not belong to this fold. These also I must lead, and they will hear my voice, and there will be one flock, one shepherd. This is why the Father loves me, because I lay down my life in order to take it up again. No one takes it from me, but I lay it down on my own. I have power to lay it down, and power to take it up again. This command I have received from my Father."

Again there was a division among the Jews because of these words. Many of them said, "He is possessed and out of his mind; why listen to him?" Others said, "These are not the words of one possessed; surely a demon cannot open the eyes of the blind, can he?"

The feast of the Dedication was then taking place in Jerusalem. It was winter. And Jesus walked about in the temple area on the Portico of Solomon. So the Jews gathered around him and said to him, "How long are you going to keep us in suspense? If you are the Messiah, tell us plainly." Jesus answered them, "I told you and you do not believe. The works I do in my Father's name testify to me. But you do not believe, because you are not among my sheep. My sheep hear my voice; I know them, and they follow me. I give them eternal life, and they shall never perish. No one can take them out of my hand. My Father, who has given them to me, is greater than all, and no one can take them out of the Father's hand. The Father and I are one."

The Jews again picked up rocks to stone him. Jesus answered

them, "I have shown you many good works from my Father. For which of these are you trying to stone me?" The Jews answered him, "We are not stoning you for a good work but for blasphemy. You, a man, are making yourself God." Jesus answered them, "Is it not written in your law, 'I said, "You are gods" '? If it calls them gods to whom the word of God came, and scripture cannot be set aside, can you say that the one whom the Father has consecrated and sent into the world blasphemes because I said, 'I am the Son of God'? If I do not perform my Father's works, do not believe me; but if I perform them, even if you do not believe me, believe the works, so that you may realize [and understand] that the Father is in me and I am in the Father." [Then] they tried again to arrest him; but he escaped from their power.

He went back across the Jordan to the place where John first baptized, and there he remained. Many came to him and said, "John performed no sign, but everything John said about this man was true." And many there began to believe in him.

PSALM 144:9-11

O God, I will sing a new song to
    you;
    with a ten-stringed lyre I will
        chant your praise,
You who give victory to kings,
    and deliver David, your
        servant.
From the evil sword deliver
    me;
    and rescue me from the hands
        of aliens,
Whose mouths swear false
    promises
    while their right hands are
        raised in perjury.

PROVERBS 30:7-9

Two things I ask of you, / deny them not to me before I die; / Put falsehood and lying far from me, / give me neither poverty nor riches; / [provide me only with the food I need;] / Lest, being full, I deny you, / saying, "Who is the Lord?" / Or, being in want, I steal, / and profane the name of my God.

DECEMBER 18

JOHN 11:1-16

Now a man was ill, Lazarus from Bethany, the village of Mary and her sister Martha. Mary was the one who had anointed the Lord with perfumed oil and dried his feet with her hair; it was her brother Lazarus who was ill. So the sisters sent word to him, saying, "Master, the one you love is ill." When Jesus heard this he

said, "This illness is not to end in death, but is for the glory of God, that the Son of God may be glorified through it." Now Jesus loved Martha and her sister and Lazarus. So when he heard that he was ill, he remained for two days in the place where he was. Then after this he said to his disciples, "Let us go back to Judea." The disciples said to him, "Rabbi, the

Jews were just trying to stone you, and you want to go back there?" Jesus answered, "Are there not twelve hours in a day? If one walks during the day, he does not stumble, because he sees the light of this world. But if one walks at night, he stumbles, because the light is not in him." He said this, and then told them, "Our friend Lazarus is asleep, but I am going to awaken him." So the disciples said to him, "Master, if he is asleep, he will be saved." But Jesus was talking about his death, while they thought that he meant ordinary sleep. So then Jesus said to them clearly, "Lazarus has died. And I am glad for you that I was not there, that you may believe. Let us go to him." So Thomas, called Didymus, said to his fellow disciples, "Let us also go to die with him."

PSALM 144:12-15

May our sons be like plants
    well-nurtured in their youth,
Our daughters like wrought
        columns
    such as stand at the corners of
        the temple.
May our garners be full,
    affording every kind of store;
May our sheep be in the
        thousands,
    and increase to myriads in our
        meadows;
    may our oxen be well laden.
May there be no breach in the
        walls, no exile,
    no outcry in our streets.
Happy the people for whom
        things are thus;
    happy the people whose God is
        the LORD.

PROVERBS 30:10

Slander not a servant to his master, / lest he curse you, and you have to pay the penalty.

DECEMBER 19

JOHN 11:17-57

When Jesus arrived, he found that Lazarus had already been in the tomb for four days. Now Bethany was near Jerusalem, only about two miles away. And many of the Jews had come to Martha and Mary to comfort them about their brother. When Martha heard that Jesus was coming, she went to meet him; but Mary sat at home. Martha said to Jesus, "Lord, if you had been here, my brother would not have died. [But] even now I know that whatever you ask of God, God will give you." Jesus said to her, "Your brother will rise." Martha said to him, "I know he will rise, in the resurrection on the last day." Jesus told her, "I am the resurrection and the life; whoever believes in me, even if he dies, will live, and everyone who lives and believes in me will never die. Do you believe this?" She said to him, "Yes, Lord. I have come to believe that you are the Messiah, the Son of God, the one who is coming into the world."

When she had said this, she went and called her sister Mary secretly, saying, "The teacher is here and is asking for you." As soon as she heard this, she rose quickly and went to him. For Jesus had not yet come into the village, but was still where Martha had met him. So when the Jews who were with her in the house comforting her saw Mary get up quickly and go out, they followed her, presuming that she was going to the tomb to weep there. When Mary came to where Jesus was and saw him, she fell at his feet and said to him, "Lord, if you had been here, my brother would not have died." When Jesus saw her weeping and the Jews who had come with her weeping, he became perturbed and deeply troubled, and said, "Where have you laid him?" They said to him, "Sir, come and see." And Jesus wept. So the Jews said, "See how he loved him." But some of them said, "Could not the one who opened the eyes of the blind man have done something so that this man would not have died?"

So Jesus, perturbed again, came to the tomb. It was a cave, and a stone lay across it. Jesus said, "Take away the stone." Martha, the dead man's sister, said to him, "Lord, by now there will be a stench; he has been dead for four days." Jesus said to her, "Did I not tell you that if you believe you will see the glory of God?" So they took away the stone. And Jesus raised his eyes and said, "Father, I

thank you for hearing me. I know that you always hear me; but because of the crowd here I have said this, that they may believe that you sent me." And when he had said this, he cried out in a loud voice, "Lazarus, come out!" The dead man came out, tied hand and foot with burial bands, and his face was wrapped in a cloth. So Jesus said to them, "Untie him and let him go."

Now many of the Jews who had come to Mary and seen what he had done began to believe in him. But some of them went to the Pharisees and told them what Jesus had done. So the chief priests and the Pharisees convened the Sanhedrin and said, "What are we going to do? This man is performing many signs. If we leave him alone, all will believe in him, and the Romans will come and take away both our land and our nation." But one of them, Caiaphas, who was high priest that year, said to them, "You know nothing, nor do you consider that it is better for you that one man should die instead of the people, so that the whole nation may not perish." He did not say this on his own, but since he was high priest for that year, he prophesied that Jesus was going to die for the nation, and not only for the nation, but also to gather into one the dispersed children of God. So from that day on they planned to kill him.

So Jesus no longer walked about in public among the Jews, but he left for the region near the desert, to a town called Ephraim, and there he remained with his disciples.

Now the Passover of the Jews was near, and many went up from the country to Jerusalem before Passover to purify themselves. They looked for Jesus and said to one another as they were in the temple area, "What do you think? That he will not come to the feast?" For the chief priests and the Pharisees had given orders that if anyone knew where he was, he should inform them, so that they might arrest him.

PSALM 145:1-7

Praise. Of David.
I will extol you, O my God and King,
and I will bless your name forever and ever.
Every day will I bless you,
and I will praise your name forever and ever.
Great is the LORD and highly to be praised;
his greatness is unsearchable.
Generation after generation praises your works
and proclaims your might.
They speak of the splendor of your glorious majesty
and tell of your wondrous works.
They discourse of the power of your terrible deeds
and declare your greatness.
They publish the fame of your abundant goodness
and joyfully sing of your justice.

PROVERBS 30:11-14

There is a group of people that curses its father, / and blesses not its mother. / There is a group that is pure in its own eyes, / yet is not purged of its filth. / There is a group—how haughty their eyes! / how overbearing their glance! / There is a group whose incisors are swords, / whose teeth are knives, / Devouring the needy from the earth, / and the poor from among men.

DECEMBER 20

JOHN 12:1-19

Six days before Passover Jesus came to Bethany, where Lazarus was, whom Jesus had raised from the dead. They gave a dinner for him there, and Martha served, while Lazarus was one of those reclining at table with him. Mary took a liter of costly perfumed oil made from genuine aromatic nard and anointed the feet of Jesus and dried them with her hair; the house was filled with the fragrance of the oil. Then Judas the Iscariot, one [of] his disciples, and the one who would betray him, said, "Why was this oil not sold for three hundred days' wages and given to the poor?" He said this not because he cared about the poor but because he was a thief and held the money bag and used to steal the contributions. So Jesus said, "Leave her alone. Let her keep this for the day of my burial. You always have the poor with you, but you do not always have me."

[The] large crowd of the Jews found out that he was there and came, not only because of Jesus, but also to see Lazarus, whom he had raised from the dead. And the chief priests plotted to kill

Lazarus too, because many of the Jews were turning away and believing in Jesus because of him.

On the next day, when the great crowd that had come to the feast heard that Jesus was coming to Jerusalem, they took palm branches and went out to meet him, and cried out:

"Hosanna!
Blessed is he who comes in the name of the Lord,
[even] the king of Israel."

Jesus found an ass and sat upon it, as is written:

"Fear no more, O daughter Zion;
see, your king comes, seated upon an ass's colt."

His disciples did not understand this at first, but when Jesus had been glorified they remembered that these things were written about him and that they had done this for him. So the crowd that was with him when he called Lazarus from the tomb and raised him from death continued to testify. This was [also] why the crowd went to meet him, because they heard that he had done this sign. So the Pharisees said to one another, "You see that you are gaining nothing. Look, the whole world has gone after him."

PSALM 145:8-13

The LORD is gracious and
    merciful,
    slow to anger and of great
      kindness.
The LORD is good to all
    and compassionate toward all
      his works.
Let all your works give you
    thanks, O LORD,
    and let your faithful ones bless
      you.
Let them discourse of the glory of
    your kingdom
    and speak of your might,
Making known to men your
    might
    and the glorious splendor of
      your kingdom.
Your kingdom is a kingdom for
    all ages,
    and your dominion endures
      through all generations.
The LORD is faithful in all his
    words
    and holy in all his works.

PROVERBS 30:15-16

The two daughters of the leech are, "Give, Give." / Three things are never satisfied, / four never say, "Enough!" / The nether world, and the barren womb; / the earth, that is never saturated with water, / and fire, that never says, "Enough!"

DECEMBER 21

JOHN 12:20-50

Now there were some Greeks among those who had come up to worship at the feast. They came to Philip, who was from Bethsaida in Galilee, and asked him, "Sir, we would like to see Jesus." Philip went and told Andrew; then Andrew and Philip went and told Jesus. Jesus answered them, "The hour has come for the Son of Man to be glorified. Amen, amen, I say to you, unless a grain of wheat falls to the ground and dies, it remains just a grain of wheat; but if it dies, it produces much fruit. Whoever loves his life loses it, and whoever hates his life in this world will preserve it for eternal life. Whoever serves me must follow me, and where I am, there also will my servant be. The Father will honor whoever serves me.

"I am troubled now. Yet what should I say? 'Father, save me from this hour'? But it was for this purpose that I came to this hour. Father, glorify your name." Then a voice came from heaven, "I have glorified it and will glorify it again." The crowd there heard it and said it was thunder; but others said, "An angel has spoken to him." Jesus answered and said, "This voice did not come for my sake but for yours. Now is the time of judgment on this world; now the ruler of this world will be driven out. And when I am lifted up from the earth, I will draw everyone to myself." He said this indicating the kind of death he would die. So the crowd answered him, "We have heard from the law that the Messiah remains forever. Then how can you say that the Son of Man must be lifted up? Who is this Son of Man?" Jesus said to them, "The light will be among you only a little while. Walk while you have the light, so that darkness may not overcome you. Whoever walks in the dark does not know where he is going. While you have the light, believe in the light,

so that you may become children of the light."

After he had said this, Jesus left and hid from them. Although he had performed so many signs in their presence they did not believe in him, in order that the word which Isaiah the prophet spoke might be fulfilled:

"Lord, who has believed our
    preaching,
    to whom has the might of
    the Lord been revealed?"

For this reason they could not believe, because again Isaiah said:

"He blinded their eyes
    and hardened their heart,
so that they might not see with
    their eyes
    and understand with their
    heart and be converted,
and I would heal them."

Isaiah said this because he saw his glory and spoke about him. Nevertheless, many, even among the authorities, believed in him, but because of the Pharisees they did not acknowledge it openly in order not to be expelled from the synagogue. For they preferred human praise to the glory of God.

Jesus cried out and said, "Whoever believes in me believes not only in me but also in the one who sent me, and whoever sees me sees the one who sent me. I came into the world as light, so that everyone who believes in me might not remain in darkness. And if anyone hears my words and does not observe them, I do not condemn him, for I did not come to condemn the world but to save the world. Whoever rejects me and does not accept my words has something to judge him: the word that I spoke, it will condemn him on the last day, because I did not speak on my own, but the Father who sent me commanded me what to say and speak. And I know that his commandment is eternal life. So what I say, I say as the Father told me."

PSALM 145:14-16
The LORD lifts up all who are
    falling

and raises up all who are
    bowed down.
The eyes of all look hopefully to
    you,
    and you give them their food in
      due season;
You open your hand
    and satisfy the desire of every
      living thing.

PROVERBS 30:17
The eye that mocks a father, / or scorns an aged mother, / Will be plucked out by the ravens in the valley; / the young eagles will devour it.

DECEMBER 22

JOHN 13:1-38

Before the feast of Passover, Jesus knew that his hour had come to pass from this world to the Father. He loved his own in the world and he loved them to the end. The devil had already induced Judas, son of Simon the Iscariot, to hand him over. So, during supper, fully aware that the Father had put everything into his power and that he had come from God and was returning to God, he rose from supper and took off his outer garments. He took a towel and tied it around his waist. Then he poured water into a basin and began to wash the disciples' feet and dry them with the towel around his waist. He came to Simon Peter, who said to him, "Master, are you going to wash my feet?" Jesus answered and said to him, "What I am doing, you do not understand now, but you will understand later." Peter said to him, "You will never wash my

feet." Jesus answered him, "Unless I wash you, you will have no inheritance with me." Simon Peter said to him, "Master, then not only my feet, but my hands and head as well." Jesus said to him, "Whoever has bathed has no need except to have his feet washed, for he is clean all over; so you are clean, but not all." For he knew who would betray him; for this reason, he said, "Not all of you are clean."

So when he had washed their feet [and] put his garments back on and reclined at table again, he said to them, "Do you realize what I have done for you? You call me 'teacher' and 'master,' and rightly so, for indeed I am. If I, therefore, the master and teacher, have washed your feet, you ought to wash one another's feet. I have given you a model to follow, so that as I have done for you, you should also do. Amen, amen, I say to you, no slave is greater than his master nor any messenger greater than the one who sent him. If you understand this, blessed are you if you do it. I am not speaking of all of you. I know those whom I have chosen. But so that the scripture might be fulfilled, 'The one who ate my food has raised his heel against me.' From now on I am telling you before it happens, so that when it happens you may believe that I AM. Amen, amen, I say to you, whoever receives the one I send receives me, and whoever receives me receives the one who sent me."

When he had said this, Jesus was deeply troubled and testified, "Amen, amen, I say to you, one of you will betray me." The disciples looked at one another, at a loss as to whom he meant. One of his disciples, the one whom Jesus loved, was reclining at Jesus' side. So Simon Peter nodded to him to find out whom he meant. He leaned back against Jesus' chest and said to him, "Master, who is it?" Jesus answered, "It is the one to whom I hand the morsel after I have dipped it." So he dipped the morsel and [took it and] handed it to Judas, son of Simon the Iscariot. After he took the morsel, Satan entered him. So Jesus said to him, "What you are going to do, do quickly." [Now] none of those reclining at table realized why he said this to him. Some thought that since Judas kept the money bag, Jesus had told him, "Buy what we need for the feast," or to give something to the poor. So he took the morsel and left at once. And it was night.

When he had left, Jesus said, "Now is the Son of Man glorified, and God is glorified in him. [If God is glorified in him,] God will also glorify him in himself, and he will glorify him at once. My children, I will be with you only a little while longer. You will look for me, and as I told the Jews, 'Where I go you cannot come,' so now I say it to you. I give you a new commandment: love one another. As I have loved you, so you also should love one another. This is how all will know that you are my disciples, if you have love for one another."

Simon Peter said to him, "Master, where are you going?" Jesus answered [him], "Where I am going, you cannot follow me now, though you will follow later." Peter said to him, "Master, why can't I follow you now? I will lay down my life for you." Jesus answered, "Will you lay down your life for me? Amen, amen, I say to you, the cock will not crow before you deny me three times."

PSALM 145:17-21

The LORD is just in all his ways
　　and holy in all his works.
The LORD is near to all who call
　　upon him,
　　to all who call upon him in
　　　truth.
He fulfills the desire of those who
　　fear him,
　　he hears their cry and saves
　　　them.
The LORD keeps all who love
　　him,
　　but all the wicked he will
　　　destroy.
May my mouth speak the praise
　　of the LORD,
　　and may all flesh bless his holy
　　　name forever and ever.

Three things are too wonderful for me, / yes, four I cannot understand: / The way of an eagle in the air, / the way of a serpent upon a rock, / The way of a ship on the high seas, / and the way of a man with a maiden. / Such is the way of a adulterous woman: / she eats, wipes her mouth, / and says, "I have done no wrong."

DECEMBER 23

JOHN 14:1-31

"Do not let your hearts be troubled. You have faith in God; have faith also in me. In my Father's house there are many dwelling places. If there were not, would I have told you that I am going to prepare a place for you? And if I go and prepare a place for you, I will come back again and take you to myself, so that where I am you also may be. Where [I] am going you know the way." Thomas said to him, "Master, we do not know where you are going; how can we know the way?" Jesus said to him, "I am the way and the truth and the life. No one comes to the Father except through me. If you know me, then you will also know my Father. From now on you do know him and have seen him." Philip said to him, "Master, show us the Father, and that will be enough for us." Jesus said to him, "Have I been with you for so long a time and you still do not know me, Philip? Whoever has seen me has seen the Father. How can you say, 'Show us the Father'? Do you not believe that I am in the Father and the Father is in me? The words that I speak to you I do not speak on my own. The Father who dwells in me is doing his works. Believe me that I am in the Father and the Father is in me, or else, believe because of the works themselves. Amen, amen, I say to you, whoever believes in me will do the works that I do, and will do greater ones than these, because I am going to the Father. And whatever you ask in my name, I will do, so that the Father may be glorified in the Son. If you ask anything of me in my name, I will do it.

"If you love me, you will keep my commandments. And I will ask the Father, and he will give you another Advocate to be with you always, the Spirit of truth, which the world cannot accept, because it neither sees nor knows it. But you know it, because it remains with you, and will be in you. I will not leave you orphans; I will come to you. In a little while the world will no longer see me, but you will see me, because I live and you will live. On that day you will realize that I am in my Father and you are in me and I in you. Whoever has my commandments and observes them is the one who loves me. And whoever loves me will be loved by my Father, and I will love him and reveal myself to him." Judas, not the Iscariot, said to him, "Master, [then] what happened that you will reveal yourself to us and not to the world?" Jesus answered and said to him,

"Whoever loves me will keep my word, and my Father will love him, and we will come to him and make our dwelling with him. Whoever does not love me does not keep my words; yet the word you hear is not mine but that of the Father who sent me.

"I have told you this while I am with you. The Advocate, the holy Spirit that the Father will send in my name—he will teach you everything and remind you of all that [I] told you. Peace I leave with you; my peace I give to you. Not as the world gives do I give it to you. Do not let your hearts be troubled or afraid. You heard me tell you, 'I am going away and I will come back to you.' If you loved me, you would rejoice that I am going to the Father; for the Father is greater than I. And now I have told you this before it happens, so that when it happens you may believe. I will no longer speak much with you, for the ruler of the world is coming. He has no power over me, but the world must know that I love the Father and that I do just as the Father has commanded me. Get up, let us go."

PSALM 146:1-4

Alleluia.
Praise the LORD, O my soul;
    I will praise the LORD all my
        life;
    I will sing praise to my God
        while I live.
Put not your trust in princes,
    in man, in whom there is no
        salvation.
When his spirit departs he
        returns to his earth;
    on that day his plans perish.

PROVERBS 30:21-23

Under three things the earth trembles, / yes, under four it cannot bear up: / Under a slave when he becomes king, / and a fool when he is glutted with food; / Under an odious woman when she is wed, / and a maidservant when she displaces her mistress.

DECEMBER 24

JOHN 15:1-27

"I am the true vine, and my Father is the vine grower. He takes away every branch in me that does not bear fruit, and everyone that does he prunes so that it bears more fruit. You are already pruned because of the word that I spoke to you. Remain in me, as I remain in you. Just as a branch cannot bear fruit on its own unless it remains on the vine, so neither can you unless you remain in me. I am the vine, you are the branches. Whoever remains in me and I in him will bear much fruit, because without me you can do nothing. Anyone who does not remain in me will be thrown out like a branch and wither; people will gather them and throw them into a fire and they will be burned. If you remain in me and my words remain in you, ask for whatever you want and it will be done for you. By this is my Father glorified, that you bear much fruit and become my disciples. As the Father loves me, so I also love you. Remain in my love. If you keep my commandments, you will remain in my love, just as I have kept my Father's commandments and remain in his love.

"I have told you this so that my joy might be in you and your joy might be complete. This is my commandment: love one another as I love you. No one has greater love than this, to lay down one's life for one's friends. You are my friends if you do what I command you. I no longer call you slaves, because a slave does not know what his master is doing. I have called you friends, because I have told you everything I have heard from my Father. It was not you who chose me, but I who chose you and appointed you to go and bear fruit that will remain, so that whatever you ask the Father in my name he may give you. This I command you: love one another.

"If the world hates you, realize that it hated me first. If you belonged to the world, the world would love its own; but because you do not belong to the world, and I have chosen you out of the world, the world hates you. Remember the word I spoke to you, 'No slave is greater than his master.' If they persecuted me, they will also persecute you. If they kept my word, they will also keep yours. And they will do all these things to you on account of my name, because they do not know the one who sent me. If I had not come and spoken to them, they would have no sin; but as it is they have no excuse for their sin. Whoever hates me also hates my Father. If I had not done works among them that no one else ever did, they would not have sin; but as it is, they have seen and hated both me and my Father. But in order that the word written in their law might be fulfilled, 'They hated me without cause.'

"When the Advocate comes whom I will send you from the Father, the Spirit of truth that proceeds from the Father, he will testify to me. And you also testify, because you have been with me from the beginning."

PSALM 146:5-10

Happy he whose help is the God
  of Jacob,
    whose hope is in the LORD, his
      God,
Who made heaven and earth,
    the sea and all that is in them;
Who keeps faith forever,
    secures justice for the
      oppressed,
    gives food to the hungry.
The LORD sets captives free;
    the LORD gives sight to the
      blind.
The LORD raises up those that
    were bowed down;
    the LORD loves the just.
The LORD protects strangers;
    the fatherless and the widow
      he sustains,
    but the way of the wicked he
      thwarts.
The LORD shall reign forever;
    your God, O Zion, through all
      generations. Alleluia.

PROVERBS 30:24-28

Four things are among the smallest on the earth, / and yet are exceedingly wise: / Ants—a species not strong, / yet they store up their food in the summer; / Rock-badgers—a species not mighty, / yet they make their home in the crags; /

Locusts—they have no king, / yet they migrate all in array; / Lizards—you can catch them with your hands, / yet they find their way into kings' palaces.

DECEMBER 25

JOHN 16:1-33

"I have told you this so that you may not fall away. They will expel you from the synagogues; in fact, the hour is coming when everyone who kills you will think he is offering worship to God. They will do this because they have not known either the Father or me. I have told you this so that when their hour comes you may remember that I told you.

"I did not tell you this from the beginning, because I was with you. But now I am going to the one who sent me, and not one of you asks me, 'Where are you going?' But because I told you this, grief has filled your hearts. But I tell you the truth, it is better for you that I go. For if I do not go, the Advocate will not come to you. But if I go, I will send him to you. And when he comes he will convict the world in regard to sin and righteousness and condemnation: sin, because they do not believe in me; righteousness, because I am going to the Father and you will no longer see me; condemnation, because the ruler of this world has been condemned.

"I have much more to tell you, but you cannot bear it now. But when he comes, the Spirit of truth, he will guide you to all truth. He will not speak on his own, but he will speak what he hears, and will declare to you the things that are coming. He will glorify me, because he will take from what is mine and declare it

to you. Everything that the Father has is mine; for this reason I told you that he will take from what is mine and declare it to you.

"A little while and you will no longer see me, and again a little while later and you will see me." So some of his disciples said to one another, "What does this mean that he is saying to us, 'A little while and you will not see me, and again a little while and you will see me,' and 'Because I am going to the Father'?" So they said, "What is this 'little while' [of which he speaks]? We do not know what he means." Jesus knew that they wanted to ask him, so he said to them, "Are you discussing with one another what I said, 'A little while and you will not see me, and again a little while and you will see me'? Amen, amen, I say to you, you will weep and mourn, while the world rejoices; you will grieve, but your grief will become joy. When a woman is in labor, she is in anguish because her hour has arrived; but when she has given birth to a child, she no longer remembers the pain because of her joy that a child has been born into the world. So you also are now in anguish. But I will see you again, and your hearts will rejoice, and no one will take your joy away from you. On that day you will not question me about anything. Amen, amen, I say to you, whatever you ask the Father in my name he will give you. Until now you have not asked anything in my name; ask and you will receive, so that your joy may be complete.

"I have told you this in figures of speech. The hour is coming when I will no longer speak to you in figures but I will tell you clearly about the Father. On that day you will ask in my name, and I do not tell you that I will ask the Father for you. For the Father himself loves you, because you have loved me and have come to believe that I came from God. I came from the Father and have come into the world. Now I am leaving the world and going back to the Father." His disciples said, "Now you are talking plainly, and not in any figure of speech. Now we realize that you know everything and that you do not need to have anyone question you. Because of this we believe that you came from God." Jesus answered them, "Do you believe now? Behold, the hour is coming and has arrived when each of you will be scattered to his own home and you will leave me alone. But I am not alone, because the Father is with me. I have told you this so that you might have peace in me. In the world you will have trouble, but take courage, I have conquered the world."

PSALM 147:1-6

Praise the LORD, for he is good;
   sing praise to our God, for he
     is gracious;
   it is fitting to praise him.
The LORD rebuilds Jerusalem;
   the dispersed of Israel he
     gathers.
He heals the brokenhearted
   and binds up their wounds.
He tells the number of the stars;
   he calls each by name.
Great is our Lord and mighty in
     power:
   to his wisdom there is no limit.
The LORD sustains the lowly;
   the wicked he casts to the
     ground.

PROVERBS 30:29-31

Three things are stately in their stride, / yes, four are stately in their carriage: / The lion, mightiest of beasts, / who retreats before nothing. / The strutting cock, and the he-goat, / and the king at the head of his people.

DECEMBER 26

JOHN 17:1-26

When Jesus had said this, he raised his eyes to heaven and said, "Father, the hour has come. Give glory to your son, so that your son may glorify you, just as you gave him authority over all people, so that he may give eternal life to all you gave him. Now this is eternal life, that they should know you, the only true God, and the one whom you sent, Jesus Christ. I glorified you on earth by accomplishing the work that you gave me to do. Now glorify me, Father, with you, with the glory that I had with you before the world began.

"I revealed your name to those whom you gave me out of the world. They belonged to you, and you gave them to me, and they have kept your word. Now they know that everything you gave me is from you, because the words you gave to me I have given to them, and they accepted them and truly understood that I came from you, and they have believed that you sent me. I pray for them. I do not pray for the world but for the ones you have given me, because they are yours, and everything of mine is yours and everything of yours is mine, and I have been glorified in them. And now I will no longer be in the world, but they are in the world, while I am coming to you. Holy Father, keep them in your name that you have given me, so that they may be one just as we are. When I was with them I protected them in your name that you gave me, and I guarded them, and none of them was lost except the son of destruction, in order that the scripture might be fulfilled. But now I am coming to you. I speak this in the world so that they may share my joy completely. I gave them your word, and the world hated them, because they do not belong to the world any more than I belong to the world. I do not ask that you take them out of the world but that you keep them from the evil one. They do not belong to the world any more than I belong to the world. Consecrate them in the truth. Your word is truth. As you sent me into the world, so I sent them into the world. And I consecrate myself for them, so that they also may be consecrated in truth.

"I pray not only for them, but also for those who will believe in me through their word, so that they may all be one, as you, Father, are in me and I in you, that they also may be in us, that the world may believe that you sent me. And I have given them the glory you gave me, so that they may be one, as we are one, I in them and you in me, that they may be brought to perfection as one, that the world may know that you sent me, and that you loved them even as you loved me. Father, they are your gift to me. I wish that where I am they also may be with me, that they may see my glory that you gave me, because you loved me before the foundation of the world. Righteous Father, the world also does not know you, but I know you, and they know that you sent me. I made known to them your name and I will make it known, that the love with which you loved me may be in them and I in them."

PSALM 147:7-11

Sing to the LORD with
   thanksgiving;
  sing praise with the harp to our
   God,
Who covers the heavens with
   clouds,
  who provides rain for the
   earth;
Who makes grass sprout on the
   mountains
  and herbs for the service of
   men;
Who gives food to the cattle,
  and to the young ravens when
   they cry to him.
In the strength of the steed he
   delights not,
  nor is he pleased with the
   fleetness of men.
The LORD is pleased with those
   who fear him,
  with those who hope for his
   kindness.

PROVERBS 30:32-33

If you have foolishly been proud / or presumptuous—put your hand on your mouth; / For the stirring of milk brings forth curds, / and the stirring of anger brings forth blood.

DECEMBER 27

JOHN 18:1-24

When he ·had said this, Jesus went out with his disciples across the Kidron valley to where there was a garden, into which he and his disciples entered. Judas his betrayer also knew the place, because Jesus had often met there with his disciples. So Judas got a band of soldiers and guards from the chief priests and Pharisees and went there with lanterns, torches, and weapons. Jesus, knowing everything that was going to happen to him, went out and said to them, "Whom are you looking for?" They answered him, "Jesus the Nazorean." He said to them, "I AM." Judas his betrayer was also with them. When he said to them, "I AM," they turned away and fell to the ground. So he again asked them, "Whom are you looking for?" They said, "Jesus the Nazorean." Jesus answered, "I told you that I AM. So if you are looking for me, let these men go." This was to fulfill what he had said, "I have not lost any of those you gave me." Then Simon Peter, who had a sword, drew it, struck the high priest's slave, and cut off his right ear. The slave's name was Malchus. Jesus said to Peter, "Put your sword into its scabbard. Shall I not drin 'k the cup that the Father gave me?"

So the band of soldiers, the tribune, and the Jewish guards seized Jesus, bound him, and brought him to Annas first. He was the father-in-law of Caiaphas, who was high priest that year. It was Caiaphas who had counseled the Jews that it was better that one man should die rather than the people.

Simon Peter and another disciple followed Jesus. Now the other disciple was known to the high priest, and he entered the courtyard of the high priest with Jesus. But Peter stood at the gate outside. So the other disciple, the acquaintance of the high priest, went out and spoke to the gatekeeper and brought Peter in. Then the maid who was the gatekeeper said to Peter, "You are not one of this man's disciples, are you?" He said, "I am not." Now the slaves and the guards were standing around a charcoal fire that they had made, because it was cold, and were warming themselves. Peter was also standing there keeping warm.

The high priest questioned Jesus about his disciples and about his doctrine. Jesus answered him, "I have spoken publicly to the world. I have always taught in a synagogue or in the temple area where all the Jews gather, and in secret I have said nothing. Why ask me? Ask those who heard me what I said to them. They know what I said." When he had said this, one of the temple guards standing there struck Jesus and said, "Is this the way you answer the high priest?" Jesus answered him, "If I have spoken wrongly, testify to the wrong; but if I have spoken rightly, why do you strike me?" Then Annas sent him bound to Caiaphas the high priest.

PSALM 147:12-20

Glorify the LORD, O Jerusalem;
  praise your God, O Zion.
For he has strengthened the bars
    of your gates;
  he has blessed your children
    within you.
He has granted peace in your
    borders;
  with the best of wheat he fills
    you.

He sends forth his command to
    the earth;
  swiftly runs his word!
He spreads snow like wool;
  frost he strews like ashes.
He scatters his hail like crumbs;
  before his cold the waters
    freeze.
He sends his word and melts
    them;
  he lets his breeze blow and the
    waters run.
He has proclaimed his word to
    Jacob,
  his statutes and his ordinances
    to Israel.
He has not done thus for any
    other nation;
  his ordinances he has not made
    known to them. Alleluia.

PROVERBS 31:1-3

The words of Lemuel, king of Massa. / The advice which his mother gave him: / What, my son, my first-born! / what, O son of my womb; / what, O son of my vows! / Give not your vigor to women, / nor your strength to those who ruin kings.

DECEMBER 28

JOHN 18:25-40

Now Simon Peter was standing there keeping warm. And they said to him, "You are not one of his disciples, are you?" He denied it and said, "I am not." One of the slaves of the high priest, a relative of the one whose ear Peter had cut off, said, "Didn't I see you in the garden with him?" Again Peter denied it. And immediately the cock crowed.

Then they brought Jesus from Caiaphas to the praetorium. It was morning. And they them-selves did not enter the praetor-ium, in order not to be defiled so that they could eat the Passover. So Pilate came out to them and said, "What charge do you bring [against] this man?" They an-swered and said to him, "If he were not a criminal, we would not have handed him over to you." At this, Pilate said to them, "Take him yourselves, and judge him ac-cording to your law." The Jews an-swered him, "We do not have the right to execute anyone," in order that the word of Jesus might be fulfilled that he said indicating the kind of death he would die. So Pilate went back into the praetorium and summoned Jesus and said to him, "Are you the King of the Jews?" Jesus answered, "Do you say this on your own or have others told you about me?" Pilate answered, "I am not a Jew, am I? Your own nation and the chief priests handed you over to me. What have you done?" Jesus answered, "My kingdom does not belong to this world. If my kingdom did belong to this world, my attendants [would] be fighting to keep me from being handed over to the Jews. But as it is, my kingdom is not here." So Pilate said to him, "Then you are a king?" Jesus answered, "You say I am a king. For this I was born and for this I came into the world, to testify to the truth. Everyone who belongs to the truth listens to my voice." Pilate said to him, "What is truth?"

When he had said this, he again went out to the Jews and said to them, "I find no guilt in him. But you have a custom that I release one prisoner to you at Passover. Do you want me to release to you the King of the Jews?" They cried out again, "Not this one but Barabbas!" Now Barabbas was a revolutionary.

PSALM 148:1-6

Alleluia.
Praise the LORD from the
    heavens,
    praise him in the heights;
Praise him, all you his angels,
    praise him, all you his hosts.
Praise him, sun and moon;
    praise him, all you shining
    stars.
Praise him, you highest heavens,
    and you waters above the
    heavens.
Let them praise the name of the
    LORD,
    for he commanded and they
    were created;
He established them forever and
    ever;
    he gave them a duty which
    shall not pass away.

PROVERBS 31:4-7

It is not for kings, O Lemuel, / not for kings to drink wine; / strong drink is not for princes! / Lest in drinking they forget what the law decrees, / and violate the rights of all who are in need. / Give strong drink to one who is perishing, / and wine to the sorely depressed; / When they drink, they will forget their misery, / and think no more of their burdens.

DECEMBER 29

JOHN 19:1-42

Then Pilate took Jesus and had him scourged. And the soldiers wove a crown out of thorns and placed it on his head, and clothed him in a purple cloak, and they came to him and said, "Hail, King of the Jews!" And they struck him repeatedly. Once more Pilate went out and said to them, "Look, I am bringing him out to you, so that you may know that I find no guilt in him." So Jesus came out, wearing the crown of thorns and the purple cloak. And he said to them, "Behold, the man!" When the chief priests and the guards saw him they cried out, "Crucify him, crucify him!" Pilate said to them, "Take him yourselves and crucify him. I find no guilt in him." The Jews answered, "We have a law, and according to that law he ought to die, because he made himself the Son of God." Now when Pilate heard this statement, he became even more afraid, and went back into the praetorium and said to Jesus, "Where are you from?" Jesus did not answer him. So Pilate said to him, "Do you not speak to me? Do you not know that I have power to release you and I have power to crucify you?" Jesus answered [him], "You would have no power over me if it had not been given to you from above. For this reason the one who handed me over to you has the greater sin." Consequently, Pilate tried to release him; but the Jews cried out, "If you release him, you are not a Friend of Caesar. Everyone who makes himself a king opposes Caesar."

When Pilate heard these words he brought Jesus out and seated him on the judge's bench in the place called Stone Pavement, in Hebrew, Gabbatha. It was preparation day for Passover, and it was about noon. And he said to the Jews, "Behold, your king!" They cried out, "Take him away, take him away! Crucify him!" Pilate said to them, "Shall I crucify your king?" The chief priests answered, "We have no king but Caesar." Then he handed him over to them to be crucified.

So they took Jesus, and carrying the cross himself he went out to what is called the Place of the Skull, in Hebrew, Golgotha. There they crucified him, and with him two others, one on either side, with Jesus in the middle. Pilate also had an inscription written and put on the cross. It read, "Jesus the Nazorean, the King of the Jews." Now many of the Jews read this inscription, because the place where Jesus was crucified was near the city; and it was written in Hebrew, Latin, and Greek. So the chief priests of the Jews said to Pilate, "Do not write 'The King of the Jews,' but that he said, 'I am the King of the Jews.' " Pilate answered, "What I have written, I have written."

When the soldiers had crucified Jesus, they took his clothes and divided them into four shares, a share for each soldier. They also took his tunic, but the tunic was seamless, woven in one piece from the top down. So they said to one another, "Let's not tear it, but cast lots for it to see whose it will be," in order that the passage of scripture might be fulfilled [that says]:

"They divided my garments
    among them,
    and for my vesture they cast
    lots."

This is what the soldiers did. Standing by the cross of Jesus were his mother and his mother's sister, Mary the wife of Clopas, and Mary of Magdala. When Jesus saw his mother and the disciple there whom he loved, he said to his mother, "Woman, behold, your son." Then he said to the disciple, "Behold, your mother." And from that hour the disciple took her into his home.

After this, aware that everything was now finished, in order that the scripture might be fulfilled, Jesus said, "I thirst." There was a vessel filled with common wine. So they put a sponge soaked in wine on a sprig of hyssop and put it up to his mouth. When Jesus had taken the wine, he said, "It is finished." And bowing his head, he handed over the spirit.

Now since it was preparation day, in order that the bodies might not remain on the cross on the sabbath, for the sabbath day of that week was a solemn one, the Jews asked Pilate that their legs be broken and they be taken down. So the soldiers came and broke the legs of the first and then of the other one who was crucified with Jesus. But when they came to Jesus and saw that he was already dead, they did not break his legs, but one soldier thrust his lance into his side, and immediately blood and water flowed out. An eyewitness has testified, and his testimony is true; he knows that he is speaking the truth, so that you also may [come to] believe. For this happened so that the scripture passage might be fulfilled:

"Not a bone of it will be broken."

And again another passage says:

"They will look upon him whom they have pierced."

After this, Joseph of Arimathea, secretly a disciple of Jesus for fear of the Jews, asked Pilate if he could remove the body of Jesus. And Pilate permitted it. So he came and took his body.

Nicodemus, the one who had first come to him at night, also came bringing a mixture of myrrh and aloes weighing about one hundred pounds. They took the body of Jesus and bound it with burial cloths along with the spices, according to the Jewish burial custom. Now in the place where he had been crucified there was a garden, and in the garden a new tomb, in which no one had yet been buried. So they laid Jesus there because of the Jewish preparation day; for the tomb was close by.

PSALM 148:7-14

Praise the LORD from the earth,
    you sea monsters and all
        depths;
Fire and hail, snow and mist,
    storm winds that fulfill his
        word;
You mountains and all you hills,
    you fruit trees and all you
        cedars;
You wild beasts and all tame
    animals,
    you creeping things and you
        winged fowl.
Let the kings of the earth and all
    peoples,
    the princes and all the judges
        of the earth,
Young men too, and maidens,
    old men and boys,
Praise the name of the LORD,
    for his name alone is exalted;
His majesty is above earth and
    heaven,
    and he has lifted up the horn
        of his people.
Be this his praise from all his
    faithful ones,
    from the children of Israel, the
        people close to him. Alleluia.

Open your mouth in behalf of the dumb, / and for the rights of the destitute; /
Open your mouth, decree what is just, / defend the needy and the poor!

DECEMBER 30

JOHN 20:1-31

On the first day of the week, Mary of Magdala came to the tomb early in the morning, while it was still dark, and saw the stone removed from the tomb. So she ran and went to Simon Peter and to the other disciple whom Jesus loved, and told them, "They have taken the Lord from the tomb, and we don't know where they put him." So Peter and the other disciple went out and came to the tomb. They both ran, but the other disciple ran faster than Peter and arrived at the tomb first; he bent down and saw the burial cloths there, but did not go in. When Simon Peter arrived after him he went into the tomb and saw the burial cloths there, and the cloth that had covered his head, not with the burial cloths but rolled up in a separate place. Then the other disciple also went in, the one who had arrived at the tomb first, and he saw and believed. For they did not yet understand the scripture that he had to rise from the dead. Then the disciples returned home.

But Mary stayed outside the tomb weeping. And as she wept, she bent over into the tomb and saw two angels in white sitting there, one at the head and one at the feet where the body of Jesus had been. And they said to her, "Woman, why are you weeping?" She said to them, "They have taken my Lord, and I don't know where they laid him." When she had said this, she turned around and saw Jesus there, but did not know it was Jesus. Jesus said to her, "Woman, why are you weeping? Whom are you looking for?" She thought it was the gardener and said to him, "Sir, if you carried him away, tell me where you laid him, and I will take him." Jesus said to her, "Mary!" She turned and said to him in Hebrew, "Rabbouni," which means Teacher. Jesus said to her, "Stop holding on to me, for I have not yet ascended to the Father. But go to my brothers and tell them, 'I am going to my Father and your Father, to my God and your God.' " Mary of Magdala went and announced to the disciples, "I have seen the Lord," and what he told her.

On the evening of that first day of the week, when the doors were locked, where the disciples were, for fear of the Jews, Jesus came and stood in their midst and said to them, "Peace be with you." When he had said this, he showed them his hands and his side. The disciples rejoiced when they saw the Lord. [Jesus] said to them again, "Peace be with you. As the Father has sent me, so I send you." And when he had said this, he breathed on them and said to them, "Receive the holy Spirit. Whose sins you forgive are forgiven them, and whose sins you retain are retained."

Thomas, called Didymus, one of the Twelve, was not with them when Jesus came. So the other disciples said to him, "We have seen the Lord." But he said to them, "Unless I see the mark of the nails in his hands and put my finger into the nailmarks and put my hand into his side, I will not believe." Now a week later his disciples were again inside and Thomas was with them. Jesus came, although the doors were locked, and stood in their midst and said, "Peace be with you." Then he said to Thomas, "Put your finger here and see my hands, and bring your hand and put it into my side, and do not be unbelieving, but believe." Thomas answered and said to him, "My Lord and my God!" Jesus said to him, "Have you come to believe because you have seen me? Blessed are those who have not seen and have believed."

Now Jesus did many other signs in the presence of [his] disciples that are not written in this book. But these are written that you may [come to] believe that Jesus is the Messiah, the Son of God, and that through this belief you may have life in his name.

PSALM 149:1-9

Alleluia.

Sing to the LORD a new song
  of praise in the assembly of the
  faithful.
Let Israel be glad in their maker,
  let the children of Zion rejoice
  in their king.
Let them praise his name in the
  festive dance,
  let them sing praise to him
  with timbrel and harp.
For the LORD loves his people,
  and he adorns the lowly with
  victory.
Let the faithful exult in glory;
  let them sing for joy upon their
  couches;
let the high praises of God be in
  their throats.
And let two-edged swords be in
  their hands:
  to execute vengeance on the
  nations,
  punishments on the peoples;
To bind their kings with chains,
  their nobles with fetters of iron;
To execute on them the written
  sentence.
  This is the glory of all his
  faithful. Alleluia.

PROVERBS 31:10-24

When one finds a worthy wife, / her value is far beyond pearls. / Her husband, entrusting his heart to her, / has an unfailing prize. / She brings him good, and not evil, / all the days of her life. / She obtains wool and flax / and makes cloth with skillful hands. / Like merchant ships, / she secures her provisions from afar. / She rises while it is still night, / and distributes food to her household. / She picks out a field to purchase; / out of her earnings she plants a vineyard. / She is girt about with strength, / and sturdy are her arms. / She enjoys the success of her dealings; / at night her lamp is undimmed. / She puts her hands to the distaff, / and her fingers ply the spindle. / She reaches out her hands to the poor, / and extends her arms to the needy. / She fears not the snow for her household; / all her charges are doubly clothed. / She makes her own coverlets; / fine linen and purple are her clothing. / Her husband is prominent at the city gates / as he sits with the elders of the land. / She makes garments and sells them, / and stocks the merchants with belts.

DECEMBER 31

JOHN 21:1-25

After this, Jesus revealed himself again to his disciples at the Sea of Tiberias. He revealed himself in this way. Together were Simon Peter, Thomas called Didymus, Nathanael from Cana in Galilee, Zebedee's sons, and two others of his disciples. Simon Peter said to them, "I am going fishing." They said to him, "We also will come with you." So they went out and got into the boat, but that night they caught nothing. When it was already dawn, Jesus was standing on the shore; but the disciples did not realize that it was Jesus. Jesus said to them, "Children, have you caught anything to eat?" They answered him, "No." So he said to them, "Cast the net over the right side of the boat and you will find something." So they cast it, and were not able to pull it in because of the number of fish. So the disciple whom Jesus loved said to Peter, "It is the Lord." When Simon Peter heard that it was the Lord, he tucked in his garment, for he was lightly clad, and jumped into the sea. The other disciples came in the boat, for they were not far from shore, only about a hundred yards, dragging the net with the fish. When they climbed out on shore, they saw a charcoal fire with fish on it and bread. Jesus said to them, "Bring some of the fish you just caught." So Simon Peter went over and dragged the net ashore full of one hundred fifty-three large fish. Even though there were so many, the net was not torn. Jesus said to them, "Come, have breakfast." And none of the disciples dared to ask him, "Who are you?" because they realized it was the Lord. Jesus came over and took the bread and gave it to them, and in like manner the fish. This was now the third time Jesus was revealed to his disciples after being raised from the dead.

When they had finished breakfast, Jesus said to Simon Peter, "Simon, son of John, do you love me more than these?" He said to him, "Yes, Lord, you know that I love you." He said to him, "Feed my lambs." He then said to him a second time, "Simon, son of John, do you love me?" He said to him, "Yes, Lord, you know that I love you." He said to him, "Tend my sheep." He said to him the third time, "Simon, son of John, do you love me?" Peter was distressed that he had said to him a third time, "Do you love me?" and he said to him, "Lord, you know everything; you know that I love you." [Jesus] said to him, "Feed my sheep. Amen, amen, I say to you, when you were younger, you used to dress yourself and go where you wanted; but when you grow old, you will stretch out your hands, and someone else will dress you and lead you where you do not want to go." He said this signifying by what kind of death he would glorify God. And when he had said this, he said to him, "Follow me."

Peter turned and saw the disciple following whom Jesus loved, the one who had also reclined upon his chest during the supper and had said, "Master, who is the one who will betray you?" When Peter saw him, he said to Jesus, "Lord, what about him?" Jesus said to him, "What if I want him to remain until I come? What concern is it of yours? You follow me." So the word spread among the brothers that that disciple would not die. But Jesus had not told him that he would not die, just "What if I want him to remain until I come? [What concern is it of yours?]"

It is this disciple who testifies to these things and has written them, and we know that his testimony is true. There are also many other things that Jesus did, but if these were to be described individually, I do not think the whole world would contain the books that would be written.

PSALM 150:1-6

Alleluia.

Praise the LORD in his sanctuary,
  praise him in the firmament of
  his strength.
Praise him for his mighty deeds,
  praise him for his sovereign
  majesty.
Praise him with the blast of the
  trumpet,
  praise him with lyre and harp,
Praise him with timbrel and
  dance,
  praise him with strings and
  pipe.
Praise him with sounding
  cymbals,
  praise him with clanging
  cymbals.
Let everything that has breath
  praise the LORD! Alleluia.

PROVERBS 31:25-31

She is clothed with strength and dignity, / and she laughs at the days to come. / She opens her mouth in wisdom, / and on her tongue is kindly counsel. / She watches the conduct of her household, / and eats not her food in idleness. / Her children rise up and praise her; / her husband, too, extols her: / "Many are the women of proven worth, / but you have excelled them all." / Charm is deceptive and beauty fleeting; / the woman who fears the Lord is to be praised. / Give her a reward of her labors, / and let her works praise her at the city gates.

Personal Reflections

JANUARY

Personal Reflections

_____
_____
_____
_____
_____
_____
_____
_____
_____
_____
_____
_____
_____
_____
_____
_____
_____
_____
_____
_____

FEBRUARY

Personal Reflections

_____

_____

_____

_____

_____

_____

_____

_____

_____

_____

_____

_____

_____

_____

_____

_____

_____

_____

_____

_____

_____

MARCH

Personal Reflections

_____

_____

_____

_____

_____

_____

_____

_____

_____

_____

_____

_____

_____

_____

_____

_____

_____

_____

_____

_____

_____

_____

_____

APRIL

Personal Reflections

_____
_____
_____
_____
_____
_____
_____
_____
_____
_____
_____
_____
_____
_____
_____
_____
_____
_____
_____
_____
_____

<u>MAY</u>

Personal Reflections

_____
_____
_____
_____
_____
_____
_____
_____
_____
_____
_____
_____
_____
_____
_____
_____
_____
_____
_____
_____

JUNE

Personal Reflections

_____

_____

_____

_____

_____

_____

_____

_____

_____

_____

_____

_____

_____

_____

_____

_____

_____

_____

_____

_____

_____

JULY

Personal Reflections

_____

_____

_____

_____

_____

_____

_____

_____

_____

_____

_____

_____

_____

_____

_____

_____

_____

_____

_____

AUGUST

Personal Reflections

_____

_____

_____

_____

_____

_____

_____

_____

_____

_____

_____

_____

_____

_____

_____

_____

_____

_____

_____

_____

SEPTEMBER

Personal Reflections

_____

_____

_____

_____

_____

_____

_____

_____

_____

_____

_____

_____

_____

_____

_____

_____

_____

_____

_____

OCTOBER

Personal Reflections

_____
_____
_____
_____
_____
_____
_____
_____
_____
_____
_____
_____
_____
_____
_____
_____
_____
_____
_____
_____
_____

NOVEMBER

Personal Reflections

_____
_____
_____
_____
_____
_____
_____
_____
_____
_____
_____
_____
_____
_____
_____
_____
_____
_____
_____
_____

DECEMBER

Personal Reflections

_____

_____

_____

_____

_____

_____

_____

_____

_____

_____

_____

_____

_____

_____

_____

_____

_____

_____